Special Edition

USING
NETSCAPE™ 3

Special Edition

Using
Netscape™ 3

Written by Mark R. Brown with

Steven Forrest Burnett • Tim Evans • Heather Fleming • Galen Grimes • Raymond C. Gronberg • David Gunter • Derek H. Hamner • Jerry Honeycutt • John Jung • Peter Kent • Greg Knauss • Margaret J. Larson • Lori Leonardo • Bill Nadeau • Paul Robichaux • Andrew Bryce Shafran • Todd Stauffer • Ian Stokell • Michael Thomas • Paul Wallace • John Williams

que®

Special Edition Using Netscape 3

Credits

PRESIDENT
Roland Elgey

PUBLISHER
Joseph B. Wikert

ACQUISITIONS MANAGER
Cheryl D. Willoughby

ACQUISITIONS EDITOR
Stephanie Gould

EDITORIAL SERVICES DIRECTOR
Elizabeth Keaffaber

MANAGING EDITOR
Sandy Doell

DIRECTOR OF MARKETING
Lynn E. Zingraf

PUBLISHING MANAGER
Jim Minatel

PRODUCT DEVELOPMENT SPECIALIST
Mark Cierzniak

PRODUCTION EDITOR
Elizabeth A. Bruns

EDITORS
Kelli M. Brooks
Mitzi Foster Gianakos
Patrick Kanouse

ASSISTANT PRODUCT MARKETING MANAGER
Kim Margolius

TECHNICAL EDITORS
Matthew Brown
Warren Ernst
Noel Estabrook
John Jung
Lori Leonardo
Thomas Martin

TECHNICAL SPECIALIST
Nadeem Muhammad

ACQUISITIONS COORDINATOR
Jane Brownlow

OPERATIONS COORDINATOR
Patricia J. Brooks

EDITORIAL ASSISTANT
Andrea Duvall

BOOK DESIGNER
Ruth Harvey

COVER DESIGNER
Dan Armstrong

PRODUCTION TEAM
Marcia Brizendine
Jason Carr
Erin M. Danielson
Trey Frank
Brian Grossman
Julie Searls
Kelly Warner
Donna Wright

INDEXERS
Chris Barrick
Ginny Bess

Composed in *Century Old Style* and *ITC Franklin Gothic* by Que Corporation.

About the Authors

Mark R. Brown has been writing computer magazine articles, books, and manuals for over 13 years. He was managing editor of *.info* magazine when it was named one of the six Best Computer Magazines of 1991 by the Computer Press Association, and was nominated by the Software Publisher's Association for the 1988 Software Reviewer of the Year award. He is currently the manager of Technical Publications for Neural Applications Corporation, a major player in applying cutting-edge artificial intelligence techniques to industrial control applications, such as steel making and food processing. A bona fide personal computing pioneer, he hand-built his first PC in 1977, taught himself to program it in hexadecimal, and has since dabbled in dozens of different programming languages. He has been telecomputing since 1983, and is currently Webmaster of two World Wide Web sites: **http://www.neural.com**, and a personal Web site on the topic of airships, which will have moved to a new URL by the time this is published. (Chapters 5, 10-14, 19, 26, and 30)

Steven Forrest Burnett is a technical writer, editor, and teacher of artificial linguistics, with a master of science in technical communication from North Carolina State University. Having dealt with Internet issues for several years, Steve also contributed to the book *Programming Client/Server Applications with RPC and DCE*. (Chapters 6, 10, 16, and Appendix C)

Tim Evans is a UNIX system administration and network security consultant. Employed by Taratec Development Corporation, his full-time contract assignment for the past three years has been at the DuPont Company's Experimental Station in Wilmington, Delaware. Tim pioneered development of DuPont's own World Wide Web, known as DuPont-Wide Web, widely used within the company for information sharing via its worldwide network. Previously, Tim worked for the U.S. Social Security Administration in various staff jobs for more than 20 years. In 1991, before the Internet got hot, he brought that government agency onto the Internet. At both DuPont and SSA, he provided support for large numbers of UNIX users, running UNIX on a variety of computer systems ranging from PCs to workstations to mini-computers. He can be reached via Internet e-mail at **tkevans@dupont.com**. (Chapter 10 and Appendix D)

Heather A. Fleming received her first lessons on a computer when she was given an Apple IIe for a Christmas present at the age of 12. Working her way to a Stephens College graduation with a B.A. in Mathematics and Computer Science, she landed a job working at a lumber mill in Oregon, where, besides pulling green chain, she studied machinery automation. The next year spent studying Human and Computer Interaction at the University of Nebraska-Lincoln, University of Missouri-Columbia, and Stephens College set her on a career path that has kept her in mid-Missouri writing training manuals for Datastorm Technologies, Inc. (Appendix B)

Galen Grimes lives in a quiet, heavily wooded section of Monroeville, Pennsylvania, a suburb of Pittsburgh, with his wife Joanne, and an assortment of deer, raccoons, squirrels, possums, and birds, which are all fed from their back door. Galen is also the author of several other Macmillan Computer Publishing books, including Sams' *First Book of DR DOS 6*, Que's *10 Minute Guide to NetWare* and *10 Minute Guide to Lotus Improv*, and Que's *Windows 3.1 HyperGuide*. Galen has a master's degree in Information Science from the University of Pittsburgh, and by trade, is a project manager and NetWare LAN administrator for a large international bank and financial institution. (Chapters 1 and 17)

Ray Gronberg is a journalist in Chapel Hill, North Carolina, where he specializes in government and public affairs reporting. He has an M.A. in journalism from the University of North Carolina and a B.A. in political science from the University of North Carolina at Charlotte. His practical experience with computers, as a hobbyist, dates from the late 1970s and early 1980s, when the gee-whiz operating system was CP/M and "mass storage" was a cassette deck. He uses Internet Web and e-mail services heavily in the course of his daily reporting. Ray can be reached via e-mail at **gronberg@nando.net**. (Chapter 7)

David Gunter is a consultant and computer author based in Cary, North Carolina. His areas of interest include UNIX systems management and network and systems programming. David holds a master's degree in computer science from the University of Tennessee. During his free time, David enjoys traveling, reading, and spending as much time as possible with his wonderful wife. (Chapter 28 and Appendix A)

Derek Hamner is a senior in computer science at the University of North Carolina at Chapel Hill. He is currently the Webmaster at UNC-General Administration, performing Web site development and maintenance. His duties also include designing Web-based applications for automating general office activities. In his spare time, Derek provides consulting services to commercial Web sites, and is working on several large networked applications in Java. Derek can be contacted via e-mail at **hamner@sunsite.unc.edu**. See **http://sunsite.unc.edu/hamner/** for more information. (Chapter 27)

Jerry Honeycutt is a business-oriented, technical manager with broad experience in software development. He has served companies such as The Travelers, IBM, Nielsen North America, and most recently, Information Retrieval Methods, as director of Windows Application Development. Jerry has participated in the industry since before the days of Microsoft Windows 1.0, and believes that everyone must eventually learn to use the Internet to stay in touch with the world.

Jerry wrote *Using Microsoft Plus!* and was a contributing author on *Special Edition Using Windows 95* for Que. He has also been printed in *Computer Language Magazine* and is a regular speaker at the Windows World and Comdex trade shows on topics related to software development and corporate solutions for Windows 95.

Jerry graduated from the University of Texas at Dallas in 1992 with a B.S. degree in computer science. He currently lives in the Dallas suburb of Frisco, Texas, with Becky, two Westies, Corky and Turbo, and two cats, Scratches and Chew-Chew. Please feel free to contact Jerry on the Internet at **jerry@honeycutt.com**, on CompuServe at **76477,2751**, or on The Microsoft Network at **Honeycutt**. (Chapters 2 and 8)

John Jung is an alumnus of the University of Southern California with a degree in computer science. He became interested in computers over 16 years ago and has been on the Net for over eight years. He wastes his time watching TV, surfing the Net, and playing video games. John can be reached at **jjung@netcom.com**. (Chapters 22 and 25)

Peter Kent lives in Lakewood, Colorado. He's been training computer users, documenting software, and designing user interfaces for the last 14 years. Working as an independent consultant for the last nine years, Peter has worked for companies such as MasterCard, Amgen,

Data General, and Dvorak Development and Publishing. Much of his consulting work has been in the telecommunications business.

Peter is the author of *Using Microsoft Network* (Que) and *Using Microsoft Internet Explorer* (Que), and the best-selling *The Complete Idiot's Guide to the Internet* (Que). He's also written seven other Internet-related books—including *The Complete Idiot's Guide to the Internet for Windows 95* and *The Complete Idiot's Guide to the World Wide Web*—and a variety of other works, such as *The Technical Writer's Freelancing Guide* and books on Windows NT and Windows 3.1. His articles have appeared in many periodicals, including *Internet World*, *Dr. Dobb's Journal*, *Windows* Magazine, *The Dallas Times Herald*, and *Computerworld*. Peter can be reached via CompuServe at **71601,1266** and the Internet at **pkent@lab-press.com**. (Chapter 18)

Greg Knauss lives in Los Angeles with his wife, Joeanne, and works as a UNIX and Windows programmer. He graduated from the University of California, San Diego with a degree in political science, but has been programming and writing about computers for over 15 years. He has previously worked on *Using HTML* for Que. (Chapter 24)

Margaret Larson is a founding partner of Wintergreen Associates, located in Western Massachusetts. She has worked as a computer programmer and software designer for 15 years. Originally from Ohio, Peg (as she is commonly called) got her B.A. in economics from UMass/ Amherst and spent 5 years in graduate school focusing on computerized economic forecasting and simulation models. Her work has involved software design, testing, documentation, technical writing, statistics, and data analysis.

In late 1994, when the company for which she worked was sold and moved to Boston, she and her husband, Bill Nadeau, reorganized their consulting business and founded Wintergreen Associates. They specialize in design and maintenance of commercial Web sites with a focus on forms/CGI programming, management and analysis of large databases, and market research. You can find a link to Peg's résumé at Wintergreen's Web site—**http://www.wintergreen. com/**. (Chapter 5)

Lori Leonardo is owner of L. Leonardo Consulting, a computer services company that provides Internet consulting and training. She is also an instructor at Brown University Learning Community where she teaches "Personal Finance: How to Capitalize on the Web" and "For KIDS Web Ventures—Cyber Out on the Web." Lori can be reached at **lorileo@aol.com**. (Chapter 26)

Bill Nadeau is a founding partner of Wintergreen Associates, and develops Web sites with his wife and partner, Peg Larson. Bill is a designer, writer, and programmer, and has worked as a consultant and contractor on a variety of projects with over 15 years experience in the field. Peg and Bill coauthored the *FreeThink Users Guide* and developed tutorials in multi-dimensional data modeling for clients such as The World Bank while working at Power Thinking Tools before FreeThink was purchased by Praxis International in late 1994. Bill has a B.S. in regional planning & environmental design, and some graduate training in architecture, as well as some schooling in music and visual arts. He is currently enmeshed in developing multimedia/CGI applications. (Chapter 5)

Paul Robichaux, who has been an Internet user since 1986 and a software developer since 1983, is currently a software consultant for Intergraph Corporation, where he writes Windows NT and Windows 95 applications. In his spare time, he writes books and Macintosh applications. He still manages to spend plenty of time with his wife and young son. He can be reached via e-mail at **perobich@ingr.com**. (Chapter 29)

Andrew Bryce Shafran is a full-time writer and computer consultant living in Columbus, Ohio. He is a student at The Ohio State University, and might actually graduate some year. He loves writing books and magazine articles, especially about CompuServe and the WWW. His other Que books include *Creating Your Own Netscape Web Pages*, *Enhancing Netscape Web Pages*, and *The Complete Idiot's Guide to CompuServe*. You can visit his home page at **http://www.cis.ohio-state.edu/~shafran**. (Chapters 19 and 20)

Todd Stauffer has been writing nonstop about computers and the computer industry since he graduated from Texas A&M University, where he studied a bizarre combination of English literature, managment information systems, and entirely too much golf. A die-hard fan of the Macintosh, Todd is the author of *Using Your Mac*, *Easy America Online*, and the coauthor of *Special Edition Using the Internet with Your Macintosh*—all Que publications.

Todd has recently finished a stint as editor of *Texas Computing* Magazine and is currently a freelance writer and author. He has worked previously as an advertising, technical, and magazine writer—all in the computer industry. He can be reached by Internet e-mail at **TStauffer@aol.com**. (Chapters 3, 18, and 23)

Ian Stokell is a freelance writer and editor living in the Sierra Foothills of northern California with his wife and three young children. He is also Managing Editor of *Newsbytes News Network*, an international daily newswire covering the computer and telecommunications industries. His writing career began with a 1981 article published in the U.K.'s *New Statesman* and has since encompassed over 1,500 articles in a variety of computing and non-computing publications. He wrote the Networking chapter of Que's *Special Edition Using the Macintosh*, and has also written on assignment for such magazines as *PC World* and *MacWeek*. He is currently seeking representation for two completed novels and a screenplay. (Chapter 4)

Michael D. Thomas graduated from the University of North Carolina in December 1995 with a concentration in computer science. Since August 1994, he has worked extensively with the World Wide Web. While a student, he acted as UNIX System Administrator on a campus Web server. In addition to running Web servers, he also has done extensive writing of CGI programs and formatting of Web pages. In May 1995, he added Java to a repertoire of programming languages, which also includes Perl, C, and C++. Michael's home page, which includes current links to Java information, can be found at **http://sunsite.unc.edu/mdthomas/**. (Chapter 27)

Paul Wallace lives in Knoxville, Tennessee, where he is pursuing a Ph.D. in instructional technology at the University of Tennessee. He is an Internet consultant specializing in content development, interface design, and interactive programming for the World Wide Web. In his diminishing free time, Paul can be found relaxing with friends in one of Knoxville's coffee shops, visiting the animal shelter, swimming laps, or patiently awaiting the next Dinosaur Jr. album. Paul is an accomplished surfer who has traveled to many of the world's best point breaks and hopes to visit the coast of South Africa. Paul can best be reached via his home page at **http://www.clever.net/wallace**. (Chapters 21, 22, and 25)

John F. Williams began his work with multimedia and personal computers after purchasing Director's predecessor, VideoWorks. At about the same time, he created one of the first commercial programs demonstrated for HyperCard's release in 1987. John continued to work in the infant multimedia industry, founding the startup development company Midnight Design in 1989, speaking at universities and conferences on multimedia, and honing his skills while working with some of the best multimedia design firms in the business. Since then, he has gone on to help create dozens of commercial and private CD-ROMs, as well as over 30 interactive demo disks for various companies (most recently the Director 4.0 Guided Tour for Macromedia). Today, John is working on a variety of next-generation CD-ROM "titles" that Apple Computers, and some as-yet-to-be-found companies, will publish for Midnight Design. (Chapter 30)

For my parents, Robert and Margaret Brown, who brought me up right.

Acknowledgments

It takes a lot of hard work to put together a book of this size and scope in such a short time.

All the writers associated with this project put forth a tremendous effort and deserve all the laurels we can heap upon them. The editors and staff at Que books certainly earned their kudos as well; special thanks go to Cheryl Willoughby, Mark Cierzniak, and Benjamin Milstead for their invaluable assistance and infallible guidance. And I'd like to add a special "thank you" to Oran J. Sands at Que for bringing me into this project.

Of course, we wouldn't have a book at all if it weren't for the excellent product produced by the programmers, planners, and management of Netscape Corporation. And the authors and developers of all the Netscape support programs mentioned in this book deserve our thanks, as well.

Then there are "all those wonderful people out there in the dark" who make up the World Wide Web. Certainly, to the people at CERN in Switzerland who first conceived and implemented the Web, our thanks. But the Web is made up of the efforts of literally millions of people, many of whom selflessly contribute the thoughts, ideas, articles, stories, graphics, movies, sound clips, and all the other elements that make up the multinational, multilingual, multimedia stew that is the World Wide Web. To all of them, our thanks for making Web surfing such an entertaining, enlightening, and engaging activity!

Finally, I'd like to thank my friends and family for their patient understanding of all the hours I had to spend away from them while working on this book. A special thanks goes to my wife, Carol, who has supported me wholeheartedly in this and all my other writing projects, with more patience than anyone could ever ask for or expect from another human being.

—Mark R. Brown

We'd Like to Hear from You!

As part of our continuing effort to produce books of the highest possible quality, Que would like to hear your comments. To stay competitive, we really want you, as a computer book reader and user, to let us know what you like or dislike most about this book or other Que products.

You can mail comments, ideas, or suggestions for improving future editions to the address below, or send us a fax at (317) 581-4663. For the online inclined, Macmillan Computer Publishing has a forum on CompuServe (type **GO QUEBOOKS** at any prompt) through which our staff and authors are available for questions and comments. The address of our Internet site is **http://www.mcp.com** (World Wide Web).

In addition to exploring our forum, please feel free to contact me personally to discuss your opinions of this book: I'm **76245,476** on CompuServe, and **mcierzniak@que.mcp.com** on the Internet.

Thanks in advance—your comments will help us to continue publishing the best books available on computer topics in today's market.

Mark Cierzniak
Product Development Specialist
Que Corporation
201 W. 103rd Street
Indianapolis, Indiana 46290
USA

Contents at a Glance

Table of Contents

11 CoolTalk 285

VII | Appendixes

Introduction

Everywhere you turn you find people talking about the World Wide Web. Corporations now include Web addresses in their TV commercials. Television show and movie debuts are accompanied by the launch of promotional pages on the Web. Newspapers and magazines supplement their readership with an online presence. Celebrity fan clubs set up houses of worship on the Net. TV news shows blare excited warnings about kids accessing pornography on the Web.

In just a few short years, the World Wide Web has become a part of daily life. Every day, millions of people all over the world browse the Web for news, product information, entertainment, and even good, hard data. And the browser of choice for the majority of them is Netscape Navigator.

People have always liked Netscape for its solid reliability, generous allotment of features, and free preview offer. And now, with the release of version 3.0, Netscape is even more useful and powerful than before.

Of course, there's more to learn, too—like JavaScript, the Netscape scripting language, and plug-ins, which allow multimedia files to display right in the Netscape window without launching helper applications.

That's why we're here. *Special Edition Using Netscape 3* gently guides you through all the steps to get Netscape set up and working to its full potential on your machine. ■

Who Should Use This Book?

This book is intended for anyone and everyone who wants to get the most out of Netscape and the World Wide Web.

Novices will find information on how to obtain, install, and configure Netscape. Intermediate users will discover tips, tricks, and techniques to make Netscape even more fun and useful. And advanced users will learn the nuts and bolts of Netscape operation, including how to use powerful Netscape 3.0 features like plug-ins and the JavaScript scripting language.

How This Book Is Organized

Special Edition Using Netscape 3 is organized into six logical sections.

Part I, "Internet Fundamentals," explains what the Internet and World Wide Web are, and what they are likely to become in the future. It explains how the Web is organized and how it works.

Part II, "Mastering Netscape," tells you how to navigate the Web using links, online search engines and indexes, and bookmarks. You'll also find information on how to use online forms, including a discussion of security. The section wraps up with information on using Netscape to access Internet services other than the World Wide Web, like e-mail, FTP, Gopher, and UseNet news.

Part III, "Plug-Ins and Helper Applications," guides you through the process of finding and configuring Netscape plug-ins and helper applications for audio, graphics, and video. There's a chapter apiece on Netscape 3.0's new CoolTalk phone utility and the new Power Pack 2.0 collection of Netscape add-ons and plug-ins. You'll also be introduced to VRML (Virtual Reality Modeling Language) and how to view VRML worlds using Netscape plug-ins and helper applications, as are compressed files and how to deal with them.

Part IV, "Building World Class Home Pages for Netscape," gets you started with HTML (HyperText Markup Language), the language used to create Web pages. You'll learn how to create links and use advanced graphics techniques like imagemaps to make your Web pages dynamic. You'll even learn about Netscape-specific and proposed future HTML commands. Finally, you'll discover how to work with the Web's most advanced page development tools, forms, and CGI-bin scripts.

Part V, "Building World Class Web Sites and Servers for Netscape," builds on the knowledge you gained in Part IV, tying together Web page creation techniques to help you build an excellent Web site. There's a chapter on LiveWire, Netscape's integrated Web site creation and management tool. Then you'll ride along on a test-drive of the Netscape Commerce server, the software for the "other end" of the Web that delivers Web pages to users.

Part VI, "Advanced Netscape Customization," delves into the depths of Netscape 3.0's most powerful new features, with chapters on Sun's Java language for C, C++, and JavaScript customization of Netscape.

Appendixes finish out the book with information on how to connect to the Internet, how to install and configure Netscape Navigator on a variety of platforms, and what you'll find on the book's CD-ROM.

The Book's CD-ROM

Inside the back cover of this book you'll find a CD-ROM containing multi-megabytes of helper applications, links, tips, and programs that will help you get the most out of Netscape.

Whenever we mention a program in this book that is included on the book's CD, you'll see the icon at the right. Keep an eye out for it.

Conventions Used in This Book

This book uses various stylistic and typographic conventions to make it easier to use.

Keyboard shortcut key combinations are joined by + signs; for example, Ctrl+X means to hold down the Ctrl key, press the X key, then release both.

Menu items and dialog box selections often have a mnemonic key associated with them. This key is indicated by an underline on the item on screen. To use these mnemonic keys, you press the Alt key, then the shortcut key. In this book, mnemonic keys are underlined, like this: <u>F</u>ile.

This book uses the following typeface conventions:

Typeface	Meaning
Italic	Variables in commands or addresses, or terms used for the first time
Bold	Text you type in, as well as addresses of Internet sites, newsgroups, mailing lists, and Web sites
`Computer type`	Commands, HTML tags

N O T E Notes provide additional information related to the topic at hand. ■

T I P Tips provide quick and helpful information to assist you along the way.

CAUTION
Cautions alert you to potential pitfalls or dangers in the operations discussed.

TROUBLESHOOTING

Troubleshooting boxes address problems that you might encounter while following the procedures in this book.

On the Web Site

Netscape is constantly undergoing changes. In fact, you may find that Netscape releases new versions of software more often than you want to buy a book to find how to use new features. While we'd be happy to see you buy every new Netscape book we publish, we realize that a book is not a minor investment and should be something that has lasting value.

With that in mind, we've set up a special Netscape section on our Web site (The Information Superlibrary). This section will include new chapters and coverage of new or changed features in Netscape. The address for this Web site is **http://www.mcp.com/que/et/netscape**. So you can connect to this site and get all of the latest information you need and this book will never go out of date. Then, when you find that enough features in Netscape have changed that you need a whole new book, we'd encourage you to back to your favorite bookstore or retailer and pick up the lastest Netscape book from Que.

Internet Fundamentals

World Wide Web and Netscape 3

The explosive proliferation of Internet usage and Web browsing has led many new users to freely exchange the terms Internet and World Wide Web, as if they are the same entity. Well, let's begin by setting the record straight—the Internet and the World Wide Web are not the same!

Internet is a collective term used to describe an interconnection of worldwide computer networks. Operating on the Internet are a variety of computer services such as e-mail, UseNet newsgroups, FTP, Telnet, Gopher, and the World Wide Web.

Even though the World Wide Web (most often referred to simply as the Web or WWW) has only been around since 1992 (the first Web server prototype was developed in 1990 at CERN, the European Laboratory for Particle Physics in Geneva, Switzerland), its growth on the Internet has been nothing short of phenomenal. In 1993, when the alpha version of Mosaic—the first graphic Web browser— was initially released, there were a total of 130 Web servers. Today, there are more than 13,000 Web servers worldwide, displaying more than 10 million Web pages!

The release of a version of Mosaic for Windows in late 1993 was one of the milestones that spurred Internet and Web activity. Netscape, a second generation Web browser, appeared on the scene not long after the PC version of Mosaic. Netscape forced open the door that Mosaic had been knocking on. Netscape's improved performance and added features helped create the near stampede to the Internet that has occurred in the last year or two.

Before diving into Netscape 3.0, to help give you an overall better idea of how we've gotten this far and what's going on behind the scenes, this chapter covers the history and operation of the Internet and the World Wide Web in addition to the following topics:

- Understanding the evolution, structure, and operation of the Internet
- What URLs are and how they are used to locate Internet resources
- How the World Wide Web works
- What future projects are being planned for the Web
- What's new in Netscape 3.0

N O T E   Throughout this chapter you will see references to certain publications such as RFC-1738 or RFC-1173. RFCs (Requests For Comment) are informational documents that describe policies, procedures, and protocols on the Internet. If you're interested in reading the in-depth discussions that have taken place on various aspects of the Internet (from "soup-to-nuts" as the saying goes), this is your ticket. RFCs can be referenced from various locations on the Internet, but to save you the time of locating them, here's one reference point: **http://www.uwaterloo.ca/uw_infoserv/ rfc.html**. ■

Who Uses the World Wide Web

The World Wide Web is one of the most accessible places because it is available to virtually anyone worldwide who has access to a computer and a modem. For this reason, the Web has literally become "the kiosk for the entire planet." Because of the potential for getting a message to a very large and diverse audience, it's no wonder that there are now more than 10 million Web pages available for your viewing, all posted on the Web in just the last three years.

As I stated earlier, the initial release of Mosaic for Windows was one of the keys to the success of the Web because Mosaic on the "common" PC made the Web accessible to the masses of ordinary PC users.

So who are these masses of ordinary PC users who have posted those 10 million Web pages? The answer is literally anyone and everyone. Major corporations, small businesses, government agencies, politicians, social organizations, historical societies, and a burgeoning industry of would-be Web authors are among those who have Web pages they are trying to get you to view.

Many Web authors are simply trying to supply information over the Web, but more often you will see businesses either advertising their presence and products, advertising their services, or directly trying to sell you their wares.

When you look out on the Web, you will see Coca-Cola, IBM, CNN, the National Football League, the World History Archives, and the Virtual Quilt home page, just as an example of some of the diversity you'll find (see figs. 1.1 through 1.6).

FIG. 1.1
The Coca-Cola home page.

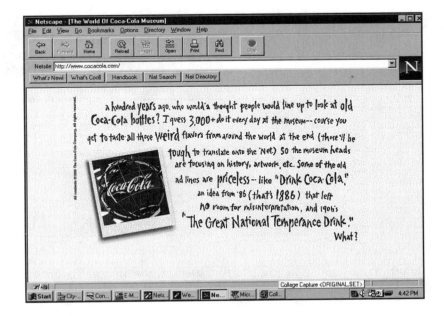

FIG. 1.2
The IBM home page.

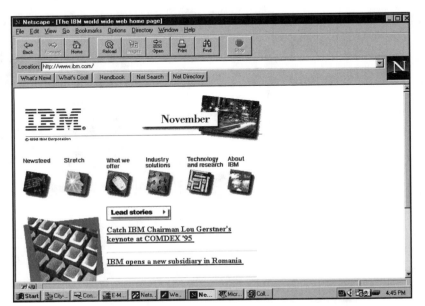

FIG. 1.3
The CNN Interactive
home page.

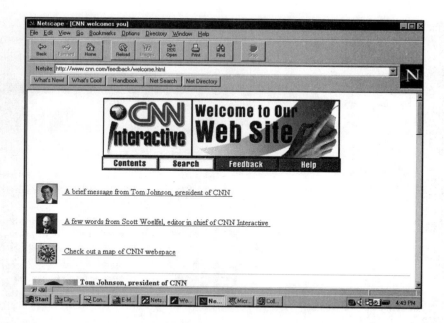

FIG. 1.4
The NFL home page.

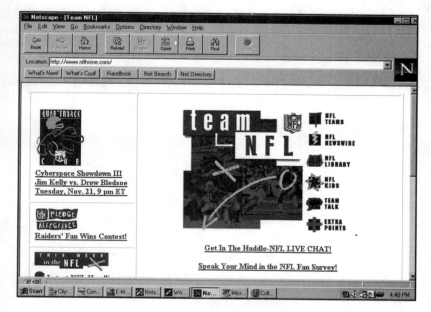

FIG. 1.5

The World History Archives home page.

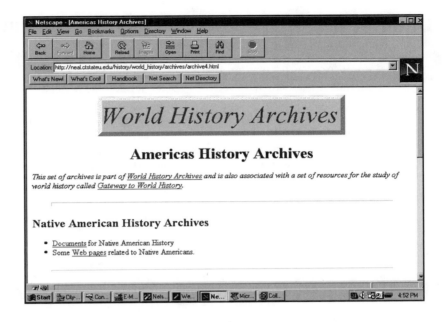

FIG. 1.6

The Virtual Quilt home page.

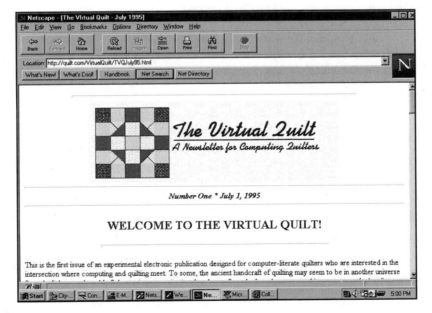

Understanding the Evolution of the Internet

To understand how the Internet functions, you need to know something of its history.

In the 1960s following the Cuban Missile Crisis, the RAND Corporation, America's foremost think tank, first proposed the idea of a decentralized computer network spanning this country. The proposal envisioned linking together military and academic computers in a network that could survive a nuclear attack. The key to this design was to decentralize the control and authority of this network, so that failure or destruction of one or more segments of the network would not result in the network's collapse. This design could only be accomplished if multiple pathways existed between each computer (node) on the network.

The original proposal, released in 1964 by RAND staffer Paul Baran, simply stated that each node in the network would be equal in status to all other nodes. Each node would have the authority to originate, pass, and receive messages from any other node. The messages would be broken down into smaller, standardized units for transmission called packets. Packets would be individually addressed to their destination node, and because each node would be capable of passing or forwarding (or routing) packets along the network to the designated address, each message was guaranteed to reach its destination. The network's multiple pathway design ensured that there would always be one or more pathways available for message transmission.

Creation of the Early ARPANET

In the late 1960s, the RAND Corporation, MIT, and UCLA experimented with the concept of a decentralized, packet-switching computer network, as did the National Physical Laboratory in Great Britain. In 1968, the Pentagon's Advanced Research Projects Agency (ARPA) began funding a project in the U.S. By the fall of 1969, the infant ARPANET came into being with its first four nodes:

- An SDS SIGMA 7 at UCLA
- An SDS940 at the Stanford Research Institute
- An IBM 360 at the University of California at Santa Barbara
- A DEC PDP-10 at the University of Utah

The early tests conducted on ARPANET proved highly successful. Scientists at the test institutions were able to transfer data and share computer facilities remotely. By 1971, ARPANET expanded to 15 nodes, and included links to MIT, RAND, Harvard, CMU in Pittsburgh, Case Western Reserve, and NASA/Ames. By 1972, there were a total of 37 nodes on ARPANET. In 1973, the first international connections to ARPANET were made to the University College of London and to the Royal Radar Establishment in Norway.

Despite the fact that the early makeup of ARPANET consisted of connections between this country's most prestigious research institutions, and that the earliest proposals for ARPANET stressed its importance as a means of allowing remote computing, the main traffic on ARPANET in its early days did not fit its intended role. At first scientists were using it to collaborate on research projects and exchange notes on work. But very quickly it became the equivalent of a high-speed, computerized "party-line." Many of its users were sending personal messages and gossip, and eventually using it mainly to just "schmooze."

Growth and Change of ARPANET in the '70s

Nevertheless, despite what it was being used for, ARPANET and the concept of a packet-switching, decentralized network were a huge success. During the 1970s, this decentralized structure made expansion easy and resulted in tremendous growth. Its decentralized structure, vastly different from corporate computer networks at the time, allowed connection of virtually any type of computer as long as it could communicate using the packet-switching protocol NCP, Network Control Protocol (the forerunner to TCP/IP, Transmission Control Protocol/Internet Protocol).

As early as 1974, Vint Cerf and Bob Kahn, both of NSF, published their first specifications for a transmission control protocol, which was being used by other networks to attach to the ARPANET by 1977.

TCP/IP, released into public domain, differed from NCP in that it converted messages into packets at the source, and then assembled them back into messages at the destination. IP, or Internet protocol, was used to establish the addressing for the packet, and was able to ensure that packet addressing guided packets through multiple nodes and, more importantly, across multiple networks even if the standards differed from ARPANET's early NCP standard. TCP/IP was the impetus in the late 1970s and early 1980s that led to further expansion of ARPANET, because it was fairly easy to implement on most any computer and allowed easy expansion from any existing node.

By 1983, ARPANET (which by then was commonly referred to as the Internet because of the vast array of interconnected computers and networks) officially dropped NCP and replaced it with the more advanced and more widespread TCP/IP, which had been officially adopted by the Department of Defense (DOD) the year before.

Expansion in the '80s and '90s

The 1980s was a period of tremendous growth for the Internet. The pattern established in the U.S. of interconnecting remote computer systems via a decentralized network was spreading worldwide, and many of those foreign computer networks wanted to become connected to the U.S. network. The Internet's reach broadened by the inclusion of:

- EUnet—the European UNIX Network in 1982
- EARN—the European Academic and Research Network in 1983
- JUNET—the Japanese UNIX Network in 1984
- JANET—the Joint Academic Network in the United Kingdom in 1984

It was also during the 1980s that the major players in this country, through funding from the National Science Foundation, established the NSFNET—five supercomputing centers at Princeton, CMU, UCSB, UIUC, and Cornell that loosely became known as the "Internet backbone in the U.S." The original speed of NSFNET in 1986 was a blazing 56 Kbps. In less than two years the continued expansion of the Internet and demand for computing services led to an upgrade of the NSFNET backbone in 1988 to T1 speed (1.544 Mbps). In 1987, there were more than 10,000 host computers interconnected on the Internet. By 1989, the number of hosts reached 100,000.

The 1990s and the Coming of the Web

The 1990s saw continued expansion of the Internet along with the invention of several Internet services and programs. In 1990, Archie was released by Bill Heelan, Alan Emtage, and Peter Deutsch. In 1991, the NSFNET backbone was upgraded to T3 status (44.736 Mbps), and Brewster Kahle invented WAIS. Also in 1991, Paul Lindner and Mark McCahill of the University of Minnesota released Gopher, followed in 1992 by the release of Veronica from the University of Nevada. In 1992, the number of host computers on the Internet broke the one million mark.

But by far the greatest advancement to the Internet in the 1990s (some might even say in its entire existence) was the creation of the World Wide Web. In November of 1990, Tim Berners-Lee of CERN created the first Web server prototype using a NeXT computer. The Web as an actual functioning system did not go online until 1992. In February of 1993, the alpha version of Mosaic was released by NCSA. By September 1993, the first working version of Mosaic was released and WWW traffic was already one percent of NFSNET. By October 1993, there were already 200 Web servers in operation.

In the years following, Internet and Web expansion continued at even greater levels. Actual statistics on the number of host computers and Web servers are hard to measure because they change almost daily. A good guess on the number of host computers on the Internet (averaged from several sources) as of June 1995 would be about 6.5 million, with the largest concentration, as you might expect, in the United States.

Internet Administration

The Internet, despite its initial development, support, and funding by ARPA and NSF, does not really belong to anyone, even though it has had a number of agencies and groups "overseeing" its operation. In 1979, ARPA first established the ICCB (Internetwork Configuration and Control Board). The ICCB was replaced in 1983 by the IAB (Internet Activities Board). In 1987, the NSF contracted with Merit Network, Inc. to manage the NSFNET backbone. Ordinarily, the management of the Internet would not warrant much mention, except that in 1993 NSF began laying the plans for a new U.S. Internet backbone as a total replacement for NSFNET. The new backbone went into operation in 1995 as Internet traffic was transitioned from the NSFNET, which ceased backbone operations on April 30, 1995. The new backbone is composed of the following:

■ A very high-speed Backbone Network Service (vBNS) OC3 line (155 Mbps) funded by NSF; its use is restricted to organizations requiring high speeds for scientific calculations or visualizations

■ Four regional Network Access Points, NAPs (located in San Francisco, Chicago, New York City, and Washington, D.C.) that interconnect the vBNS, other backbone networks, both domestic and foreign, and network service providers

■ A routing arbiter (also funded by NSF) that arbitrates high-speed and low-speed band-width requests

Hypertext and Hypermedia Concepts

With an understanding of how the Internet has grown and evolved to its present state, under-standing what URLs (Uniform Resource Locators) are and how they function is key to under-standing how the Internet and the Web function and how Internet resources are located and accessed.

URLs are a very convenient method of identifying the location of devices and resources on the Internet. As defined in RFC-1738, all URLs follow this format:

<scheme>:<scheme-dependent-information>

Some examples of <scheme> are http, FTP, and Gopher. This scheme tells you the application you are using:

■ What type of resource you are trying to locate (for example, a Web page, a file, or a Gopher menu or Gopher document)

■ What mechanism you need to access the resource (for example, a Web browser, an FTP utility to download the file, or a Gopher client)

The <scheme-dependent-information> usually indicates:

■ The Internet host making the file available

■ The full path to the file

A more recognizable pattern for most users is:

scheme://machine.domain/full-pathname-of-file

Here we see the scheme describing the type of resource separated from the computer and its Internet address by two slashes (//) and then the Internet address separated from the path and file name by one slash (/). URLs for http, FTP, and Gophers generally fit this pattern.

To make this example a bit clearer, let's use a real-world URL as an example. Here is the URL for my home page:

http://www.city-net.com/~gagrimes/galen1.html

Figure 1.7 shows you how my home page appears.

FIG. 1.7
The Galen Grimes Most
Excellent Home Page.

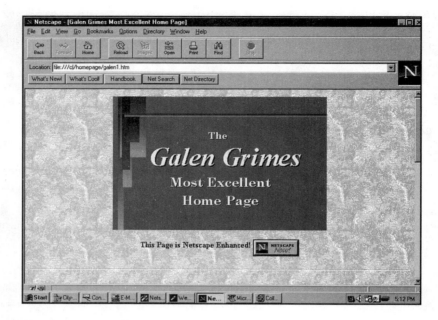

Here's the scheme for this URL broken down into its component parts:

- http:—indicates that you are using the HyperText Transfer Protocol to access the resource, which usually means you want to use your Web browser
- www.city-net.com—identifies the host computer and its Internet address (its domain name to be precise)
- /~gagrimes/galen1.html—identifies the path and file name on the host computer for the desired resource

Most Web pages follow this scheme. You may have noticed that when accessing http, FTP, or Gopher URLs, the "full pathname" sometimes ends in a single slash (/). This is used to point the URL to a specific directory instead of to a specific file. In this case the host computer will usually return what is called the default index for that directory. In http the default index file is usually named index.html, but can also be named home.html, homepage.html, welcome.html, or default.html.

So, let's say you're sitting in front of your PC in Phoenix (or anywhere for that matter) and decide to visit my Web page. You start Netscape, and enter **http://www.city-net.com/ ~gagrimes/galen1.html** in the location window, press Enter, and in a few seconds my home page appears.

How the Domain Name Service Works

One of the key components responsible for helping Netscape run on your computer and locate my home page file, galen1.html (which is stored on the Web server of my service provider, City-Net) is a program, or more precisely, a series of programs called the domain name service.

Here's how the domain name service, or DNS for short, works its magic. When you initially set up your connection to your Internet Service Provider (if you used Microsoft Plus! you did it using the Internet Setup Wizard) you were asked to enter the IP address of your DNS Server. The IP address you entered, which your service provider supplied you with, looked something like the IP address shown in figure 1.8.

Part

I

Ch

1

FIG. 1.8
Entering the IP address of your DNS Server in Microsoft Plus! Internet Setup Wizard.

> **N O T E** An IP address is a unique number, in the format nnn.nnn.nnn.nnn (where nnn is a number between 0 and 255) that is assigned to every physical device on the Internet. Your service provider is assigned a block of IP addresses (by the InterNIC Registration Services) that are in turn assigned to each user who is provided access to the Internet. Your provider either assigns you a permanent IP address that doesn't change, or each time you log in to your provider, you are assigned a dynamic IP address, which could be any number in your provider's assigned block of IP address numbers. ■

When you enter the URL for my home page, **http://www.city-net.com/~gagrimes/ galen1.html**, Netscape parses the domain name from this URL according to the URL scheme explained previously. The domain name Netscape gets from this URL is city-net.com. Netscape, working in conjunction with Windows and your TCP/IP protocol stack, passes the domain name, **city-net.com**, to your domain name service.

> **N O T E** You may have noticed that domain names often end in .com, .edu, or .org. These identifiers are used with the domain name to help identify the type of domain. The most common identifiers are shown here, along with examples of each:
>
> - .com for commercial organizations; for example, netscape.com, ibm.com, fedex.com
> - .edu for educational institutions; for example, psu.edu for Penn State Univ., cmu.edu for Carnegie-Mellon Univ., mit.edu for the Massachusetts Institute of Technology
> - .gov for government agencies; for example, whitehouse.gov for the White House, fbi.gov for the FBI
> - .mil for the military; for example; army.mil for the Army, navy.mil for the Navy

- .org for nonprofit organizations; for example, red-cross.org for the American Red Cross, oneworld.org for Save the Children Fund

- .net for network service providers; for example, internic.net for InterNIC, si.net for Sprint International

There are also identifiers for countries:

- .uk for United Kingdom

- .ca for Canada

- .ch for Switzerland (Confoederatio Helvetica); you may have noticed that the domain name for CERN is cern.ch

- .li for Liechtenstein

- .cn for China

- .jp for Japan

- .br for Brazil

The lack of a country identifier usually indicates the domain is in the United States. ▪

Your domain name service in one sense is a very large database program running on one of your service provider's computers (other computers are running other services such as mail service, news service, and FTP to name a few). When the domain name is passed to the domain name service, the DNS returns the corresponding IP address.

N O T E If by some chance your DNS does not contain the domain name, your DNS will attempt to locate the IP address by requesting the domain name from another DNS, in this case a centralized DNS containing .com domain names. If the domain name is still not located, the DNS will finally return an error message indicating the requested domain name does not exist. ▪

In the previous example using my home page, the domain name 21city-net.com is passed to your DNS, and your DNS should return 199.234.118.2. The IP address is not only used for identification, it is also used to route the request to the appropriate host computer. The starting sequence of this IP address, 199., routes the request to North America. Additional routers connecting various Internet segments in North America, and containing routing tables for the segments they connect, eventually route the request to Pittsburgh and to City-Net. Once the request arrives at the domain city-net.com, it is routed to the appropriate host computer and finally to the appropriate directory path until the file galen1.html is located.

Because the request for galen1.html was made using http, the host computer, a Web server, returns the requested file for display by the requesting client, which in this case is Netscape, a Web browser.

The Web Metaphor Hypertext Links

Now you have an understanding of how URLs work, and how URLs are used to help route files to the computers that request them. Figure 1.9 does a good job of illustrating Internet connections in the U.S. and how requests to various host computers could possibly be routed over the various interconnected Internet segments.

FIG. 1.9
Map of the U.S. illustrating how Internet network segments are interconnected.

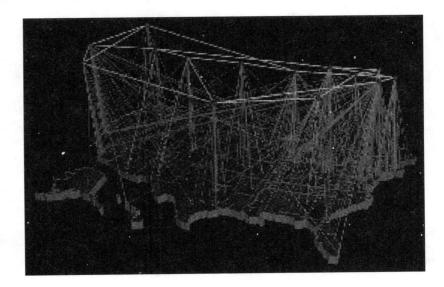

The World Wide Web is a means of supporting hypertext across the Internet. Hypertext is simply text that contains links, and these links provide additional information about certain keywords or phrases. Links are just what they sound like, and on Web pages, these links are used to connect one page (or file) to another page. We can use my home page as an example of Web page hypertext links. Figure 1.10 shows three links on my home page. These links are references to three additional Web pages, which also happen to be located on the same computer as my home page, which is the Web server of my service provider, City-Net.

N O T E You can easily identify links when using Netscape because links will usually appear as either blue or magenta <u>underlined text</u>. ▉

Selecting the link Author Stuff will send another request from your PC across the interconnected segments of the Internet to the City-Net Web server, requesting the file galen-a.htm, which is the file name of the Author Stuff Web page. The URL for the Author Stuff page is included in this link. In a few seconds the page shown in figure 1.11 appears.

FIG. 1.10
Galen's home page links.

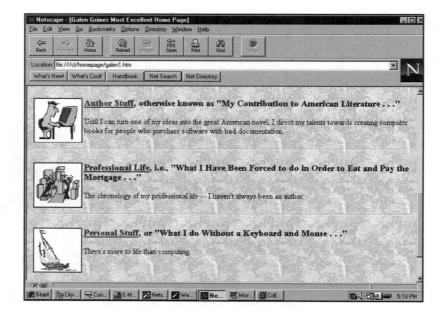

FIG. 1.11
Author Stuff page link from Galen's home page.

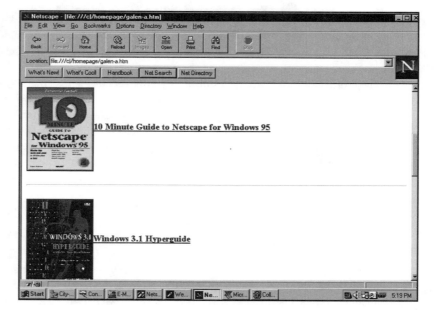

Scroll down this page and you will see additional links to more Web pages. These links, however, are to Web pages on the Web server operated by Macmillan Computer Publishing, the owner of Que, and this Web server is located in Indianapolis.

Selecting any of these links will send a request from your PC across the interconnected segments of the Internet to the Macmillan Web server in Indianapolis, requesting the file referenced in the URL in this link.

N O T E Netscape will let you see the URLs in links even before you select the link. Use your mouse and place the pointing finger Netscape cursor on the link without clicking your mouse. Look down at the status bar and you'll see the URL for that link. ▩

You should have a much better understanding now of how the hypertext metaphor applies to the Web and to Web pages. You can see that the World Wide Web resembles a spider's web with connections from any one point or Web page, branching outward to various other connection points, or other Web pages, which in turn can also contain connections to even more Web pages.

Other Internet Services Accessed Through the Web

In the past year or so, many Web browsers have exceeded their original purpose of simply displaying HTML pages. Many Web browsers are becoming all-purpose Internet tools that can also be used for accessing non-Web Internet services such as FTP, e-mail, newsgroups, and Gophers.

FTP

FTP, short for file transfer protocol, is an Internet protocol that allows you to upload or download text or binary files. FTP is most often used to download files from an archival storage site. In the past few years, numerous FTP sites have sprung up all over the Internet as repositories for shareware, freeware, and general PC utilities and various support files.

It has also become fairly common for computer hardware and software manufacturers to set up FTP sites for customer support. These FTP sites are stocked with software updates and hardware support drivers, which are free for customers to download.

FTP sites that are used for hardware and software support are usually advertised so users who need access to their contents can easily find the sites and the files they store. Unfortunately, many FTP sites do not fall in this category and largely remain unknown, except when passed from user to user, or when these sites are included in a list of FTP sites in books like this. Fortunately, there is another way to locate files on FTP sites. In 1990 Peter Deutsch, Alan Emtage, and Bill Heelan created a program they called Archie, which can be used to locate files stored (or archived, hence the name Archie) on FTP sites. A listing of Archie servers can be found at **http://pubweb.nexor.co.uk/public/archie/servers.html** (see fig. 1.12).

Until you become more familiar with using Archie servers, go to this Web site for a listing of FTP sites you might find helpful: **http://hoohoo.ncsa.uiuc.edu/ftp/** (see fig. 1.13).

For more information on FTP and how to use this protocol, especially in Web browsers, see chapter 6, "Accessing Other Internet Services with Netscape."

FIG. 1.12
NEXOR List of Archie
Servers.

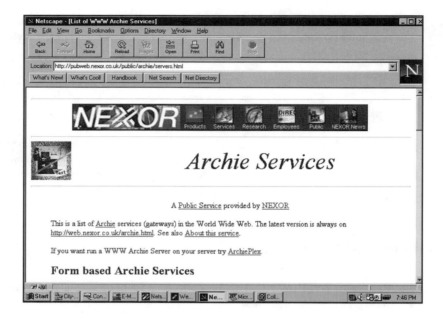

FIG. 1.13
The Monster FTP Sites
List.

E-mail and UseNet Newsgroups

E-mail, short for electronic mail, is a simple system designed to allow the sending and receiving of messages across a network. For most of its history on the Internet, e-mail has been used primarily by businesses and academicians, but in the past few years a large percentage of e-mail messages have been created and read by individuals.

E-mail access is another traditional non-Web service that Web browsers are starting to encroach on. E-mail was one of the earliest services available on the Internet, having been invented in 1972 by Ray Tomlinson to send messages across the early distributed networks. E-mail today, probably the widest used of all Internet services, is still used primarily for sending messages, but an increasing percentage of e-mail messages now include some sort of file attachment.

UseNet newsgroups are strikingly similar in operation to e-mail, since both involve sending messages that often have file attachments, and like e-mail, newsgroup functionality is also starting to turn up in Web browsers.

The first UseNet newsgroup was set up in 1979 by Tom Truscott and Steve Bellovin using UUCP (UNIX-to-UNIX Communication Protocol) between Duke University and the University of North Carolina.

E-mail and UseNet both suffered early on from the same problem—how to attach a non-text file to a text-based message. This chapter explains how the problems were solved in UseNet. (To understand how files are attached in e-mail, see chapter 7, "E-mail with Netscape.")

Gophers

Accessing Gopher servers is another non-Web function being taken over by Web browsers. Gopher servers, or simply Gophers, first appeared on the Internet in 1991, and were originally created and released by the University of Minnesota by Paul Lindner and Mark P. McCahill. (Gophers were named after the UM mascot, the Golden Gopher.)

Gophers are similar in operation to FTP sites in that they are established as repositories for files. Gopher files, however, are largely academic and informational text documents, and are meticulously arranged by subject under a hierarchical menu structure. Accessing a Gopher server to search for documents by subject is similar to using a Web search engine such as Lycos or WebCrawler. The only problem is that Gophers differ in the subjects they contain documents for. To solve this problem, developers at the University of Nevada in 1992 devised a Gopher database search program, which they dubbed Veronica. Veronica works to create its database of Gopher documents and menus like the robot search tools used in many Web search engines. It continuously scans Gopher servers to see what menus and documents are being stored.

If you want to see how Gophers and Veronica work, point your (Gopher-functioning) Web browser to **Gopher://veronica.scs.unr.edu/11/veronica**.

You can also get more information on Gophers in chapter 6, "Accessing Other Services with Netscape."

The Future of the Web

The Web, just like the Internet, is still growing, and more importantly, still evolving. As you might expect, numerous groups and organizations are developing new projects to assist in the evolution of the Web, most notably, the World Wide Web Consortium, or W3C for short, at CERN in Geneva, Switzerland. The W3C has posted on its Web server a list of some of the projects it currently has under development. If you want more information on these projects, go to **http://www.w3.org/hypertext/WWW/Bugs.html** to see the entire listing. The following sections are a sampling of some of the projects.

HTML Style Sheets

Most high-end word processors have some sort of style sheet capability, as do some HTML editors, but until recently there was no HTML standard for style sheets. The style sheet standard is so new that it has yet to be included in this version of Netscape or, indeed, in any major Web browser. You can find much information about style sheets at **http://www.w3.org/hypertext/WWW/Style/Welcome.html**.

SGML and the Web

SGML, Standard Generalized Markup Language, is another HTML discussion hot button at W3C. The focus of the discussion is on extending HTML to encompass more of the SGML standard language.

To get more information on this discussion and project:

> **http://www.w3.org/hypertext/WWW/MarkUp/SGML/**

Internationalization of Character Sets

This will likely be one of the hot areas to watch for future HTML and Web development. Everyone now agrees that the Web has a severe bias toward English and the western-European/Latin writing system. There are several factors that have contributed to this bias, primarily 7-bit ASCII.

N O T E ASCII is the American Standard Code for Information Interchange. The 7-bit ASCII code, which most computer manufacturers recognize, allows for the creation of only 128 characters and symbols, which does not include foreign or non-Latin-based characters. There are several 8-bit character sets that allow for 256 characters, but not an agreement on which one will be universally accepted. ▪

Currently the greatest concentrations of Internet computers and domains are in the U.S. and Western Europe (see fig. 1.14).

FIG. 1.14
Internet domain
concentrations
worldwide.

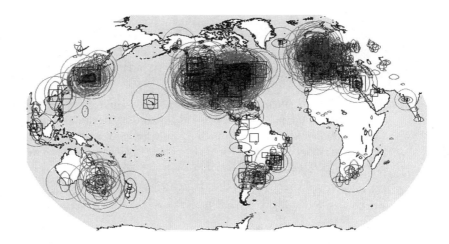

With the Internet spreading into more countries that do not use the ISO-8859 Latin-1 character set (an 8-bit character set), there is pressure to approve a 16-bit character set (which would permit a total of 65,536 characters) standard, which will provide character sets for Eastern Europe, Asia, and the Pacific rim.

For more on this discussion see **http://www.w3.org/hypertext/WWW/International/**.

Virtual Reality

This is a hot topic, not just at W3C, but all over the Web. Virtual reality is considered the next step for multimedia on the Web, and there are several proposals for how best to handle 3-D VR graphics. Much of the discussion extends to how best to implement VR on the Web—should it be through VRML, Virtual Reality Markup Language; should it be through PostScript extensions; or should a new VR platform be done "from the ground up." The discussion in W3C can be found at **http://www.w3.org/hypertext/WWW/Bugs/GraphicalComposition.html**.

(For more information on VRML and how VRML is implemented, see chapter 16, "Using VRML.")

Emerging Technologies

Several emerging technologies that could have an impact on the Web and the Internet in the next few years are just on the horizon—specifically ISDN and cable modems.

ISDN   ISDN, Integrated Services Digital Network, simply stated is digital telephone. ISDN's main advantage over the current analog telephone system is speed. With ISDN your connection to the Internet will be 4 1/2 times faster (128 Kbps) than the current top speed using analog telephone lines and 28.8 Kbps modems.

ISDN's main drawbacks now are availability and cost. As of November 1995, ISDN was available to only about 70 percent of available telephone service areas in the U.S., with the heaviest concentrations in the northeast. Also, many Internet service providers are not set up to provide ISDN connections to their subscribers but are scrambling to offer ISDN connection.

The other drawback is cost. Each of the Regional Bells in the U.S. has established a separate pricing scheme for ISDN service. Through Bell Atlantic, there is a one-time installation charge of only $169.00, but there is a monthly charge of $39.00, plus an online charge of $0.02 per minute per channel ($0.04 per minute if you're multiplexing the two 64 Kbps channels into one 128 Kbps channel). Other Bell service providers have dropped the online charge but charge upwards of $500–700 for installation.

The other cost for ISDN is in the equipment. Equipment prices are dropping as more companies begin offering ISDN equipment, but costs for an NT-1 terminal adapter are still in the $300–500 range.

Cable Modems   The other emerging technology, which many experts feel is still several years away, is what is being called cable modems. Cable modems are, in effect, 2-way digital communications lines tied in over the same line used for cable TV. With many cable TV operators upgrading their service line to fiber optic, the potential here is for communications connections to the Internet in the 1–10 Mbps range. Cost will be another factor driving this technology as well, both for the user and the provider. Early speculation for cable modems estimates prices in the $500–700 range. Also, cable operators will have to install fiber optic hubs and routers at an estimated cost of $2,000–5,000 for every 30–50 users.

Obviously there are problems associated with both of these technologies, but once these are solved and either (or both) of these technologies is more widespread, the Internet backbone could begin to face serious bandwidth constraints. Apparently, this concern is being addressed. In April 1995 the NFSNET backbone was phased out and replaced with a new "very high-speed Backbone Network Service" (vBNS). The vBNS is currently running at 155 Mbps. In 1996, it is scheduled to be upgraded to operate at 622 Mbps. While no mention is made of upgrading other segments of the Internet backbone in this country, this example clearly shows that bandwidth concerns remain a high priority.

Exploring the WWW with Netscape 3.0

Netscape has managed to remain the leader of the pack among Web browsers due in large part to the fact that Netscape has most often been the first Web browser to incorporate new features and new extensions to HTML.

Version 3.0 pushes the limits of a Web browser even further by incorporating new features both for end-users who will use Netscape primarily as a Web browser, and for HTML authors and developers who will be incorporating many of the proposed HTML 3.0 features into their Web sites.

The following gives a cursory overview of some of the new features you'll be seeing in Netscape 3.0.

LiveAudio

LiveAudio is a new plug-in (this plug-in is discussed in detail in chapter 13) that is included with Netscape. This plug-in allows you to hear music and voice audio directly within Web pages (see fig. 1.15). This plug-in plays the most popular audio file formats that you'll find on the Web and it's likely that it's the only audio player you'll need.

FIG. 1.15
You can see the controls for the audio player here embedded in this web page but you'll need speakers to hear the sounds.

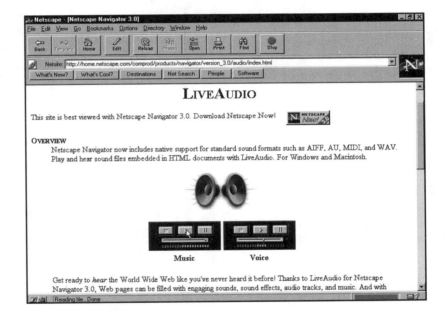

LiveVideo

LiveVideo is Netscape's built-in player for AVI movie files. AVI is Microsoft's popular Video for Windows movie file format. With LiveVideo you no longer need a separate player to see AVI videos embedded in Web pages, like the one shown in figure 1.16. However, there are many other popular file formats for video that you will still need plug-ins (see chapter 9) or helper applications (chapter 10) to use.

FIG. 1.16
Near the upper left side of this page is a video of a sculture in Italy. This AVI movie file is a part of the Web page it is in.

Live3D

VRML is supposed to be the interactive future of the Web. The Virtual Reality Markup Language (VRML) is used to make 3D "worlds" that you can travel through and interact with through your computer. Live3D is Netscape's built-in support for VRML. VRML can be used to create separate Web pages that are "worlds" or to embed VRML objects in a standard Web page as shown in Live3D in figure 1.17.

FIG. 1.17
These Netscape cubes are a simple collection of VRML objects that rotate in the left side of this web page.

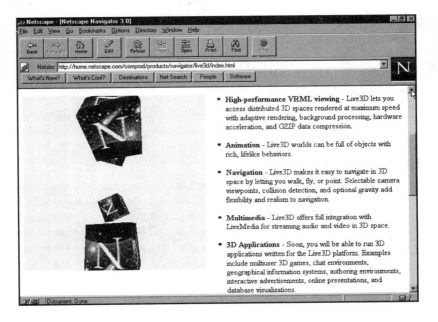

CoolTalk

If you've heard about people using the internet for chat or to make long-distance phone calls for free, CoolTalk is Netscape's way for you to do this and more. With CoolTalk you can "chat" via text-based messages along with a shared whiteboard where you and a friend can edit an image together over the internet. With the audio portion of CoolTalk, you and a friend (who will also need a computer using Netscape and CoolTalk) can talk over the Internet just like a telephone, except there are no charges beyond your Internet connection costs. CoolTalk is explored in detail in chapter 11.

Enhanced Security

With the new security features in Netscape, you can have your own "personal certificate" in Netscape. With personal certificates you can identify yourself from everybody else. This is particularly useful when you're submitting a form, so that the recipient will know for sure the information is from you, and nobody else. Personal certificates are described in detail in chapter 5.

Frame Navigation

Netscape introduced frames in version 2. Frames make it possible to divide Web pages into several sections on-screen called frames. While these made for some nice Web pages, many users soon found that navigating Web pages with frames had some hidden surprises. With version 3, Netscape has made it easier to navigate frames as you'll see in chapter 2.

Mail and News Improvements

Both the mail and news windows in Netscape can now be customized more than before so that you can view them in a way that suits the way you work.

Netscape Gold

The biggest improvement in Netscape Gold is its ability to create and edit tables. Tables can be very difficult to code with HTML manually so this is a welcome improvement.

Other Improvements

There are some other improvements that work primarily behind the scenes in Netscape. Java and JavaScript have been improved to work better together and with plug-ins. Caching has been improved to allow developers to include "pre-cached" web pages on CD-ROM to speed up access. There is support for some new HTML tags and network administrators have an administration kit to facilitate installing Netscape in a corporate setting with common setup preferences. ●

Moving Around the Web

Some people characterize the Web as confusing. They complain that it's not linear. It doesn't present you with a logical sequence of choices that you must make in order to move forward. You'll find through your own experience, however, that this is precisely why the Web is so intuitively easy. It's free-form, not linear. It more closely matches how people think: jumping from topic to topic as we see fit, as opposed to having order forced upon us.

Do you watch television, read the news, or listen to your technically adept friends talk about the Web? If so, you've probably encountered a variety of metaphors that people use to explain how the Web works. Here are two examples:

- The Web is like our national highway system. It connects countless destinations together in a web.

- The Web is similar to a spider's web. Nodes are joined together by tiny strands of silk.

The one concept that both of these metaphors have in common is that of joining, or linking, things together. This is, in fact, what the Web is all about, and represents one of the most important things you need to know about it. For example, you need to know that you can jump from one Web page to another by clicking a link. You also need to know some other ways to get to a Web page without using links.

In this chapter, you learn about all these things and much more, including:

- Understanding how links work and how they look
- Learning about what a link can do
- Getting around with and without links
- Making Netscape load Web pages faster
- Configuring the way Netscape works with links ■

Understanding Links

By now, you've noticed the references in the margins of this book. They serve a similar purpose as links do on a Web page—albeit a little low-tech. They refer you to other places in this book that might be useful or interesting to read. Without these references, you would have to resort to flipping through the pages looking for what you need.

Links on a Web page are even more vital. You have all the pages of this book right in front of you. At least you would know where to start looking. On the other hand, you have no idea where to find all the Web pages on the Internet. And there are too many to keep track of, anyway. Therefore, links are the only reasonable way to go from one Web page to another related Web page.

N O T E Hypertext and hypermedia are two terms you'll frequently hear associated with the Web. A hypertext document is a document that contains links to other documents—allowing you to jump between them by clicking the links. Hypermedia contains more than text, it contains multimedia such as pictures, videos, and sounds, too. In hypermedia documents, pictures are frequently used as links to other documents. ■

A link really has two different parts. First, there's the part that you see on the Web page—called an anchor. There's also the part that tells Netscape what to do if you click that link—called the URL reference. When you click a link's anchor, Netscape loads the Web page given by the link's corresponding URL reference. You'll learn about both parts of a link in the following sections. You'll also learn about the different resources to which a link can point.

Anchors

A link's anchor can be a word, a group of words, or a picture. Exactly how an anchor looks in Netscape depends largely on what type of anchor it is, and how the person who created the Web page used it. There are only two types of anchors though: text and graphical. You'll learn about both types in this section.

TIP When you move the mouse cursor over a link's anchor, it changes from a pointer to a hand.

Text Anchors   Most text anchors look somewhat the same. A text anchor is one or more words that Netscape underlines to indicate that it represents a link. Netscape also displays a text anchor using a different color than the rest of the text around it.

TIP Click and drag a link's text anchor onto your desktop. You can return quickly to that Web page by double-clicking the shortcut.

Figure 2.1 shows a Web page that contains three text anchors. In particular, notice how the text anchors on this Web page are embedded in the text. That is, they aren't set apart from the text, like the references in this book, but are actually an integral part of it. Clicking one of these links will load a Web page that is related to the link. You'll find many text anchors used this way.

FIG. 2.1
You'll find Vogon's Hitch-Hiker's Guide to the Galaxy Page at **http://www. metronet.com/ ~vogon/hhgttg.html**.

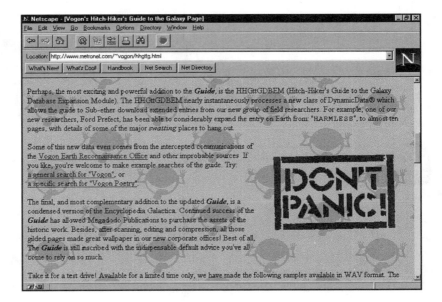

Figure 2.2 shows another Web page with a lot of text anchors. These anchors aren't embedded in the text, however. They are presented as a list or index of links from which you can choose. Web page authors frequently use this method to present collections of related links.

FIG. 2.2
Yahoo (**http://
www.yahoo.com**) is one
of the most popular
indexes on the Web. To
learn more about Yahoo,
see chapter 8, "Finding
Information on the Web."

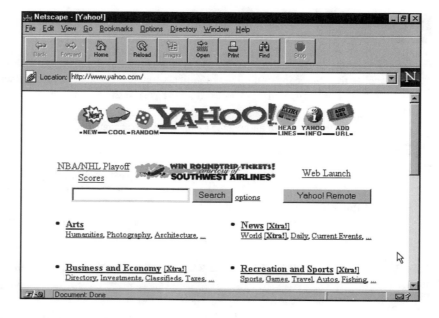

Graphical Anchors   A graphical anchor is similar to a text anchor. When you click a link's graphical anchor, Netscape loads the Web page that the link references. Graphical anchors aren't underlined or displayed in a different color. And no two graphical anchors need to look the same. It depends entirely on the picture that the Web page's author chose to use.

 Right-click a graphical anchor, and choose Save This Image As to save the image in a file on your computer.

Versatility is the strong suit of graphical anchors. Web page authors effectively use them for a variety of reasons. Here are some examples of the ways you'll find graphical anchors used on a Web page:

- Bullets. Graphical anchors are frequently used as list bullets. You can click the picture to go to the Web page described by that list item. Frequently, the text in the list item is also a link. You can click either the picture or the text.

- Icons. Many Web sites use graphical anchors in a similar manner to the way Windows 95 uses icons. They are common on home pages, and represent a variety of Web pages available through that site. Figure 2.3 shows a Web site that uses graphical anchors in this manner. Click the ProShop icon to open the ProShop Web page, for example.

- Advertisements. Many Web sites have sponsors that pay to advertise on the site. This keeps the Web site free to you and me, while the site continues to make money. You'll usually find advertisements, such as the one shown in figure 2.4, at the top of a Web page. Click the advertisement, and Netscape will load the sponsor's Web page.

FIG. 2.3
You'll find GolfWeb at **http://www. golfweb.com**. GolfWeb's home page uses graphical anchors to represent a variety of its pages you can load.

Graphical anchors used as icons

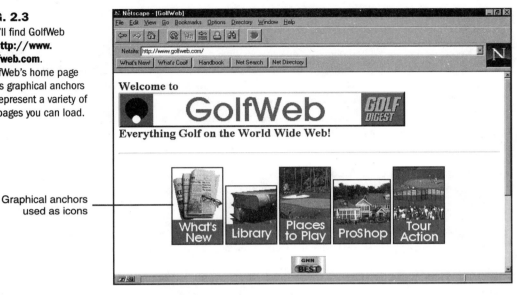

FIG. 2.4
Excite (**http:// www.excite.com**) is an up-and-coming Web search tool that uses sponsors to keep the service free to you and me.

Graphical anchor used as an advertisement

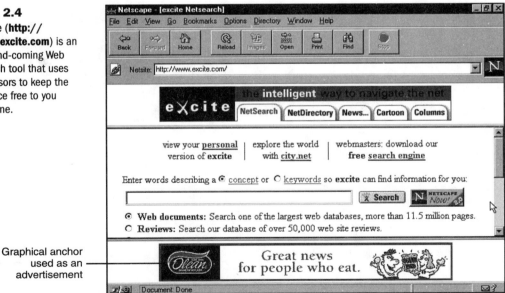

URL References

The other part of a link is the URL reference. This is the address of the Web page that Netscape will load if you click the link. Every type of link, whether it uses a text or graphical anchor, uses either a relative or absolute reference. You'll learn about each type in this section, but when you're "surfing" the Web it really doesn't matter which type of URL reference a link is using—as long as Netscape loads the Web page you want.

 TIP Choose View, Document Source to tell for sure if a link is using relative references.

An URL reference to a file on the same computer is also known as a relative reference. It means that the URL is relative to the computer and directory from which Netscape originally loaded the Web page. If Netscape loads a page at http://www.mysite.com/page, for example, then a relative reference to /picture would actually refer to the URL http://www.mysite.com/page/picture. Relative references are commonly used to refer to Web pages on the same computer. Figure 2.5 shows a Web page that contains relative references to other Web pages on that site.

FIG. 2.5
Netscape's Web site is at **http://www.netscape.com**. You can find various information about Netscape and its products.

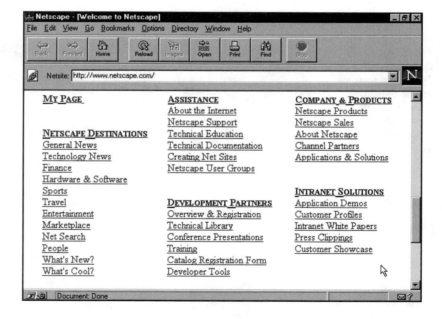

The primary reason Web authors use a relative reference is convenience. It's much simpler to just type the file name instead of the entire URL. It also makes it easier to move Web pages around on a server. Since the URL references are relative to the Web page's computer and directory, the author doesn't have to change all the links in the Web page every time the files move to a different location.

Corporate Bulletin Boards

Many corporations, such as Hewlett Packard, have created corporate bulletin boards that their associates view with Web browsers such as Netscape. These Web pages aren't on the Web, however. They're stored on the companies' internal network servers. They contain a variety of information that is useful to their associates such as the following:

- Meeting schedules and meeting room availability
- Announcements about corporate events
- Information about policies and benefits
- Recent press releases and financial statements
- Technological information

You can easily create a bulletin board for the corporation you work for, too. Part IV, "Building World Class Home Pages for Netscape," shows you how to build pages for the Web. The only difference between that and building a corporate bulletin board is in the type of information you choose to include on the page.

Absolute References An URL reference that specifies the exact computer, directory, and file for a Web page is an absolute reference. Whereas relative references are common for links to Web pages on the same computer, absolute references are necessary for links to Web pages on other computers.

TIP

Hold your mouse over a link and look at Netscape's status line to see its URL reference.

N O T E You'll learn about HTML (Hypertext Markup Language) in chapter 26, "HTML Primer." If you're curious about what a link with an absolute reference looks like in HTML, however, here's an example:

<A HREF="**http://www.yahoo.com/**">Yahoo</A>

The first part of this link, the bit between the left (<) and right (>) brackets, is the URL reference. The word yahoo is the text anchor that Netscape underlines on the Web page. The last part ends the link.

Resources to Which Links Can Point

Links can point to more than just Web pages. They can point to a variety of files and other Internet resources, too. A link can point to a video, pictures, or even a plain text file. It can also point to an FTP server, Gopher server, or a UseNet newsgroup. Table 2.1 describes the other types of things a link can point to, and shows you what the URL looks like.

Table 2.1   Resources to Which a Link Can Point

Type	Sample URL
Web Page	http://www.mysite.com/page.html
Files	file://C:/picture.bmp
Multimedia	http://www.mysite.com/video.avi
E-mail	mailto:info@netscape.com
FTP	ftp://ftp.mysite.com
Gopher	gopher://gopher.mysite.com
Newsgroup	news:alt.fan.que
Telnet	telnet://mysite.com

How to Move Around the Web

You didn't buy this book to learn how to load a Web page in Netscape, then sit back and look at it all day. You want to "surf" the Web—jumping from Web page to Web page, looking for entertaining and useful information.

In fact, surfing is such an important part of the Web that both Netscape and the Web itself provide many different ways to navigate. You can use the links and imagemaps that you find on a Web page, for example. You can go directly to a Web page if you know its URL. You can also use some of the more advanced Netscape features such as bookmarks and frames. In this section, you'll learn how to use those features to move around the Web like a pro.

Clicking a Link

You learned about links earlier in this chapter. They are the primary method you use to go from the Web page you're viewing to another related Web page. All these links are provided by the Web page's author, and are usually accurately related to the context in which you found it (see fig. 2.6).

Client Pull On The Web

You'll eventually run across a Web page that says something like "We've moved" or "This Web page has a new location." It'll display a link that loads the Web page at its new location if you click it. If you wait long enough, however, Netscape may automatically load the Web page at its new location.

Client pull is the technology behind this behavior. Client pull allows the Web server to tell Netscape to reload the current Web page or load a different Web page after a set amount of time. One of the most common uses for client pull is the situation described previously. It's also used for simple sequences of Web pages, however, that work just like slide shows.

FIG. 2.6
This Web page (**http://www.netscape.com/comprod/index.html**) has a complete list of Netscape products and services at the bottom.

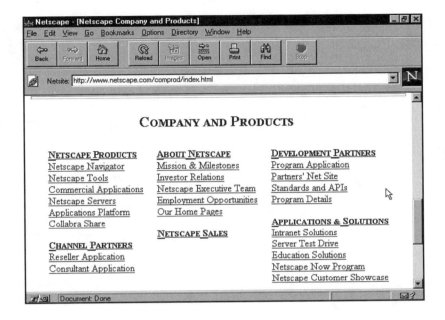

Clicking an Imagemap

Imagemaps are similar to graphical anchors, in that if you click an imagemap, Netscape will load another Web page. Imagemaps can load more than one Web page, however, depending on what part of the image you click. The image itself usually indicates the areas you can click to load a particular Web page.

Figure 2.7, for example, shows the imagemap that Microsoft uses at its Web site. Each region of the imagemap is clearly defined so that you know where you need to click, and you know what Web page Netscape will load as a result.

 If you're having trouble deciphering a button bar, look for text links just below it.

A common use for imagemaps on the Web is button bars. Button bars are similar to the toolbars you've used in Windows 95 and other windowing environments. They don't appear to toggle in and out like buttons, however. They are, after all, just imagemaps. You'll find them at the top or, more frequently, the bottom of a Web page. Figure 2.8 shows a button bar from Netscape's Web site. Just like any other imagemap, each area you can click is clearly defined. You can click different areas to load different Web pages. You can click the Netscape Search button to search Netscape's Web site, or you can click the Table of Contents button to get a roadmap of Netscape's site.

FIG. 2.7
Microsoft's Web site
is at **http://www.
microsoft.com**.

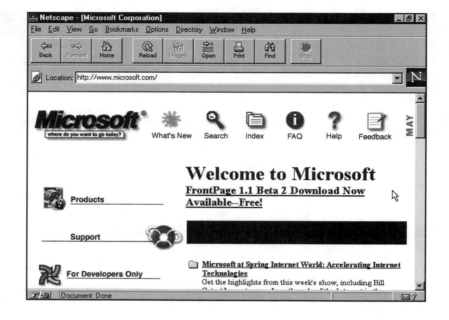

FIG. 2.8
You'll find this button
bar at the bottom of all
Netscape Web pages.

Search clickable area

Going Directly to a Resource

Which came first, the link or the Web page? If the only way to load a Web page was by clicking a link, you'd never get anywhere. If a friend gives you an URL, for example, you need a way to tell Netscape to open that Web page without having to use a link. That's why Netscape lets you go directly to a Web page by specifying its URL in either the location bar or Open Location dialog box.

TIP URLs are case sensitive. If you can't open a Web page, check for strangely capitalized letters such as **http://www.MywEbsiTe.com**.

Figure 2.9 shows the Netscape location bar with the drop-down list open. Type the URL of a Web page in Netscape's location bar, and Netscape will load the Web page. Netscape keeps the addresses of all the Web pages you've opened this way in the location bar's drop-down list. It keeps this list from session to session, too. That way you can always go back to a previous site by dropping down the list, and clicking the Web page's URL.

N O T E You don't have to type the http:// part of an URL for a Web address in the location bar, because Netscape will add this for you. ∎

FIG. 2.9
The drop-down list keeps track of only those Web pages you've opened using the location bar.

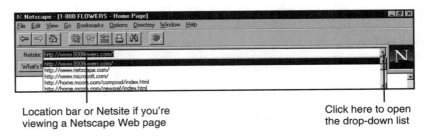

Location bar or Netsite if you're viewing a Netscape Web page

Click here to open the drop-down list

The Open button requires a few more mouse clicks, but it's just as easy to use. Click the Open button on the Netscape toolbar. Type the URL of a Web page in the Open Location dialog box, and click Open. Netscape loads the Web page that you specified.

Moving Forward and Backward

After you've clicked a few links and opened a few Web pages, you may want to go back to a Web page you looked at earlier. Maybe you forgot something you just read, or something didn't seem that interesting then, but it does now. Netscape provides two useful features to look at previously viewed Web pages: the history list and the Back/Forward buttons on the toolbar.

 In the History window, select a Web site from the list, and click Create Bookmark to add it to your bookmarks.

■ The history list keeps track of all the Web pages that you've visited during the current session. You can access the history list in one of two places: the Go menu, shown in figure 2.10, shows the last 15 Web pages that you've loaded in Netscape. Choose Go from the Netscape main menu, and then choose any of the Web pages on the menu. If you want to see a list of all the Web pages that you've visited during the current session, choose Window, History from the Netscape main menu. Figure 2.11 shows the History window. You can scroll up and down the list, and double-click a Web page to open it in Netscape.

■ The Forward and Back buttons move you up and down the history list shown in figure 2.11. If you click the Back button, Netscape moves the highlight down the list and opens that Web page. If you click the Forward button, Netscape moves the highlight up the list, and opens that Web page. Once you've reached the bottom of the list, the Back button is disabled. Likewise, when you reach the top of the list, the Forward button is disabled.

Going to Your Home Page

If you start feeling a bit lost, it's sometimes easier to get your bearings by going back to your home page. Netscape lets you configure a home page that it uses for two purposes:

■ Netscape loads your home page every time Netscape starts. It usually loads it from the cache so that you don't have to wait for Netscape to transfer it from the Internet.

■ At any time, you can click the Home button on the Netscape toolbar to return to your home page.

FIG. 2.10
The checkmark in this menu indicates the current Web page.

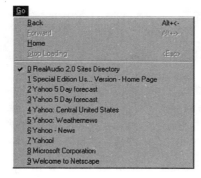

FIG. 2.11
The highlight in this list indicates the current Web page.

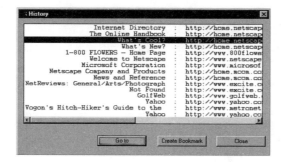

 TIP Configure your home page to point to your favorite Web index such as www.excite.com. Then it'll be only one click away.

Here's how to change your home page in Netscape:

1. Choose Options, General Preferences from the Netscape main menu.
2. Click the Appearance tab, and Netscape displays the dialog box shown in figure 2.12.

FIG. 2.12
See the section "Changing the Way Netscape Works with Links" later in this chapter to learn more about this dialog box.

Type your home page URL here

3. Select <u>H</u>ome Page Location, and type the URL of your home page as shown in figure 2.12.

4. Click OK to save your changes.

N O T E　The term home page has two different meanings these days. First, a home page is usually a personal Web page where you would store links to your favorite Web pages, and maybe express yourself a bit. Second, many people refer to the opening page of a Web site as that site's home page. Hewlett Packard's home page contains links for computers and peripherals, for example. ■

Saving Bookmarks to Web Pages

The easiest way to get back to a Web page that you visit frequently is to use Netscape bookmarks. Bookmarks let you save and organize links to your favorite Web pages. Unlike Netscape's history list, the bookmarks hang around from session to session. They are always easily accessible. Choose Bookmarks from the Netscape main menu. Figure 2.13 shows you what the <u>B</u>ookmarks menu looks like.

FIG. 2.13

Open a submenu or click a Web site to load it in Netscape.

Navigating a Web Site with Frames

Frames are a feature that is currently specific to Netscape. They allow the Netscape window to be split into multiple sections. Each frame on the window can point to a different URL. Figure 2.14 shows a Web page that uses a frame to present a button bar that's always available to you.

With the addition of frames, Netscape added an extra bit of complexity in navigation. Each frame was treated independent of each other, which meant that you couldn't easily go to a previous frame. With Netscape 2.0, you had to put your mouse cursor in a particular frame, click the right mouse button, then select Back in Frame. If you had pressed the Back button, it would've loaded the previous complete page. Netscape Atlas greatly simplifies navigation with frames by making the Back button smarter. Now, when you press it, you automatically go back to the most recently modified frame.

N O T E　You'll run across many Web sites that say "Netscape Enhanced," "Best Viewed with Netscape," or something similar. They mean it. Many Web sites implement Netscape specific features that can't be viewed with other Web browsers. Frames are a typical example. ■

Many Windows 95 programs divide their windows into panes. They do it to make the organization of the windows' contents more obvious. A program that makes the résumés of a list of people available might have two panes: one to display a list of people and another to display the résumé of the currently selected person. Netscape frames can serve a similar purpose as well.

Figure 2.15 shows a Web page that does the same thing as the résumé program. It has three frames: one that shows a list of people, another for the résumé of the currently selected individual, and a pane at the bottom to select a category.

FIG. 2.14

At this site, the button bar will always be available in the left frame, regardless of which Web page the right frame is displaying.

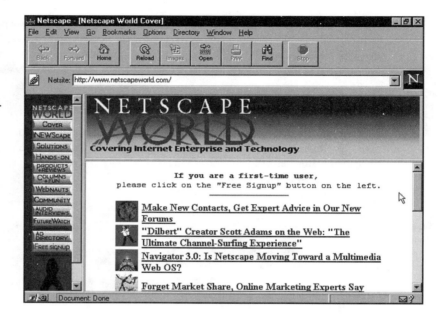

FIG. 2.15

Frames make a Web site easier to use by organizing its contents in a logical fashion.

Résumé of selected person ────

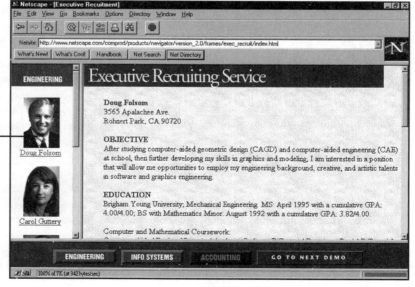

Watching Netscape's Status

Netscape gives you a lot of feedback about what's happening after you click a link or open an URL. Stars shoot past the Netscape logo while Netscape is transferring a Web page or file, for example. It also updates the status bar with information that'll help you keep track of what Netscape is doing. Here are some of the messages you'll see in the status bar:

Message	Description
http://server/file	The URL reference of the link to which you are currently pointing.
X% of YK	Netscape has completed X percent of a Y kilobyte transfer.
Contacting hostserver:	Netscape is trying to contact the given server.
Connect:	Netscape has contacted the server and is waiting for reply.
Document: Done.	The Web page is finished loading.

Getting Around Faster

If you're using a 14.4Kbps or slower modem, you'll eventually become frustrated with how long it takes to load some Web pages. Many Web pages have very large graphics that take a long time to download. Unfortunately, the use of large graphics is becoming more common as Web authors take it for granted that everyone on the Internet is using at least a 28.8Kbps modem.

 TIP Many Web sites provide links to text-only versions. Look for a text link that says "Text Only."

Fight back. Netscape provides a few features that make Web pages containing too many graphics more tolerable:

- You don't have to wait for the entire Web page to finish loading before you can click a link. Click the Stop button, and Netscape will stop transferring the Web page. If you change your mind and want to reload the page, click the Reload button. Also, most of the text links are available before Netscape has finished transferring the images for the Web page. You can click any of these links. Netscape will stop loading the current page, and start loading the Web page referenced by the link.

- Most of your time is spent waiting for inline images to load. The irony is that the images on many Web pages aren't really worth the time if you have a slow connection. If you don't want Netscape to automatically load inline images, make sure that Options, Auto Load Images is not checked. If you want to view the images on a particular Web page, and you've disabled Auto Load Images, click the Load Images button on the Netscape toolbar. Figure 2.16 shows what a Web page looks like when it's loaded without inline images. Notice that Netscape displays placeholders where it normally displays the images. Netscape also displays alternative text to help you figure out what the link points to.

FIG. 2.16

You can click one of the placeholders to load the Web page it refers to, or you can click the Load Images button to see the inline images.

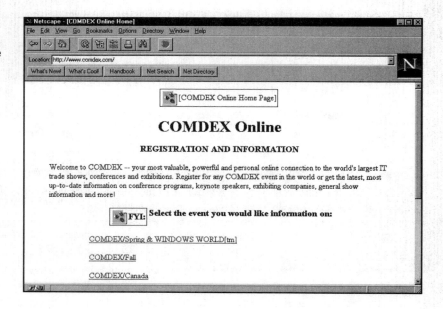

Changing the Way Netscape Works with Links

Netscape gives you a bit of control over how it displays links. It lets you choose whether or not they're underlined and what color it uses to display them.

Underlining Links

You learned earlier in this chapter that Netscape underlines a link's text anchor on a Web page. You can change that. Here's how to configure Netscape so that it doesn't underline a link's text anchor:

1. Choose Options, General from the Netscape main menu.
2. Click the Appearance tab, and Netscape displays the dialog box shown in figure 2.17.
3. Deselect Underlined, and click OK.

Beginning with the next Web page that Netscape loads, text anchors won't be underlined. You can still figure out where the links are, however, because they are displayed in a different color than the text around them.

Using a Different Color for Links

If you don't like the colors that Netscape uses for links, you can change them. If the default colors are hard to tell apart on your computer, for example, you'll want to change the colors so you can easily see the links. Use the following steps to change the colors Netscape uses for a text link's anchor:

FIG. 2.17
The Appearance box allows you to change the toolbar, start up options, and link styles.

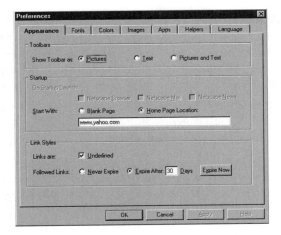

Part

I

Ch

2

FIG. 2.18
Most of Netscape's options can be configured on one of this dialog box's tabs.

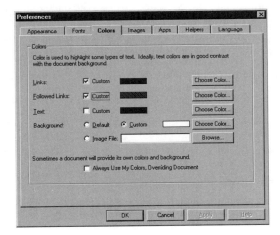

1. Choose Options, General from the Netscape main menu.
2. Click the Colors tab, and Netscape displays the dialog box shown in figure 2.18.
3. Select Links, and click the corresponding Choose Color button. Choose a color from the Color dialog box, and click OK.
4. Select Followed Links, and click the corresponding Choose Color button. Choose a color from the Color dialog box, and click OK.
5. Click OK to save your changes.

Beginning with the next Web page that Netscape loads, Netscape will display text anchors that you've never visited using the color you chose in Links, and text anchors that you've already visited using the color you chose in Followed Links.

Controlling Link Expiration

Netscape caches Web pages so they'll load faster the next time you visit that Web page. It takes much longer to load a Web page from the Internet than it takes to load it from the hard drive. So, Netscape stores every Web page it loads to your hard drive. The next time you point Netscape to that URL, it loads it from the hard drive instead of the Internet.

The problem is that if Netscape is loading Web pages from your hard drive instead of the Internet, you may be looking at a Web page that's out of date. Even if the Web page's author changes it, you'll still be looking at the older version.

Netscape lets you configure how long it will continue to get a Web page from the cache before it loads it from the Internet again. This is called the expiration. By default, Netscape expires a link after 30 days. If you find that the Web pages you use are updated more frequently, you can easily change it. Here's how:

1. Choose Options, General Preferences from the Netscape main menu.
2. Click the Appearance tab, and Netscape displays the dialog box shown earlier in figure 2.17.
3. Type the number of days you want Netscape to wait before expiring each link in Days. Alternatively, you can expire all of the links in the cache by clicking Expire Now.
4. Click OK to save your changes. ●

Mastering Netscape

## CHAPTER 3

Finding Information on the Web

You've probably heard some of the staggering numbers associated with the rise of the Internet and the World Wide Web: 40 million global users increasing by millions each month, millions of Web pages containing countless documents—hundreds of new servers popping up almost daily. Just realizing that the enormous resources of sites like the Library of Congress are only one small part of all this vastness does a lot to explain the phrase "information age."

How do you navigate such a universe? As a diligent infonaut perched at your computer—modem screaming, hard drive whining—you may begin to feel like a small spaceship drifting from one planet's gravitational pull to the next, with only the occasional burst from a new Web page's thrusters to point you in a new direction.

What we need is a map. All of this clicking around on links is great; but when you really need to find something (for instance, because your boss wants you to), surfing is about the last thing you want to do. But what if the Web had a table of contents—and some really strong search engines? Well, it does—sort of. And, Netscape makes the best of these engines easily accessible from the directory buttons on the browser window.

In this chapter, you learn how to:

- Use Netscape's home page
- Specify your own home page
- Use the What's Cool and What's New buttons
- Perform category searches with Yahoo and other subject-search tools
- Find information using the most powerful Internet search engines ■

The Home Page

The home page, as you've likely discovered, is simply the first Web page that you see when you launch Netscape Navigator. By default this is Netscape Communications Corporation's Web site, but you have the option of changing your home page to just about any Web page on the Internet you want, as well as to a local (on your computer) HTML file.

 When upgrading from Netscape version 1.x or 2.x to 3.0, install Netscape in the same directory as the previous version (the Windows 95 default is c:\Program Files\ Netscape\Navigator). This will retain your current home page settings, as well as your bookmarks file and any shortcuts you have in your Start menu or on your desktop. If you've not yet installed Netscape or you install to a different directory, Netscape automatically sets your home page to its Web site. For more information on downloading and installing Netscape, see the appendixes.

You'll also see the term "home page" used in a general sense to describe the main, or first, Web page of other people's and organizations' Web sites on the Internet. In my opinion, this is really the wrong way to use the term but it's fairly well entrenched, so there's not much chance of changing it. If a page is the first page of a particular site, it's more correct to call it the index page or default page for that site. As far as Netscape (the application) is concerned, your home page is the first page that loads when you start your browser.

Selection of a home page is personal, and it depends on how you use the Web. Whether your interests are business, pleasure, or both, you'll have little problem finding a Web page out there that will suit your needs as you begin each browsing session. There are, however, some important things to know about the home page:

- You may return to your designated home page at any time by clicking the Home Page button.
- Netscape's own home page (**http://home.netscape.com**) is a great place to begin, especially if you're new to the Web.
- Netscape doesn't load the home page from cache on start-up (though it does cache after loading), so expect lag-time if you set your home page to a heavily accessed server or URL that has specific time constraints.
- If you copy the source file for a Web page from another site and use it as your home page (loading it off your hard drive), you won't see any changes or updates from the original Web site.

- You may set your bookmarks file as the home page; however, your history file will not work as a home page.

- You may set your home page to bring up any number of files, including Windows 95 applications, helper programs, plug-ins, and Java applets.

Let's look at this in a bit more detail.

The Home Page Button

Clicking the Home Page button once takes you to your home page at any time during a browsing session. Alternatively, you may also select Go, Home from the drop-down menu bar.

You can think of the Home Page button as a mini-bookmark that contains only one hyperlink—a very important link with which you begin your Web session. Loading that page from the Home Page button is a bit different, though, than loading it at the start of a session, because of the way Netscape stores the home page in its cache.

Regardless of how you have your cache configured, the first time you load in your home page it does not use the files on your hard drive's cache. Netscape always travels to that first URL, updates the Web page, and then caches its contents in memory. This is especially important if you decide to change your home page to a site other than Netscape Corp.'s pages. Since Netscape must download all the files from your home page without the speed and support of the cache, connecting to a heavily used site or a Web page with a slow server can be frustrating.

N O T E How Netscape uses its cache memory is a fully configurable option. See chapter 3 for more information on how to set up your cache.

Fortunately, the Home Page button—unless you've designated otherwise—acts as a regular URL, and uses the files from your cache.

The Home Page button is a little deceptive—it's a bit more powerful than it lets on. Though you can't move it, assign a macro to it, or change its appearance, you can use it to launch a number of Windows 95 files, as well as files that use a helper application, plug-ins, or Java applets. We'll see more about that in a moment. For now, let's take a close look at some of the benefits to using Netscape's own (default) home page.

Using Netscape's Home Page

As a veteran of the World Wide Web, Netscape has had the time and resources to put together an informative, flexible, and useful Web site (**http://home.netscape.com**), shown in figure 3.1.

Netscape's home page offers a variety of resources and features a clickable imagemap with the following six options:

Part

II

Ch

3

■ Exploring the Net duplicates the same options that are reachable from the Netscape Directory buttons, namely, What's New, What's Cool, Handbook, Net Directory, and Net Search.

■ Company Products divides itself into links about Netscape Products, Development Partners, About Netscape, Netscape Sales, Channel Partners, and Business Solutions.

■ Netscape Store keeps you informed about Netscape software and publications with four links to Software, Publications, Support, and Bazaar, which allows you to buy t-shirts and boxer shorts sporting the Netscape Mozilla logo.

■ Assistance points to sources that teach you more about the Internet.

■ Community includes links to user groups and White Pages directories.

■ News & Reference gives you access to a variety of news and information links, including Internet Headlines, Netscape Press Releases, Standards Docs, and Reference Material. A lot of technical information is available here.

FIG. 3.1

Netscape's opening page is now even easier to return to or reload, thanks to client-side imagemaps.

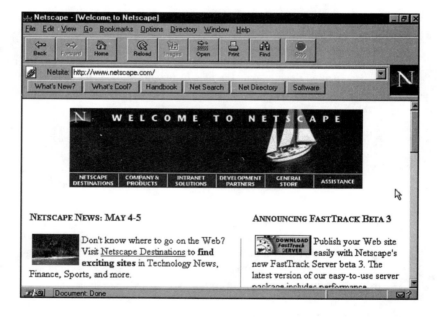

NOTE Reloading Netscape's home page is faster than ever, since the main imagemap that contains the most important links is now stored in your cache. For more details on client-side imagemaps, see chapter 23, "Using Imagemaps." ■

One of the most important links on this page is to the latest version of Netscape Navigator. You'll find it at the bottom of the Company & Products page under Netscape Products. You'll want to check this from time to time as Netscape updates the speed, reliability, and functions of its browser. Be aware, though, that the process of obtaining the latest version will take you through several pages of links to get to the download. You may be able to circumvent this to some extent by going directly to Netscape's FTP site. Do this by typing **ftp.netscape.com** in the address box, or use File, Open Location on the menu bar. Netscape's FTP server is often overloaded, but don't worry; if you get an error message you'll also get a list of dozens of mirror sites—FTP sites that contain the same files as Netscape's—that you can immediately access.

The Netscape Directory Buttons

Built into Netscape's interface are links to certain pages on its Web site that can be of particular use to almost any Netscape user. Netscape, by default, displays these five buttons near the top of the browser. If you don't see these buttons, go to the Options menu and make sure that the Show Directory Buttons option is checked. Save your selection by clicking Options, Save Options.

Later in this chapter we look at the Net Directory and Net Search options for our discussion of search engines and techniques; right now let's look at the other three buttons.

What's Cool   The What's Cool button brings you to a collection of favorite Web pages, compiled and updated by Netscape. This is a good starting point for finding interesting Web sites. Figure 3.2 shows you what to expect.

FIG. 3.2
The Netscape Cool team is on the job, so there's some great surfing here!

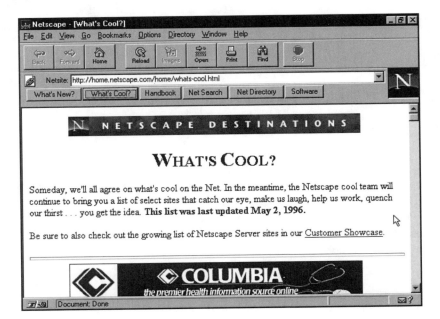

Also, check out the growing list of Netscape Server sites from the Galleria link; sites that use Netscape's Server software have native security features built-in for special use with Netscape Navigator.

Be on the lookout for other cool-sites listings as you travel the Internet—many other Web sites compile, post, and update their favorite Web pages. You'll find a number of sites that also follow Netscape's practice of requesting you to submit your own cool links for inclusion in their pages. If you have some really cool Web sites you'd like to see in Netscape's What's Cool, submit them via Netscape's online form.

What's New!   The What's New! button takes you to an assortment of new Internet resources, archived monthly. This is an excellent place for introducing you to new Web sites; it will give you a good feel for just how fast the surface of the Web is spinning. Just as with the What's Cool pages, Netscape is interested in any new Web sites you want to tell them about. Of course this area is updated quite often, so your version of figure 3.3 will most certainly be a bit different.

FIG. 3.3
Netscape lists a "What's New" section of links to its own site.

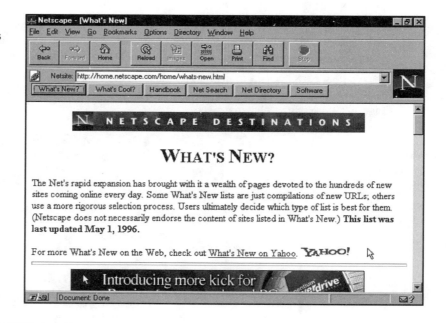

 Want some other examples of What's New sites? To keep up with the latest software on the Net, point your browser to Stroud's WSApps List, at **http://www.cwsapps.com**, and Tucows, at **http://www.tucows.com/**. Both of these sites are meticulously maintained and updated daily, include reviews of the newest and best programs, and have direct links to FTP sites to download the freeware and shareware.

Using the Netscape Handbook   You may already have noticed that the Netscape browser really doesn't have much in the way of an online help file. That's because most of the documentation for the program is actually provided in Web format on Netscape Corp.'s Web site. The Netscape Handbook button takes you to all the information Netscape provides about the most current version of Navigator. In addition to the basics of using the Netscape browser, some elementary concepts of the Internet are explained (see fig. 3.5).

Perhaps among the most important links available from the Handbook button are links to the Release Notes for the current version of Navigator. It's on these pages that you can see what advances (and what problems, if any) have been introduced with the latest version of the program.

Software

Netscape Atlas also sports a new addition to the directory toolbar. The Software button is linked to Netscape's Web page on software products, and upgrades (see fig. 3.4). From here, you can purchase Netscape Navigator directly from Netscape, or download the latest version. This makes it easier for you to keep up-to-date with the latest software happenings of Netscape.

Part

II

Ch

3

FIG. 3.4

The new Software button takes you to Netscape's page that lets you purchase Netscape, or get the latest version.

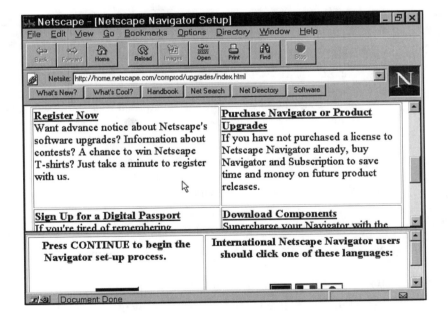

FIG. 3.5
Netscape's own list of
some of the latest sites
to appear on the Web.

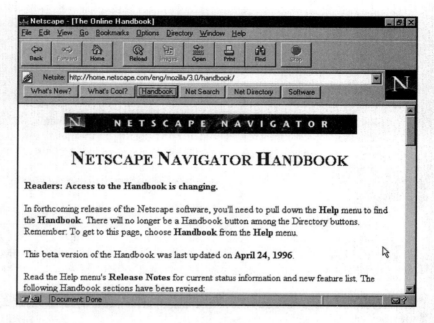

Using Another Home Page

As comprehensive as Netscape's home page is, you'll probably, at some point, find another you like better. You may discover that you change your home page as your needs change. For example, if you're heavily into e-mail, you may want your home page to be set to Netscape's e-mail window. If you become interested in a particular newsgroup, you may find yourself specifying the Newsgroups window as your starting point.

In fact, you can set your home page to load any valid, accessible URL on the Internet. And it's as easy as a few clicks. Just remember to watch out for slow servers or heavy Web sites—otherwise you'll become more intimate with the Stop button than you probably want to be.

To change your home page settings, select Options, General Preferences and then the Appearances tab (it's the default tab). The dialog box shown in figure 3.6 pops up.

Midway down you'll see the Start With text box. Enter the new URL there. You don't have to enter the protocol tag for most URLs, though some will require it. For example, if I'm setting my home page to Que's Web site, I type in

http://www.mcp.com/que or just www.mcp.com/que

Notice that there is no Browse button that allows you access to your history file, bookmarks file, or address box. You'll also find that Netscape doesn't allow you to paste a copied URL into this text box. This is an annoying setup that Netscape should eventually fix in later releases. For now—unless you have a photographic memory—you have to resort to pen and paper to write down the URL, and then type it directly into the box.

FIG. 3.6
Enter your new home page in the Start With text box.

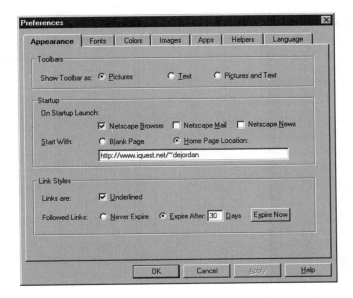

Part
II

Ch
3

Notice the two radio buttons above the box. The first one, labeled Blank Page, should be checked if you don't want a start-up page to begin your Web sessions. Why do this? It keeps Netscape from loading anything when it starts up. Perhaps you have different URLs you like to load first, depending on the work at hand. Sometimes, for instance, I know I want to go straight to the WebCrawler Web site to search for something. Other times I might want to set off for Netscape's home pages or some other site I often call home.

The second radio button is the one you'll need to check if you're specifying a home page other than Netscape's site.

Above the radio buttons are three checkboxes where you can specify whether you want to start up with your home page, with Netscape's built-in e-mail, or with the Newsgroups browser.

Using a Local File as Your Home Page

There are some distinct advantages to using a local HTML file on your hard drive as your home page. A local file will load fast, and will always load (barring a badly fragmented hard drive or other local system problem). Again, a heavily accessed site sometimes means it takes quite a while for a remote home page to load. And, even if you specify a URL on the Web that's not heavily accessed, it's always possible that the site's server is down.

Perhaps the most important advantage to a local home page, however, is the control it gives you over the content of your start page. Write your own home page, and you can include exactly what you need and want—your own favorite links and graphics.

Finding the Internet—On Your Own Computer

When we talk about a local file, we're talking about a client-side file. If your computer is capable of only connecting to other computers, but cannot be accessed by any other machines, it is a client. If your computer can be accessed by other machines via the Internet or any network, it is referred to as a server.

Part of the evolution of the Web is its move toward an environment where its computers can be both clients and servers. As technologies like ISDN, wireless systems, coaxial cable, and optical fiber evolve—as bandwidth increases—a stronger server base emerges. Still, applications run much faster on your own system than if the bytes are moving through a data link. And, however quickly they grow, the faster access speeds will never be faster than your computer's processor.

The need for a large client-based cache that's only updated at user-specified intervals makes a lot of sense, then, while larger storage devices allow you, as a server, to make more interactive, snazzier content available to everyone else out there. This is especially feasible now, when storage devices (hard drives and CD-ROMs) sell for a tiny fraction of what they did a decade ago. For both clients and servers, the ready availability of electronic storage results in less reliance on the bandwidth of the connection.

What does this mean? It means that in the future in order to support new ways of finding and using the information and resources on the Internet, you'll store more and more HTML (Web) pages, graphics, videos, audio, applets, and so on, on your own computer. As directories and indexes evolve, and as search engines and the like become more intelligent, interactive, and flexible, you'll need more and more of your own client computing power and storage to make your search for information as painless and fun as possible.

Of course, in order to specify a local file for your home page, you've got to have a file. One option is to create your own HTML page and use it as your home page.

N O T E   Controlling just how you want to display your home page is an exciting idea—and a lot easier to do than you may realize. Part IV of this book shows you how to design and create your own world-class home pages. ■

Another option is to save the source code to any one of the millions and millions of URLs your browser can access. If you spend even a few minutes a day on the Web—and many of you spend far more time than that—you'll have already lost count of the number of Web pages you've visited. Just point your browser to the Web page you want to save, and:

1. With the page you want saved displayed in Netscape, open the File menu and choose Save As. The Save As directory box appears (see fig. 3.7).

FIG. 3.7
Save the downloaded
file using the Save As
option in the File menu.

2. Select the directory or subdirectory where the file will reside using the Save in: drop-down menu.

3. Enter a name for the file.

4. Select the file type in the Save as type drop-down menu. In this case, you want source (*.htm, *.html) option.

5. Click the Save button and the file will be downloaded to the location you specified.

To verify that the page was downloaded successfully, go ahead and load it into Netscape Navigator. From File, Open File, click the Browse button and find the folder you saved it in, highlight the file and double-click it or click Open. Look first in the address box after the file is loaded. Netscape, by default, displays your local file structure with UNIX specifiers:

file:///c|directory/subdirectory/filename.htm

where c represents the name of the drive the file is located on.

You'll notice, too, that your Web page has changed; the background and any inline graphics are now replaced by Netscape's little broken picture icons. We'll talk about this later in this chapter in the section "Starting Other Files with Your Home Page."

Specifying a Local File as Your Home Page   To change your home page to a local file, select Options, General Preferences, and the Appearances tab. Place your cursor inside the text box. Type the letter of the drive where the file is located, followed by a colon, backslash, the appropriate directories or subdirectories, and the file name. The file can be from any drive and any directory on your system.

For example, if I'm setting my home page to a file in the windows directory on my hard drive C, all I need to enter is:

c:\windows\myhome.htm

Ensure that the .htm extension is used (see fig. 3.8).

Not surprisingly, you may also enter the older UNIX version of the file name, which is a protocol handler file:/// followed by the letter of the hard drive, a vertical line or "pipe" (Shift+backslash key on a 101 or 102 standard keyboard), and forward slashes. The previous example would mutate into this:

Part

II

Ch

3

file:///c|windows/myhome.htm

You can use either the DOS parameters or the UNIX specifiers; however, you may not mix the two styles.

FIG. 3.8
Setting up a local file for your home page is no more difficult than setting up a URL.

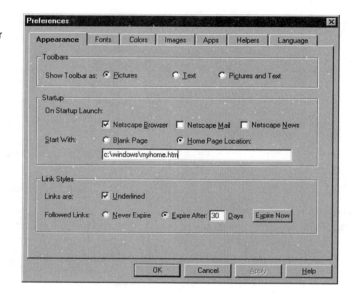

Specifying the Bookmarks File as Your Home Page   You can also set your Bookmarks file as your home page. After you've been on the Web for a while and catalogued many of your favorite sites, this is a quick and easy option—it's also less clunky than fiddling with Netscape's View Bookmarks window. The file is located in your Navigator subdirectory and is simply named bookmarks.htm. Netscape's default installation for Windows 95 sets up the directory structure like this, where c is the letter of the hard drive:

c:\Program Files\Netscape\bookmarks.htm

You may be tempted to try to use your History file as your home page. This would make some sense—the History file makes it easy for you to remember some of those dynamite Web sites you visited during your last session, but forgot to put in your Bookmarks file. Unfortunately, the file, netscap.hst, located in your navigator subdirectory, is just a text file that's used for reference to your cache, and is useless as a home page.

Starting Other Files with Your Home Page

As we saw earlier, if the Web page you saved from the Internet has any graphics or other media besides text, you get a surprise when you load that file—Netscape will not load in the other media with your home page. There's a simple reason for this.

The file you saved, of course, is an HTML file. Within the file are references to other files—graphics files—that were stored at the original server you downloaded from. The tags—the codes that HTML uses to display a document—within the HTML page gave the location of these files so that Netscape would know where to find them when displaying the page.

Unfortunately, when you saved the HTML file, Netscape did not save the graphics as specific files in the same directory, nor did Netscape do anything to change the code so the references would be renamed to work correctly on your hard drive. There are two ways to fix the problem:

- Return to the Web page at its original URL. While holding down the Shift key, click each graphic within that page one at a time, and save each picture to the same directory that holds the HTML file.

- Open up Netscape's Cache subdirectory in Windows Explorer and find the files. This will be hit-or-miss because the files are not saved with their original file names, but with a Netscape specific name that looks something like MO0#####. You can narrow your search by showing file extensions in Explorer—any graphics files will have an extension of either .JPEG or .GIF. Rename each file with the name referenced in the HTML document (you have to view the HTML code in Notepad or Wordpad to find the references to graphics files) and save each one in the same directory you used for your HTML file.

If this sounds a bit complicated, don't worry, it won't make much sense until you read Part III of this book to learn how graphics are referenced in HTML files. But, since HTML is not much more difficult than using your favorite word processor, you shouldn't have much trouble.

Launching Netscape Helpers, Plug-ins, and Other Files   As you become experienced with the Web and begin to drool over some of its exciting new ways to deliver information, you may want to spruce up your home page with other applications. However, there's not much practicality in using a video or audio file to start your Web session (remember though, the file is also tied to your Home Page button, and you can click the button any time you choose), you may find a plug-in or Java applet works better than a regular HTML page, depending upon your particular needs.

For example, if you play the stock market and there's an available Java applet that updates a small spreadsheet to keep you informed of the daily averages, you may want to begin each session with this important information. Or, you may want to start your Web session off in three dimensions—using a VRML plug-in, you may intuitively find your favorite links quicker, easier, and a lot more fun. With the functionality and level of interactivity that Java and VRML promise to offer the Web, the possibilities are literally endless.

Part
II

Ch
3

Run Your Other Windows 95 Apps from the Home Page Button

As it turns out, you can specify a number of other local files in Windows 95 to load from your Home Page button. More specifically, since Netscape communicates directly with the registry in Windows 95, it recognizes file extension associations located there—with the exception of executable files—and loads the associated application that supports your file. (Actually, Netscape will also recognize the EXEs directly, but you have to disable the Octet-stream MIME that still doesn't work exactly right. The result is not worth the effort.)

For example, if I want to launch a Microsoft Word document (and, by association, Microsoft Word) from my Home Page button, all I need to enter into the text box located in the Options, General Preferences, Appearances tab is:

```
c:\directory\subdirectory\filename.doc
```

where c is the name of the drive the file is located in.

Netscape recognizes the file extension and has Windows launch Microsoft Word along with my document. Of course, it will not only load when I hit the Home button, but will also load at my home page every time I start Netscape.

Let's do a quick example with the WebFX VRML plug-in, which is freeware from Paper Software, Inc. You can find the latest version of the plug-in on the Netscape home page (**http://home.netscape.com**) or at **http://www.paperinc.com**, Paper's Web site. Download the WebFX plug-in into a temporary directory and launch its installation program. It will automatically configure and attach itself to Netscape. Make sure you have no other windows programs running while you're performing the setup.

 TIP   It's always a good idea to close the MS Office shortcut bar, too, whenever you set up new applications.

Both Netscape and Paper, Inc. have links to a number of VRML sites and pages. Alternatively, and the most fun, you can create your own VRML pages with the software on the CD-ROM included with this book. Once you've loaded in a VRML file, the look of the plug-in should be similar to figure 3.9.

Unlike an HTML file, a saved VRML file includes all its graphics and hyperlinks together in the same file. You'll find this to be true with Java applets, as well. Simply bring up the Appearances tab under Options, General Preferences again, and enter the name of the file as either a local file or the URL, depending on whether you've saved the file or you're accessing it from a remote system. Be sure to label the file extension as .WRL.

FIG. 3.9
Mark Pesce's "Zero Circle" (**http:// www.hyperreal.com/ ~mpesce/circle.wrl**) looks great in the WebFX plug-in.

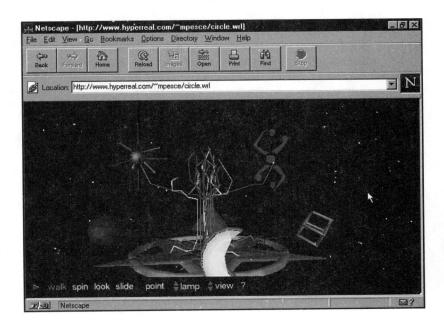

Net Directory Searching the Internet by Subject

There's no question that using Netscape and the World Wide Web is the wave of the immediate future on the Internet, and it's an amazing tool for gathering information. The Web metaphor, in fact, with its links spiraling out into the unknown, is an ingenious method of information retrieval— if only because it mimics the way most humans think—relationally.

But, sometimes things can feel a little disorganized. Especially when you're on a deadline or sick-to-death of surfing to find something. If you've ever used Gopher for information retrieval, then maybe you're feeling a bit nostalgic. Isn't there some way this silly Web can be organized?

Enter the Net Directory pages provided by Netscape. Click once on the Net Directory button on Netscape's interface and you're presented with a listing of available Internet directories scattered around the Web. This page is almost guaranteed to save you hours of surfing frustration more than once in your Web life.

What do we mean by directory? Directories generally provide an editorial service—they determine the best sites around the Web and include them in categorized listings to make finding information easier. Some directories actually combine two features—a directory of categorized sites and a search engine for searching both the category listing and the Internet.

There are a number of directories listed in Net Directory, the most well-known of which is Yahoo, known by many as the most outstanding attempt at organizing the Web yet.

The following are the options currently available in Net Directory:

- Yahoo is the grandfather of Internet guides. Easily the most comprehensive attempt at creating a table of contents for the Internet, Yahoo lets you get directly at listings of Web sites by category. Internet users send submissions to Yahoo, whose editors screen the sites for suitability. There are a lot of sites that aren't covered in Yahoo, but many of the quality sites are.

- The McKinley Internet Directory lists a database of World Wide Web, Gopher, FTP, Telnet, UseNet and mailing-list links that are divided into categories. The database is searchable, and the sites are rated by an editorial team.

- Point offers reviews of what they consider to be the top five percent of Internet sites. Sites are also allowed to submit their own selling copy, which is edited.

- World Wide Arts Resources offers a digital outlet for more than 2,000 artists. This index page for the arts features links to galleries, museums, arts sites, an antiques database, and arts-related educational and government sites.

- World Wide Web Servers offers a huge listing of Web servers. United States servers are listed by state.

- Virtual Tourist is similar to the World Wide Web Servers information, but presented as a clickable graphical map.

The Yahoo Directory

The Yahoo Internet directory (**http://www.yahoo.com**) was created in April 1994 by David Filo and Jerry Yang, two Ph.D. candidates in electrical engineering at Stanford University, as a way to keep track of their personal interests on the Internet. The directory grew quickly in popularity after they made it available to the public and spent more and more time organizing sites into their hierarchy. In early 1995, Netscape Corp. invited Filo and Yang to move their files from Stanford's network to computers housed at Netscape.

Using Yahoo is a little like shopping for the best Internet sites. Instead of blindly following links to different Web sites, hoping that you'll eventually come across one that's interesting, you deal with Yahoo's pages for a while. As you move deeper through Yahoo's menu-style links, you get closer to Web sites that interest you.

 Although Yahoo's primary role is as a directory for the Web, it also offers access to breaking Reuters NewMedia newswire stories. If you're a newshound, click the Headlines button at the top of Yahoo's index page.

First you need to get to Yahoo. From the Net Directory page, click the link to Yahoo once. Starting at the top-most level, you choose the category of Web site you're interested in seeing, for instance, Computers and Internet (see fig. 3.10).

FIG. 3.10
Yahoo offers a directory listing of subjects from the Internet.

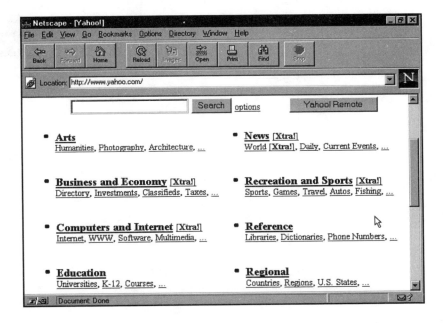

 Yahoo's direct URL is **http://www.yahoo.com**. I'd even go so far as to recommend creating a Bookmark for Yahoo (or using it as your home page)—sometimes Netscape's Net Directory page is a bit slow to respond.

From there, it's as easy as clicking your way through the hierarchy as you get closer and closer to the type of site you're trying to find. In figure 3.11, for instance, I've moved the line down a little bit, having chosen to view Connectivity, Access Providers, Regional and U.S. States. Now I'm looking at a listing of different parts of the country. Pick one, and I'll get a list of links to the Web pages of Internet providers in that part of the country.

FIG. 3.11
Digging a little deeper into Yahoo gets you closer to the Web sites you're seeking.

This is how far down into the hierarchy I am.

This is another category level that I can dig into.

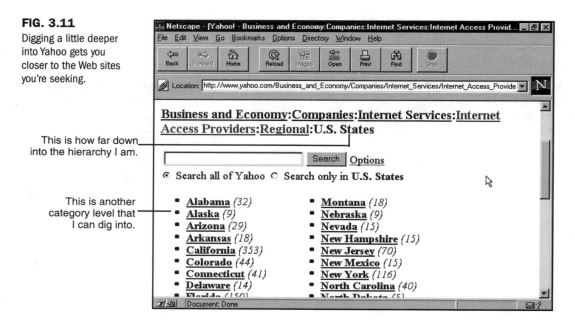

How Yahoo Works What you first notice about the Yahoo directory is its 14 top categories. These categories, determined by the folks who designed Yahoo, are the basic structure of the table of contents approach. But how do you get your Web site included in this hierarchy?

Web site creators decide what category they feel is most appropriate for their Web site's inclusion in the directory. Once you get to the part of the directory you'd like your site to appear in, you click the Add URL button at the top of Yahoo's interface. You're then asked by Yahoo to fill out a Web form with information on their site, the URL, a contact's address, and other tidbits (see fig. 3.12). After reviewing the entry, Yahoo's staff decides if the site merits inclusion.

Why is this important? Two reasons. First, whether you're a Web user or a Web creator, it's significant to recognize that being included in the Yahoo directory is something of a make-or-break proposition. That's not to say that you can't have a successful site if you're not in the Yahoo directory (or, that it will be successful just because it does get included). But being in the Yahoo directory does, at least in a sense, suggest that you've arrived.

Second, it's important to note that being in the Yahoo directory is something you generally have to actively seek. These are, then, sites that want to be accessed. A lot of these sites are high-traffic areas with broad appeal—in fact, a good percentage of them are commercial sites. That is by no means always bad, but you should recognize that it is a limitation to what you'll find using the Yahoo directory.

FIG. 3.12
Submitting your own
Web site for inclusion in
the Yahoo directory.

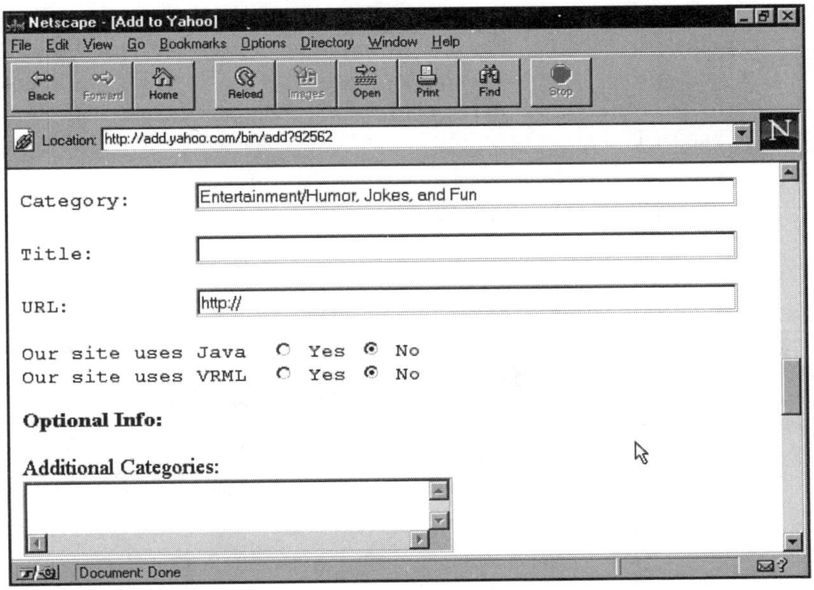

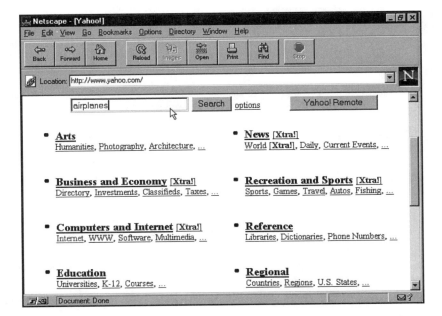

Searching with Yahoo   Clicking through the directory isn't the only way to get at Yahoo's
listed sites. There's also a basic search engine that uses keywords to find interesting pages for
you. Where do you do this searching? From Yahoo's main index page, enter a search phrase in
the text box that sits above the category listings (see fig. 3.13).

FIG. 3.13
Yahoo lets you search
its database for
relevant sites.

By search phrase, I simply mean a few keywords to help Yahoo limit the search. This takes some experimentation (as it does with all of the Internet search engines), and we'll discuss that later in this chapter in the section "Searching on the Web." This simple search from the Yahoo index page assumes you want to find all the keywords you enter. By default it searches the names, URLs, and descriptions of all its Web pages.

What results from this search is a list of possible matches in Yahoo's database, with hypertext links to the described pages (see fig. 3.14). This gives you an opportunity to look at a number of different pages that may or may not include the information you're seeking.

FIG. 3.14
The Yahoo Search Results page. Each of these results is actually a link to the site that's being described.

Click here to see a page that may be what you're trying to find.

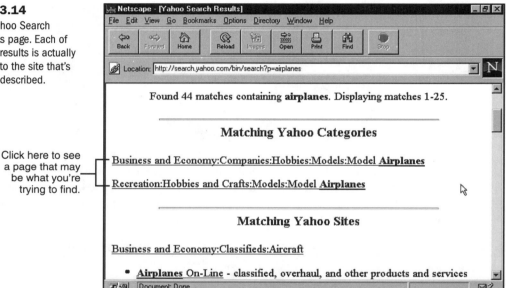

This is a pretty basic search, and, as I pointed out, it's based on a number of default assumptions about the type of search you want to use. If you're not having much luck, you may want to try taking a little more control over the search variables. For a more advanced search, follow these steps:

1. From the basic Yahoo index page, click the Options link next to the Search button. The advanced Yahoo Search page appears (see fig. 3.15).

2. Type your search phrase or keywords into the text box.

3. Put a check in the boxes next to the type of information you want Yahoo to examine as it performs the search. The more checkboxes you have selected, the more results you'll probably get.

4. If you'd like to see more results, click the radio button that allows results that contain less than all of your search phrases. To narrow the search even further, you can click the

radio button for All keys as a single string, which looks for all of the words you entered in the text box—in exactly that order, with no words.

5. Then determine whether or not Yahoo treats your keywords as substrings (potentially parts of larger words) or only complete words.

FIG. 3.15
If you don't get good results from the simple Yahoo search, you can take more control of the variables.

Enter the search phrase here.

Radio buttons that help you widen or narrow the search

Radio buttons determine what will be searched.

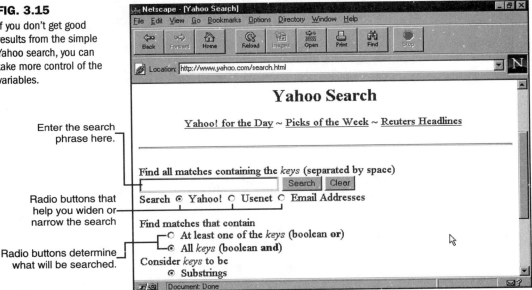

> **TIP** You can eliminate a lot of erroneous results by telling Yahoo to assume your keywords should be complete words only. Why? Consider the keyword "net." As a substring, it may appear as Net, Internet, and Netting. It may also, however, result in pages referencing the Netherlands and garnets.

6. Finally, choose the number of results you want shown. You can choose 100, 200, 300, or Unlimited. The more results you ask for, the longer it takes to get through them all.

7. Click the Search button to initiate the search.

What results is a page very similar to the search results page we saw with the simple Yahoo Search except, hopefully, it's more likely to have links to the sites you need to access. If not, you might want to keep trying if you feel like you can narrow or widen the search with the advanced options. If you feel like you've done all you can, it might just be that Yahoo doesn't have what you're interested in.

Don't worry, though. We've got plenty more directories and Internet search engines to consult.

The McKinley Internet Directory—Magellan

Offered by the McKinley Group, Magellan (**http://www.mckinley.com**) is another Internet directory and search service available from Netscape's Net Directory page (see fig. 3.16).

Magellan offers a listing of over 1,000,000 sites—30,000 of which are reviewed, evaluated, and rated Web, Telnet, Gopher, and FTP sites. Like Yahoo, Magellan allows you to search its database directly for links that match certain keywords. You can also access the staff's recommended sites through a hierarchy of menus.

FIG. 3.16

From Magellan's index page you can search over 1,000,000 sites or browse around 30,000 reviewed sites.

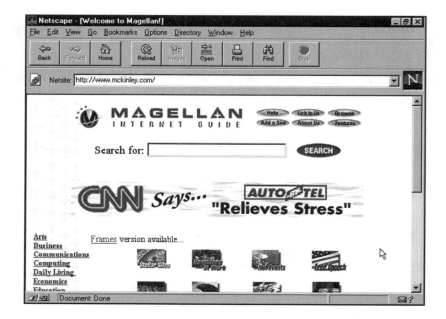

Magellan isn't quite identical to Yahoo—it's both less and more of a directory than Yahoo is. While searching is more tightly integrated into the directory portion of Magellan, it does offer more description and recommendations than Yahoo does—at least for a limited number of sites.

Browsing the Magellan Directory   If you're looking for some of the best possible sites on the Internet, choose the Browse Categories link on Magellan's index page. This gives you a listing of categories to choose from, much like Yahoo's directory. Eventually, you'll dig deep enough to find some sites that have been reviewed by the McKinley Group staff (see fig. 3.17). You'll see in figure 3.18 that many of these sites have been given a star rating to let you know how useful and impressive that particular site is.

Notice also that you can limit the number of reviewed sites that appear in the listing by entering keywords at the top of the page and clicking the Focus Search button. This results in fewer listings in a particular category—most of which, hopefully, will include information that interests you.

FIG. 3.17
After choosing a category and a subcategory, here's a list of possible sites.

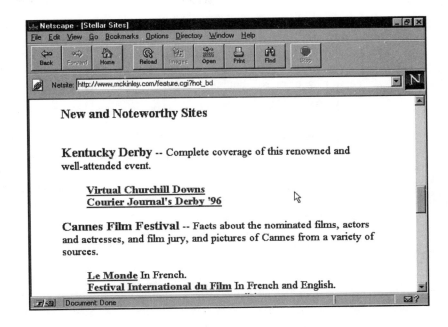

Searching Magellan As I mentioned before, you can also search Magellan for interesting Web sites. For a simple search, enter a search phrase in the text box on Magellan's index page and click the Search Magellan button. For a more advanced search, click the graphic marked Advanced Search. That presents you with the page in figure 3.18.

FIG. 3.18
Magellan's advanced search page helps you find exactly what you're seeking.

How much description should the results list give?

Click this link to visit the recommended sites.

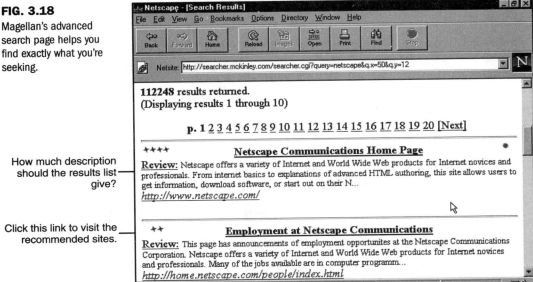

Part
II
Ch
3

Enter your search keywords in this box, then you've got some choices to make. Magellan allows you to do a straight keyword search or a concept search. For a concept search, Magellan generates a series of words that are related to the keywords you enter, and also searches for these. This generates resulting Web sites that don't necessarily include the specific keyword you entered, but may contain related information.

You are also asked to choose whether AND or OR should be assumed between your keywords (to, respectively, broaden or limit your search), the minimum rating for the pages to be returned, and how much description you want to see in the resulting list. Once you've made these decisions, click the button marked Search the Magellan. Now you're off and running.

  The advanced Magellan search engine can actually accept very involved (and somewhat complicated) keyword phrases. For more on Magellan's searching abilities, choose Help from Magellan's graphical interface, then click the Search the Magellan link.

Point

Point (**http://www.pointcom.com**) is another widely recognized repository of Internet site reviews. Claiming to have links to the "top 5 percent" of Internet sites, Point is a great place to find some of what's cool on the Web (see fig. 3.19). To see a directory of the reviews that Point has to offer, click once on the Top 5% Reviews graphic in the top-left corner of Point's index page interface.

FIG. 3.19
Point offers reviews of what it considers to be the best Internet sites in various categories.

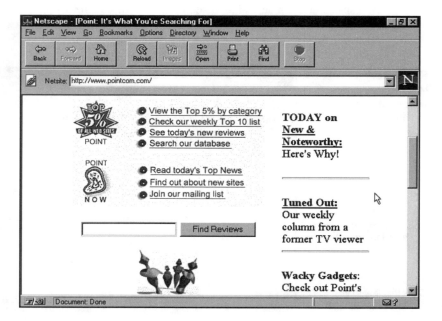

The reviews can sometimes be a little irreverent, fun and, as the Netscape Net Directory page puts it, pointed. Internet sites can also submit their own descriptions, which are duly edited. You search the reviews using keywords via the Point Search feature. If you want to submit your site for inclusion in Point's listing, you use the Submit feature.

NOTE Interestingly, Point Communications, which puts out the Point directory and ratings, has recently been acquired by Lycos, one of the premier search engines on the Internet. According to the Point index page, this gives you access not only to the top 5 percent of sites, but, through Lycos, access to 90 percent of all the Internet sites around the world. We'll discuss Lycos in the "Net Search: Searching on the Internet" section of this chapter. ■

The Best of the Rest

Part
II

Ch
3

There are a few other Internet directories available behind Netscape's Net Directory button. They're a little more specialized, but, if you're interested, you may find tons of links to the kinds of sites you want to visit.

World Wide Arts Resources   For anyone interested in the arts, the World Wide Arts Resources (**http://www.concourse.com/wwar/default.html**) offers access to galleries, museums, an antiques database, related arts sites, as well as arts-related educational and governmental sites. The directory also presents the digital work of over 2,000 artists. There are a variety of resources within the directory, which have been actively compiled for well over a year now.

For example, if you are looking for the work of a particular artist, then use the Artist Index. Other resources include: Art Galleries & Exhibits; Museums, for international listings; USA Museums, which features a 20-page preview and has categorized both the museums and what is available at those museums; Important Arts Resources, which lists related arts sites; and Arts Publications, which features both electronic and conventional publications.

World Wide Web Servers   The World Wide Web Servers directory (**http://www.w3.org/ pub/DataSources/WWW/Servers.html**) is a huge list of available Web servers from the CERN educational institution. The servers are presented alphabetically by continent, country, and state. Clicking the top-level country, for instance, lets you "drill-down" to the next geographic level, where you find listings of individual servers according to region.

North America is subdivided into states, which are listed alphabetically. Also available is a listing of federal government servers for North America. The directory is actually a listing of HTTP (HyperText Transmission Protocol) servers whose administrators have sent requests to **www-request@w3.org**, and other sites.

Virtual Tourist   The Virtual Tourist (**http://www.vtourist.com**) is similar in content to the World Wide Web Servers directory, but is presented in a visually appealing clickable map (see fig. 3.20).

When you click a specific area of the map, another screen appears to help you narrow down your search for geographically sited Web servers.

FIG. 3.20
Virtual Tourist offers a clickable map listing of Web servers around the world.

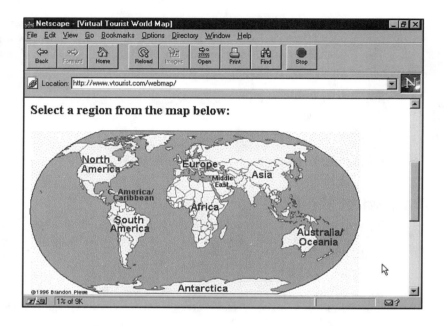

N O T E Information about individual countries and states is not provided by Virtual Tourist. That sort of information is evidently available in The Virtual Tourist II, which is operated in cooperation with City.Net. ■

Net Search Searching on the Internet

Now for that other button on Netscape's browser window, Net Search. Although some of these services overlap with the directories we found on Netscape's Net Directory page, you'll find that all of these are a little more oriented toward searching—and a little less interested in editorializing. For the most part, these search engines are here to help you find keywords in titles of Web pages. You won't see many reviews in these pages. You will, however, see hundreds of results to your queries—chosen from among millions and millions of possible Web pages.

The Net Search directory button takes you to the Internet Search page at Netscape Corp.'s Web site. Here you'll find a collection of easy-to-use search engines that allow you to find information and documents on the Internet.

There are a number of useful search engines listed, offering a variety of search techniques—for example, some search headers and document titles, some search their own extensive indexes of Internet documents and pages, and others rummage through the Internet itself.

The different search options available in Net Search are discussed in the next section. Here are some of the more popular engines:

■ InfoSeek Search allows you to search the Web using plain English or keywords and phrases. Special query operators let you customize your search. Results include the first few lines from each Web site—often making it clear how your keyword is used, and thus, whether or not a site is actually interesting to you.

■ The Lycos Home Page is an extremely comprehensive search engine that reportedly features a database of millions of link descriptors and documents. The engine searches links, headings, and titles for keywords you enter. It also offers different search options.

■ WebCrawler lets you search by document title and content using words you enter into the search box. It's not as comprehensive as Lycos, but it's a quick and easy way to find a few hundred sites that match your keywords.

■ Deja News Research Service allows you to search UseNet newsgroups in, what the company claims is, the world's largest UseNet news archive. A variety of search options are available.

■ Excite allows you to search a database with over one million Web documents. You can also search through the past two week's worth of classified ads and UseNet news. Internet site content quality evaluations are also available through Excite.

■ W3 Search Engines offers a variety of topics and subjects from the University of Geneva, although the list is not updated as often as the more mainstream search engine databases.

■ CUSI (Configurable Unified Search Interface) features a single form to search different Web engines, provided by Nexor U.K.

How These Search Engines Work

Each one of these search services on the Net Search page is designed to give you access to a database of information related to Internet sites around the world. Some are Web-specific (like Lycos and WebCrawler) while others, like InfoSeek and Excite, allow you to search not only Web pages, but also UseNet newsgroups, online publications, and other archives of information.

What all of these do have in common is that they require you to come up with keywords to facilitate the search. There's definitely an art to this search—the more you try it, the more you'll see that it takes some patience and creativity. Let's discuss some of the basic concepts.

The key to a good search is good keywords. What you're trying to do is come up with unique words or phrases that appear only in the documents you want to access. For instance, one thing to definitely avoid are common terms, such as www, computer, Internet, PC, Mac, and so on. These terms come up time and again on pages that may or may not have material that interests you. Also consider that words like Mac not only appear in words like Macintosh, but also in Mace, Mach, Machine, Macaroni—you'll probably get a lot of bizarre results with such a common keyword. Articles and common English words like a, an, the, many, any, and others are generally unnecessary.

Most of these search engines also give you a choice of Boolean operators to use between keywords (AND, OR, NOT). Take care that you understand how these operators work. If you enter them yourself (in the search phrase text box), then an example might be:

Part
II
Ch
3

> **Windows AND shareware NOT Mac**

This results in pages that discuss shareware programs for Microsoft Windows, while it eliminates pages that include the word Mac, even if they also discuss Windows shareware. Remember that AND and NOT are used to limit searches; OR is used to widen them. Notice, for instance, that

> **Ford OR Mustang**

generates many more results than either

> **Ford AND Mustang**

or

> **Ford NOT Mustang**

Presumably, the first only returns pages that have references to both, while the second returns pages that do reference Ford, but do not reference Mustang.

InfoSeek Search

InfoSeek (**http://www.infoseek.com**) is a very popular search engine that generates not only search results but also offers the first few lines from pages to help you determine if a Web site may have what you need before you leave InfoSeek to view it. While this can often save you time, the way InfoSeek reports its results (a maximum of 100 results, ten to a page) can take a little while to flip through. InfoSeek, therefore, is really designed for digging deep for a subject—perhaps when you've had less luck with other search engines.

What Is InfoSeek Search?   You access InfoSeek by clicking the InfoSeek Search button on the Internet Search page at Netscape. You can also start searching straight away by entering search words in the text box under InfoSeek Search and pressing the Search button on Netscape's Net Search page. This is a quick way to get results. The InfoSeek index page offers this same text box, but also includes a quick directory of popular sites (see fig. 3.21).

InfoSeek is very easy to search. Simply enter keywords in the text box and click the Search button. InfoSeek assumes an AND between each of your keywords, although it returns pages that don't include every keyword. Capitalization is important, though, so only capitalize words that you want recognized as proper nouns.

InfoSeek offers this ability to search the Internet as a free service to the Internet community; however, free searches are limited to 100 results per search, and they don't cover the breadth of services that InfoSeek offers. InfoSeek's commercial searching accounts may end up being something that interests you, and more information is provided on their Web site.

FIG. 3.21
InfoSeek's index page is a little Spartan, but it gets the job done.

Here are some links to InfoSeek's directory.

Enter search keywords here.

Click the Search button to begin.

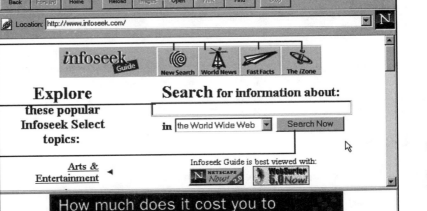

Advanced InfoSeek Searches

At its most basic, InfoSeek is a quick and easy way to search the Internet. In fact, it's one of the few search engines that doesn't offer an advanced page with more control over the results. What you see is basically what you get with InfoSeek.

That is, at least, until you dig a little deeper. Then you realize that there is some customizing you can do to your searches. It all takes place in your search phrase (what you enter in the text box). The following little tidbits may help you get faster, and more reliable, results.

- Before authorizing any search for documents on the Internet, make sure there are no misspelled words and typographical errors in the text box.
- Don't use characters such as an asterisk (*) as wildcards.
- Unlike some other search engines such as Lycos, don't use Boolean operators such as AND and OR between search words, as InfoSeek looks at all words as search terms.
- When searching for documents, try both word variations (plural, adjective, and noun forms of the same word) and synonyms.
- If you want both the upper- and lowercase occurrences of a term, use only the lowercase word in the search text box.
- You need to separate capitalized names with a comma (for example, Bill Gates, Microsoft). You can also use a comma to separate phrases and capitalized names from each other.

continues

continued

- Quotation marks and hyphens can be used to identify a phrase.
- You can use a plus sign (+) to distinguish terms that should appear in every document. The + appears at the beginning of the term, with no space before the first letter of the first word (for example, +skiing Colorado, Utah).
- As an alternative to a plus sign, you can use a minus sign (-) to designate phrases or words not to be included in any document. This is useful if you have a word that is often used with another word in unison, but you want only documents containing the word and not both words to be retrieved (for example, desktop-computer).

Lycos

Lycos (**http://www.lycos.com**) is a very comprehensive and accurate search engine that is also very popular. It consists of a huge catalog that, as of August 1995, claimed to include more than 90 percent of the Web. As a result, you may find it often too busy to let you use it, especially during peak business hours. However, it is worth the wait; Lycos claims to already have included more than 7.98 million URLs and is adding to that number every day.

Lycos was developed at Carnegie-Mellon University, Pittsburgh. However, in June 1995, Lycos, Inc. was formed to develop and market the Lycos technology. Lycos, Inc. says that Lycos will remain free to Internet users, although, as a commercial venture, it will gain revenue from advertising and licensing the Lycos catalog and search technologies. Nonexclusive license holders of the Lycos technology already include Frontier Technologies and Library Corp., as well as Microsoft Corp. for use in the company's newly introduced Microsoft Network online service.

Searching with Lycos   The Lycos interface is similar to InfoSeek's in that you can just enter words and click the Search button. However, Lycos includes more options and contains a much larger database of indexed Web documents. You can begin by selecting the Lycos link on Netscape's Net Search page. That brings up the Lycos index page, where your search begins. A simple Lycos search works just like most of the other search engines. Enter your search keywords in the text box and click the Search button. Lycos finds any pages or documents matching any of the words you type into the search box.

For a more advanced search, choose the Search Options button next to the text box on Lycos' index page. Now you're presented with a new page, where you can spend a little more time tailoring your search (see fig. 3.22).

Here is where you can take a little more control of the search phrase. For instance, if you enter a number of keywords and you'd like to expand the search to show pages that match any of your keywords, pull down the first Search Options menu and choose Match Any Term (OR). You can also choose to match a certain number of keywords with this same menu.

FIG. 3.22

The Lycos Search Options page for a more advanced search.

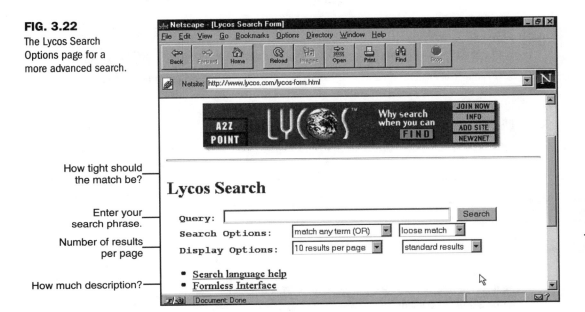

How tight should the match be?

Enter your search phrase.

Number of results per page

How much description?

TIP If you're unsure how a keyword is spelled, type in a couple of different ways you think it might appear, then choose to match the number of terms that you know are spelled correctly. For instance, entering Heron Hearon Huron senate candidate, then selecting to match three terms would give me a good chance of finding information about this public figure whose name I'm not sure how to spell.

The second Search Options pull-down menu allows you to specify if you want close or not-so-close matches. If you are really just "fishing" for some leads as to where to concentrate your next search, make sure the "loose match" option is selected from the second Search Options menu. If you are pretty sure of the search criteria you typed in the Query box, then select "strong match." There are a number of choices in between, each becoming about 20 percent more lenient as they move down the list.

There are two Display Options pull-down menus—one dictates how many results are displayed on the page, and the second determines the level of detail for the specified search.

Although Lycos always allows you to access all the "hits" that resulted from your search, obviously all of them cannot be displayed at once. You can choose to display between 10 and 40 links on a page at any one time. This is done using the first of the two Display Options pull-down menu. To specify how many search results are displayed on the page at any one time, pull down the first menu and select the number you'd like to see.

The second pull-down menu lets you determine the level of information detail to be displayed about each search result. With this menu there are three levels of detail, each one on the list being a little more detailed than the one above it. The level of detail you specify will probably change with each search you do, depending on the documents you are seeking and the research you are trying to accomplish. If you don't specify any level, the default "standard results" takes the middle ground, reporting with a reasonable amount of detail.

How Lycos Works   So how does Lycos manage to cover so much ground on the Internet? There are actually three parts to Lycos, all of which are interconnected, and each requires the others to work properly. The first part of Lycos are groups of programs, called spiders, that go out and search the Web, FTP, and Gopher sites every day.

The results are added to the second part of Lycos—the "catalog" database—which contains such things as the URL address of each site found, along with information about the documents found at that site, the text, and the number of times that site is referenced by other Web addresses. As a result of the advanced search performed by the spiders, the most popular sites are indexed first. Whatever information and new sites are found by the spiders is added to the existing catalog.

The final element is the "search engine" itself. It's the real strength of the system for the end-user (us) because it can manage to access all of this information so smoothly and accurately. The engine sorts through the catalog and produces a list of hits according to your search criteria, listed in descending order of relevance. This means that, according to the search engine, the best and most accurate hits are at the top of the Lycos results list. So, the deeper you dig into Lycos' results, the less likely you are to find what you want—at least, according to Lycos.

WebCrawler

WebCrawler is one of the best search engines on the Web, not least because it is so easy to use and very fast. It is owned and maintained by America Online, which provides it as a public service to the Internet community. It's a great search engine to use when you're fairly sure that what you're looking for will appear in the title of a Web page—WebCrawler only searches titles of Web pages, not all text. For direct access, its URL is **http://www.webcrawler.com/**. You can, of course, also access it from the Net Search page.

 WebCrawler is also a great way to start out on a directed surfing expedition—that is, when you're not searching too closely. If you want to see 500 hits with the word Microsoft in the title, you'll find them the most quickly and easily with WebCrawler.

WebCrawler's interface is designed to be as uncomplicated as possible (see fig. 3.23).

Instead of searching the entire World Wide Web for instances of your typed keywords, WebCrawler searches its own index of documents. This makes for quicker searches, although with documents and pages being added to the Web at such an astounding rate, newer resources can be missed.

The result of your WebCrawler search is a list, with each item on the list underlined and colored indicating it is a hypertext link that you can click to retrieve that page from the Internet.

Down the left side of the search results is a list of numbers, with one number corresponding to each item on the list. The highest number is next to the first item on the search results list.

FIG. 3.23
WebCrawler allows for
easy searching and
quick results.

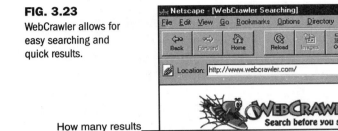

How many results
per page?

Decide whether to
find pages with ALL or
ANY of the keywords.

Enter search
phrase here.

Click Search when
you're ready.

Part

II

Ch

3

This indicates that the first item is the most relevant according to your search keywords, which is why the numbers (from 100 to 001) are called relevance numbers. As you move down the list you notice that the number along the left side decreases for each item on the list—indicating that each of these pages offers fewer occurrences of your keywords than the previous item.

With a large search, not all the results are necessarily displayed on the first page. In fact, WebCrawler limits the results to 10, 25, or 100, depending on how many pages you specified in your search criteria. But if WebCrawler finds, for example, 500 pages that correspond to your search keywords and you chose to view 25 at a time, only 25 are going to be shown on the Netscape screen.

That doesn't mean you can't view the rest of the search results. To view the next 25 items in the resulting search list, click the Get the Next 25 Results button under the resulting list, and the next 25 items in the search are displayed. Keep doing that until you have viewed all the items in the list, if you need to see them. But don't forget, the further down the list you go, the less relevant the search results, according to your keywords.

Other Search Engines

There are a variety of other search engines available on the Internet, and some of the best have also been made available to users of Netscape's Internet Search page. These engines tend to be either more specialized—focusing on searching UseNet newsgroups instead of the entire Internet, for instance— or simply convenient ways to access the search engines we've already talked about.

Deja News Research Service   If you want to search UseNet newsgroups exclusively, then the Deja News Research Service (**http://www.dejanews.com**) is the place for you. Currently claiming over four gigabytes of searchable data, Deja News is updated every two days. You can even follow an entire newsgroup thread by just clicking the subject line when it appears at the top of your screen.

To get to the search engine page, choose Deja News from the Net Search page. Then, click the Search link on Deja News' index page. The Deja News query form page appears (see fig. 3.24).

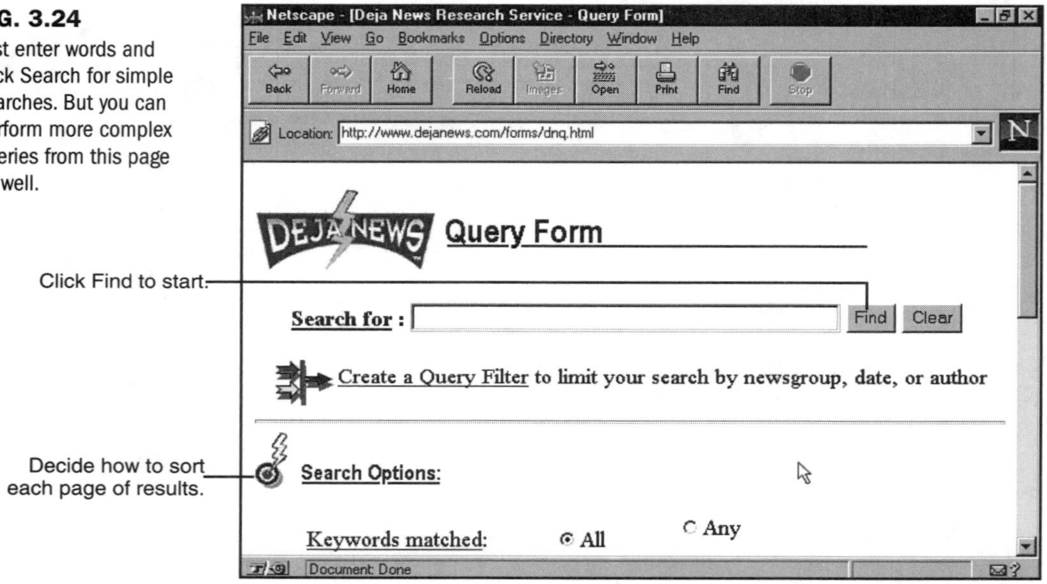

FIG. 3.24

Just enter words and click Search for simple searches. But you can perform more complex queries from this page as well.

Click Find to start.

Decide how to sort each page of results.

For the simplest search, just type search words into the text box, click the Search button, and use the default options. However, for the best results, you should customize your search a little by following these steps:

1. Type your search words into the text box. You don't need to worry about capitalizing words because the search engine isn't case-sensitive. The engine automatically assumes there is an OR between multiple words.

2. Choose the maximum number of hits you want retrieved by checking either 30, 60, or 120 in the Maximum Number of Hits option. The default is 30. If more than the number specified is returned, a link appears at the bottom of the screen allowing you access to the next set of hits.

3. The amount of information retrieved about each site is determined by the Hitlist Format option. Click Terse for less information, or Verbose for more.

4. The Sort By option lets you emphasize score, group, date, or author.

N O T E Score is just another way to say relevance number, as we discussed earlier. It's how Deja News determines how close each result is to your search phrase. ■

5. You can choose between default Boolean operators using the Default Operator: OR or AND option.

6. Use the Create a Query Filter option if you want to use a filter to narrow down your search. A filter can be used to specify a date range, if you only want postings from a specific author, or if you know which newsgroups you want to retrieve (refer to fig. 3.20).

7. The age of the record can also be a factor in your search. If you want newer postings, check the Prefer New box, or if you want older ones, check the Prefer Old box. In addition, you can use the Age Matters option to tell Deja News how important it is that a message is relatively recent or a few months old.

There are some groups that are not included in the indexing, such as *alt., *soc., *talk., and *.binaries. Deja News says that this is either because they contain a large volume of postings that are mostly "flames," or else they don't lend themselves well to text searchings, such as binary groups.

In any event, Deja News is worth using if you want to search the enormous amount of UseNet newsgroups available. There are reportedly as many as 80MB of traffic posted on newsgroups each day! Newsgroups can be very useful for retrieving information if you know how to search and where to look.

Excite   Excite (**http://www.excite.com**) allows you to search through more than a million Web documents and the past two weeks-worth of UseNet newsgroups and classified ads. The user interface is as simple as other search engines available (see fig. 3.25).

FIG. 3.25
The Excite database lets you search Web documents, UseNet newsgroups, and classified ads.

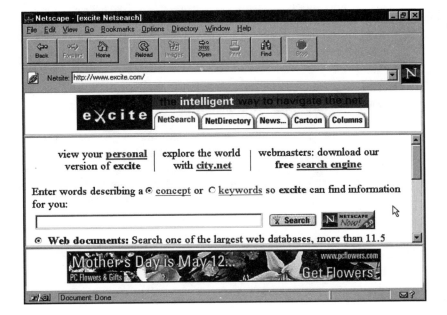

Searching Excite is only slightly different from the other search engines. You start by selecting the type of search you want Excite to carry out—click the Enter Keywords box if you want documents retrieved using regular keywords. You can also click the Enter Words Describing a Concept box if you want the search engine to retrieve documents that seem to involve a subject that's related to the words you typed in the search box, and not just those documents that contain those words.

After you type in your keywords, you have another set of checkbox options. Check Web Documents if you want Excite to search its database of Web documents. Check UseNet Discussion Groups if you want to search through the last two weeks-worth of UseNet messages, or select Classifieds if you want Excite to search the last two weeks-worth of classified advertisements.

Excite uses both color-coded icons and percentage-style scores to indicate the relevance of retrieved results. When there's a red icon at the beginning of the result line, that is an indication that Excite thinks it's a good search match. On the other hand, a black icon means that it may not be such a good match. The colors are a quick way of identifying good matches at a glance.

The percentage is a better way of identifying the relevance of a search result, relative to the next search result. Obviously, the higher the percentage score, the better the match—at least in Excite's eyes.

The title of each result depends on whether it is a Web page or site, or a UseNet article. If it is a Web page, the page's title is displayed, or (if there is no title) it may just show the URL. If it is a Web site, then an Excite editor-selected site title is displayed. With UseNet listings, things are different. If a UseNet group is indicated, the name of the group is displayed. If a UseNet article is referenced, its Subject text is shown.

Excite also offers NetReviews (some of the best Web sites as chosen by the Excite staff) along with its database of Web pages and UseNet newsgroups. In fact, that's why you'll find Excite both on the Net Search and Net Directory pages. To access these reviews, click the NetReviews tab on the Excite index page.

AltaVista

AltaVista (**http://www.altavista.digital.com/**) is another up and coming Web search engine, backed by Digital Equipment Corp. DEC, well known for their powerful Alpha chip, has provided a very powerful Web search engine. Superficially, it functions the same as most other Web search engines (see fig. 3.26). But under the hood, is an extremely fast and powerful Web indexer. Speed is easily AltaVista's strongest suit. In the middle of a work day, AltaVista found over 8,000,000 matches on the word "Netscape." All in under a second.

FIG. 3.26
AltaVista is a remarkably fast and powerful Web search engine.

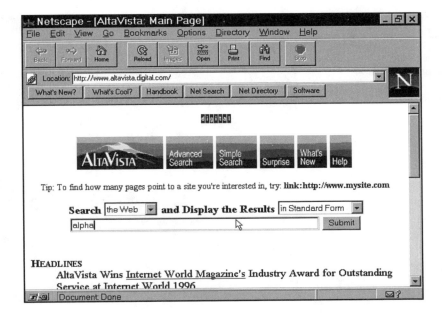

OpenText

OpenText (**http://www.opentext.com/**) is yet another Web search engine available. It's pretty much like any other search engine (see fig. 3.27), in that all you have to do is type in some keywords, then press the Submit button. If you want a more sophisticated search, simply select the "Search the World Wide Web" button. This will allow you to refine your search on OpenText's database to narrow down your search options.

Probably the most notable aspect of OpenText is that it's linked into Yahoo! search results. With the list of matching Yahoo categories and sites, you have the ability of performing the same search with OpenText. Because OpenText is much more automated than Yahoo, there's a good chance it'll find more matching Web pages.

FIG. 3.27
OpenText is a Web search engine that is automatically updated, unlike other engines.

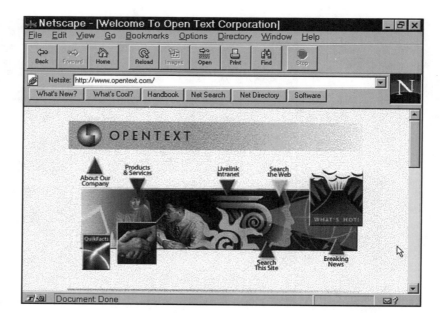

W3 Search Engines There are, in fact, many more searching services available on the Internet than we've even begun to touch on in this chapter. While InfoSeek, WebCrawler, and Lycos are some of the largest and most popular, that won't always mean they're the best for what you need to find. If you're not having much luck with the big name engines, head over to the W3 Search Engines page.

The W3 Search Engines page (**http://cuiwww.unige.ch/meta-index.html**) is basically an interface to many different types of search engines around the world (see fig. 3.28). You can search information servers (Web and Gopher, primarily), UseNet news, publication archives, and software documentation. You can even use these pages to search for people on the Internet in a variety of ways.

To use the individual search engine, just type in your search words in its text box and click the Search button next to that engine's description. You'll notice that you really don't have many options for these engines, but it is a convenient way to initiate simple searches for many different services.

CUSI (Configurable Unified Search Index) The Configurable Unified Search Engine (**http://web.nexor.co.uk/susi/cusi.html**) allows you to quickly check related resources, without retyping search keywords.

This configurable search interface for a variety of searchable World Wide Web resources was developed by Martijn Koster in 1993 and is now provided as a public service by Nexor, which can be contacted at **webmaster@nexor.co.uk**.

CUSI offers a search text box for both manual Web indexes and robot-generated Web indexes, such as Lycos and WebCrawler.

FIG. 3.28
Here are a few of the search engines you can use from the W3 Search Engines page.

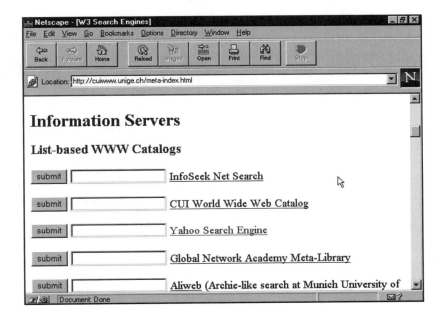

Saving and Printing Copies of a Web Page

Because the Web is used as a source of information on a myriad of topics, you often need to keep a copy of the material that you read. Sometimes you need to incorporate some of this information in another document, or you may simply need a hard copy to give to someone else. In either case, Netscape allows you to retain that Web site permanently with a click of your mouse.

Saving an HTML File for Future Reference   All Web pages are created from a text file that has special key commands stored in it that the Web browser reads. These codes allow us to see graphics, colorful backgrounds, bold text, and brightly colored links to other sites. You can save a copy of the original HTML file for future reference by following these steps:

1. Open the File menu and select Save As (Save Frame As, if you are visiting a site that uses Frames) or press Ctrl+S.
2. The Save As dialog box appears, which allows you to direct Netscape to save a copy of the HTML code to a directory of your choosing. The default directory is c:\Program Files\Netscape\Program.
3. Select the directory in which you want to save this page.
4. Place your cursor in the File Name: field and enter a name for this HTML document.
5. Click Save. You have now saved a copy of this World Wide Web page that you can view at any time without actually connecting to the Internet.

Because you are saving pages, you must need to look at them at least every once in a while. The following steps assist you in reading a saved HTML document.

Part
II

Ch

3

1. Open the File menu and choose the Open File option, or press Ctrl+O.

2. The Open dialog box appears. Change to the c:\Program Files\Netscape\Programs directory, if you are not already there.

3. Click your mouse pointer on the name of the file that you want to open.

4. Click Open.

Netscape opens the file, allowing you to continue working with that Web site. You do not have to retrace your steps. You can forge ahead finding the information you need to complete your tasks.

Printing Web Pages   Sometimes you simply need to capture the information that is on a Web page in the fastest way possible and you do not necessarily have to be able to look at it in electronic form. That is where Netscape's printing feature enters the picture.

1. Open the File menu and select the Print option (Print Frame if you are looking at a site that uses Frames), or press Ctrl+P.

2. Select the name of your printer from the Name drop-down list.

3. Set the number of Copies and the Print Range options to meet your needs.

4. When you're done setting up the printer, click the OK button.

A window appears telling you that your document is being retrieved from the main Web site and that it is being formatted for the printer. This process should only take a few moments, and you can resume your search of the World Wide Web.

If you end up with a stack of printed pages and you're not sure where they are from, you will find the URL for that Web page located in the upper-right corner of the printout. This URL also allows you to go back to that site to get more or updated information.

Displaying Information on a Web Page

Netscape 3.0 allows you to look at a Web page in three different views. The first, and most common, is through the browser with all the HTML tags activated. This is the way you are going to automatically see all sites when you first jump to them.

The second method involves looking at the text file that makes up the body of the Web page. This is viewing the document source, and it is useful if you want to know how the Webmaster at that site achieved a specific look in his or her Web page. Of course, if you are just starting to program with HTML, you will want to look at a lot of Web sites in this view. It helps you learn the language, and the conventions that are used when writing HTML documents.

To view the source document of any Web page, open the View menu and select the Document Source option. This opens a document viewer, generally the Netscape viewing utility that comes with Netscape, unless you have asked the program to use another. In this view, you see the source code that is interpreted by the Web browser to create the graphical pages that you see on your screen.

The third method shows you specific information about the Web page. Open the File menu and select the Document Info option. This opens another Netscape window using a frame. In the top half of this window you see a copy of the main document. In the bottom half of this screen you see a summary listing about that Web page, as you can see in figure 3.29.

FIG. 3.29
The Netscape browser window showing both the main Web page and the appropriate summary information on that file.

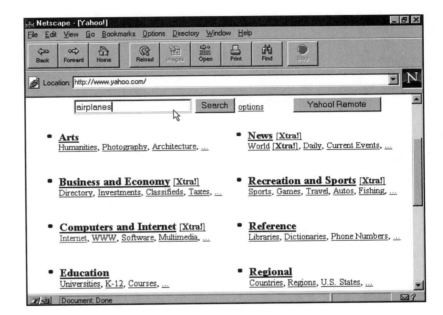

Part
II

Ch
3

Netscape Bookmarks

This chapter covers the use of Netscape's Bookmark feature. You can use Bookmarks to keep track of your most visited Internet sites. Placing them in your Bookmark list makes the site address instantly accessible from the Bookmarks pull-down menu in the menu bar.

In this chapter you learn about the following:

- Using Bookmarks and why they are useful

- How to create and delete Bookmarks

- Creating Bookmarks from your History list

- How hierarchical menus work

- Effective menu management

- How to turn your Bookmark list into a Web page ■

What Are Bookmarks?

The World Wide Web is a tapestry of millions of different documents and sites, all linked via references from other sites and documents. It is no surprise then that help was considered necessary for those exploring the links. One option available to all end users of Netscape is the Bookmarks feature.

Bookmarks are an extremely useful feature of Netscape. They basically allow Netscape to remember whatever places on the Web you tell it to remember. Having taken note of the Internet address of a site, Netscape lists it in a pull-down menu that you access from the menu bar.

When you select an item on the list, Netscape enters the item's URL that it has saved in your Bookmark file and tries to connect to the site, document, graphic, or whatever it corresponds to.

Because of the complexity of Web URLs, it would be enormously tedious if you had to remember and manually enter every page's address each time you wanted to read it. And while you should always try to save a document or image on your local drive so as not to have to connect to it over the Internet, you will likely have a great many remote pages that you will want to access on a regular basis, because they will be continually updated with new information by the remote site's administrator.

Bookmarks take away that tedious task of having to write down or otherwise save each page's or document's URL address.

When you add an item to your Bookmark list, you are essentially keeping a record of that item's address on the Internet, along with a description of that item; however placing it in a pull-down menu that you can quickly access from the menu bar in Netscape.

When you want to go to that site or document or graphic, pull down the Bookmarks list, and select the item. Netscape automatically enters the item's URL and tries to access the address. Chances are you will be able to access the item without any problems; however, the Internet is a global network and difficulties do sometimes occur.

 The Bookmark list contains all the elements that go into making a normal Web page. However, when viewed as a hypertext document, the special HTML coding takes over and displays it with enlarged fonts and a visually pleasing composition that is easy on the eyes.

 If a link doesn't work, one reason may be that the filename on the remote server has changed or it has been moved to another directory. Instead of using the entire URL, type in a truncated version listing just the main server address. That should get you into the remote server from which you can rummage around and look for the old file.

Saving Web Pages

Before you can begin to categorize and separate your Bookmarks into different sections, you need to create them by notifying Netscape that you want to save the URL of a specific Web page. Fortunately, Netscape makes adding a Bookmark to your Bookmark list a simple matter of pulling down a menu.

Creating a Bookmark

There are two ways to add a Bookmark to your Bookmark list. The first involves just pulling down a menu, while the second requires an extra step or two. Let's take the simple way first.

The easiest way to add a Bookmark to your existing Bookmark list is to just select Add Bookmark (Ctrl+D) from the Bookmarks pull-down menu. The current page is added to the bottom of the list.

> **N O T E** Just as you can use your Bookmark file as your home page, you can also use it as any other Web page. This is because it is actually a normal hypertext document just like any other you come across when you go "Web crawling." ▨

The second way of adding a Bookmark allows you to add a Bookmark without having to be at the actual site on the Internet in question.

To add a new Bookmark the long way, follow these steps:

1. Select Bookmarks from the Windows menu. The Netscape Bookmarks list window appears (see fig. 4.1).

Part
II

Ch
4

FIG. 4.1
The Netscape Bookmarks list includes all your saved Bookmarks with their addresses.

2. Select a current item in the Bookmark list window. The new Bookmark appears directly below the current selection in the list. Alternatively, you can skip this step and go straight to step 3. Then, when the bookmark has been added to the list, drag and drop the bookmark in the appropriate folder.

3. Select Insert Bookmark from the Item menu. The Bookmark Properties General sheet appears (see fig. 4.2).

FIG. 4.2

To add a new Bookmark's details, select Insert Bookmark from the Item menu in the Netscape Bookmarks list window.

4. Name the Bookmark in the Name: text box.

5. Enter the URL address of the new link in the Location (URL): text box.

6. You can include a lengthy description of the Bookmark in the Description: text box.

7. The Select Aliases button lets you select all aliases (or copies) of this bookmark in the Bookmark file. If there are no Aliases, the button is dimmed.

8. The Last Visited field shows when the site was last visited.

9. The Added On message shows the date that you added the Bookmark.

10. When all the particulars of the new Bookmark have been entered, click OK. The new Bookmark appears in the Bookmark list.

To go directly to your new Bookmark, either double-click the item in the list, or make the item the current selection and select Go To Bookmark from the Item menu, or drag the bookmark to the Netscape content area. Alternatively, if you want to exit, click the close box in the upper-right corner of the Netscape Bookmarks window.

The newly added Bookmark now appears in the Bookmark list each time it is shown, or it can be accessed via the lower section of the Bookmarks menu. By default, the bookmark list file is called Bookmark.htm.

N O T E After you begin categorizing a large Bookmark list by adding headers and separators, for example, make sure you make a backup copy of the resulting file. If you get a hard disk crash and you have not saved the file, you will have to start constructing the Bookmark file again from scratch, which can be a very time-consuming process. ▪

Deleting a Bookmark

Deleting a Bookmark from your Bookmark list is just as easy as adding it. Follow these steps to delete a Bookmark from your list:

1. Select Bookmarks (Ctrl+B) from the Window menu. The Netscape Bookmarks list window appears.
2. Select the item to be deleted from the Bookmark list.
3. Select Delete from the Edit menu, or press the Del button. The item disappears from the Bookmark list, or click the right mouse button over the bookmark. Choose Delete from the pop-up menu.
4. Click the close (x) box in the upper-right corner to exit.

Creating Bookmarks from Your History List

Your History list keeps a record of the most recently visited Internet sites in case you want to return to a specific site while you are still in the Internet session. The History list disappears when you quit Netscape and end your current Internet session.

The History window consists of two columns, one displaying the title of the page visited, and the other showing the full URL. The most recently visited page is at the top of the list.

You may decide that you want to add an item from your History list to your Bookmark list, but for some reason or another, you neglected to do it when you visited the site and had the page displayed in the main Netscape screen. However, don't fret, you can still create a Bookmark from the current History list by following these steps:

1. Select History from the Window menu. The History window appears (see fig. 4.3).

FIG. 4.3

You can create a Bookmark from the History list.

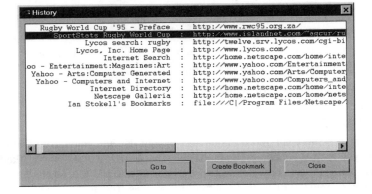

2. Select the History item you want to make a Bookmark.

3. Click the Create Bookmark button under the list window. The selected item is added to your permanent Bookmark list.

4. Click the Close button to exit the History window.

 You can access a numbered History list from the Go menu. Just click the numbered item you want to return to.

Changing Bookmark Properties

You may decide to change any number of Bookmark properties after you have placed the Bookmark in your Bookmark list. This next section tells you how to change such properties as the name, the URL link address, and the description. It also explains how to create a Bookmark shortcut using a function key.

Changing Bookmark Names

At some point, you may decide to change the name of a Bookmark. For example, the site name may change on the Web and you may want to have your Bookmark name correspond to the current name, or you may have organized your Bookmark list into categories and you want the name to reflect the category name.

 When you initially save a bookmark using the Add Bookmark option from the Bookmarks menu, the bookmark is saved as per the original file or document name. You rename it via the Properties option of the Item menu in the Netscape Bookmarks list window.

Whatever the reason, changing the name of a Bookmark list item is a simple procedure; follow these steps:

1. Select Bookmarks (Ctrl+B) from the Window menu. The Netscape Bookmarks list window appears.

2. Select the item from the Bookmarks list.

3. Select Properties from the Item menu. The Bookmark Properties list appears.

4. Change the name of the Bookmark in the Name field.

5. Click OK when you have finished.

Adding a Description

As you add more and more Bookmarks to your list, and you find additional interesting sites that you want to return to, remembering what exactly it was that you liked at the site becomes more difficult. As a result, it is always a good idea to add a description to your Bookmark in order to remember exactly what the site includes. To add a description, follow these steps:

1. Select <u>B</u>ookmarks (Ctrl+B) from the Window menu. The Netscape Bookmarks list window appears.
2. Select the item from the Bookmarks list.
3. Select <u>P</u>roperties from the <u>I</u>tem menu. The Bookmark Properties dialog box appears.
4. Add or change the description of the Bookmark in the Description field.
5. Click OK.

Changing a Bookmark Link

The Internet is a continually changing environment. Every day there are tens of thousands of documents added. In addition, documents are often moved from server to server, or directory to directory on the same server.

When this happens, the remote server administrator often places a note where the document used to be, telling anyone that comes to that address hoping to find the document that it has moved. In this case, there is usually a referring Web URL for you to change in your Bookmark list. Make a note of the new address and do the following to change the Bookmark URL:

1. Select <u>B</u>ookmarks (Ctrl+B) from the Windows menu. The Netscape Bookmarks list window appears.
2. Select the item from the Bookmark list.
3. Select <u>P</u>roperties from the <u>I</u>tem menu. The Bookmark Properties dialog box appears.
4. Change the URL address in the Location (URL) text box.
5. Click OK.

The new URL is now in effect.

 T I P Make sure you have included all the different sections of the URL correctly—the protocol used, the server name, the directory path, and finally, the filename. Without all these parts you may not be able to access the desired file.

 T I P Instead of trying to remember or physically copy an URL from the Go to: location text box in the main Netscape screen, use Netscape's cut and paste features to cut it from the Go to: box and paste it into the Bookmark properties dialog box.

Organizing Bookmarks

Bookmark lists are an extremely useful feature of Netscape. However, after you have added more than a dozen Bookmarks to your list, it needs to be organized in some way or else you will find that it is difficult to retrieve saved Bookmarks. The next few sections include advice on how to organize your Bookmark lists.

Hierarchical Bookmark Menus and Menu Management

A Bookmark list is extremely simple to use if all you do is keep adding Bookmarks to it and know exactly where each book item is in the drop-down list when you want to return to it on the Web. Unfortunately, things get a little more complicated than that.

As you travel the Web, you keep adding Bookmarks to your list, and before you know it, the list is long and cluttered. At this point, you need to think about organizing and categorizing the list into a hierarchical one, most likely with different subject categories divided into sections using headers and separators.

A well planned Bookmark list, with common sense headers and categories, and a visually un-complicated setup using separators, can take a lot of the frustration out of navigating the Web. A few seconds of forethought can save you many minutes in search time when you mislay that just-added Bookmark somewhere in your list of 300 items.

A Netscape hierarchical Bookmark list works much the same way as the Mac's folder-nested-within-another-folder, or the Windows 3.x/DOS subdirectory-within-a-directory format. With a hierarchical listing, you have top-level items, within which are at least one other sub-level category of Bookmarks.

That's how hierarchical Bookmark lists work. They have categories of items contained beneath headers or category titles. The items on the second-level appear indented in the Bookmark list to show they are on a sublevel (see fig. 4.4).

FIG. 4.4

A hierarchical Bookmark list contains indented items beneath higher-level folders.

A major benefit of a hierarchical system is that it allows you to display only the items that you want. You can just display the top-level headers by clicking each one header folder in turn. Top-level folder icons are shown as either closed or open. When the folder is closed, the items within it are hidden. When the folder is open, items are displayed in the Netscape Bookmarks window in a hierarchical listing.

If you want only the main folders displayed, just close all the folders in the window. Then, when you want to open up a specific header folder and access a particular Bookmark item, just double-click the top-level folder and the indented items appear in the list window.

If you have a lot of nested items within your Bookmark list and you want to locate one that is not immediately visible, use the Find Bookmark dialog box, which you access by selecting the Find option from the Netscape Bookmarks list in the Bookmark list window.

Organizing and Categorizing Your Bookmark List

When you get so many Bookmarks in your list that it overruns the list window, it is time to think about categorizing and organizing it. You can use headers and separators to visually distinguish between the different sections.

The categories you choose, of course, depend on the Bookmarks that you have listed, and the emphasis you want to place on the Bookmarks themselves; maybe you want them listed in order of importance, for example.

Bookmark items should be grouped in logical categories wherever possible, so you don't have to hunt through a large number of header folders in order to locate them, which defeats the purpose of organizing the Bookmark list in the first place. The next sections cover using header folders and separators.

Header Folders and Separators

Having decided what form your Bookmark list is going to take, one way to divide it up into easily recognizable sections is by using headers and separators. A header is essentially the title of a specific category group within your Bookmark list, and is represented in the newer versions of Netscape for Windows as a folder icon, while a separator is a physical line separating categories.

With both, you need to strike a balance between using too many headers and separators and not enough. Too many separators, for example, break up the flow of the Bookmark list and make you scroll further down the list to get where you want. Not enough separators, on the other hand, can make deciphering a long list more difficult.

> **NOTE** You will typically be accessing your bookmark list from the Bookmarks menu, which displays only second-level folders. Scrolling down the list from the Bookmarks menu allows you to open up submenus. ■

Not enough header folders can also lead to you having to scroll down long lists of unrelated files in order to find the one you are looking for. Too many folders can also be a problem, as it often means you have to keep opening folders and subfolders in order to display multiple lists and sublists, looking for the one item you need.

Part
II
Ch
4

Bookmark list organization and planning are very important for efficient management once your list begins to get long.

Creating Header Folders   In the Netscape Bookmarks list window, folders represent category headers, into which you place individual Bookmark items. You should have a new header folder for each category in your Bookmark list.

Headers appear as folder icons, each with its own name, and are either open or closed. When open, an indented list of items within that folder is displayed in the Netscape Bookmarks window. When you double-click the opened folder, it closes and all items within it become hidden from view. To reopen that folder and display the enclosed list of Bookmarks, double-click the closed folder.

Creating a new folder header is a simple process; follow these steps:

1. Select Bookmarks (Ctrl+B) from the Windows menu. The Netscape Bookmarks list window appears.

2. Select the current item in the list, under which the new header folder is to appear.

3. Select Insert Folder from the Item menu. The Bookmark Properties General sheet appears (see fig. 4.5).

FIG. 4.5

The Bookmark Properties General sheet is where you fill in the details of the new folder header.

4. Name the new folder in the Name field.

5. Add a general description of the contents of the folder in the Description text box.

6. Click OK.

The new folder header appears in the Bookmark list, directly beneath the current item previously selected.

TIP If you move or delete a header folder, all those items contained within that folder are also affected. Moving a folder is less cumbersome if you first hide the contents by double-clicking the open folder icon.

Just as you can have Bookmark items contained within header folders, so you can have folder icons within folders. To add a folder inside a folder, or indented beneath a folder in the Bookmark list window, just make the top-level folder the current item before selecting Insert Folder from the Item menu. The result will be a folder within a folder in the Bookmark list (see fig. 4.6).

FIG. 4.6
You can have folders nested within header folders in your Bookmark list.

The more Bookmarks you add to your list, the more useful nested folders become. Without the header folders, a long Bookmark list quickly becomes unmanageable.

In addition, because the bookmark list appears at the bottom of the Bookmarks menu, higher-level folders containing sublists of bookmarks are vital to maintaining order. Without folders, the Bookmarks menu can become unwieldy very quickly.

Drag-and-Drop Bookmarks   One of the primary benefits of upgrading to the Windows 95 operating system/graphical user environment is the ability to drag-and-drop files on the desktop. This is also true for using Netscape. It is a feature that is particularly useful for managing your Bookmark list.

To move Bookmark items within the list, just click the item to be moved and, while still holding down the mouse button, drag the icon to the new location. When you get to the new location, release the mouse button and the icon moves.

Part
II

Ch
4

If you are moving an item into a folder nested within another folder, make sure the sub-folder is displayed in the list. To do this, just double-click the top-level folder and the item/folders in the level immediately below the top-level folder are displayed.

If the current selection to be moved is a folder header, the header alone does not move. Everything belonging to that header—the sub-items attached and indented underneath it—also move up or down the list. In this way, you can save large amounts of time if you want to move entire categories of Bookmarks up the list. Think how long it would take to move everything individually after you have moved the header if drag-and-drop wasn't a feature of Netscape! Not to mention the time it takes indenting all the items that belong to the header!

Additionally, you can rearrange your Bookmark list items in the same way, simply by clicking the item and then dragging it to a new position in the same folder, or to another folder altogether.

 Before moving items up the Bookmark list, it may be a good idea to collapse all the header items by clicking the individual headers, so just the headers and not their subitems are visible. Then you don't have so far to move the item.

Adding Items to a Specific Header   Having established your header category, you now need to indicate what items belong to it. You can specify which Bookmark items belong to a specific folder header by dragging and dropping them within that folder.

Dropping an item on a folder indents that item directly beneath the folder. This signifies that the item belongs to that folder. To hide the list of items in the folder, double-click the folder icon.

Adding and Deleting a Separator   Adding a separator is a similar process to adding a header, except you obviously don't get to name it! But be careful not to add too many. Separators can be very visually effective when used in the right amount, but too many can make a list look messy—especially if you want to use the list as a regular Web page as well as within the Bookmark menu.

To add a separator, follow these steps:

1. Select Bookmarks (Ctrl+B) from the Windows menu. The Netscape Bookmarks list window appears.
2. Select the current item in the list, under which the new separator is to appear.
3. Select Insert Separator from the Item menu.

The separator appears directly beneath the item you selected as the current list item.

If you want the separator to appear directly beneath a header folder, and not as the first item in that folder's list, you need to close that folder icon, then make it the current item, before selecting Insert Separator from the Item menu. If the folder is open and selected as the current item when you click Insert Separator, the separator appears as the first item in that folder's list.

There will often come a time when you need to delete a separator from your Bookmark list. Deleting a separator is a simple two-step process; follow these steps:

1. Click the separator that needs to be deleted from your Bookmark list, making it the current selection.

2. Select <u>D</u>elete from the <u>E</u>dit menu, or press the Delete key on the keyboard.

The separator is immediately deleted.

Using the Find Option in Netscape Bookmarks   When you first start saving Bookmarks, it's pretty easy to find items that you have added to the list. However, as time goes by and you begin to organize your Bookmark list into categories with headers, finding the Bookmark you want can get a little time-consuming. Sometimes you have to scroll through pages of items to get the one you want. Fortunately, Netscape includes a Find feature in the Netscape Bookmarks window that helps solve that very problem.

The Find feature allows you to search for titles in the Bookmark list. Found items match whatever you type into the Find dialog box, except that the word or letters are not case sensitive unless you enable the Match Case checkbox. To use the Find feature, follow these steps:

1. Select <u>B</u>ookmarks (Ctrl+B) from the Windows menu. The Netscape Bookmarks list window appears.

2. Select Find from the <u>E</u>dit menu. The Search Headers dialog box appears.

3. Enter the word, phrase, or letters that you want to find in the Find what box.

4. Select Find <u>A</u>gain in the <u>E</u>dit menu, or press F3.

When you click the Find Next button, the search begins with whatever is the current selection and works its way down the list.

Obviously, if you want to search the entire list, it is best to make the topmost Bookmark item the current selection. That way the search begins from the top and works its way right through the list.

The item found becomes selected, at which point you can press the Find Next button again and wait for the next instance of the requested word, phrase, or letters to be located. The text you typed in the Find what box becomes selected if there is no match in your list.

The search also locates matches even if they are found within folder headers. If this happens, the header's folder list automatically unfolds, and the item that matches the search parameters becomes selected.

Using the What's New? Option

Instead of hunting through your entire list of bookmarks each time you sign onto the Web to see if there is anything new at the sites, you can have Netscape do it for you using the What's New? option. Here's how:

1. Select <u>B</u>ookmarks from the Windows menu.

Part

II

Ch

4

2. In the resulting Bookmarks window, select the What's New? option from the File menu. The What's New? window appears.

3. If you want to check all the bookmarks on the list, click the All bookmarks radio button.

4. If you want to choose individual bookmarks from your list, check the Selected Bookmarks radio button.

5. Click the Start Checking button.

Netscape will check the selected sites and report any new changes.

Importing/Exporting Bookmark Files

There may come a time when either you want to let someone else use your Bookmark list—especially if you are involved in a workgroup project at work—or you want to use someone else's Bookmark list. This next section covers importing and exporting Bookmark lists.

Importing and Exporting Bookmarks

You can make your Bookmarks available for exporting to other users, just as they can make their Bookmarks available to you.

As you travel around the Web looking for information or research locations pertaining to your collective interest, you will no doubt run across a variety of sites you want to share with a group of friends or co-workers. If you create a Bookmark list for that day's search, for example, or update an existing Bookmark category list, you will then be in a position to export that list to other users.

Because documents on the Web are formatted using the platform-independent HTML language, the Bookmark list you save and want to export can be read on another platform without any converting. You just have to save it in the HTML format and pass it on, either via "sneakernet" across the workspace, over a local area network within your building, or over the Internet as an e-mail message.

How to Import a Bookmark List   You can import another Bookmark list via the Netscape Bookmarks window. This is a particularly useful feature for office or education environments where a number of people are working on the same project and need to share research and information.

If your PC is connected to a local area network, you will probably be able to access other team members' hard drives, or at least a centralized server that can act as a holding pen for information collected by the different team members.

To import a list, follow these steps:

1. Select Bookmarks from the Windows menu. The Netscape Bookmarks window appears.

2. Select the current item from the Bookmark list window. The imported Bookmark list is added to the list directly under the current item selected.

3. Select Import from the File menu. The Import Bookmarks File dialog box appears (see fig. 4.7).

4. From the Import Bookmarks File dialog box, select the file you are interested in from the list of available folders, drives, and file types. The selected file's name appears in the File name field at the bottom of the dialog box.

5. When you have the desired file listed under File name, click Open. The imported file appears in the Bookmark list immediately below the current item.

FIG. 4.7
You can import a
Bookmark using the
Import Bookmarks File
dialog box.

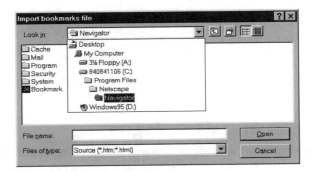

How to Export or Save a Bookmark List   After you have completed a new search or updated an old Bookmark list file, you can either send the file directly to other users using the company e-mail system, connect to their hard drives and place it in a place where they will find it, store it on the central information repository server, or leave it in a place on your own drive where those users will be able to retrieve it. Of course, the latter means you will have to keep your PC on all the time to allow them to access the new file.

 TIP   Because your bookmark list is already in the form of an HTML file called Bookmark.htm, you can save it as a straight text file and send it to someone else on the Internet via e-mail.

Turning your current Bookmark list into an export file for use by someone else is just as simple as importing a file.

To export your Bookmark list file, follow these steps:

1. Select Bookmarks from the Windows menu. The Netscape Bookmarks window appears.

2. Select Save As from the File menu. The Save Bookmarks File dialog box appears (see fig. 4.8).

3. Type the name of the file as it will appear to others in the File name field.

4. Select the type of file it will be saved as (for example, .htm for hypertext markup language) from the Save As type drop-down menu.

5. Select the drive where the exported file is to reside from the Save In drop-down menu. If you are connected to a local area network, this can either be your own local drive, a drive on a distant user's PC, or a server on the network.

6. Select the folder where the exported file is to reside from the folder list.

7. Click the Save button. The file has now been exported to the specified location.

FIG. 4.8
Use the Save
Bookmarks File dialog
box to export your
current booklist to
another location.

Bookmark Lists and Web Pages

Bookmark lists are actually Web pages in that they are already hypertext documents containing links to an item's URL address. Because they already contain the HTML special codes that allow a Web browser to arrange the text in the document as it was originally intended, you can use your Bookmark list as a Web page. The next few sections explain Web and home pages as they relate to Bookmark lists.

A home page is a sort of welcome mat to a server or a person's presence on the Web. It is the initial contact that an Internet user has to a remote server, and, as a result, contains a number of related documents that can be accessed from the home page. You can have a personal home page as well, and you can either store it on a remote server or on a local drive.

Your personal home page then should contain links to your favorite and most-used documents.

Storing your home page on a remote server has its drawbacks, though. If you configure Netscape to retrieve that document each time you log onto the Web, the server might be too busy to accommodate you, or the server might be down for maintenance.

However, if you want other people to be able to access your home page, for whatever reason, it should be placed on an easily accessible server that is available to other Internet users 24 hours a day.

But if you are going to be the only one using the home page, store it on your local drive in your PC. Then, when you start up Netscape, all the browser has to do is pull it up from your hard drive and won't need to go across the Internet to display it. It can save you time and trouble if you have your home page stored on your own hard drive.

A personal home page then, should feature a list of your most frequently accessed Internet sites for it to be of practical value. One way of doing this is to turn your Bookmark list into your home page.

To turn your Bookmark list into your home page, follow these steps:

1. Take note of the name of your Bookmark list file and the directory where it is stored.
2. Select General Preferences from the Options menu.
3. In the resulting Preferences dialog box, select the Appearance tab (see fig. 4.9).

FIG. 4.9
The Appearance
Preferences sheet
allows you to specify
your home page.

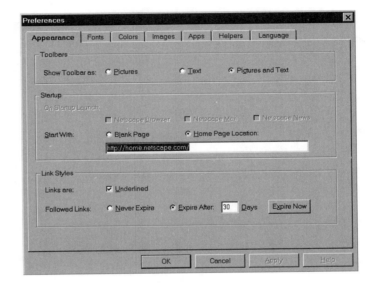

4. In the Start With: section, click the Home Page Location: radio button.
5. Enter the path to your Bookmarks list file stored on your local hard drive. For example, type file:///C:|/PATH/BOOKMARK.HTM, where PATH is the path from your C drive to the Bookmark directory, and BOOKMARK.HTM is the name of your Bookmark file.
6. Click OK.

   ▶ **See** "Moving Around the Web," **p. 31**

Your Bookmark file is now your home page and will appear on your screen each time you start Netscape, click the Home button on the toolbar, or choose Home from the Go menu. ●

Forms and Transaction Security

Browsing the Web is mostly a matter of downloading files
from a Web server to view with your browser. But when
you fill out an online form, you're sending data the other
way—from your computer back to the server you're connected to.

Web forms are like paper forms; they are comprised of
data entry fields, checkboxes, and multiple-choice lists.
They open the electronic door to all kinds of exciting
transactions on the Web. You can sign a guest book, sign
up for a service, ask to be added to a mailing list, join an
organization, request a catalog or brochure, and even
make purchases by submitting forms over the World
Wide Web.

We'll look at all of these possibilities in this chapter. You'll
also learn the following:

- What different kinds of forms there are on the Web

- What the parts of a form are

- How to fill out and submit an online form

- What happens when you submit a form

- What security issues are associated with submitting Web forms

■ How to make sure that your transactions (including credit card purchases) are secure and safe

■ What the future holds for Web security ■

What Are Forms Good For?

Forms are the Web's standard method for letting you submit information to a World Wide Web server. They are used for four major functions:

■ Searching for information in an online database

■ Requesting a user-customized action, such as the creation of a custom map or table

■ Registering for a service or group

■ Online shopping

In each of these cases, forms give you the means to send specific information to the server you're connected to, so that you can receive a customized response.

N O T E How does a Web site send a customized response when you submit a form? Usually by running an associated program on the server called a CGI-BIN script. This specially written program analyzes information provided by the form and performs the action(s) you request. Chapter 26, "Netscape Forms and CGI-BIN Scripts," covers how to write custom CGI-BIN programs to run on your own Web server. ■

In contrast, normal page links only allow you to click a link from a list to retrieve a "canned" response from the server. Forms let Web page creators send you information and services that are tailored to your specific needs, rather than broad, generic responses built for an audience constrained by "least common denominator" considerations.

Let's take a look at four real-world examples from the Web, one for each of these common uses of forms.

Searching

The most popular site on the World Wide Web is Yahoo at Stanford University. Yahoo is a combination Web index/search engine that lets you find just about any site on the Web in seconds. There are two different methods built into Yahoo for finding specific Web sites.

T I P You can also find some interesting sites by clicking the New, Cool, Popular, and Random buttons in the Yahoo title bar, though these are more for Web surfers than for anyone trying to find specific information on the Web.

One search method is a standard hierarchical index. While you can find a site by following the index through its ever-narrowing lists of topics and subtopics, this is definitely the brute-force approach, especially when you consider the tens of thousands of sites that are contained in Yahoo's index space!

The superior way to search Yahoo is to let it build a custom index to your personal specifications. You do this by filling out and submitting the simple one-line form near the top of the page (see fig. 5.1). You just click in this data entry field and type a list of keywords, then click the Search button. Yahoo then searches its database of Web site information and builds a custom index composed only of the entries that contain your keywords. This takes only a few seconds. Finally, Yahoo builds and transmits a custom Web page that contains an index that has been generated "on the fly" just for you.

FIG. 5.1

Yahoo lets you search for Web sites in two very different ways. The best, shown here, is to use its online form to search for keywords.

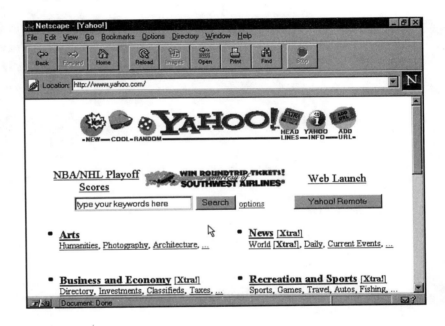

There are literally thousands of sites like Yahoo on the Web that let you use forms to search online databases and retrieve custom pages containing information on a myriad of topics. Just about every kind of information you can imagine (and some you can't imagine!) is available on the Web somewhere in a forms-searchable database. The following are a few good examples:

- Search UseNet postings with DejaNews (**http://www.dejanews.com/**)
- Look up drugs on the Pharmaceutical Information Network (**http://pharminfo.www.com/**)
- Find interesting biographical notes in Britannica's Lives (**http://www.eb.com/calendar/calendar.html**)
- Do a keyword search for jobs (**http://www.occ.com/occ/SearchAllJobs.html**)

Requesting

Forms can also be used to ask a server to run a program to perform a specific task for you (see fig. 5.2). This is one of the most open-ended (and fun!) examples of interactivity on the Web.

Part

II

Ch

5

FIG. 5.2

The Earth Viewer form lets you specify latitude and longitude for your point of view, as well as which satellite data to use. You can even generate a custom view from the sun or the moon!

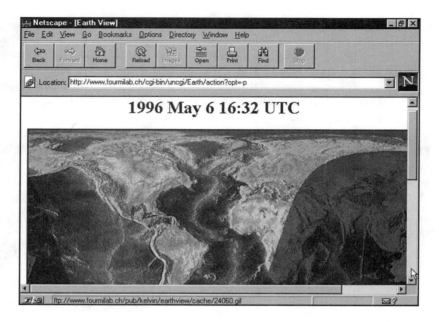

Because a Web server is a computer just like any other, it is fully capable of running any program that any other computer can run. So the types of actions you can request of a Web server are limited only by what the server is willing to let you do. The following is a quick list of a few of the actions you can request on the Web by submitting a form to the right site:

- Display an up-to-the-minute satellite view of the earth's cloud cover from a user-definable viewpoint using the Earth Viewer (**http://www.fourmilab.ch/earthview/ vplanet.html**)

- Say something over the speech synthesizer in Rob Hansen's office at Inference Corporation (**http://www.inference.com/~hansen/talk.html**)

- Operate a model train at the University of Ulm in Germany (**http:// rr-vs.informatik.uni-ulm.de/rrbin/ui/RRPage.html**)

- Generate custom tables of 1990 census data (**http://www.census. gov/cdrom/ lookup**)

While some of these activities are definitely more useful than others, they serve to illustrate what it is possible to do over the Web if the server you are connected to provides the right forms and support programs.

Registering

You can use online forms to sign up for just about anything somewhere on the Web (see fig. 5.3). You can enter contests and sweepstakes, join organizations, apply for credit cards, subscribe to e-mail lists on hundreds of different topics, and even sign a guest book at some of the sites you visit.

FIG. 5.3
Many sites, like this one, ask that you fill out a registration form before you are allowed to access the rest of their site.

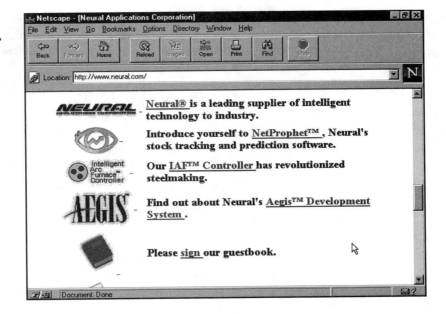

Most online registration forms ask you for the same information you'd supply on a paper registration form: name, address, phone, and—since this is the Internet, after all—e-mail address. Many places also require user registration before they allow you into the deeper, and hopefully most interesting, regions of their Web site. (Some may charge you for this privilege, some not.)

Some of the places on the Web that ask you to fill out a registration form are the following:

- Neural Applications Corporation wants you to fill out a short registration form before you take a look at their home page (**http://www.neural.com**).
- Follow the links and enter your personal information and some keywords to win a new Toyota from Oxyfresh (**http://www. oxyfresh.com/Oxyfresh/Contest/**).
- Apply for an AT&T "universal card" credit/phone card (**http://www.att.com/ucs/app/ app_intr.html**).
- Subscribe to an e-mail list of properties for sale in San Francisco (**http:// www.starboardnet.com/form.html**).

Shopping

You can shop 'til you drop without ever leaving home by cruising the electronic malls on the World Wide Web (see fig. 5.4).

Web shopping generally involves filling out an order form (or registering as a shopper) with your name, address, and credit card information. Many sites now even include an electronic "shopping cart." This allows you to browse a site, reading product descriptions and price information; when you find something you like, you just click the checkbox (an online form, of course) next to the item you want and it is added to your cart. When you get ready to leave the online store, you go through a "checkout" where your items are totaled and you are presented with a bill, which you can then pay with your credit card or "electronic cash." For more information on electronic cash, see the "Digital Money" section later in this chapter.

By "shopping" we really mean the process of requesting goods, "hard copy" information like catalogs or brochures, or services that require either the action of human beings or the transfer of physical objects through delivery services. Though this certainly can involve buying things, it also includes many other services. The following is a list of some more or less random examples: (Please note that we are not endorsing or recommending any of these products or services. Use at your own risk!)

- Enter Liechtenstein's $1,000,000 InterLotto lottery (**http://www.interlotto.li/**).

- Order free and low-cost government pamphlets from the Consumer Information Center (**http://www.pue.blo.gra.gov/**).

- Click checkboxes to receive hundreds of free catalogs at the Mall of Catalogs (**http://www.csn.net/marketeers/mallofcatalogs/**).

- Request books or research services from a library. Though you'll have to check with your local or university library to see if they offer such services via the World Wide Web, Jim Robertson maintains a list of links to the kinds of forms commonly used by libraries at **http://hertz.njit.edu/~robertso/LibForms.html**.

FIG. 5.4
You can enter Liechtenstein's national lottery directly through their secure server connection by filling out an online form.

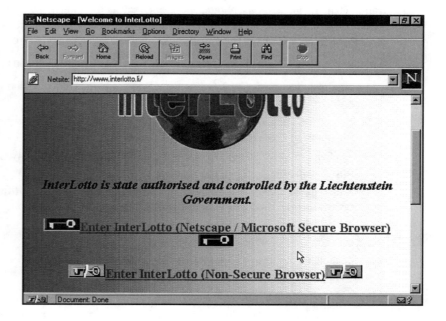

A Generic Online Shopping Trip

Just so you'll know the steps that are involved, let's take a quick virtual shopping trip on the World Wide Web.

The first question is "Where to go?" A good place to begin is the All-Internet Shopping Directory at **http://www.webcom.com/~tbrown/**. It lists hundreds of online malls, catalogs, and stores.

From this list, a good choice might be The Awesome Mall of the Internet (**http://malls.com/awesome/**). How could you pass by a place with a name like that?

The Awesome Mall lists the CyberWarehouse online store (**http://www2.pcy.mci.net/marketplace/cyber/**); it's intriguing because they list a 28.8 modem for only $99.99, if you're tired of your slow 14.4 kilobit-per-second dial-up connection to the Web.

Scrolling down to the bottom of the page, you find a short form that lets you specify your preferred Delivery method, and Quantity to purchase (see fig. 5.5 for a look at CyberWarehouse). Normal delivery is okay, and you only want one unit, so you can accept the default answers by clicking the button marked Add to Basket. This adds the item to your virtual shopping basket. Though you could add more items, you decide to be done for now. Selecting Shopping Basket from the bottom-of-page menu lets you examine your shopping basket's contents.

The shopping basket is private. Netscape pops up a Security Information dialog box to warn you that you're about to enter a secure space, and that all data transmissions from here on will be encrypted. Note that you haven't accessed any secure data yet, which means that the key icon in the lower-left corner of the screen will still look broken.

Part
II

Ch

5

FIG. 5.5

You can use an online order form like this one to buy things on the Web.

The shopping basket screen lists what you've purchased. At this point, the key icon is unbroken, reminding you that this page is secure. (And you didn't have to do a thing to get a secure connection—Netscape did it all for you!) You could change your order now, but you decide you're happy so you just click the button marked Checkout.

That takes you to an online form where you fill out your shipping and credit card information (see fig. 5.6). The process is very similar whether you use a credit card or digital money, though many more sites take credit than "ecash." The key shows you still have a secure link.

Scrolling down to the bottom of this page, you find the credit card information part of the form. You know you can fill this out safely because your link is secure, and the data you send will be safely encoded by Netscape. When done, you press the Continue Checkout button, proceed though a couple of final messages, and you're done.

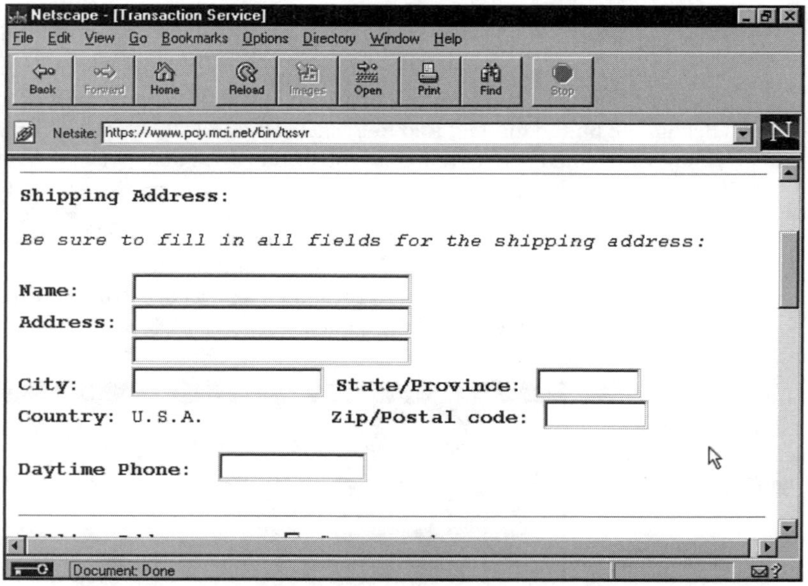

FIG. 5.6
When ready to make an online purchase, you are asked to fill out an order form through a secure connection (note unbroken key in lower-left corner of screen).

Form Formats

Web forms are created using the <FORM></FORM> HTML tag. Within this structure, many options are available to the Web forms designer to create a wide range of form elements. Online forms can include data entry fields, checkboxes, scrolling lists, and even push buttons.

You'll run into a wide variety of form formats on the Web. Among them are inline forms, full-page forms, multiple forms on a single page, and even hidden forms.

Inline Forms

If the Web page you're visiting needs only a single item of information from you, it's likely to present you with a much simplified form called an inline form.

The Lycos search engine is a good example of an inline form (see fig. 5.7). There is only one field to fill in and a single button to push when you're done. In fact, most forms that have only a single field don't even require that you push a button to submit the information you've filled in; if you just hit the Enter key when you're done, the information is sent to the server automatically.

FIG. 5.7
Lycos uses a single inline form field to ask for a list of keywords to search for.

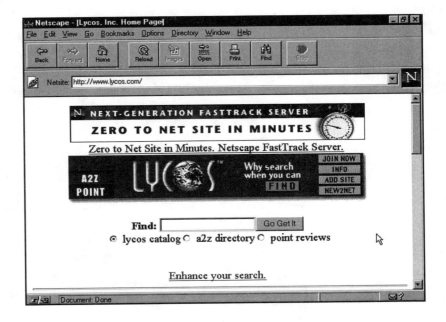

Full-Page Forms

You'll find many examplesof full-page forms on the Web. These ask for a variety of information, and may make use of all the available form elements (push buttons, checkboxes, fields, scrolling menus, and so on). However, they probably also incorporate many other HTML design elements like style tags, formatted text, inline images, hypertext links, links to objects that launch helper applications, and even links to other sites. Sometimes it's hard to sort out which parts are the form and which parts are collateral material.

Yahoo's Search Options form is a good example of a full-page form with a variety of input field types (see fig. 5.8).

Multiple Forms

You can also put several separate forms on a single Web page. If there are multiple forms on one page, they are independent, each with its own SUBMIT button.

Each individual form has its own associated program or script that is invoked when its SUBMIT button is pressed. Only the data from the associated form is passed to the server. Figure 5.9 shows an example of a Web page with multiple forms.

FIG. 5.8

Yahoo's Search Options screen is a good example of a full-page form, and it includes most of the input field types you'll see on online forms.

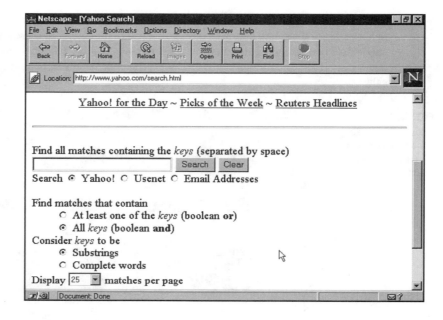

FIG. 5.9

Multiple forms occupy William D. Cross's All-in-One Search Page at http://www.albany.net/allinone.

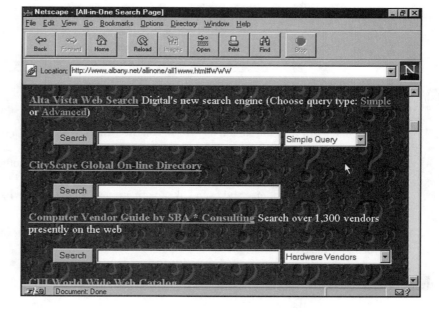

N O T E If you put more than one form on a Web page, make sure you don't nest one <FORM> </FORM> construct within another. Forms cannot be nested within forms. According to proposed HTML 3.0 specifications, forms can only be nested within the following "parent" elements on an HTML page: BANNER, BODYTEXT, DD, DIV, FIGTEXT, FN, LI, NOTE, TD, and TH. Some older browsers have reportedly had problems displaying forms within tables; similar problems might arise from nested constructs. ■

Hidden Forms

You may have used forms without even knowing it. Sometimes forms are completely hidden. Forms can consist of nothing but hidden fields that send predefined data when an associated button, image, or link is clicked. Since there is nothing to see on a hidden form, we won't show an example here; however, we will discuss how they work a little later in this chapter.

Filling Out a Form

Now that we've covered what forms are good for, and what different kinds of forms you're likely to run into on the Web, let's step through filling out a form page. We'll choose as our example a form that contains almost all of the different elements you're likely to encounter in real life.

Within a <FORM></FORM> form definition, most of the visible parts of a form are defined by three HTML tags: INPUT, SELECT, and TEXTAREA. These tags are discussed from a programmer's point of view in chapter 26, "Netscape Forms and CGI-BIN Scripts." For now, we'll concentrate on what they look like on the Web page, and how to fill them in.

Our sample form as displayed in figure 5.10 is defined in the short HTML script shown in listing 5.1:

Listing 5.1 HTML Source for a Sample Form

```
<HTML>
<HEAD>
<TITLE>Forms Test Page</TITLE>
</HEAD>
<BODY>
<H1>Forms Test Page</H1>
<FORM ACTION="http://www.test.com/cgi-bin/binfile" METHOD=POST>
Type text in this field:
<INPUT NAME="SomeText" TYPE="TEXT" SIZE="15" MAXLENGTH="30">
Enter Password:
<INPUT NAME="passw" TYPE="PASSWORD" SIZE="5" MAXLENGTH="10"><br>
Check all that apply:
<INPUT NAME="checkb1" TYPE="CHECKBOX" VALUE="check1" CHECKED>Checkbox #1
<INPUT NAME="checkb2" TYPE="CHECKBOX" VALUE="check2">Checkbox #2
<INPUT NAME="checkb3" TYPE="CHECKBOX" VALUE="check3">Checkbox #3<br>
Select "Yes" or "No" (or "Maybe"):
```

continues

Listing 5.1   Continued

```
<INPUT NAME="rad" TYPE="radio" VALUE="yes" CHECKED>Yes
<INPUT NAME="rad" TYPE="radio" VALUE="no">No
<INPUT NAME="rad" TYPE="radio" VALUE="maybe">Maybe<br>
[Here's a HIDDEN field...]
<INPUT NAME="hidd" TYPE="hidden" VALUE="secret!">
Here's an IMAGE:
<INPUT NAME="coord" TYPE="image" SRC="formtest.gif"><P>
<INPUT TYPE="submit" VALUE="Click Here to SUBMIT the form">
<INPUT TYPE="reset" VALUE="Click Here to RESET the Form"><P>
What's your name?
<SELECT NAME="Name" MULTIPLE>
<OPTION> Mary
<OPTION> Pete
<OPTION> Pamela SELECTED
<OPTION> John
<OPTION> Louise
</SELECT>
Enter comments:
<TEXTAREA NAME="address" ROWS=5 COLS=40>
I love what you've done with this page!
You are the Master of Web page design.
And I really, really mean this.
</TEXTAREA>
</FORM>
</BODY>
<HTML>
```

FIG. 5.10

Examples of the most visible parts of an HTML form as defined by <FORM> tags. These parts are explained in the following sections.

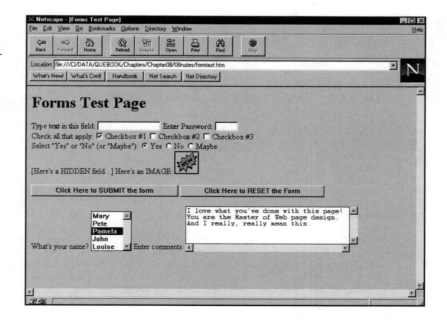

The INPUT Tag

The <INPUT> HTML tag is what is used to define most of the input areas of a Web page form. It has eight commonly used TYPE options, each of which looks and acts differently on-screen.

The TEXT type is used for entering a single line of text. The SIZE attribute specifies the visible width of a text field, while the MAX attribute specifies the actual maximum number of characters that can be typed. (Though our example doesn't show it, you can also define a default value for input text that appears automatically in the text field by assigning VALUE="default text" in the INPUT tag line.) For example:

```
<INPUT NAME="SomeText" TYPE="TEXT" SIZE="15" MAXLENGTH="30">
```

To fill in a TEXT field, point and click in the field, then type. To move from one TEXT field to the next, use the Tab key.

 TIP When any form field is "active," your cursor and page up/down keys don't work to scroll the Netscape window anymore. Instead, they work to move around in the form field. To use them for scrolling the window again, just click anywhere in the window background.

A PASSWORD field is the same as a TEXT field, but for security purposes the screen doesn't display what you type. Instead, you see a string of asterisks (*). For example:

```
<INPUT NAME="passw" TYPE="PASSWORD" SIZE="5" MAXLENGTH="10">
```

You fill in a password field the same way you fill in a text field.

The CHECKBOX type is for Boolean variables, which can take only one of two values. When a box is checked, the value of its VALUE attribute is assigned to the variable specified in its NAME attribute. If present, the CHECKED attribute indicates that the checkbox is checked by default. Example:

```
<INPUT NAME="checkb1" TYPE="CHECKBOX" VALUE="check1" CHECKED>
<INPUT NAME="checkb2" TYPE="CHECKBOX" VALUE="check2" >
<INPUT NAME="checkb3" TYPE="CHECKBOX" VALUE="check3" >
```

You check a checkbox by clicking it; you uncheck a checked checkbox by clicking it again.

The RADIO input type is for variables that can take any one of several different specified values. This is done by giving several (at least two) radio buttons the same NAME attribute with different VALUEs. Selecting one of the buttons causes any previously selected button in the group to be deselected, and assigns the VALUE to the NAMEd variable. The CHECKED attribute indicates which radio button is checked by default. For example:

```
<INPUT NAME="rad" TYPE="radio" VALUE="yes" CHECKED>
<INPUT NAME="rad" TYPE="radio" VALUE="no">
<INPUT NAME="rad" TYPE="radio" VALUE="maybe">
```

You select a radio button by clicking it. If the radio button you click has the same variable NAME as a radio button that has already been selected, the previous button will automatically be unselected when you select the new one.

Part

II

Ch

5

TIP Want to know which radio buttons share the same variable NAME, or what the default VALUE of a variable is? If the Web page creator hasn't been nice enough to tell you on-screen, the only way to know is to choose View, Document Source (Alt+V,S) from the Netscape menu and comb through the HTML code.

An input field of the HIDDEN type does not appear anywhere on a form, but the VALUE specified is transmitted along with the other values when the form is submitted. HIDDEN fields are not usually used on predefined Web page forms. They usually only appear on customized forms that are created "on the fly" by the a Web server you're connected to. They are used to keep track of information specific to your request. For example, if you request information from a server and it sends back a form asking for additional details, that form might include a hidden field type that defines a request number. When you submit the second form, the server is then able to tell which request number your second form referred to. Here's a simpler example from our test page, which simply returns the value secret in the variable named hidd:

```
<INPUT NAME="hidd" TYPE="hidden" VALUE="secret">
```

You don't (and can't) fill out a HIDDEN field. Its value is predefined. In fact, you probably won't even know it's there.

The IMAGE type is an advanced form of the SUBMIT type. (See the following line of code.) Instead of providing a push button, the IMAGE type lets you use a bitmapped image to submit a form. When clicked, the IMAGE field submits the entire form to the Web server, and can also be used to transmit the coordinates of exactly where the image was clicked. For example, if the IMAGE variable is named coord and the bitmap is 100×100 bits in size and you click the pixel at location 50,62, the server receives all of the form data, including the two clicked-coordinate values, coord.x=50 and coord.y=62.

```
<INPUT NAME="coord" TYPE="image" SRC="formtest.gif">
```

If the INPUT type is IMAGE, you'll probably be asked to "Click somewhere on this image to submit this form," or something similar. If it is set up to transmit the coordinates of your mouseclick (that is, if it has a variable NAME), you'll probably be asked to click in different specific spots depending on what you want to do. In any event, you shouldn't click the IMAGE bitmap until you have filled in all the other fields on the form.

The SUBMIT input type creates a push button which, when selected, activates the ACTION specified in the FORM definition. In most cases, this means it sends the data from all of the form fields on to the server. The VALUE attribute of the SUBMIT type is actually the label that appears on the button. For example:

```
<INPUT TYPE="submit" VALUE="Click Here to SUBMIT the form">
```

When you are done filling out a form, click the SUBMIT button to finish.

TIP SUBMIT buttons are often labeled something else, like "Done" or "Send." Don't let labels fool you. If it's a push button and it sounds like something you should only click when you're finished, it's probably a SUBMIT button.

RESET also manifests itself as a push button, but selecting it resets all of a form's fields to their initial values as specified by their VALUE attributes. Like the SUBMIT button, the VALUE attribute defines the button label text. For example:

```
<INPUT TYPE="reset" VALUE="Click Here to RESET the Form">
```

If you've totally mucked up filling out a form, click the RESET button to reset all the fields to their default values so you can start over.

There are other less-often-used or proposed-for-future-versions types for INPUT, but the types just covered cover 99 percent of what you'll run into on the Web. For information about other INPUT options, check out chapter 26, "Netscape Forms and CGI-BIN Scripts."

There are two other common HTML tags besides INPUT that are used to create online forms: SELECT and TEXTAREA.

The SELECT Tag

RADIO and CHECKBOX fields can be used to create multiple choice forms. But the <SELECT> </SELECT> element pair can be used to produce a neat multiple-choice field in the form of a pull-down list. If more than one choice is valid, the MULTIPLE attribute enables the selection of more than one option. Each choice is specified in a separate OPTION element. For example:

```
<SELECT NAME="Name" MULTIPLE>
<OPTION> Mary
<OPTION> Pete
<OPTION> Pamela SELECTED
<OPTION> John
<OPTION> Louise
</SELECT>
```

To choose a SELECT option, click it. To select more than one option in a MULTIPLE-enabled list, click one option and drag to select more. To select non-contiguous options, hold the Ctrl key when you click additional items. Selected items are highlighted; if you can only highlight one option, then the MULTIPLE attribute isn't enabled.

The TEXTAREA Tag

The <TEXTAREA></TEXTAREA> HTML construct lets you type in multiple lines of text in a scrolling text box. As usual, the NAME attribute defines the variable. The ROWS and COLS attributes specify the width and height of the text area in characters. Default text (if any) is entered line by line between the <TEXTAREA> and </TEXTAREA> tags. For example:

```
<TEXTAREA NAME="address" ROWS=6 COLS=60>
I love what you've done with this Web page!
You are definitely the God of Web page design.
And I really, really mean this.
</TEXTAREA>
```

To fill in a TEXTAREA field, just click it and type. You can use all of the standard editing keys (arrows, Delete, Page Up/Down, etc.) to move around and edit in the TEXTAREA box.

Part

II

Ch

5

Filling Out a Form by Uploading a File

Netscape adds the ability to upload the data for a form, rather than having to fill it all out online. This can save you lots of connect time when filling out long online forms. (Unfortunately, you can't upload data for just any old form—the Web form you're looking at has to be specially configured to accept a file as input.)

This is accomplished through the use of a new value for the <FORM> tag ENCTYPE, which defines the MIME type of a form submitted using the POST method. In the past, there has been only one valid value for ENCTYPE, application/x-www-form-urlencoded. The new value defined for input files is multipart/form-data.

A new INPUT TYPE has also been defined for FILE type input.

Here's an example of a short form that accepts file input (see fig. 5.11):

```
<FORM ENCTYPE="multipart/form-data" ACTION="http://www.site.com/cgi-bin/getfile"
METHOD=POST>
File to process? <INPUT NAME="file1" TYPE="file">
<INPUT TYPE="submit" VALUE="Send File">
</FORM>
```

FIG. 5.11
A short example of a
Web form that accepts a
file as input.

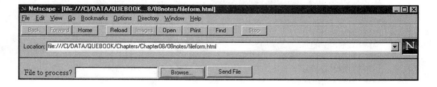

The new INPUT TYPE="file" not only lets you upload a file in response to the form request, it even adds a BROWSE button that, when clicked, brings up a standard Windows file requester dialog box. It couldn't be much easier.

For Every Action

Every FORM definition has an associated ACTION that determines how the server deals with the information it receives from the form. There are two possible form actions: GET and POST.

GET

The form GET action is no longer recommended, but you still see it used in forms on older sites. It's functionally identical to the POST action described later, but sends form data appended to the URL rather than as separate MIME urlencoded data. The following is an example:

```
<FORM ACTION="http://www.server.com/cgi-bin/doit" METHOD=GET>
```

When submitted, this sample form actually asks the server for a URL called **http://www.server.com/cgi-bin/doit&data&moredata&etc.**, where the items separated by ampersands at the end of the URL address are the various data fields you filled in on the form.

Don't worry if you see some strange-looking URLs containing lots of ASCII "garbage" in the location box on the Netscape Navigator screen. Some POST instructions (and all GET instructions) append form data to the URL. The server will know what it means, even if you don't.

Somebody somewhere decided this was sloppy, and came up with the POST action as an alternative. It keeps the URL request and the form data neatly separated.

POST and CGI-BIN Scripts

The form POST action sends form data back to the Web server you're connected to and (usually) launches a program called a CGI (Common Gateway Interface) script. The following is an example:

```
<FORM ACTION="http://www.server.com/cgi-bin/doit" METHOD=POST>
```

When submitted, this form launches a program called doit on the server, which processes your form data and performs the requested action(s).

CGI scripts may be written either in scripting languages like Perl, or in any other programming language, like C, Pascal, or BASIC (in which case they are more properly called CGI programs).

 On many HTTP servers, CGI scripts are stored in a separate directory called cgi-bin, so if you see a pathname in Netscape's URL address line that includes /cgi-bin/ after submitting a form, it's almost a certainty that your submission has launched a CGI script or program.

Data sent to the CGI script by the POST action is MIME-encoded using the MIME data type application/x-www-form-urlencoded. URL encoding is not for security purposes; in fact, it's easily read by human eyes, if a bit strange looking. URL encoding is just a way for the server to identify POSTed data and receive it reliably.

URL encoding simply runs all the form data together as a single string. It then replaces spaces with "+" characters; replaces non-alphanumeric characters with their ASCII hexadecimal equivalent, preceded by a percent (%) sign; includes NAME= in front of every field; and puts an ampersand (&) between fields.

Here's an example. Let's say the form you are submitting (which uses the POST action, of course) asks you for values for variables named YOURNAME, YOURCITY, and CHOICE. You fill it out with the following data:

> Mary Jones
>
> Oklahoma City
>
> Y

When you press the SUBMIT button, here's how the data is transmitted back to the server:

```
YOURNAME=Mary+Jones&YOURCITY=Oklahoma+City&CHOICE=Y
```

Part
II

Ch
5

This line would be preceded by a MIME notice that the message is encoded in the MIME type/ subtype application/x-www-form-urlencoded. Because the data is in a known format, the server can make some sense out of it.

Fortunately, all of this is totally invisible to you. You don't have to worry about how it works at all, because the process is fully automatic.

POST and MAILTO

The form POST action can also simply mail form data to a specified address through the MAILTO command. The following is an example:

```
<FORM ACTION="mailto:mbrown@neural.com" METHOD=POST>
```

Rather than launching a CGI-BIN script, the MAILTO command mails the same URL-encoded data string to the specified Internet mail address. Though not all browsers support the MAILTO command, Netscape does, and you'll find it used quite often on the Web.

The Form Submission Process Flowchart

So what really happens when you submit a form? The whole process is summarized in the flowchart shown in figure 5.12.

The following is the step-by-step process that occurs when you submit a form.

1. While filling out the form, you can move around and edit, and even press the RESET button to clear the form back to its default VALUE settings.

2. When you are satisfied with the data you've entered, pressing the SUBMIT button sends the form data to the server you got the form from via the Internet.

3. The server receives the data and performs the ACTION defined in the FORM statement.

4. If the METHOD is POST and the ACTION references a CGI-BIN script (or program), the CGI-BIN is run with the form data as input. If the ACTION is MAILTO, the form data is mailed to the address specified in the ACTION statement.

5. The server then sends a response to you. If the action was successfully completed, you get a confirmation message or custom page, depending on the actions defined in the CGI-BIN script. If unsuccessful, you (hopefully) are sent an error message. If the action was MAILTO, the only feedback you get may be a Document Done message in Netscape's status bar at the bottom of the screen.

TROUBLESHOOTING

I pressed the SUBMIT button, but all I got back was some weird error message that I couldn't interpret. What gives? There are a number of things that can happen when you press the SUBMIT button that result in an error message. The following are just a few:

- Between the time you received the form and the time you submitted it, the server you were connected to may have gone down.

- The server you're connected to may submit its CGI scripts to another server to be run, and that server may be down. (Hey—nobody said this would be easy!)

- The CGI program may be buggy, and might have choked on your particular data.

- The CGI program may be telling you that you filled out the form incompletely or incorrectly. Read the error message carefully to see if it's specific about the problem.

The fix is often no more complicated than pressing the Back button on the Netscape toolbar and filling out the form correctly. If you continue to get errors, your only solution may be to e-mail the Webmaster of the site where you're experiencing the problems. There's usually an address or link on most home pages for this purpose.

FIG. 5.12
This diagram shows the sequence of events when submitting a form.

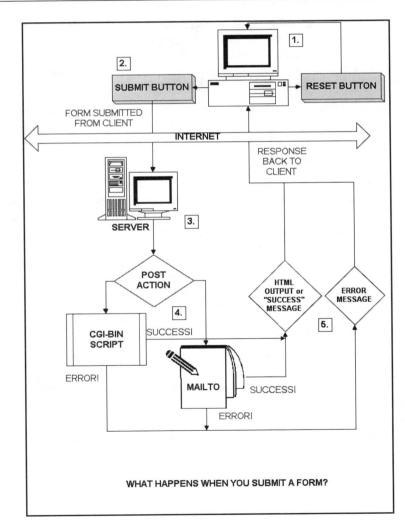

WHAT HAPPENS WHEN YOU SUBMIT A FORM?

Part

II

Ch

5

Forms and Security

The first time you click the SUBMIT button to order something using an online form, you may wonder if you should be afraid to use your credit card on the Web. But you might also wonder why no one seems to care about how much "insecurity" there is in more traditional uses of credit cards in stores, by mail order, and over the phone. It's really much more likely that someone will pull a receipt out of the trash at a store and steal your credit card number than it is that some hacker will latch onto it on the Web.

The real issue is this: How trustworthy is the party you're dealing with? Your major worry should probably be the chance of running into a dishonest employee or a bogus company— online or not—that wants to steal your number outright.

That being said, it should also be noted that there really are a few dishonest hackers out there who revel in gathering information through any means possible. Some of them even go on to use it for personal gain. When this happens, it doesn't matter that the percentages are low if it's your credit card number they're playing with! And, as commerce increases on the Web, it's likely to draw larger numbers of out-and-out professional thieves, too.

If nothing else, business and government are extremely concerned about security, and they won't trust their transactions to the Web until they're convinced that no one else can illegally tap in and see what's going on.

Clearly, the security of online transactions is not an issue that can simply be ignored.

Enter encryption. Public-key encryption, to be exact. Encryption uses a "key" number to change readable text into unreadable code that can be sent and decrypted back into a legible message at the receiving end. A public key system uses two keys: a public key number and a private key number. Messages encrypted with the public key can only be decrypted with the associated private key, and messages encrypted with the private key can only be decrypted with the public key. You keep the private key private and make the public key as public as you want, and you've guaranteed that all of your communications will be secure. Netscape incorporates public-key cryptography as part of its built-in Secure Sockets Layer (SSL) security.

(For more on public-key encryption, see the discussion on Netscape's Secure Sockets Layer technology later in this chapter.)

Of course it's more complicated than that, or this chapter would end right here.

 TIP Point your Netscape newsreader to the comp.security newsgroups for the latest discussions of security on the Web.

The following are some of the other issues involved in making sure your online communications are really secure:

- Is your computer (the client in the transaction) set up in a secure manner?
- Is the server you're connected to secure?

■ Is the connection between the two systems secure?

■ Is there some way you can be sure your transaction is secure?

We'll address all four of these concerns (see fig. 5.13) in this chapter.

FIG. 5.13
This diagram illustrates
the four areas of
security concern.

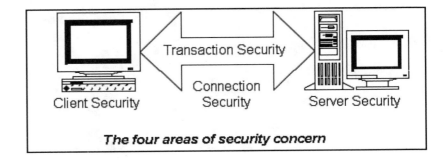

Client Security

Frankly, client security is the only area in which you have much say. Your computer is yours, and you can choose how to set it up. The chain being only as strong as its weakest link, you want to make sure that your link in the security chain is not the one that's going to snap first.

There are three areas where you have can have some major effect on the security process: how you configure helper applications, how you set up proxy servers, and how carefully you keep your passwords.

Configuring Helper Applications You can get into some real security problems if you configure helper applications without first thinking about security issues (see fig. 5.14). (See chapter 10, "Configuring Helper Applications," for detailed information on using the Netscape Helpers dialog box to set up helper applications.)

For example, if you configure Microsoft Excel as a helper application to view files with an extension ending in .XLS, what happens if a spreadsheet file you view while you're browsing the Web has an auto-execute macro that runs some hidden (and sinister) procedures? At that point, your system has been breached.

You expose your PC to a great many security risks if you configure helper applications that aren't simply passive viewers or players, unless you are certain that downloaded files can never contain any malicious content.

Be careful about helper applications. Don't configure fancy helper applications that can be programmed to run sinister macros via the Web.

Part

II

Ch

5

FIG. 5.14

You get to this dialog box for configuring Helpers by selecting Options, General Preferences (Alt+O,G) from the Netscape menu.

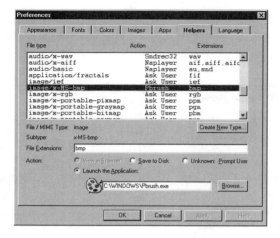

N O T E Concern about sinister macros is no mere bugaboo. Recently, Microsoft addressed the issue of what it called a "prank macro" that was being distributed via a MS Word document on the Web. Though all this macro did was display a "playful" message, it could easily have done something much more harmful.

Microsoft immediately issued a prank-macro-swatter program that would kill the macro and scan all Word documents for it, to eliminate it from your system completely.

If nothing else, this real-world example illustrates how seriously Microsoft takes this issue. ■

Proxy Servers   Proxy servers—also called application gateways or forwarders—are programs that handle communications between a protected network and the Internet. Most proxy programs log accesses and authenticate users (see fig. 5.15).

If you run Netscape from a machine on a network that is protected with a firewall (see "Firewalls" later in this chapter), you'll need to set up a different proxy server for each Internet application you want to use in conjunction with Netscape—for example, one for FTP, one for Telnet, one for UseNet news, and so on. (See appendix B, "Loading and Configuring Netscape," for information on how to configure proxies.)

Your major responsibility in this area is to make sure the proxies you use are secure and a good match to your network's firewall. In short, you should never use a proxy application that hasn't been approved by your system administrator.

If you connect to the Web via a commercial dialup service like America Online or CompuServe, you don't need proxies and don't need to worry about them.

Passwords   If you ever want to rob a bank, just walk in at noon and check around the computer terminals of people who are out to lunch. The odds are very, very good that you'll find at least one person who has left their system password on a sticky note in public view.

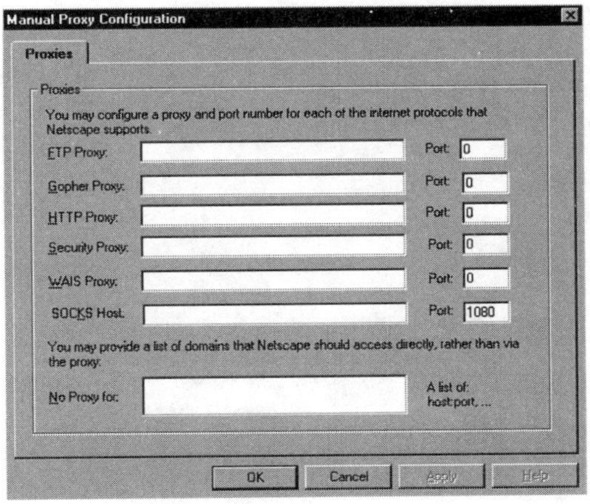

FIG. 5.15

You get to this dialog box for configuring Proxies by selecting Options, Network Preferences from the Netscape menu.

Manual Proxy Configuration

Proxies

Proxies

You may configure a proxy and port number for each of the internet protocols that Netscape supports.

FTP Proxy:	Port: 0
Gopher Proxy:	Port: 0
HTTP Proxy:	Port: 0
Security Proxy:	Port: 0
WAIS Proxy:	Port: 0
SOCKS Host:	Port: 1080

You may provide a list of domains that Netscape should access directly, rather than via the proxy.

No Proxy for: A list of: host:port, …

OK   Cancel   Apply   Help

Of course, you'll never have to worry about anyone stealing your password, because you follow the Five Basic Rules of Password Security, which are as follows:

1. Choose a password that isn't obvious.
2. Commit your password to memory.
3. Never write your password down anywhere that's accessible by anyone but you.
4. Change your password often.
5. Don't ever share your password with anyone.

If you're on a network, you already have a password for network access. Odds are, you'll register for additional access passwords on many Web sites, as well.

But there's also a password you can set for access to Netscape itself. To set your password, follow these steps:

1. Select Options, Security Preferences from the Netscape menu.
2. Click on the Passwords tab to bring it to the front (see fig. 5.16).
3. Click the Use a Password radio button.
4. Under the Ask for Password option, click one of the following buttons, depending on your preference:
    - Once per session
    - Every time it's needed
    - After __ minutes of inactivity

    If you select the last option, enter an appropriate number in the minutes field.
5. Select the Change Password push button. You'll see the screen as shown in figure 5.17.
6. Click the radio button that indicates you want a password, then select the Next> button.

Part

II

Ch

5

FIG. 5.16

Netscape's Preferences dialog box lets you set access password options.

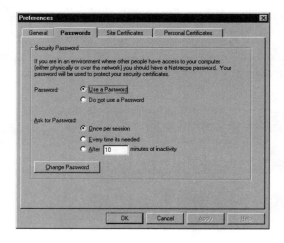

FIG. 5.17

This box lets you confirm that you really want to use a password.

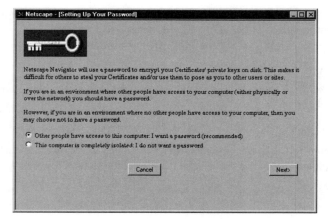

7. You are prompted to enter a password of more than eight characters, then retype it to confirm (see fig. 5.18). REMEMBER YOUR PASSWORD!!! Netscape cannot tell you what it is if you forget.

8. Choose the Next> button.

9. When the last window appears, select Finished. You'll be sent back to the Password window.

10. Choose OK to end.

FIG. 5.18

Entering a password.

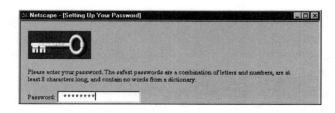

Server Security and Firewalls

A poorly managed Web server can be the source of many security compromises. For example, a poorly written CGI script can accidentally allow malicious intrusions into a system. The Web server administrator is responsible for managing the server in such a way as to prevent such security compromises.

It's also important that the Web server software installed on the server machine be capable of handling secure transactions over the Internet. For example, the Netscape Commerce Server (Netscape's server software package) incorporates SSL (Secure Sockets Layer) security, with support for acquiring a server certificate and communicating securely with SSL-capable browsers like Netscape Navigator. (For more on the Netscape Commerce Server, see chapter 29, "Testing the Netscape Commerce Server.")

But perhaps the most important security concern regarding servers is the installation of a good firewall.

A better name for firewall might be traffic cop, because the main function of the group of programs that comprise a firewall system is to block some Internet traffic while allowing the rest to flow. There are a variety of ways that this can be implemented on a server system, but all firewalls perform similar functions.

Some allow only e-mail traffic, which limits security concerns to "mail bombs" and other e-mail-based attacks. Others allow a full range of Internet accesses. In any event, a firewall performs two major functions: user authentication and access logging. The first keeps out intruders; the second provides an accurate record of what happened in case one gets through.

Since all firewalls provide a single access point between the Internet and a network, they make it relatively easy to monitor communications should there be any suspected breaches of security.

Without some kind of firewall installed, a network system hooked up to the Internet is open to all kinds of security attacks.

 T I P For more information on firewalls, point Netscape to ftp://ftp.greatcircle.com/pub/firewalls, which contains the Firewalls mailing list archives.

Connection Security

Between point A (your computer) and point B (the Web server you're connected to on the Internet), there may be dozens of other computers handling the communications link. Obviously, the more computers in the chain, the more chances for some unknown person to break into your transmission and steal your data.

Unfortunately, you don't have much control over your Internet connection. That's even more reason to make sure you do as much as you can to make the things you do have some control over as solid and secure as possible.

Part

II

Ch

5

Transaction Security

Transaction security is the area that most people think of when they think of security on the Web. Maybe it's because it's the area that encompasses the most high-tech and dramatic aspect of computer security: cryptography.

There is, of course, much more to transaction security than just data encryption. Message verification and server identification are at least as important, if not even more so. After all, what difference does it make if a message is securely encoded if its source is someone impersonating you and trying to use your credit card or steal your data, or if a message that you legitimately sent has been intercepted and altered in transit?

N O T E What if your major concern is not making sure that data is transmitted securely, but making sure that it doesn't get transmitted at all? Many parents are concerned about (admittedly overblown) media reports about pornography and other objectionable materials that are available on the World Wide Web. They don't want their children to be able to access such data.

Parental lock-out systems can work in much the same way as the security measures employed in ensuring secure transactions. For example, a Web browser might have different accounts set up with different passwords and different encryption keys for parents' and kids' accounts. The parents' account might allow unlimited access, while the kids' account wouldn't properly decode transmissions from restricted sites. Such sites could be defined by looking for specific "ratings" tags sent by the Web server, or by setting up a list of forbidden sites.

There are many ways that parental lock-out could work. Netscape and two other leading Internet software companies (Microsoft and Progressive Networks) have formed the Information Highway Parental Empowerment Group to work on the problem. ■

The rest of this chapter is devoted to the topic of transaction security and how Netscape handles it.

Netscape Security

N O T E Additional information on Netscape security is just a couple of mouse clicks away. From the Netscape menu, select Help, On Security for access to the following helpful documents from Netscape Corporation's World Wide Web site:

- Netscape Navigator Handbook: Security
- Netscape Data Security
- Using RSA Public Key Cryptography
- The SSL Protocol ■

The Cracking of SSL

You may have read about it in the papers: Two University of California-Berkeley students and a researcher in France almost simultaneously posted messages to the Internet detailing their success in decoding a message that had been posted as a "Netscape security challenge." They discovered how Netscape 1.2 generates session encryption keys, enabling them to replicate the keys for that specific message with a moderate amount of computing power and, within a few days, they had deciphered it.

What was the problem? In a nutshell, Netscape was using a relatively small set of pseudo-random data (the number of processes running on the client computer, process ID numbers, the current time in microseconds, and so on) to generate a relatively large random number encoding key. This meant that the hackers didn't have to try every possible random 40-bit number to find the key.

The researcher in France used 120 workstations and two parallel supercomputers at three major research centers for eight days—approximately $10,000 worth of computing power. While this seems like a lot of effort to put into decoding just one simple little one-page message (and it is), it did serve to show that Netscape's security was crackable. If the same techniques had been applied to a security-critical message (for example, a hostile takeover bid for a major corporation), the consequences could be substantial.

The 40-bit key used in the "challenge" message is the international encryption mode used in export versions of Netscape Navigator. The 128-bit key encryption used in the U.S. version is export-restricted under government security regulations. It is much more robust; it would have taken many years to break the challenge message if the same amount of computing power had been encoded with the U.S. version.

While no actual thefts of real-world information have ever been reported to Netscape Corporation, they worked quickly to provide updated software for free downloading from their home page on the Web. The new version 1.22 security patch increased the amount of random information used to generate keys from 30 bits to approximately 300 bits. With 10 times as much pseudo-random data to start with, keys in the latest versions of Netscape Navigator are now effectively immune from similar "brute-force" attacks.

The security features built into Netscape Navigator (and the Netscape Commerce Server) attempt to protect your Web transactions in the following three important ways:

- Server authentication (thwarting impostors)
- Encryption (thwarting eavesdroppers)
- Data integrity (thwarting vandals)

Netscape's Visual Security Cues

Netscape Navigator includes some visual security indicators to let you know about security conditions. These indicators include identification of secure URLs, changing color bars, a broken/solid key icon, and the ability to view identification and security information associated with a Web page. You'll also see various warning dialog boxes from time to time, depending on how you have your security options set.

URL Identification   You can tell whether a Web page comes from a secure server by looking at the URL (location) field at the top of the Netscape window. If the URL begins with https:// instead of http://, your connection is secure (see fig. 5.19). Similarly, a news URL that begins

Part
II

Ch
5

with snews: instead of news: indicates that a document comes from a secure news server. In both cases the s stands for secure, of course, and in both cases it requests are traveling through a Secure Sockets Layer.

FIG. 5.19

If the server you're connected to is secure, Netscape's URL bar shows the address as beginning with https:// instead of http://.

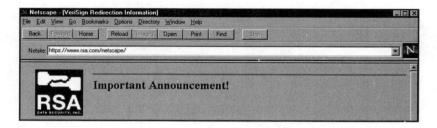

The Key and the Color Bar   To the left of the status message at the bottom of the Netscape screen, you'll find a key icon. The status of this key indicates whether or not you are viewing a secure document. A broken key icon on a gray background indicates an insecure document; a solid key on a blue background indicates a secure document (see fig. 5.20). The secure key icon varies slightly depending on the grade of encryption: The key has two teeth for high-grade and one tooth for medium-grade. A mixed document with insecure information omitted is shown as secure; if the insecure information is included, the status is displayed as insecure.

Likewise, a blue color bar above the Netscape display window indicates a secure document, while a gray color bar indicates an insecure document.

Netscape Security Dialog Boxes   Several notification dialog boxes (or alerts) inform you of the security status of documents.

When entering a secure document space, you are notified that the secure document is encrypted when it is transferred to you, and any information you send back is also encrypted (see fig. 5.21).

When leaving a secure document space, you are notified that the insecure document can be observed by a third party when it is transferred to you, and any information you send back can also be read by a third party.

When viewing a document with a mix of secure and insecure information, you are notified that the secure document you just loaded contained some insecure information that will not be shown. If an insecure document contains secure information (either inline or as part of a form), this alert is not displayed. The document is simply considered to be insecure.

When you submit a form using any insecure submit process, you are notified that the submission process you are about to use is insecure (see fig. 5.22). This means that the information you are sending could be compromised by a third party.

FIG. 5.20
The key in the lower-left corner of the Netscape window is broken (top) if your connection is insecure or mixed, and solid (bottom) if your connection is secure.

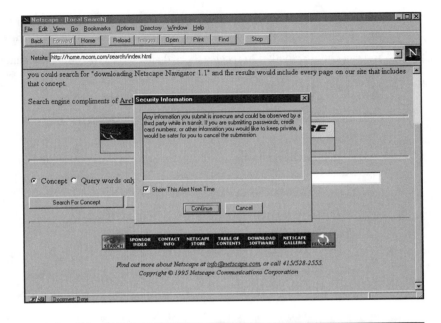

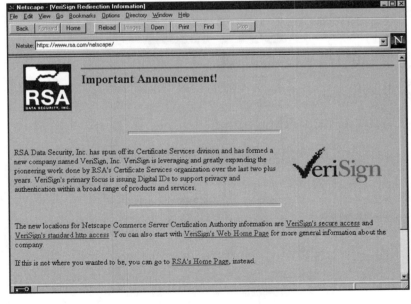

You are notified if the document was expected to be a secure document but is actually an insecure document (the document location has been redirected to an insecure document).

You can choose whether to receive these dialog boxes by setting the panel items in the Netscape Options menu.

Here's how to turn Netscape's security alert dialog boxes on or off:

1. Select Options, Security Preferences from the Netscape menu.
2. Click the General tab to bring it to the front (see fig. 5.23).
3. You'll see the following four different Security Alerts selections, labeled Show a Security Alert Before:

   - Entering a Secure Document Space (Server)
   - Leaving a Secure Document Space (Server)
   - Viewing a Document With a Secure/Insecure Mix
   - Submitting a Form Insecurely

   Click the appropriate spaces to select or deselect the dialog boxes you want to see.
4. Choose OK to finish.

You can also simply uncheck the dialog box's Show this Alert Next Time checkbox if you decide you never want to see it again.

FIG. 5.21

One of Netscape's security alert dialog boxes; this one is to notify you of encrypted data transfers.

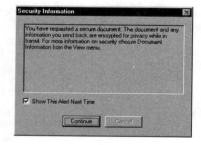

FIG. 5.22

If a form you submit is insecure, you'll see this alert.

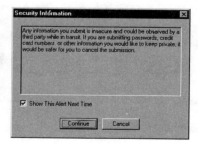

View Document Information   To view information about a displayed Web page, choose View, Document Info from the Netscape menu. A new Netscape window (see fig. 5.24) displays the document title, the URL of the file, and document info, which includes file type, source, modification date, file length, expiration date, character set, and security level. This information is taken from the header of the document and from the server that supplied the page.

FIG. 5.23

You use Netscape's Preferences dialog box to set alert display options.

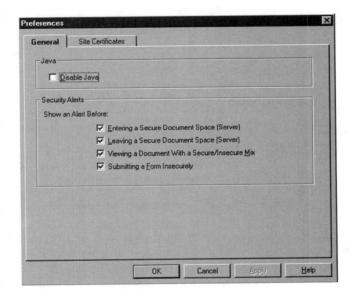

The Document Info window displayed in Netscape uses another new feature, Frames, which enables independent sub-windows, or frames, within one page display window. In the Document Info window, the top frame shows the document title and its URL, and the bottom frame shows a list of information about the document. If you click the link to the document in the lower frame, the document itself is shown in the lower frame. If you then click the link in the upper frame, the lower frame displays the document information again. You can resize the relative sizes of the frames in the window: just put the mouse on the boundary until you see the mouse icon change into a split pair of arrows, then click and drag the boundary between frames.

N O T E   Depending on where the Document Info window appears on your screen when it is invoked, you may need to move it (click and drag the title bar) to be able to use the scroll bar in the lower frame. You may need to scroll the lower frame down to where the security information line is, at the bottom of the list of document information, so you can see the lines of security information for the document. ▨

Part
II

Ch
5

FIG. 5.24
Netscape displays document information using its new Frames capability. This info is for a page at RSA, Inc.'s secure WWW server.

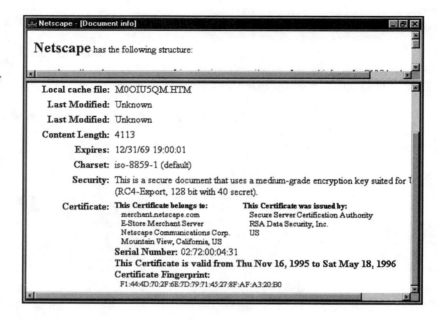

If a document is insecure, the security information panel notifies you that encryption is not used and there is no server certificate. If a document is secure, the security information panel notifies you of the encryption's grade, export control, key size, and algorithm type, and, in a scrolling field, the server certificate presents coded data identifying the following:

- Certificate version and serial number
- Issuer of the certificate
- Subject (organization) that is being certified

To ensure that you are communicating with the organization you want, examine the subject of the server certificate. The organization should identify itself with the name and location you expect.

Certificate information is protected by encryption to ensure authenticity and integrity. You can interpret the coded data as follows:

- Country: Two-character country code
- State or Province (ST): Unabbreviated state/province name
- Organization (O): Legal, registered organization name
- Organizational Unit (OU): Optional department name
- Locality (L): City the organization resides or is registered in
- Common Name (CN): The server's fully qualified host name (such as hostname.netscape.com)

To return to the main Netscape window, choose File, Close to close the Document Info window, or use the window Close button.

Personal Certificates

Netscape Atlas now provides for the ability to definitely identify who you're sending data to. Previously, you could never be sure that the Web page you're looking at was created or maintained by the person who said it was. That is, somebody could've put up a Web page and claim to be somebody else, and you'd never have been able to tell the difference.

Personal certificates allow you to identify yourself from everybody else. This is particularly useful when you're submitting a form, so that the recipient will know for sure the information is from you, and nobody else. You can control your personal certificates by selecting Options, Security Preferences, and choosing the Personal Certificates tab. This dialog box (see fig. 5.25) lists your existing personal certificates.

FIG. 5.25
The Personal Certificates tab is used to help you control how you identify yourself to others.

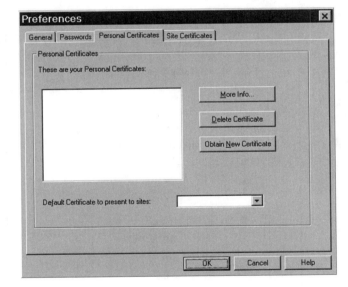

Part
II

Ch
5

Site Certificates

Certification for an entire domain or company is performed in a manner similar to personal certificates. The only difference is that it's applied to a larger entity, rather than an individual. As with personal certificates, all site certificates must be issued from a Certifying Authority (CA). A CA can be any trusted central administration, a person or a computer, willing to acknowledge the identities of those to whom it issues certificates. For example, a company would probably be the Certifying Authority for any certificates it issues its employees.

SSL

The Secure Sockets Layer (SSL) protocol is Netscape's answer to transmission security over the World Wide Web. SSL is application protocol-independent and provides encryption, which creates a secured channel to prevent others from tapping into the network; authentication, which uses certificates and digital signatures to verify the identity of parties in information exchanges and transactions; and message integrity, which ensures that messages cannot be altered en route.

The Netscape Commerce Server and Netscape Navigator incorporate SSL technology, and both (or compatible programs) are needed in order to establish a secure SSL connection.

SSL is layered beneath application protocols such as HTTP, Telnet, FTP, Gopher, and NNTP, and layered above the connection protocol TCP/IP (see fig. 5.26). This strategy allows SSL to operate independently of the Internet application protocols. With SSL implemented on both the client and server, your Internet communications are transmitted in encrypted form, ensuring privacy.

FIG. 5.26
This diagram shows how SSL fits into transactions on the Internet.

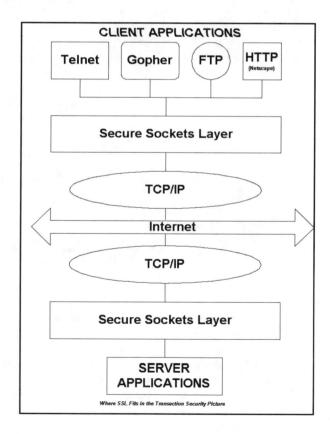

SSL uses authentication and public-key encryption technology developed by RSA Data Security, Inc.

Server authentication uses RSA public key cryptography (see the "RSA Public Key Cryptography" sidebar that follows) in conjunction with ISO X.509 digital certificates. Netscape Navigator and the Netscape Commerce Server deliver server authentication using signed digital certificates issued by trusted third parties known as certificate authorities. A digital certificate verifies the connection between a server's public key and the server's identification (just as a driver's license verifies the connection between your photograph and your personal identification). Cryptographic checks using digital signatures ensure that information within a certificate can be trusted.

RSA Public Key Cryptography

RSA (Rivest-Shamir-Adleman) public key cryptographic technology is at the heart of most Web security schemes, including Netscape's built-in Secure Sockets Layer protocol. The following is how it works, in a nutshell.

Encoding and decoding of messages is accomplished by using two large random numbers. One is called the public key, and is made public. The other is the private key, and is kept secret. Messages encoded with the public key can be decoded only using the private key, and vice versa. So messages sent to you can be decoded only by you, and messages you send can be verified as coming from you, because only your public key decodes them.

Because encryption is considered a national security issue by the federal government, U.S. products can't be exported to foreign countries with really high-level security built in. That's why the international version of Netscape uses only 40-bit keys, while the domestic version uses 128-bit keys.

The RSA encryption technology used in Netscape is owned by RSA, Inc., which also makes a stand-alone security product for Windows called RSA Secure. RSA Secure integrates into the Windows File Manager to provide RSA encryption for the Windows file system. The company offers a trial version for 30-day evaluation, and checking it out is a good way to learn more about RSA encryption. For more information on RSA, Inc., or to download the free evaluation version of RSA Secure, go to their secure (naturally) WWW server at **http://www.rsa.com**.

Public key cryptography has been around only a couple of years longer than the World Wide Web. Pretty Good Privacy (PGP) is a stand-alone public-key encryption program from MIT for multiple platforms that lets you play around with and learn about public key cryptography. You can also use it for serious purposes, like encrypting mail and files on your hard disk.

The latest version of PGP for Windows can be downloaded from **ftp://net-dist. mit.edu/pub/PGP**.

To learn more about PGP and public-key cryptography, point Netscape to **http://bs.mit.edu:8001/ pgp-form.html**.

Part

II

Ch

5

N O T E The security of this system comes from the fact that the numbers used are very large. Though the numbers can be discovered by factoring, the amount of computer time required to do so is highly impractical, often running into hundreds of years. ■

Server Certificates

To operate using security features, the Netscape Commerce Server requires a digitally signed certificate, which is a kind of trustworthy "electronic driver's license"—it's a unique identifier. Without a certificate, the server can only operate insecurely. If you are a server administrator and want to obtain a signed certificate, you need to submit a certificate request to a certificate authority, a third-party organization that issues certificates, and pay an associated service fee.

When you request a server certificate from an online service, your server software generates a public key/private key pair and you choose a distinguished name. Online forms guide you through the process of submitting the form to the certificate authorization company.

The authenticity of each certificate request is verified (making sure requesters are who they claim to be). Upon approval, the certifier digitally signs the request and returns the unique digitally signed certificate through e-mail. You can then install the signed, valid certificate to enable security.

Setting Certificate Options in Netscape   You can examine and change Netscape's installed security certificates through the Options, Security Preferences section on the menu bar.

Select the Site Certificates tab for a scrolling list of server certificates that Netscape is configured to handle (see fig. 5.27).

FIG. 5.27
You can set Site Certificate preferences through this Preferences dialog box.

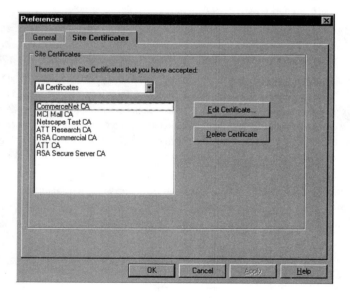

You can highlight an entry and select Delete Certificate to remove a certificate from the Netscape setup. You'll probably want to do this only if there is some major flap over bugs or breaches of a particular certification authority's certificates.

The Edit Certificate button brings up the certificate information dialog box shown in figure 5.28. Clicking checkboxes here lets you choose to allow or disallow connections to sites using the chosen certificate. You can also elect to see an alert dialog box when you encounter a site with the specified certification.

N O T E Cookie files seem to be mentioned in passing in a lot of discussions having to do with security, without much associated definition or clarification.

Briefly, a cookie file is a small amount of data sent back from the server to be stored on your computer, which the server can access later. This might be account information or any other information associated with your specific session that the server doesn't want to keep on hand, but needs to refer to later.

Cookie files may be transmitted to your computer and back to the server in a secure or insecure manner (that is, with or without SSL security). So security with cookie files is, as with any data transfer, a separate issue to itself.

There are two things you can say about cookie files and security in general: There might be some extra measure of security in keeping your personal information on your machine rather than on the server, but there is also some additional security risk involved in transferring cookie file data back and forth between your machine and the server every time it's needed. ■

FIG. 5.28
Netscape displays detailed information about a site certificate.

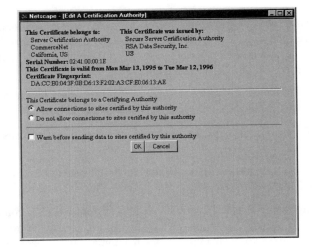

Business Transactions

First there was television, which from the very beginning included commercials. Then there were those late-night infomercials for Ginsu knives and the Popeil Pocket Fisherman. Finally, with the advent of cable TV, there was the Home Shopping Network (and its many clones).

Though the Internet began life as an infrastructure for the exchange of scholarly information, it didn't take long for someone to figure out how to turn a quick buck online with mass postings and mailings. And it took even less time for those annoying all-text "spam" messages to give way to a plethora of Web-based online shopping malls.

Not that there's anything wrong with that (though some old-timers whine all night about the commercialization of the Web). Let's face it—people like to buy things. And buying things on the Web is no worse than buying them on the Home Shopping Network, or even at Wal-Mart. It's just different.

One of the toughest things to work out is how to pay for something you've ordered electronically. Cash and checks can't be squeezed down the wires, and most people are leery about posting their credit card numbers where they might be grabbed by unscrupulous hackers.

But enterprising Web entrepreneurs have already figured out how to take the electronic equivalents of credit cards and money electronically.

There are differences between using credit cards and using electronic cash, but the range of services available blurs the lines of distinction between the various methods of conducting financial transactions electronically on the Internet. Some schemes deal directly with banks, while some use second-tier arrangements, bonding-houses, or third-party secure-server services.

Digital Money

Digital money is a totally new concept. Even more radical in concept than the once preposterous idea that paper bills could represent real gold, in its most basic form, digital money involves transmitting an encoded electronic packet of information that is as secure and difficult to counterfeit as a dollar bill. (More so, really.)

Digital money is based on the same security encoding schemes as other secure transactions on the Web—encryption and authentication. But some of the proposed schemes go a step beyond.

For example, the two companies examined next have very different ideas of how digital money should work.

CyberCash CyberCash has set up both debit and credit systems, but we're mostly interested here in the debit, or "cash" system.

In the CyberCash scheme, participating banks let a customer open accounts that amount to "electronic purses." Using the company's software, a customer moves money from the checking account into the electronic purse. As with an automatic teller machine, the customer then withdraws digital tokens from the purse and uses them to make purchases on the Net. Upon receipt, the seller queries the CyberCash computer to verify the token is valid and instructs CyberCash where to deposit the money.

To use the CyberCash system, you must install the client version of CyberCash software to work with your browser. It also requires that the Web server handling the transaction form must use the CyberCash system to decrypt order information.

CyberCash believes that most consumers want to have a record of their transactions to budget and account for their spending.

For more on CyberCash, visit its Web site at **http://www.cybercash.com/**.

DigiCash DigiCash operates a debit system that is similar to an electronic checking account. To set up a DigiCash account, you deposit money in a bank that supports the DigiCash system, and you are issued Ecash that can be used to purchase things through the Web.

But DigiCash has a philosophy that is much different than CyberCash's. DigiCash sees records as a threat to privacy, and has developed a method to create completely untraceable, anonymous digital cash. Without anonymity, they say, electronic transactions leave a detailed trail of activity that could enable governments, personal enemies, or commercial marketers to easily trace an individual's activities, preferences, and beliefs.

DigiCash, based in the Netherlands, has created electronic tokens that can be trusted as valid money regardless of who is spending them. An ingenious double-blind encryption method makes it impossible to trace transactions unless there is mathematical proof that fraud has occurred.

But the idea of total anonymity has scared off most bankers and has government officials worried as well. Total anonymity, they fear, could provide a haven for money launderers, arms dealers, and kidnappers.

For more info on DigiCash, check it out on the Web at **http://digicash.support.nl/**.

 For more information on digital money and the companies making it happen, check out the Yahoo index on the topic at **http://www.yahoo.com/Business_and_Economy/Electronic_Commerce/ Digital_Money/**.

Part II

Ch 5

Credit Card Transactions

If you're concerned about security risks when using your credit card over the Web, then you also should be concerned about giving out any personal information through a Web page. But then again, maybe you shouldn't buy raffle tickets from the neighborhood kids, either. Who knows what people will do with your personal information?

Using your credit card anywhere poses risks. Those risks are certainly more complex in the realm of Internet servers, browsers, and complex multi-functional systems. Secure communications does not eliminate all of an Internet user's concerns. The situation is analogous to telling someone your credit card number over the telephone. You may be secure in knowing that no one has overheard your conversation (privacy) and that the person on the line works for the company you wish to buy from (authentication), but you must also be willing to trust the person and the company.

That being said, let's look at a few of the schemes that are surfacing on the Web that claim to make using your credit card online as secure as (or even more secure than) using it at your local supermarket.

Netscape's Secure Courier Netscape's Secure Courier protocol builds on their existing Secure Sockets Layer (SSL) protocol. Secure Courier observes the MasterCard and Visa security specification for bank card purchases on open networks.

While SSL encrypts data passing along the network between a client system and a server, Secure Courier keeps a transaction encrypted in a secure digital envelope when it arrives at a merchant's server or at other intermediate points on the Net. This means that the data remains wrapped, or protected, at any site at which it stops.

To find out more, connect to Netscape's Web page for the Secure Courier protocol at **http:// home.netscape.com/newsref/std/credit.html**.

First Virtual First Virtual Corporation is an online transaction handling company that operates a system that is designed for selling downloadable products, such as executable software files and information in text files. To get an account, you call them and give them your credit card information, and they issue you a First Virtual account number.

Whenever your First Virtual account number is used to purchase something online, you are notified by e-mail, and you must confirm the transaction before your credit card is charged. Once you verify, your card is charged for the purchase and the money is deposited in the vendor's First Virtual checking account.

The First Virtual method needs no software or hardware on either end of the transaction. It's designed to be simple, fast, and efficient.

For more detailed information, go to **http://www.fv.com/** on the Web.

VeriSign VeriSign, a spin-off of RSA, Inc., is collaborating with Netscape to provide Digital IDs (digital certificates) for direct online transactions through the Netscape Commerce Server and Netscape Navigator version 3.0. The following four classes of ID are available:

- Class 1—A low level of assurance, to be used for secure e-mail and casual browsing. Noncommercial and evaluation versions are offered for free, with a VeriSign-supported commercial version for $6 per year.

- Class 2—Provides a higher degree of trust and security. Used for access to advanced Web sites. $12 per year.

- Class 3—A higher level of assurance for valued purchases and inter-company communications. $24 per year.

- Class 4—Said to provide "a maximum level of identity assurance" for high-end financial transactions and trades. Pricing is by quote.

The Digital ID system from VeriSign is being marketed as "The Driver's License for the Internet." RSA has the good fortune to own the patents on the encryption schemes used by SSL and SHTTP, so this gives the VeriSign system a boost.

For more info, see **http://www.verisign.com/**.

Open Market   Open Market acts as its own credit card company in a scheme that relies on their own Open-MarketPlace Server. It is unique in that it depends on the end-user having a browser that supports the S-HHTP protocol, not Netscape's SSL protocol. They'll be worth watching, if just to see whether a company other than Netscape can help set security standards on the Web.

You can check out their Web site at **http://www.openmarket.com/**.

For lots of links relating to credit cards, point Netscape to the Credit Card Network Home Page at **http://www.creditnet.com**.

For an excellent detailed discussion of how credit card transactions work on the Web, check out this Netscape page: **http://www.netscape.com/newsref/std/credit.html**.

The Future of WWW Security

For a lengthy discussion of current Web security issues, check out **http://www-genome.wi.mit.edu/ WWW/faqs/www-security-faq.html**.

With a topic as hot as security, it's about as easy to get an agreement on the question of what's secure as it is to get two politicians to agree on a plan to balance the federal budget.

Though Netscape Corporation is in a powerful position, it's not powerful enough to simply dictate security standards for the World Wide Web. There are a lot of people out there—powerful, influential, and monied people in banking and credit and the government—who simply aren't convinced that Netscape's SSL protocol can protect their important transactions over the Internet.

That's why there are dozens of alternative proposals for security protocols for WWW transactions. Because of Netscape's position in the Web community, it's likely that SSL will be with us well into the future, but you're still likely to start running into some sites that want you to use another protocol. The following pages offer an overview of some of the most likely contenders for real-world implementation as WWW security protocols in the months and years to come.

S-HTTP

S-HTTP (Secure HTTP) has emerged as the major competitor to Netscape's SSL security protocol. In fact, it has gained such a following that most commerce on the Web will be supporting both protocols—including Netscape Navigator!

Developed by EIT, CommerceNet, OpenMarket, and others, S-HHTP extends the Web's standard HTTP data transfer protocol by adding encryption and decryption using paired public-key encryption, support for digital signatures, and message authentication.

Several cryptographic message format standards can be incorporated into S-HTTP clients and servers, including PKCS-7, PEM, and PGP. S-HTTP clients can also communicate with non-secure standard HTTP servers, though without security.

S-HTTP doesn't require (though it does support) client-side public key certificates or public keys, which means that you can initiate spontaneous transactions without having an established public key first.

S-HTTP also provides for simple challenge-response freshness authentication—that is, an "are you really you" and "yes, I'm really me" secure message exchange—to make sure no one is intercepting and changing transmitted messages. It can even consider HTTP's DATE header when determining freshness.

For more information on S-HTTP, visit the following sites: **http://www.eit.com/**, **http://www.openmarket.com/**, or **http://www.commerce.net/**.

Shen

CERN (the organization in Switzerland that created the World Wide Web) is developing a new high-level secure protocol called Shen. It approaches security by providing for weak authentication with low maintenance and no patent or export restrictions, or strong authentication using public key encryption. Since it's coming from CERN, which has the ear of the whole Web, Shen is bound to become a standard itself, or at least influence the development of other security standards.

For more info on Shen, point Netscape to **http://www.w3.org/hypertext/WWW/Shen/ref/shen.html**.

Fortezza

One of Netscape Corporation's latest security additions is integrated support for the Fortezza security card, which is based on U.S. government standard cryptography. Developed by the National Security Agency, Fortezza is a cryptographic system delivered in a PCMCIA card format, and is now mandatory for use in many government agencies. Fortezza cards are already being used by the Department of Defense and the U.S. intelligence community.

Support for Fortezza has been added to Netscape's Secure Sockets Layer (SSL) open protocol, and Netscape Corp. will be upgrading Netscape Navigator and other Netscape products to support the use of Fortezza cards.

Netscape is currently working with Litronic Industries to further develop the Fortezza cryptographic interface.

Because of its status as a top-secret government security protocol, information on Fortezza is difficult to come by. I know of no site on the Web that offers more than just a terse sentence or two on the subject.

Security is a hot topic on the Web. A good place to find out more about security online is the Virtual Library Subject Catalogue entry on the topic at **http://www.w3.org/hypertext/DataSources/ bySubject/Overview.html**.

For more details on Netscape's security technologies, see **http://home.netscape.com/newsref/ref/ netscape-security.html**.

An excellent source of links to security sites on the Web is at Xenon Laboratories WWW site: **http:// www.xe.net/xenon/security.htm**.

Part
II
Ch
5

## CHAPTER 6

Accessing Other Services with Netscape

The World Wide Web was only created in 1991, and has since experienced explosive growth. However, the Internet was more than 20 years old when the Web was first developed as a graphical, point-and-click interface that would reduce the learning curve associated with navigating it. Finding anything on the Internet then was associated with understanding UNIX, and the tools developed for searching the Internet were only marginally more intuitive than being a systems administrator yourself.

This chapter will discuss some of Netscape's other capabilities besides looking at World Wide Web pages. One of the newest tools for navigating the Internet, Netscape incorporates many of the Internet access techniques that formerly required separate tools. In this chapter, you will learn:

- How to access an FTP site

- How to use Gopher to find information

- How FTP and Gopher are integrated into Netscape

- How to search FTP sites and Gopherspace with comic book characters

- The ancient art of Telnet

Accessing and Downloading from an FTP Site

FTP (File Transfer Protocol) lets you examine the directories of remote systems on the Internet, and lets you transfer files between your computer and other computers. Almost as old as the Internet itself, FTP was designed to work with the systems of the time. You can think of FTP as being very much like using the CD and Dir commands in DOS to move from one directory to another, and to see what's in that directory only when you get there. FTP lets you transfer both text files and binary files (programs).

Using Netscape for FTP

As a Netscape user, you have FTP incorporated into Netscape so that you really don't notice any difficulty. Netscape displays FTP information as a single column of links, each link being either a file or a directory link. An FTP directory viewed with Netscape looks very similar to the File Manager in Microsoft Windows. Each line of the FTP directory displays a small icon (either a file or a directory), the name of the file, the size of the file, and the date that file was added to the directory. FTP directories may include a README or an INDEX text file, which describes the contents of the directory, or the policies of FTP access for that site.

To reach an FTP server in Netscape, type the URL of the FTP server. If a link to an FTP server is on a Web page, select that link to jump to that FTP server. Netscape 3.0 reduces the effort needed to access an FTP site if the hostname starts with ftp. For example, typing the hostname ftp.foobar.com into the location field (without ftp:// before it) takes you to the URL **ftp://ftp.foobar.com/**. For example, typing ftp.kli.org into Netscape's Location field takes you to the FTP archive of the Klingon Language Institute shown in figure 6.1, just as **ftp://ftp.kli.org/** does.

FIG. 6.1

The Klingon Language Institute's FTP server.

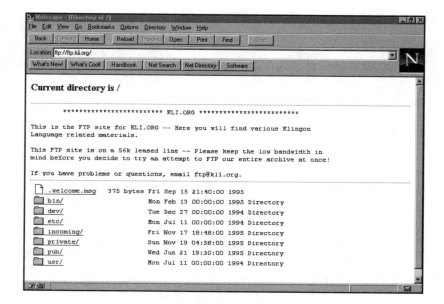

If, for whatever reason, a Web site you are trying to reach has named its Web server as ftp.whatever.com/, you can avoid the new default by specifying the protocol identifier. So typing the URL as ftp.foobar.com/ or as ftp://ftp.foobar.com/ starts an FTP session with the FTP server ftp.foobar.com/, but typing the URL as http://ftp.foobar.com/ attempts to retrieve a Web page from the Web server. When you have found the file you want, downloading from an FTP archive with Netscape is as simple as selecting the appropriate link, and the file is transferred to your local system.

 TIP FTP directories and subdirectories almost always have a link at the top of the page named "Up to higher level directory." Clicking this link takes you one step higher in that FTP site's directory hierarchy—not back one Web page as the Back button in Netscape does.

Most FTP servers are set up to allow anonymous access—meaning that you do not need a login and password account set up specifically for that server. Typically, an anonymous FTP server accepts "anonymous" as the login, and your e-mail address as your password. Netscape is designed to try to log in anonymously when it encounters an FTP server.

NOTE Because Netscape tries to log in anonymously, you need to have your electronic mail preferences set up in the Mail and News window of Netscape's Options window before you try. Most anonymous FTP servers request that you use your e-mail address as your password. ▪

Downloading Files

Downloading a file (getting a file from an FTP site to your computer) is as simple as clicking a link in Netscape. When an FTP site is displayed in Netscape, you can click any of the directory links to see the contents of that directory. When you click the link for a file, Netscape will prompt you to see what you want to do with the file. You'll see the same dialog box that you see when Netscape encounters any file type it doesn't have a helper or plug-in for. (See chapters 9 and 10 for a discussion of plug-ins and helper applications.) Generally, you'll want to click the Save File button and then choose a location to save the file.

For files such as text and graphics that Netscape can display, Netscape will display them if you simply click on them. You can do this and then choose the File, Save As command to save it. Or, you can save it directly by clicking the link with the right mouse button and choosing Save Link As from the shortcut menu.

Uploading Files

There may be times when you need to upload a file (send a file to an FTP site from your computer). Not all FTP sites allow uploading so you'll need to check to see if you have permission to upload files. If you do have permission,

1. Click the directory links until you are in the directory where you want the file uploaded.
2. Choose the File, Upload File command.
3. Find and select the file to upload in the dialog box and click Open.

Part
II
Ch
6

This uploads your file. You can also use drag and drop to upload a file. To do this, drag a file from your desktop, file manager (or Explorer) to the Netscape window. Netscape will ask you to confirm that you want to upload the file to this location.

Using Netscape to FTP Non-Anonymously

In some instances, you have a username and password for a network, and need to log in to that network and download files. Netscape does support FTP access with a username and password. To start a non-anonymous FTP session with Netscape, add your username and the at (@) symbol before the FTP server's hostname. For example, if you had access to the servers at startup.com, and the FTP server's name started with ftp, you would type the following URL into the Location field at the top of the Netscape window:

> **ftp://username@ftp.startup.com/**

The next window Netscape displays is a prompt asking for your password. After you type in your password, you are logged into the FTP server, and may start downloading files.

Archie How to Search for Files to Remotely Transfer

The original problem with FTP was that, while FTP let you transfer a file from a remote computer system, you had to go to that remote directory with FTP first and find what you wanted. If the person administering the FTP server had not included an index text file describing the files in the directory, you had to guess if the file name you were reading was the one you wanted.

Archie was designed to create a centralized indexed list of files that are available on anonymous FTP sites. The Archie database, which as of this writing indexes over 1,000 anonymous servers and an aggregate of 2.4 million files, is mirrored at several locations around the world to reduce the load on individual systems. Over 50,000 queries are made to Archie databases every day. Many of the Archie servers now support inquiries using the Web forms capability discussed earlier in this chapter. Archie is accessible in three ways:

- Netscape
- Archie-specific client software
- Telnet

The Telnet protocol will be discussed later in this chapter. Archie clients are available for almost every platform, and may be found with the Web interfaces to the Archie database. To use Netscape to conduct Archie searches, use the URL **http://pubweb.nexor.co.uk/public/archie/servers.html** (see fig. 6.2).

This Web page presents you with links to many of the mirror sites of the Archie database. One Archie server you can use is located at **http://www.lerc.nasa.gov/archieplex/doc/form.html**, which gives you the form shown in figure 6.3.

N O T E Whenever you are presented with a choice of multiple sites to connect to, it is polite to try the one closest to you first. International connections are often heavily loaded, and you may get a faster response from a host computer on the same continent that you are. However, if closer hosts don't respond, try the other hosts from the menu. ■

FIG. 6.2

The central index of Archie servers on the World Wide Web.

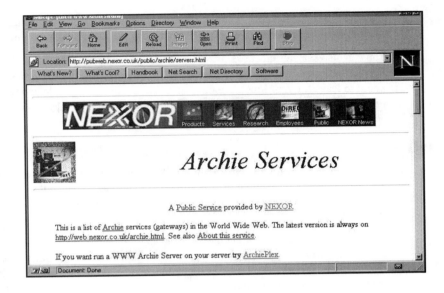

FIG. 6.3

The Archie form for searching FTP servers, as provided by the NASA Lewis Research Center.

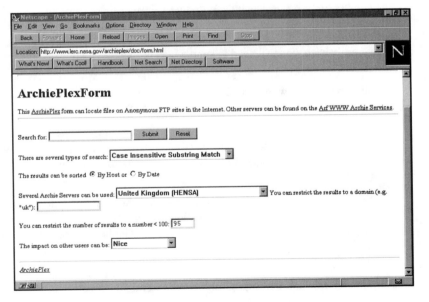

Part

II

Ch

6

You may choose many ways to customize your Archie search. The default setting for matching your entry is a case-insensitive substring match, but you may choose other options from the drop-down list box. The results of your search may be given to you sorted by host or by date of the files, and you may choose a specific server from the next list box, or enter a domain in the field below that list box to restrict the search to only part of the world. To speed up your reply, you can reduce the number of answers. This is helpful if you have a good idea of what you're looking for. For example, if you know the exact name of the file you want, you probably don't need to receive the location of more than the first ten or so files matching that exact file name.

You can also set the "niceness" of your Archie search, from "Nicest" to "Not Nice at All." Niceness is a priority tag that determines how fast your Archie query is processed. If you are just about to leave for your lunch break, be considerate of other people and set your query as lower priority than normal ("Nice"), because you don't need your query answered immediately.

Gopher Burrowing Through the Internet

Gopherspace is a common way to refer to the interlinked set of Gopher menus. Gopherspace, with its individually designed menus and no unifying taxonomy, but with frequent links from one Gopher menu to others, is generally considered to be the forerunner to the World Wide Web.

Gopherspace lacks some of the most visible features of the Web. Firstly, Gopher is text-based only, so there are no cool pictures, no odd little images usable as buttons or dividing rules on pages, and no large images used as menus. Second, Gopher servers don't know how to accept anything back from the Gopher client program you are running on your computer, so Gopherspace is one-way only. With no CGI-BIN support, nothing like a Webform for shopping or surveys exist in Gopherspace. With no e-mail capability, there are no hypertext links for sending e-mail with a single click. If you want to interact with someone or some site in Gopherspace, you will need to send e-mail or use the telephone.

However, Gopherspace has some strong points. The World Wide Web didn't exist five years ago, so anybody who wanted to set up a Web-like access before 1991 that didn't require the user to have a thorough understanding of UNIX had to use Gopher.

For you, the Netscape user, the biggest advantage Gopherspace has is that you don't have to do anything special. Netscape has full Gopher capability integrated into the point-and-click graphical interface of Netscape. A Gopher page appears to be a plain, but ordinary, Netscape page (see fig. 6.4).

Netscape displays a Gopher page as a single column of text links. Each entry in a Gopher menu consists of a small icon indicating the type of the file, and a description of the file. One major distinction between FTP directories and Gopher menus is that Gopher descriptions are typically in plain text, whereas FTP directories look like a directory listing from an operating system.

Some of the common Gopher link types you might see are:

- Menu—Another Gopher menu or directory
- Text—A text file
- Binary—An application (transferred via FTP if you select it)
- Telnet—Starts a Telnet session
- Search—Starts a simple Gopher search

FIG. 6.4
A Gopher page viewed
with Netscape.

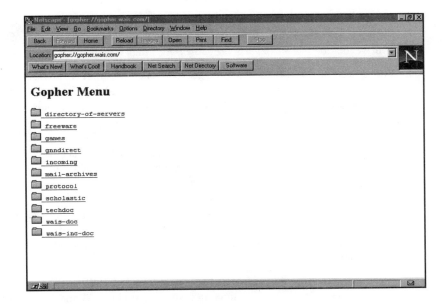

A full list of Gopher document types is presented in table 6.1, in the section "How to Ask
Veronica a Question: Search Strategies."

Veronica—a Gopher Search Tool

Gopherspace is too large to search randomly. In addition to the fact that Gopher has been
around for several years longer than the World Wide Web, every Gopher menu was organized
by the individual who created it, and there are no particular standards for organizing menus.
"Tunneling through Gopherspace" may be almost as much fun as surfing the Web, but you are
likely to take longer to find what you're looking for if you don't take advantage of some additional tools.

N O T E   The name Veronica is a crowning example of Silly Acronym Syndrome (SAS). Just as the
UNIX variant GNU means GNU's Not UNIX, and the name of the e-mail reader PINE is an
acronym meaning Pine Is Not Elm, Veronica's creators were inspired to create a somehow-meaningful
acronym around the name of one of Archie's cartoon girlfriends. Officially, Veronica means:

Very Easy Rodent-Oriented Net-wide Index to Computerized Archives.

You be the judge of whether you believe the words, or the acronym, came first. ■

Remember how Archie searches directories and file names available on anonymous FTP servers? Veronica is like Archie, but Veronica searches Gopher servers. While Archie is a good
search tool to use if you know the exact file name you are looking for, Veronica can find items
where Archie can't. Veronica's success derives from the fact that, while Gopher menus may be
descriptive names, FTP shows just the file and directory names. For example, giving Veronica
the words "martial arts pictures" may find you a GIF of Bruce Lee. On the other hand, Archie

won't find the same picture of Bruce Lee unless you ask Archie to search for GAM_DTH2.GIF. If you don't know exactly what you're looking for, but have a good idea of what kind of thing you're looking for, Veronica is probably better than Archie.

Using Veronica is simple. After you get to a Veronica server from a Gopher server, you can enter keywords to search for. Veronica searches its index of Gopherspace looking for matches to your keywords. When Veronica's done, you receive a Gopher menu consisting of all the matches to your search.

N O T E A Veronica menu of Gopher items is the same as an Archie page of FTP files and directories: you may not get the same result twice. If you run a Veronica search today and then again tomorrow, new files may have been made available by tomorrow, old files may have been removed, whole servers may be offline (or back online) tomorrow, and so on. The Veronica page you get today is an answer to your question today; the exact details of the answer may change tomorrow. ▪

The following steps demonstrate a search from the home Gopher site at the University of Minnesota:

1. Once you have your Internet connection up and Netscape is running, enter the URL gopher.micro.umn.edu to jump to the University of Minnesota's Gopher server, as shown in figure 6.5.

N O T E Remember that Netscape 2.0 allows you to skip entering the gopher:// portion of the URL if you are jumping to a Gopher server whose hostname starts with gopher. ▪

FIG. 6.5
The home of Gopher.

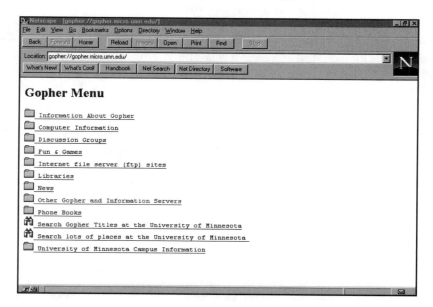

2. Select the Other Gopher and Information Servers item and the Gopher menu displayed in figure 6.6 appears.

3. Select the Search Titles in Gopherspace Using Veronica item to see the Gopher menu shown in figure 6.7.

FIG. 6.6

Other Gopher and Information Servers menu.

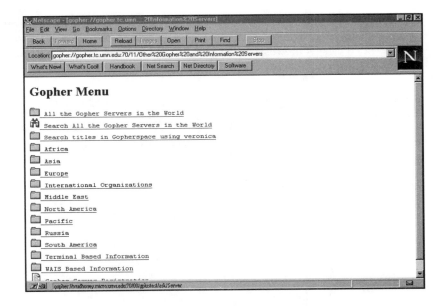

FIG. 6.7

Several Veronica servers.

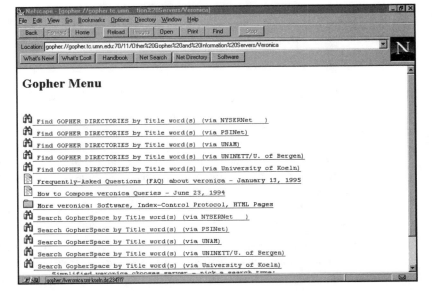

Part

II

Ch

6

You should notice the two text file items in the middle of figure 6.7. The Frequently-Asked Questions (FAQ) about Veronica and How to Compose Veronica Queries text files can provide additional information on this search tool.

4. Select the Search Gopherspace by Title words (via PSInet) item to retrieve an Index Search dialog box as shown in figure 6.8.

5. Place the cursor in the text entry field and type anything you like. You may get a message that looks like too many connections, please try again soon, or some variation. If you get this response, try another Veronica server, or just try again in a minute or two. Some servers may be busy at different times of the day or week.

FIG. 6.8

A Veronica search input page.

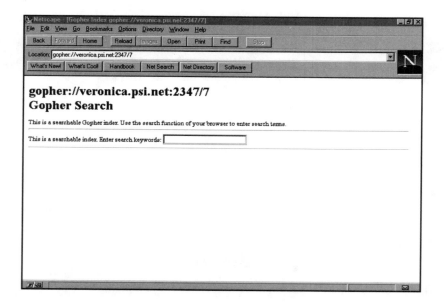

How to Ask Veronica a Question Search Strategies

Veronica, like a hammer, extends your ability. A hammer lets you put nails into wood. However, a hammer also lets you hit your other hand (the one holding the nail) REALLY hard if you miss. Like any tool, Veronica can be used correctly or incorrectly. Because Veronica servers are always busy, search results can take time. If your search criteria are too narrow or just not quite right, you can eliminate the material you are looking for. If your search criteria is too wide, you can get a huge result (huge searches take even longer) that is not much better than tunneling through Gopherspace until you find the right file yourself. (What's the right file? The one you think fits the answer.) Here is some advice on how to ask Veronica the right question.

Remember that Gopher servers are set up individually—sometimes very individually. You can be creative in your search keywords as long as you are creative in the way others might have been creative before. You can use multiple words to quickly narrow your search. Veronica supports the Boolean operators NOT, AND, and OR. For example, the search TELEVISION AND DRAMA NOT DAYTIME gives you Gopher items for evening drama television shows, but TELEVISION AND DRAMA increases the size of the search result to include all Gopher items also relating to daytime soap operas.

You can use an asterisk (*) as a wild card at the ends of words. A Veronica search for the keyword "director*" returns Gopher items for director, directory, directories, directorate, and so on.

A useful way to narrow your search is by file type. To narrow your search to return only results of a specific file type, add -t# to your Veronica search keywords, where the number sign (#) is a character representing a Gopher file type. The official Gopher document types and their signifying characters are presented in table 6.1.

Table 6.1   Official Gopher Document Types

Type Value	Description
0	Text file
1	Directory
2	CSO name server—read as text or HTML
3	An error of some sort
4	.HQX (also called BinHex, a Macintosh compression format)
5	PC binary (an uncompressed application)
6	UUEncoded file (a UNIX compression format)
7	Full text index (a Gopher menu)
8	Telnet session—if you have a Telnet application configured, it will launch
9	Binary file
s	Sound (an audio file)
I	Image (any format that's not GIF)
T	TN3270 session—if you have a TN3270 application (a fancy Telnet) configured, it will launch
g	GIF image
;	MPEG (a video file)
h	HTML (HyperText Markup Language)—a Web URL (Universal Resource Locator)
H	HTML URL Capitalized
i	Information (text) that is not selectable (like a comment line in a program)

Part

II

Ch

6

continues

Table 6.1 Continued	
Type Value	**Description**
w	A World Wide Web address
e	Event (not supported by Netscape)
m or M	Unspecified MIME (multi-part or mixed message)

For example, if you want to find Web pages on paleobotanical research in Turkey, you could use the Veronica search string `paleobotany AND Turkey -th`. If you know the Bruce Lee movie photo mentioned earlier was in GIF format, you could search for it using `bruce AND lee -tg`.

Jughead Another Gopherspace Search Engine

Another Gopherspace search tool is Jughead, which was written by Rhett "Jonzy" Jones at the University of Utah. In keeping with the Archie comics motif for Internet search engine names, the acronym came first, and the name Jughead was justified as

> Jonzy's Universal Gopher Hierarchy Excavation And Display

Like Veronica, Jughead is a Gopherspace search engine. However, Veronica searches widely, over all of Gopherspace. Jughead is most commonly configured to search only the one Gopher server it is installed on, but Jughead can search that one Gopher server very thoroughly.

Jughead: If It's There, Use It

System administrators rarely bother to install Jughead on a Gopher server with a small file collection. If you find a Jughead search engine on a specific Gopher server, it's because someone thought it was better to install Jughead than to do without it.

FIG. 6.9
North Carolina State University's Jughead search index.

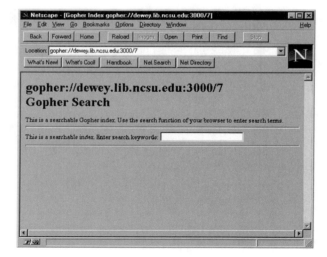

For an example of how Jughead works, go to North Carolina State University's library Gopher server at gopher://dewey.lib.ncsu.edu:300/7. The Jughead search index of NCSU's library is shown in figure 6.9. Because the server's hostname does not start with gopher, you have to type the gopher:// portion of the URL.

Entering search text into the field and pressing the Enter key gives you a Gopher menu made up of all matching items in the site that the Jughead server indexes.

How to Ask Jughead a Question

Jughead accepts the same kind of Boolean search requests Veronica does, but Jughead has some special commands. The generic form for these commands is a question mark followed by the command (no spaces between the question mark and the command), followed by the string of characters to search for.

The special Jughead commands are as follows:

Command	Result
?all string	Returns all matches to the string
?help string	Returns the Jughead help document, as well as any matches for the string
?limit=x string	Returns up to x matches for the string
?range=x1-x2 string	Returns the matches between x1 and x2

The ?range command is useful if the string matches a very large number of Gopher files.

N O T E You can use only one special command per query. However, you can limit your Jughead queries to improve the response time. (It's also polite; other people may want to use that server, and asking Jughead for all matches to "IBM" may be a waste of processor time if the item you want turns out to be the third one returned.) ▪

Jughead also restricts special characters for its own use. Almost all of the standard special characters are treated as a space. These special characters are:

!"#$%&'()+,-.?/\[@]{^}'~

This entire line is read as 24 spaces. Jughead treats a space as a Boolean AND, so it's probably best to use letters and numerals only in your search string.

Accessing a Telnet Site

Telnet is an ancient (as old as the Internet) way to access services on the Internet. When people speak of the Internet, they are generally referring to those computers that are on and connected to the Internet all the time.

Part
II

Ch
6

N O T E If you have a SLIP or PPP dial-up connection, your computer has an IP (Internet Protocol) address and is "part of the Internet." However, this only lasts as long as the connection. Generally, you need to have at least a leased-line connection before you can consider your local system as part of the Internet. ■

Telnet, like the World Wide Web, works because all the computers of the Internet are on and connected all the time, barring system crashes, backhoes accidentally cutting the T1 cable, and other things system administrators don't really like to think about.

You can think of Telnet as making your computer a dumb terminal for the system you are "telnetting" to. A dumb terminal was called such because it was only a keyboard and screen, directly wired into the host computer. Dumb terminals are called dumb because they have no processor inside. Terminals were manufactured in standard designs so they would be compatible with many different computers. A common type of terminal was the VT series manufactured by Digital Equipment Corporation. VT terminals came in several models (VT100, VT102, VT220, and so on). Your personal computer is enormously more powerful than a VT100 terminal, so a Telnet terminal emulator acts like a terminal in order to let your computer communicate with computers that are set up to connect to VT100 terminals. In other words, every time you run Telnet, you are reducing your high-end state-of-the-art personal computer to the level of a keyboard and screen.

What you get for lobotomizing your great workstation is the ability to connect to many computer systems that, in some cases, don't have any other connectivity available. Also, because Telnet is the lowest common denominator of computer power, almost everyone can participate. Windows 95 and Windows NT include Telnet applications in the Windows folder.

You can configure Netscape to launch a Telnet application as a supporting application. Telnet applications are available from Netscape's Helper Applications Web page at URL **http://home.netscape.com/assist/helper_apps/index.html**. To use these applications with Netscape, you need to download and uncompress the files, then configure the application as a helper application in the General window of the Options menu. You can find information on how to configure helper applications for Netscape in Part III, "Plug-Ins and Helper Applications," of this book.

N O T E One specific Telnet application is Wintel, NCSA's Telnet application for Windows. Wintel is available through Netscape's Helper Applications Web page as listed earlier, or it may be downloaded directly from the FTP site **ftp://gatekeeper.dec.com/pub/micro/msdos/win3/winsock/wintelb3.zip**.

Remember that, because the FTP site does not start with ftp, you have to type the URL type (ftp://) before the hostname.

If you have Windows 95 or Windows NT installed on your machine, you already have a Telnet application installed in C:\WINDOWS\ folder as TELNET.EXE. ■

Because Telnet and Gopher are both early Internet tools, many Telnet sites are most easily found through Gopher menus. For example, use Netscape to view the Gopher menu at URL gopher://gopher.micro.umn.edu, as you did earlier in this chapter. The Gopher menu shown in figure 6.5 is displayed. As you did earlier, choose the Other Gopher and Information Servers item and the Gopher menu displayed in figure 6.10 appears. Choose the Terminal Based Information from the bottom of the Gopher menu.

FIG. 6.10
Choose Terminal Based Information on this Gopher menu to see a menu of Telnet applications.

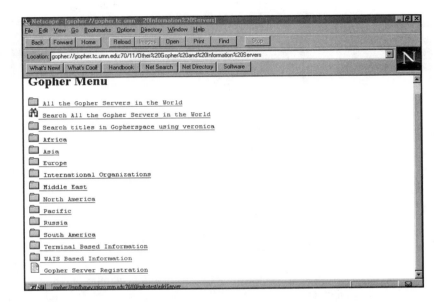

When you choose the Terminal Based Information item, a Gopher menu appears as shown in figure 6.11.

FIG. 6.11
Netscape displays Telnet session links in Gopher menus as small terminals.

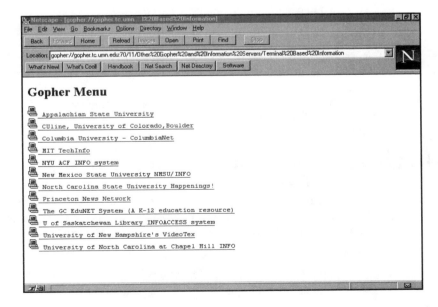

Part
II

Ch
6

Select the Telnet connection for Appalachian State University. If you have Netscape configured correctly, your Telnet supporting application launches, and the informational message Log in as 'info' appears before the Telnet window displays. When you see the "Enter username" prompt appear in the Telnet window, type INFO as your username. The main menu for Appalachian State University's information distribution server will appear, as shown in figure 6.12.

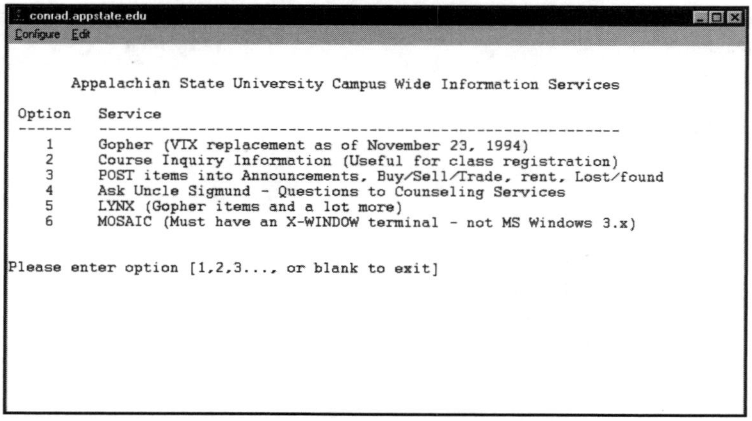

FIG. 6.12

A Telnet session with Appalachian State University.

```
conrad.appstate.edu                                                    _ □ ×
Configure  Edit


            Appalachian State University Campus Wide Information Services

   Option   Service
   ------   ---------------------------------------------------------------
     1      Gopher (VIX replacement as of November 23, 1994)
     2      Course Inquiry Information (Useful for class registration)
     3      POST items into Announcements, Buy/Sell/Trade, rent, Lost/found
     4      Ask Uncle Sigmund - Questions to Counseling Services
     5      LYNX (Gopher items and a lot more)
     6      MOSAIC (Must have an X-WINDOW terminal - not MS Windows 3.x)


  Please enter option [1,2,3..., or blank to exit]
```

Appalachian State University provides a great deal of information to its students via its Telnet host computers. However, not all Telnet sessions are used for information gathering. Multi-User Dungeons (MUDs) are computer programs that people can explore by adopting a character and typing commands for the character to move, talk, and do other things. MUDs are commonly used for social interaction between people. There are many different types of MUDs, both in types of programming involved in their creation and extension, and in the types of interaction typically occurring. Some MUDs are socially oriented chat discussion, some are fantasy role-playing in nature, and others are oriented to foreign language practice. While Telnet applications may be used for MUDs, many of the various types of MUDs have specific client applications that were created to optimize some aspects of performance on a given type of MUD. For more information on multi-user games, see Yahoo's directory of multi-user games at **http://www.yahoo.com/Recreation/Games/Internet_Games/ MUDs_MUSHes__MOOs_etc_/.**

Troubleshooting Connection Problems

Sometimes you do not get where you want to go on the Internet. A site may be down, or a connection may have exactly too much interference in the lines to connect. A Web page you looked at yesterday may be deleted or moved today. This last section of the chapter offers some advice to improve your ability to get where you want to go.

Any address embedded in a link may be entered directly in the Locations field of your Netscape application. If the Web link is not the full link text, you can always see the link by moving your cursor over the link and not clicking the link. The full link description can be seen in the bottom edge of your Netscape window.

Normally, if the full URL (example: **http://www.yahoo.com/Recreation/**) has a slash at the end indicating the last part of the URL is a directory, Netscape adds the slash for you as it loads the default page there. If Netscape gives you an error Not Found, your first action should be to select the Reload command (either from the View menu, or the Reload button to the right of the Home button on the Netscape toolbar).

N O T E An immediate Reload is not just an impatient, "Why won't this thing do what I want?" behavior, it's often the solution. Small errors happen all the time, and reloading may work more often than you think. Reloading is an especially good idea if images on a page are downloading badly and Netscape displays a "broken picture" image where the picture should have been.

Reloading is exactly the right answer if you get a Too busy, try again later message when attempting to start an FTP or Gopher session. Gopher and FTP servers are often busy, and trying again is the same as redialing a telephone after you get a busy signal. ▪

Your second attempt (if you were using a link from another page) is to look at the destination link displayed in the Location field between the two rows of buttons in the toolbar, and see what it looks like. Leaving the closing end off an anchor causes the rest of the page—from the beginning of the anchor, including the text label (if it was one), the image (if you used an image as the visible part of the link), and everything else to the end of the page—to become part of the destination address. If the location looks like a URL followed by words or file names, select the part of the address that doesn't look like a URL, and delete it. Try again.

Similarly, if you are typing in the address yourself, proofread the destination address. Fix any problems you see such as spaces accidentally inserted into the middle of the URL or capitalization errors, then select the Reload command. I recently encountered a non-functional link in a large Web site discussing HTML authoring. The Web page builder had typed /hyperext/ in the directory path where he meant to type /hypertext/. If a reload of the page doesn't work, or if you saw no problems with the URL, retype the URL, and try again anyway. If you got the URL from e-mail or an article you have electronically, try to copy the URL from where it is and paste it into the Location field in order to reduce interference from typing errors. ●

Part

II

Ch

6

E-mail with Netscape

Netscape started life as a dedicated Web browser, and there's never been a doubt that it's a superior piece of software for that purpose. Netscape has also bent over backwards, for the most part successfully, to make other Internet services like FTP and Gopher accessible from Netscape.

But in one key area—e-mail—Netscape fell short. Early, 1.x versions of Netscape provided only the most rudimentary capability to access the Internet's most popular service. Users could only send mail with Netscape; they couldn't receive it. Needless to say, the designers of dedicated e-mail managers didn't find Netscape a threat to their business.

This is changing fast. In a bid to make its flagship program a full-service Internet client, Netscape has given version 3.0 a powerful mail manager that many users—particularly those at home—may find suits their needs.

In this chapter, you learn how to:

- Configure Netscape 3.0's e-mail servers and preferences

- Send and receive mail

- Organize your mail using folders

- Create an address book to speed your correspondence ■

Netscape's New E-mail Manager

In their first attempt to make their Web browser a full-service Internet client, Netscape's programmers have done a pretty fair job. The new e-mail manager provides most of the functionality that veteran Net users have come to expect from their software. It also offers a couple of very useful, Netscape-only twists.

The feature that, above all others, sets Netscape's mail package apart from its established competitors is the fact that it treats incoming messages basically as HTML documents. The mail reader is able to detect any URL mentioned in the text of a message and highlight it for one-click access by the user. Your mail becomes a separate, hotlinked gateway to the World Wide Web and the rest of the Internet.

Netscape doesn't stint on the standard stuff, either. You've always been able to use it to write and send messages, but now you'll find that you can easily reply to, forward, and carbon copy messages, just as users of third-party mail packages can. Message management is a snap because you have the ability to transfer your traffic to a set of custom, user-defined mail folders. Within those folders, you can tell Netscape to sort your mail by subject, sender, or date. You can also keep and maintain a list of your most frequently used addresses.

If you're a casual e-mail user, you'll likely find that Netscape's new built-in mail capabilities are all you need. And if it's important that you have the ability to tap into the Web directly from your message traffic, you'll find Netscape's mail manager indispensable.

But if you're accustomed to using other mail packages, programs like Eudora and cc:Mail, you'll soon see that Netscape's package isn't quite complete. Although some rough edges present in the Address Book and file attachment features of Netscape's early betas have been smoothed over, power users will miss high-end features like automatic message filtering.

All in all, if you're happy with your current mail program, you'll have to make the call as to whether you want to switch to Netscape just yet. You'd be well-advised, however, to watch carefully as it evolves in the future. It's quite clear that Netscape is serious about making its leading program the only Internet client most people will ever need.

But if you're a new mail user, or if you haven't found a package quite to your liking just yet, you'll probably want to give Netscape's e-mail facility a try. You may find that it meets your needs completely.

Setting Mail Preferences

Before attempting to use Netscape's mail facility, you must provide some basic information about yourself, your Internet provider, and your computer. Begin by choosing Options, and then select Mail and News Preferences. Netscape responds with a tabbed dialog box.

The best way to familiarize yourself with Netscape's mail settings is to step through each of the five tabs sequentially as you set up the program for the first time.

Appearance

The options on this tab, seen in figure 7.1, affect the way Netscape displays message text. Under Messages and Articles Are Shown With, your choice tells Netscape whether to use a fixed-width or variable-width font when it displays the text of your mail. The default is Fixed Width Font; in most cases you'll want to stick to that setting because Variable Width Font can ruin the formatting of many Internet messages. The settings under Text Beginning With > (Quoted Text) Has the Following Characteristics affects the display of message excerpts included in a mailing to establish its subject and context. They're largely self-explanatory; change them to suit your taste.

FIG. 7.1

The settings on the Appearance tab give the user control over the fonts Netscape uses to display the text of mail messages.

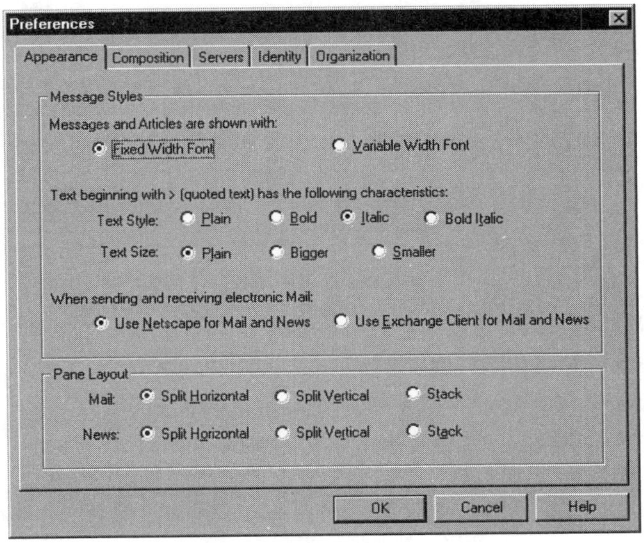

The remaining buttons on this tab, found under heading When Receiving Electronic Mail, tell Netscape whether to use its own built-in e-mail capabilities or those provided with every copy of Windows 95 by Microsoft Exchange. If you want to use Netscape's, click Use Netscape for Mail and News.

New to Netscape is the ability to configure the window layout of Netscape Mail. You can have Netscape Mail's window panes use one of three basic configurations. The default, Split Horizontal, lists your mail folders in the upper-left pane, the mail headers in the upper-right pane, and the letters themselves in the bottom pane. The Split Vertical option (see fig. 7.2) has the folders in the upper left, the headers in the lower left, and the messages on the right.

Finally, the Stack option puts the folders on top, the headers in the middle, and the mail body at the bottom. Just choose the window pane layout you want and click the OK button. The new layout won't be used until you quit out of Netscape Mail, and start it up again.

Part
II

Ch
7

FIG. 7.2

This is one of the new Netscape Mail window pane layouts that's available with Netscape.

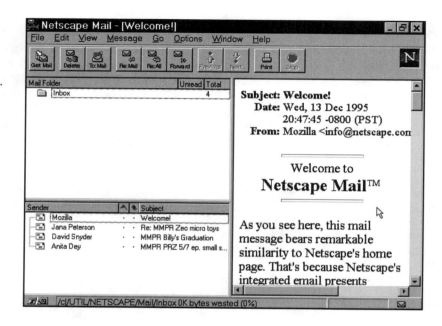

Composition

There are several key settings on this tab, seen in figure 7.3:

- The Send and Post setting determines how file attachments are coded. Allow 8-bit is the default and is recognized by most mail programs.

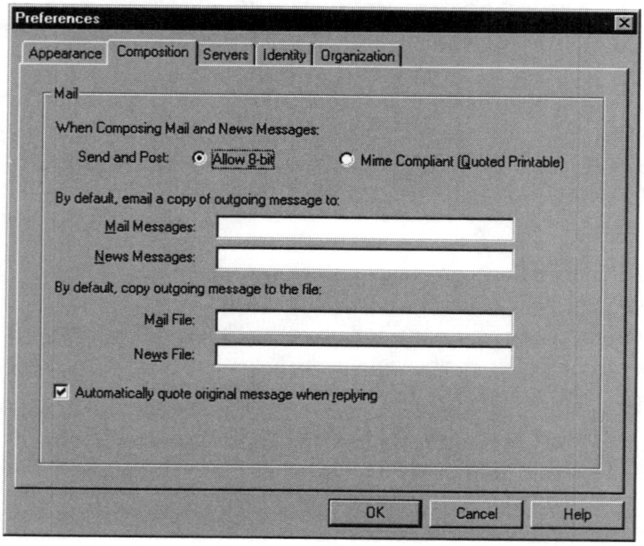

FIG. 7.3

The Composition tab controls key settings for file encoding and message queuing.

- The Deliver Mail setting tells Netscape whether you want to send each message when you're done writing it, or to hold it on disk. Choosing Automatically tells Netscape to send when you're done writing; Queue for Manual Delivery holds your message.

TIP You'll probably want to queue your messages on disk if you do most of your work offline, as a dial-in Internet user. Send them by clicking File and choosing Deliver Mail Now.

- You can have Netscape send a copy of all your outgoing messages to a single address by entering that address in the Mail Messages field.
- The entry in the Mail File field tells Netscape where to store copies of your outgoing messages on disk. This is a key setting; in the following discussion of the Directories tab, we'll tell you how to avoid problems by reconciling it with that tab's Mail Directory field. If you don't care to keep copies of your outgoing traffic, you can avoid problems entirely by leaving this field blank.
- Checking Automatically Quote Original Message When Replying tells Netscape to insert the text of any message you answered with the Message menu's Reply option into the body of your answer.

Servers

This tab is probably the most important of the five on the Mail and News Preferences dialog box. On this tab, seen in figure 7.4, you tell Netscape how to get to your mail.

FIG. 7.4
Many of the controls that affect your use of Netscape's e-mail features are on the Mail and News Preferences dialog box. Here we're using it to enter information about our mail server.

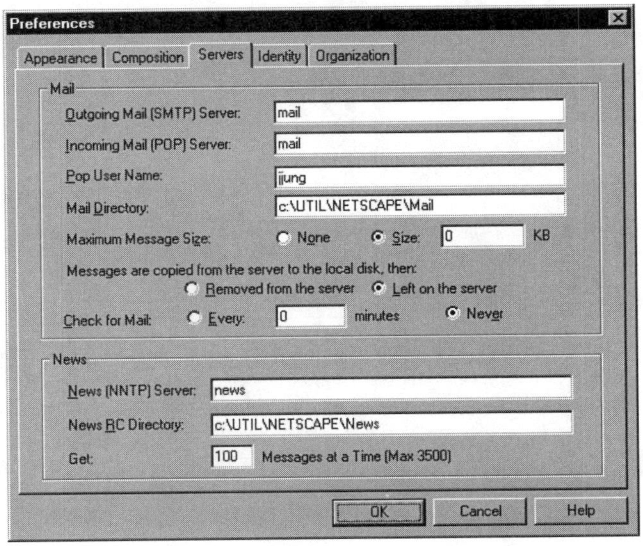

Do the following:

1. Type the Internet addresses for your service provider's SMTP (send mail) and POP3 (receive mail) clients in the Mail (SMTP) Server and Mail POP Server fields, which are

near the top of the tab. Get this information from your service provider if you don't already have it.

2. Type your e-mail name (in all likelihood, the one you use when you log into your Internet provider) in the Pop User Name box.

3. You should make sure Netscape's setup routine has provided access to the directory where your mail folders are stored by looking in the Mail Directory field. There should be some entry like C:\Program Files\ Netscape\Navigator\Mail, as seen in figure 7.3. The actual listing will vary depending on your Netscape setup.

4. If there's no path in the Mail Directory field, or you have reason to believe the path is incorrect, open Explorer, find the folder Netscape's installed in, and then find the Mail subfolder. Note the Windows 95 path, go back into Netscape, and type the path into the Mail Directory field.

T I P   You can use the Mail Directory field to tell Netscape to store your mail in any Windows 95 folder you want. Simply type its path in place of the one provided by Netscape.

5. Click the Composition tab. Look in the Mail File field, near the bottom of the tab. The Windows 95 path listed there should match that in the Mail Directory field, with the addition of the characters, \Sent (see fig. 7.5). Netscape stores a copy of your outgoing messages in this file.

FIG. 7.5
Make sure the Composition tab's Mail File field refers to the same path as the Directories tab's Mail Directory field.

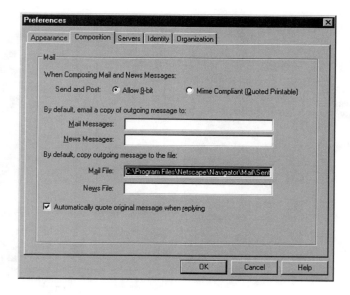

6. If it doesn't match, type the path in yourself. For example, if your Mail Directory is C:\Program Files\Netscape\Navigator\Mail, type C:\ Program Files\Netscape\ Navigator\Mail\Sent in the Mail File field.

TROUBLESHOOTING

When I try to send mail, Netscape responds with an error message that says Can't open FCC file. I've searched the Netscape directories and the rest of my hard drive and can't find an FCC file. Should I create one? No. This cryptic message is Netscape's way of telling you that the Composition tab's Mail File field isn't referring to the same Windows 95 path as your Mail Directory field. The Sent file has to be located in the same folder as the rest of your mail files.

This problem originally cropped up because the installation routines for the early betas of Netscape 3.0 wouldn't update the Mail File field when asked to install the program to any folder other than their default settings.

There are three ways to fix the resulting mess. Check the Mail Directory field, and then enter this path in the Mail File field, tagging the characters "\Sent" on the end. Alternatively, open Windows 95's Registry Editor and, using its search facility, find the phrase "Default FCC." It'll turn up among the HKEY_CURRENT_USER settings, as in figure 7.6. Click Edit, choose Modify, and enter the proper path in the field provided.

Your remaining option, if you don't consider it important to keep copies of your outgoing messages, is to leave the Composition tab's Mail File field blank. If you do, Netscape won't save any copies, but it won't pop up an error message either.

7. After you're comfortable with Netscape's mail features, you'll likely want to click the Removed from the Server button so old mail doesn't clutter your Internet provider's disk.

FIG. 7.6
You can use Windows 95's Registry Editor to reconcile the Mail Directory and Mail File fields. The path to the Sent file listed beside Default FCC should match the path beside Mail Directory.

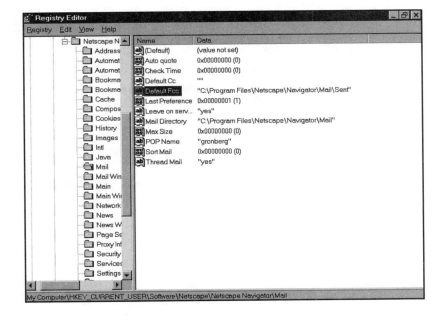

Part

II

Ch

7

Identity

Netscape personalizes your outgoing messages by adding bits from the settings on this tab. You'll want to do the following:

1. Type your real name in the Your Name field.

2. Type your e-mail address in the Your Email field.

3. If you want replies to your outgoing messages sent to an address other than the one listed in Your Email, type it in the Reply-to Address field.

4. Fill in Your Organization if you want the name of your employer or the group you represent to appear on your mail.

5. If you want Netscape to append a signature file to your outgoing messages, use the Browse key next to Signature File on the Identity tab to search for and select a signature file from your hard drive. Your signature must be an ASCII text file. It should be hard-formatted and less than 80 characters wide. Internet etiquette would also suggest that you keep it short.

6. If you're concerned about retaining your privacy on the Internet, click either the Nothing: Anonymous User or A Unique ID Number button at the bottom of the tab. In most cases, however, you'll want your messages identified with Your Email Address.

Organization

The threading and sorting features of Netscape's mail manager are fully controllable from the mail window, but the program does allow you to designate their default settings. They're available on the Organization tab, seen in figure 7.7.

■ If you think you'll want your message traffic threaded (that is, with messages and replies on the same topic grouped together for easy reading), click the Organization tab and make sure the Thread Mail Messages box is checked.

■ You may also want to change the default sort order for your incoming message traffic. If so, click the Organization tab and choose one of the Sort Mail By selections. The available sort options are by Date, Subject, and Sender.

 TIP For now at least, ignore the fields and buttons that control Netscape's newsreader functions. Read about them in chapter 8, "Reading UseNet Newsgroups with Netscape."

When you're satisfied with the changes you've made to the various tabs on the Mail and News Preferences dialog box, click OK to save your work. Clicking Cancel abandons it.

Using the Mail Package

At first glance, Netscape 3.0 appears no more a sophisticated mail package than its predecessors. The picture begins to change, though, when you click the Window menu and select Netscape Mail.

FIG. 7.7

The settings on the Organization tab tell Netscape how to sort and thread your message traffic.

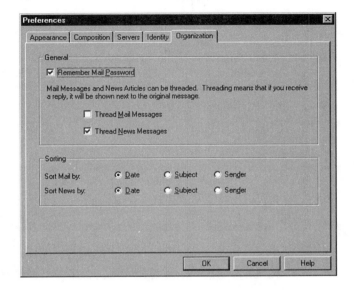

The program responds first by asking you to enter a password. In the Password Entry dialog box, enter verbatim the phrase your Internet provider told you to use when logging on to your mail server (see fig. 7.8).

FIG. 7.8

Netscape demands that you enter the password for your Internet e-mail account every time you want to access its mail window.

If you click OK, Netscape immediately tries to log on to your mail server. If it finds that you're not online, or that it can't log on to your server, eventually it will give up and flash an error message. If you've opened a mail window to work offline, you can avoid this problem by clicking Cancel in the Password Entry dialog box.

Understanding the Screen

Once in the program, you're confronted by a screen that reminds some users of the Microsoft Exchange e-mail client that comes with every copy of Windows 95. Don't be fooled: Netscape's mail facility is nowhere near as sophisticated as Exchange and nowhere near as resource-hungry. In actual use Netscape's mail facility compares favorably with such light-footed freeware and shareware packages as Eudora and Pegasus.

Part
II

Ch
7

Let's get oriented.

■ On the top left of Netscape's mail screen, you see a listing of your personal mail folders (see fig. 7.9). At minimum, this listing contains your inbox and your trash folder. After you've sent your first message with Netscape, you should see a Sent folder that holds copies of your out-going traffic.

■ On the top right, you see a scrollable listing of the message headers for every piece of mail in the folder you're looking at. The inbox opens by default when you first open Netscape's mail facility.

N O T E   Netscape highlights unread messages in bold. Folders that contain unread messages are also highlighted in bold. You open folders by double-clicking them. ■

■ On the bottom of the screen, you see the text of the open message, along with headers indicating the message's subject, sender, sender's reply-to address, and the date it was sent.

FIG. 7.9

Netscape's clean mail layout provides easy access to your message traffic and your personal mail folders.

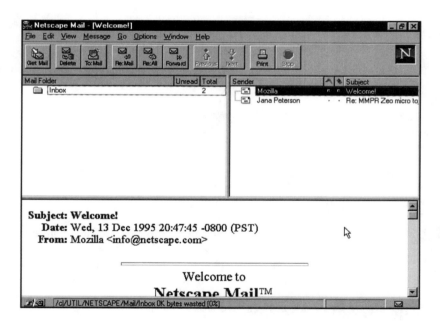

One feature you'll learn to like may not be immediately obvious: If the message contains a URL, Netscape treats it as such, recognizing and highlighting it for immediate use. By clicking a URL, you can jump immediately to the Web page, FTP site, or other Internet service that it points to.

T I P   Netscape gives you one-click access to any URL embedded in an e-mail message displayed on-screen.

N O T E You may notice at low screen resolutions that Netscape's mail display is a bit cramped. You can adjust the sizes of the various panes by clicking and dragging their frames. You'll find that the only real way to see what you're doing, video card permitting, is to use a higher screen resolution. Open Control Panel's Display properties, click the Settings tab, and set the Desktop Area slider to at least 800 × 600 pixels for a better look. ■

Netscape now has the ability to show you a variety of e-mail headers. Typically, all e-mail you send or receive has a lot of information stored in its headers. The information is often technical and not intended for most people to figure out. However, some mail headers can be useful to the casual person. Whether it's because of a cute quote that somebody put in, or a particular e-mail address, some header information is useful.

You can determine how much, or how little, of the e-mail header you want to see. Simply click on Options, Show Headers, and select between All, Normal, or Brief. The All option shows you every single bit of header information in the letter body. The Normal option only shows you the subject of the letter, the date it was sent, who it's from, and who it's to. The Brief option shows you pretty much the same information as the Normal option, but puts it into a compact, one-line format.

Composing and Sending Mail

Netscape 3.0's mail and news clients use the same front end for message composition. In the case of the mail client, you begin a message either by clicking the New Mail button on the toolbar or by clicking the File menu and selecting New Mail Message. A message form like the one shown in figure 7.10 opens.

FIG. 7.10
Netscape uses a standard form for outgoing e-mail and UseNet articles. Here's an e-mail message ready to go.

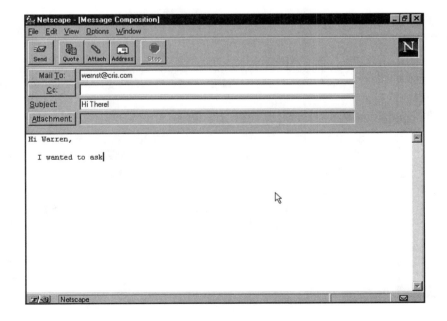

Part
II

Ch
7

Netscape inserts the text of your signature file, if you use one, in the section of the screen reserved for message text. Fill out the rest of the message by following these steps:

1. Type the address of the person or organization you're writing to in the Send To field.

2. Type a short phrase in the Subject field describing the content of your message.

T I P You don't have to open the Netscape Mail window to create a message. Click Netscape's File menu and choose New Mail Message to open a Composition window.

3. If you want to send copies of your message to third parties, click the View menu and select either Mail Cc or Mail Bcc. This adds a blank address field of the same name to your message header. Type the addresses of the additional recipients. Use Cc if you want to publicize the fact you've sent copies; use Bcc (blind copy) if you don't.

4. Click once in the main text box to set the cursor at the beginning of your message, and begin writing your text. Standard Windows 95 Cut, Copy, and Paste commands are available on the Edit menu.

N O T E If the recipient of your message is using Netscape's e-mail manager also, you can pass along interesting and useful URLs in one of two ways. First, you can simply type the URL into a message. Or, if you're viewing a Web page or some other resource in the browser, you can click the File menu and select Mail Document. When you do, Netscape opens a new message window with the URL listed in the body of the mailing. In either case, when the person viewing your message opens it in Netscape's mail manager, the URL will appear as a hotlink. You need do nothing more than type; Netscape detects the presence of the URL automatically. ■

5. When finished, make sure you're online and then click the Send button on the Composition window's toolbar.

Netscape sends a new message as soon as you click Send if its Composition preferences are set to deliver mail automatically. If they're set to queue messages, eventually you'll have to click the File menu and select Deliver Mail Now to send your outgoing traffic to your server.

Attaching Files and URLs to Mail

Most e-mail packages provide the capability to transmit binary files over the Internet by attaching ASCII-coded copies of them to your message traffic. Netscape is no exception. In fact, its attachment facility is one of the most versatile around.

You can attach files to a message any time before sending it. Open the Attachments dialog by clicking the Attachments button, which you'll see just below the Subject field. You may also click the Attach button on the message composition window's toolbar. Figure 7.11 shows the Attachments dialog box.

T I P If the Attachment button is grayed out, you can enable it by clicking any of the message's header boxes.

FIG. 7.11

You can attach a binary file to any outgoing message. Netscape will translate it using an ASCII coding scheme intelligible to most mail readers.

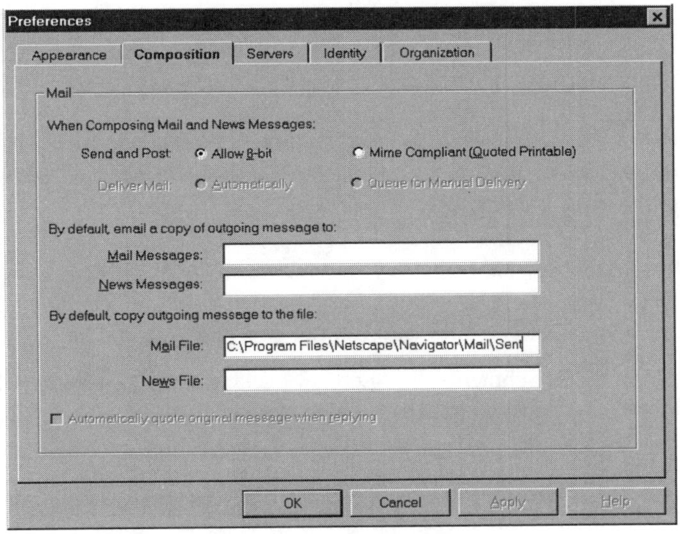

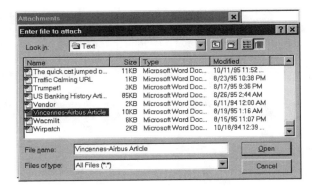

Once the Attachments dialog opens, you may add files to your message by clicking the Attach File button. Use the Enter File To Attach dialog box to select the file you want to transmit (see fig. 7.12).

FIG. 7.12

The Enter File To Attach dialog box looks and works like any other Windows 95 file-handling dialog box.

Once you've actually selected the file, you have a decision to make:

- You'll want Netscape to code and transmit true binary files like a spreadsheet or a compressed archive using MIME rendering. Make sure it does so by highlighting the name of the file in the Attachments dialog and clicking the As Is button. Most e-mail software available automatically decodes and stores the attachment when it arrives on the receiving end.

- You may ask Netscape to incorporate ASCII text files, such as those created with Notepad, into the body of the message itself. You do this by clicking the Convert to Plain Text button. Netscape does not, however, let you control where this insertion takes place. It always adds the new text to the bottom of the message. You will not see the text displayed in Netscape's message window, but as long as the file's visible in the Attachments dialog box it will appear in the finished message seen by your correspondent.

TIP Bear in mind that you can always send an ASCII file As Is. If you do, Netscape will treat it as a binary file. This is perhaps the best way to handle heavily formatted plain-text files. Sending them in the body of a message could badly disrupt their formatting.

The Attachments dialog box also gives you the ability to e-mail a copy of an entire Web page—not just its Internet address. This new and exciting feature is unique to Netscape. If the recipients are using Netscape, they can view the Web page you're sending within a mail window.

Begin from the Attachments dialog box by clicking Attach Location (URL). Netscape opens the Please Specify a Location to Attach dialog box; type the full Internet address of the page you want to send (see fig. 7.13).

FIG. 7.13
Enter the URL of the Web page you want to send.

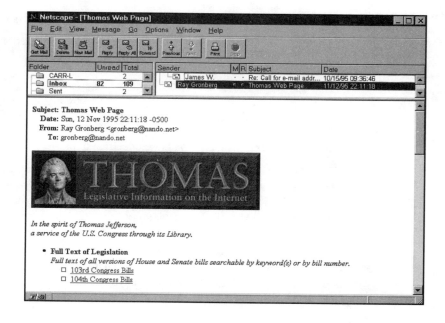

As with files, you have to decide whether to send the attachment as is or as plain text. If you know that the person to whom you're sending the URL is using Netscape 3.0 as a mail reader, click As Is. The result on the receiving end will be rather extraordinary (see fig. 7.14).

FIG. 7.14
Your friends don't have to seek out Web pages like this one from the Library of Congress. If they're using Netscape as a mail reader, you can send them a copy.

What you basically did is ask Netscape to mail the HTML source code of the URL to your correspondent. Because Netscape's mail facility treats every message as an HTML document, it is able to reconstruct a fully formatted and hotlinked Web page. Whatever you can do with that page from within a normal browser window, your friends can emulate within a Netscape mail window.

If your friends don't have Netscape, all is not lost. By clicking Convert to Plain Text, you instruct Netscape's mailer to strip the HTML codes out of the page and send the remaining text. You may send it As Is anyway; they'll see pure HTML, but after saving a copy to disk they can always open and view the page in any Web browser. Bear in mind that they won't get any of the artwork that gives a Web page its distinctive look and feel.

Receiving and Replying to Mail

As explained earlier, Netscape tries to log on and retrieve messages from your mail server the first time you open the Netscape Mail window.

TROUBLESHOOTING

When Netscape tries to deliver my mail, it responds with a message that it's unable to locate the server. What's wrong? One of four things—three of which you can do something about.

The first thing you want to do is note the name of the server Netscape's trying to access. It'll be listed in the error message. It should be the name of your Internet provider's mail server. If it isn't, open the Preferences dialog box, click the Directories tab, and correct the entry in the Mail (SMTP) Server field.

If Netscape has the right address but can't get through, you may be working offline or you may have another program open that's got the mail server tied up. Get on-line by dialing in or logging on. Close any other program that uses SMTP or POP service before you try to use Netscape's mail manager.

The remaining possibility is that your Internet provider's mail server is down. If that's the case, you can do little but wait. If your provider has a help desk, you may want to call to let them know there's a problem.

You can also retrieve messages any time while the Netscape Mail window is open either by clicking the File menu and selecting Get New Mail, or by clicking Get Mail button on the toolbar. If you haven't already entered your mail server's password, Netscape requests it.

Netscape dumps all new mail into the inbox. Unlike some mail software, it can't automate the sorting of messages into user-specified folders. That's a job you have to handle yourself.

Like most e-mail packages, Netscape lets you respond directly to a message without having to address a new one from scratch. You do this by using the Reply, Reply All, and Forward buttons on the mail screen's toolbar.

By clicking either Reply or Reply All, you can tell Netscape to create a preaddressed message. You can include the text of the message you received by clicking the mail window's File menu and selecting Include Original Text (see fig. 7.15). The Quote Icon on the Netscape Mail Composition Toolbar performs the same function. Trim the length of your quotation using the Edit menu's Cut, Copy, and Paste commands.

Part

II

Ch

7

FIG. 7.15
By using the Reply and
the Include Original Text
commands located on
the mail window's File
menu, you can draft
understandable answers
to your mail quickly and
easily.

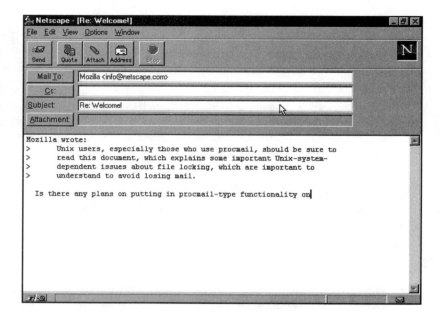

The Forward button works a bit differently. As with Reply and Reply All, clicking it creates a
new message. This time, however, you supply the address of your intended recipient. But you'll
notice that Netscape has filled in the Attachment field for you. By doing so, it tacks a copy of
the text open in Netscape Mail window to the bottom of the message you're creating, including
it for the benefit of your correspondent.

Organizing Your Mail

Fortunately, Netscape doesn't make mail sorting hard. You can add and name an unlimited
number of folders and shift messages between them at your discretion (see fig. 7.16).

FIG. 7.16
User-created message
folders simplify the task
of organizing your mail.

Create a folder by clicking the Netscape Mail window's File menu and selecting New Folder. A
Netscape mail folder is nothing more than a Windows 95 file, so you can give it a name up to 255
characters long. You may want to keep your names shorter than that, though. As it displays your
folders, Netscape truncates the names of any that are too long to fit in the available window.

N O T E Unlike many full-featured e-mail packages, Netscape does not offer any method of nesting
folders within folders. High-volume mail users may find this a serious limitation that argues
for keeping their current software. Low-volume users should be able to get along fine, but they may find
it advisable to keep their filing system short and understandable. ■

Conversely, you kill an unused folder by clicking it once to highlight its name, and then selecting Delete Folder from the Edit menu.

The commands for shifting mail between folders—Move and Copy—are at the bottom of the Message menu (see fig. 7.17). Highlight either, and you'll find a list of your folders nested beneath them.

FIG. 7.17
The Move and Copy commands take only a single click. Highlight the directory you want to send the message to and release the mouse button.

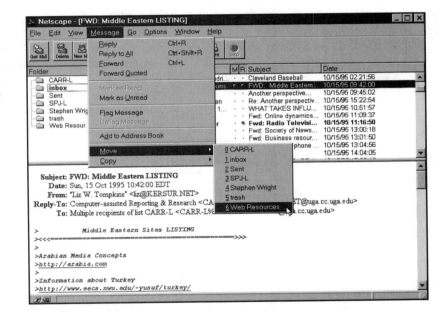

The Move and Copy commands work the same way:

1. Highlight the message you want to move or copy in the Message Headers pane by clicking it.

2. Click the Message menu and select Move or Copy.

3. A list of your folders will pop up next to the Message menu. Select the folder you want the message transferred to.

Choosing Move places the selected message into the destination folder and deletes it from the source. Copy puts a copy in the destination folder while leaving the contents of the source folder unchanged.

Within folders, Netscape gives users several options for sorting messages. All are accessible by clicking the View menu and highlighting Sort.

The three major options—Sort by Date, Sender, and Subject—are largely self-explanatory. Toggling the Ascending command tells Netscape to arrange messages in ascending or descending order.

Part
II

Ch
7

Netscape's capability to organize messages into threads is both unusual and powerful. By toggling Thread Messages, you're ordering the mail client to override normal sort order in cases where a single message has inspired at least one reply. It groups the original and any replies, making the conversation easy to follow as it develops over time (see fig. 7.18).

FIG. 7.18
The Windows Explorer-like tree structures indicate message threads.

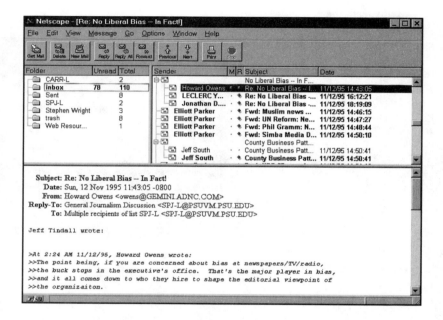

You can send any highlighted message to the trash folder by clicking the Delete button on the toolbar, by clicking Edit and selecting Delete Message, or by transferring it there using the Message menu's Move command. Trash stays on your disk, however, until you click the File menu and select Empty Trash Folder. Unlike many mail packages, Netscape provides no way of automating deletions.

Using the Address Book

Any good e-mail software provides some quick and simple way of storing and retrieving the addresses of your most frequent correspondents. Most are very easy to use. See figure 7.19.

Setting up an address book isn't difficult. In fact, Netscape gives you a couple of ways to do it. The easiest method is to open a message from someone you want to correspond with regularly, click the Message menu, and select Add to Address Book.

Netscape responds by opening a Windows 95 property sheet that has four fields (see fig. 7.20). If you're adding to your Address Book using the Message menu command, you'll find that two of them, Name and E-Mail Address, are already filled in.

FIG. 7.19
Netscape's address book simplifies mailing chores by storing the names and addresses of the people you write the most.

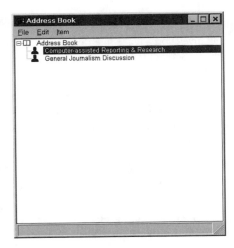

FIG. 7.20
Use the Address Book properties sheet to create and maintain your address list.

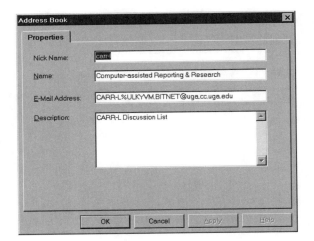

TROUBLESHOOTING

Netscape's Add to Address Book function filled out the properties sheet for the addition incorrectly. It didn't use the name and address of the person who wrote the original message. Why not?
There's an entry in the message's Reply To field. When it's creating an Address Book entry, Netscape always takes the name and address listed in Reply To. This avoids problems with mailings to a list or to a person who takes return mail at a different address. But it means more work for you; you have to take the time to enter the correct name and address yourself. Always check the entries in these fields the first time you create an Address Book entry.

The Description field gives you a place to write a short note about your correspondent.

The remaining field, Nick Name, gives you a place to enter a short, one-word phrase that can serve as a shortcut to your Address Book entry. Be sure to use lowercase characters only; Netscape won't accept a Nick Name that contains uppercase characters.

You can also create Address Book entries from scratch. Click the Window menu and select Address book. Once the address book opens, click the Item menu and select Add User. Netscape will open a blank Address Book properties sheet. You can also modify any existing entry in the Address Book by right-clicking the entry and selecting Properties.

Once you've created your Address Book, Netscape gives you three ways to use it. They work with any of the available address fields, Mail To, Cc and Bcc:

- The simplest way, once you've placed the cursor in the Message Composition window's Mail To field, is to click the toolbar's Address button. Netscape opens a dialog box called Select Addresses (see fig. 7.21). Highlight the address you want to use, and then click the button that corresponds to the field you want it placed in. Click OK when you're done.

FIG. 7.21

Clicking either the toolbar's Address button or a message's Send To, Cc, or Blind Cc button opens the Select Addresses dialog box. Highlight your choice, click the button for the field you want it placed in, and click OK.

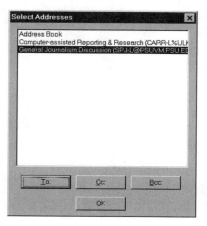

- You may also open the Select Addresses dialog box by clicking any of the labels next to your message's various address fields. Unfortunately, once you've highlighted the address you want to use, you still have to place it in the proper field by clicking the corresponding button on the dialog box. You can't just click OK and expect the address to pop up where you want it.

- If your memory is good, you can address a message quickly merely by typing an Address Book entry's Nick Name property in Mail To, Cc or Bcc. Netscape will automatically fill the box with the name and e-mail address associated with the Nick Name as soon as you move the cursor elsewhere.

You may notice that Netscape fills the message address boxes differently, depending on an Address Book entry's properties. If you've given the entry a Nick Name, it will use that until you close the Select Addresses dialog box. Once you do, it will fill a field with both the name and the address of your intended correspondent. This is nothing to be alarmed about. As long as the e-mail address itself is bracketed by the < and > symbols, your mail server will be able to find it.

If you haven't given an address book entry a Nick Name, Netscape will only list the e-mail address in the proper field. The recipient's name won't appear. Again, no harm is done.

Because an address book is an HTML document—just like your Bookmarks file—Netscape gives you one other way of getting at it quickly. Just as with your Bookmarks file, you can load your address book directly into your browser.

Close your mail window, and then open the File menu and select Open File. You should find address.htm somewhere in your Netscape folder structure, most likely in the Program subfolder. If it doesn't open readily, use Windows 95's Find Files or Folders utility to search for it. When you find it, double-click to load it in Netscape (see fig. 7.22).

FIG. 7.22

Your address book is an HTML document you can see within Netscape. Load it, and you have the ability to address mail with a single click, just as you would from any Web page.

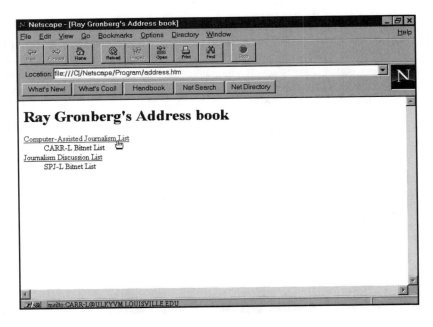

Once the file is there, you can create a new message, complete with precompleted address information, merely by clicking one of the highlighted links. Because it's HTML, clicking a link opens a message composition window, just as it would if you had clicked an e-mail link embedded on a Web page.

And, again because it's HTML, you can also add your Address Book to your Bookmarks menu, putting it one click away any time you're using your browser.

Setting Up the Microsoft Exchange Client

There's more than one way to manage e-mail with Netscape 3.0. Starting with version 1.2, Netscape has shipped a connection to Microsoft Exchange with every copy of Netscape. Until recently, the Exchange client was the only thing that gave Netscape users full access to Internet e-mail services.

It was, and is, by no means a perfect solution. Exchange is a notorious resource hog that gulps RAM and virtual memory by the megabyte. It's also slow. For all that, it offers the Internet e-mail users little more than freeware programs like Eudora Light. You'll look high and low in Exchange, for example, and never find a high-end feature like automatic message filtering, which in a package like Eudora Pro, lets you tell the program to pre-sort incoming message traffic into mail folders.

Exchange shines as a corporate network messaging client. If you're not part of such a network, you're probably better off using Netscape 3.0's e-mail service, or acquiring a third-party mail package.

But if you are part of a corporate network, and if you're an Exchange user, you'll probably want Internet mail routed to your Inbox instead of relying on another program.

You don't necessarily need Netscape to use Exchange for handling your Internet mail. Microsoft provides its own POP3 client for Exchange as part of Microsoft Plus! You can find instructions for setting it up in many publications, including Que's *Special Edition Using Windows 95*. The same references will tell you more about using Exchange on a day-to-day basis, which we also don't cover.

But we do tell you how to enable the connection to Netscape in the event you don't have Plus! Just follow these steps:

1. From Windows 95's Start menu, open the Control Panel.
2. Double-click on the Mail and Fax icon.
3. On the Services tab, click the Add button.
4. Highlight Netscape Internet Transport and click OK (see fig. 7.23). A tabbed dialog box labeled Netscape Transport Configuration appears.
5. On the User tab, type your name in the Display Name box and your e-mail address in the Internet Address box.

FIG. 7.23

Click OK to add the Netscape Internet Transport to your Microsoft Exchange user profile.

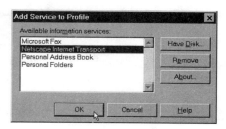

6. On the Hosts tab, enter the addresses supplied by your Internet Provider in the SMTP Host and POP3 Host boxes (see fig. 7.24). These should match exactly those you entered in Netscape's Mail and News Preferences dialog box.

FIG. 7.24

Enter mail server and login information in the indicated boxes.

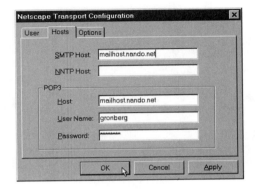

7. Also on the Hosts tab, enter your login name and password in the POP3 User Name and Passwords boxes.

8. On the Options tab, be sure to clear the Send RTF Text check box.

9. Click OK twice and close Control Panel.

10. Open Netscape's Mail and News Preferences dialog box by selecting it from the Options menu.

11. On the Appearance tab, click to put a check in the Use Exchange Client for Mail and News box. ●

Reading UseNet Newsgroups with Netscape

CompuServe calls them forums. The Microsoft Network calls them BBSs (bulletin board systems). At your office, they're possibly known as cork boards. They are all places where people come together to exchange ideas and opinions, post public notices, or look for help. The Internet has such a place, too. On the Internet, it's called UseNet newsgroups, or just newsgroups for short.

You learn all about how newsgroups work and how to access newsgroups in this chapter. Here are some of the topics you'll find:

- How newsgroups work

- The different types of newsgroups on UseNet

- The organization of UseNet newsgroups

- Using Netscape's newsreader to access newsgroups

- Accessing newsgroups without using the newsreader ■

A UseNet Primer

Newsgroups are a bit more complicated than forums, BBSs, and cork boards—not in a technical sense, but in a cultural sense. Newsgroups don't have official rules that are enforced by anyone in particular. They have unofficial rules that newsgroup peers enforce. Newsgroups concentrate cultures, from all over the world, in one place—a source of a lot of conflict as you can imagine.

So, take a few moments to study this section before you dive into newsgroups head first. Make sure that you understand how newsgroups and the UseNet culture works. Then, you'll learn how to use Netscape's newsreader to access one of the most dynamic parts of the Internet—newsgroups—later in this chapter.

> **CAUTION**
>
> If you're particularly sensitive or easily offended, newsgroups may not be right for you. Unlike the forums and BBSs on commercial online systems, no one is watching over the content on newsgroups. The material is often very offensive to some folks. You'll find plenty of nasty language and abusive remarks in some newsgroups, just like you'd expect to find in some pubs.

The Basics of Using Newsgroups

If you've ever used a forum or BBS on a commercial online service, you're already familiar with the concept of a newsgroup. Readers post messages, or articles, to newsgroups for other people to read. They can also reply to articles that they read on a newsgroup. It's one way for people like yourself to communicate with millions of people around the world.

Newsgroups are a bit looser, however. A newsgroup doesn't necessarily have a watchdog—other than the readers themselves. As a result, the organization is a bit looser, and the content of the messages is often way out of focus. The seemingly chaotic nature of newsgroups, however, produces some of the most interesting information you'll find anywhere.

Newsgroup Variety Is Good The variety of content is exactly what makes newsgroups so appealing. There are newsgroups for expressing opinions—no matter how benign or how radical. There are other newsgroups for asking questions or getting help. And, best of all, there are newsgroups for those seeking companionship—whether they're looking for a soul mate or longing to find someone with a similar interest in whittling. The following is a sample of the types of newsgroups you'll find:

- alt.tv.simpsons contains a lot of mindless chatter about *The Simpsons*.
- comp.os.ms-windows.advocacy is one of the hottest Windows newsgroups around. You'll find heated discussions about both Windows 3.1 and Windows 95.
- rec.games.trading-cards.marketplace is the place to be if you're into sports trading cards.
- rec.humor.funny is where to go to lighten up your day. You'll find a wide variety of humor, including contemporary jokes, old standards, and bogus news flashes.

Alternative and Regional Newsgroups   Not all the newsgroups available are true UseNet newsgroups. Some newsgroups are created to serve a particular region or are so obscure that they wouldn't make it through the rigorous UseNet approval process. If something looks like a newsgroup and acts like a newsgroup, however, it can find its way onto your news server.

Here are some examples:

- Regional—Many localities, such as Dallas or San Francisco, have their own newsgroups where people exchange dining tips, consumer advice, and other regional bits of information.

- Alternative—The alt newsgroups are responsible for most of the variety on UseNet. Some of these groups have a reputation for being downright nasty (for example, pornography), but also have groups dedicated to your favorite TV shows, books, or politicians.

N O T E   If you have a child who will be using newsgroups, you might consider finding a service provider that makes the pornographic newsgroups, such as alt.sex.pictures and alt.binaries.pictures.erotica, unavailable. ■

Moderated Newsgroups   Moderated newsgroups are a bit more civil, and the articles are typically more focused than unmoderated newsgroups. Moderators look at every article posted to their newsgroup before making it available for everyone to read. If they judge it to be inappropriate, they nuke it.

So what are the advantages of a moderated newsgroup? You don't have to wade through ten pounds of garbage to find one ounce of treasure. Check out some of the alternative newsgroups and you'll get the picture. Most the alternative newsgroups are unmoderated. As such, they're a free-for-all—profanity, abusiveness, and childish bickering. The value and quality of the information that you'll find in moderated newsgroups is much higher than their unmoderated cousins.

The disadvantages, on the other hand, are just as clear. Some people believe that moderating a newsgroup is the equivalent of censorship. Instead of the group as a whole determining the content of a newsgroups, the judgment of a single individual determines the content of the newsgroups. Another significant disadvantage is timeliness. Articles posted to moderated newsgroups can be delayed days or weeks.

Participating in a Newsgroup   Every Internet resource that you want to use requires a client program on your computer. Newsgroups are no exception. The program that you use to read newsgroups is called a newsreader.

A newsreader lets you browse the newsgroups that are available, reading and posting articles along the way. Most newsreaders also have more advanced features that make using newsgroups a bit more productive. Later in this chapter, you'll learn how to use Netscape's newsreader to access the news. You'll also find other ways to read the newsgroups without using a newsreader.

So How Do Newsgroups Work, Anyway?

NNTP (Network News Transport Protocol) is used to move the news from one server to another. It's very similar to e-mail in a lot of respects. Instead of all the messages sitting on your machine, however, they are stored on an NNTP news server that many other people can access. Therefore, the news only has to be sent to the server, instead of each user. Each user is then responsible for retrieving the articles she's interested in.

UseNet news makes its way to your news server using a process called flooding. That is, all the news servers are networked together. A particular news server may be fed by one news server, while it feeds three other news servers in turn. Periodically, it's flooded with news from the server that's feeding it, and in turn floods all of its news to the servers that it feeds.

Wading Through UseNet

Sometimes, you'll feel like you're knee-deep in newsgroups. There are over 10,000 newsgroups available. Wading through them all to find what you want can be a daunting task. What's a new user to do?

It's all right there in front of you. There's a lot of logic to the way newsgroups are named. Once you learn it, you'll be able to pluck out a newsgroup just by how it's named. You'll also find tools to help you locate just the right newsgroup, as well as a few newsgroups that provide helpful advice and pointers to new users.

Newsgroup Organization   Newsgroups are organized into a hierarchy of categories and subcategories. Take a look at the alt.tv.simpsons newsgroup discussed earlier. The top-level category is alt. The subcategory is tv. The subcategory under that is simpsons. The name goes from general to specific, left to right. You'll also find other newsgroups under alt.tv, such as alt.tv.friends and alt.tv.home-imprvment.

 T I P   alt.tv.* is a notational convention that means all the newsgroups available under the alt.tv category.

There are many different top-level categories available. Table 8.1 shows some that you probably have available on your news server.

These categories help you nail down exactly which newsgroup you're looking for. A bit of practice helps, as well. If you're looking for information about Windows 95, for example, start looking at the comp top-level category. You'll find an os category, which probably represents operating systems. Under that category, you'll find an ms-windows category.

N O T E   Exactly which newsgroups are available on your news server is largely under the control of the administrator. Some administrators filter out regional newsgroups that don't apply to your area. Some also filter out the alt newsgroups because of their potentially offensive content. ■

Table 8.1   Internet Top-Level Newsgroup Categories

Category	Description
alt	Alternative newsgroups
bit	BitNet LISTSERV mailing lists
biz	Advertisements for businesses
clarinet	News clipping service by subscription only
comp	Computer-related topics; hardware and software
k12	Educational, kindergarten through grade 12
misc	Topics that don't fit the other categories
news	News and information about UseNet
rec	Recreational, sports, hobbies, music, games
sci	Applied sciences
soc	Social and cultural topics
talk	Discussion of more controversial topics

Searching for Newsgroups on the Web   Scouring the categories for a particular newsgroup may not be the most efficient way to find what you want. Here are a couple of tools that help you find newsgroups based upon keywords that you type:

- Point Netscape at **www.cen.uiuc.edu/cgi-bin/find-news**. This tool searches all the newsgroup names and newsgroup descriptions for a single keyword that you specify.
- Another very similar tool is at **www.nova.edu/Inter-Links/cgi-bin/news.pl**. This tool allows you to give more than one keyword, however.

Newsgroups for New Users   Whenever I go someplace new, I first try to locate a source of information about it. Likewise, the first few places that you need to visit when you get to UseNet are all the newsgroups that are there to welcome you. It's not just a warm and fuzzy welcome, either. They provide useful information about what to do, what not to do, and how to get the most out of the newsgroups. Table 8.2 shows you the newsgroups that you need to check out.

N O T E   Don't post test articles to these newsgroups. Don't post articles asking for someone to send you an e-mail, either. This is a terrible waste of newsgroups that are intended to help new users learn the ropes. See the section "Practice Posting in the Right Place" later in this chapter to learn about a better place to post test articles. ■

Table 8.2   Newsgroups for the Newbie

Newsgroup	Description
alt.answers	A good source of FAQs and information about alt newsgroups
alt.internet.services	This is the place to ask about Internet programs and resources
news.announce.newsgroups	Announcements about new newsgroups are made here
news.announce.newusers	Articles and FAQs for the new newsgroups user
news.newusers.questions	This is the place to ask your questions about using newsgroups

news.announce.newusers

The news.announce.newusers newsgroup contains a lot of great articles for new newsgroup users. In particular, look for the articles with the following subject lines:

- What is UseNet?
- What is UseNet? A second opinion
- Rules for posting to UseNet
- Hints on writing style for UseNet
- A Primer on How to Work with the UseNet Community
- Emily Postnews Answers Your Questions on Netiquette
- How to find the right place to post (FAQ)
- Answers to Frequently Asked Questions about UseNet

Getting Real News on UseNet

UseNet is good for a lot more than just blathering and downloading questionable art. There's a lot of news and great information coming from a variety of sources. You'll find "real" news, current Internet events, organizational newsgroups, and regional newsgroups as well—all of which make newsgroups worth every bit of trouble.

ClariNet   You can be the first kid on the block with the current news. ClariNet is a news service that clips articles from sources such as the AP and Reuters news wires. They post these services to the clari.* newsgroups. These newsgroups aren't free, though. They sell these newsgroups on a subscription basis. You wouldn't want to pay for them, either, because they can be expensive. Many independent service providers do subscribe, however, as a part of their service.

ClariNet has more than 300 newsgroups from which to choose. My favorite ClariNet newsgroups are shown in table 8.3. You'll come up with your own favorites in short order. One

ClariNet newsgroup that you definitely need to check out is clari.net.newusers. It's a good introduction to all the newsgroups that ClariNet offers.

Table 8.3   Popular Clarinet Newsgroups

Newsgroup	Description
clari.biz.briefs	Regular business updates
clari.local.State	Your own local news
clari.nb.online	News about the online community
clari.nb.windows	News about Windows products and issues
clari.news.briefs	Regular national and world news updates

For your convenience, table 8.4 describes each ClariNet news category. You'll find individual newsgroups under each category. Under the clari.living category, for example, you'll find arts, books, music, and movies.

Table 8.4   ClariNet News Categories at a Glance

Category	Description
clari.news	General and national news
clari.biz	Business and financial news
clari.sports	Sports and athletic news
clari.living	Lifestyle and human interest stories
clari.world	News about other countries
clari.local	States and local areas
clari.feature	Special syndicated features
clari.tw	Technical and scientific news
clari.matrix_news	A networking newsletter
clari.nb	Newsbytes, computer industry news
clari.sfbay	San Francisco Bay Area news
clari.net	Information about ClariNet
clari.apbl	Special groups for the AP BulletinLine

Net-happenings   If it seems that the Internet is moving too fast to keep up with, you're right—without help, anyway. The comp.internet.net-happenings newsgroup helps you keep track of new events on the Internet, including the World Wide Web, mailing lists, UseNet, and so on.

The subject line of each article tells you a lot about the announcement. Take, for example, the following announcement:

WWW>Free Internet service for first 100 visitors

The first part tells you that the announcement is about a World Wide Web site. You'll find many other categories such as FAQ, EMAG, LISTS, and MISC. The second part is a brief description about the announcement. Most of the time, the description is enough to tell you whether you want to see more information by opening the article. The article itself is a few paragraphs about the announcement, with the address or subscription information near the top.

Regional Newsgroups   Is your geographical region represented on UseNet? A lot are. The Dallas/Fort Worth area has a couple of newsgroups, such as dfw.eats, dfw.forsale, and dfw.personals. Virtually every state has similar newsgroups. Other states might have special needs. For example, California users might be interested in the ca.environment.earthquakes newsgroup.

Using Netscape to Read the News

All that news is out there, just sloshing around on the news server, and you need a program to get it. There are a lot of newsreaders out there, but you already have Netscape's newsreader. It's one of the cleanest and easiest to use newsreaders available.

Starting the Netscape newsreader is easy. Choose <u>W</u>indow, Netscape <u>N</u>ews from the Netscape main menu. Figure 8.1 shows the Netscape newsreader, and table 8.5 shows what each of the buttons on the toolbar do.

FIG. 8.1
The Netscape newsreader window is divided into three panes: groups list, article list, and article body.

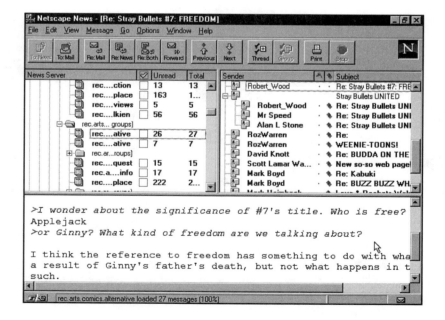

Table 8.5   Buttons on the Netscape Newsreader Toolbar

Button	Name	Description
	Post new	Post new article to newsgroup
	New message	Create a new e-mail message
	Reply	Reply using an e-mail message
	Post reply	Post reply to newsgroup article
	Post and reply	Post and e-mail a reply
	Forward	Forward article to e-mail address
	Previous Unread	Previous article in a newsgroup
	Next Unread	Next article in a newsgroup
	Mark thread read	Mark entire conversation as read
	Mark all read	Mark entire newsgroup as read
	Print	Print the current article
	Stop	Stop transferring from news server

Configuring Netscape to Read the News

To configure Netscape for your service provider, use the following steps:

1. Choose Options, Mail and News Preferences from the Netscape newsreader main menu, and click the Servers tab. Netscape displays the dialog box shown in figure 8.2.

2. Fill in your NNTP (Network News Transfer Protocol) and SMTP (Simple Mail Transfer Protocol) servers as shown in figure 8.2, and click the Identity tab. Netscape displays the dialog box shown in figure 8.3. You can also control how many UseNet messages Netscape will retrieve using the Get test field. If you're paying toll charges to access your UseNet server, or your computer is a bit on the slow side, you'll want to set this to a low number.

FIG. 8.2
Your service provider should have given you the NNTP news server and SMTP mail server.

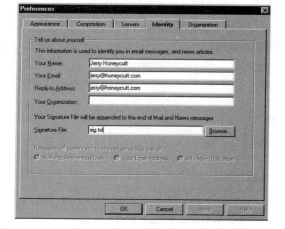

3. Fill in Your Name, Your Email, and Reply-to Address as shown in figure 8.3. If you want to attach a signature file to the end of your postings, select a text file by clicking Browse. Click OK to save your changes.

FIG. 8.3
You need to provide a name and e-mail address so that other people can respond to your postings.

TROUBLESHOOTING

Why do I get an error message that says Netscape couldn't find the news server? First, make sure that you have a connection to your service provider. If you're definitely connected, make sure that you correctly configured your NNTP news server. Don't remember the exact address your provider gave you? Try this: If your domain name is provider.net, then add news to the front of it like this: news.provider.net.

Can I use Netscape to access UseNet through CompuServe? Yes. The CompuServe news server is news.compuserve.com and the SMTP mail server is mail.compuserve.com.

A Note about Signatures

You can easily personalize your postings with a signature. Save about three lines that say something about yourself, such as your address and hobbies, into a text file. Then, in step 3 of "Configuring Netscape to Read the News," select the text file you created. Here's an example of a signature file:

> Jerry Honeycutt | jerry@honeycutt.com
> | (800) 555-1212
> | Buy Using the Internet, Now!

Your signature can communicate anything that you want about yourself including your name, mailing address, phone number, address, or a particular phrase that reflects your outlook on life. It is considered good form, however, to limit your signatures to three lines.

Subscribing to Newsgroups

After you've configured the Netscape newsreader for your service provider, you need to download a complete list of the newsgroups available on your news server. Highlight your news server in the groups pane, and choose Show All Newsgroups from the Options menu. Netscape displays a dialog box warning you that this process can take a few minutes on a slow connection. Click OK to continue.

Before you can read the articles in a newsgroup, you have to subscribe to it. When you subscribe to a newsgroup, you're telling Netscape that you want to read the articles in that newsgroup. Normally, Netscape only displays the newsgroups to which you've subscribed. Thus, subscribing to a handful of newsgroups keeps you from having to slog through a list of 15,000 newsgroups to find what you want.

 Categories are indicated with a file folder icon; newsgroups are indicated with a newspaper icon.

Earlier you learned that newsgroups are named in a hierarchical fashion. Netscape takes advantage of this by organizing newsgroups the same way, using folders in the groups pane. Initially, all you see under a news server is the top-level categories. If you click one of the top-level categories, you see the subcategories underneath it. Continue clicking categories until you see a newsgroup to which you can subscribe.

If you want to subscribe to alt.tv.simpsons, for example, follow these steps:

1. Click the alt top-level newsgroup.
2. Find alt.tv in the list under alt, and click it.
3. Find alt.tv.simpsons in the list under alt.tv, and check the box that is to the right of the name to indicate that you want to subscribe to that newsgroup.

After you subscribe to all the newsgroups you want, you can tell Netscape to display only those newsgroups to which you've subscribed. Choose Options, Show Subscribed Groups from the main menu.

N O T E You can sample the articles in a newsgroup before subscribing. If you click a newsgroup to
which you haven't subscribed, Netscape displays that newsgroup's articles in the article
pane. If you like what you see, subscribe to the group by checking the box next to the name of the
newsgroup. ■

Browsing and Reading Articles

Select a newsgroup in the groups Pane and Netscape displays all the current articles for that
group in the articles pane. You can scroll up and down the list of articles looking for an interesting article. When you click an article in the article pane, Netscape displays the contents of that
article in the body pane.

T I P Articles that you haven't read have a green diamond in the R column.

Notice that some of the articles are indented under other articles. These are replies to the
articles under which they are indented. All the messages indented under an article, including
the original message, are called a thread. Netscape indents articles this way so you can visually
follow the thread. Figure 8.4 shows what a thread looks like in Netscape.

FIG. 8.4
The top portion of the
message's body tells
you who posted the
message and what other
groups they posted the
message to.

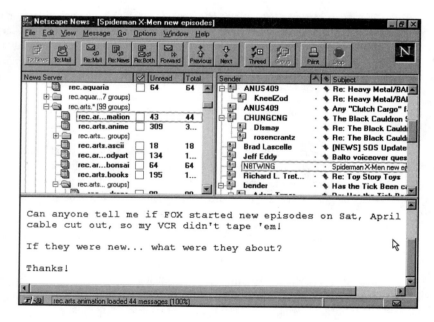

TROUBLESHOOTING

What happened to the articles that were here a few days ago? It's not practical to keep every article posted to every newsgroup indefinitely. Your service provider deletes the older articles to make room for the newer articles. Another way of saying this is that a message scrolled off. The length of time that an article hangs around varies from provider to provider, but is usually between three days and a week.

Moving Around the Article Pane   When you click an article header in the article pane, the article's contents are automatically displayed in the body pane. After you read the article, you can click another article, or you can use the following options from Netscape's toolbar and menu to move around:

- Choose <u>G</u>o, Ne<u>x</u>t Unread from the main menu to read the next message you haven't read.

- Choose <u>G</u>o, Pre<u>v</u>ious Unread from the main menu to read the previous message you haven't read.

- Click the Next button to read the next article in the newsgroup—whether you've read it already or not.

- Click the Previous button to read the previous article in the newsgroup—whether you've read it already or not.

- Choose <u>G</u>o, <u>F</u>irst Unread to read the first message in the newsgroup that you haven't yet read.

TROUBLESHOOTING

I opened an article, but its contents were all garbled. You've probably opened an article that is ROT13-encoded. ROT13 is an encoding method that has little to do with security. It allows a person who is posting a potentially offensive message to place the responsibility for its contents on you—the reader. It essentially says that if you decode and read this message, you won't hold me responsible for its contents. To decode the article, right-click in the body pane, and choose Unscramble (ROT-13).

Downloading Files from Newsgroups   Posting and downloading files from a newsgroup is a bit more complicated than your experience with online services. Binary files can't be posted directly to UseNet. Many methods have evolved, however, to encode files into text so that they can be sent.

The downloading process works as follows:

1. A file is encoded, using UUEncode, to a newsgroup as one or more articles.

2. While you're browsing a newsgroup, you notice a few articles with subject lines that look like this (headings are provided for your convenience):

Lines	File name	Part	Description
5	HOMER.GIF	[00/02]	Portrait of Homer Simpson
800	HOMER.GIF	[01/02]	Portrait of Homer Simpson
540	HOMER.GIF	[02/02]	Portrait of Homer Simpson

These articles are three parts of the same file. The first article is probably a description of the file because it is part zero, and because there are only five lines in it. The next two articles are the actual file.

3. To download a file from a newsgroup, you retrieve all the articles belonging to that file. Then, you UUDecode the articles back into a binary file. See chapter 17, "Using Compressed/Encoded Files," to learn how.

Replying to an Article   You'll eventually want to post a reply to an article you read in a newsgroup. You might want to be helpful and answer someone's question. You're just as likely to find an interesting discussion to which you want to contribute. Either way, the following are two different ways you can reply to an article you have read:

■ Follow up—If you want your reply to be read by everyone who frequents the newsgroup, post a follow-up article. Your reply is added to the thread. To reply to an article, click the Post Reply button on the toolbar. Fill in the window shown in figure 8.5, and click the Send button.

FIG. 8.5
The text that starts with the greater-than sign (>) is the original article. Delete everything that you don't need to remind the reader of what he posted.

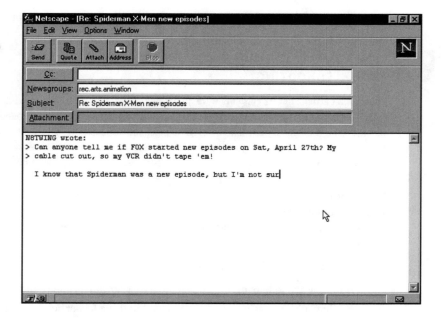

Part
II

Ch
8

■ E-mail—If your reply would benefit only the person to whom you're replying, respond with an e-mail message instead. That person gets the message faster, and the other newsgroup readers aren't annoyed. To reply by e-mail, click the Reply button on the toolbar. Fill out the window shown in figure 8.6 and click the Send button.

FIG. 8.6
Look carefully—the only difference between this window and the window in figure 8.5 is this window has the Mail To field and the previous window has the Newsgroups field.

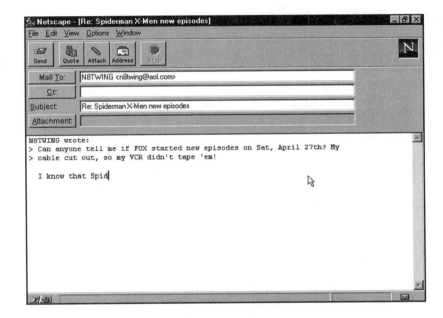

Stay out of Trouble; Follow the Rules

Etiquette, as Miss Manners will tell you, was created so that everyone would get along better. Etiquette's rules are not official rules, however; they're community standards for how everyone should behave. Likewise, netiquette is a community standard for how to behave on the Internet. It's important for two reasons. First, it helps keep the frustration level down. Second, it helps prevent the terrible waste of Internet resources by limiting the amount of noise.

● Post your articles in the right place. Don't post questions about Windows 95, for example, to the alt.tv.simpsons newsgroup.

● NEWSGROUP READERS REALLY HATE IT WHEN YOU SHOUT BY USING ALL CAPS. It doesn't make your message seem any more important.

● Don't test, and don't beg for e-mail. There are a few places where that is appropriate, but this behavior generally gets you flamed (a flame is a mean or abusive message).

● Don't spam. Spamming is posting an advertisement to several, if not hundreds, of newsgroups. Don't do it. It's a waste of Internet resources.

● Don't cross-post your article. This is a waste of Internet resources, and readers quickly tire of seeing the same article posted to many newsgroups.

Posting a New Article

It's no fun being a spectator. You'll eventually want to start a discussion of your own. To post a new article, click the Post New button on the toolbar. Fill in the window shown previously in figure 8.5, and click the Send button.

 N O T E   Lurk before you leap. Lurking is when you just hang out, reading the articles and learning the ropes without posting an article. You'll avoid making a fool of yourself by learning what's acceptable and what's not before it's too late. ■

Practice Posting in the Right Place   You'll find a special newsgroup, called alt.test, that exists just for test posting. You can post a test article to that newsgroup all day long and no one will care.

In fact, you should go ahead and post a test article just to make sure that everything works. You'll get a good idea of how long it takes your article to show up, and you'll also learn the mechanics of posting and replying to articles.

T I P   Test your file uploads in the alt.test newsgroup, too, instead of testing them in productive newsgroups.

Posting a File   Netscape makes posting a file easy. Post a new article as described earlier in the section "Posting a New Article." Before you click the Send button, however, follow these instructions:

1. Click Attachment. Netscape displays the Attachments dialog box as shown in figure 8.7.

FIG. 8.7
You can attach more than one file to an article.

2. Click Attach File, choose the file you want to attach in the Enter File to Attach dialog box, and click Open.

3. Repeat step 2 for each file you want to attach to your article. Then, click OK to save your attachments.

After you've selected the files you want to attach to your posting, you can continue editing it normally. Click the Send button when you're finished.

Other Ways to Read the News

If browsing newsgroups with a newsreader seems like too much trouble, the tools described in this section might be just what you need. You'll learn to use DejaView, which lets you search UseNet for specific articles. You'll also learn how to use SIFT, a tool that filters all the newsgroup postings and saves them for you to read later.

Searching UseNet with DejaNews

DejaNews is a Web tool that searches all the newsgroup articles, past and present, for terms that you specify. Point your Web browser at **http://www.dejanews.com/forms/dnq.html**. Figure 8.8 shows you the DejaNews search Web page. To search UseNet, fill in the form as shown in figure 8.8, and click Search.

FIG. 8.8
Click the Create a Query Filter link to specify exactly which news-group, author, or date range to search.

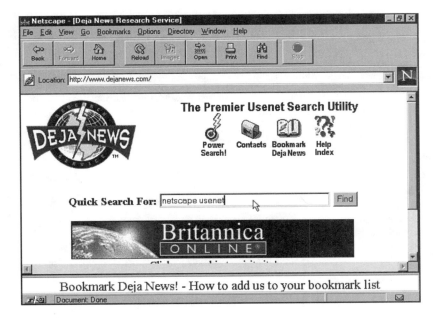

DejaNews displays another Web page that contains a list of the newsgroup articles it found. You can click any of these articles to read them, or click Get Next 30 Hits to display the next page full of articles. The following are a couple of other things you should know:

- The author's name is the last item on each line. You can click it to see what other newsgroups they typically post to.

- You can click the subject line of an article to display the complete thread that contains that article.

Filtering UseNet with SIFT

SIFT is a tool provided by Stanford that filters all the articles posted to UseNet. As an added bonus, it filters a lot of public mailing lists and new Web pages, too. You tell SIFT the keywords in which you're interested, and it keeps track of all the new documents on the Internet that match those keywords. Like DejaNews, this is a Web tool, so point your browser at **http://sift.stanford.edu**.

The first time you access SIFT, it asks you for an e-mail address and password. You don't have one, yet. That's OK. Type your e-mail address and make up a password. You'll need to use the same password the next time that you access SIFT. Click Enter to go to the search form.

The most effective way to use SIFT is as follows:

1. Figure 8.9 shows the SIFT search form. Select the Search radio button, and type the topics you're looking for. If you want to make sure that some topics are not included, type them in Avoid.

2. Click Submit. SIFT displays a page containing all of today's new articles that match your keywords. The most relevant line is at the top; the least relevant is at the bottom. Read some of the articles, Web pages, and mailing list messages by clicking them.

3. If you're happy with these test results, click Subscribe at the bottom of the Web page. Then, click Submit. The next time you log on to SIFT, you'll see additional lines at the bottom of the Web page, as shown in figure 8.9, that let you delete subscriptions or review the current day's hits.

FIG. 8.9
You won't see the Read and Delete Topic choices until you've submitted at least one subscription.

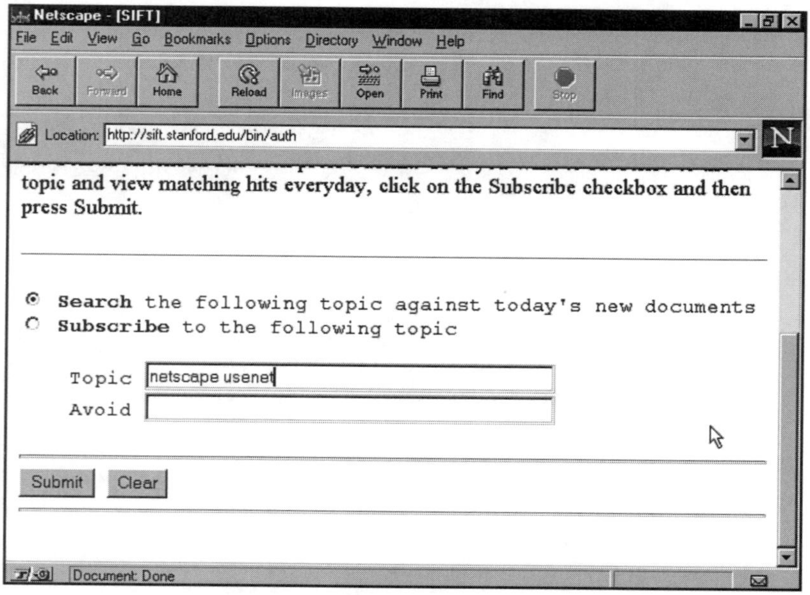

4. If you're not happy with the results, click Search at the bottom of the Web page. Then, adjust the keywords in Topic and Avoid, and click Submit. SIFT displays a similar Web page using your new search keywords.

The Pros and Cons of Netscape's Newsreader

There's a wide variety of newsreaders available on the Internet. They range from the most basic (Qnews) to complex (Free Agent). Netscape's newsreader is at the basic end of this spectrum. It doesn't have the features that an avid UseNet junkie needs to be productive. Netscape doesn't let you choose a UUEncoded file, for example, then download and UUDecode it automatically. If you need more advanced features such as this, you should consider some of the freeware and shareware newsreaders available. Free Agent is available on the Web at **www.forteinc.com/forte/agent/dlmain.htm**.

Netscape's newsreader does have everything that a casual user needs, however. You can easily post, reply, and view articles—possibly easier than with the other newsreaders available. You can also view UUEncoded images on UseNet just by selecting the article in the list. This is about all most people use UseNet for anyway. Incidentally, the most important feature of Netscape's newsreader is how solid and well thought out it appears to be. For example, Newsgroups are organized using an outline metaphor, and the article list is easy to navigate. ●

Plug-Ins and Helper Applications

Netscape Browser Plug-Ins

Though a wide variety of plug-in modules are now available for Netscape (more than 100 are described in this chapter alone), and more are under development, they fall roughly into three categories. In this chapter, you will learn about all three types:

- Multimedia—including viewers for video (AVI, MOV, and MPEG movies), audio (speech, music, and digitized sound), and graphics (including vector objects and super-compressed images), as well as multimedia presentation formats like Macromedia Director and Astound

- VRML—Virtual Reality Modeling Language 3D world display plug-ins (sometimes with extra features)

- Business Applications—this includes viewers for application files like Excel spreadsheets and Word documents, Web navigation tools, and plug-ins that link to OLE objects to call other programs, embed applications, or provide custom controls, as well as some interesting miscellaneous applications.

We won't list every plug-in ever created for Netscape—some have been merely testbed projects or fun demos ("Animated Widgets" comes to mind). But we *will* try to list all of the most useful plug-ins released so far. Of course, plug-in development proceeds apace, and it's almost impossible to keep up-to-date, even if you're online checking every day. Over 50 were released in the three months which immediately preceded the writing of this book! ■

 TIP   Look for the icon at the left, which indicates that the plug-in under discussion is one of the fifteen plug-ins included on Netscape's Power Pack 2.0 CD-ROM.

 ▶ **See** chapter 12, "Power Pack 2.0," **p. 305,** for more about the Power Pack 2.0 CD-ROM.

What Is a Netscape 3.0 Plug-In?

Plug-ins are feature add-ons designed to extend the capabilities of Netscape 3.0, much the way plug-ins extend the capabilities of other products such as Adobe Photoshop. In more technical terms, plug-ins are dynamic code modules that exist as part of Netscape's Application Programming Interface (API) for extending and integrating third-party software into Netscape 3.0. The creation of (and support for) plug-ins by 5Netscape is significant primarily because it allows other developers to seamlessly integrate their products into the Web via Netscape, without having to launch any external helper applications.

For Netscape users, plug-in support allows you to customize Netscape's interaction with third-party products and industry media standards. Netscape's plug-in API also attempts to address the concerns of programmers, providing a high degree of flexibility and cross-platform support to plug-in developers.

What Plug-Ins Mean for End Users

Because plug-ins are platform-specific, you must have a different version of each plug-in for every operating system you use, such as Windows or the Mac OS. Regardless of your platform, however, Netscape plug-ins should be functionally equivalent across all platforms.

 TIP   Many plug-ins ship with the copy of Netscape you purchased, already designed for your platform. However, if you find other plug-ins that you want to either purchase and/or download from the Internet, make sure the plug-in is designed for your specific platform.

For most users, integrating plug-ins is transparent. They open up and become active whenever Netscape is opened. Furthermore, because most plug-ins are not activated unless you open up a Web page that initiates the plug-in, you may not even see the plug-in at work most of the time. For example, after you install the Shockwave for Director plug-in, you will notice no difference in the way Netscape functions until you come across a Web page that features Shockwave.

Once a plug-in is installed on your machine and initiated by a Web page, it will manifest itself in three potential ways:

- Embedded
- Full-screen
- Hidden

An *embedded* plug-in appears as a visible, rectangular window integrated into a Web page. This window may not appear any different than a window created by a graphic, such as an embedded GIF or JPEG picture. The main difference between the previous windows supported by Netscape and those created by plug-ins is that plug-in windows can support a much wider range of interactivity and movement, and thereby remain live instead of static.

In addition to mouse clicks, embedded plug-ins may also read and take note of mouse location, mouse movement, keyboard input, and input from virtually any other input device. In this way, a plug-in can support the full range of user events required to produce sophisticated applications.

An example of an embedded plug-in might be an MPEG, Video for Windows, or QuickTime movie player, or the Shockwave for Macromedia Director player discussed later in this chapter.

A *full-screen* plug-in takes over the entire current Netscape window to display its own content. This is necessary when a Web page is designed to display data that is not supported by HTML. An example of this type of plug-in is the Adobe Acrobat viewer.

If you view an Acrobat page using the Netscape plug-in, it pulls up just like any other Web page, but it retains the look and functionality of an Acrobat document viewed in Adobe's stand-alone viewer. For instance, you might find an online manual for a product displayed on a Web site with Acrobat, and you'd be able to scroll, print, and interact with the page just as if it were being displayed by the stand-alone Acrobat Reader program.

A *hidden* plug-in doesn't have any visible elements, but works strictly behind the scenes to add some feature to Netscape that is otherwise not available. An example of a hidden plug-in might be a MIDI player or a decompression engine. A MIDI player plug-in could read MIDI data from a Web page whenever it's encountered, and automatically play it through your local hardware or software. Similarly, a decompression engine could function much the way it does on commercial online services, decompressing data in real-time in the background, or saving decompression until the user logs off the Internet.

TIP For more information on Netscape 3.0 plug-ins, point Netscape to **http://home.netscape.com/comprod/products/navigator/version_2.0/plugins/index.html**.

Regardless of which plug-ins you are using, and whether they are embedded, full-screen, or hidden, the rest of Netscape's user interface should remain relatively constant and available. So even if you have an Acrobat page displayed in Netscape's main window, you'll still be able to access Netscape's menus and navigational controls.

What Plug-Ins Mean for Programmers

For programmers, plug-ins offer the possibility of creating Netscape add-on products or using development plug-ins to create your own Internet-based applications. Creating a custom plug-in requires much more intensive background, experience, and testing than actually using a plug-in (such as Shockwave for Director). If you are a developer, or are interested in creating a plug-in, the following discussion will be useful.

The current version of the plug-in Application Programming Interface (API) supports four broad areas of functionality. Plug-ins can:

- Draw into and receive events from a native window element that is a part of the Netscape window hierarchy.
- Obtain MIME data from the network via URLs.
- Generate data for consumption by Netscape or other plug-ins.
- Override and implement protocol handlers.

Netscape plug-ins are ideally suited to take advantage of platform-independent protocols, architectures, languages, and media types such as Java, VRML, and MPEG. While plug-ins should be functionally equivalent across platforms, they should also be complementary to platform-specific protocols and architectures, such as OLE 2.

N O T E Netscape Corporation has a wealth of information online for programmers who want to create their own Netscape plug-ins. For starters, you can read the online documentation for the Plug-Ins SDK (Software Developers' Kit) for both Macintosh and Windows at **http:// home.netscape.com/comprod/development_partners/plugin_api/index.html**. You can also download the SDKs themselves from this page. ■

When the Netscape client is launched, it makes note of any plug-ins available, but does not load any into RAM. This way, a plug-in is only resident in memory when needed, although because many plug-ins may be in use at any one time, you still need to be aware of memory allocation. Plug-ins simply reside on disk until they are needed.

Integration of plug-ins with the Netscape client is quite elegant and flexible, allowing the programmer to make the most of asynchronous processes and multithreaded data. To further this claim, Netscape makes note of plug-ins based upon the MIME type they support, since all plug-ins are associated with a MIME type not native to the Netscape client. Plug-ins may be associated with multiple MIME types, and Netscape may in turn create multiple instances of the same plug-in.

By allowing many instances of many plug-ins to be readily available, without taking up any RAM until just before the time they are needed, the user is able to seamlessly view a tremendous amount of varied data. A plug-in is deleted from RAM as soon as the user moves to another HTML page that does not require the plug-in.

At its most fundamental level, a plug-in can access a URL and retrieve MIME data just as a standard Netscape client. This data is streamed to the plug-in as it arrives from the network, making it possible to implement viewers and other interfaces that can progressively display information.

For instance, a plug-in may draw a simple frame and introductory graphic or text for the user to comprehend, while the bulk of the data is streaming off the network into Netscape's existing cache. All the same bandwidth considerations adhered to by good HTML authors need to be accounted for in plug-ins.

Of course, plug-ins can also be file-based, requiring a complete amount of data to be down-loaded first before the plug-in can proceed. This type of architecture is not encouraged due to its potential user delays, but may prove necessary for some data-intensive plug-ins.

If more data is needed by a plug-in than can be supplied through a single data stream, multiple, simultaneous data streams may be requested by the plug-in, so long as the user's system supports this.

While a plug-in is active, if data is needed by another plug-in or Netscape, the plug-in can generate data itself for these purposes. Thus, plug-ins not only process data, but they also generate it. For example, a plug-in can be a data translator or filter.

Plug-ins are also provided a random-access model of network data, via the proposed Byte Range extension to HTTP.

To embed a plug-in in an HTML document, you use the EMBED tag.

The Netscape page at **http://home.netscape.com/comprod/development_partners/ plugin_api/win_avi_sample.html** presents this example: If you were to compile and install the program they present, you'd get a plug-in that can serve as an AVI (Video for Windows) player. You initialize it from your HTML document with the EMBED tag and two parameters, "autostart" and "loop." The autostart parameter specifies whether the AVI movie starts playing right away or whether it waits for user input, and the "loop" parameter dictates whether play-back repeats back to the beginning of the movie when the movie finishes. In this example, the EMBED tag in your HTML document might look like this if you wanted to display the AVI file "myavi.avi" in a 320×200 window:

```
<embed src=myavi.avi width=320 height=200 autostart=true loop=true>
```

In the example above, the EMBED tag serves as a command line for the plug-in, allowing you to pass different values as parameters. This tag also allows you to specify where in your HTML page the AVI window appears. Of course, you can create larger, even full-screen versions of this plug-in as well by implementing a full-screen plug-in that puts the AVI window in the center of the Netscape window.

T I P   To view actual C++ code for the sample AVI player plug-in discussed here, check out the "NPAVI32.DLL" page on the Netscape Web site at **http://home.netscape.com/comprod/development_partners/ plugin_api/win_avi_sample.html**.

> **N O T E**   While creating a plug-in is much easier to do than, say, writing a spreadsheet application, it still requires the talents of a professional programmer. Some third-party developers may soon offer visual programming tools or BASIC environments that provide plug-in templates, making the actual coding of plug-ins much less tedious. However, most plug-ins are, and will be, developed in sophisticated C++ environments, requiring thousands of lines of code. ■

Downloading, Installing, and Using Plug-Ins

Downloading Netscape plug-ins couldn't be much easier—Netscape maintains a page which lists many of the currently available plug-ins, with links to the pages from which they can be downloaded, at **http://home.netscape.com/comprod/products/navigator/version_2.0/ plugins/index.html**. There's also the Plug-Ins Plaza site, which seems to be consistently more up-to-date than Netscape's own site. It's at **http://www.browserwatch.com**. For your convenience, we've included the URL of the download site for all of the plug-ins that are listed in this chapter.

You should download a plug-in file into its own temporary directory before installing it. I usually keep a directory called C:\INSTALL on my hard drive just for this purpose. I download a single plug-in to the INSTALL directory, install it, then delete the files in C:\INSTALL so that the directory is empty and available for my next installation. (I usually make sure that the plug-in is actually installed correctly and working properly before I delete the installation files.)

Each plug-in downloads as a single file. Installation involves one of two procedures:

1. If the file is called Setup.exe, you simply have to run it. It will automatically install itself as a Netscape plug-in. You may be given the option to determine which directory the plug-in will be installed to. Don't change the default unless you already have a directory by that name which contains something else.

2. If the file has some obscure name like xx32b4.exe, it's a sure bet that it's a self-extracting archive. In this case, double-clicking the file in Win95 (or opening a DOS shell in Windows 3.1, CD-ing to the INSTALL directory, and typing the filename) will extract the archive into a whole bunch of files in your INSTALL directory. Then close the DOS window and run the program called Setup.exe. From here, the process is identical to (1) above.

In any event, the download page for a plug-in always contains complete instructions on downloading and installation. Read and follow these instructions carefully. They might just do something different, and you don't want to be caught by surprise. (For example, you can optionally download a bare-bones version of the Crescendo MIDI player plug-in without a setup program, but if you do, you have to unpack and copy the file into the Netscape Plug-ins directory yourself.)

CAUTION

Make sure you have the latest version of Netscape Navigator properly installed before you install any Netscape plug-in. The plug-ins in this chapter will not work at all with versions of Netscape earlier than 2.0, and some may require 3.0.

TROUBLESHOOTING

I've been playing around with plug-ins, and have installed several. Now I can't remember which ones I have, and which ones I don't! Worse, I had a nice plug-in installed for playing audio [or video, or multimedia, etc.] plug-ins, but some plug-in I installed later seems to have taken over this function, and I don't like it near as well! How can I figure out which plug-ins I have installed, and which ones I still need? Is there any way to get my old plug-in back? Unfortunately, Navigator has no easy menu selection or pop-up dialog that just tells you exactly which plug-ins you have installed. However, there are three places you can go to get some good clues.

One is to pick <u>H</u>elp, About <u>P</u>lug-ins from the Navigator menu. You'll get a screen with a list formatted like this:

```
File name:
Types:
      Description: data
      MIME Type: x-world/x-vrml
      Suffixes: wrl
etc…
```

This is a list of the MIME types that are registered to launch plug-ins. Each entry on this list was entered when you installed a plug-in. While this list is a good indicator of which file types will launch plug-ins when they're encountered, it won't tell you exactly which plug-ins will be launched.

If the list includes two or more entries documenting the same MIME type and/or Suffixes, then you've installed one plug-in over another, and the more recent one is handling that type of file display.

You can also check out <u>O</u>ptions, <u>G</u>eneral Preferences and select the Helpers tab from the dialog box that appears. This box includes a scrolling list of registered MIME types. Look under the Action column, and you'll see either the word "Browser" (which means that file type is handled by Netscape itself), "Ask User" (which means it'll bring up a dialog to ask the user what to do), or the name of a helper application that has been set up to handle that type of file for Netscape. If the Action field is blank, it means that there's a plug-in configured for that MIME type. Though you still don't know *which* plug-in is associated with that file type, at least you know there is a plug-in of some kind handling it.

Note that in the version of Netscape 3.0 that I'm currently working with, this list has a bug that could throw you off. If you click on an entry with a blank Action field, you may see a filename in the <u>L</u>aunch the Application text box. Don't be fooled. This box should be blank; if there's a filename there, it's

continues

Part

III

Ch

9

continued

left over from a previous list selection. Don't make the mistake of thinking it's a helper application configured for that MIME file type. If the Action field is blank, a plug-in is handling that file type. Period. This bug may be fixed in future versions.

The last thing to try is to use Explorer to look in the folder c:\program files\netscape\navigator\ program\plug-ins (this is the default folder; if you installed Netscape elsewhere, you'll have to find the path to the plug-ins folder yourself). This folder contains the .dll libraries and other files used by the plug-ins you've installed. Unfortunately, most of them have obscure names like "Npskwav.dll" or "Micrdate.dll." Right-click on a .dll filename under Win95 and select Properties from the pop-up menu, and you'll get a variety of information about the file, including what company created it and any developer's notes associated with it. There's usually enough information for you to be able to figure out which plug-in it is.

By combining the knowledge you glean through your explorations with your memory of which plug-ins you *think* you remember installing, you should be able to figure out which plug-ins you actually have installed and enabled.

If you can manage to figure out what you've got installed, all you need to do to re-enable a plug-in that has been superseded by another is to delete the offending plug-in. Once it's gone, the older one will take over again, provided it's still in the plug-ins directory. If it isn't, you'll have to reinstall it.

Running a plug-in is a piece of cake—you don't have to run a plug-in at all.

They run themselves whenever a Web page or link contains the proper kind of embedded file. You don't have to decide when to run them, you don't have to figure out how to load in the data file, nothing.

However, you do have to learn how the controls work. Many of these programs put a set of specialized controls on the screen for zooming, printing, panning, scrolling, or what have you. Each plug-in comes with detailed documentation explaining what its specific controls are and how they work. (In some cases there may be a separate manual file to download, or the documentation will be online in the form of Web pages—pay close attention so you get the documentation along with the plug-in itself.) Make sure you read the documentation so you know all about a plug-in *before* you encounter any files it'll be called upon to display. That way you won't spend valuable online time trying to figure it out.

Multimedia Plug-Ins

It's not an overstatement to say that interest in delivering multimedia content on the Web and on corporate intranets is what's driving plug-in development. Though there are plug-ins for things other than playing audio, video, and multimedia content, these types of plug-ins are, by far, the most pervasive.

This section lists and describes the sound, graphics, video, multimedia, and animation plug-ins currently being distributed for Netscape Navigator.

Sound

Internet audio is growing like gangbusters. It seems like there are more live audio programs, digitized sound files, and MIDI music files on the Web every day. And with the explosion of plug-ins development in this area, it's sure to move even faster in the near future.

In the beginning, the Web was mute. Eventually, some sites began to add a few digitized sounds, which had to be downloaded and played using helper applications. Now there are several sound plug-ins that let Netscape play live audio data streams in real-time. Audio plug-ins are available for several varieties of digitized sound, as well as MIDI music and speech.

LiveAudio   Netscape's LiveAudio plug-in is shipped with Netscape 3.0, so you could call it the "official" Netscape audio player. Unlike the other audio plug-ins discussed here, LiveAudio doesn't use a proprietary sound file format; it plays standard AIFF, AU, MIDI, and WAV files. Sound files can be either embedded in or linked to a Web page. LiveAudio features an easy-to-use console with play, pause, stop, and volume controls.

▶ For an in-depth look at LiveAudio, **see** "Configuring Netscape for Sound," **p. 327.**

Real Audio   Progressive Networks' RealAudio plug-in provides live, on-demand, real-time audio over 14.4 Kbps or faster Internet connections. Users with 28.8 or better connections can now hear true FM-quality tunes. Its controls are like a CD player—you can pause, rewind, fast-forward, stop, and start play with on-screen buttons.

RealAudio is getting a lot of support on the Net from big companies like ABC broadcasting, small independent radio stations, and individual users alike. It's almost a necessity for browsing the Web. The latest version even has synchronized multimedia playback capabilities.

You create RealAudio format sound files using the RealAudio Encoder 2.0 program. It's available as part of the RealAudio Player 2.0 Standard Edition CD-ROM, which is $29. To deliver RealAudio content, your Web server will also have to be set up with the RealAudio Server software.

Available for Windows 95, Windows NT, Windows 3.1, UNIX, and Macintosh, the RealAudio Version 2.0 player plug-in is included on Netscape's Power Pack 2.0 CD-ROM. It can also be downloaded directly from the RealAudio Web site at **http://www.realaudio.com/products/ra2.0/.**

TrueSpeech   If nothing else, TrueSpeech is convenient. If you're using Windows 3.1 or Windows 95, the supplied Sound Recorder program can digitize sound files and convert them to TrueSpeech format. The TrueSpeech Player can then be used to listen to them on the Web in real-time. Despite its name, TrueSpeech can be used for any type of audio file. No special server is needed. From the DSP Group's home page at **http://www.dspg.com** you can download TrueSpeech players for Windows 3.1, Win95/NT, Mac, and PowerMac.

Crescendo & Crescendo Plus   Most sound cards go a step beyond merely digitizing and playing back sounds. They can also generate their own. If your sound card is MIDI-compatible (and most are), you've got more than a passive record-and-playback system—you've got a full-fledged music synthesizer in there. And with a MIDI plug-in, you can experience Web sites with a full music soundtrack.

LiveUpdate's Crescendo plug-in lets Navigator play inline MIDI music embedded in Web pages. With a MIDI-capable browser, you can create Web pages that have their own background music soundtracks. And don't forget that MIDI instruments can be sampled sounds, so it's possible to create sound effect tracks, too.

Crescendo requires an MPC (MIDI-capable) sound card and Netscape Navigator version 2.0 or above. It launches automatically and invisibly and is a fun addition to Web browsing.

Crescendo is a 10K self-extracting archive file for Windows 95 and Windows NT, or a 50K file for Windows 3.1. The Win95/NT version is super-tiny—I had to check twice to make sure it had downloaded! A Mac version is now also available. Download Crescendo from **http://www.liveupdate.com/midi.html**. An enhanced version called Crescendo Plus (see fig. 9.1) adds on-screen controls and live streaming (you don't have to wait for a MIDI file to completely download before it starts playing), and can be purchased from LiveUpdate's Web site.

FIG. 9.1
Crescendo Plus features a CD-player style control panel and a convenient pop-up menu.

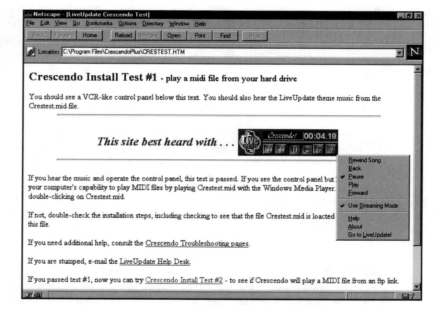

More Music Plug-ins   Can't get enough music on the Web? Here are a few more Netscape music plug-ins.

RapidTransit decompresses and plays music that has been compressed up to 40-to-1. It can provide full 16-bit, 44.1kHz, It's available for Windows 95, Windows NT, and Macintosh from **http://monsterbit.com/rapidtransit/**.

Arnaud Masson's MIDI Plugin is for the Mac and PowerMac only. Get it from **http:// www.planete.net/~amasson/**.

Another Mac-only plug-in for MIDI files is MidiShare from GRAME at **http://www.grame.fr/ english/MidiShare.html**.

Do you prefer the sound of the Orient? Then Sseyo's Koan (**http://www.sseyo.com/**) might better fit your preferences. It plays real-time, computer-generated Japanese Koan music on Win95 and Win3.1 versions of Netscape.

Part

III

Ch

9

ToolVox   If speech is all you need, there are a variety of speech plug-ins for Netscape. Under this category there are really three kinds of plug-ins:

- Players for digitized audio that is of less-than-music quality
- Text-to-speech converters, currently available only for the Macintosh
- A speech recognition plug-in, also Mac-only

ToolVox provides audio compression ratios of up to 53:1, which means very small files that transfer quickly over the Internet. Speech can be delivered in real-time even over 9600 baud modems. One unique feature is that you can slow down playback to improve comprehension, or speed it up to shorten listening times without changing voice pitch.

Like the higher-fidelity RealAudio, ToolVox streams audio in real-time, so you don't have to wait for a file to download before you can listen to it.

ToolVox doesn't need special server software to deliver audio content from your Web server. Buffering and playback are controlled by the player, in the form of a Netscape Navigator 2.0 add-in. As a result, any standard HTML server can act as a streaming media server. Even the encoder is free. It compresses a speech file from WAV format to an 8kHz, 2400 bps VOX file.

Netscape Communications Corporation has become a part-owner of Voxware, the makers of ToolVox, so expect to hear a lot more about it. Netscape has also licensed key elements of Voxware's digital voice technology, including the Voxware RT24 compressor/decompressor (codec) and ToolVox, for incorporation into the Netscape LiveMedia multimedia standard.

Voxware has also announced plans to release an enhanced version of ToolVox, called ToolVox Gold.

ToolVox Navigator plug-ins are available for Win 95 and Windows 3.1, and Mac and PowerMac versions are promised. Download them from the Voxware site at **http://www.voxware.com/ download.htm**.

EchoSpeech   EchoSpeech compresses speech 18.5 to 1. This means that 16 bit speech sampled at 11025 Hz is compressed to 9600 bits per second. Even people with 14.4 Kbps modems can listen to real-time steaming EchoSpeech audio streams. Because EchoSpeech was designed to code speech sampled at 11025 Hz rather than 8000 Hz, it sounds better than ToolVox.

Real-time decoding of 11kHz speech requires only 30% of a 486SX-33 CPU's time. EchoSpeech plug-ins are also small—40-50K when decompressed.

No server software is required to deliver EchoSpeech content; your ISP or server administrator only needs to declare a new MIME type and pay a one-time $99 license fee. To add EchoSpeech files to your Web pages, you compress them with the EchoSpeech Speech Coder (available for evaluation via free download) then use the HTML <EMBED> tag to include them in your documents.

Echospeech is available for Windows 95 and Windows 3.1, and a Mac version is promised. You can get it at **http://www.echospeech.com**.

Talker & Other Mac Speech Plug-ins   MVP Solutions' Talker plug-in is just for the Macintosh. It uses the Mac's built-in PlainTalk speech synthesis technology to create text-to-speech voice messages—in other words, it "reads" text files to you out loud. Of course, this uses much less bandwidth than recorded audio, and you can change the words your Web page speaks by editing a text file.

This is one place where Mac owners can claim a real edge over Windows and Win95 Netscape users—this plug-in just will never work on those platforms because they lack the speech synthesis technology of the Mac. Talker can be had at **http://www.mvpsolutions.com/ PlugInSite/Talker.html**.

If Apple's "English Text-to-Speech" software is not installed on your Macintosh yet, you can download a copy of the English Text-to-Speech installer from Apple's site at **ftp:// ftp.info.apple.com/Apple.Support.Area/Apple.Software.Updates/US/Macintosh/ System/PlainTalk_1.4.1/English_Text-to-Speech.sea.hqx**.

William H. Tudor's Speech Plug-In for the Mac and PowerMac does essentially the same thing as Talker. You can get it at **http://www.albany.net/~wtudor/**.

But Mac plug-ins aren't limited to just talking to you—they can also listen to you and understand what you say!

Bill Noon's ListenUp is for the PowerMacintosh running System 7.5 or above. It also needs the PlainTalk Speech Recognition v1.5 program. You can find out all the gory details and download the plug-in at **http://snow.cit.cornell.edu/noon/ListenUp.html**.

Digital Dream's ShockTalk speech recognition plug-in isn't a Netscape plug-in at all; it's a plug-in for the Shockwave for Director plug-in! Available for Mac and PowerMac you can get it at **http://emf.net:80/~dreams/Hi-Res/shocktalk/**.

Graphics

Though Netscape Navigator displays inline GIF and JPEG images just fine, there's more to graphics than those two file formats. Besides other bitmap formats like TIFF and PNG, Navigator is completely ignorant of vector graphics formats like CGM and Corel's CMX. Graphics plug-ins fill that void. The real-time demands of the Net are also pushing graphics compression to the limit, with new high-tech encoders coming out all the time. Some of the very latest compression techniques can be handled via Netscape plug-ins.

FIGleaf Inline   Bitmaps are the canvas of computer graphics. Every image you see on your screen is a bitmap, a collection of colorfully lit pixels in a grid. Computers generally store screen images in bitmap format, too. That is, after all, the easiest way; there is a one-to-one relationship between the dots in the picture and the dots on the screen. Netscape can handle GIF and JPEG bitmap images all by itself, but they are not the be-all and end-all of bitmaps. There are dozens—perhaps hundreds—of different bitmap formats available on the Web. To view them, you'll need to install the appropriate Netscape plug-ins.

Carberry Technology's FIGleaf Inline plug-in lets you zoom, pan, and scroll both vector (CGM format) and bitmap graphics, including GIF, JPEG, TIFF, CCITT GP4, BMP, WMF, Sun Raster, PNG, and other graphics file formats. It even handles Encapsulated PostScript (EPS) files, as well as the new proposed standard PGM and PBM file types. It'll even provide improved display of your GIFs and JPEGs.

FIGleaf Inline adds rotation of all images to 0, 90, 180, or 270 degrees, as well as the ability to view multipage files. Scrollbars are available when zoomed in on an image, or when the image is too large to be displayed in the default window.

The version shown in fig. 9.2 is for Win95, though Macintosh and Windows 3.1 versions are planned. The self-extracting archive is 1.5MB big including sample files, but in one fell swoop it practically eliminates the need for other Netscape graphics plug-ins or helper applications. If the file size disturbs you, a smaller version called Figleaf Inline Lite is also available.

FIG. 9.2

This tight zoom on two graphics being displayed inline by the FIGleaf plug-in demonstrates the superiority of CGM vector graphics (left) versus GIF bitmap graphics (right). Note that, since FIGleaf is now handling the display of Netscape's inline GIFs, they are zoomable as well. This is an excellent example of how plug-ins can even improve Netscape's built-in capabilities.

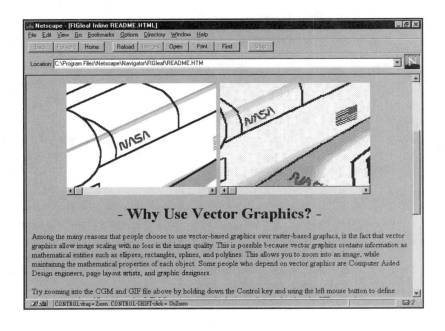

FigLeaf Inline is available for free evaluation at **http://www.ct.ebt.com/figinline/ download.html**. You can buy it for $19.95.

ViewDirector   The ViewDirector Imaging plug-in from TMS displays black-and-white, grayscale and color raster images in TIFF (uncompressed, modified Huffman, G3 1&2D, and G4), CALS Type 1, JPEG, PCX/DCX, BMP, and other image formats. With it, you can zoom, pan, and rotate images embedded in Web pages. ViewDirector even lets you enhance image quality by turning on scale-to-gray and color smoothing functions. A professional version adds the ability to view multipage images, magnify them, and more. Available for Windows 95 and Windows NT, you can download ViewDirector from **http://www.tmsinc.com**.

Autodesk's WHIP!   Most architects, engineers, and designers create their masterworks in AutoCAD, the de facto computer aided drafting program. Just about every manufactured thing or constructed edifice you encounter started out somewhere as an AutoCAD drawing. With the rise of the corporate intranet, there is increased interest in making these drawings available for viewing in Web browsers. Thanks to a handful of Netscape plug-ins, this is now possible.

Autodesk is the publisher of AutoCAD. Though they were not the first to come out with a Netscape plug-in for viewing 2D AutoCAD drawings on the Web, they are almost certain to end up being the most popular. Their WHIP! plug-in is based on the same rendering technology as the WHIP driver in AutoCAD Release 13. It allows for panning, zooming, and embedding URLs in AutoCAD drawings.

WHIP! uses a new DWF (Drawing Web Format) file type, which will be supported in future versions of AutoCAD. Though WHIP! won't view current DXF AutoCAD files, the new file type is said to be highly compressed and optimized for fast transfer over the Internet. Autodesk is publishing the new DWF file format as an open standard, and other software vendors who use 2D vector data are being encouraged to adopt the DWF file format as well. The DWG file format is the actual editable AutoCAD drawing, so DWF files offer a form of security in that they are not editable by the end user. However, if you want you can bundle the DWG data in a DWF file (for use over a secure corporate intranet, for example) so that the end user can drag and drop the file into a copy of AutoCAD for modification. Though there will be a time lag as existing AutoCAD files are converted to the new format, with Autodesk pushing it it's bound to become very popular very soon.

The compressed WHIP! Plug-In is less than 1.4 megabytes, so it will fit on a single floppy, and requires Windows NT 3.51 or Windows 95. A stand-alone file conversion utility is promised soon. Also available will be a free WHIP! Development Kit for other software vendors who plan to support the DWF file format. You can download WHIP! from Autodesk's Web site at **http:// www.autodesk.com/**.

DWG/DXF Viewer   SoftSource's DWG/DXF plug-in (see fig. 9.3) was the first Netscape plug-in to make it possible to view AutoCAD and DXF drawings on the Web. Zoom, pan, and layer visibility controls make it simple to explore complex CAD drawings online. Its advantage over WHIP! is that it can view standard AutoCAD DXF format display-only or even editable DWG format drawing files, so existing libraries of AutoCAD drawings don't have to be translated before they can be viewed.

FIG. 9.3
SoftSource's DWG/DXF plug-in makes viewing AutoCAD format drawings an online activity.

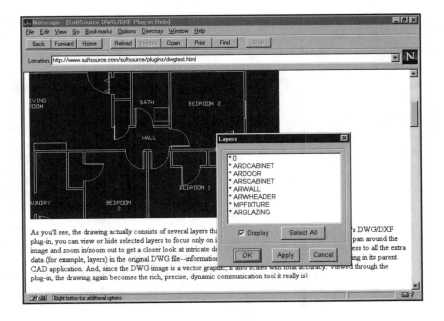

Part
III

Ch
9

Available for Windows 95 and Windows NT, you can download this plug-in from **http://www.softsource.com/softsource/plugins/plugins.html**.

NOTE European users especially might want to check out NetSlide 95 by Alessandro Oddera, an AutoCAD file plug-in for Win95 available from **http://www.archserver.unige.it/caadge/ao/first.htm** in Italy. ▪

Corel CMX The problem with bitmaps is that they're chunky. Because they're made up of square pixels arranged in a grid, they aren't really scalable. Where a bitmap is an actual map of a picture, vector graphics are more of a description of how to draw a picture. A vector graphic file tells a drawing program how to use lines, curves, fill patterns, rectangles, and other elements to re-create an image. How big to make it is an entirely different question. For this reason, vector graphics can be rescaled to any size and retain their good looks, without losing detail.

There are a plethora of vector graphics formats out there, and with the following plug-ins, Netscape can display a good number of them.

CorelDRAW! is perhaps the most popular vector graphics creation program for both the PC and the Mac.

Corel's CMX Viewer plug-in for Navigator lets you view Corel CMX vector graphics in Web pages inline (see fig. 9.4). The CMX viewer is, so far, available only for Win95 and WinNT, though a Mac version is promised.

There are no special controls or considerations with the CMX Viewer—when installed, it simply displays CMX images when they are encountered. It's a kick to see them "draw" in pieces on-screen in real-time, rather than coming in like a window shade, as bitmap graphics do.

FIG. 9.4
Corel's CMX vector graphics viewer lets you view smooth Corel format vector graphic images inline in Navigator.

You can download the Corel CMX viewer from **http://www.corel.com/corelcmx/**.

Other Vector Graphics Viewers SoftSource, the creator of the DWG/DXF AutoCAD plug-in, also has its own vector graphics drawing program. The SVF plug-in for Netscape Navigator lets you view those images on the Web. SVF (Simple Vector Format) uses an officially registered MIME type and features single-download navigational capabilities and scalable vector graphics. You can pan and zoom an SVF image, and hide and display layers. In the way it works, it is unsurprisingly similar to their DWG/DXF plug-in. The SVF plug-in also lets you include HTML hyperlinks (either URLs or textual annotations) in an SVF file. You can download the SVF plug-in, one of Softsource's Vdraft (Virtual Drafter) suite of Internet CAD Tools, for Windows 95 or Win 3.1 from **http://www.softsource.com**.

CGM (Computer Graphics Metafiles) can be created and used by a wide variety of programs; they're an industry standard. The InterCAP InLine plug-in from Intercap Graphics Systems is an online adaptation of their MetaLink RunTime CGM viewer. With it, you can view, zoom, pan, and magnify an image. Animation of intelligent, hyperlinked CGM graphics is also possible. A Windows 95/NT version is available at **http://www.intergraph.com/icap/**.

FutureSplash's CelAnimator is software for creating vector-based drawings and animations for multimedia and Web pages. CelAnimator can be used for creating static or fully animated cartoons, logos, technical drawings, and interactive buttons. You can export these animations as FutureSplash, animated GIF, Windows AVI, or QuickTime files. You can download a free trial version of CelAnimator for Macintosh or Windows 95/NT from their Web site at **http://www.futurewave.com/**. Since this isn't a plug-in, why should you care? Well, besides the fact that you can use AVI, animated GIF, and QuickTime files with other plug-ins, the FutureSplash plug-in for Netscape (available for Macintosh and Windows 3.1/95/NT) will let you view FutureSplash format animations as well. "Wait," you ask, "what's an animation plug-in doing in this section?" Read those last few lines again, and you'll see that these animations are vector graphics-based, which means they're zoomable and scalable. This is a truly unique product. FutureSplash animations can even be displayed as they are downloaded, which allows long animation sequences to begin playing immediately. It even supports antialiasing for the elimination of jagged edges, and scalable outline fonts. Interactive buttons let you get URLs and play animations. The plug-in in small (90–150K uncompressed), and UNIX and a Java versions are planned. All are available from **http://www.futurewave.com/**.

Lightning Strike   Graphics are big. Huge, in fact. Graphics files can take up multi-megabytes of hard disk space in no time, and can seemingly take an eternity to load over the Web. JPEG images are better than most, compressing some images dozens of times smaller than they started out. But JPEG has its limitations, and the bandwidth demands of Web browsing have people searching for even better solutions. There are at least three Netscape plug-ins that improve graphics transfer times considerably.

Infinet Op's Lightning Strike plug-in is meant to compete directly with JPEG image compression. Images compressed with Lightning Strike are said to have higher compression ratios, smaller image files, faster transmissions, and improved image quality.

Infinet Op says that JPEG uses a Fourier analysis-based method, such as discrete cosine transform (DCT), while it uses a form of the wavelet transform. Okay. All I know is that the images look every bit as good as JPEG and come down the line fast. Will they gain a following? Hard to say. But if you are into graphics, you'll definitely want to install Lightning Strike and take a look at some of the sample compressed images on Infinet Op's site. They're awesome.

Macintosh and Windows 3.1/95/NT plug-ins are available from **http://www.infinop.com/html/extvwr_pick.html**.

FIF Viewer   Iterated Systems' FIF (Fractal Image Format) viewer plug-in for Navigator displays fractally compressed images inline in the Netscape window. FIF images are smaller and load faster than JPEGs, and can be scaled and zoomed on the page. One typical 768 × 512 image in the Iterated Systems gallery compressed from 1.15MB to only 47KB with remarkable fidelity.

The FIF plug-in is available for Windows 95/NT, Macintosh, and Windows 3.1. You can download the FIF Viewer plug-in from **http://www.iterated.com/cnplugin.htm**.

Summus Wavelet Viewer   Summus' Wavelet Viewer is another plug-in for decompressing images inline which have been compressed using its proprietary wavelet technology.

Versions of this plug-in are currently available for Win95/NT and Windows 3.1. at **ftp://ftp.scsn.net/software/summus/**.

Special Graphics Formats   Sometimes a "standard" graphics format is just not good enough. When you need a graphic to do something special, you turn to proprietary formats.

For example, Freehand. Freehand is the major competitor to CorelDRAW! as the top-of-the-heap illustration program. If your studio or company uses Freehand, you'll be glad to know that the Shockwave for Freehand plug-in from Macromedia will let you put your Freehand drawings on the Web or on your company intranet. Don't be confused by the name—Macromedia calls *all* of its plug-ins "Shockwave." The first was for Macromedia Director; this one is for Freehand. The Shockwave for Freehand plug-in lets users view compact 24-bit vector graphics with panning and zooming up to 25,600 percent. These can contain irregularly shaped hot objects that link to other Web pages. There are actually three modules involved here: the Shockwave for Freehand plug-in for Netscape; the Shockwave Afterburner Xtra module, which is installed into the Freehand drawing program to compress FreeHand images by up to 50% for distribution on the Web; and the Shockwave URL Managers, which lets the designer add URL references to hot spots on drawings. Windows 95/NT, Windows 3.1, and Macintosh versions are available at **http://www.macromedia.com/Tools/Shockwave/Info/index.html**.

Though its end result is a graphic image, the Chemscape Chime plug-in from MDL Information Systems is more of a scientific and chemical engineering tool than a graphics plug-in. Chemscape Chime plug-in lets scientists and engineers display "chemically significant" (that is to say, scientifically accurate) 2D and 3D structures within an HTML page or table. MDL Information Systems supplies chemical information-management solutions to the pharmaceutical, agrochemical, and chemical industries, so it knows what they're about. Windows 95/NT, Windows 3.1, Macintosh, and PowerMac versions can be downloaded from **http://www.mdli.com/chemscape/chime/download.html**.

Micrografx's QuickSilver is a highly popular business graphics tool, and now its ABC QuickSilver plug-in for Netscape makes QuickSilver files usable over the Web or corporate intranets. You create these vector images with ABC Graphics Suite, which can make drawings move, display messages, or link to URLs. The plug-in uses a 32-bit vector graphics rendering engine for fast display. Available for Windows 95/NT you can download the plug-in from **http://www.micrografx.com/download/qsdl.html**.

Johnson-Grace's ART Press program creates ART image format files, which can be viewed online using its ART press plug-in from **http://www.jgc.com/aip/artpub.html**. ART compression is already being used in America Online's TurboWeb browser. Johnson-Grace says ART Press images download and display three times faster than GIF and JPEG images.

Vertigo from Lari Software displays pictures in GX format, which can be created using LightningDraw GX or any other application that saves in GX format. This plug-in performs automatic smoothing (antialiasing), and allows pictures to be animated using HTML tag spin, stretch, move, loop, and time attributes. PowerPC and Mac versions can be downloaded from **http://www.larisoftware.com/Products/WebPlugin.html**.

There are two Mac-only plug-ins now available for viewing Apple QD3D (QuickTime VR) files in Netscape. WurlPlug by John Louch is available from the Apple site at **ftp:// ftp.info.apple.com/Apple.Support.Area/QuickDraw3D/Test_Drive/Viewers/**. WebActive 3D (which promises a Windows version) can be had at **http://www.3d-Active.com/pages/WebUtilities.html**. QuickTime VR scenes can be made from photographs, video stills, or computer renderings. Most scenes are made from photographs using a series of photos taken at 30 degree increments while turning the camera in a full circle. These are organized into a panorama and combined with multi-frame photos of real objects taken at a variety of angles. The experience of viewing these scenes is said to be very realistic. You can find out more about the technology from Apple at **http://qtvr.quicktime.apple.com/**.

Part
III

Ch
9

Video

Video plug-ins let Netscape Navigator play inline videos in real-time. Video for Windows, MPEG, and QuickTime movies can all be played with the right plug-in.

LiveVideo   Video for Windows is the standard for PC platforms. There are a number of programs and video boards that let you create AVI format animations or digitized scenes. With the following plug-ins, you can deliver them as Web page content in Netscape.

Netscape's official plug-in for AVI video is LiveVideo, which is included with the Netscape 3.0 distribution. It automatically installs and configures as your Video for Windows player of choice. You click on a movie image to play it and click again to stop. A right mouse click on an image pops up a complete menu of controls including Play, Pause, Rewind, Fast Forward, Frame Back, and Frame Forward. If you didn't get it with Netscape, you can download it by following the links from Netscape's home page at **http://www.netscape.com**.

▶ For the full story on LiveVideo, **see** the sidebar on **p. 354** in chapter 15, "Configuring Netscape for Video."

VDOLive   The VDOLive Plug-in for Netscape 3.0 enables inline Video for Windows (.AVI) clips to be included in HTML pages and played back in real-time (see fig. 9.5).

If you are operating over a slow connection, VDOLive will intelligently download a video file, skipping over enough information to retain real-time playback. In cases of severe bandwidth shortage (such as 14.4 Kbps PPP connections) you'll get a low frame rate (approximately one frame each 1–3 seconds) but you'll still be able to view videos. In other cases, the VDOLive Player and the VDOLive Server will try to converge at the best possible bandwidth, which may sometimes result in blurry display and/or low frame rate. While this can result in jerky playback (especially over a slow modem SLIP or PPP connection), it sure speeds up viewing video over the Web!

FIG. 9.5
VDOLive displays video files inline, and can deliver reasonable performance over even a very slow Internet connection.

Autostart, Stretch, Width, and Height options let HTML designers customize inline Web page video for just about any purpose.

The VDOLive Personal Server is required to deliver motion video from your Web server. The VDOLive Personal Server and Tools 1.0 enable you to deliver up to two streams of video, capture, compress, and serve up to one minute of video and audio, and will scale up to 256 Kbps connections.

VDOLive is available for Windows 3.1 and Windows 95/NT from VDONet's site at **http://www.vdolive.com/download/**.

CoolFusion   Iterated Systems' CoolFusion is a plug-in for Navigator which plays inline Video for Windows (.avi) movies. It lets you view videos at any size all the way up to full-screen, and you can stop, replay, and save them using a full set of controls.

The self-extracting archive I looked at (cf_b6_32.exe) is for Windows 95 or Windows NT. It requires only a 256-color graphics card, though a 24-bit or high-color graphics adapter is recommended. You'll also need at least 8MB of RAM.

You can downlaod CoolFusion at **http://webber.iterated.com/coolfusn/download/cf-set32.htm**.

Quicktime Plug-Ins   Where Microsoft's standard video format is Video for Windows (AVI files), Apple's video standard is QuickTime. Because a lot of creative types use the Mac, there are a lot of QuickTime movies out there on the Web.

Apple (**http://www.apple.com**) has had a QuickTime movie player plug-in for Netscape in the works for some time, though it still wasn't available at presstime for this book. However, there are quite a few third-party plug-ins available that can play QuickTime movies in Netscape.

Knowledge Engineering's MacZilla is a Mac-only Navigator plug-in that's a sort of Swiss Army knife of plug-ins. Besides QuickTime movies, it plays or displays: MIDI background music; WAV, AU, and AIFF audio; MPEG; and AVI movies. Using its own plug-in component architecture, MacZilla can extend and update itself over the Net with the click of a button. You even get a built-in "MacZilla" game! Download it from Knowledge Engineering, **http://maczilla.com**.

MovieStar by Intelligence at Large is less ambitious—it's only for QuickTime movie playback. Using its MovieStar Maker, a multimedia editing application also available for download, Webmasters can optimize QuickTime movies so that Navigator users can view them while they download. You can also use autoplay, looping, and many other settings. This one is available for Windows, Windows 95, and Macintosh at **http://www.beingthere.com/**.

Need more choices? There are at least three more QuickTime player plug-ins for Netscape: Iván Cavero Belaúnde's ViewMovie for Win95 and Macintosh at **http://www.well.com/~ivanski/**; TEC Solutions' TEC Player, also for Win95 and Mac, at **http://www.tecs.com/TECPlayer_docs**; and Kevin McMurtrie's Mac-only Multimedia Plugin at **ftp://ftp.wco.com/users/mcmurtri/MySoftware/**.

MPEG Plug-Ins   MPEG is the bright and shining star of multimedia right now. The MPEG2 movie compression standard is destined to give us full-screen, full-motion movies on a highly compressed CD-ROM, among other things. Because of its high compression ratios, it's also a good choice for delivery of movies over the Internet.

Of course, it works best with a video board capable of doing hardware decompression. But even running in software on fast Pentium systems, MPEG shows promise.

There are at least four Netscape plug-ins available for playing inline MPEG videos.

Open2U's Action MPEG player plug-in can also play included synchonized soundtracks, or sound-only files that have been compressed using MPEG. Action doesn't require special hardware or even a special Web server. Available for Windows 95/NT, you can download it for trial at **http://www.open2u.com/action/action.html**.

InterVU's PreVU plug-in also plays streaming MPEG video without specialized MPEG hardware or a proprietary video server. It gives you a first-frame view inline, streaming viewing while downloading, and full-speed cached playback off your hard drive. PreVU requires a 486 or Pentium processor and Windows 95/NT; a Mac version is also available. PreVU can be downloaded from **http://www.intervu.com/download.html**.

Xing (**http://www.xingtech.com**), well-known for its MPEG applications, will be providing a Navigator plug-in to support live streaming MPEG and LBR (low bitrate) audio and full-motion MPEG video from Xing StreamWorks Web servers. Check out its Web site for availability information.

Sizzler Pictures that move—that wonderful concept has brought millions of children (and adults who hold onto their childlike wonder) untold hours of entertainment and enjoyment. When computers got powerful enough, animation made the move to the computer. With powerful animation player plug-ins for Netscape, its making the transition to the World Wide Web, and even to corporate intranets.

Totally Hip Software's Sizzler plug-in and companion converter program let you create and display Web animation. The Sizzler converter (currently available only in a version for the Macintosh) takes PICS files or QuickTime movies and converts them into sprite files that can be played in real-time in Navigator.

However, Totally Hip's core technology (called Object Scenario) allows for streamed delivery of several media types including text, animation, video, sound, and interactivity. It plans to add all of these to Sizzler in the near future.

The Sizzler plug-in is available as a free download for Windows 95/NT, Windows 3.1, and the Macintosh from **http://www.totallyhip.com/tools/Win/2f_tools.html**.

Emblaze GEO Interactive Media Group's Emblaze plug-in is a real time animation player. It plays a proprietary animation format that GEO says needs only 3MB to 4MB of disk space for approximately 30 minutes of play time. The animations can be displayed at a rate of 12 to 24 frames per second in 256 colors in real-time over a 14.4 Kbps connection. Animations must be created using the commercial Emblaze Creator program.

Windows 3.1, Macintosh, PowerMac, and Win95 versions can be had at **http:// www.Geo.Inter.net/technology/emblaze/index.html**.

Other Animation Plug-Ins Here are a few more Animation plug-ins for Netscape:

Deltapoint's Web Animator, for the Macintosh only (a Windows version is promised), combines animation, sound, and live interaction. The authoring tool for creating animations to add to your own site is also available from its Web site at **http://www.deltapoint.com/animate/ index.htm**.

Heads Off's Play3D plug-in supports real-time interactive 3D, 2D sprites, and WAVE and MIDI sound playback. Objects can be linked to URLs, media files, or Play3D "scene" files. The free demo version allows for authoring and playback without leaving Netscape. For Win95 only, Play3D is downloadable from **http://www.headsoff.com**.

Shockwave for Macromedia Director "Multimedia" is a good buzzword, but what does it really mean? Literally "more than one medium." When most people use the term they mean a presentation that includes some combination of sound, graphics, animation, video, and even interactivity. Interactivity is an important part of multimedia. It's the part that puts the flow of the whole thing under the user's control. Though this can be as simple as an on-screen button that you have to click to move to the next slide, more often it involves making selections from multiple choices.

Multimedia is the hottest topic on the Web right now, so it's not surprising that there are a dozen or more multimedia player plug-ins already available for Netscape.

Perhaps one of the most significant and awe-inspiring plug-ins supported directly by Netscape 3.0 is Macromedia Shockwave for Director (see fig. 9.6), which allows you to view Director "movies" directly on a Web page. Director movies are created with Macromedia's Director (don't confuse Director "movies" with other file types of the same name, such as QuickTime movies), a cross-platform multimedia authoring program that gives multimedia developers the ability to create fully interactive multimedia applications, or "titles." Because of its interactive integration of animation, bitmap, video, and sound media, and its playback compatibility with a variety of computer platforms including Windows, Mac OS, OS/2, and SGI, Director is now the most widely used professional multimedia authoring tool.

Using Shockwave for Director, a Director movie run over the Internet can support the same sort of features as a Director movie run off a CD-ROM, including animated sequences, sophisticated scripting of interactivity, user input of text right into the Director window (or "stage"), sound playback, and much more. Developers can even include hot links through URLs.

FIG. 9.6

The Shockwave for Director plug-in for Netscape 3.0 plays interactive multimedia Director files inline in the Netscape window. These can range from simple animations to complex interactive games, like this "concentration" game from the Toy Story Web site.

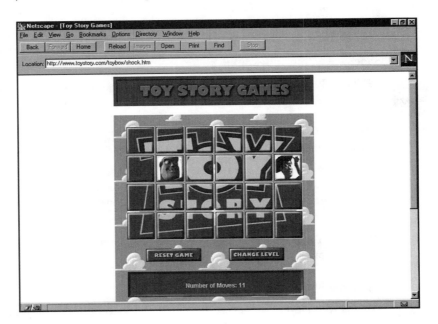

Shockwave for Director consists of two main components, the Shockwave plug-in itself, and Shockwave Afterburner, a compressor program that squeezes a Director file by 40–50% for faster access over the Net. You can download it from Macromedia at **Shockwave http://www-1.macromedia.com/Tools/Shockwave/Plugin/plugin.cgi**.

Part
III

Ch
9

Shockwave for Authorware   Another in the series of "Shockwave" plug-ins from Macromedia, its Shockwave for Authorware plug-in lets users interact with Authorware interactive multimedia "courses" and "pieces" right in the Netscape Navigator window. Animation, clickable buttons, links to other Web pages, hybrid layout and delivery, streaming PICS movies and sound, and more can be integrated within a piece to deliver an interactive multimedia experience.

Intended for the delivery of large, content-rich multimedia presentations, such as courseware and training materials, Authorware can also write viewer data back to a Web server using FTP, so it's useful for creating market surveys, tests and quizzes, and customer service applications.

Like all Shockwave plug-ins, this one includes an "Afterburner" module for compressing files for delivery on the Web. Authorware developers package their multimedia pieces without the usually included Runtime Projector, then drag and drop this file onto the Authorware Afterburner program. Afterburner compresses the Authorware file by 50 to 70 percent and creates one map file and multiple segment files. Developers can optimize the number and size of segment files to the bandwidth of the network. Developers also are able to create a single map file referencing both Macintosh and Windows segment files for display in the same Web page, making this transparent to the viewer.

Windows 95/NT, Windows 3.1, and Macintosh versions of Shockwave for Authorware can be downloaded from the Macromedia Web site at **http://www.macromedia.com/Tools/ Shockwave/Info/index.html**.

ASAP WebShow   Software Publishing Corporation's ASAP WebShow is a Netscape Navigator plug-in presentation viewer for viewing, downloading, and printing presentations created with ASAP WordPower. Similar to PowerPoint presentations, WordPower presentations can contain tables, organization charts, bullet lists, and other graphic and text elements, in a slide show format. Since the files are compressed, they can be transmitted very quickly over the Net.

Presentations and reports can be embedded as icons, as live thumbnails, or in a window on a Web page. Each slide can be viewed in a small, live area window, enlarged to fill the current Web page, or zoomed to full screen. You can select one slide at a time or watch a continuously running show.

A Win95/NT version is available, with Window 3.1 promised. You can download a fully functional copy of ASAP 1.0 or ASAP WordPower 1.95, for a free 30-day trial for creating your own WebShow-compatible presentations. It's available at **http://www.spco.com/asap/ asapwebs.htm**.

Astound Web Player   Gold Disk's Astound Web Player displays multimedia "greeting cards" and other interactive documents created with Gold Disk's Astound or Studio M programs. These presentations can include sound, animation, graphics, video, and even interactive elements.

I took a look at Version 1.0 of the Astound Web Player for Win95 and Navigator 2.0. Versions are also available for Windows 3.1 and for Navigator 1.1. You can even get a stand-alone version for use with browsers other than Netscape.

You can choose to download a "slim" version of the player without chart, texture, and animation libraries if you already own Studio M or Astound. If you plan on including movies in your presentations, you'll need QuickTime for Windows, which is also available from the Gold Disk site.

The Astound Web Player lets you actively view one multimedia slide while it downloads the next one in the background. But the main appeal of Studio M and Astound is that they let non-programmers create multimedia presentations by using pre-designed templates that integrate animations, graphics, sound, and interactive elements. If you've thought that multimedia might be too difficult to integrate into your site, you might want to check the specs for Studio M and Astound on Gold Disk's site at **http://www.golddisk.com/awp/index.html**.

Other Multimedia Plug-Ins   Though the above four are arguably the "hottest" multimedia plug-ins for Netscape, here are a few more to keep you busy:

The mBED plug-in for Netscape plays multimedia "mbedlets." The MBD file format and the built-in mBED players are open and license-free. Available for Windows 95/NT, Windows 3.1, Macintosh, and PowerMac, you can find out more and download these plug-ins from **http://www.mbed.com**.

Rad Technologies (**http://www.rad.com**) has a plug-in to play back multimedia applications built in RAD PowerMedia. Designed for corporate communicators and Web designers, PowerMedia provides authoring and viewing of interactive content, presentations, training, kiosks, and demos. It's available for Windows 95/NT.

Asymetrix's ToolBook is one of the top multimedia authoring tools. Now, with its new Neuron plug-in for Netscape, you can deliver ToolBook multimedia titles over the Net. The Neuron plug-in supports external multimedia files, so you can access either complete courseware or multimedia titles, or just the relevant portions of titles in real-time. Content that is not requested is not downloaded, saving you download time and making the application more responsive. Jump to **http://www.asymetrix.com/** for more info and the download files.

The mFactory Netscape plug-in promises streamed playback of and communication between fully interactive multimedia "worlds" embedded in Web pages. Here are the supported file formats: Video: QuickTime, QTVR, Video for Windows (AVI); Graphic: PICT. Text: Dynamic and editable text; Audio/sound: AIFF, and MIDI; Animation: PICT, PICS, QuickTime. Its cel-based proprietary mToon animation format enables ranges of cels to be defined and played. Check out **http://www.mfactory.com/** for info and download availability.

7TH LEVEL has Top Gun in the works, an authoring and playback engine for both Windows and Macintosh. It's not available yet, but you can read all about it at **http://www.7thlevel.com**.

Powersoft's media.splash plug-in for Windows 3.1 and Win95 resides at **http://www.powersoft.com/media.splash/product/index.html**.

The SCREAM inline multimedia player is for Windows 3.1, Win95, and Mac, at **http://www.savedbytech.com/sbt/Plug_In.html**.

Kaleida will have a multimedia player plug-in for Navigator, too. Kaleida Labs is the developer of ScriptX, an object-oriented programming language for multimedia, and currently offers a free platform-independent Kaleida Media Player (KMP) for playback of ScriptX applications which can be configured as a helper application. To find out when you can get its plug-in, check out **http://www.kaleida.com**.

VRML

VRML (Virtual Reality Modeling Language) promises to deliver real-time virtual 3D worlds via the Web. Though it's arguable whether this has actually been accomplished yet, its promise looms great. And VRML plug-ins bring 3D worlds right into the Navigator window.

Live3D   Moving Worlds is a newly proposed extension to the VRML (Virtual Reality Modeling Language) specification which has been developed by Silicon Graphics and Sony. Netscape and many other online developers, including heavy-hitters like Adobe and IBM, are hoping it will become the VRML 2.0 standard.

Moving Worlds goes beyond the current VRML standard to include Java and JavaScript integration and support for third-party plug-ins which would allow developers to incorporate live content such as video and RealAudio into 3D VRML worlds. A key new element is the ability to link to databases.

Moving Worlds allows 3D data sets to be scaleable for viewing on a variety of computer systems ranging from low-cost Internet PCs to powerful 3D graphics workstations. Integrated Java applets can be used to create motion and enable interactivity.

Advocates say that the Moving Worlds version of VRML will finally allow the development of real "cyberspace" applications, such as 3D shopping malls, collaborative 3D design, 3D visual database and spreadsheet display, 3D interactive real-time online games, and photorealistic geographic landscapes.

Silicon Graphics will make the source code for Moving Worlds application development available to all developers.

Netscape's own Live3D Navigator plug-in is a VRML viewer that implements the proposed Moving Worlds VRML extensions. It's feature-packed, it's fun, and—most of all—it's Netscape's official VRML browser. It comes bundled with Navigator 3.0 and is automatically installed when you install NS3.0. If you missed it somehow, you can download Live3D from **http://www.netscape.com/comprod/products/navigator/live3d/index.html**.

▶ For more information about Live3D, **see** "Using VRML," **p. 361** in chapter 16.

VR Scout   Chaco ommunications' VR Scout VRML plug-in displays VRML worlds inline. Chaco's viewer implements the full VRML 1.0 standard.

I've found that with VRML viewers, as with Web browsers, the one you like is most often a matter of personal preference, not features. But VR Scout uses Microsoft Reality Lab for fast software rendering and hardware acceleration, and that can't hurt. It's multithreading, so different aspects of a scene are simultaneously downloaded. Toys include a headlight with a brightness control, and Walk/Fly/Examiner viewing modes with a heads-up toolbar. It also supports textures (GIF, JPEG, BMP, and SFImage).

The VR Scout 1.22 plug-in is for Win95/NT, and is 2.96MB big. Windows 3.1 users can download a stand-alone viewer to use as a Netscape helper application. Download if from **http://www.chaco.com/vrscout/plugin.html**.

WIRL   WIRL, VReam'S Win95 VRML plug-in for Navigator supports object behaviors (motion, rotation, gravity, weight, elasticity, throwability, and sound), logical cause and effect relationships, multimedia capabilities, and links to Windows applications.

Its "Full Object Interactivity" lets you pick up objects, and throw them around in 3D space. This goes way beyond mere passive VRML viewing. Of course, a VRML world has to include the code to enable all these behaviors—you won't get to handle things in a "normal" VRML world. In a nutshell, WIRL supports VRML worlds with VREAMScript interactive extensions. It uses Microsoft's Reality Lab for Super-Fast Performance—100,000 polygons/sec on a 90Mhz Pentium. If you're into computer graphics and programming, you might be impressed to know that WIRL uses real-time Gouraud and Phong Shading, real-time Z-buffering, real-time perspective corrected texture wrapping, and multiple light sources and lighting models. You get full DDE, OLE, and MCI support under Windows 3.1. It promises support for multiple interface devices (mouse, head-mounted displays, gloves, etc.) for an ultra-realistic VR experience.

WIRL is currently available only for Win95 from **http://www.vream.com/3dl1.html**.

Other VRML Browser Plug-Ins   There are more VRML plug-ins than any other type and, frankly, most of them are pretty much "me too." Still, some offer a few special features, and since VRML browsers (like Web browsers) are pretty much a personal preference thing, here's a list of some others you might want to check out:

SuperScape's Viscape lets you grab objects, do walkthroughs, and hear sounds in VRML worlds. It's available for Windows 95/NT at **http://www.superscape.com**.

Integrated Data Systems' VRealm VRML plug-in also adds some features to VRML worlds, like object behaviors, gravity, collision detection, autopilot, and multimedia support. For Windows 95/NT, it can be downloaded from **http://www.ids-net.com/ids/downldpi.html**.

Topper supports the VRML VRBL extensions, for dynamic 3D interactive worlds with keyframe animations and proximity triggers. Topper also supports 3DS and DXF file formats. Windows 95/NT users can download it from **http://www.ktx.com/products/hyperwire/download.htm**.

Template Graphics Software's WebSpace/VRML plug-in is adapted from Silicon Graphics' VRML browser. WebSpace supports the complete Open Inventor 2.x feature set plus the VRML 1.0 subset. For Windows machines, you can download WebSpace from **http://www.sd.tgs.com/~template**.

Express VR for the Mac resides at **http://www.cis.upenn.edu/~brada/VRML/ExpressVR.html**.

Part

III

Ch

9

Liquid Reality for Win95, Win 3.1, and Mac is located at **http://www.dimensionx.com/products/lr/index.html**.

Cybergate for Win95 supports multiuser interaction, chat, and "Avatars" in VRML worlds delivered by servers equipped with their Cyberhub server. It can be found at **http://www2.blacksun.com/beta/c-gate/download.html**.

Paragraph 3D for Win95 allows users to view ParaGraph Virtual Home Space Builder Files, which are VRML worlds that can include animations, sounds, and behaviors. Find it at **http://russia.paragraph.com/vr/d96html/download.htm**.

Virtus Voyager, at **http://www.virtus.com/voyager.html**, is currently a stand-alone VRML viewer, but a plug-in is promised for Netscape.

Finally, Terraform Free is a VRML browser plug-in for Internet Explorer. (However, we understand that many plug-ins are interchangable between the two programs.) For more info, check out the Brilliance Labs home page at **http://www.brlabs.com/files/terraform.zip**.

Productivity Plug-Ins

"Productivity" is a nebulous category which includes real-world tools like word processors and spreadsheets, development systems that let you create your own integrated controls and programs, and miscellaneous tools like clocks and calculators. Most of these are already available as Netscape plug-ins, and I'm sure the rest will come along in time.

Acrobat Amber Reader   If you're like most Web users, you've got a lot of files sitting around that you'd like to put up on the Web. Problem is, they're in a wide variety of formats, and the prospect of translating that much content into HTML files is intimidating, if not impossible.

Never fear. There are a wide variety of document viewer plug-ins becoming available for Netscape. No matter if your information is in the form of Word documents, Excel worksheets, Adobe Acrobat portable documents, or what-have-you, the odds are good that there is—or soon will be—a Netscape plug-in that can display it.

Adobe's "Amber" version of the Acrobat Reader lets you view and print Acrobat Portable Document Format (PDF) files. What are "PDF" files? In a nutshell, they are viewable documents that have the visual integrity of a desktop-published document that has been printed on paper. PDF viewers are available for UNIX, Macintosh, and Windows platforms, and each displays PDF documents identically. If the integrity of your documents is important to you (as it is, say, to the IRS, which uses Acrobat to distribute accurate tax forms over the Web), then PDF files are for you.

Amber differs from the stand-alone version of the Acrobat reader in that it will, under the right conditions, display PDF pages in real-time, without waiting for the entire file to download. This requires that the server sending the document be able to "byteserve" the PDF files a page at a time to the Amber reader plug-in. The PDF files themselves must also be "optimized" for progressive display and maximum file compression.

Barring all this, Amber will also happily wait for a non-optimized, non-byteserved standard Acrobat file, and display it as a piece when it's done downloading.

Progressively displayed PDF files let you see the text first, then the images, then embedded fonts—it's similar to the way Web pages appear in "pieces." Fonts are displayed in a substituted format first, then the proper outline font is blitted over the substitute for final display. The final text is antialiased for a crisper on-screen appearance.

The Amber plug-in itself has a plug-in called Weblink, which, when added in, allows PDF files to include hyperlinks to URLs. In other words, it lets you create Acrobat files that act, in many ways, like HTML Web pages.

When the Amber plug-in is activated, it creates a dockable Toolbar in the Netscape window (see fig. 9.7) with controls for zooming, printing, and navigating the Acrobat document.

Part

III

Ch

9

FIG. 9.7
The Adobe Acrobat Amber PDF reader plug-in in action in Netscape Navigator 2.0. It brings up a full set of Acrobat navigational and viewing controls.

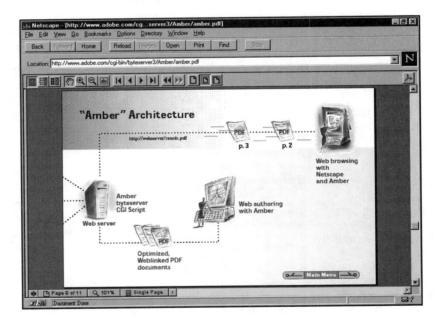

The Amber plug-in is available for Windows 95. Macintosh, and Windows 3.1, with a UNIX version in the wings. It can be downloaded from the Adobe Web site at **http://www.adobe.com/Amber/Download.html**.

Envoy   Chapter 17 told you how to configure Novell's stand-alone Envoy viewer as a Netscape helper application. Now, with Tumbleweed Software's Envoy plug-in you can view Envoy portable documents in Navigator inline. Envoy documents, like Acrobat PDF files, maintain their look and feel no matter where or how they are displayed, and an Envoy document is generally much smaller than the original document.

So what can the Envoy plug-in do? Live Hypertext links allow you to jump to other URLs. Zoom features let you fit your document to the width or height of the browser, and move in and out of the document from 3% to 2000% magnification. You can scroll or pan the display, and jump to different areas of the document using buttons or the scrollbar. Envoy even lets you search for text strings within a document. You can use any application to create your document; you publish it in Envoy format using a custom printer driver that translates the content into an Envoy format file.

You can download the Envoy plug-in from **http://www.twcorp.com/plugin.htm**.

Formula One/NET Visual Components' Formula One/NET is an Excel-compatible spreadsheet plug-in for Navigator. It allows you to display fully functional worksheets which can include live charts, links to URLs, formatted text and numbers, calculations, and clickable buttons and controls. (See fig. 9.8.) It's absolutely amazing—I am blown away that they can place the functionality of a full spreadsheet program inline in Navigator! This thing has all the fancy formulas, all the formatting options, and even all the charts and graphs you need to do everything from simple forms to the quarterly taxes for General Motors.

Formula One/NET is the plug-in for viewing spreadsheets, and Formula One/Net Pro adds a pop-up inline designer for creating them. The pro package also comes with a stand-alone version of the program that adds the ability to read, write, and work with Excel workbook files, all for $39. A professional version of the whole works with OLE controls is available for $249.

Formula One/NET is available for Windows 3.1, Windows95, or Windows NT. It can be downloaded from **http://www.visualcomp.com/f1net/download.htm**.

FIG. 9.8
This embedded spreadsheet displayed by the Formula One/NET plug-in looks and acts just like an Excel spreadsheet. Unlike a form, data doesn't have to be transmitted back and forth to a server if you make changes and want to update your calculations.

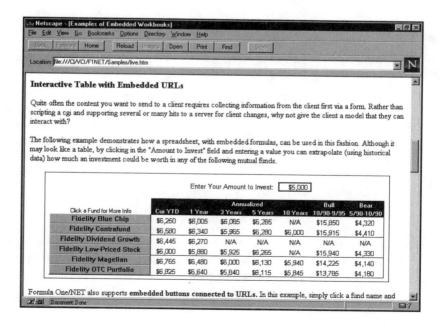

Word Viewer   Inso's Word Viewer plug-in displays Microsoft Word 6.0 or 7.0 documents in Netscape Navigator 2.0 inline. Based on Inso's Quick View Plus viewer, this plug-in lets you copy and print Word documents with all original formatting intact.

Versions for Win95/NT, Win 3.1, and Macintosh can be found at **http://www.inso.com/ plug.htm**.

KEYview (Win95)   The KEYview Netscape plug-in from FTP Software lets you view, print, and convert nearly 200 different file formats. That's right: 200 formats. Name one, and I'll almost guarantee you, as they say on TV, "it's in there." Microsoft Word, WordPerfect, Microsoft Excel, EPS, PCX, compressed files, you name it. Windows 95/NT and Win 3.1 evaluation versions can be downloaded from **http://www.ftp.com**. The upcoming KEYviews version 5.0 promises to display even more file types, including popular multimedia formats.

Other Document Viewers   Here's a roundup of some of the other document viewers available as Netscape plug-ins:

PointPlus displays Microsoft PowerPoint presentations within the Netscape browser window. You can view slide-by-slide manually, or presentations can be displayed hands-free on auto-play. For more info, check out the PointPlus Home Page, **http://www.net-scene.com**.

Not to be outdone by a third party, Microsoft has its own Powerpoint plug-in for Windows 95 at **http://www.microsoft.com/mspowerpoint/internet/player/default.htm**. This special viewer is for compressed Powerpoint files which can include audio. It has also made the publisher for these files available, so if you have Powerpoint95 you can save slides in this new format. Even though this plug-in is from Microsoft and intended for Internet Explorer, it seems to work great with Netscape!

Texture Viewer plays interactive files created with the Texture program. For Win95, this one's at **http://www.futuretense.com/viewdown.htm**.

Techexplorer is an exciting new Netscape plug-in from, of all places, IBM. Techexplorer processes and displays a large subset of TeX/LaTeX, the professional markup language used for typesetting and publishing in education, mathematics, and many of the sciences. Tuned for on-screen readability, Techexplorer provides many options for formatting and customization. Because it formats on the fly, Techexplorer source documents are small, often just one-fourth the size of documents in Acrobat format. Techexplorer can help authors and publishers rapidly and if you publish in TeX, this plug-in will let you put your files right on the Web. It's available at **http://www.ics.raleigh.ibm.com/ics/techexp.htm**.

Navigational Aids   The Web is huge, and it's easy to get lost. What was that site you visited early this morning that was so funny? Where did you find that info on the new model Ford cars? You read a great inside scoop on your competitor's new product, but where?

What you need is a plug-in that will help you track, organize, and recall the sites you've visited. And the more automatic it is, the better. Brother, are you gonna *love* the following plug-ins!

ISYS HindSite by ISYS/Odyssey Development remembers everywhere you've been and everything you've seen. You can perform full-text, plain-English searches on the contents of all the

Part
III
Ch
9

Web pages you've visited. For example, to find previously accessed Web documents relating to bananas, type in "Where did I see bananas?". HindSite indexes and saves the text content of all Web pages visited in a timeframe you set—a week, a month, or six months, for example. Menu-assisted query lets you quickly build accurate queries with push button operators. ISYS HindSite can also display a structured tree outline of every previously accessed URL. It's available for Windows 95/NT and Windows 3.1 from (let's see, where is that URL? Oh, yeah, here!) **http://www.isysdev.com.**

Iconovex (**http://www.iconovex.com**) will be releasing an AnchorPage Client plug-in, which will automatically index and abstract all HTML documents read by Navigator. AnchorPage is built from ICONOVEX's Syntactica engine that incorporates the semantic and syntactic rules of the English language to analyze HTML documents. AnchorPage then extracts the significant phrases and concepts and automatically creates the HTML links from those phrases and concepts to their occurrences within the source document. Finally, AnchorPage generates four Content-Driven Navigation views of the documents (Table of Contents, Abstract, Phrase, and Concept views). Check its Web site for availability.

HistoryTree for Windows and Win95 records your web explorations in a tree, not just a list. It can be had from **http://www.smartbrowser.com/.**

DocuMagix's HotPage captures, organizes, and manages World Wide Web and Intranet information and content. With DocuMagix HotPage, you can view saved Web pages offline, link back to the original sites without needing to remember the exact URL, organize Web pages, and merge them with other Windows documents. You can search for a particular Web page that contains references to a particular topic, forward a Web page document by fax or e-mail inside your company, mark annotations on a Web document, or even add URL links to any Windows documents. Available for Windows or Windows 95, you can get it at **http://www.documagix.com/.**

Remote PC Access Lots of companies use Carbon Copy, Timbuktu, or other remote access programs to let their field service personnel log into remote computers for troubleshooting or control. These programs require a modem on each end and dialup access. Now, there are Netscape plug-in versions of both programs that work with any computers connected to the Internet. No more long distance dialup charges, no more dedicated modem lines, no more dialing hassles. I know guys would be willing to kill to get these programs; they'll make their lives that much easier. Fortunately, you don't have to kill anyone to get them. You can download them right off the Web.

Carbon Copy/Net is Microcom's plug-in version of its extremely popular Carbon Copy remote access program. In brief, it lets you remotely control another PC over the Internet. You can run applications, access files, and view or edit documents on a remote PC as though they were on the PC in front of you. Your screen looks like their screen; what you type goes to their computer. Carbon Copy/Net is an ideal tool for remote access to Windows applications, collaboration, remote software demonstrations, remote support, and remote file transfer access to CD-ROMs and other data. The only requirement is that both machines must be running a copy of Carbon Copy/Net, and (for security reasons, of course) the machine being accessed must be set up to allow remote access. It is currently available for Windows 95 and Windows 3.1 at **http://www.microcom.com/cc/ccdnload.htm**.

Not to be outdone, Farallon has released a plug-in based on its equally useful Timbuktu Pro remote access package. It's called Look@Me (cute name!). Look@Me gives you the ability to view another Look@Me user's screen anywhere in the world in real time. From within Navigator, you can view a remote computer screen and watch the activity taking place. You can edit documents, go over presentations, review graphics, or provide just-in-time training and support via Netscape Navigator and the World Wide Web. Look@Me is also available as a stand-alone application for use outside a browser in Win95, Win 3.1, or on a Macintosh. The plug-in is available for Windows 95 only at **http://collaborate.farallon.com/www/look/ download.html**.

Miscellaneous Tools   There's no end of things that can be implemented as Netscape plug-ins. I'm sure we'll see quite a few that make us wonder just what their creators had in mind. But until then, here are a few of the miscellaneous plug-ins available for Netscape 3.0.

Starfish Software's *EarthTime* plug-in (see fig. 9.9) is a world clock that displays the local time and date in eight cities of your choice. It features a dynamic world map that shows the day and night regions, and it automatically adjusts for daylight savings time. EarthTime also includes a conversion calculator that translates distances, weights, volumes, power, and other measurements between U.S. and metric measurement systems.

You invoke EarthTime from Navigator by selecting File, Open File (Ctrl+0) from the menu, selecting the new filetype "EARTHTIME, .ETC", and loading file:///C|/Program Files/ Netscape/Navigator/Program/PLUGINS/EarthTime/Earthtim.etc. This brings up the World Map shown in figure 9.9. While I might have preferred something a little more intuitive (like a button on the toolbar), this does keep the world clock just a few keystrokes away. The best thing to do is to set it up once, then bookmark it. Then all you need to do is select EarthTime from the Bookmark menu and it comes up quickly and easily.

For the Win95/NT version of Netscape 3.0 only, EarthTime is a self-installing file. It's handy for determining just what time of day it is in that far-off place you're browsing through. You can get it at **http://www.starfishsoftware.com/getearth.html**.

The *PointCast Network* is a free online service that broadcasts up-to-the-minute news and other information via the Internet. Its PointCast Network plug-in lets this content be delivered inline in Netscape. This service provides headline news stories, sports, financial news (including stock indices), and lifestyle stories, as well as weather forecasts for 250 cities and business news covering both individual companies and entire industries. The PointCast Network also includes Time-Warner's Pathfinder channel, which presents daily news from *Time, People*, and *Money* magazines. If you live in New England you can also see stories from the *Boston Globe* newspaper, and those in Southern California have access to the *Los Angeles Times*. The PointCast Network supports live URL links in all news stories, so you can jump right to relevant Web sites. Available for Windows 95 and Windows 3.1, with a Mac version under development, you can download the PointCast Network plug-in from **http://www.pointcast.com**.

FIG. 9.9
EarthTime is a cool
world time clock plug-in
for Navigator 2.0 from
Starfish Software.

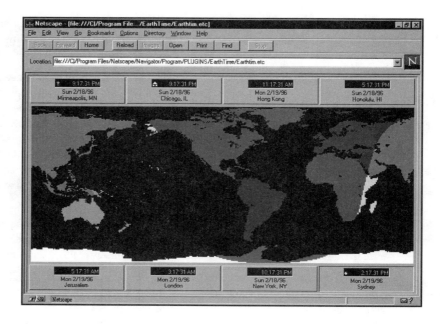

The *Argus Map Viewer* displays vector-based maps composed of multiple layers of information. These are dynamic, interactive, scalable maps which change based on your inquiries. With ARGUS Map Viewer, you can zoom in on items of interest and the map in front of you is automatically redrawn to display new and more detailed information matching the scale of view. Each item on the map is a dynamic object which is selectable. Information on selected objects can be viewed in reports. URL links attached to map objects can be activated taking you directly to other maps, documents, images, and web sites. If you go to **http:// www.argusmap.com/mbr_main.htm**, you'll find versions for Win 3.1 and Win95.

Globalink provides translation services and software, and now they've added a set of Netscape plug-ins that are truly impressive. These perform bidirectional translations that convert between English and French, Italian, German, or Spanish. Yes, that means you can jump into a site written in German and see it translated into English on your screen. This is a tremendous step in making the World Wide Web truly worldwide. When you encounter a foreign site, just clicking a button will get you a translated page. Translated pages maintain all graphics, hotlinks, and formatting. These translations can be created online, while surfing, or alternatively, pages can be downloaded and saved to be translated and viewed offline. The dictionaries for Web Translator have been specially prepared for use on the Web and include Internet terminology which enhances the accuracy of the translation. Globalink comes on a single CD-ROM which includes both domestic and localized versions. Though not available as a downloadable demo, the price is right at $49.95. You can get further information from Globalink's Web site at **http://www.globalink.com**. (Now, Globalink, how about Japanese?)

The *JetForm Filler* plug-in lets users fill out online forms designed with JetForm Design. Windows, Win95, and Macintosh versions are planned. Check out **http://www.jetform.com/** for more information on this product.

It's interesting to note that Netscape Corporation's official IRC (Internet Relay Chat) solution isn't a plug-in, but a helper application. Though its Netscape Chat application auto-configures, it's a separate program. If you want to do your IRC chatting inline in the Netscape window, you need the *ICHAT IRC* Plug-in for Windows from **http://www.ichat.com/**. With ICHAT installed, Web pages can become chat rooms. When you visit a chat-enabled Web page, the plug-in opens a frame in the lower part of the browser window. Within that frame, ICHAT displays a real-time, on-going chat session among all the visitors to that page. Users can enter the conversation and communicate with each other simply by typing. This is a hot product, and I think we can expect to see Netscape trying to play "catch up" soon.

Groupware Applications   Groupware is software that allows people in groups (usually on corporate intranets) to exchange information and to collaborate on projects. It's one of the hottest areas of software development right now. There are already a couple of Netscape plug-ins that can be classified as legitimate, powerful groupware applications.

Lotus Notes is the best-established groupware solution for corporations. Brainstorm Technology's *Groupscape* is a visual, object-oriented development tool for building and extending Lotus Notes workgroup applications to the Web. This lets organizations standardize on Netscape clients as the integrated front-end to the World Wide Web and their existing Lotus Notes infrastructure. Groupscape provides corporate users with the ease-of-use of Netscape clients combined with the security and replication strengths of Lotus Notes.

As a demo of what Groupscape can do, Brainstorm has released the free Groupscape Notes Browser, an interactive Netscape/Groupscape application which lets corporate users view, browse, and surf internal Lotus Notes networks. This plug-in provides a sample of the types of applications that can be built using Groupscape. The Groupscape Standard development system is priced at $995.00 per developer with no run-time fees, but the Notes Browser is free for the downloading from **http://www.braintech.com/gscape.htm**.

Galacticomm Worldgroup, for Windows 3.1 and Windows 95, is a Netscape plug-in that supports dozens of off-the-shelf groupware applications. These can range from real-time video conferencing to online fax-back services, questionnaires with graphed results, and more. In fact, its focus is on information, commerce, multimedia databases, and other real-world, corporate-level solutions. Secure buying and selling via the Web is supported, as is forms management, powerful document searching, etc. **http://www.gcomm.com/wgsupb4.exe**. Galacticomm has an impressive list of high-profile clients in business, industry, and the government. If you're looking to bring your big business onto the Web in a big-time way, with more than just a set of Web pages for the public to peruse, it looks like you should look into Worldgroup. You can find out more and download the plug-in from **http://www.gcomm.com/show/plugin.html**.

ActiveX What if there isn't a plug-in that does what you want it to do? Well, you can always write your own from scratch. There's info about the Netscape plug-ins SDK (Software Developer's Kit) online at the Netscape site at **http://www.netscape.com**. But there are other solutions. If you're mainly concerned about delivering to Windows platforms (all types), there are four plug-ins that let you launch OLE applications inline in Netscape.

ExCITE's NCompass division has created a Navigator plug-in for Windows 95 that lets you embed OLE controls as applets created using standard programming languages and development tools like Visual C++, Visual Basic, and the MS Windows Game SDK.

With the OLE Control plug-in, a software developer can create a version of any Windows standard OLE-compliant program that is customized for use with Netscape and the Web. For example, games, investment programs, multimedia players, and just about anything else can be created for Windows, then compiled in a version for the Web.

Because OLE plug-ins use compiled native Windows code, Internet applications can run just as fast as stand-alone Windows 95 applications while also supporting data exchange and data updating over the Web.

NCompass provides several examples on its Web site, including a multiplayer DirectX game, a real-time OpenGL rendering of a robot arm (see fig. 9.10), inline AVI movie player control, and more.

The OLE plug-in requires a 486 DX33 with 8MB RAM, 14.4KB Internet connection, and Windows 95 or NT. You can download it from **http://www.excite.sfu.ca/NCompass/nchome.html**.

FIG. 9.10

That's a Windows 95 program running in the Netscape window, courtesy of NCompass's OLE Control plug-in.

OpenScape   Business@Web's OpenScape plug-in is similar to NCompass's OLE Control plug-in in that it lets developers create OLE/OCX-compatible applications that run inline in Netscape over the Web. However, OpenScape applications must be created using the OpenScape development system rather than Visual Basic or C++.

There are four versions of the OpenScape product for actually creating the applications that the OpenScape plug-in runs. OpenScape is for individuals who want to build Web pages using Visual Basic-style tools. It lets you create reusable and customizable OCXs with a Visual Basic-compatible scripting language. OpenScape can also be used to create stand-alone desktop applications with embedded OCXs, OLE 2.0 servers, and DLLs. OpenScape Professional adds the ability to actually create OCXs and OLE 2.0 servers. OpenScape Workgroup is for creating applications that can be distributed securely across a network. Finally, OpenScape Enterprise is for large, corporate development work.

The OpenScape Navigator plug-in is currently downloadable for both Window 95/NT and Windows 3.1. You can get it at **http://www.busweb.com/download/f_down.html**.

QuickServer   QuickServer, by Wayfarer Communications, is for high-performance intranet and Internet client-server applications developed with Visual Basic, PowerBuilder, C++, and Java. Applications developers can build the client component of Internet applications using the leading development tools and run them inside Netscape Navigator using this plug-in. QuickServer reduces development time by leveraging the leading client/server development tools, such as Visual Basic, PowerBuilder, Visual C++, Delphi, and Java, and by eliminating the complexity of communications programming.

You can download the 30-day evaluation version of the QuickServer SDK (Software Developer's Kit), and you can download StockWatcher, a demo application in Visual Basic using Wayfarer's plug-in, to see live, dynamic stock quotes inside Netscape Navigator. For Windows 95/NT, both are available at **http://www.wayfarer.com/**.

WinFrame   Citrix Systems' WinFrame plug-in for Windows 3.1 and Windows 95 actually allows you to execute Windows programs over the Internet. With the WinFrame client, you can publish applications as easily as you publish Web documents. Just download this plug-in, run the setup program, and you can try it for yourself on standard Windows applications like Microsoft Access, Lotus Notes, and Adobe Acrobat. Check it out at **http://www.citrix.com**. ●

Part
III

Ch
9

## CHAPTER 10

Configuring Helper Applications

We can't always single-handedly manage everything that comes our way—sometimes we need a little help from our friends. Netscape is no different. It can't handle every single file type that it encounters on the World Wide Web. Sometimes it needs a little help from helper applications.

Fortunately, it's pretty easy to configure helper applications for Netscape. The hard part is figuring out which ones you need and where to get them. This chapter should help with that first dilemma, the enclosed CD-ROM should help you with the second.

In this chapter, you learn:

- Which file types require helper applications, and which don't
- What kind of helper applications are right for you
- Where to get helper applications
- How to configure helper applications to work with Netscape

The following sections will help you choose the best Netscape helper applications for:

- Sound
- Graphics
- Video
- VRML (Virtual Reality Markup Language)
- SGML (Standard Generalized Markup Language)
- Adobe Acrobat and other Portable Document Formats
- File decompression ■

What Are Helper Applications?

Though Netscape 3 is a pretty versatile Web browser, you'll still run into files on the Web that it can't display. Although this newest release of Netscape incorporates support for more file types and includes plug-ins (see chapter 9) to use even more, there are still some video files, audio files, odd graphics files, strange document formats, and even compressed files that Netscape can't display. To display or play these files, you need to set up helper applications.

A helper application is simply a program that can understand and interpret files that Netscape can't handle itself. Almost any program can be configured to act as a helper application for Netscape. The trick is figuring out which ones will be the most useful to you.

All Web browsers need helper applications. There are simply too many different file types on the Web for a browser to be able to handle them all internally.

Think about this: On a daily basis, you probably use a dozen or more different programs for word processing, spreadsheets, database management, electronic mail, graphics, and many other different applications. Each of these programs produces a different kind of data file, yet only a few of your applications are able to import even a limited number of different file types from other applications. And we're only talking about one person's files on a single computer. It's just not possible for Netscape to handle all the thousands of different file types it might encounter on the Web all by itself.

There is a key difference between helper applications and plug-ins. Plug-ins can display or use the files they work with directly in Netscape. A plug-in becomes almost like a part of Netscape. When using helper applications, the helper application is started and runs as a separate application, in its own window just as if you had started it from the Program Manager or Windows 95 Start Menu.

For that reason, plug-ins are really the preferred way to work with the extra file types in Netscape. Where you have a choice, you are better off to install a plug-in application (as described in the previous chapter) than to use a helper application. As more plug-ins are written, the need for helpers will decrease even further.

Configuring a Helper Application

No matter what helper applications you choose to add, they all configure the same way. It takes only a few simple steps to set one up.

If you look at table 10.1, you'll notice that Netscape can't display .BMP and .PCX image files. These are pretty ubiquitous file types, and you'll run into them fairly often on the Web. A helper application is definitely in order.

Fortunately, Microsoft includes a program in Windows 95 that does a great job of displaying .PCX and .BMP files: Microsoft Paint—called Paintbrush in Windows 3.1 (see fig. 10.1).

FIG. 10.1

Microsoft's Paint comes with all versions of Windows. It makes a dandy Netscape helper application for viewing .BMP and .PCX image files.

Part
III

Ch
10

To configure Paint as your .PCX/.BMP helper application for Netscape, follow these steps:

1. Open Netscape's Options menu, and select General Preferences.
2. Click the Helpers tab to bring it to the front (see fig. 10.2).
3. Scroll down the list of MIME types until you see the image/x-MS-bmp entry. Click it to highlight it. The extension "bmp" appears in the file Extensions field (see fig. 10.3).
4. Click the Browse button. A dialog box appears. Find your Windows directory and double-click Pbrush (see fig. 10.4).
5. The full path name for the Paint program appears in the application box beside the Paint icon, and the Launch the Application radio button is auto-selected. If you choose OK now, Paint will be configured as Netscape's helper application for .BMP files. But we want to use it to view .PCX files, too, so we'll go on.

FIG. 10.2

The Helpers tab.

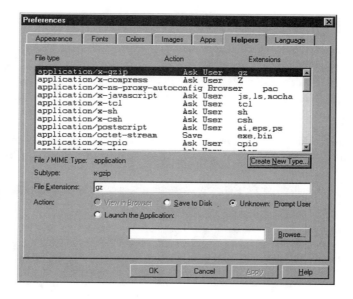

FIG. 10.3

Select the file type from the variety of types available.

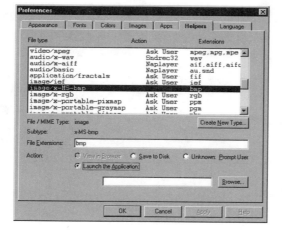

FIG. 10.4

Find the Pbrush.exe file and double-click it.

6. Scrolling up and down through the list of MIME file types reveals that there is no entry for a file type with a .PCX extension, so we have to define our own. Click the Create New Type button to bring up the Configure New Mime Type dialog box. We can enter only one of the seven official MIME types in the Mime Type windows, so choose Image. We must make up our own MIME subtype because none is listed. Any "unofficial" MIME subtype must begin with "x-", and we need to follow that prefix with something unique, so let's just use the file name extension. Type x-pcx into the Mime SubType box and then click OK (see fig. 10.5).

FIG. 10.5

The Configure New Mime Type dialog box.

7. In the File Extensions box, type pcx. Because you already know the full path name for Paint, just type it into the File Path box, or enter it like you did before by Browsing. If the radio button labeled Launch the Application isn't auto-checked, check it manually (see fig. 10.6).

8. Click OK to finish.

FIG. 10.6

Choose your file extension here.

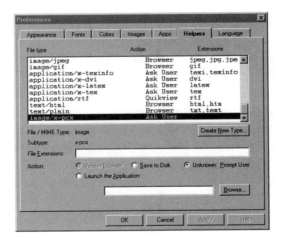

That's it. Paint is officially a Netscape helper application. The next time Netscape encounters a .PCX or .BMP image, it will automatically launch Paint to view it (see fig. 10.7).

FIG. 10.7
Paint, now fully
configured as a
Netscape helper
application, displays the
flag.

 T I P   You can also tell Netscape to automatically save a particular file type to disk whenever it is encountered, rather than configuring a helper application to display it. During the configuration process, just
click the radio button labeled Save to Disk instead of the one marked Launch Application. You'll
probably want to pick Save to Disk for files with an extension of .EXE (MIME: application/octet-stream)
because these are usually executable programs.

What Kinds of Files Are on the Web?

Just about every type of file you can imagine exists somewhere on the World Wide Web (see
table 10.1 for some examples). But this doesn't mean you'll run into them all.

Web pages themselves are almost always composed of just two elements: HTML-formatted text
and inline graphics. All Web browsers can handle these, including Netscape; you don't need to
worry about configuring helper applications just to be able to read Web pages. The problem
comes when you try to access an external file by clicking a link to something other than a Web
page.

Even then, the problem does not loom as large as you might fear, because the Web is mostly a
compendium of hypermedia documents. That is, the hyperlinks on most Web pages jump to
files with some sort of multimedia content: text, audio, graphics, or video. Even if these are in
formats that Netscape doesn't speak natively, once you've configured helper applications for
the half dozen or so most common multimedia file types, you may be able to go for months
without encountering anything your Netscape configuration can't handle. (For some great
online info about multimedia file types, follow the link in fig. 10.8.)

However, even if you do your best to avoid exotic file types, the day will come when you'll find a
site that provides a link to some killer, must-have file that exists only in some weird format that
you've never heard of before. Never fear. By configuring the proper Netscape helper application on the spot, you'll be able to play or display it properly. That's the beauty of helper applications. They make Netscape infinitely open-ended, extensible, and expandable.

FIG. 10.8

An excellent reference to the kinds of files you'll run into on the World Wide Web is Allison Zhang's online book Multimedia File Formats on the Internet at http://ac.dal.ca/~dong/contents.html.

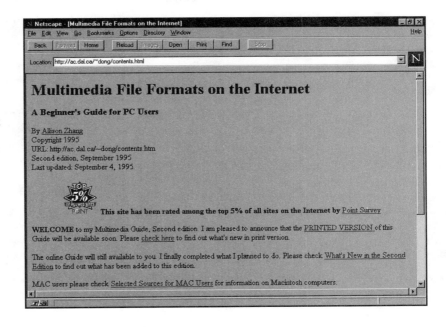

Netscape's Built-In Capabilities

Before we get into the topic of the helper applications you need, let's take a moment to find out which ones you don't need. Netscape already includes the built-in ability to display the three most-used graphics file formats on the Web, and bundles a plug-in that plays the most popular audio file types, as well.

Built-In GIF, JPEG, and XBM Image Display

You don't have to configure helper applications for GIF, JPEG, or XBM images. Netscape displays all three of these graphic file formats just fine all by itself.

There are good reasons for having graphics support built right into Netscape, though (see fig. 10.9). Web pages are more aesthetically pleasing if they combine text with inline graphics. But you'd be stuck with separate windows for text and graphics if Netscape had to launch a helper application every time it displayed an image. All Web browsers have to be able to display at least one graphic image format internally if text and graphics are to stay together on the page.

TIP Have you ever wished that Netscape could display an inline graphic in its own window instead of inline? It can! Right-click the image and you'll see the menu of options shown in figure 10.10. Select View this Image and it will be displayed in its own window. You can also choose Save this Image As to save the image to disk, or choose Copy this Image Location to copy the URL of the image to the Windows Clipboard.

Part

III

Ch

10

FIG. 10.9
Netscape 3.0 doesn't need a helper application to display inline GIF, JPEG, and XBM images like these.

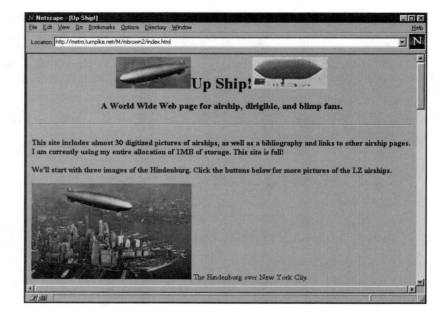

FIG. 10.10
Click the right mouse button on an inline image to open this helpful menu of options.

Most of the inline graphics on Web pages are GIF (Graphics Interchange Format) images, because that's what early Web browsers could display. Like all Web browsers, Netscape has built-in support for GIFs. But by today's image compression standards, GIF image files are just plain big. And when you're talking about a time-intensive medium like the Web, smaller is better.

JPEG images are much smaller than GIFs—in fact, a 16-million color JPEG graphic can be as little as 1/4 the size of the same GIF image in only 256 colors. That's why Netscape added built-in JPEG image display capability to its browser a couple of revisions back. Due in no small part to Netscape's support for the JPEG format, many Web sites now include inline JPEGs on their pages, which result in faster page downloads and much better-looking Web sites.

T I P   Look for sites with JPEG images in the new Progressive JPEG format supported by Netscape 3.0. They load up to three times faster than GIFs, and preview faster, too!

What about XBM images? Well, XBM is a monochrome image format used mostly on X Window systems running under UNIX. Frankly, these days you'll only run into XBMs on older UNIX sites where they haven't bothered to convert their images to GIFs or JPEGs yet. Because most Web servers are UNIX machines (with Windows NT and Windows 95 up-and-coming contenders), XBM isn't dead yet.

GIFs, JPEGs, and XBMs currently account for almost 100 percent of the inline graphic images on Web pages. With built-in support for all three, Netscape faithfully displays most of the images you encounter on the Web without requiring you to configure a single external helper application.

> **CAUTION**
>
> If you are designing your own Web pages, don't entirely abandon GIFs for JPEGs. There are still some people out there using older browsers that can't read JPEGs. And for small, simple images with few colors, GIFs can often be even smaller than JPEGs. Not only that, but GIFs support background transparency, which can improve the look of your pages—JPEG doesn't (at least not yet). For more information on how to implement graphics on your own Web pages, go to chapter 22, "Advanced Graphics."

Netscape's Included LiveAudio Plug-In

Multimedia just isn't multimedia without sound. Text, graphics, and animation only stimulate the eyes, but sound brings a whole different sense into play. By combining graphics with sound, you activate more of the brain and get your audience more involved. (Not convinced? Try watching TV with the sound muted.)

Starting with version 3, Netscape includes a new audio player in the form of a plug-in. This plug-in, called LiveAudio, is configured by default to play AIFF, MIDI, WAV, and AU sound formats. For more about this plug-in, see chapter 9.

Other Built-In Formats

Netscape also supports Microsoft's AVI Video for Windows file format for movies directly. With the Live3D plug-in included with Netscape, many VRML worlds also display without the need for any other helper applications or plug-ins.

How Does Netscape Know When It Needs a Helper Application?

Before Netscape can tell if it can handle a file internally or whether it has to launch a helper application, it has to determine what kind of data it's dealing with.

If you've been using a PC for very long, you can probably identify many file types by their file name extensions. You know that a file named foo.exe is an executable program because the file name ends in ".EXE," and that one named boo.doc is a Microsoft Word document because it ends in ".DOC."

N O T E   By default, Windows 95's file-handling dialog boxes hide file name extensions. For example, a file named "picture.gif" is listed as "picture." File types are identified by icons. To tell Windows 95 to display file name extensions in all its file dialog boxes, follow these steps:

1. Run Windows Explorer.
2. Select the View, Options menu.
3. Choose the View tab.
4. Uncheck the Hide MS-DOS File Extensions box. ■

> **CAUTION**
>
> Not every file type can be correctly identified by its file name extension. Some different file formats share the same extension, and there are also many files on the Web that have arbitrary or misleading file names. Be sure to check for "context clues" that will help you identify a file's real file type. For example, if a file has the file name extension .exe but the text identifies it as an archive file, the odds are good that it's not an executable program, but a self-extracting archive.

Netscape can identify files on the Web by their file names, too. But that is only its backup method of determining what kind of files it's dealing with. Its primary method is by referencing a file's MIME type.

A Brief Course in MIME Types

MIME is an acronym for Multipurpose Internet Mail Extensions, but this is a little misleading. MIME type definitions are not just for Internet mail; they are used to identify any file that can be transmitted over the Internet.

A MIME type definition consists of two parts:

> type/subtype

Here's a real-world example:

> image/jpeg

It's pretty easy to see that this MIME type definition describes an image file in JPEG format.

Before a Web server sends a file to Netscape, it sends the MIME type definition for that file. Netscape reads this definition and looks it up to see if it can handle the file internally, or if there is a helper application defined for it. In the case of the example above, Netscape knows that the file it is about to receive is an image in JPEG format, which, of course, it can interpret internally; it won't try to launch a helper application.

If the server doesn't send a MIME type along before transmitting the file, Netscape uses the file name extension to identify the file type.

TROUBLESHOOTING

I thought I clicked a link to a graphic, but Netscape displayed a screen of unreadable text instead. If Netscape has to identify a file by its file name extension rather than its MIME type, it can make the same kind of misidentification that a human would make with a misnamed or ambiguously named file. If Netscape tries to display a misidentified file typed in its own display or in the wrong helper application, all you see is a garbled mess.

If this happens to you, hover over the file link with the hand pointer and read the file name in the status bar at the bottom of the Netscape window. If the file name extension looks wrong for the type of file you're trying to view, that's probably the problem.

In the rare case where you get a garbled inline image, you can view the file name by right-clicking the image. The file name will be displayed in brackets beside the View this Image choice on the pop-up menu.

You can also see file names by selecting View, By Document Source from the Netscape menu and looking for the file name in the HTML code.

If you can't figure out why a link isn't working right, you can always save the suspect file by holding down the Shift key and clicking the link. Then you can work with it later.

You can see a complete list of the MIME types that Netscape recognizes by choosing Options, General from the Netscape menu, then selecting the Helpers tab (see fig. 10.11), or you can look at table 10.1 for a list of some of the more common types that you may encounter.

FIG. 10.11
Netscape can display this scrolling list of the MIME types it knows about. Just select Options, General Preferences from the menu and click the Helpers tab.

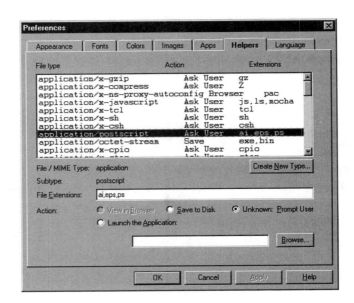

Table 10.1 MIME Types That Netscape Recognizes

Type/Subtype	Extensions	Description
application/x-gzip	.GZ	GNU Zip Compressed Data
application/x-compress	.Z	Compressed Data
application/x-javascript	.JS, .LS, .MOCHA	JavaScript
application/x-tcl	.TCL	TCL Program
application/x-sh	.SH	Bourne Shell Program
application/x-csh	.CSH	C Shell Program
application/postscript	.AI, .EPS, .PS	PostScript Program
application/octet-stream	.EXE, .BIN	Binary Executable
application/x-cpio	.CPIO	UNIX CPIO Archive
application/x-gtar	.GTAR	GNU Tape Archive
application/x-tar	.TAR	UNIX Tape Archive
application/x-shar	.SHAR	UNIX Shell Archive
application/x-zip-compressed	.ZIP	Zip Compressed Data
application/x-stuffit	.SIT	Macintosh Archive
application/mac-binhex40	.HQX	Macintosh BinHex Archive
*video/x-msvideo, video/msvideo	.AVI	Microsoft Video
video/quicktime	.QT, .MOV, .MOOV	QuickTime Video
video/mpeg	.MPEG, .MPG, .MPE, .MPV, .VBS, .MPEGV	MPEG Video
video/x-mpeg-2	.MPV2, .MP2V	MPEG Level 2 Video
*audio/x-wav	.WAV	WAV Audio
*audio/x-aiff, audio/aiff	.AIF, .AIFF, .AIFC	AIFF Audio
*audio/basic	.AU, .SND	ULAW Audio Data
application/fractals	.FIF	Fractal Image Format
audio/x-pn-realaudio	.RA, .RAM	RealAudio
audio/x-mpeg	.MP2, .MPA, .ABS, .MPEGA	MPEG Audio
audio/x-midi, audio/midi	.MID, .MIDI	MIDI Musical Instrument
image/x-png	.PNG	Portable Network Graphic

Type/Subtype	Extensions	Description
image/x-MS-bmp	.BMP	Windows Bitmap
image/x-rgb	.RGB	RGB Image
image/x-portable-pixmap	.PPM	PPM Image
image/x-portable-graymap	.PGM	PGM Image
image/x-portable-bitmap	.PBM	PBM Image
image/x-portable-anymap	.PNM	PBM Image
image/x-xwindowdump	.XWD	X Window Dump Image
image/x-xpixmap	.XPM	X Pixmap
*image/x-xbitmap	.XBM	X Bitmap
image/x-cmu-raster	.RAS	CMU Raster Image
image/tiff	.TIFF, .TIF	TIFF Image
*image/jpeg	.JPEG, .JPG, .JPE	JPEG Image
*image/gif	.GIF	CompuServe Image Format
application/x-texinfo	.TEXI, .TEXINFO	GNU TeXinfo Document
application/x-dvi	.DVI	TeX DVI Data
application/x-latex	.LATEX	LaTeX Document
application/x-tex	.TEX	TeX Document
application/rtf	.RTF	Rich Text Format
*text/html	.HTML, .HTM	Hypertext Markup Language
*text/plain	.TXT, .TEXT	Plain Text
*x-conference/x-talk	.ICE	CoolTalk real-time audio conferencing
application/x-director	.DXR	Shockwave for Director
*x-world/x-vrml	.WRL	Virtual Reality 3D Worlds/Live 3D files

Part III
Ch 10

Files that Netscape handles internally or via plug-ins included in version 3 are marked with an asterisk (*). In addition, there are plug-ins to handle QuickTime, MPEG Video, Shockwave (there is no helper application for this type), Real Audio, Portable Network Graphics, TIFF, BMP, EPS, PCX, and MIDI. You probably won't need helper applications for any of these types.

So, what you may find is that there aren't many common file types left in which your only option is a helper application. Most likely, you'd want to configure a helper for dealing with compressed files (like a software program you download).

Types and Subtypes There are only seven sanctioned MIME types: text, audio, image, video, multipart, message, and application. If somebody comes up with some hot new program or data file type, they have to fit it into one of these seven MIME types if a MIME-enabled application is going to recognize it.

However, there are both "official" and "unofficial" MIME subtypes. Official subtypes appear on the list without an "x-" prefix. That kind of gives away the fact that "x-" is the official way to label an unofficial MIME subtype. That a MIME subtype is "unofficial" in no way makes it a second-class citizen, however. It just means that the Internet Working Group, the organization that oversees the MIME standard, hasn't defined an official subtype for it yet.

Missing MIME Types Important file types that didn't make Netscape's internal list will be discussed by topic in subsequent chapters in this section.

You can create your own definitions for MIME subtypes that aren't on Netscape's list by clicking the Create New Type button in Netscape's Helper Applications dialog box, and entering a new type/x-subtype designation. Be sure to include the "x-" in the subtype name, and don't duplicate a name that's already on the list.

Of course, the rest of the world won't know about MIME types that you define, so Web browsers you connect to won't send file IDs that match your MIME types. Netscape will be stuck with identifying the file by its file name extension, which, in most cases, will work fine. If Netscape encounters a file with an unknown MIME type and a file extension that is not on its internal list, it may try to display it as text. In most cases, this is definitely not what you want it to do. If you run into this problem, you can configure Netscape so that it automatically saves files of that type to disk by following these steps (see fig. 10.12):

FIG. 10.12

You must define both type and subtype for any new MIME type you define for Netscape.

1. Select Options, General Preferences from the Netscape menu.
2. Click on the Helpers tab to bring it to the front.
3. Choose the Create New Type button.
4. Enter a MIME type in the Mime Type field, and a MIME subtype in the Mime SubType field. (This should begin with an "x-".)
5. Enter the proper file extension(s) in the File Extensions field.
6. Click the Save to Disk radio button.
7. Click OK when you're done.

> **CAUTION**
>
> Once you've set up a new MIME type/subtype, you can't get rid of it—there's no Delete button in the Helper Applications configuration window. You can change the name of the application or the file name extension, and you can change the Action to Save to Disk or Ask User, but you can't get rid of it. The only way to do so is to manually edit the NETSCAPE.INI file under Windows 3.1 or the Registry under Windows 95.

N O T E   You can find out more about MIME types by obtaining the Internet Working Group's RFC document on the topic. It can be downloaded by pointing Netscape to:

ftp://ftp.isi.edu or ftp://ds.internic.net

Look for the directory rfc/ and the file name rfc1521.txt.

You can also enter into discussions about MIME on UseNet. Just point Netscape's newsreader to the group comp.mail.mime. ▓

TROUBLESHOOTING

I configured a helper application for "type/subtype," but Netscape doesn't always seem to use it. And I sometimes get a `Warning: unrecognized encoding` **message. What's going on?** If this problem is only occasional, it's probably not Netscape or your helper application configuration that's at fault. The problem may be with the way the Web site you're connected to is sending MIME type information. Netscape may be receiving a self-contradictory or confusing MIME type identification, and it's trying to interpret the file without really knowing what it is. If you regularly run into this problem on a particular site, e-mail the Webmaster (usually webmaster@site) and inform him of the problem.

▶ **See** "E-mail with Netscape," **p. 173**

Separating the Wheat from the Chaff   So which file types do you actually need to worry about?

You can safely ignore the ones that Netscape handles internally. Though you can configure external helper applications to display the graphics files that Netscape normally handles, you generally don't want to do so; it disrupts the look and feel of Netscape's page display because helper applications don't appear inline.

The Three Philosophies of Helper Application Selection

There are three very different approaches to the process of selecting Netscape helper applications. One camp likes to configure a single monster, do-it-all helper application to juggle as many different file types as possible. Others like to use powerful stand-alone applications as helper applications so they can really manipulate the files they access. The last group prefers small, quick applications that display just one type of file. Let's look at this approach first.

The Zen Minimalist Approach

The type of helper application preferred by the minimalist is small, has very few features, and does just one thing.

The advantage to this approach is that your helper applications load and play quickly. They don't eat up much memory, so they're perfect for systems with slower processors and less RAM.

The disadvantage is that you may have to install and configure lots of helper applications to handle all the different file types you might run into on the Web.

The minimalist approach is best if you're running Netscape on a computer with limited resources (like a notebook) or if your needs are utilitarian: catching up on news, doing mostly text-based research, and so on.

The Control Freak's Preference

If you like to work "on the fly," you might prefer to use more powerful programs as helpers. For example, say you're involved in a project where you are downloading and converting hundreds of public domain graphics files to .BMP format. You could save yourself a lot of file manipulation time later if the helper application you have configured as your graphics viewer could convert and save them for you as you browse the Web.

Paint Shop Pro is a good example of a powerhouse program that also makes a good Netscape helper application. It can read and convert three dozen different file types and manipulate graphics in scores of different ways, but it's easy to use and is compact enough to load relatively quickly. (Paint Shop Pro is discussed in depth in chapter 14, "Configuring Netscape for Graphics.")

N O T E   You won't want to spend a lot of time manipulating and converting files while you're online if you are using a dial-up connection that charges you for connect time. Instead, save the files you want to keep and work with them offline later. ▪

 T I P   You can save even more time if you don't view files while you're online. Just download them directly to disk. Instead of left-clicking a file's link to display it, right-click it and select Save this Link as. The file will be saved to disk without being displayed.

TIP The true Netscape hacker knows that you never really even have to save a file you've viewed recently—it's already stored in Netscape's Cache directory (in pieces with cryptic file names). If you're patient, you can find the file content you're interested in by scanning the cache using the Find, Files, or Folders option on the Start menu in Windows 95, or by loading them one-by-one into Netscape using File, Open File. (Because older files in the cache are purged regularly, if you find something you want to keep you need to copy it elsewhere.) This process is not for the faint of heart, but if you know you looked at something just great on the Web yesterday and can't find it today, then happy hunting.

The Swiss Army Knife Solution

The advantage of having one helper application that handles everything is that configuration is quick and easy—you install one program, go through the configuration process once, and you're done.

The disadvantage is that do-it-all helper applications have a tendency to load slowly and hog system resources.

And, of course, there are no programs that will handle absolutely everything you might encounter on the Web. But you can come surprisingly close.

Take VuePrint, for example.

VuePrint is a program that is a veritable Swiss Army Knife for audio, graphics, and video. It comes in versions for Windows 3.1 and Windows 95, and can play or display all of these file types:

- Image files (.GIF, .BMP, .DIB, .RLE, .PCX, .TGA, .JPG, .TIF)
- Sound files (.MID, .WAV, .MCI)
- Movie files (.AVI, .MPG, .MMM, .MOV, .FLI, .FLC)
- Slide show files (.SLI)
- UUEncoded files (.UUE, .UU1, .01, .MSG)
- Zip files (.ZIP)

With a program like VuePrint installed on your system, you don't have to worry about running into files that Netscape can't handle. (VuePrint's capabilities are discussed at length in chapter 14, "Configuring Netscape for Graphics.")

Your Personal Setup

You'll most likely want to take an approach that's a compromise among these three extremes. Like most Netscape users, you'll end up configuring a handful of useful helper applications that expand Netscape's native capabilities without doing too much or too little.

Part
III

Ch
10

Personally, I favor a "minimalist" approach. Because I connect to the World Wide Web via a 14.4KB dial-up connection, I keep helper applications configured only for the few file types that I run into all the time, like .AU and .WAV sounds, .BMP graphics, and .MOV and .MPG movies. For everything else, I just select Save to Disk when Netscape flashes its Save/Cancel/Configure dialog box for an unconfigured file type. Then I can view them offline, when I'm not paying for the connection.

What Kinds of Programs Can You Use as Helper Applications?

Almost any program can be configured as a helper application for Netscape. But that doesn't mean you should go ahead and configure every program you own. Keep in mind effectiveness, efficiency, and utility.

Should You Use DOS, Windows 3.1, or Win95 Helpers?

If you're running under Windows 95, stick with Win95 helper applications as much as you can. If you're running Windows 3.1, use Windows 3.1 helper applications. I can't think of a single reason to ever use a DOS program as a Netscape helper, though you may discover a couple in the following chapters that are useful as offline file conversion utilities.

DOS applications don't integrate well with Windows. They don't make good use of system resources and don't multitask well with Windows applications like Netscape.

If you're running under Windows 95, you'll find that Windows 3.1 applications don't handle long file names, don't multitask efficiently, don't run as fast under Win95 as native 32-bit applications, and don't use the standard Win95 file dialog box.

Both you and Netscape will be happier in the long run if you use the most advanced, up-to-date programs your system can run as helper applications. But don't forget that you want your helper applications to be quick and resource-friendly, too.

Programs You Already Own

The first place you should look for helper applications is in the treasure trove of programs you already own. Both Windows 3.1 and Windows 95 come with a handful of small, efficient bundled applications that make excellent Netscape helper applications.

Earlier in this chapter, we discussed how to set up Paint, another program that is included with both versions of Windows, as a helper application for viewing .PCX and .BMP image files. With Netscape's native support for .GIFs, .JPEGs, and .XBMs, the addition of Paint instantly sets you up for viewing the Web's five most popular graphics image file types.

Windows 3.1's Notepad and Write can be handy helper applications for text file formats you want to display in a separate window. Windows 95 users can use QuickView or Wordpad, which also display Microsoft Word documents.

If you have Microsoft Office installed on your system, you can configure PPTView as a helper application for viewing online PowerPoint presentations (admittedly a rare thing). The Win95 version of Office includes Microsoft Imager, a graphics viewer and manipulation program that can handle seven different image file types.

All these programs are discussed in more detail in the appropriate chapters in this section. The point is, you may not have to look any further than your own system for the Netscape helper applications you need.

Freeware and Shareware Solutions

You should also be prepared to mine the Web itself for helper applications. There are literally thousands of freeware and shareware programs out there, free for the downloading. The chapters in this section discuss dozens of freeware and shareware programs that you can use as Netscape helper applications.

N O T E What's the difference between freeware and shareware? Freeware is just that: free. You can download it and use it forever without ever paying anyone a dime. Shareware, on the other hand, is software you can try for free, but if you continue to use it, you're expected to pay the author for the privilege. If you use it past the trial period stated in the program's license agreement, you are effectively stealing the program, just as if you had shoplifted it from a store shelf. Fortunately, most shareware license fees are so reasonable that they won't put much of a strain on your pocketbook. ▪

So where do you go to get freely distributed helper applications?

First of all, check out the CD included with this book. It includes most of the helper applications discussed in this section. The odds are good that you won't have to go any further to get all the helper applications you need.

You might also want to check out the helpful advice that Netscape offers on its own Web site. While you're connected to the Web, choose Help, Release Notes from the Netscape menu and you'll find information on some of the most popular Netscape helper applications, as well as directions on how to download them.

Here are some other software archive sites to try on the World Wide Web:

▶ **See** "What's on the CD-ROM," **p. 799**

- ▪ **http://vsl.cnet.com**—The Virtual Software Library
- ▪ **http://pcwin.com**—Randy Burgess's Windows 95 Resource Center
- ▪ **http://www.pcworld.com/win95/shareware**—PC World Online
- ▪ **http://www.netex.net/w95/windows95**—Unofficial Windows 95 Software Archive

- **http://www.csusm.edu/cwis/winworld/winworld.html**—CSUSM Software Archive
- **http://www.mcp.com/que/software**—Que Publishing's Software Library

For additional information on how to download files from the Web, see chapter 2, "Moving Around the Web." For more about finding files, see chapter 3, "Finding Information on the Web."

Many of the files you download from the Web will be compressed. To find out how to decompress the files you download, see chapter 17, "Using Compressed/Encoded Files."

CAUTION

Watch out for files you download that have an .EXE file name extension. Most are self-extracting archives, not usable executable files.

Commercial Programs

Of course, you could actually spend some money and buy programs to use as helper applications. If you're a real control freak, you might be considering using PhotoShop, PhotoStyler, PhotoFinish, or some other "name brand" commercial graphics, sound, or video program as a Netscape helper application.

But you should be aware that most of the programs you can buy for multimedia use are huge and eat up a lot of system resources. For most people, it would certainly be overkill to buy anything like the programs mentioned above just to use as Netscape helper applications.

But if you can find a small, elegant commercial program that you really like, there is certainly no reason why you can't buy it and configure it as a Netscape helper. If you're inclined to go this way, I advise you to read the reviews in popular computer magazines for guidance on which ones might be right for you. But try to steer clear of the huge "professional" packages. Odds are that they would just get in the way of browsing the Web.

Configure Now or Later, or Not at All

If you want, you can try to anticipate your needs and find and configure helper applications for all the file types you think you're likely to encounter in the future. Or you can just wait for Netscape to tell you that you need a helper application.

As you may have noticed when we talked about MIME types, the scrolling list of file types that Netscape maintains under the Action heading also tells you what it will do when it encounters each of them (refer to fig. 10.6). If it handles the file internally, this entry says Browser. If it has been configured to launch a helper application, it lists the name of the application. Most entries are simply labeled Ask User.

If you try to display a file that you haven't configured a helper application for (one that lists Ask User as its Action), Netscape displays the Unknown File Type alert shown in figure 10.13.

FIG. 10.13
The Unknown File Type
alert lets you configure
a helper application on
the fly.

If you want, you can simply back out at this point by choosing Cancel, which returns you to the Netscape main window without viewing the file. You can also choose Save File to load the problem file into your favorite application later. But if you select Pick App, Netscape jumps directly to the Helper Application configuration dialog box shown in figure 10.14, just as though you'd selected it from the menu.

FIG. 10.14
You'll be able to browse
for a helper application
if you choose the Pick
App button.

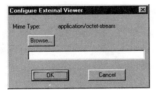

 TIP Advanced users may want to take a look at Netscape's helper application configuration settings in the Windows 95 Registry. You can do so by running RegEdit (in the Windows directory) and viewing HKEY_CURRENT_USER/Software/Netscape Navigator/Viewers.

Checking Your Work—The WWW Viewer Test Page

How can you make sure your helper applications are configured properly? Test 'em out!

The easiest way to test a Netscape helper application is to select File, Open File from the Netscape menu and try to open a file of the type you want to test from your system. If Netscape launches the right helper application and the file is displayed properly, you're in business.

If you don't have a file of the type you want to check, or if you simply prefer to test your helper application "under fire" on the Web, go to the Lawrence Livermore Labs Web Viewer Test Page at **http://www-dsed.llnl.gov/documents/WWWtest.html**. This page presents a menu of buttons that send you dozens of different files to exercise just about any helper application you can think of (see fig. 10.15).

FIG. 10.15

You can test your helper application configuration by pointing Netscape to the Lawrence Livermore Labs Web Viewer Test Page.

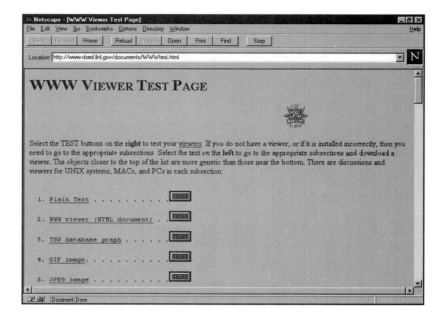

Netscape Helper Applications for UNIX

We'll cover how to set up helper applications for Windows 95 and Windows 3.1 in the following chapters. But if you're a UNIX user, read on for information on how to set up helper applications for the UNIX version of Netscape.

There's a rich set of UNIX programs that can be set up as Netscape Helper applications. Some of them are standard operating system utilities, while others are freely available on the Internet for retrieval and installation. This chapter can only cover a few of them: helper applications for viewing graphics files, displaying PostScript files, and playing audio and video files.

Setting Up a Helper Application for Viewing Graphics Files

We cover the steps of setting up helper applications in the next few paragraphs. As we set up a graphical image viewer, you'll learn important information about helper applications in general. While Netscape can handle several kinds of graphical image files, you'll encounter others; and you'll want a helper application to handle them. John Cristy's package ImageMagick contains just such an image viewer, called display.

N O T E   The ImageMagick source code is included on the CD-ROM. This package contains not only display, but also several other valuable programs for manipulating images. For more information about ImageMagick, see **http://www.wizards. dupont.com/cristy/ImageMagick.html**. Like most available UNIX software, this package is distributed in source code form, and must be compiled before you can run it on your system. It will build on virtually all UNIX systems. The following paragraphs assume you've compiled and installed the ImageMagick package on your system. ▇

Here are the steps to setting up ImageMagick's display as a Netscape helper application for viewing graphics files. As you follow them, you learn important information about helper applications in general that will be useful later.

In Netscape, pull down the Options menu and select General, and then click Helpers. Figure 10.16 shows the Helper Applications dialog box.

FIG. 10.16
The Netscape Helper Applications dialog box.

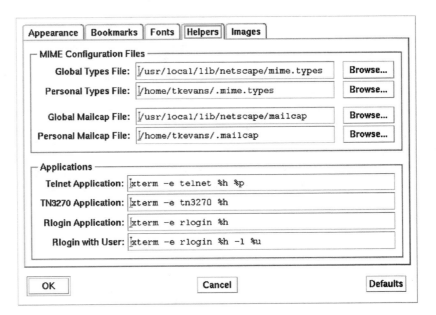

UNIX Netscape does not have the same graphical interface for setting up helper applications as do the Windows and Mac versions. In fact, this dialog box doesn't do very much of anything, but it does contain some very important information about MIME.

UNIX Netscape and MIME   Though we covered MIME basics earlier in this chapter, UNIX Netscape deals with MIME types a bit differently. While UNIX Netscape has built-in knowledge of MIME, and uses it to deal with the data it receives from a Web server, up to four MIME configuration files may be consulted by Netscape with each Web transaction. These four files, all of which need not exist on your system, are grouped into Global and Personal categories. Within these categories, Netscape uses the Types file and the Mailcap file.

In Netscape, MIME is used for linking file name extensions to types of files and, hence, from there to helper applications. Netscape already knows about the standard file name extensions and associates each with a MIME data type/subtype. For example, the file name extension XWD is associated with image files produced by the xwd (X Window Dump) program. (See your system manual for information about XWD.) Here's the entry from the Types file for XWD files:

```
image/xwd      xwd
```

As you can see, the MIME data type/subtype (on the left) is associated with the XWD file name extension, on the right. You can see the complete list of MIME data types/subtypes and associated file name extensions in the Global Types file.

Using MIME to Enable Netscape Helper Applications

You use MIME information—the association between the MIME data type/subtype and the file name extension—to set up your helper applications. For example, to enable Netscape to view graphics files with the display program as a helper application:

- Check the Global Mailcap File to see if display (or some other program) has already been set up as a helper application for images. You can use the UNIX more or pg commands to view this file on your screen. Look for a line that begins with the MIME type/subtype "image/*;". If you find it, there should be something to the right of the semicolon; if it says display %s, you're already set up to view graphics with display. You may find another image viewer (a common one is xv) defined.

- If you didn't find display in the Global Mailcap File, or the file doesn't exist, set up display in your Personal Mailcap File. Usually called .mailcap (note the leading period in the file name), this file can be created with any text editor, such as vi, emacs, or Sun's textedit editor. (As shown in the Netscape Helper Applications dialog box, this file is normally in your Home Directory.) Add the following line, making sure to include the semicolon:

```
image/*; display %s
```

Note that the asterisk here is a wild card, meaning that you want to use display as your helper application for all images in Netscape.

The Global Mailcap File sets helper applications for all users on a UNIX system, which means that you or your system administrator can set up common helper applications (such as display) and make them available to everyone on the system. This minimizes the need for users to set up and maintain Personal Mailcap Files. If both files exist, your Personal Mailcap File overrides any conflicts with the Global File. For example, if you found an xv entry in the Global Mailcap file, putting the display entry in your .mailcap overrides the system default of using xv for you, but not for anyone else on the system.

Setting Up a Helper Application for PostScript Files

PostScript is a widely used graphic format. Defined as a device-independent standard for representing the printed page, you may think of PostScript in the context of printers. It's often useful, however, to view PostScript documents on-screen, so having a PostScript viewer as a Netscape helper application is important. Some UNIX systems include PostScript viewers as a standard part of the system. These include Sun's Solaris 2.x imagetool, SunOS 4.1.x pageview, and IBM's showps. You may also have the freeware package ghostscript installed on your system. To enable imagetool as a Netscape helper application for viewing PostScript files, add the following entry to either the Global or your Personal Mailcap File:

```
application/postscript;     imagetool %s
```

The Global or Personal Types file should contain a mapping of the MIME application/post-script data type/subtype to the file name extension .PS. You may also want to add the common PostScript file name extensions .EPS and .AI.

Configuring Netscape for Sound   As with images and PostScript, you use MIME information to configure a Netscape helper application to play sound files. Here are the steps; we'll use Sun's audiotool in this example. (You can substitute your system's audio player program—SGI's sfplay, for example—for audiotool.)

Check the Global and Personal Types files for an audio/basic entry. It should look something like this, with the MIME type/subtype and file name extension information:

```
audio/basic     au snd
```

As you'll recall, the Types file maps MIME data types/subtypes with file name extensions; in this case audio/basic is mapped to the file name extensions .AU or .SND. Add the entry to the Types file, if necessary.

Next, check the Global and Personal Mailcap files for an audio/basic MIME types/subtype entry, and add it, if necessary. It should look like this:

```
audio/basic;     /usr/openwin/bin/audiotool
```

Part
III

Ch
10

Other Audio Types

So far, the discussion of audio has dealt only with the basic audio file format defined by Sun Microsystems and supported on other UNIX systems. You'll find, however, other kinds of audio files on the Web. One of the most common is the PC WAV format (audiotool doesn't support this audio format). To support this and other audio formats, you need to install another audio helper application. A no-cost audio player that works on most UNIX systems is AudioFile, which is on the CD-ROM in the back of this book. Alternatively, you can set up a custom Netscape helper application that uses an audio file conversion utility to convert the foreign audio format on-the-fly and pass it off to audiotool. SGI's sfconvert and Sun's audioconvert are two examples.

Netscape Helper Applications for Macintosh

The Helpers screen of the General Preferences window lets you choose which applications installed on your Macintosh are designated as helper applications for Netscape. Helper applications are used to process file types that Netscape is not designed to handle by itself. One example is Aladdin Software's StuffIt Expander. If Netscape is configured to pass received StuffIt files to StuffIt Expander, StuffIt Expander will launch, unstuff the .SIT file, expand the unpacked file further (if the unstuffed file is compressed in one of the several formats StuffIt Expander can process) until done, then close itself. Other helper applications are used to process sound or video that Netscape itself doesn't process natively.

Helper applications are discussed in detail in chapters 9 through 17 of this book. However, Netscape has a Web page that presents links to many of the most popular helper applications for Netscape for the Macintosh at

http://home.netscape.com/assist/helper_apps/ machelpers.html.

Configuring Netscape for Full-Motion Video

As you might guess from the last few pages, configuring a Netscape helper application for viewing video files involves adding the correct MIME information to the Types and Mailcap files. Most UNIX systems, however, don't yet have video player software, so you'll need a helper application for this too. The most widely used MPEG (Motion Picture Experts Group, a widely used video data format) viewer for UNIX is called mpeg_play, and is available on this book's CD-ROM, where you'll find documentation on how to compile and install it, as well as the source code.

After you've installed mpeg_play in a directory that's accessible to you, you're ready to configure it as a Netscape helper application. First, check the Global Types file for a video entry, and add one if necessary. It should look like this:

```
video/mpeg          mpeg mpg mpe
```

Next, look for an MPEG viewer set up in the Global Mailcap file. It should look like this:

```
video/mpeg;         mpeg_play %s
```

If there's no entry, you or your system administrator can add one to the Global Mailcap file so everyone can access it, or you can add one to your Personal Mailcap file.

Other Kinds of Video

If you've ever used a Macintosh, you probably know about QuickTime videos. mpeg_play can't handle QuickTime or other video types. A good all-purpose video player for UNIX systems that handles QuickTime is Mark Podlipec's xanim, which is on the CD-ROM. You can set up xanim as your video helper application in the same way you do with mpeg_play. Because it can play several kinds of video, you may want to use xanim for all video, including MPEG video, and not use mpeg_play at all. To do this, add a wild card video entry to the Global Mailcap file.

```
video/*;           xanim %s
```

Check your Global Types file for the MIME type/subtype information for the other video types:

```
video/quicktime    qt mov
```

Configuring Helper Applications on UNIX

In prior releases of Netscape, the configuration of helper applications was very minimal and simplistic. All the MIME types for every file had to be stored in a particular file. There was little documentation or explanation on what was supposed to be in the file, and how to configure it. This also made it impossible for plug-in support, as was available on Windows 95 and Macintosh.

That has all changed dramatically with Atlas on the various UNIX platforms. Now, when you select Options, General Preferences, and choose the Helpers tab, you get a new dialog box (see fig. 10.17). This dialog box strongly resembles the helper configuration dialog box from Windows 95. The scrollable list shows you two important aspects of MIME types. The left-hand side shows you a description of the MIME type in plain English. The right-hand side of the list shows you the action that should be taken.

FIG. 10.17
Configuring helper applications for Netscape on UNIX is greatly improved.

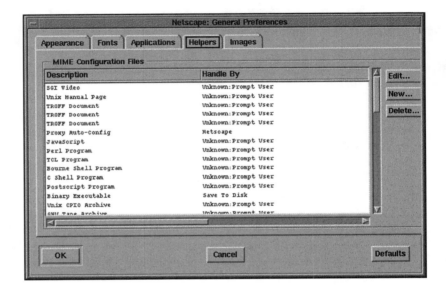

Part
III

Ch
10

Typically, the action to be performed on a particular file type will be "Save To Disk," "Prompt User," "Netscape" or the name of the program to execute. You can edit, delete, or add helper applications and file extensions with the buttons on the right of the dialog box. The Edit and Delete buttons will only work when you've selected an entry from the list.

When creating a new file type you'll be presented with another new dialog box (see fig. 10.18). Simply type in a plain English description of the MIME type you're adding in the Description text field. The actual MIME type and sub-type should be typed into the Type field, while the Suffix field indicates the file extension.

Finally, you can choose the action you want performed on that particular file type. The Navigator option will have Netscape load the file into the browser window. When you enable the Application option, you can specify which program to run by typing in its name in the text field. If you're not sure where the program resides, simply click the Browse button. If you're unsure what to do with a particular file type simply choose either the "Save to Disk" option, or the "Prompt User" option.

FIG. 10.18
Just specify the
necessary information
on the file type you want
to add.

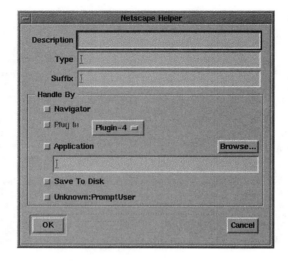

> **N O T E**   You cannot define a helper application to be a plug-in just by choosing the Plug-in option,
> and specifying the program. Plug-ins must be installed separately, and they will automati-
> cally configure Netscape themselves. ▪

## CHAPTER 11

CoolTalk

How would you like to have free long-distance telephone service for life? "Wow! Is this a prize in the lottery," you ask? Not exactly. All you need is Internet access and a sound card to be able to call anyone, anywhere, anytime, for free.

Of course, there are a few catches. The people you call also have to have Internet access and a sound card. They need to be connected to the Internet when you try to call. They have to be running the same Internet telephony software you are. It's not as easy as just picking up a phone and dialing. (Though if you think about it, the requirements are similar; you can't call someone on the phone if they're not connected to the phone system or don't own a telephone.) If you have a cousin in France, a fiancé in Alaska, or you just like to talk to your Mom back home in Biloxi for a couple of hours every night, these shortcomings may not mean much compared to the savings you'll realize.

In this chapter you'll discover:

- Whether or not it's realistic to use the Internet for voice communications
- The hardware requirements for setting up your computer to talk on the Internet
- How to get and configure CoolTalk, which is the official, Netscape-sanctioned program you need to use the Internet for phone conversations
- Some alternatives to CoolTalk ■

Using the Internet for Phone Calls

The whole purpose of the Internet is to transfer data from one computer to another. The Net is blithely unaware of what that data represents. Text, graphics, audio—all are the same to the Net. So holding a phone conversation over the Internet is mostly a problem of turning your voice into digital data at one end and turning that data back into audio at the other. In between, it's just data, and the Internet can transfer that just fine no matter what it represents.

System Requirements

If your computer is capable of browsing the Web, the odds are excellent that you already have the one additional component that you need to be able to digitize your voice to transmit, and then to convert the data you receive from the Net back into voice—a sound card.

Of course, besides a sound card you'll need a dialup or direct connection to the Internet. You'll also have to have:

- At least a 50 MHz CPU
- 12-16 MB of RAM
- A set of self-amplified speakers
- A microphone, preferably with an on/off switch
- A relatively fast connection to the Internet

> **CAUTION**
>
> Real-time voice communication on the Internet is a real system hog. It uses a lot of CPU time, hardware resources, and RAM. If you're going to be talking on the Internet, it's best if you refrain from running any other tasks. Otherwise, your audio feed is likely to "break up."

N O T E   Contrary to popular belief, you don't have to have a direct TCP/IP connection to the Internet to use CoolTalk. You can talk just fine over a SLIP or PPP dial-up connection via a 14.4 or 28.8 Kbps (kilobits per second) modem. Voice communications doesn't use nearly the bandwidth that graphics and video do, so chatting over the Internet on a dialup connection is not only realistic, but under ideal conditions is indistinguishable from communicating over a direct connection. ■

Your Sound Card

All sound cards can convert digital data to audible audio, and most can also digitize audio in real-time from a microphone input. Almost any sound card that can do both can be used with CoolTalk.

A 16-bit stereo sound card is best; though an 8-bit card may work, a 16-bit card is more likely to give you trouble-free compatibility. Creative Labs' Sound Blaster 16 is the industry standard; if you have a Sound Blaster card or compatible hooked up to a microphone and a set of speakers or headphones, you're all set for holding conversations on the Internet with CoolTalk.

> **CAUTION**
>
> Windows '95 multitasking doesn't mean you can use two programs that use the sound card at the same time. For example, you can't play MIDI music files while chatting on the Internet.

Most sound cards operate in *half duplex* mode; that is, you can record audio or play audio, but you can't do both simultaneously. This means that your Internet conversations will be limited to a one-way-at-a-time mode. Most people have experienced this type of conversation when using a CB radio or speakerphone; while one person is talking, the other listens. Participants in a conversation must take turns.

There are a few sound cards on the market that support *full duplex* mode; that is, they can record and play sound simultaneously. With such cards, CoolTalk supports full telephone-style two-way conversations. Unfortunately, *full duplex* sound cards are relatively rare and expensive. Some that are currently on the market are the Gravis UltraSound Max, the ASB 16 Audio System, and the Spectrum Office F/X (which is an all-in-one fax, modem, and sound card). As DSP (Digital Sound Processor) chip technology becomes more prevalent in the PC marketplace, we're bound to see more, less expensive *full duplex* sound cards.

Part

III

Ch

11

You can easily test your sound card to see if it supports *full duplex* operation by using Sound Recorder, an application included with all versions of Windows. Here's how:

1. Open a copy of Sound Recorder, which is located in your Windows directory. Then load in a .wav file using File, Open.
2. Open a second copy of Sound Recorder, and press the record button on the toolbar of this second copy.
3. Now press the play button on the toolbar of the first copy of Sound Recorder, the one that you loaded the .wav file into in step one.
4. If you get the warning dialog box shown in figure 11.1, you've got a half duplex sound card, like most of us. Sorry. However, if the .wav file plays okay, you're one of the lucky ones—your card is working in full duplex mode!

> **CAUTION**
>
> A few Internet telephony packages purport to provide full duplex operation with a half duplex sound card. This requires the installation of special software drivers, and can potentially result in compatibility problems with other programs that use your sound card. It's probably best to settle for half duplex operation in most cases rather than trying to "push" your sound card to do something it's not intended to do.

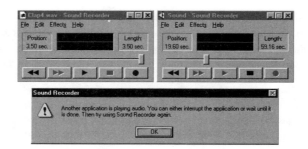

FIG. 11.1
Run two copies of
Windows Sound
Recorder to test whether
you have a full duplex
audio card. If you see
this warning dialog, your
card is only half duplex.

What CoolTalk Is

CoolTalk is a stand-alone program that lets you talk and listen to others over the Internet. Note that it is a totally independent program—it doesn't require Netscape to run. You can run it all by itself. However, when you install Netscape 3.0, CoolTalk is also installed, and is configured as a helper application for Netscape.

When you run CoolTalk—or when Netscape invokes CoolTalk as a helper application—it connects to another user on the Internet and lets you hold a conversation. It uses your computer's sound card and a microphone to digitize your speech, which is then sent via your Internet connection to the party you're talking to. At her computer, the data that represents your spoken words is translated back into sound using her sound card.

CoolTalk also has some impressive additional features. There is an Answering Machine, which can take CoolTalk messages for you when you're connected to the Internet but unable to answer. The Chat Tool option lets you communicate with another CoolTalk user by typing in text. The White Board is probably CoolTalk's coolest option—it lets you load up graphics (even snapshots of your work screens) and share them over the Net. Better yet, you can both mark up the screen and see the comments you both make. This sort of functionality is called "collaborative software" by groupware developers, and it's currently one of the hottest areas of software development.

Installing CoolTalk

CoolTalk comes with Netscape Navigator 3.0, and is included as part of the Netscape distribution file. When you run the Netscape installation program, CoolTalk is automatically installed as well.

N O T E   If you didn't get CoolTalk with your copy of Navigator—if, for example, you downloaded a "minimal distribution" version of Navigator without CoolTalk—you can download an installation file containing only CoolTalk from **http://home.netscape.com/comprod/products/ navigator/cooltalk/download_cooltalk.html**. ■

Setting CoolTalk Options

During the CoolTalk installation process, you will be asked if you want to install the CoolTalk Watchdog in your system StartUp directory. This Watchdog program runs in the background, waiting for someone to try to call you using CoolTalk. If it detects an incoming call and CoolTalk is not running, it automatically launches CoolTalk so you can receive your call.

Installing the Watchdog only makes sense if you are always (or almost always) connected to the Internet while not running Netscape. If this doesn't describe you, the Watchdog just senselessly uses up system resources. However, if you are connected to the Internet full-time, the Watchdog makes sure that you'll never miss a CoolTalk call. If you expect to be using CoolTalk a good portion of the time, it makes sense to let the setup program put a copy in your StartUp directory.

When the Watchdog is active, its icon will appear in the TaskBar Status Tray. To suspend the Watchdog, double-click on its icon. When it's suspended, a red stop sign will appear over its icon.

If you change your mind later, you can manually delete or move the file Wdog.exe from the Windows\Start Menu\Programs\StartUp directory. (You can likewise add the Watchdog at any time by moving or copying Wdog.exe from Program Files\Netscape\Navigator\Cooltalk to the StartUp directory.)

Once CoolTalk is installed, you'll want to run it and select Help, Setup Wizard from the CoolTalk menu. This brings up the CoolTalk Setup Wizard (see fig. 11.2)

Part

III

Ch

11

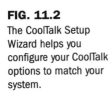

FIG. 11.2
The CoolTalk Setup Wizard helps you configure your CoolTalk options to match your system.

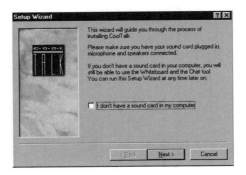

The Setup Wizard first gives you a chance to select a checkbox to tell it that you don't have a sound card, in which case you can't use CoolTalk anyway, so the setup program will abort, leaving the default settings in place.

Assuming you do have a sound card, selecting the Next button takes you to a screen which asks you to indicate whether you have a 9600, 14,400, or 28,800 baud modem. A press of the Next button then auto-detects the type of sound card you have installed, and begins a series of tests of your sound card at different playback and sampling rates. (You'll need to have a microphone connected to your sound card for these tests.)

When done with the audio tests, the Setup Wizard will check your overall system performance.

Provided your system passed all these tests, the Setup Wizard will configure CoolTalk for proper operation depending on how you answered the test questions.

When you're done with the Setup Wizard, you'll want to select Conference, Options from the CoolTalk menu. This lets you set your Conference, Answering Machine, Audio, and Business Card settings.

The Conference options tab lets you set up phonebook behavior, dialup speed, and call answering options (see fig. 11.3).

FIG. 11.3

The conference option dialog controls server settings, connection speed, and call answering setup.

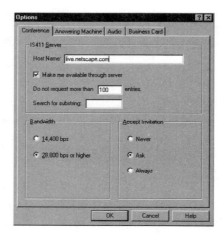

The IS411 area under the Conference tab lets you set options for the "411" or "phonebook" server for CoolTalk. The Host name field should contain the URL **live.netscape.com**. This is the default IS411 phonebook server for CoolTalk, and is hosted at Netscape Communications Corporation. Other servers may be made available, and you can select one of them instead if you know the address. If the "Make me available through server" checkbox is selected, when you run CoolTalk, you'll be entered automatically into the Host server listing so that others may call you. If you don't want to be bothered, leave this box unchecked and you won't be listed. Every time you run CoolTalk, the status field near the bottom of the CoolTalk window tells you that it's resolving your address. People with dialup connections to the Internet generally get a different IP address assigned to them each time they dial in. CoolTalk resolves this address for the current session and, if the "Make me available…" box is checked, registers your currently active IP address with the Host name listed in the dialog. This way, people can call you using CoolTalk whenever you come online, no matter what your IP address is for the current session. This is a very clever setup, and neatly bypasses the problem of floating IP addresses for dialup connections.

The "Do not request more than [n] entries" field lets you control the number of IS4111 listings you view. The "Search for substring" field limits the listings to those which contain only the substring you specify.

The Bandwidth box contains just two radio buttons, which let you select either a 14.4 or 28.8 Kbps (kilobits per second) connection. Make sure this selection matches your modem speed.

The Accept Invitation buttons let you choose to "Never" accept an invitation to chat, or to "Ask" or "Always" accept.

Click on the Answering Machine tab to set up your answering machine, which can record messages for you whenever you're connected to the Internet, but unable to take calls personally (see fig. 11.4).

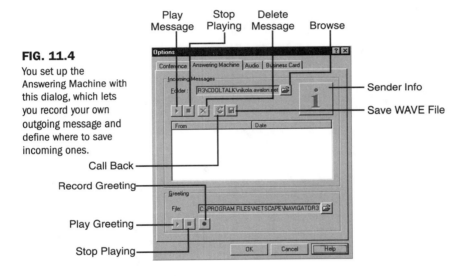

FIG. 11.4

You set up the Answering Machine with this dialog, which lets you record your own outgoing message and define where to save incoming ones.

Part

III

Ch

11

 T I P You'll have to have either CoolTalk or the Watchdog program running in order for your Answering Machine to work properly.

The Incoming Messages field lets you browse to set a Folder which will contain your incoming messages. Below the Folder field is a set of message playback buttons. The large window in the middle of the dialog displays your list of incoming messages. The buttons let you play, stop playing, delete, call back, or save a WAVE file of any messages on your machine. Near the bottom of the dialog are buttons to play, stop, and record your outgoing greeting; there is also a browse button for selecting the filename under which your greeting will be saved to a disk.

Selecting the Audio tab brings up a dialog for setting your sound card options. While it's unlikely you'll have more than one Recording Device or Playback Device set up under Windows, this dialog will let you choose which to use if you do. The Sliding control bars let you adjust Recording Sensitivity and Playback Amplification. Both can also be adjusted in the main CoolTalk window by using the up and down arrow buttons on the right end of the bar graph displays. Also in this dialog is the "Recording/Playback Autoswitch" checkbox. If checked, CoolTalk will automatically switch back and forth from transmitting to receiving audio, determined only by the setting of your Silence Level slider. If this box is checked, you can't manually select to transmit or receive.

The Business Card tab lets you input personal information, which can be displayed by you or your partner by selecting Conference, Participant Info from the CoolTalk menu during a conversation (see fig. 11.5).

FIG. 11.5
Sharing your personal information by filling out the Business Card fields makes you a real cool cat!

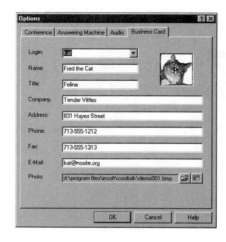

Using CoolTalk

The CoolTalk window is small and well-organized, with only a few easy-to-use buttons and tools (see fig. 11.6).

FIG. 11.6
The CoolTalk window is unobtrusive and uncluttered but it packs a lot of power in a small space.

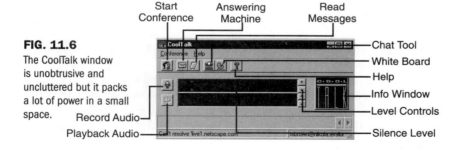

The Start Conference button is equivalent to the menu selection Conference, Start. It is, logically enough, the control you'll use to initiate conversations.

CoolTalk's Answering Machine can be set to answer and log messages when your computer is connected to the Internet but you're not available to answer calls. It's turned on or off using the Answering Machine button. The Read Messages button is used to retrieve messages that have been left on your Answering Machine.

The Chat Tool button brings up the text chat window, and the White Board button invokes the collaborative graphical white board tool. These handy tools augment CoolTalk's voice chat with real-time collaborative text and graphic tools.

The Help button—which corresponds to selecting Help, Help Topics from the CoolTalk menu—brings up CoolTalk's extensive help system.

The little microphone is, as you'd expect a push-to-talk button. You click on it when you want to talk, unless you've configured CoolTalk to work in automatic mode, where it decides when to automatically kick in the microphone. That's what the arrows on the bar graph are for—they set a "silence level" that determines when your mike kicks in if you're in automatic mode.

The speaker button is what you press to listen to the party you're conversing with, if you're not in automatic mode.

Up and down audio level control buttons on the right end of the bar graph displays let you set amplification for recording (top) and playback (bottom) sound levels. It's important to adjust these properly for each conversation, as you're likely to run into a wide variety of quality in your CoolTalk connections. I've had good quality hookups with people overseas who are connected with a 486 computer and a 14.4 dialup connection, and bad-to-the-point-of-unintelligible talks with folks hooked up with a T1 line and a Pentium 166. A lot of external factors can affect your connection, including the other person's CoolTalk settings. If you're both willing to play with these a bit, you can usually achieve a very good connection.

Finally, the box at the right center of the CoolTalk screen shows you the image of the person you're speaking to, if they've set it up in their business card settings.

Part

III

Ch

11

Calling With CoolTalk

You begin a CoolTalk chat session by calling someone up in one of two ways. Clicking on the Start Conference button (or selecting File, Start from the menu) brings up the Open Conference dialog shown in figure 11.7.

FIG. 11.7
The Open Conference dialog lets you call someone using your internal address book or an IS411 server.

From this dialog you can select your internal Address Book, which includes a list of people you've called before, as well as those you've added to the list manually. Picking a name from the list and choosing OK (or simply double-clicking on the name) will dial that person. If the person isn't on your list, you can simply type in their address manually.

From this dialog, you can also select an IS411 Directory. Picking a recipient from this list works in the same manner as the Address Book.

From either list, you can highlight a name and choose Add to Speed Dial to add the recipient to your speed dial bar near the bottom of the CoolTalk main window (see fig. 11.8).

FIG. 11.8

Speed dialer buttons (along the bottom of the CoolTalk window) give you instant access to frequently called addresses.

Speed dialer buttons

The second way to call someone makes use of the fact that CoolTalk is configured as a Netscape helper application. You use Netscape to connect to **http://live.netscape.com**, the home page for the IS411 Directory (see fig. 11.9).

Clicking on a link in this alphabetical listing of CoolTalk users will launch CoolTalk and attempt to link you to the listed user.

FIG. 11.9

The IS411 Directory page, hosted by Netscape, lists all currently active CoolTalk users who have made their presence known.

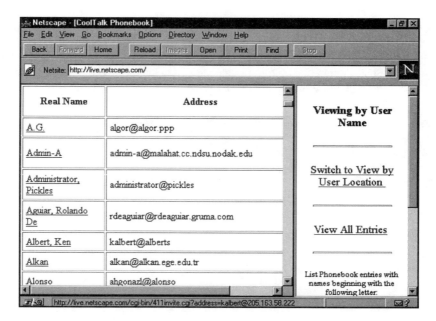

N O T E "Hey," you may be saying about now, "This is a bit of a fraud! CoolTalk doesn't seem to have much to do with Netscape at all!"

You're right. It doesn't. It's really just a stand-alone program, configured to work as a Netscape helper application. Perhaps a future version of CoolTalk will be more integrated into Netscape (as a plug-in, for example), but for the time being, Netscape's Internet telephony application of choice is, indeed, a totally separate program. ■

The CoolTalk Answering Machine

We've already covered many of the CoolTalk Answering Machine's features, but it might help to go through the process of using it step-by-step, since its features are really located in different places in CoolTalk.

First, you have to determine if you can realistically use the CoolTalk Answering Machine. It's important to understand that this is not a *telephone* Answering Machine, but a CoolTalk message Answering Machine. That is, it takes CoolTalk calls for you when you're not available to answer them yourself. To be able to do this, you must be connected to the Internet whenever you want it to answer for you. If you're paying for a dialup connection by the minute, obviously the CoolTalk Answering Machine is not for you.

But if you have unlimited access, either through a flat-fee dialup connection or a dedicated line, the CoolTalk Answering Machine can make sure you don't miss important CoolTalk calls.

Once you've decided to set it up, you need to select File, Options from the CoolTalk menu, then click on the Answering Machine tab in the dialog that pops up. Set up a directory to hold your incoming messages and record your outgoing message, as explained in a previous section, "Setting CoolTalk Options."

Back in the main CoolTalk window, click on the Answering Machine button to turn it on.

If you receive any messages while you're away from your computer, the Read Messages button will show you how many you received. Clicking on it will let you play back your messages, and you can choose to delete, save, or respond to them as you wish.

CoolTalk's Chat Tool

Collaboration is a hot word in groupware, intranet, and Internet application circles. All it means, of course, is "working together," and CoolTalk incorporates a couple of great tools for working together over the Internet—the Chat Tool and the White Board.

CoolTalk's Chat Tool is easy to bring up—you just press the Chat Tool button on the CoolTalk Window. Though the Chat Tool button looks like a little telephone, it actually brings up a text-based chat box (see fig. 11.10).

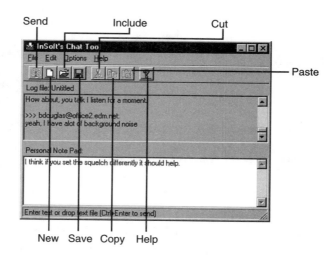

FIG. 11.10

The CoolTalk Chat Tool lets you type messages back and forth, or send text files.

You simply type your messages into the lower text box. You can send them by typing a Ctrl+E, clicking on the Send button, or selecting File, Post NotePad from the CoolTalk menu. These notes appear on your conversation partner's screen, as well as in the upper Log window of your Chat Tool window. Her messages appear on your screen too, of course. You can save a log file of your Chat session by selecting Save or Save As from the File menu, or clicking on the Save button. Clicking on the New button will clear the text windows and start a new log. Picking File, Include or clicking on the Include button brings up a file browser that lets you send along a text file (though unfortunately not binaries). There are buttons and menu selections for cut, copy, and paste, and the File menu includes Print Setup and Print options.

There is just one selection under the Options menu in the Chat Tool—this is "Pop Up On Receive." If checked, this option will automatically launch the Chat Tool when a text message is transmitted to you.

The Chat Tool is great for exchanging pre-written notes, meeting minutes, etc., and is a handy backup means of communication if you're having problems with voice transmissions.

CoolTalk's White Board

Clicking on the White Board button brings up CoolTalk's White Board, which at first seems to be simply an elementary drawing program (see fig. 11.11). However, a little experimentation reveals it to be an immensely powerful collaboration tool.

Of course, you can use the line, rectangle, circle, text, and freehand tools to draw simple illustrations that can be seen by your collaborator. But they can draw on the same workspace. This means you can work on the same image together, trading off one another's ideas. Not only that, but the menus reveal that there are actually two layers to the White Board—one for an image, and one for markups. Either can be changed independently of the other. You can load an image, mark it up, and delete just the markups or the entire white board. You can use the eraser on just markups, too, so you can change your markings any way you wish. At any time, either of you can load in a new image. Zoom controls and even an option to "float" the menu bar give you excellent control over your workspace.

FIG. 11.11
CoolTalk's White Board is a sophisticated collaboration tool with many surprising features.

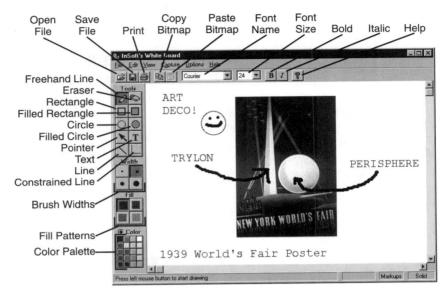

Collaboration software is the hot topic among "groupware" developers right now. But modest little CoolTalk gives you some fine collaboration tools already.

The CoolTalk White Board can load a variety of bitmapped images, including:

■ Windows Bitmap

■ Compuserve GIF

■ ZSoft Paintbrush PCX

■ TIFF Revision 5.0

■ JPEG

■ Sun Raster

■ Truevision TARGA

It can also snapshot your desktop, a window, or a dragged-out region of your screen. This means you can load up just about any software program while you're online (CAD, spreadsheet, etc.), capture an image of it with a single CoolTalk menu selection, and share it with your collaborator over the Internet. You can both talk about it, exchange text notes about it, mark it up, and change your markups as you work. Then you can quickly move on to the next image under consideration.

I strongly suggest you link up with another CoolTalk user and experiment with the collaboration features embodied in the CoolTalk Chat Tool and White Board. I guarantee you'll fall in love with them. It's a whole new way to communicate.

Part
III

Ch
11

> **N O T E**   CoolTalk comes with an extensive set of help files. To find answers to any CoolTalk questions not answered here, select <u>H</u>elp Topics from the CoolTalk <u>H</u>elp menu. You can also find out more at **http://www.netscape.com**. ▓

Other Internet Telephone Programs

Though CoolTalk enjoys the distinction of being distributed with Netscape (its parent company, Insoft, has even been acquired by Netscape Communications Corp.), it is not the only Internet phone software available. There are at least a half dozen such programs that can claim some measure of fame, from being the "first" to being the "latest." But which is the "best?" As always, that's a matter of personal opinion. CoolTalk certainly holds the edge in terms of distribution and acceptance, if only because of its position with Netscape. It also has features that most others lack, such as text chat and white board collaboration.

But this chapter would not be complete without presenting at least a quick overview of some of the other Internet phone applications.

> **N O T E**   At least one online company is doing its best to provide one-stop shopping for Internet telephony products. Direct Image's Web pages at **http://www.directimage.com/** provide links to most of the freely downloadable Net telephone applications, and you can buy commercial software and necessary hardware from them online. ▓

TIP   Most of the Internet voice applications discussed in this chapter can be downloaded from the Consummate Winsock Applications List site at **http://cwsapps.texas.net**.

Internet Voice Chat

Internet Voice Chat was the very first program to use the Internet for voice communications. Written by a student at the University of Pennsylvania named Richard Ahrens, IVC was fairly easy to use and simple to install. There was even a very primitive answering machine embedded in the program.

Ahrens was bought out by a Canadian company that planned to develop its own version of his software. When IVC was bought, Ahrens was prohibited from further developing or supporting the shareware version. Literally overnight, people who were using it could not get support or register their software. Since you can't use IVC until you register it, this made it impossible for new users to get set up with the program. Though it can still be downloaded from a few places on the Net, it's impossible for new users to run it since they can't register it.

The sudden disappearance of IVC annoyed many Internet users. Now in certain Usenet newsgroups, there are "crack codes" floating around to unlock the program for general use. The legality of this behavior is, to say the least, questionable. Besides, it has now been surpassed by many other programs.

It seems a sad ending for a pioneering program.

The Internet Phone

The Internet Phone by VocalTec was the first commercially marketed Internet telephony software package (see fig. 11.12). Internet Phone 4.0 includes voice messaging, simultaneous voice and data connections, document conferencing, text chat mode, Web integration, file transfer, and other capabilities. With a full duplex sound card, the Internet Phone allows full duplex voice conversations.

The Internet Phone can be downloaded from VocalTec's home page at **http://www.vocaltec.com/** for a free 30-day evaluation. Though it does not expire after a trial period, the trial version limits you to just 60 seconds of chatting before you get unceremoniously kicked out of a conversation. The license fee is $49.95. Internet Phone is also available in a boxed version on software store shelves.

FIG. 11.12

Internet Phone's ten "tiles" keep track of the last ten people you talked to. With one touch, you can automatically reconnect to them if they are online.

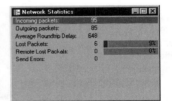
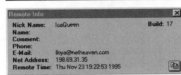

Digiphone

Another major Internet phone application is Obicom's Digiphone, distributed by Third Planet Publishing (see fig. 11.13). Where Internet Phone uses IRC (Internet Relay Chat) servers to provide a communications link, Digiphone uses direct point-to-point connections to other users who own Digiphone software.

FIG. 11.13

Using Digiphone, you contact a user by typing in their E-mail name in the "Remote Site" box. From this box, Digiphone resolves their IP address.

Digiphone is a commercial application without a downloadable demo. The Digiphone Web site at **http://www.planeteers.com/** tells you where you can buy it; the retail price for the Digiphone CD-ROM is $59.95. Digiphone Deluxe adds conference calling, call record and playback, call mute, speed dial, text/voice caller ID, and other features to Digiphone's basic features for $89.95.

Speak Freely

Speak Freely supports three forms of data compression as well as secure communications using data encryption with DES, IDEA, and/or a key file (see fig. 11.14). If the PGP (Pretty Good Protection) program is available on your system, it can be invoked automatically.

FIG. 11.14

Though it looks plain, Speak Freely packs a lot of power under the hood, including built-in data encryption and several compression options.

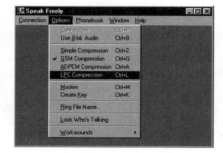

There are Windows and UNIX versions of Speak Freely, and users of the program for both platforms can find one another by communicating with a phone book server.

Multicasting is also implemented, which allows you to create multi-party discussion groups which users can subscribe to or drop at their discretion. For those without access to multicasting, a broadcast capability allows transmission of audio to multiple hosts (at least, it does on a fast local network).

Speak Freely was written by John Walker, the founder of Autodesk and the programmer who created AutoCAD. The latest version of Speak Freely can be downloaded from his home page at **http://www.fourmilab.ch/**.

WebTalk

WebTalk was the first Internet voice communications program to come from a major established player in the software industry: Quarterdeck, the publishers of the QMosaic WWW browser. A downloadable demo version of the program is available from Quarterdeck's home page at **http://www.quarterdeck.com/**. The commercial version includes two licenses (so you can speak to someone else right away) and the QMosaic browser.

WebPhone

If there were an award for "Flashiest User Interface Design for an Internet Voice Communications Program," WebPhone would win it hands-down. This program is configured to look and work like a sexy high-tech cellular telephone (see fig. 11.15).

FIG. 11.15
If looks were everything, WebPhone would have it all. The user help is just as classy looking, and is complete and genuinely helpful as well.

Because its user interface is based on a common everyday item, WebPhone is uncommonly easy to use. What you can't figure out right away is clearly explained in WebPhone's truly helpful (and downright fun to use) online help pages.

WebPhone (from the Internet Telephone Company—honest!) gives you a plethora of user options, plus four phone lines. It offers full duplex operation with the right sound card and half duplex for the rest of us.

ITEL's Directory Assistance Server connects you to other WebPhone users worldwide, and you also have a local phone book. Voice mail is promised for the final release.

You can try out the latest version of this program for free by downloading it from ITEL's home page at **http://www.itelco.com**. WebPhone's one-time "activation fee" is $49.95.

PowWow

"Unique" is an overused word, but PowWow really is a unique personal communications program for the Internet (see fig. 11.16). Besides voice chat (our topic at hand), PowWow lets you chat with up to seven people by keyboard (as well as voice), send and receive files, play .wav format sound files, and browse the World-Wide Web together as a group. Though its voice communications are delayed, not real-time, it is probably the most "sociable" Internet application you have ever seen.

Perhaps it should come as no surprise that this program is of Native American origin. It was created through the auspices of Tribal Voice, an organization run by Native Americans from many tribes which is dedicated to providing a Native American presence in the high-tech industry through free and low-cost computer software and services. All Tribal Voice products are "Native American in concept, architecture, and implementation."

FIG. 11.16
PowWow is optimized for friendly use by small groups.

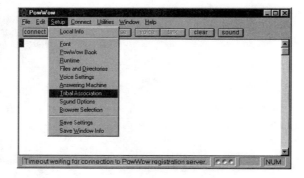

PowWow connects to users through their e-mail addresses. All that's necessary is that they be running PowWow, too.

PowWow is tremendously easy to personalize. You can send the URL of your home page to the people you're chatting with, and they can click the link to view it. You can set it up to send a JPEG image of yourself along to those who want to view it. You can chat with one or many, using voice or text. You can ask others to tag along with you as you browse the Internet as a group—a really neat feature that I haven't seen in any other software, anywhere.

There's even an Answering Machine mode where you can enter a message (up to 255 characters) that you would like displayed to those who try to connect to you when you have the Answering Machine mode turned on.

This program is well worth a look, if only to check out its truly unique features. The latest version can be downloaded from **http://www.tribal.com/**. This site also includes a comprehensive phone book of PowWow users.

TeleVox

It's a little tough to figure out just what's going on with TeleVox (see fig. 11.17). Originally called Cyberphone, this product was acquired by Voxware and upgraded with their high-compression technology. Then Netscape bought an "equity interest" in Voxware. Netscape is distributing CoolTalk as its official Internet phone software, but TeleVox is available for free download (totally free—no license fee) from the Voxware site at **http://www.voxware.com**.

Voxware is partnering with Netscape to provide some of the principal technology components of the LiveMedia standard, which will allow telephone products from multiple vendors to talk to one another. As this standard is published, they say they will provide their users with a free upgrade to the new technology.

So which Internet telephone software is the "official" Netscape standard: TeleVox or CoolTalk? The vote has to go to CoolTalk for now, since that's the program Netscape is bundling with

Navigator. But keep an eye out for TeleVox. Netscape could switch horses, or may decide that both have a place in their future plans.

FIG. 11.17
TeleVox is part of Netscape's Internet Telephony strategy. It's easy to use and the voice quality is excellent.

TS Intercom

Telescape's TS Intercom not only allows you to talk over the Internet, it also lets you view images and transfer files while you talk (see fig. 11.18).

FIG. 11.18
The TS Intercom program window displays two images, one specified by you, and one by the person you're chatting with.

Your "signature" image file can be in GIF, JPEG, or BMP format. While this picture can be of you (if you're of the type who wants everyone to know what you look like), it can also be an image of a project, design, or other topic under discussion.

Setting up a chat session is pretty easy. You can e-mail your intended recipient using a built-in link to your favorite mail program before starting up. TS Intercom maintains a phone book of people you've chatted with in the past.

Perhaps TS Intercom's most useful feature is its ability to send and receive files during a chat session. This has its fun aspects (sending picture and sound files, etc.) but it can also be very useful when you need to exchange documents, CAD files, or spreadsheets in a business environment.

The latest version of TS Intercom can be downloaded from **http://www.telescape.com/**.

The Impact of Internet Voice Communication

Speaking by way of the Internet is still in its infancy, but there is a tremendous amount of potential in such technology. Just as the telephone revolutionized conversation early in this century, Internet talk software could initiate another revolution in the way we converse. Voice communications on the Internet is still in its "hobbyist" stage, much as radio was in the Twenties. Though it is currently not practical to make initial contact with people in the business world with Internet phone utilities, that day may come sooner rather than later.

For personal communications, where price is a major factor in limiting long distance calls, Internet voice chat utilities are already unmatched in economy, if not usefulness. Long distance phone companies have indicated that they are not amused with this emerging technology, and have made their first challenges to it in the courts. Time will tell if they'll be able to shut down Internet telephony before it even gets completely off the ground.

The Future

In the near future, we'll see new data compression techniques that will let standard phone twisted pair and CATV coax lines handle phone, live video feeds, cable TV, and Internet WAN (Wide Area Network) connections and still be ready to accommodate lots more data. Fiber optic lines are also being laid in many areas, which will expand these capabilities a thousand-fold.

Provided it can survive the legal hurdles, the future of Internet telephony includes these possibilities:

- Conference calling in full duplex
- Call forwarding to other terminals
- Sending files to each other as you talk about something
- Remote talking, so you don't have to be sitting in front of your computer

Voice communications on the Internet has the potential to become as popular as the World Wide Web itself. It is a very possible that on business cards, people will someday have Internet voice contact information right under their e-mail address.

N O T E For more information on the topic of voice communications on the Internet, check out the Internet Phone FAQ (Frequently Asked Questions) file on Usenet. This file is posted on the 5th and 19th of each month to the Usenet newsgroups **alt.internet.services, alt.bbs.internet, alt.culture.internet, alt.winsock.voice, alt.winsock.ivc, comp.sys.mac.comm, comp.os.ms-windows.apps.comm, alt.answers, comp.answers**, and **news.answers**. the latest version is also available on the World Wide Web at **http://www.northcoast.com/~savetz/voice-faq.html**. ■

## CHAPTER 12

Power Pack 2.0

Netscape Navigator is a great program, but it doesn't do everything. You can't use it to view inline movies, or listen to live audio streams, or check download files for viruses. You can't chat with other people on the Internet in real-time, and there is no way to monitor Web sites so that you'll be notified when they change.

Of course, that whole introductory paragraph is really just a set-up, because you can do all of those things with Netscape. But you can't do them with Netscape alone. You need helper applications or plug-ins to add these features to Netscape.

Netscape Corporation, with an eye to enhancing your overall Netscape Web browsing experience, has bundled some of the best helper applications and plug-ins into a commercial product on CD-ROM that it calls the Netscape Power Pack.

In this chapter you'll find out:

- Which plug-ins and helper applications have been included in Power Pack 2.0

- How to obtain and install Power Pack 2.0—including information on how to download the free evaluation version

- How to use the four major add-ons included in Power Pack 2.0
- Where to go in this book for information on using the fifteen additional plug-ins included in the Power Pack 2.0 CD-ROM—and where to download them all for free! ■

What's in Power Pack 2.0?

Netscape's Power Pack 1.0 CD-ROM included five add-on applications for Netscape: Netscape SmartMarks 1.0, Netscape Chat 1.0.1, Adobe Acrobat Reader 2.1, Apple QuickTime 2.0.3, and RealAudio Player 1.0. Of these, SmartMarks, Chat, and RealAudio have survived into the 2.0 release. The Adobe Acrobat Reader and Apple QuickTime aren't on the new CD-ROM, but can be downloaded from the Web for free.

N O T E The Adobe Acrobat Amber plug-in for Netscape can be downloaded from the Adobe Web site at **http://www.adobe.com**.

Apple's QuickTime player is available at **http://www.apple.com**. (Note that this is only a system-level QuickTime player. To actually play QuickTime movies using Netscape, you'll also need to install a QuickTime player plug-in or helper application. See chapter 9 for information on where to download QuickTime player plug-ins.) ■

Where the Power Pack 1.0 CD-ROM included only these five Netscape add-ons, Power Pack 2.0 includes a "main suite" of four add-ons, plus a collection of fifteen other Netscape plug-ins. With a total of nineteen Netscape enhancements, you could say that there are nearly four times as many useful additions included in the 2.0 package.

The main suite of four major applications in Power Pack 2.0 includes:

- INSO CyberSpell for Netscape Mail
- Norton AntiVirus Internet Scanner
- SmartMarks 2.0
- Netscape Chat 2.0

Note that SmartMarks and Chat have both been upgraded to 2.0 versions in this release. CyberSpell and Norton AntiVirus round out the "top four."

"Where's RealAudio," you ask? Well, you could say that it has been demoted—it's listed as one of the fifteen plug-ins also included on the CD-ROM. These are:

- ASAP WebShow
- Astound Web Player
- CarbonCopy/Net
- EarthTime/Lite
- Envoy
- FIGleaf Inline Lite
- FormulaOne/NET

- Lightning Strike
- Netscape Live3D
- RealAudio
- Shockwave for Director
- VDOLive
- VRScout
- WIRL 3D Browser
- Word Viewer

Let's take a quick look at the fifteen plug-ins first.

The Power Pack 2.0 Plug-Ins

The plug-ins included on the Power Pack 2.0 CD-ROM cover the field as far as adding new capabilities to Netscape is concerned. This set has been carefully balanced to provide at least one plug-in for just about every type of content you can name.

What follows in this section is a summary of the plug-ins included in Power Pack 2.0, with Web sites where you can download each for free, if you don't have the CD-ROM.

▶ For more information on any of the plug-ins listed in this section, turn to chapter 9, "Netscape Browser Plug-Ins," **p. 219**.

The *ASAP WebShow* plug-in from Software Publishing Corporation lets you view business presentations inline in Web pages. You can view, download, and print any document created by SPC's ASAP WordPower report and presentation software package. Available for Windows 95 and Windows 3.1, you can download the latest version from **http://www.spco.com**.

Astound Web Player by Gold Disk plays back multimedia presentations created with Gold Disk's Astound and Studio M products. These documents can include sound, animation, graphics, video, and interactivity. The Astound Web Player features dynamic streaming; the next slide in a presentation is downloaded in the background while you view the current slide. This plug-in is available for Windows 95 and Windows 3.1 from **http://www.golddisk.com**.

Microcom's *CarbonCopy/Net* lets you access and control other PCs over the Internet. You can run applications, access files, and view or edit documents on a remote PC as though they were on the PC in front of you. A plug-in adaptation of Microcom's much-used stand-alone CarbonCopy program, Carbon Copy/Net is useful for collaboration, remote software demonstrations, remote support, and remote access to CD-ROMs and other data. Available for Windows 95 and Windows 3.1, you can download the CarbonCopy/Net plug-in from **http://www.microcom.com/**.

EarthTime/Lite (see fig. 12.1) by Starfish Software is a world time plug-in that displays the local time and date for eight geographic locations from your choice of more than 400 world capitals and commercial centers. Its animated worldwide map also indicates sunrise and sunset boundaries. A Windows 95 and Windows NT version is available at **http://www.starfishsoftware.com**.

Part
III

Ch
12

FIG. 12.1
EarthTime is a great example of a unique plug-in that is both useful and fun.

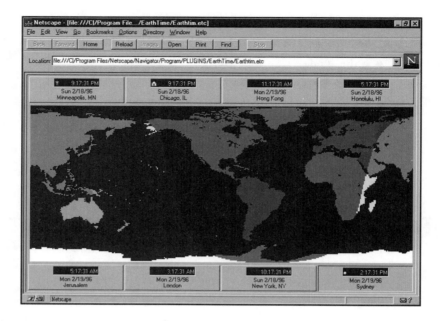

Tumbleweed Software's *Envoy* is the major competitor to Adobe's Acrobat. That Envoy is in the Power Pack 2.0 collection, while Acrobat (which was in Power Pack 1.0) is not, represents a major coup for Tumbleweed. The Envoy plug-in lets you view documents with well-defined and unchangeable fonts, graphics, and layouts. Tumbleweed Publishing Essentials is the commercial program you use for creating Envoy documents, and TW also offers an Envoy Software Developer's Kit for creating customized Envoy document viewers. Access **http://www.twcorp.com** to download versions for Windows 95, Windows NT, Windows 3.1, Macintosh, and PowerMac.

FIGleaf Inline Lite by Carberry Technology lets you view and zoom a wide variety of raster and vector graphics formats. FIGleaf Inline adds rotation of all images in 90, 180, 270, or 360 degrees, and viewing of multipage files. Scrollbars are available when zoomed in on an image, or when the image is too large to be displayed in the default window. Format support includes CGM (the first vector graphic MIME standard), GIF, JPEG, PNG, TIFF, CCITT GP4, BMP, WMF, EPSF, Sun Raster, RGB, and others. Download a Windows 95 and Windows NT version from **http://www.ct.ebt.com/**.

Visual Components' *FormulaOne/NET* lets you embed and manipulate live spreadsheets and charts on Web pages. This Excel-compatible spreadsheet's worksheets can include live charts, links to URLs, formatted text and numbers, calculations, and clickable buttons and controls. Though probably of limited use on the World Wide Web, this plug-in is sure to get a lot of use on corporate intranets. Download Formula One/NET for Windows 95, Windows NT, and Windows 3.1 from **http://www.visualcomp.com**.

Lightning Strike by InfinitOp lets you view image files compressed with the Lightning Strike optimized wavelet image codec. This alternative to JPEG is said to provide higher compression ratios, smaller image files, faster transmissions, and improved image quality. Available for

Windows 95, Windows NT, Windows 3.1, and Macintosh, you can download this plug-in from **http://www.infinop.com**.

It was probably a no-brainer for Netscape to include its own *Live3D* VRML viewer plug-in on the Power Pack 2.0 CD-ROM. This plug-in lets you fly through VRML worlds on the Web and run interactive, multiuser VRML applications written in Java. Netscape Live3D features 3D text, background images, texture animation, morphing, viewpoints, collision detection, gravity, and RealAudio streaming sound. You can download Live3D for Windows 95, Windows NT, and Windows 3.1 by following the links from Netscape's home page at **http://home.netscape.com**. It's interesting to note, however, that Live3D is not the only VRML plug-in in this collection. The third-party VR Scout and WIRL plug-ins listed below are also included.

Though a major player on the Power Pack 1.0 CD-ROM and, by comparison, relegated to "me too" status on the 2.0 collection, *RealAudio* by Progressive Networks—up to version 2.0 in this release—is an important Netscape plug-in. It lets you listen to both live and rebroadcast audio on the Internet. It works over 14.4 Kbps or faster connections, and is gaining wide acceptance on the Web. Available for Windows 95, Windows NT, Windows 3.1, and Macintosh, you can download RealAudio from **http://www.realaudio.com/**.

Shockwave for Director by Macromedia lets you play Macromedia Director animations and presentations. You can interact with Director presentations right in a Netscape Navigator window with animation, clickable buttons, links to URLs, digital video movies, sound, and more. Windows 95, Windows 3.1, and Macintosh versions reside at **http://www.macromedia.com**.

VDOLive from VDOnet is for viewing real-time Video for Windows movies over the Internet. VDOLive compresses video images, and the speed of your connection determines the frame delivery rate. With a 28.8 Kbps modem, VDOLive runs in real time at 10 to 15 frames per second. VDOLive is available for Windows 95, Windows NT, and Windows 3.1 at **http://www.vdolive.com/**.

VRScout VR Browser by Chaco Communications is one of three VRML viewers contained in this collection. Download VR Scout for Windows 95 and Windows NT from **http://www.chaco.com**.

The final VRML viewer on the CD-ROM is the *WIRL 3D Browser* by VREAM. This one adds support for object behaviors, logical cause-and-effect relationships, multimedia capabilities, world authoring, and links to Windows applications. Available for Windows 95 and Windows NT, you can download it from **http://www.vream.com**.

Word Viewer by Inso Corporation lets you embed Microsoft Word documents in Web pages. Another plug-in that's more likely to see intranet rather than Internet use, this plug-in can display both Microsoft Word 6.0 and Microsoft Word 7.0 documents. It also lets you copy and print Word documents with all original formatting intact. Download the Word Viewer plug-in for Windows 95, Windows NT, and Windows 3.1 from **http://www.inso.com**.

N O T E For the latest up-to-the-minute information on all Netscape plug-ins, check out the official Netscape list of available plug-ins at **http://home.netscape.com/comprod/ products/navigator/version_2.0/plugins/index.html** or the Plug-Ins Plaza site at **http:// www.browserwatch.com/plug-in.html**. ▪

Part
III

Ch
12

The Power Pack 2.0 Major Add-Ons

As we said before, the four major add-ons provided in the Power Pack 2.0 collection are INSO CyberSpell for Netscape Mail, Norton AntiVirus Internet Scanner, SmartMarks 2.0, and Netscape Chat 2.0. A free downloadable trial version of Power Pack 2.0 that includes only these four add-ons is available from **http://home.netscape.com/comprod/mirror/client_download.html**.

INSO's *CyberSpell* provides an integral spell checker for Netscape's Main and News composition windows. This will be a welcome addition for those to whom spelling comes hard. In addition, CyberSpell also provides some basic grammar and capitalization help. CyberSpell features a 146,000 word dictionary with U.S. and British spellings, as well as 13,000 specialized legal, business, and technical terms.

The *Norton AntiVirus Internet Scanner* is an online adaptation of Symantec Corporation's famed Norton AntiVirus stand-alone program. It protects your system from viruses that may come attached to downloaded files or e-mail messages. In addition, it can do a virus scan of your entire system, to make sure that you start with a clean slate.

Netscape Smartmarks 2.0 is an update of the Smartmarks program on the Power Pack 1.0 collection. It represents Netscape's own attempt to build a better bookmark program. It seamlessly integrates into Navigator's Bookmark menu, providing not only improved bookmark management, but the ability to track Web site changes. You can even automatically download and browse Web sites offline, saving connect time charges. There's also an integrated search tool for searching multiple online search engines with a single query. The whole works is powered by a third party engine from First Floor Software called "Smart Catalog" technology.

Netscape Chat 2.0 is also an in-house Netscape project, and is, again, an update of a program included on the first Power Pack CD-ROM. This package lets you participate in IRC, or Internet Relay Chat. IRC, a live online chat system, has been around for years, but the Netscape Chat program makes IRC easy to use. If you've made the move from CompuServe or America Online to a standard ISP (Internet Service Provider) and miss the real-time conferences, then IRC is for you. You can initiate one-on-one chats, participate in group conferences, or visit moderated "auditoriums." Netscape Chat includes a special function that lets you share interesting URLs with others in your chat room, launching Navigator automatically so they can browse the Web right along with you. Netscape is even hosting its own IRC server, so you can get online right away.

Installing Power Pack 2.0

You can purchase the Power Pack 2.0 CD-ROM online from the Netscape General Store or you can download the trial version which contains just the four main add-on programs. **http://www.netscape.com** is the place to go for either choice.

You'll need at least 8MB of RAM, a 14.4 Kbps or faster modem, and several megabytes of available hard disk space to install these applications—how much hard drive space depends on how many you choose to install. Let's just say that installing the whole works is another good reason to upgrade to that one gigabyte hard drive you've been wanting.

Power Pack 2.0 uses the familiar InstallShield Wizard under Windows 95 (see fig. 12.2). Installation on other platforms follows a similar process. You'll need at least version 2.0 of Netscape before you can use these programs—since this book covers Netscape 3.0, we'll assume that's the version of Netscape you own, so you probably won't have any problems.

FIG. 12.2

The Power Pack 2.0
InstallShield Wizard
steps you gently through
the installation process.

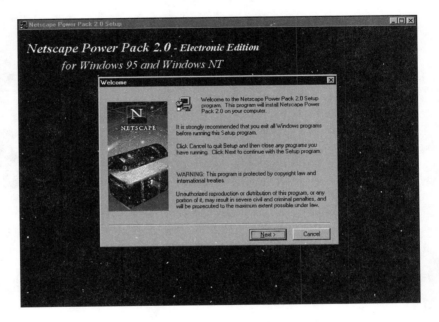

The first thing you'll see is a license window. Read the legalese carefully, then click on the "I Agree" button. If you don't agree to the stated terms and conditions, you won't be able to install any of the Power Pack 2.0 programs.

Once you've been agreeable, you'll see the screen shown in figure 12.3. Here you can choose which of the four applications to install. All are checked by default; uncheck any you don't want installed, then use the Next> button to move on to the installation process for each individual program.

Part

III

Ch

12

CAUTION

Heed the warning on the program selection window in figure 12.3! The InstallShield Wizard is really a shell program that ties together four *separate* and unrelated installation programs, one for each add-on. Some of these will ask you to reboot your computer so that their changes can take effect. *Do not do this!* Instead, always choose the "Do Not Reboot" selection. At the end of the string of installations, you'll be returned to the InstallShield Wizard where you can do a "once for all" reboot to activate the changes.

FIG. 12.3
You can install all of the Power Pack 2.0 applications or none by checking the appropriate boxes in this window.

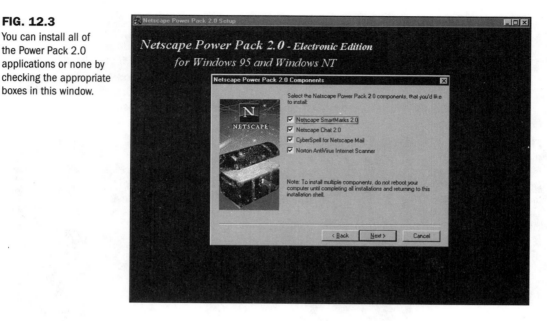

We'll only step through the installation for SmartMarks here. The installation process for each of these add-ons is similar enough that this should get you by. However, be aware that they do vary some in the details, so be careful to follow the on-screen instructions for each individual program.

The SmartMarks installer first asks you for some personal identification information. Enter your info and select Next> to proceed.

You're then asked to choose a Typical, Compact, or Custom installation (see fig. 12.4). The default choice is "Typical," and this is the choice you should make unless there is an overpowering reason to do otherwise. For example, if you're a power user you might want to go through the Custom setup; if you're installing on a laptop with limited resources, you might want to pick Compact.

Finally, you'll be asked to pick a directory in which to install SmartMarks. Again, pick the default unless you have an overpowering reason not to. If that directory doesn't exist, the installer will create it for you. Finally, you review your settings and the SmartMarks files are decompressed and put in their proper place.

> **CAUTION**
> Do not install SmartMarks 2.0 into your SmartMarks 1.0 directory, or you may suffer dire (though unspecified) consequences!

FIG. 12.4
The SmartMarks installer can customize your installation for you.

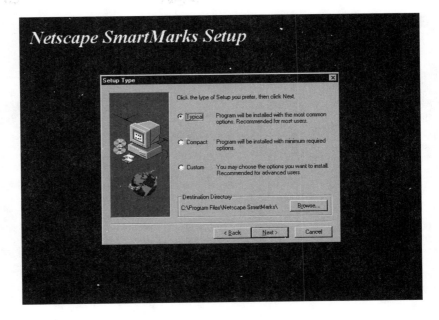

Once SmartMarks has been installed, the InstallShield Wizard moves on to install the other programs. At the end, you'll be asked to approve the restarting of your computer. Once rebooted, your add-ons are ready to use.

Netscape SmartMarks 2.0

Like Netscape's built-in bookmarks, Netscape SmartMarks 2.0 lets you organize bookmarks listing the URLs of interesting sites on the Web. However, SmarkMarks does a lot more for you. It offers more organizational choices, sure. But it also lets you automatically monitor your favorite sites for changes, alerting you when it's time to go back for new information. You can also tell SmartMarks to automatically download a copy of a Web site for you onto your hard drive for offline browsing. If you pay for your Web access, this can save you a lot of connect time charges (albeit at the cost of multi-megabytes of hard disk space). There is an integral search feature that queries many of the most popular online search engines—including Web Crawler, Yahoo, Lycos, InfoSeek, Excite, OpenText, DejaNews, and Alta Vista—with a single form. SmartMarks even intelligently imports your own set of personal bookmarks and integrates them seamlessly with its own humongous set of predefined bookmarks.

Much of the magic is accomplished using the licensed Smart Catalog technology from First Floor, Inc.

CAUTION

Note that if you are running Windows 3.x or Windows for Workgroups, you must use the 16-bit SmartMarks even if you have Win32s installed. If you are running Windows 95 or Windows NT, use the 32-bit SmartMarks. To run the 32-bit SmartMarks, you must have a 32-bit TCP/IP stack.

Getting Started with SmartMarks

Figure 12.5 shows the SmartMarks main window.

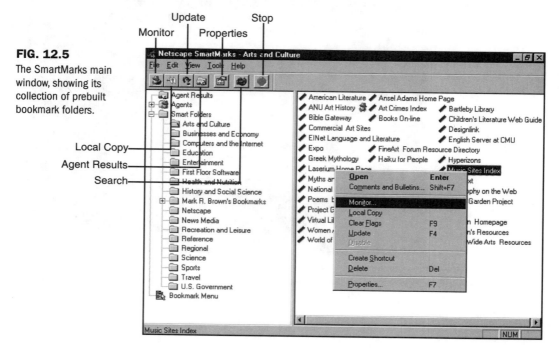

FIG. 12.5
The SmartMarks main window, showing its collection of prebuilt bookmark folders.

For version 2.0, the main window has been simplified and redesigned to look and work like the Windows Explorer. Your catalog, or collection of bookmarks, is shown as a tree in the left side of the window. Clicking on a folder displays its contents in the right-hand window, which the SmartMarks documentation refers to as the "grid." Standard Win95 elements include a menu and toolbar at the top of the screen, and a status bar at the bottom. You can turn off all but the grid window through options under the View menu.

TIP Windows 95 integration extends to the ability to create a shortcut to your favorite bookmarks to place on the Win95 desktop. Just right-click on a bookmark and select Create Shortcut from the popup menu. Now, right from the desktop, you can monitor your favorite Web sites.

The toolbar has buttons for (from left to right) monitoring a site for updates; making a local copy of a Web site for offline browsing; updating a site's listing; displaying Agent Results; changing Properties; performing a Search; and stopping an action.

As you can see from figure 12.5, right-clicking the mouse over an item brings up a popup menu from which you can choose to open, monitor, or create a local copy of a Web site. These choices are also available from the menus.

SmartMarks starts up with a predefined catalog, comprised of folders containing bookmarks for hundreds of interesting Web sites. As you can see from the tree list in figure 12.5, SmartMarks automatically grabbed my bookmarks and integrated them into its own collection when it was first installed.

Working with the Catalog

At its core, SmartMarks is a sophisticated bookmark cataloging system. Because it integrates with Netscape, selecting Add SmartMark from the Netscape Bookmarks menu is all you have to do to add a new Web site to your SmartMarks catalog. Deleting a bookmark can be accomplished by simply right-clicking the mouse on a bookmark and selecting the Delete item, or by clicking and selecting it and pressing the Delete key. Moving bookmarks is as simple as dragging them and dropping them in a new folder.

NOTE SmartMarks is only available from the Netscape menu if you have enabled it. To do so, select Tools, Preferences from the SmartMarks menu, then check the "Load with browser" item under the Options tab.

It's surprising that there's no toolbar button for searching for a bookmark, but it's done easily enough by right-clicking in a blank spot in the grid window and selecting Find, Bookmark from the popup menu. You can accomplish the same thing by selecting Tools, Find, Bookmark from the main menu.

To create a new folder, right-click the mouse in a blank spot on the grid window. To delete one, select it and press the Delete key, or right-click on it and select Delete from the popup menu. Folders can be moved with a simple drag-and-drop.

In general, if you can use Windows Explorer, SmartMarks 2.0 is a snap. Many of the same commands are available from the menu, toolbar, and right-mouse button popup menus.

You Gotta Have an Agent

Agents are a hot topic in programming these days. Basically, an agent is a user-configurable program that will go off and do something you've told it to do in the way you told it to do it, then report back to you with the results. SmartMarks uses agents to tell you when your favorite Web sites have been updated, and to make local copies of them for offline viewing, if you wish.

Agents are listed in the left-hand tree window just like folders. Selecting one lists the Web sites it targets in the grid window on the right, just like opening a folder. However, agents are programmable.

SmartMarks comes with three predefined agents: List/Searches, Local Copy, and What's New? Right-clicking on any of them in the tree list and selecting Properties (or selecting one and pressing the F7 key) brings up the dialog shown in figure 12.6.

FIG. 12.6

Agents can be programmed using this dialog to perform a surprising variety of online functions automatically.

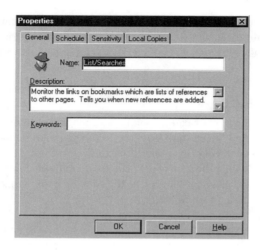

Options for an agent include Keywords you can search for, times at which the agent should automatically update its information, how sensitive it should be to changes, and whether or not it should save a copy for local browsing (as well as how much it should save). If you want to keep your current agents' settings, instead of editing an existing agent you can create a new one by selecting File, New, Agent from the main menu.

> **CAUTION**
>
> Don't go crazy setting agents up to make local copies of Web sites. Depending on your agent settings, each local copy can eat up an horrendous amount of hard disk space. Whole copies can also take a lot of time to download. Keep both factors in mind when using the Local Copy option.

To associate an agent with a bookmark, right-click the bookmark in the grid window and choose Monitor from the popup menu. You'll get a dialog with a list of available agents that you can pick from, as well as buttons that let you change an agent's settings or define a new agent on the spot.

N O T E   If a Web site uses the HTML feature "bulletins," SmartMarks will tell you more than just the fact that a monitored page has changed—it will tell you *what* has changed! If you're interested in checking out this feature, you will find a SmartMarks-importable list of sites that use bulletins at **http://www.firstfloor.com/catalogs/bulletin.htm**. ∎

Searching the Web with SmartMarks

Another of SmartMarks' nifty features is its ability to perform a search of the most popular Web search engines using a single, simple dialog (see fig. 12.7).

You can search the contents, title, URL, or comments of any of the search engines listed for a match of any combination of keywords. Included in the drop-down list of supported search engines are all the most popular Web search sites: Yahoo!, Lycos, InfoSeek, Webcrawler, Excite, DejaNews, OpenText, and Alta Vista.

FIG. 12.7
SmartMarks' all-in-one search dialog not only saves you time, it simplifies searches by making the interface the same for all.

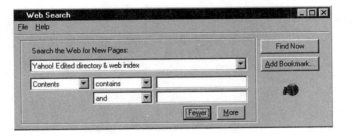

SmartMarks is a very useful and sophisticated program. Though it can take some time to get comfortable with the controls, if you are a serious Web user the time you invest in learning to use it right can pay off in time savings later on. SmartMarks' extensive Help system can help you flatten the learning curve considerably.

Netscape Chat 2.0

Netscape Chat is, like SmartMarks, a product of Netscape Communications Corporation. Also like SmartMarks, Netscape Chat makes a repeat appearance in the Power Pack 2.0 collection as a v2.0 revision of a program from the original Power Pack CD-ROM.

Netscape Chat lets you participate in IRC—Internet Relay Chat. This is a live text-based chat system that predates the World Wide Web. By logging onto an IRC server computer system, you can enter discussion "rooms" and hold real-time conversations with other Internet users. These types of services have long been a favorite on CompuServe, America Online, and other for-pay services. But IRC has until recently largely been reserved for those willing to learn how to use the relatively complex UNIX tools you needed to hook up to IRC servers.

Netscape Chat changes all that. It's easy to install, use, and set up. And it integrates with Navigator so you can enter into discussions right from Web page links. Not only that, it adds an option to "share" Web page URLs with others in an IRC room, so you can all effectively browse the Web together! This is not only fun, it can be a great collaboration tool for coworkers, either in the same building or continents apart.

N O T E One of the best sites on the Net for information about IRC is at **http://www.irchelp.org/**. Here you'll find lots of hand-holding help and a complete set of IRC documents, including the IRC FAQ (Frequently Asked Questions list). ■

Getting Set Up with Netscape Chat

When you first run Netscape Chat, you'll be asked for a few items of personal information (see fig. 12.8).

FIG. 12.8
The Server Connection dialog lets you set up your connection information so you can get online.

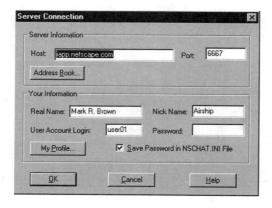

IRC works through a series of IRC host computers. You can pick a Host by selecting one from the Address Book, or you can enter one yourself. A good choice is **iapp.netscape.com**, which is Netscape's own IRC server. The Port number for IRC chat is almost always 6667 or, occasionally, 7000—if it's not, you'll be told by your host provider. Table 12.1 lists some of the more popular IRC hosts in the world. Try to pick one close to you.

Table 12.1   IRC Hosts

Location	Server Name	Port
North America		
Montreal, Quebec	montreal.qu.ca.undernet.org	6667
Netscape Communications	iapp.netscape.com	6667
Austin, TX	austin.tx.us.undernet.org	6667
Bloomington, IN	bloomington.in.us.undernet.org	6667
Charlotte, NC	uncc.dal.net	6667
Chicago, IL	chicago.il.us.undernet.org	6667
Davis, CA	davis.ca.us.undernet.org	6667
Davis, CA	davis.dal.net	7000
Detroit, MI	rochester.mi.us.undernet.org	6667
Hoffman Estates, IL	cin.dal.net	6667
Manhattan, KS	manhattan.ks.us.undernet.org	6667
Marblehead, MA	xanth.dal.net	6667
Minneapolis, MN	skypoint.dal.net	6667
University of Oklahoma, OK	norman.ok.us.undernet.org	6667

Location	Server Name	Port
Phoenix, AZ	phoenix.az.us.undernet.org	6667
Phoenix, AZ	phoenix.dal.net	6667
Pittsburgh, PA	pittsburgh.pa.us.undernet.org	6667
Rohnert Park, CA	groucho.dal.net	6667
San Jose, CA	sanjose.ca.us.undernet.org	6667
San Jose, CA	mindijari.dal.net	6668
Tampa, FL	tampa.fl.us.undernet.org	6667
Washington, D.C.	washington.dc.us.undernet.org	6667
Europe		
Amsterdam, Netherlands	amsterdam.nl.eu.undernet.org	6667
Bristol, England	liberator.dal.net	7000
Caen, France	caen.fr.eu.undernet.org	6667
Delft, Netherlands	delft.nl.eu.undernet.org	6667
Espoo, Finland	xgw.dal.net	7000
Gothenburg, Sweden	gothenburg.se.eu.undernet.org	6667
Ljubljana, Slovenia	ljubljana.si.eu.undernet.org	6667
Oslo, Norway	oslo.no.eu.undernet.org	6667
Oxford, England	oxford.uk.eu.undernet.org	6667
Vienna, Austria	vienna.at.eu.undernet.org	6667
Australia and New Zealand		
Auckland, New Zealand	auckland.nz.us.undernet.org	6667
Brisbane, Australia	brisbane.qld.au.undernet.org	6667
Wollongong, New South Wales	wollongong.nsw.au.undernet.org	6667

Part III

Ch 12

The Server Connection dialog is also where you enter personal information. The most important item here is your Nick Name, which is what you'll be known as in your online chats. You can enter additional personal information by clicking on the My Profile button. People can view this information by using IRC's Info function, so don't list anything you don't want people to know about you.

TIP The User Account Login and Password fields may or may not be optional, depending on the requirements of the Chat Server you are connecting to.

The Option menu includes a Preference selection that lets you customize the way Netscape Chat acts. You can use it with the default settings, but after you've got a bit of experience you're bound to want to play with the settings. The Help menu includes extensive documentation on how each of the Preferences settings works.

Going Online with Netscape Chat

The Netscape Chat main window (see fig. 12.9) includes a menu and toolbar, a chat window, and a console window (shown in fig. 12.10).

FIG. 12.9

The Netscape Chat main window is clearly laid out and easy to use.

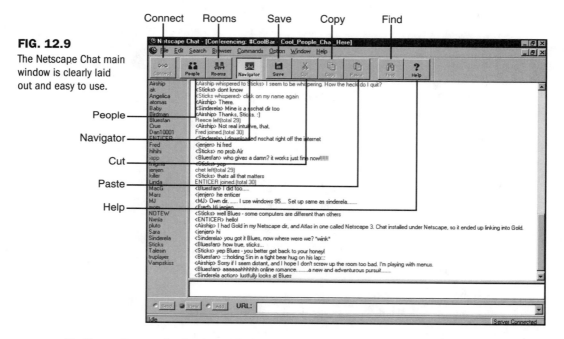

Starting a chat session begins with the Connect button on the toolbar. Click it to open the Server Connection dialog we talked about in the previous section. You can change your Host or personal information if you wish, then click OK to connect to the specified IRC server. If everything goes well, the Console window will display a series of messages to let you know you've gotten connected okay, and the Quick Join dialog box will appear (see fig. 12.10).

FIG. 12.10

The Console window displays important connection information. The Quick Join dialog gets you chatting right away.

To join the selected chat room, click OK. To pick a different room, click on the List button and a list dialog will appear listing all available chat rooms. Pick one and you're online! You can bring up the room list at any time by clicking on the Rooms button on the toolbar. Netscape Chat will let you join up to 10 or more rooms at once, depending on the server, but switching among that many conversations can get pretty confusing. To leave a room, select Command, Leave Room from the menu.

You can also create your own chat rooms by simply clicking on the Rooms toolbar button and typing a new room name into the Room: name box. You'll be asked to specify if you want this to be a conference room or auditorium. You'll usually specify a conference. An auditorium is a moderated discussion group that you administer—details are available through the Netscape Chat Help menu.

You type messages into the window above the URL field. Everyone's input is displayed in the large central window. At the left is a list of room participants. You can "whisper" a private message to anyone in a room by clicking on their name on the list to highlight it, then typing your message. To turn off whisper mode, click their name again to un-highlight it. Right-clicking on a name lets you choose to initiate a private conversation (Talk), turn off their messages (Ignore), or find out more about (Info) that person. All of these options are available for a scrolling list of all persons on the server by selecting the People button from the toolbar.

Because Netscape Chat is linked to Netscape Navigator, you can share an URL with others in the room by typing it into the URL field at the bottom of the window. You can also just click the "Send" button to transmit the URL of the Web page currently displayed in Netscape. Either way, everyone in the room will see the URL and, if they have this feature enabled, their copy of Netscape will jump to the URL you've sent. (Choose Option, Preference, Navigator from the menu and check the Auto View box to activate this feature on your system.) Shared URLs can even be loaded and saved via the Browser, URL List menu selection.

The Navigator button on the toolbar jumps you right to Netscape. The Cut, Copy, Paste, Save, and Find buttons can be used to find and manipulate text you've highlighted in the chat window. To save an entire session, turn logging on using the Edit, Logging menu selection, then choose Save Transcript from the same menu when done.

When you're done with a session, choose File, Disconnect from the menu.

Netscape Chat includes a thorough and well-organized Help file that will quickly acclimate you to the program and help you figure out all the niceties and custom settings.

 TIP If you're an IRC old-timer, you'll be happy to know that Netscape Chat fully supports access to all standard IRC "slash" commands, as defined in RFC 1459.

CyberSpell

You've probably done it a million times—created a mail message or Usenet news post and only realized after it's gone that you probably misspelled a slew of words. Even so, until now there was no way to spell check your mail and news messages. But CyberSpell changes that. When installed, it integrates seamlessly into your mail and news composition windows, providing you with a new Spelling menu that not only gives you flexible spell checking, but a degree of grammar, punctuation, and capitalization checking as well.

CyberSpell has been optimized for use on the Web, and knows about URLs, FTP addresses, newsgroup names, e-mail addresses, and specialized Net terminology, so it won't flag them as "errors" like most spell checkers. It even recognizes many "emoticons" (smiley faces).

When you install CyberSpell, it is automatically included in the Windows StartUp group. Under Win95, it appears as an icon in the taskbar. It has no window of its own. If active, CyberSpell appears only as a menu in the mail and news composition windows (see fig. 12.11).

FIG. 12.11

The CyberSpell menu lets you select either of two spell checkers, set options, or get help.

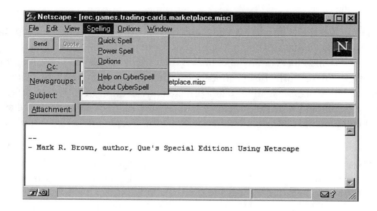

 TIP To display the extensive CyberSpell help file, right-click on the CyberSpell icon in the Win95 taskbar and select Help on CyberSpell.

CyberSpell has two modes of operation. They work alike, and differ only in power. Quick Spell checks spelling only, while Power Spell also checks for punctuation, formatting, spacing, and grammar.

The CyberSpell dictionary has over 159,300 words, including:

- 2,600 technical and computer-related words
- 2,200 names of well-known companies and products
- 8,500 legal, financial, business, and insurance terms

Using CyberSpell should be easy if you've ever used any spell checker. To spell check a composed message, select either Quick Spell or Power Spell from the message composition window's Spelling menu. You'll get the dialog shown in figure 12.12.

Quick Spell or Power Spell will scan the document for errors, which you can choose to ignore, correct, or add to a custom dictionary. You can edit or add custom dictionaries by selecting Options from the Spelling menu and selecting the Dictionaries tab (see fig. 12.13).

FIG. 12.12
Quick Spell and Power
Spell look alike, but
Power Spell (shown
here) lets you check
grammar, punctuation,
and capitalization.

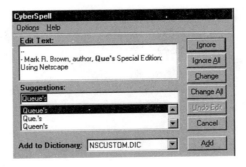

FIG. 12.13
You can Edit, Add,
Remove, or create a
New custom dictionary
from the Options
dialog. Other tabs
allow you to adjust
CyberSpell's overall
behavior.

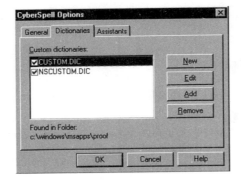

CAUTION
CyberSpell distinguishes between uppercase and lowercase letters in custom dictionaries. In other words, if
you add "Tuna" to a custom dictionary, CyberSpell flags "tuna" as a misspelling.

When you've run CyberSpell for awhile, you may get an offer from its Spelling and Proofing
Assistants to custom CyberSpell's behavior to match your historical use. For example, if you
customarily allow the word "ain't," after three consecutive approvals CyberSpell will ask if you
want it to ignore this word all the time. (I wish all spell checkers had this feature!)

Norton AntiVirus

Viruses are always a concern for computer users, especially when you download a lot of files
from the Internet. You always wonder where that file's been, and whether it could have picked
up a virus somewhere that will infect your system.

Symantec's Norton AntiVirus Internet Scanner may suffer from an overly long name, but it can
help ease your virus worries. It incorporates the same virus hunting and killing technology that
has made the stand-alone version of Norton AntiVirus a standard industry tool.

You can run this version of AntiVirus in stand-alone mode. If you do, you'll see the window
shown in figure 12.14.

FIG. 12.14

Norton AntiVirus can be used to scan for viruses on your floppies, hard drives, or network drives.

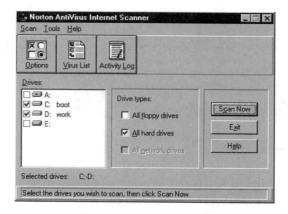

In stand-alone mode, Norton AntiVirus can scan any or all of your disks for viruses. Pick the disks you want to scan and click Scan Now to do so. This takes quite awhile, so pick a time when you don't need your system for anything else. If you suspect something in an individual Folder, or even a single File, you can scan these by selecting them from the Scan menu.

The Virus List and Activity Log buttons or menu items (under Tools) fill you in on which viruses AntiVirus knows about and how much scanning you've done, respectively. Though the Tools, Options menu selection (or Options button) gives you a lot of control over the virus checking process, I suggest you leave it alone until you know more about the program. A healthy dose of help from the Info Desk under the Help menu will get you going, as Norton AntiVirus has one of the best and most extensive help systems you'll find anywhere.

Norton AntiVirus is a Netscape helper application, and it automatically sets itself up to check .exe executables, .zip compressed files, and several other file types when it is installed. To see which file types have been configured for automatic checking by Norton AntiVirus, select Options, General Preferences, from the Netscape menu and click on the Helpers tab. Then look down the scrolling list of MIME types.

When operating in conjunction with Netscape, Norton AntiVirus is almost invisible. Whenever you download a file or encounter an e-mail attachment, it kicks in invisibly, only popping up briefly to let you know everything's okay, then prompting you where to save the file (see fig. 12.15)

Of course, all this is assuming that it doesn't detect any viruses. But what if it does?

Never fear. Norton AntiVirus can automatically eliminate most viruses. If it can't, it'll tell you so and give you the option of trashing the file instead. Either way, your system is safe from infection.

FIG. 12.15
Norton AntiVirus at work, protecting you from nasty viruses in the files you download using Netscape Navigator.

N O T E How Norton AntiVirus Works

Symantec engineers track reported outbreaks of computer viruses to identify new viruses. Once identified, information about the virus (a virus signature) is stored in a virus definitions file. When Norton AntiVirus scans your disk and files it is searching for these telltale signatures. If a file is found that has been infected by one of these viruses, Norton AntiVirus eliminates the virus automatically.

A new virus signature file is available monthly from the Symantec Web site at **ftp://ftp.symantec.com/public/win95_nt/nav/**. You can tell the current virus signature file by the filename, which takes the form mmNAVyy.ZIP, where "mm" is the month and "yy" is the year. ■

 For more info on Netscape Power Pack 2.0, check out **http://home.netscape.com/comprod/power_pack.html**.

Part
III

Ch
12

## CHAPTER 13

Configuring Netscape for Sound

Netscape is mute; by itself, it can't play sound or music files. But by setting it up with the right helper applications, you can turn Netscape into a veritable Caruso.

Of course, you not only need the right sound software—you also need the right hardware. Then you'll be ready to find some noisy places to visit on the Web. Fortunately, these are in ample supply.

In this chapter, you learn:

- How Netscape works with sound

- What kinds of audio file formats you're likely to run into on the World Wide Web

- What Netscape's Live Audio Plug-In does with audio files ■

Hardware Requirements for Netscape Sound

Back in the "old days" of personal computing—when "PC" was always followed by "XT," processor numbers were only four digits long, and software ran directly off floppy disks—every PC shipped with a tinny little AM-radio quality speaker that beeped nastily at you any time you did something wrong. Some masochists (the kind who like to scrape their fingernails on blackboards) even wrote a few annoying DOS programs that played what they claimed to be digitized sounds on that little speaker. But no normal human being ever heard a single recognizable sound in the cacophonous din that emanated from a PC when those programs ran.

Now we're in the high-tech age of multimedia computers—complete with 24-bit True Color animations, 16-bit stereo music soundtracks, and digitized CD-ROM voice-overs by the likes of Patrick Stewart—but all PCs still ship with that same nasty, tinny little speaker.

Sure, Microsoft has a Windows driver that purportedly plays music and audio using only the internal PC speaker, but it freezes up your system when it runs, and everything still sounds like it's being fed through a weather-beaten drive-in movie speaker with a shorted connection.

To get real audio out of your PC, you need a sound card. If you bought your computer recently, or if you've spent a few bucks upgrading, the odds are good that you already have a sound card. But if you don't, you can pick one up for anywhere between $30 and $800, depending on what you want it to do.

A good 16-bit stereo Sound Blaster Pro (or compatible) sound card does just about everything the average person needs done audio-wise, and does it for under $100. If you haven't invested in a sound card yet, drop this book right now, scan a few computer magazine reviews and ads, run to your local computer store, buy a sound card, and plug it in. You'll be glad you did, because PC speaker sound is almost worse than no sound at all.

How Computer Audio Works

Most of the sounds you hear coming from your PC are digitized. That is, the waves that make up the sound have been converted into a stream of digital bits and bytes by feeding them through some kind of analog-to-digital converter. You can do this yourself using the software that came with your sound board on any audio source, such as a microphone or tape player. Once digitized, the sound data is saved as a file on disk.

Digitized sound files vary in at least three important ways. First is the sampling rate, or the number of times each second the audio wave form is sampled as it is converted to digital data. PC sound file sampling rates generally range from 8,000 to 44,100 samples per second. (More samples = higher quality sound.)

Second is the way the data is organized in the file. For example, a digitized sound file may or may not include header information, which describes the file; may interleave the data from multiple sound tracks (i.e., 2 tracks for stereo); or may be comprised of a library of different instrument sound samples followed by a "play list" for using them to play a song.

Finally, the data in a sound file may be compressed in some way to save both disk space and transfer time. For example, MPEG audio files are compressed at a 6:1 ratio.

There are a dozen or more relatively popular sound file types, each of which varies in the way it stores sound data. Most programs only play one or two kinds of sound files. Fortunately, if you have Netscape helper applications configured to play the three or four most popular types, you won't run into many audio problems cruising the Net. You don't have to worry about the rest unless you're a real sound freak or have some specialized application.

N O T E You can find out more about audio file formats by checking out the Audio FAQ (Frequently Asked Questions) list on UseNet. You can retrieve the latest version by pointing Netscape to **ftp://ftp.cwi.nl/pub/audio**. Look for the files AudioFormats.part1 and AudioFormats.part2. More information can also be obtained by reading the UseNet newsgroup **alt.binaries.sounds**. ■

How Netscape Works with Sounds

Web pages don't generally include audio files inline because Web browsers like Netscape can't play them without launching a plug-in or helper application. Most Web pages that have an audio component make sounds optional; they ask you to click a link to load an external sound file.

N O T E Plug-ins are a relatively new feature introduced back in Netscape 2.0 that expand its multimedia capabilities in new directions. Plug-ins are basically add-on viewer modules for "live objects" that can be placed inline on Web pages. In the case of audio files, this means that they could be played automatically without having to launch a helper application when the page is loaded or when the user clicks a link. This doesn't necessarily mean that you don't need audio helper applications anymore, but it is an exciting new capability of Netscape. For a detailed look at plug-ins, see chapter 9, "Netscape Plug-Ins." ■

▶ **See** "Netscape Browser Plug-Ins," **p. 219**

Previous versions of Netscape came bundled with a stand-alone sound player helper application called *NAPlayer* (see fig. 13.1). When Netscape was installed, it automatically configured NAPlayer as your helper app for two digitized audio file formats: Sun/NeXT (.AU, .SND) and Mac/SGI (.AIF, .AIFF). NAPlayer was small, quick, and unspectacular.

 To cope with other sound file types, you needed to configure additional audio helper applications. Because NAPlayer was so limited in what it could do, you often configured a different player for .AU and .AIF sounds, as well.

FIG. 13.1
NAPlayer, the audio helper application that once came bundled with Netscape.

Part
III

Ch
13

The LiveAudio Plug-In

Netscape is now shipping the LiveAudio audio player plug-in with Netscape 3.0. It is automatically installed when you install Netscape 3.0.

If your system is equipped with a sound card, LiveAudio lets you listen to audio tracks, sound effects, music, and voice files that have been embedded in Web pages. You can also use it to listen to stand-alone sound files both on the Web and on your own computer system.

LiveAudio is a huge improvement over the NAPlayer audio helper application that Netscape shipped with previous versions of Netscape Navigator. Where NAPlayer only played Sun/NeXT (.au, .snd) and Mac/SGI (.aif, .aiff) sound files, LiveAudio automatically identifies and plays four of the most popular standard sound formats:

- AIFF—Mac/SGI format sounds
- AU—Sun/NeXT format sounds
- MIDI—Musical Instrument Digital Interface music files
- WAV—Microsoft Windows system sound files

LiveAudio is also a plug-in, not a helper application, which means it doesn't launch a separate window to play back audio—audio playback is done inline in the Netscape window.

When you encounter a sound file embedded or linked on a Web page, LiveAudio creates the on-screen control console shown in figure 13.2.

FIG. 13.2

The LiveAudio plug-in expresses itself as a minimalist inline audio player control console, shown here on a Netscape Web site demo page.

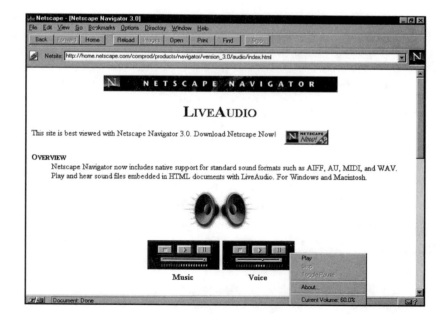

The LiveAudio plug-in works with both embedded sound files, like the two it encountered in figure 13.2, and with stand-alone sound files. In the case of stand-alone files, a blank Netscape window is displayed containing only a LiveAudio console.

The LiveAudio console controls are intuitive and easy to use (see fig. 13.3).

FIG. 13.3

The LiveAudio audio player control box features four manual controls and a simple drop-down menu.

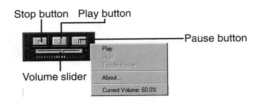

Stop button   Play button

Pause button

Volume slider

The Stop, Play, and Pause buttons work just as they do on a tape or CD player. Clicking Play plays the sound, selecting Stop stops it, and choosing Pause pauses audio playback. Pressing the Pause button a second time resumes play from the point at which the sound was paused.

Click to the right or left of the Volume slider knob to increase or decrease volume. The volume can only be jumped in increments of 20%—you can't slide the volume smoothly from 0% to 100%. The LED bargraph below the Volume slider indicates the current volume level. The dark green LEDs are for the 0%–40% range; light green LEDs refer to the 100% range.

Clicking the LiveAudio console brings up the pop-up menu shown in figure 13.4. This menu includes selections that duplicate the Play, Stop, and Pause buttons. There is also a selection that displays the program's "About" dialog box, and a final non-selectable menu item that tells you the volume level as a percent of maximum volume.

There is a single keyboard hotkey for the LiveAudio player—the spacebar. Pressing it will cause whatever button you pressed last (Stop, Play, or Pause) to be reactivated. Restopping an already stopped playback is of limited use, to say the least. But if you last pressed Pause, the spacebar becomes an unpause/repause toggle. And if you last pressed Play, it becomes a handy replay key.

LiveAudio is included with the Windows 3.1, Windows 95, Macintosh, and PowerPC versions of Netscape 3.0. The Windows 3.1 and Windows 95 versions require a minimum of a 386 processor and a compatible sound card. The Macintosh version requires at least a Mac 68030 with System 7.1. The PowerPC version needs a PPC 601 (66MHz) with System 7.1.2. Both Mac versions also require QuickTime 2.1 with Musical Instrument Plug-in and Sound Manager 3.1.

Part
III

Ch
13

Sound File Formats

Netscape recognizes audio files the same way it identifies all the files it accesses on the Web: first by MIME type, and then (if it doesn't receive a valid MIME type from the Web server) by file name extension. (For more about MIME types, see chapter 10, "Configuring Helper Applications.")

The audio file MIME types and file name extensions that Netscape knows are listed in table 13.1.

Table 13.1   The Three Audio File Types Recognized by Netscape

Type/Subtype	Extensions	Description
audio/basic	.AU, .SND	ULAW Audio Data
audio/x-wav	.WAV	Windows RIFF
audio/x-aiff	.AIF, .AIFF, .AIFC	AIFF Audio

This is certainly not a very extensive list. In fact, Netscape only acknowledges the three file types that LiveAudio can play. There are over a dozen other sound file types on the Web.

Table 13.2 lists some of the other audio formats you're likely to encounter while browsing the Web.

Table 13.2   Other Audio File Types You'll Find on the World Wide Web

Type/Subtype	Extensions	Description
audio/x-fssd	.SND, .FSSD	Mac, PC
audio/x-iff	.IFF	Amiga
audio/x-midi	.MID, .MIDI, .RMI	MIDI music
audio/x-mod	.MOD, .NST	Amiga, Atari ST
audio/x-sf	.SF	IRCAM
audio/x-ul	.UL	US telephony
audio/x-voc	.VOC	Sound Blaster

You'll probably want to configure helper applications for underlined file types right away.

You'll probably want to configure a helper application or plug-in right away for MIDI music files (.MID).

Wave Files

The wave format is Windows' own standard file format. All Windows' warning beeps, whistles, and clangs are in your Windows directory as files and have .WAV extensions. Because it is such a standard fixture on Windows computers, thousands upon thousands of wave files have made their way onto the World Wide Web.

MIDI Music Files

MIDI music files (.MID, .MIDI) are completely different than other sound file formats. Originally developed to control electronic musical instruments, the MIDI file format has become extremely popular on PCs since the advent of MIDI-capable sound cards.

MIDI files combine sound definitions called *instruments* with MIDI sequence control commands that tell a MIDI device (like your PC's sound board) which instruments to play when, for how long, and at what settings. In a way, a MIDI file is more like a music score than a digitized sound file. In fact, MIDI files don't contain digitized sounds at all, unless the file uses custom instrument definitions. ●

## CHAPTER 14

Configuring Netscape for Graphics

If the World Wide Web was a box of raisin bran, text would be the bran flakes and graphics would be the raisins. While most of the Web's "nutritional content" may be in the text, the graphics are what make the Web tastier and just plain more fun than the rest of the Internet.

Netscape handles the most popular Web graphics file formats on its own, inline, but to view all the graphics on the Web, you need to set up a couple of helper applications.

In this chapter, we talk about:

- How Netscape works with graphics
- What kinds of graphics file formats you're likely to run into on the World Wide Web ■

Hardware Requirements for Netscape Graphics

Many older desktop PCs and notebook computers are limited in their graphics capabilities. If your machine can't display any more than 16 colors, this chapter probably isn't for you.

The minimum for cruising the Web these days is a 640 × 480 screen capable of displaying 256 colors. If your computer can do at least this well, you'll be able to view 85 percent of the graphics you find on the Web with no problem.

Of course, the real cutting-edge sites out there have pages that look good only on an 800 × 600 (or larger) screen, with 16-bit (65,536) or 24-bit (16,777,216) color palettes. Personally, I try to avoid such sites. They are a real killer on a 14.4KB dial-up connection.

 Trying to view a big page on a small screen? No problem! Just use the scroll bar at the bottom of the Netscape window to move horizontally. Most people don't pay any attention to it on "normal" size screens, so they forget it's there when viewing pages that are a little wider than normal.

Still, some of those images are well worth waiting for. And once you've got them, you've got to have some way to display them.

I suggest you check the manual for your PC's display card and see what it's capable of. If your display card is more than a couple of years old, you may want to upgrade so you can handle those big, beautiful images. If your pocketbook says "no," don't despair. You can still look at them—if you're willing to compromise a bit.

 Read your display card carefully! Even if your display isn't what you'd like it to be, it may be possible for you to plug in more video RAM and bring it up to speed. Sometimes, just checking with the manufacturer can lead to an even more economical solution: Merely upgrade your video drivers. Netscape is designed to call to the most updated drivers, so often this is a simple remedy. Most manufacturers post the updated drivers on their WWW sites. These are much cheaper solutions than buying a whole new graphics card.

How Computer Graphics Work

Computer graphics are bitmapped images; that is, they consist of a grid of dots called pixels that are mapped to a color palette. For example, the minimum Windows 95 display screen is 640 pixels wide by 480 pixels high (640 × 480), with a palette of 16 colors.

Many of the graphics images you'll encounter on the Web come in one of four "standard" sizes, which happen to match the screen sizes of common computer displays: 320 × 200, 640 × 480, 800 × 600, and 1024 × 768. However, you'll find bitmaps on the Web in sizes ranging from tiny "thumbnails" with dimensions of only a few pixels to images so huge your computer can't even load them, much less display them.

The number of colors in an image is dependent on how many bits are used to define the color for each pixel (see fig. 14.1). Table 14.1 shows how many bits are required for the five most common color palette depths.

Table 14.1   The Number of Bits Needed to Define Different Image Color Palettes

Number of Bits	Colors in Palette
1	2
4	16
8	256
16	65,536
24	16,777,216

FIG. 14.1
The scenic Grand Tetons in eight bitplanes, four bitplanes, and one bitplane.

 TIP Don't forget that black, white, and gray are colors, too. A 2-color image (1 bit) is always monochrome (black and white). But 4- and 8-bit images are sometimes grayscale images, with each pixel's value indicating brightness, not color.

An image's color palette is generally defined in one of two ways.

For images with 16, 256, or 65,536 colors, the number that defines each pixel's color is usually a pointer into a table of predefined or user-definable colors. For example, a bit with the color "233" would point to the 233rd color defined in the color palette table. A color palette table defines colors using more bits than are used to indicate the color for each pixel. In this way, you can have images that, for example, use 256 colors out of a possible 24-bit color palette of 16 million.

But images with 24-bit color definitions usually indicate color values directly. This is done on a pixel-by-pixel basis using the same scheme that defines color palettes for entire low-color images—by splitting the number of bits for each color value into RGB (red, green, blue) values. (This is because a video monitor builds up an image from red, green, and blue dots.) For example, a 24-bit image splits the palette into 8 bits each for red, green, and blue values. That is, each color is made up of 256 different shades, each of the three colors, for a total of 16,777,216 possible colors in a single image.

Part
III

Ch
14

How Netscape Works with Graphics

Most computer graphic images do not share the same set of colors. This can result in color "thrashing" if, for example, your computer tries to display two 256-color images with different color palettes on the same 256-color screen. You can also run into problems trying to display an image with more colors than your display can handle, like a 16-million color JPEG on a 256-color screen. Fortunately, Netscape is very clever about how it displays inline graphics. It handles these problems by using a process called dithering.

Dithering uses a pattern of available colors to create a visual illusion of displaying more. For example, if the Netscape screen palette had no orange available to it, it might try to "fake" orange by displaying a grid of yellow and red pixels. Your eye interprets the area as orangeish, if you don't look at it too closely.

▶ **See** "Advanced Graphics," **p. 483**

N O T E Netscape actually does a very good job of dithering images. The dithering selection is automatic in Netscape, though you can change it manually.

To change Netscape's setting for dithering images, follow these steps:

1. Open the Netscape menu and choose Options, General Preferences.

2. Select the Images tab (see fig. 14.2).

3. The Automatic (Alt+U) radio button is checked by default. If you leave it checked, Netscape will continue to decide when it does and doesn't need to dither an image.

FIG. 14.2
Setting Netscape's dithering options.

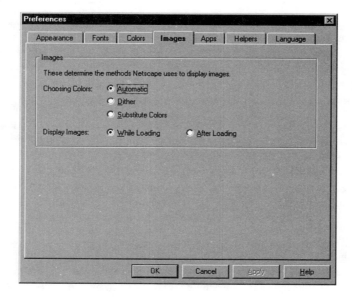

4. Choose Dither to Color Cube (Alt+D) to cause Netscape to always dither images to its internal "Color Cube" of reference colors.

5. Choose Use Closest Color in Color Cube (Alt+S) to turn off dithering altogether; Netscape will always pick the closest solid color it has available.

6. Click OK to end. ▣

N O T E   Plug-ins are a new feature in Netscape 2.0. Plug-ins are basically add-on viewer modules for "live objects" that can be placed inline on Web pages. In the case of graphics files, this means that "foreign" image formats could be displayed inline just like GIFs, JPEGs, and XBMs, without having to launch a helper application. This doesn't mean that you'll never need another graphics helper application for Netscape, but it is an exciting new capability. For a discussion of plug-ins, see chapter 9, "Netscape Plug-Ins." ▣

Graphics File Formats

There are three different ways that images can be stored in files.

Most computer graphics file formats store image information as bitmaps. After all, that's how a computer displays them. All three of the image types that Netscape can display—GIFs, JPEGs, and XBMs—are bitmapped images (see fig. 14.3).

FIG. 14.3
JPEG compression at its worst. The rose on the left is a GIF image. On the right is a JPEG version of the same image compressed to the maximum possible degree (a compression setting of 1 out of 100, with optimized Huffman encoding).

N O T E   Okay, okay, we're lying. GIFs and JPEGs aren't really bitmapped image files; they're compressed bitmapped image files.

GIFs are 256-color (or fewer) images that are compressed using LZW compression, a technique similar to the file compression algorithms used in various archive file formats.

A JPEG image begins life as a 24-bit bitmapped image, then a very sophisticated image compression algorithm takes over. This analyzes the picture and compresses it to a very high ratio. JPEG compression is actually "lossy"—that is, it usually doesn't care if it throws away some picture detail in order to make the image a whole lot smaller.

Part
III

Ch
14

XBMs are monochrome bitmapped images, but XBM files aren't binary bitmaps—they are C language source files, which represent images as numeric (hexadecimal) arrays; they can be read by C compilers, as well as Netscape and a few image display programs.

It just goes to show you that, when it comes to graphics image file formats, there are a lot of extremely different ways to store an image. ▪

Vector image files take a different approach—they actually describe how an image is drawn. When a computer displays a vector image file, it follows the instructions in the file to redraw the image. While it sounds tedious, vector images are much easier to rescale to different sizes, because the image doesn't have a hard-and-fast correlation between its definition in the file and the pixel-by-pixel image on the screen.

Metafiles use a combination of bitmapped and vector image definition. Windows Metafile (.WMF) format images are used quite often under Windows for clipart images that frequently need to be resized.

> **N O T E** You can find out more about graphics file formats by checking out the four-part Graphics FAQ (Frequently Asked Questions) list on UseNet. You can retrieve the latest version by pointing Netscape to **ftp://rtfm.mit.edu/pub/usenet/news.answers/graphics/fileformats-faq** or **http://www.smartpages.com/faqs/graphics/fileformats-faq/part[1-4]/faq.html**. This FAQ is also distributed monthly on the UseNet newsgroups comp.graphics, comp.answers, and news.answers as four separate files.
>
> More information on graphics files can also be obtained by reading the UseNet newsgroup comp.graphics.misc. ▪

TROUBLESHOOTING

I downloaded an image that looks just fine in [insert the name of your favorite generic graphics display program here], but the program I have configured as my Netscape helper application doesn't display it properly. You're probably running into an older (or newer) version of that particular image file format. Though most image display and manipulation programs can handle older versions of various file formats just fine, some will "choke" on unknown variations. And standards groups are always updating file format definitions, sometimes coming up with variations that "break" older viewers. Because of the real-time nature of the Internet, these changes will often show up first on the Web. Make sure your Netscape graphics helper applications can always handle the latest versions of a graphics file format.

Netscape recognizes graphics files the same way it identifies all the files it accesses on the Web: by MIME type first, then (if it doesn't receive a valid MIME type from the Web server it's connected to) by file name extension.

▶ **See** "Configuring Helper Applications," **p. 257**.

CAUTION

There are several very different image file formats that share the file extensions .PIC ("picture") and .IMG ("image"). The only way to properly identify what kinds of images these really are is by MIME type or to use a program that actually reads and interprets the file's header information. Don't assume that either of these (or any other) file extensions can be used to accurately identify an image's real file type.

Netscape can display inline GIF, JPEG, and XBM images. These three formats account for almost 100 percent of the inline images on the Web. But external images are another matter. If you click a link and it leads to a file in a format that Netscape can't handle, you'll have to configure a helper application for it.

The graphics file MIME types and file name extensions that Netscape knows about are listed in table 14.2.

Table 14.2 The Graphics File Types Recognized by Netscape

Type/Subtype	Extensions	Description
image/ief	.IEF	
image/x-MS-bmp	.BMP	Windows Bitmap
image/x-rgb	.RGB	RGB Image
image/x-portable-pixmap	.PPM	PPM Image
image/x-portable-graymap	.PGM	PGM Image
image/x-portable-bitmap	.PBM	PBM Image
image/x-portable-anymap	.PNM	PBM Image
image/x-xwindowdump	.XWD	X Window Dump Image
image/x-xpixmap	.XPM	X Pixmap
*image/x-xbitmap	.XBM	X Bitmap
image/x-cmu-raster	.RAS	CMU Raster Image
image/tiff	.TIFF, .TIF	TIFF Image
*image/jpeg	.JPEG, .JPG, .JPE	JPEG Image
*image/gif	.GIF	CompuServe Image Format

Images it can display internally are marked with an asterisk (*). You will want to configure a helper application right away for the file type underlined above.

Part
III

Ch
14

Of course, there are dozens more graphics image file formats in use on the World Wide Web. Table 14.3 lists some of these, though it is by no means an exhaustive list.

Table 14.3   Some of the Other Graphics File Types You'll Find on the World Wide Web

Extension	Description
.CGM	Computer Graphics Metafile
.DEM	Digital Elevation Model
.DXF	Autodesk Drawing Exchange Format
.IFF	Interchange File Format
.NAPLPS	North American Presentation Layer Protocol Syntax
<u>.PCX</u>	ZSoft Paint
.PIC	Pegasus Imaging Corporation Format
.PNG	Portable Network Graphics
.PSD	Adobe Photoshop
.RIFF	Microsoft Resource Interchange File Format
.SGI	Silicon Graphics Image File Format
.SPIFF	Still Picture Interchange File Format
.TGA	Truevision (Targa) File Format
.WMF	Windows Meta File
.WPG	WordPerfect Graphics Metafile

The one you'll probably want to configure a helper application for right away is <u>underlined</u>.

N O T E   The hottest new graphics file type on the World Wide Web is the Portable Network Graphics (.PNG) format, which was created mostly as a response to the Unisys/CompuServe GIF graphics copyright controversy (which we won't go into here). According to the first drafts of the PNG specification, "The PNG format is intended to provide a portable, legally unencumbered, simple, lossless, streaming-capable, well-compressed, well-specified standard for bitmapped image files which gives new features to the end user at minimal cost to the developer." Look for PNG graphics to carve a major niche for itself on the Web in the months to come. ■

Note that in each of these tables we've underlined a file type that you'll probably want to configure a Netscape helper application for right away. The two we've targeted are Windows Bitmap (.BMP) and Zsoft Paint (.PCX) files. Though the GIFs and JPEGs that Netscape can handle internally are much more popular on the Web, you'll run into enough BMPs and PCXs to make configuring helper applications for these two file formats worthwhile.

Windows Bitmaps

Because BMPs are the native graphics file format of Microsoft Windows, you'll find quite a few of them on the Web. (And if not on the Web itself, on the rest of the Internet, at the very least.)

TIP In the Windows directory in both Windows 3.1 and Windows 95 is a little program called Paintbrush that displays both .PCX and .BMP images. For a step-by-step guide to setting up Paintbrush to work with Netscape, see chapter 10, "Configuring Helper Applications."

Zsoft Paint Files

.PCX (Zsoft Paint) format files were really popular on the PC when all it could run was MS-DOS. Using .PCX files on PC platform is still very popular —.PCX files just don't seem to be fading away.

N O T E Has Microsoft Office been installed on your Windows 3.1 or Windows 95 system? Then you also have a little program available called Microsoft Imager (see fig. 14.4). (It may not have been installed automatically when you installed Office. If not, you can add it easily by running the Office Setup program again.) Imager can handle seven different graphics file formats: .BMP, .DIB, .GIF, .JPG, .PCD, .PCX, and .RLE. You can configure it as a Netscape helper for any of these file types (though you won't want to do so for .GIF or .JPG, since Netscape handles those inline). Microsoft Imager can also manipulate images in many different and interesting ways, since it's based on the popular graphics processing program HALO Desktop Imager. ▨

FIG. 14.4
Microsoft Imager is included in the Microsoft Office package.

Graphics Helper Applications for Netscape

With GIF, JPEG, and XBM support built into Netscape, you already have direct access to the most popular graphics file types on the Web. But by adding helper applications for a few more, you'll never be caught by surprise by some weird file off a server in the backwaters of Timbuktu. For up-to-date information about the latest versions of these and other graphics programs for Windows 3.1 and Windows 95, check out Brian Stark's excellent Graphic Utilities site on the World Wide Web at **http://www.public.iastate.edu/~stark/gutil_sv.html**. ●

## CHAPTER 15

Configuring Netscape for Video

Arguably the hottest computer term these days is "multimedia," which means "more than one medium." With its combination of audio and animated graphics, computer video is what most people have in mind when they say that trendy word.

With the right helper applications, Netscape is perfectly capable of pulling down and playing video files directly from the World Wide Web. While it won't replace the television quite yet, video from the Web foreshadows even more exciting developments to come.

In this chapter, you learn:

■ How Netscape works with video

■ What kinds of video file formats you're likely to run into on the World Wide Web

■ What the future holds for Netscape and multimedia ■

Hardware Requirements for Netscape Video

Video combines audio and graphics, so the hardware requirements for Netscape video are basically a combination of those spelled out in the previous two chapters (a 16-bit stereo sound card, plus a display card capable of displaying at least 640 × 480 pixel resolution in 256 colors).

▶ **See** "Configuring Netscape for Sound," **p. 327** and "Configuring Netscape for Graphics," **p. 335**

However, because video files play sound and display graphics simultaneously, and because the images in video files move, you also need a fast processor and lots of RAM to keep things running at a smooth pace in real time. You'll want a big hard drive, too, if you're planning to keep many video files on hand—it's not unusual for a computer movie file to run 1MB or more, and I've seen plenty of them top 6MB and 7MB!

 With videos more than with any other multimedia element, it's extremely easy to overrun your hard drive with downloaded files. At a megabyte or more apiece for the typical MPEG, .AVI, or .MOV file, it doesn't take long for your drive to fill up. If you regularly save video files to disk, make sure you also regularly purge unused files.

 If you'd like to take a look at the self-proclaimed "biggest video on the Internet today," it's a 640 × 480 MPEG promo video for Television Associates that runs 15 minutes and 28 seconds. The file is 161.5MB, and it's located at **http://www.netvideo.com/netvideo/whatsnew.html**. Make sure your viewer (and system) can handle such a large file before you take the time to download it—most shareware video viewers have a built-in file size limit of 1MB. (You'll find that there are lots of good videos and excellent links on the netvideo site, too.)

Though the minimum requirements for PC video are often stated to be something along the lines of a 386SX20 with 4MB of RAM and a 40MB hard drive, if your system doesn't have at least a 486DX33 processor, 8MB of RAM, and a 540MB hard drive, playing video files may prove to be more of an exercise in frustration than an enjoyable experience.

Because video files are so huge, they take a long time to download. You want the quickest possible Internet connection if you want to get serious about video on the Web. This means you'll do best if you connect from work or school over a fast leased line, and if you're dialing up from home you'll want a 28.8 modem (even if you're a very patient person, you'll certainly want nothing less than 14.4).

MPEG, a popular video format covered later in this chapter, has special requirements. It incorporates file compression technology that works best with a dedicated MPEG decoder board. If you get serious about video on your PC, you may want to look into buying an MPEG board or a video card with MPEG built in.

How Computer Video Works

N O T E   Feel free to use the terms "video" and "movie" interchangeably when talking about moving images on the computer. (I certainly do in this chapter.) You can even throw in "animation" every once in a while and be totally correct, though most purists use that term only for motion graphics that are built up of hand-drawn or computer-generated images, rather than frames that are digitized from live-action footage. ■

Video plays back under Windows and is usually handled though MCI (Media Control Interface) software drivers in your Windows\System directory, which can be called by any application. This means that you only need to install a driver for a particular video format once, and it can be called by any number of different viewer programs.

N O T E   You can find out more about PC video by checking out the video newsgroups on UseNet. Point your Netscape newsreader to comp.multimedia, comp.graphics. animation, comp.os.ms-windows.video, rec.video.desktop, and comp.publish.cdrom.multimedia.

There are also many excellent multimedia resources on the Web. One good example is the University of Geneva's multimedia documentation directory at **http://tecfa. unige.ch:80/pub/documentation/ multimedia/**. On this site you'll find a load of informative files, FAQs, demos, and so on. Check it out! ■

How Netscape Works with Video

Netscape needs helper applications to display video. You'll have to install two things for each video file format you want to handle:

- A video driver that will handle the format
- An application that can call the driver and display the video

You may need a different helper application or plug-in for each of the different movie formats you'll find on the Web, or you may be able to find just one player you like that will handle them all. Viewers for a single video file format are often smaller, and sometimes have features and controls that are specific to that file type. Configuring an all-in-one viewer may mean having to load a bigger program at run time, but it also means you'll only have to learn the controls and quirks of a single viewer.

You may not even want to configure any real-time video helper applications for Netscape at all, especially if you're paying for connect time. Instead, you may want to set up all video files to be downloaded automatically to disk (see fig. 15.1). This lets you view them offline, where you can take your time playing them without incurring charges.

To set up your video files to be downloaded automatically to disk, follow these steps:

1. Select <u>O</u>ptions, General <u>P</u>references from the Netscape menu bar.
2. Click the Helpers tab to bring it to the front.

FIG. 15.1

You can use the Preferences dialog box to configure Netscape to save all videos to disk automatically, for leisurely offline viewing.

3. Scroll to the video/mpeg line and click it. It becomes highlighted, and mpeg,mpg,mpe appears in the File Extensions field.

4. Click the Save to Disk radio button. It becomes highlighted.

5. Repeat steps 3 and 4 for the video/quicktime and video/x-msvideo file types.

6. If you also want to save Autodesk animation files to disk automatically, click the Create New Type pushbutton. Enter video for the Mime Type and x-fli for the Mime Subtype, and select OK. Enter fli in the File Extensions field, and click the Save to Disk radio button.

7. Click OK to finish.

 Netscape's disk cache (which is usually located in the Netscape/Navigator/Cache subdirectory) contains all the files you've viewed recently on the Web, with obscure file names but recognizable file name extensions. For example, if you recently viewed fishing.mov while browsing the Web, it might appear in the cache as something like MOOAAN4J.MOV. While it's almost impossible to figure out which specific file in the cache might be one you're interested in finding again, at least the file name extensions give you a clue. What's more, the file is still fully loadable into your regular video viewer. Happy prospecting!

N O T E Plug-ins were a new feature introduced in Netscape 2.0 that expand Netscape's multimedia capabilities. They are basically add-on viewer modules for live objects that can be placed inline on Web pages. In the case of video files, this means that they could be played automatically when the page is loaded or when the user clicks a link. Plug-ins won't make video helper applications become extinct overnight, but they are an exciting new addition to Netscape. For more information, see chapter 9, "Netscape Plug-Ins." ■

Video File Formats

Netscape recognizes video files the same way it identifies all the files it accesses on the Web: by MIME type first, then (if the Web server it's connected to doesn't send one) by file name extension. (See chapter 10, "Configuring Helper Applications," for more on MIME.)

The video file MIME types and file name extensions that Netscape recognizes are listed in the following table. (If you plan to watch movies on the Web, you'll want to configure plug-ins or helper applications for all three of these file types.)

Type/Subtype	Extensions	Description
video/x-msvideo	.AVI	Microsoft Video
video/quicktime	.QT, .MOV	QuickTime Video
video/mpeg	.MPEG, .MPG, .MPE	MPEG Video

This next table lists the only other major video format that Netscape doesn't know about that you're likely to encounter while browsing the Web:

Type/Subtype	Extension	Description
video/x-fli	.FLI, .FLC	Autodesk Animation

You'll probably want to configure helper applications or plug-ins right away for all three of the formats that Netscape recognizes: Video for Windows, QuickTime, and MPEG. You may also want to configure a viewer for .FLI files, especially if you're into animation or CAD/ engineering.

MPEG Files

MPEG (MIME: video/mpeg, Extensions: .MPEG, .MPG, .MPE) is an acronym for Moving Pictures Expert Group, the body in charge of the MPEG standard. Though it sounds like JPEG, the only thing they really have in common is that their standards groups are part of the same ISO (International Standards Organization) subcommittee, and the committees meet in the same place at the same time.

 TIP I've gleaned lots of helpful information like this from Frank Gadegast's useful and entertaining MPEG FAQ (Frequently Asked Questions) list on UseNet. The latest version can be read online by pointing Netscape to **http://www.powerweb.de**. (The .de means it's in Germany.)

MPEG exists because video files are big. The MPEG format compresses video files to a more reasonable size. Unfortunately, MPEG compression at its best requires a dedicated hardware decoder board. However, there are some MPEG software-only players that work pretty well on a fast processor.

There is no standard MCI driver for MPEG, though some players install their own and Microsoft has promised to provide one eventually. Many MPEG movie viewers choose to do their own internal decoding. Fortunately, you don't have to sort this out yourself; if a driver is needed for an MPEG viewer program, it's always included in the distribution file.

Video for Windows Files

Video for Windows (MIME: video/x-msvideo, Extension: .AVI) is Microsoft's own native video format for Windows.

The most recent versions of the Video for Windows (including Windows 95) drivers incorporate several advanced codec (compression/decompression) algorithms for both audio and video. The latest are Intel's Indeo codec and Supermac's Cinepak codec, which allow for playback of color video images up to 320 × 240 at up to 30 fps (frames per second).

N O T E   A codec (compression/decompression) algorithm actually does most of the work in a video driver. Most video formats incorporate several different codecs, and different video files in the same format can use different codecs, depending on whether quality, speed, or some other factor is most important. Some codecs that you may see references to in various video file format specifications are the following:

- Animation
- Cinepak
- Component Video
- Graphics
- Intel Indeo
- Intel-RAW
- None
- Photo-JPEG
- TrueMotion
- Video

In general, you don't have to worry about which codec a video file uses. Your driver will sort it all out and use the decompression scheme that matches the file's compression scheme without human intervention. ■

There are also hooks in Video for Windows that allow programmers to capture video sequences, add custom user interfaces, integrate text, music, and still graphics with videos, and so on. While this might not mean much to you directly, it does mean that it's relatively painless for programmers to create really nice video playback programs for the rest of us.

Video for Windows started out as Microsoft's answer to Apple's QuickTime, but it has become so popular on the Net that there are now Mac players for Video for Windows, too.

The Video for Windows Driver   If you're running Windows 95, a 32-bit version of Video for Windows has already been automatically installed on your system. You only need to configure a viewer program to be able to play videos with Netscape.

If you're a Windows 3.1 user and you haven't played videos before, you may have to install the right driver first. To check, open the Drivers icon in the Control Panel and check the list. If the

[MCI] Microsoft Video for Windows driver isn't there, refer to your Windows manual for details on how to install it from your Windows 3.1 installation disks.

If for some reason you don't have the Video for Windows driver available on your Windows 3.1 system, it can be downloaded from Microsoft's pages on the Web. Point Netscape to **http:// www.microsoft.com/kb/softlib/mslfiles** and download the file wv1160.exe. This is version 1.1 of the Video for Windows driver—if there is a more recent version in the Microsoft library, grab that instead. Follow the instructions in the file for installation.

Once the Video for Windows driver is correctly installed, you can go ahead and find a suitable viewer to use as a Video for Windows helper application.

QuickTime Files

Apple's QuickTime video format (MIME: video/quicktime, Extensions: .QT, .MOV) was originally developed for the Macintosh, but quickly migrated to the PC platform. As the original microcomputer video format, QuickTime is very popular among creative types (who tend to prefer the Mac anyway) and it is the format of preference for many of the most experienced videographers on the Web. This means that many of the best Net movies out there are in QuickTime format.

TROUBLESHOOTING

I clicked on the link for a QuickTime movie, and it seemed to download and launch my viewer, but all I got was an error message. I've played QuickTime movies successfully before. What's going on? Not all QuickTime movies are viewable under Windows. In order for a QuickTime file to be viewable on anything but a Macintosh, it has to be flattened; that is, it must be run through a converter program on the Mac that builds a cross-platform compatible file. (Unfortunately, there is currently no such converter for Windows or UNIX.) While most QuickTime videos you'll run into on the Web have been converted, you may run into one occasionally that has not been. If you find a QuickTime movie that won't play for you, this may be your problem.

Like Video for Windows, QuickTime also includes the Indeo and Cinepak codecs (among others), and can mix audio, still images, and text with video. The latest QT driver can even handle integrated MIDI music and—with a hardware card—MPEG compression.

However, the current Windows version of QuickTime (2.0.3, as this is written) lacks some of the more esoteric features of the Apple version, most notably support for capture, compression, PhotoCD display, SMPTE time codes (for tightly syncing audio and video tracks), and data references. These are promised soon for Windows.

The QuickTime for Windows Driver   The QuickTime for Windows video driver is not freely distributable. However, it has been licensed for distribution with many products, so you may already own a copy without knowing it. Check video collections on CD-ROM, CD-ROM magazines, or Windows graphics and animation programs. One of these may have even already secretly installed the QT driver on your machine. (Look for the file mciqtw.drv in your Windows/System directory.)

QuickTime can also be purchased online directly from Apple Computer at **http://quicktime.apple.com**. The current price is $10 for personal use. Upgrades are available on Apple's World Wide Web site at **ftp://ftp.support.apple.com/.www.html**.

Apple also occasionally makes QuickTime available free for the downloading. Check its site to see if now is one of those times. (It was at the time this book was written.)

The QuickTime Viewers

If you get Apple's QuickTime video driver from the archive file mentioned earlier, when you decompress the archive you also get two stand-alone viewer programs, one for still images and one for QuickTime videos.

The Picture Viewer displays Macintosh PICT (.PIC) and JPEG (.JPG) still images (see fig. 15.2). Though it can display more than one image at a time in scalable, zoomable windows, its lack of support for more than two file formats makes it pretty wimpy. You might consider using it as a helper application, though, if you regularly need to view Macintosh format images—if, for example, you're heavily into Mac desktop publishing and need to access Mac files from an online photo service.

FIG. 15.2

Apple's Picture Viewer for Windows comes archived with the QuickTime video driver, but can display only Mac PICT and JPEG format images.

The Movie Player plays QuickTime and MPEG movies (see fig. 15.3). The menus give you some control over image size and looping, and you can bring up a window that tells you some information about the movie you're playing. It can even handle multiple videos at once. Even though it's from the Enemy Camp (Apple), I've got to admit it's a pretty slick little video player.

Autodesk .FLI Animation Files

Autodesk is the publisher of AutoCAD, which is the most popular Computer Aided Design program for the PC. Unlike traditional CAD programs, AutoCAD is not limited to producing flat, monochrome, two-dimensional images. It can also generate them in glorious 3D color, with realistic lighting and shading. Not only that, but with the assistance of a couple of different AutoCAD add-on programs, you can create 3D animations from AutoCAD drawings.

FIG. 15.3

Apple's Movie Player for Windows can play both QuickTime and MPEG movies.

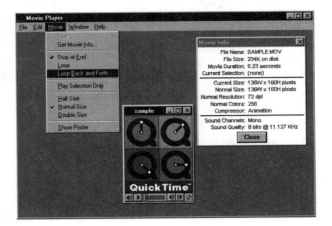

Needless to say, engineers have had a lot of fun with the 3D animation capabilities of the AutoCAD system. This means that there are more than a few animations available on the World Wide Web in the native AutoCAD .FLI file format (MIME: video/x-fli, Extension: .FLI, .FLC).

If you're into CAD, engineering, or animation, you may find that you want to set up a Netscape helper application to view .FLI animations. To do so, you need the Autodesk Animator add-on driver and AAPlay player (see fig. 15.4) in the file aawin.zip, which is available from many online FTP file download sites, including **ftp://ftp.netnet.net/pub/mirrors/truespace/utils** and **http://hyperreal.com/tools/win3/graphics/video**. .FLI animations allow a surprising number of options, including associating sound files, using scripts to tie together strings of animations, looping, color cycling, and much more. You can even preload an animation into memory for smoother playback, and hide the animation until it begins playing. There's an option for setting the number of times the animation loops, and you can specify a transition at the beginning and end of play. Soundtracks can be from CD or videodisc audio, .WAV files, or MIDI sequences. In short, you get a lot of options.

The only downside to all this is that the Autodesk software for creating .FLI animations is in the "professional" price category. But I suppose we should be thankful that we can, at least, play them back for free.

FIG. 15.4

AAPlay from Autodesk lets you play .FLI animations and edit animation scripts using a built-in editor.

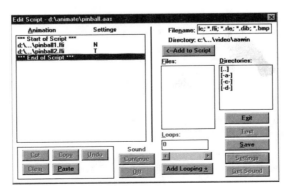

Video Helper Applications for Netscape

The LiveVideo Plug-In

Netscape Navigator 3.0 includes a bundled plug-in for displaying Video for Windows movies. It's called LiveVideo.

LiveVideo installs automatically side-by-side with Netscape 3.0. You don't have to do anything to install, set up, or configure it. Since it's a plug-in, you don't have to do anything to launch it, either. It sits there blithely waiting until you encounter a Web page with an embedded AVI format video, then plugs its video player into the Netscape window, as shown in figure 15.5.

FIG. 15.5

LiveVideo launches invisibly, without any visible controls, and plays AVI videos inline in the Netscape window.

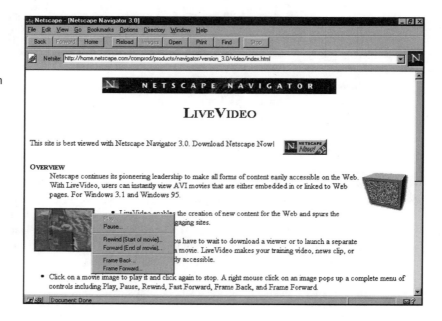

You simply click on the embedded video frame to start it playing, click again to pause, then click to resume, etc.

T I P You can also use LiveVideo to play stand-alone AVI videos, either from the Web, your corporate intranet, or your hard drive—just use File, Open File (Ctrl+O) from the Netscape menu and pick a file of type .avi.

To access the LiveVideo player controls, you click the right mouse button on the displayed video frame. You'll get the pop-up menu shown in figure 15.6.

There are six basic controls available from the LiveVideo pop-up menu. You can Play, Pause, Rewind to the start of the movie, and Fast Forward to the end.

FIG. 15.6
LiveVideo's pop-up control menu gives you a minimal but easily understood set of controls.

Like a VCR, once you've played a video through to the end, you have to rewind it before you can play it again.

You can also select Frame Back or Frame Forward to step backwards or forwards through the movie a frame at a time.

LiveVideo is included in the Windows 3.1 and Windows 95 versions of Netscape 3.0. Both require a system with at least a 386 CPU and a compatible sound card. Win 3.1 also requires the Video for Windows driver. (Video for Windows is automatically installed in Win95.)

N O T E Netscape has announced an Apple QuickTime movie player plug-in, too, but it was still unavailable as this was written. Though it is said to include esoteric features like sprite-based animation, streaming input, MPEG, Motion-JPEG, sound, music, text, and 3D support, considering that this "official" Apple QuickTime plug-in has been promised since before the release of Netscape 2.0, it might be best to pick up one of the third party QuickTime player plug-ins rather than wait for Apple's. Try *MovieStar* at **http://www.beingthere.com**, the *TEC Player* at **http://www.tecs.com**, or *ViewMovie* at **http://www.well.com/ivanski/download.html**. ▨

Assuming you've found and installed the video drivers you need, you now need to find just the right video viewer programs. Fortunately, they're not hard to come by in the multimedia-crazy computing community.

N O T E You'll run into the same options over and over when previewing Windows video players. Here are the most popular:

- Looping—This option determines whether a video stops at the end of play, or loops back and replays forever. Some viewers allow a specified number of loops, or add the option to simply rewind at the end of play.

- Color—Many players let you choose to play videos back in monochrome, grayscale, colors dithered to a set palette, or full original color.

- Scaling—Most videos are created to play back at a resolution of approximately 1/4 the size of a "standard" 640 × 400 computer screen size, or about 320 × 200 pixels. Most viewers let you choose other playback sizes, from 1/16 to full screen.

- Information—You can usually pick a menu option to view information about the file you're playing, such as resolution, number of colors, and so on.

- Playback Controls—Most viewers have a Play button. Some have a Pause button, though this may be the same as the Play button. Others may include Fast Forward, Rewind, and Step by Frame Forward and/or Backward buttons. There may be a slider to select the current frame. If the player can play back sound, you may find a volume control as well.

- File Options—All of the viewers mentioned here let you load and save videos to disk. If you have a viewer you have configured as a helper application that automatically exits when the video is done playing, you may have to be fast with the mouse on the Pause button to stop the player so you have time to pick Save from the File menu.

- Additional Options—Look for the ability to save individual frames, print a frame to the printer, and so on. Some players offer a surprising number of additional options. ▧

> **N O T E** For information on where to find helper applications and how to configure them once you've found them, see chapter 10, "Configuring Helper Applications." ▧

The Future of Video on the Web

The major limitation to viewing killer video on the World Wide Web is bandwidth. Data compression, cable television network connections, ISDN lines, and new technologies like Novell's NEST (Novell Embedded Systems Technology)—which promises to make computer networks available to a billion users by the year 2000—could make bandwidth a dead issue. Until it does, viewing video on the Internet is at best an exercise in patience.

> **T I P** For more on NEST—Novell's billion-user network that promises to interconnect everything from Coke machines to automobile factories to babies' crib monitors by the year 2000—check out Novell's NEST site at **http://nest.novell.com/**.

But there are always exciting new developments that foreshadow what video on the Web might be like in the near future.

Multimedia Plug-Ins

Plug-ins are an innovative way that Netscape 3.0 can expand its multimedia capabilities. Plug-ins are basically add-on viewers that allow Netscape to display multimedia content inline in real-time. This means that sound, video, and even interactive multimedia can be added to Web pages and Netscape won't have to launch external viewers to display them; they can all appear together on one page. Plug-ins for QuickTime video and Macromedia Director interactive multimedia presentations have already been announced by Netscape. Innovations like this will definitely change forever the look and feel of the Web.

▶ **See** "World Wide Web and Netscape 3," **p. 7**

▶ **See** "Netscape Browser Plug-Ins," **p. 219**

Video Conferencing

Video conferencing involves two or more participants who transmit live video and audio to each other simultaneously. Most of the video conferences held today are between business people who use dedicated software and secure links.

However, that may end soon. Though there are still bandwidth problems with Internet video conferencing, some brave pioneers are testing the waters. One of the first "open-air" video conferencing experiments is Cornell University's CU-SeeMe Project (see fig. 15.7). With free software for PCs (and Macs), CU-SeeMe can link up two to eight participants at a time for black-and-white, push-to-talk video conferencing through Internet "reflector sites" that take care of all the routing and trafficking problems. Hardware costs for hooking up can be as low as $100 for a cheap black-and-white CCD video camera with built-in interface, and view-only kibitzing is free.

FIG. 15.7

The CU-SeeMe site at Cornell tells you all about cheap (practically free) video conferencing. That could be your face in one of those little windows!

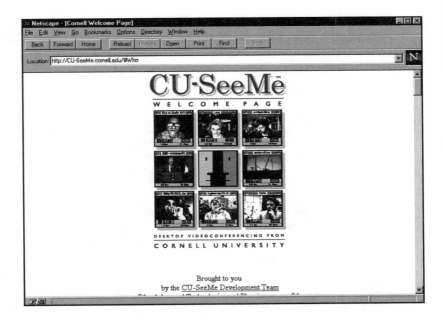

While it's far from a mature discipline, expect video conferencing to become a major player in the future of Internet communications.

For more information, point Netscape to Cornell's CU-SeeMe site at **http:// CU-SeeMe.cornell.edu**. Or you can check out White Pine Software's site for information on the commercial version of CU-SeeMe at **http://goliath.wpine.com/cu-seeme.html**.

MBONE Live WWW Video Broadcasts

The MBONE (Multicast Backbone) is a network of computers on the Internet that form a backbone network for the transmission of live video and audio broadcasts. So far, it has been used for experimental broadcasts of events as disparate as scholarly meetings and a portion of a Rolling Stones concert. It is also capable of supporting live multipoint, real-time audio and video conferencing.

The MBONE is a "virtual network" that is layered on top of the physical Internet. It packages real-time multimedia in such a way that normal networks (like Ethernet) pass it along without noticing that anything is other than normal. The MBONE network is composed of a string of network routers at different locations on the Internet, all running the MBONE software. These "islands" are linked by virtual point-to-point links called tunnels, through which pass the video and audio data packets of a live MBONE multicast.

N O T E   The MBONE is a more-or-less permanent arrangement, and requires a commitment at the network administration level. If you want your workstation-based LAN to become part of the MBONE, the IP multicast software is available by anonymous FTP. To find out how to download and set up the MBONE software, get the document mbone-connect from ftp://genome-ftp.stanford.edu/pub/ mbone/. But first, read the MBONE FAQ (Frequently Asked Questions) list at **http://www.best.com/ ~prince/techinfo/** for more details about how MBONE works. ▓

Though setting up an MBONE connection requires a real commitment of time and resources, and though there is not much live broadcast traffic on MBONE yet, it certainly shows that there is a lot of potential for video to grow and become a more important part of the World Wide Web. Look for MBONE (or a technology much like it) to make a real impact on the Web in a couple of years.

StreamWorks

StreamWorks, developed by Xing Technology, is a new commercial product for delivering live and on-demand video and audio (see fig. 15.8). The National Broadcasting Company (NBC) and Reuters news service are already using this technology for broadcast delivery of financial news programming to subscribers in the U.S. and Europe. New applications are being developed with StreamWorks for distance learning, corporate communications, news delivery, and computer-based training in corporate, educational, government, and health care markets. Xing says that it can even allow Internet providers to effectively get into the cable-TV-via-the-Web business.

FIG. 15.8
StreamWorks, Xing Technology's answer to delivering real-time multimedia via the Web and other networks.

StreamWorks can deliver live or on-demand multimedia content to multiple simultaneous users over local and wide-area networks like the Web. Xing's approach is built around international standards like UNIX and Windows NT servers, TCP/IP connections, MPEG video and audio compression, and HTTP/HTML client/server communication.

Expect many, many more players to get into the video-via-the-Web market in the coming months. There's a lot of money to be made in Web video, and there's no leader yet.

For more information on StreamWorks, point Netscape to **http://www.xingtech.com/streams/index.html**. ●

## CHAPTER 16

Using VRML

Netscape has mapped out an impressive horizon on the Cyber-landscape, and they haven't ignored Cyber*space*. VRML (Virtual Reality Modeling Language), the industry-standard scene description language for 3D worlds, has been integrated into Netscape's Live3D viewer—an open VRML framework for creating and viewing VRML worlds rich with text, images, animation, sound, music, and video. Live3D is based on the proposed Moving Worlds VRML 2.0 specification. Though VRML 1.0 browsers support worlds with simple animations, VRML 2.0 browsers have already begun to explore more complex 3D simulations and behaviors through VRMLScript, Java, and JavaScript.

In this chapter, you learn about:

- The origins of VRML
- Netscape's Live3D VRML Plug-in
- Integrating VRML 2.0 browsers with Netscape
- Sample VRML Worlds on the Internet

What Is VRML?

The Virtual Reality Modeling Language (VRML) is a scene description language—at its simplest a text file much like HTML, and at its best nothing less than the building block of cyberspace. To be more specific, VRML's designers intend it to be used for the creation of three-dimensional, multi-person, distributed interactive simulations. Not much younger than the Web itself, VRML is well on its way to realizing its designers' dreams.

How It Started

The explosion of the World Wide Web was caused by its ease of use: anything reachable on the Web is accessible by one unique address, the URL (Uniform Resource Locator). This flattening of the Internet has had the effect of making the Web very much like a single, enormous hard disk. The Web's advantages can be seen in its rapid growth as people convert their Internet resources to HTML format, the enormous popularity of Netscape as a tool to access the Web, and the very existence of this book.

However, the Web is based on HTML (HyperText Markup Language), which was developed from the SGML (Standard General Markup Language) standard. SGML and HTML are fundamentally designed as two-dimensional text formatting toolsets. Mark Pesce, Peter Kennard, and Tony Parisi presented a paper called "Cyberspace" at the First International Conference on the Web in May 1994 in which they argued that, because humans are superb visualizers and we live and work in three dimensions, extending the Web with a third dimension would allow for better organization of the masses of data already on the Web. They called this idea Virtual Reality Markup Language. The concept caught on quickly, and a new crop of VRML enthusiasts immediately began searching for a format to use as a data standard. A mailing list was started by Brian Behlendorf at Wired magazine, with Mark Pesce as the list moderator. About this time, the M in VRML was changed from Markup to Modeling to accentuate the difference between the text-based nature of the Web and VRML.

N O T E The paper Cyberspace is available over the Web at **http://www.hyperreal.com/~mpesce/www.html**.

After months of intense discussion, a draft specification for VRML was presented at the Second International Conference on the World Wide Web, held in October 1994 in Chicago. VRML 1.0 bore a lot of similarity to a format called OpenInventor, a 3D developer's toolkit originally developed at Silicon Graphics (a maker of high-end computer workstations). The specification was written by Gavin Bell of Silicon Graphics, Mark Pesce, and Tony Parisi.

VRML's design specifications were guided by three goals:

- Platform independence
- Extensibility
- The ability to work over low-bandwidth connections

All three of these are characteristics, already possessed by HTML and the Web, which the designers of VRML felt would be required if their standard was to have any popular acceptance.

N O T E The VRML 1.0 final specification can be found on the Web at **http://vrml.wired.com/ vrml.tech/vrml10-3.html**.

Instructions on how to join any of the several mailing lists on the Web that affect the decisions for the next version of the VRML standard are also on the Web at **http://www.sdsc.edu/vrml**.

The VRML FAQ can be found at **http://vag.vrml.org/VRML_FAQ.html**. ■

VRML has indeed become accepted. While a WORM search for "VRML" in the summer of 1994 might have yielded a number you could count on your fingers and toes, today a Lycos search will point you to over 30,000 Web pages about VRML on the Internet. Currently, over two dozen VRML 1.0 browsers are available for download on the Internet, including Live3D, not to mention a number of VRML world-building and object-creating toolkits.

Moving Forward with Moving Worlds

VRML 1.0 is not the cyberspace of pop culture and science fiction: it defines the parameters for defining three-dimensional models (worlds) and hyperlinking them by using the Web.

On the other hand, VRML 1.0 was foreseen from the beginning to be the minimal starting point for a much larger vision. That larger vision is VRML 2.0, also named Moving Worlds, the original name of the proposal that was chosen by the VRML community as the working document for VRML 2.0. It was created by Silicon Graphics, in collaboration with Sony and Mitra, though a number of other people in the VRML community were actively involved with Moving Worlds and contributed numerous ideas, reviews, and improvements. The VRML Architecture Group (VAG) made Moving Worlds official on March 27, 1996.

N O T E The VRML 2.0 specification can be found at the VAG's Web site (**http://vag.vrml.org**) at **http://vag.vrml.org/VRML2.0/**. ■

Moving Worlds moves VRML to something a little closer to the cyberspace of William Gibson's *Neuromancer*, going beyond simple navigation of 3D worlds by providing these extensions and enhancements to VRML 1.0:

- Enhanced static worlds, for adding backdrops, fog, terrain, and 3D spatial sound to VRML worlds
- Interaction, for event sensors, time sensors, and collision detection
- Animation, for the creation of animated objects called Interpolators
- Scripting, for giving VRML-created creatures and objects behavior—a kind of intelligence
- Prototyping, for encapsulating a group of nodes together as a new node type, making VRML even more open and extensible

Each of these are characteristics which the designers of Moving Worlds feel will be necessary if VRML is to truly become that building block of cyberspace. We'll take a look at two VRML 2.0 browers—Sony's Cyber Passage and SGI's Cosmo, later in this chapter.

Netscape's Live3D Viewer

That VRML is becoming an important part of the Web is clearly demonstrated by the fact that Netscape is bundling a VRML 3D world viewer with Navigator 3.0 Live3D (see fig. 16.1).

FIG. 16.1
Live3D is Netscape's "official" 3D VRML world browser, and sports a number of nifty features.

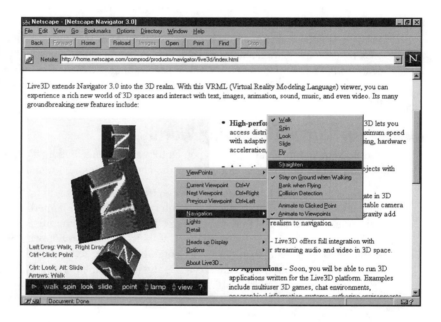

Live3D, strictly speaking, is a VRML 1.0 browser with special extensions added—namely an animation extension and support for Java—for use in Netscape Navigator. Though Live3D is based on elements of VRML 2.0, it's not fully complaint, not yet anyway.

Still, Live3D supports a number of cool features:

- 3D text
- Background images
- Texture animation
- Morphing
- Viewpoints
- Collision detection
- Gravity

- RealAudio streaming
- Multiple light sources
- Texture mapping

While you'll find other VRML 1.0-capable browsers and Netscape plug-ins with much of the same capability, Live3D's integration with LiveMedia for streaming audio and video in 3D space, selectable camera viewpoints, collision detection, and optional gravity add flexibility and realism to navigating any VRML world (see fig. 16.2).

Part
III

Ch
16

FIG. 16.2
Integration of LiveAudio, LiveVideo with Live3d will give you a true interactive window on the world.

Netscape promises support in future releases for special 3D applications written for the Live3D platform. Examples include multiuser 3D games, chat environments, geographical information systems, authoring environments, interactive advertisements, online presentations, and database visualizations.

Using the Live3D Viewer

Live3D has an intuitive interface; you'll get the hang of it in no time. After you click on a link to a VRML file (designated by the file extension .wrl), Netscape Navigator will download the file just like an html file. Depending on how the file is coded, you'll either get an HTML page with VRML objects inserted into it or just the Live3D window (containing the VRML world) by itself.

The toolbar along the bottom of a Live3D window gives you control over your movement in the displayed 3D world (see fig. 16.3).

T I P If the navigation bar doesn't appear after your VRML file has loaded, right-click anywhere in the scene and select Options, Navigation Bar to display it.

FIG. 16.3
Live3D's Navigation Bar is located at the bottom of the window.

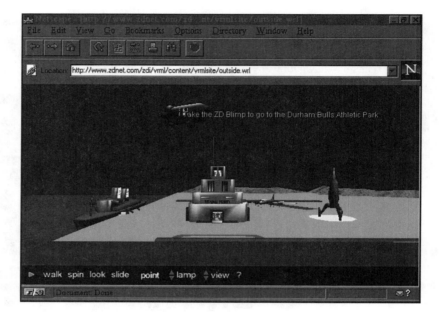

Clicking on the arrow at the left pauses any animated movement. Each selection will be highlighted when you click on it; click and move the mouse in the display to move after selecting a mode. Live3D gives you five options:

- *Walk* will allow you to move forward, backward, left, and right
- *Spin* will let you tilt the scene 360 degrees horizontally and vertically

N O T E You can access the spin control at any time by right-clicking. ■

- *Look* moves your viewpoint (not the scene!) 360 degrees horizontally or vertically
- *Slide* moves the scene (not your viewpoint!) up, down, or side-to-side
- *Point* automatically moves you to any point in the scene you click

N O T E *Point* can be selected at any time with any other option. You can also use the arrow keys (on a standard 101 or 102 keyboard or better) at any time to invoke *Walk* mode. ■

Clicking the up and down arrows by the Lamp selection changes the brightness of the illumination of the scene. Clicking the arrows by the View item changes your point of view if different views are available.

Right-clicking the mouse button anywhere in the scene brings up the pop-up menu shown in figure 16.4.

FIG. 16.4
This pop-up menu gives you a full complement of 3D movement and scene adjustment controls.

The Viewpoints selection brings up a submenu which lets you pick other points of view, if available (this is the same as clicking the arrows by the View item). The next three menu items let you pick the Current (Ctrl+V), Next (Ctrl+Right), or Previous (Ctrl+Left) viewpoint.

Performance

You'll notice that the Navigation, Lights, and Detail menu items each bring up submenus with a variety of controls for modifying the way you move, the scene lighting, and how much detail you see. The best way to find out what these selections do is to play with them. VRML worlds are very dynamic environments, and half the fun is changing things and seeing what happens!

After you've played with the different options, though, you may begin to see that how you choose to render a scene (and the complexity of the scene itself) will have an impact on your computer's performance. This has to do with the nature of 3D rendering in general.

3D Objects are generally one of two types: primitives or polygons. In VRML, these two types are lumped together in a category called *shape nodes*. Polygon rendering offers the most flexibility for a VRML designer; a polygon is any flat area enclosed by straight lines—and they can be manipulated in almost endless ways. If a sufficient number of coordinates were plotted, for example, polygons could produce quite a realistic version of a human being.

Primitives, on the other hand, deal with three simple parameters: height, width, and depth. Boxes, cones, cylinders, spheres, and text make up the primitives in VRML geometry.

What does all this mean? Primitives don't require as much processing time, since the processor only has to deal with fairly easy calculations. But if you are browsing a complex VRML scene with a lot of polygons, then you'll move much slower through the scene depending upon the capability of your processor and/or its math chip support (you'll also have noticed that the file size is considerably larger). Live3D has several options to help you increase perfomance without sacrificing too much scene-quality.

Adjusting the Detail   Right-click anywhere on the scene and select Detail. The three modes are Solid, Wireframe, and Point Cloud:

- *Solid* takes the longest time to process because it fully renders all primitives and polygons

- *Wireframe* takes less time to render since it only shows the straight lines of polygons or the outlines of primitives

- *Point Cloud* takes the least time since it only shows polygon coordinates

Generally speaking, if navigation is very slow, try switching to Wireframe mode. When you arrive at an area of scene that you want to view, switch back to Solid mode to see the fully-rendered objects. You'll probably find that using the Point Cloud mode is worthless (see fig. 16.5), since you can see so little of the scene—and that kind of ruins the whole idea of VRML to begin with! However, you may find it useful for extremely large worlds.

FIG. 16.5
Stay in Point Cloud mode for very long and you may get lost!

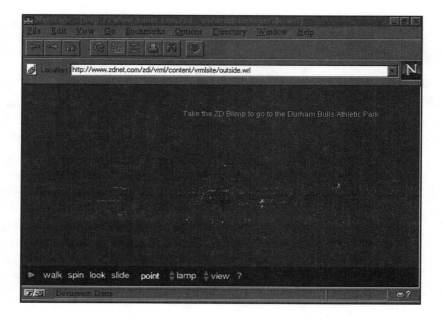

Other Options for Speed   You may also find that deselecting any or all of the following items will increase your rendering speed and hence improve Live3D's performance:

- *Collision Detection.* This is a great feature that makes navigating any room or scene easier. The option is always turned off by default, and you have to re-select it with each new VRML scene you load.

- *Smooth Shading.* Choosing Flat Shading instead of Smooth shading may help you if you have a slow video card or a 486 machine.

- *Back Faces and Motion Blur.* Your won't see a major jump in speed, but turning these off may help. The default for both is off.
- *Optimize Window Size.* Keeping the browser window as small as possible won't help the processor much, but it will help your video speed.

The aforementioned are less dependent on processor speed and more closely tied to the size of your RAM and DRAM. Realistically, the minimum amount of memory required to use VRML effectively is 16 MB. Any less than that and your computer will have to continually swap to its hard disk to compensate for the lack of RAM. You may want to consider adding more memory if you find yourself becoming a serious VRMLer.

Another option is to get a graphics accelerator card. These cards have their own memory and processors for taking over processor-intensive functions like polygon rendering. Though still fairly new, a few cards have been available commercially since the latter part of 1995, and, like everything else in the hardware biz, prices have continued to drop. For more information on graphics accelerator boards there's an FAQ at **http://www.cs.columbia.edu/~bm/ 3dcards/3d-cards1.html**.

Other VRML Browsers

While VRML 1.0 is skeletal in design, and is missing many features that are looked on as mandatory for "true" VRML, a number of 1.0-compliant browsers are still readily available on the Internet. You can find a listing of all them at **http://www.sdsc.edu/SDSC/Partners/vrml/ repos_software.html**.

This section, though, will focus on the two (nearly) compliant VRML 2.0 browsers—SGI's Cosmo Player and Sony's Cyber Passage. Both of these browsers can run stand-alone or as a helper application in Netscape.

Cosmo Player

Cosmo Player from SGI (Silicon Graphics) isn't just based on Moving Worlds—it supports VRML 2.0 as defined by the VAG. It also supports VRML 1.0 so you can view many of the VRML 1.0 worlds still on the Web. It's available for Windows95, WindowsNT, and IRIX 5.3 or 6.2, and also requires—yes, you guessed it—Netscape Navigator (2.0 or greater).

The fact that Cosmo player is a true VRML 2.0 browser is particularly important if you are interested in building your own VRML worlds. With SGI committed to maintaining Moving Worlds future refinements, any content you create for Cosmo Player now will continue to be supported cross-platform and cross-browser according to industry standards.

Cosmo seamlessly integrates itself into Netscape, much like Live3D, but its interface is a bit different. The difference is a feature Cosmos inherited from its VRML 1.0 father (a VRML browser called Webspace) called the dashboard.

The dashboard pops up by default whenever you use Cosmo Player, in the lower part of the view window (see fig. 16.6). All you need to do is click on the control you want and move your mouse in the desired direction.

FIG. 16.6

Three on-screen controls, from left to right, control your movement: The first moves you forward, back, left or right; the second (the sphere) pans you left, right, up, and down; the third tilts you up or down.

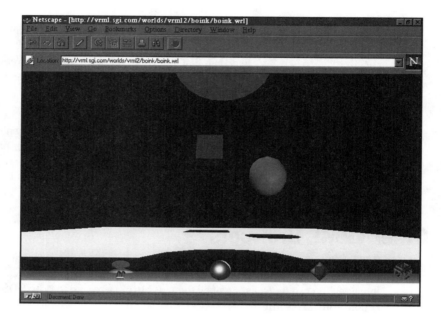

Cosmo supports a number of customizable options, including the ability to pick a traveling speed (by default Cosmo will choose the speed based upon the size and scale of the scene you load) or change the speed that may have been defined by the author of the VRML world you're viewing (see fig. 16.7).

FIG. 16.7

A simple click will allow you to travel slower or faster—or just use Cosmo's default

For more information on Cosmo, SGI provides a dedicated online help site at **http://vrml.sgi.com/cosmoplayer/beta1/help/index.html**.

Sony's Cyber Passage

Sony has done an impressive job so far of integrating VRML 2.0 into their browser. The result is a product that can be used either as a stand-alone world viewer or as speedy helper application in Netscape.

Though Cyber Passage is based on the enhanced-VRML of Moving Worlds, it will still handle any VRML 1.0 worlds you want to view. In addition to VRML 3D models, the Browser can support:

- Autonomous moving objects using Script Language
- Sound
- 3D Video or motion pictures
- Interactive object, sound, and motion picture capability by script
- Netscape NCAPI and loading of files/display of HTML files in Netscape Navigator
- Collision detection

In addition to the VRML file format, Cyber Passage also reads a number of other files, including BMP, RAS, GIF, and JPEG for textures; BMP movies; WAV and MOD for sound; and TCL scripting. Future releases promise to include support for AVI movies, MIDI music, and JavaScripting.

Probably the most interesting aspect of Sony's foray into VRML 2.0 is some of the work they're doing with servers. A server product, called Cyber Passage Bureau, uses Avatars (much like World's Chat, which you'll see later) to track all users who are sharing a space using the Cyber Passage browser.

Latest releases of Cyber Passage, Cyber Passage Bureau and Cyber Passage Conductor (a VRML authoring tool) can be downloaded from Sony's "Virtual Society on the Web" page at **http://vs.sony.co.jp/VS-E/works/downld1.html#CP**.

Part
III

Ch
16

Configuring and Using VRML Browsers

Detailed explanations of how to set up all types of helper applications are provided in chapter 10, "Configuring Helper Applications." For those of you who feel comfortable with setting Netscape's parameters, see table 16.1 for the MIME types, subtypes, and extension types required to configure the various VRML viewers with Netscape.

Table 16.1 Settings for Configuring Netscape to Use VRML Browsers as Helper Applications

Platform	MIME Type	Subtype	Extension
Windows95	x-world	x-vrml	.WRL
WindowsNT, UNIX	x-world	x-vrml	.WRL
	application	x-inventor	.IV
	application	x-gzip	.GZ
	x-world	x-vrml	.WRL
Macintosh	x-world	x-vrml	.WRL
	x-world	x-3dmf	.3DMF

For all of these helper applications, you should choose the option to launch the application.

Worlds for Exploration

This section is comprised mostly of sample VRML worlds—pointers to interesting worlds on the Web as well as some files we've included on the CD-ROM. But we begin with a pointer to an interactive, multiuser area of the Web that you can experience today—loosely based on VRML—that will give you a nice taste of some of what's to come with both Live3D and VRML 2.0.

Worlds Chat—VRML+izing IRC

Worlds Chat is basically a three-dimensional version of the Internet's IRC (Internet Relay Chat) service. IRC was initially developed as an improvement to the UNIX talk program, allowing many people to communicate in real-time by typing. To communicate on IRC, you must have an IRC client, connect to an IRC server, and choose a channel. All users' input scrolls up your screen, and you can join in as appropriate. Mostly, IRC is used as a recreational communications service.

The Worlds VRML+ incorporates three features absent in the VRML 1.0 standard:

- Avatar definitions (of yourself visible to others and vice versa)
- Motion (of others, visible to you)
- Text communication (between yourself and others)

Avatars are described using VRML. Each client sends a message to the Worlds Multiuser server that contains the description for that client's avatar. Due to packet size limitations, the avatar description message size is relatively small. One way to work around this packet size limitation is to send an avatar description message that consists of a WWWInline node pointing to a file containing a more fully detailed image of the avatar. This could eventually be extended so the avatar file includes sound, animation, and so on.

N O T E Avatar is originally a term from mythology, and meant the embodiment of a god come down to Earth. Neal Stephenson used the word in his 1993 novel *Snow Crash* to describe the visual representations of the characters as they interacted in a three-dimensional, worldwide, decentralized visual environment called the Metaverse. Stephenson's definition of avatar has already been adopted by many of those involved with VRML creation. ▪

Motion data contains information about the most recent positions of avatars in the three-dimensional space visible to the client, regardless of the physical location of the other clients. Motion has to be time-sensitive or it is meaningless information.

Simple text-based communication similar to the "chat" mode on many networks is the third major distinction between VRML+ and VRML. The ability to broadcast a message to multiple users, or just some of the multiple users within a range, may be added later.

More information on Worlds, Inc., and its products can be found via the Web at **http://www.worlds.net/**.

In any case, World's Chat shows very well what to expect from a multiuser VRML world. World's, Inc., has even taken their paradigm one step further, with the creation of another world called AlphaWorld. AlphaWorld is much like World's Chat, except that users get to "build" their "home spaces" in AlphaWorld's Cyber-domain. Your starting point to Alphaworld is **http://www.worlds.net/alphaworld**.

Worlds on the Web

Example VRML 1.0-compliant worlds are installed in a \worlds\ folder. These world files may be loaded directly into Live3D, with Netscape's File, Open File command.

> **N O T E** VRML worlds are substantially larger than Web pages. Some of the worlds mentioned below are more than 500KB. As the transferred files are so much larger than the average Web page, you will become painfully aware of the speed of your Internet connection. The VRML specification calls for adequate performance over a 14.4 modem dial-up connection, which is a bare minimum. A more realistic assessment of the minimum connection speed for VRML browsing is as fast as you can possibly afford. ■

On the Web, the place to start, for a large selection of VRML worlds (both 1.0 and 2.0) is at **http://www.sdsc.edu/SDSC/Partners/vrml/examples.html**. The page is arranged by subject and includes links to personal and organization home spaces as well.

The WWW Viewer Test Page at **http://www-dsed.llnl.gov/documents/WWWtest.html** provides sample URLs for a wide variety of content, which allows you to test your browser and how it hands data off to helper applications. It also has some other MIME pointers.

In 1991, David Blair created a surrealistic film called *WAX: Or the Discovery of Television Among the Bees*. WaxWeb (at **http://bug.village.virginia.edu**) is Blair's entire feature-length film (2,000+ hypertext documents, roughly 1.5 gigabytes) accessible as a hypertext narrative. The VRML portion of the site consists of approximately 250 rooms worth of VRML, and will give you a feel for what other people might do later.

Serch is a searchable index of VRML sites, which may be viewed in HTML or VRML. The URL for Serch is **http://www.virtpark.com/theme /serch.html**.

> **N O T E** Appropriately, you can access Serch in VRML mode by using the above URL and replacing the .HTML extension with .WRL. ■

DOOM Conquers the World?

One enterprising project is a parser that converts a .WAD file (a map file from Id Software's incredibly popular first-person marine-kills-demons game DOOM) to an .IV (Open Inventor) file. So, those of you who played DOOM and DOOM II on DOS, UNIX, and Macintoshes until carpal-tunnel syndrome set in, in a short time might be surfing a 3D shopping mall and thinking to yourselves, "This floor plan looks familiar_ there's a pig-demon around the corner here! Don't go in!" To those of you who spent days designing fascinating layouts for others, don't wipe those .WAD files—they might be your VRML architecture portfolio.

Information on the wadtoiv project (and the source code) can be found at **http:// www-white.media.mit.edu/~kbrussel/wadtoiv.html**.

Now That You're Hooked on VRML

If you're interested in learning more about VRML, perhaps your best starting point is at **http://vrml.wired.com**. The original VRML forum, it has information on the history of VRML, proto-VRML proposals, and archives of the www-vrml mailing list. You can subscribe to the mailing lists to see what has changed since yesterday. You can examine the archives of the mailing lists to backtrack conversational threads and see how the participants got to their current stage of a given discussion.

From there, go to the VRML Repository at the San Diego Supercomputer Center (SDSC) at **http://www.sdsc.edu/vrml**. This site is meticulously updated and has resources and pointers to resources on just about anything VRML-related.

If you are interested in doing anything serious with VRML, get the fastest Internet connection you can find. While the designers of VRML have set their goals to be "acceptable performance on low-bandwidth connections," their specification of low-bandwidth is a 14.4 dial-up modem connection. This minimum requirement means that anything less than that is going to be almost totally unusable by any but the most patient.

Finally, this chapter has focused on VRML browser software. However, someone must build the VRML world before you can travel through it. VRML authoring software is being written almost as fast as browsers are. Silicon Graphics' WebSpace Author, Caligari's Fountain and World Builder products, Paragraph's Homespace Builder and products from Virtus are all good choices. VREAM (**http://www.vream.com**) also has a product called VRCreator, in addition to their WIRL browser. For more current information on the VRML authoring field, check the VRML Repository at **http://www.sdsc.edu/SDSC/Partners/vrml/software/ modelers.html**. ●

## CHAPTER 17

Using Compressed/ Encoded Files

File compression and encoding are not two of the most exciting topics you'll encounter on the Internet. Both are file conversion operations you'll likely perform sooner or later, but let's face it, they are about as exciting as watching grass grow.

You might be able to avoid binary file encoding if you have absolutely no interest in newsgroups, but you'll find it nearly impossible to escape using compressed files, especially considering the number of examples of .ZIP archive files that are used just in this book.

In this chapter, you learn:

■ How Netscape works with compressed and encoded files

■ The distinction between compressed and encoded files and their uses

■ How to convert compressed and encoded files

■ Where to find (or how to locate) the Netscape helper applications you need ■

What Is File Compression and How Is It Done?

Explaining file compression is relatively easy. Simply stated, it is a method of reducing the size of one or more files so the files can either be stored in a smaller space, or transmitted in a shorter time and later returned to their "normal" size. The .ZIP files (also called archive files) that are mentioned through this text are examples of one type of compressed archive file.

File compression works by examining a file for repeating characters (or bytes) or repeating sequences of characters, removing those repeating characters, and replacing them with a symbol representing how many characters were in the original sequence.

Here is a highly simplified example of how basic file compression works. For example, suppose a compression program examined a file and found the following sequence of characters:

XmmP XmmP XmmP AAAA AAAA XmmP XmmP XmmP AAAA AAAA AAAA

This sequence of characters could be replaced with the following representation:

3(Xmmp) 2(AAAA) 3(Xmmp) 3(AAAA)

Or, it could be replaced with this representation:

2(3(Xmmp) 2(AAAA)) 4(A)

In this example, the original character sequence is 55 characters (bytes) long (counting the trailing space). The first representation is only 32 characters long, and 58 percent as large as the original sequence. The second representation is only 24 characters long, and 43.6 percent as large as the original sequence.

Either of these "compressed" representations of the original character sequence can be used to recreate the original. This is a highly simplified description of what is correctly referred to as a substitutional compression scheme.

What's important to remember is that you don't have to understand how compression schemes work their magic in order to use compression utilities. If, however, you have a greater interest in file compression and want more detailed information, check out the FAQs in the newsgroup comp.compression. (For more information on reading FAQs in newsgroups, see chapter 8, "Reading UseNet Newsgroups with Netscape.")

Compression Applications

Since Netscape is totally incapable of working with compressed archive files, you need another program to decompress archive files you download from FTP sites.

There are numerous programs you can set up in Windows, either 3.1 or 95, or DOS, to work with Netscape to compress and decompress files. One of the best is WinZip, a Windows-based version of the popular PKZIP file compression utility.

WinZip

WinZip, by Nico Mak Computing, is a shareware product patterned after the highly successful and ubiquitous DOS-based file compression utility PKZIP. Without a doubt you will find WinZip to be a highly useful and versatile Windows-based application for many of the following reasons:

- The vast majority of compressed files you are likely to download from FTP sites are in a .ZIP archive format.

- WinZip supports the native .ZIP format without the need for PKZIP or PKUNZIP, and also supports the .ARJ, .LZH, and .ARC file compression formats in the PC environment.

- WinZip is a Windows application and easily integrates into your Windows environment.

- WinZip 6.0 is a 32-bit application designed to work in the Windows 95 32-bit environment and supports numerous Windows 95 features, including long file names.

- WinZip also decompresses other popular Internet compression formats such as TAR, gzip, and UNIX compress.

In figure 17.1, you see the main operating screen for WinZip, version 6.0.

Part
III

Ch
17

FIG. 17.1
WinZip 6.0 is the Windows 95 version of the popular file compression utility.

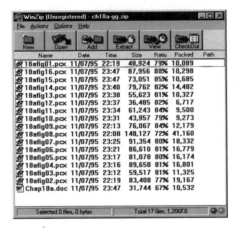

You can find WinZip on the CD-ROM with this book or on the WinZip page at **http://www.winzip.com/winzip/index.html** (see fig. 17.2).

Installing WinZip   Because WinZip is a Windows-based program, you install and use it the same way as most other Windows programs. To install the Windows 95 version of WinZip 6.0:

1. Copy the self-extracting archive file WinZip95.EXE into a temporary folder and run the file to extract the installation files from the archive.

2. Run SETUP.EXE to install WinZip.

   ▶ **See** "Configuring Helper Applications," **p. 257**

FIG. 17.2

The WinZip home page.

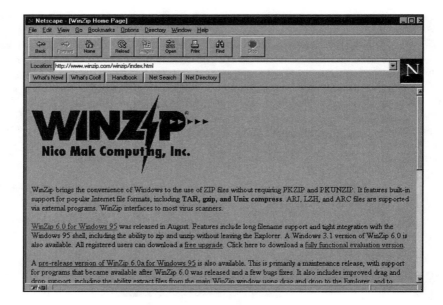

Using WinZip   Using WinZip to compress files into an archive is fairly simple:

1. Start WinZip and select File, New Archive, press Ctrl+N, or select the New icon.
2. Give the archive a name and select the folder (or directory) where you want the archive file stored.
3. Select the files you want to compress and place them in the archive. Select OK.

You can also configure it in Netscape to work as a helper application. (For more information on helper applications, see chapter 10, "Configuring Helper Applications.")

You will want to use the following types:

- application/zip
- application/tar
- application/gzip
- application/x-compress

You will also want to create the following types:

- application/arc
- application/arj
- application/lzh

N O T E Even though WinZip performs basic archiving operations without outside help, some advanced archiving features do require PKZIP and PKUNZIP from PKware, Inc., LHA.EXE from Haruyasu Yoshizaki, or the Shareware ARJ product from Robert Jung. Mainly these advanced archiving features center around creating archives rather than decompressing or extracting files from archives. ■

You can also create what are called self-extracting archive files using the WinZip Self-Extractor utility. A self-extracting archive file decompresses the files stored in its archive without the need for WinZip. This is becoming a popular method for distributing software. Netscape distributes its software products over the Internet in self-extracting archive files.

Self-extracting archive files have an .EXE extension instead of the .ZIP extension and are "run" the same as you would any other executable program to decompress the files stored in its archive. The WinZip Self-Extractor utility can also be downloaded from the WinZip home page.

LHA

Another competitor still in the PC/DOS file compression race is LHA, shown in figure 17.3, by Haruyasu Yoshizaki. LHA still maintains a small, loyal following, mainly because LHA is small, fast, and free. It is distributed as freeware, not shareware. You can download a copy of LHA version 2.13 from **http://www.mid.net/MSDOS_A/00-files.html**. The file name to download is LHA213.EXE, which is a self-extracting archive file.

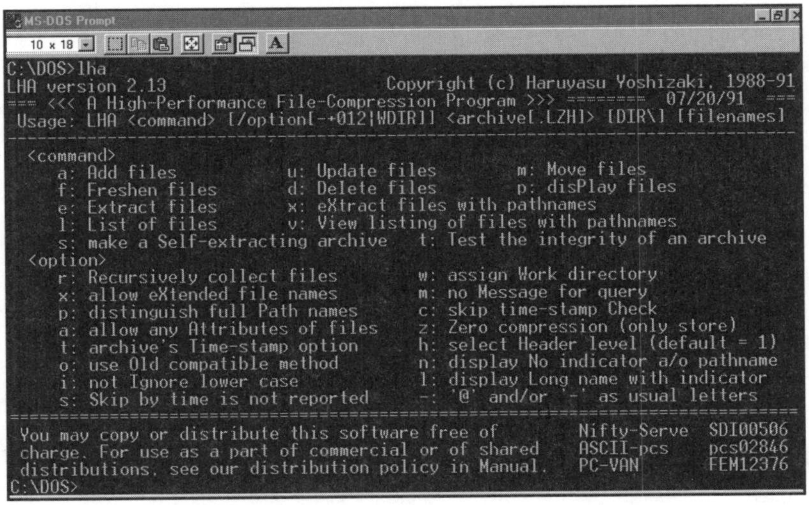

FIG. 17.3
The LHA file compression utility.

Part
III

Ch
17

The Hows and Whys of File Encoding and Decoding

While file compression can be viewed as a convenience (you really don't have to save time and space), file encoding and decoding are a necessity. File encoding grew out of the need to be able to post binary files on UseNet newsgroups.

The first UseNet was created in 1979 between Duke and the University of North Carolina using UUCP (UNIX-to-UNIX Communications Protocol, also called UNIX-to-UNIX CoPy). Then, as now, UseNet was only set up to copy 7-bit ASCII files, since originally only text files (messages) were intended to be posted and sent between UseNet systems. Posting binary files presented a problem. Binary files, such as programs, graphic files, and even compressed archive files, require 8 bits. So in order to post binary files to newsgroups, either you change newsgroups to work with 8-bit files, or you need a means of converting 8-bit binary files to 7-bit ASCII files. The solution is what has been termed UUEncoding—encoding 8-bit binary files to a 7-bit ASCII text file format (and UUDecoding to convert the ASCII files back into their original binary format). Figure 17.4 shows what an encoded binary looks like.

FIG. 17.4

A binary file encoded into 7-bit ASCII.

TIP   As you might guess, whenever you encode a binary file to ASCII, the result is a larger file since it often takes several "text" characters to represent binary information. For this reason, it is a common practice to compress binary files before encoding them.

Another limitation of UseNet carried over from its earlier days is a 32KB limit on file and message size because some early computers could only handle files up to this size. This file and message size limitation is why you often see long messages and large files broken into two or more parts.

> **N O T E**   Even though many newsgroup users still adhere to the 32KB limit on file and message size, many newer systems are not restricted by this limitation, so you still see files and messages exceeding 32KB. ▓

Initially (back in the old days of UNIX shell accounts), separate utility programs were used for encoding (UUEncode) binary to ASCII, and decoding (UUDecode) ASCII back to binary. This also meant that if you received the encoded file in several pieces, you had to edit the text file pieces back into one file before you could decode the ASCII file back into a binary format. You were lucky if the encoding program you were using had enough smarts to be able to put the pieces back together. Fortunately, now many newsreaders have built-in UUEncode/UUDecode functionality, allowing you to download/view or upload/attach binary files on-the-fly (and put the pieces back together). Netscape has thoughtfully included this functionality in its newsreader.

Encoding/Decoding with Netscape's Newsreader

In this chapter, we concentrate on encoding and decoding binary files using Netscape's newsreader and not on how to use Netscape's newsreader. (For more information on using Netscape's newsreader, see chapter 8, "Reading UseNet Newsgroups with Netscape.")

Many of the binary files you see posted in newsgroups are pictures—pictures of animals, pictures of places and things, pictures of outer space, and lots and lots of pictures of people, mostly famous. A large percentage of the pictures you see posted are in either JPEG format (.JPG, .JPE, .JPEG) or in GIF format (.GIF).

Decoding a Binary File   Netscape's newsreader, like the Netscape Web browser, is configured to display JPEG and GIF files without using a helper application. This means that whenever you see a JPEG or GIF file posted, you can download the file by double-clicking it, and when the download completes, the Netscape news-reader immediately displays the file (see fig. 17.5).

Encoding a Binary File   Just as the Netscape newsreader is configured to decode binary files on-the-fly, you can also use it to encode binary files you want to post to newsgroups. You create a message the same as you normally would and click Attach. When you attach the file, select the Convert to Plain Text radio button (see fig. 17.6).

FIG. 17.5

The Netscape newsreader displaying the USS Enterprise NCC-1701D.

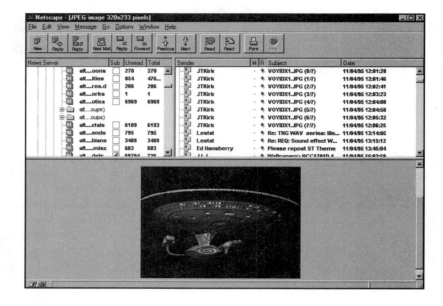

FIG. 17.6

Encoding an attached binary (.JPG) file.

Getting Your Encoded Files Decoded

Netscape in its current incarnations (versions 2.x and 3.x) only supports decoding and encoding of one-part binaries. It does not handle so-called "multi-part" binary files (larger UUencoded files broken down into several smaller sections). So, if viewing binaries is a major part of your Internet activities or if you have another newsreader you are absolutely in love with and refuse to switch to Netscape's newsreader no matter what, there are a number of encoding/decoding utilities available that let you encode and decode files manually. There are a few you can find on FTP sites, and as we stated earlier, encoding and decoding files are not flashy or sexy, and may just be slightly more exciting than watching paint dry.

WinCode   WinCode is a Windows-based encoding/decoding program, which you can use to manually encode or decode binary files (see fig. 17.7). WinCode is distributed as freeware, but the author charges $5.00 if you want the Help file.

FIG. 17.7

WinCode, a simple
Windows-based
encoding/decoding
application.

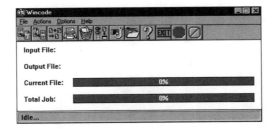

Install WinCode from the CD that accompanies this book. You can accept the defaults during
the installation.

Start WinCode to open its main operating screen. From WinCode's main operating screen, you
perform all basic encoding and decoding operations as well as set options for both. WinCode
creates a status report after each file coding operation you perform so you can see if there
were any problems (see fig. 17.8).

FIG. 17.8

WinCode's file operation
status report.

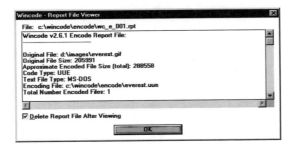

Part
III

Ch
17

Building World Class Home Pages for Netscape

## CHAPTER 18

Planning Your Web Site

Like the desktop publishing revolution of the last decade, computers are once again changing the way the written word is published and presented to readers. Last time, it meant everybody with a computer and a decent printer could develop a newsletter for their organization, advertising for their business, or their own greeting cards.

In the electronic publishing revolution, everyone now has the ability to create their own pages for the World Wide Web. And, just as with the early years of desktop publishing, Web publishing is growing easier by the day. As more of the big name companies start to include Web development tools in their products—and as a few smaller companies come to the forefront with their own revolutionary tools—Web page development will become something nearly anyone can do in the very near future.

For now, though, it still takes a little effort and education—hence the success of Web development firms and consultants. And, frankly, just because desktop publishing allowed more people than ever to dabble in the world of page layout, that didn't mean they all became commercial artists overnight. Most of the best stuff on the Web will continue to be developed by professional ad and design people. But the rest of us can put a page on the Web, too. In fact, that's what this and the next seven chapters are all about. ■

In this chapter, you learn the following:

- The role of HTML and HTML standards in Web development
- What's currently possible with HTML on the Web
- How to set up your own personal Web site
- What a Web site should cost you
- Which tools you need to get started with HTML ■

What Is HTML and What Are the Standards?

The HyperText Markup Language, or HTML, is the standard by which documents on the Web are presented in browsers like Netscape. As the name implies, HTML is a method for taking standard text and marking it up in such a way that the browser knows what styles, sizes, and emphases to use when displaying the text.

In addition to text styles, HTML is also responsible for telling the browser when text on the page should be considered a link, where to insert graphical elements, and when to insert special elements like imagemaps, background graphics, mail-to commands, and other special features on the page. Figure 18.1 shows the behind-the-scenes HTML code for a sample Web page.

FIG. 18.1

The plain-text HTML codes behind a typical Web page. If you saw this in a browser, it would be pretty attractive.

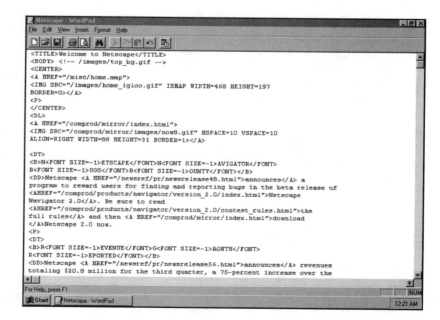

In figure 18.1, you might have noticed that HTML is all ASCII text. True to form for the Internet, we don't transmit a binary file from the Web server computer to the browser. HTML is all ASCII, which is then interpreted by the browser into formatted text and links.

Why Is HTML So Drab Looking?

If you're a veteran of DOS-based computing, you might notice that a raw HTML document looks a lot like a word processing document from a decade ago—like WordPerfect with reveal codes selected. And that's basically what HTML is. Because it's an emerging technology, we're basically seeing a new file format (like WordPerfect's .WPD format or MS Word's .DOC format) as it develops.

And since it's ASCII (instead of binary, like .WPD or .DOC files), we can see all the special codes used to format the text. In fact, we can even enter them ourselves to create our own Web pages.

The HTML Standards

The key to the World Wide Web, in fact, is the HTML standard. By sticking to this predetermined markup language, all Web browsers are capable (in varying degrees) of translating HTML codes into attractive Web pages. And, although it seems like the whole world is using Netscape, that's hardly true. There are many different browsers available for Windows, Mac, X Windows, and even command-line UNIX. In order for all these different browsers to see something relatively similar, it's important to stick to the standards.

The Current HTML Standard   Of course, as with any good computer industry standard, HTML has gone through a few different incarnations. Each new version builds on the previous; although some HTML commands have fallen into disuse while others have gained popularity, most browsers will theoretically accept any standard HTML command, starting with the original HTML, referred to (by some folks) with hindsight as HTML 1.0.

The first real coherent standard was HTML 2.0, as defined by the Internet Engineering Task Force (IETF) in July 1994. This is really an ongoing process, and technically the standard hasn't been formally set in stone. The point is moot, however, since the HTML 3.0 standard is already being worked on (and implemented) by IETF, various application developers, and Netscape.

HTML 2.0 at its essence defines a fairly basic set of HTML commands that leaves most of the formatting of a page to the individual browser. As the Web moves more toward a medium for graphic design (as opposed to just text-based document distribution), the standards are becoming increasingly more layout conscious.

The Emerging Standard HTML 3.0   It's difficult to know exactly what additions the HTML 3.0 standard will make to HTML 2.0, but it's clear that the standard will be more design-focused. Very likely to be included are some of the elements that are already included in Netscape versions 2.0 and above, including table formats, flowing text around figures, and math functions within HTML code.

HTML 3.0 is a clean superset of HTML 2.0, according to the IETF's documentation of the standard. This means that, as long as your documents adhere to the HTML 2.0 standard, browsers will continue to be able to read them, even as HTML 3.0 elements are introduced. This can be seen now, in fact, as Netscape has implemented many probable HTML 3.0 elements, while still being able to cleanly display HTML 2.0 formatted documents.

Fortunately, the bottom-line mentality (and, ironically, what is probably slowing the standard-building process) is loyalty to the simplicity of HTML and HTML 2.0. While Web development is becoming an increasingly sophisticated and professional pursuit, it's difficult to maintain the universal goal of the original HTML—that just about anyone can learn it.

The Non-Standard Netscape-Specific Commands   The fact that Netscape holds an estimated 70 percent of the browser market is a source of delight for some and heartache for others. With that sort of power in the market, Netscape Corp. has found it fairly easy to introduce its own extensions to HTML without suffering much backlash. Netscape's commanding lead in the browser market gives it a strong voice in formulating the standard while allowing it to react more quickly to customer desires (see fig. 18.2).

FIG. 18.2

Although some of these elements may eventually be part of the HTML 3.0 standard, they are currently Netscape-specific.

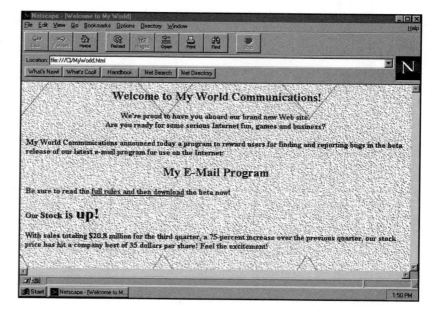

HTML features like blinking text and centered paragraphs are often confused for HTML 3.0 standard elements, but they're not. In fact, many of the HTML elements commonly found on the Web today—like different font sizes, flexible numbered lists, and background graphics—require Netscape or Netscape-compatible browsers to view. (You'll often come across Web sites that recommend using Netscape 1.1 or above for viewing.)

The question is, should you use Netscape commands in your HTML pages? You'll have to decide that for yourself. For the most graphical appeal, strongest layout, and flexibility, I'd have to say yes to Netscape commands. If your goal is to reach all Web users, you probably want to offer alternatives to Netscape commands on your Web pages.

What's Possible with HTML?

HTML documents can be enticingly simple to create—only slightly more difficult than typing text into a word processor or text editor. And, as you get started with HTML development, that may be all that interests you. If your goal is to put something as straightforward as your resume, your academic papers, or just a clean little ad for your company on the Web, then nothing particularly advanced is necessary (see fig. 18.3).

FIG. 18.3
An example of a simple HTML page. You can get your point across, even without heavy formatting or special elements.

Part IV
Ch
18

At the same time, it's possible to make a career of HTML development (and many folks do). As you move up to more and more advanced concepts, though, you begin to see that HTML really does have some of the trappings of a programming language—as well as some concessions to the world of the commercial artist. It's never mandatory that you get this involved with HTML—just as no one is forcing you to use advanced mail-merge functions in your word processing program. But, in both cases, the functionality is there if you need it.

Text Formatting, Links, and Simple Graphics

At its most basic, the goal of HTML is to present formatted text, hypertext links, and simple graphics that help make the text more readable or more communicative. The HTML 2.0 standard allows you to accomplish all of this; no further knowledge of HTML, Netscape commands, or computer programming is necessary.

If your goal is to simply get on the Web, you really don't have that much to worry about. You should be up and ready after three chapters of reading and a few hours of work.

▶ **See** "HTML Primer," **p. 433**

▶ **See** "Adding Links, Graphics, and Tables," **p. 459**

Serious Graphics and Clickable Maps

From the artist's point of view, one of the most popular advanced HTML elements is the imagemap. But don't let the name confuse you—these don't have a whole lot to do with maps of the world or road maps.

Imagemapping is a process by which specific parts of a particular graphic are designated as links to different Web pages or URL addresses. This allows the more advanced HTML creator to devise clever interface elements that make his Web pages more intuitive, more appealing, or, perhaps just more graphical (see fig. 18.4).

▶ **See** "Using Imagemaps," **p. 505**

Perhaps you can see why this technique is so important and popular for Web development. Suddenly links can be hidden behind graphical interfaces that look a lot like multimedia kiosks or other graphics presentation mediums. Instead of drab underlined text and single-graphic links, the possibilities for a creative interface become boundless. Netscape's recent addition of support for client-side imagemaps makes this an increasingly enticing prospect, because now imagemaps are an even more efficient way to create stunning interfaces.

FIG. 18.4

Creating your own
interface with
imagemaps.

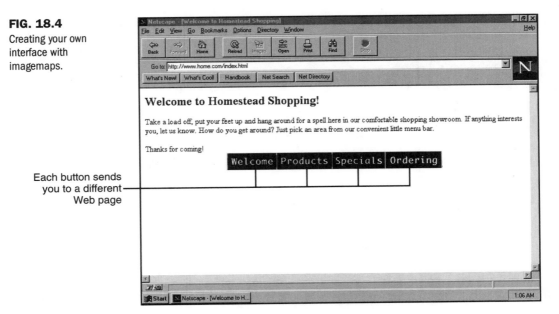

Each button sends
you to a different
Web page

The High End of HTML

At its most extreme, HTML becomes a programming language—or, at least, it invites programming languages into the fray. With HTML we can also create forms for getting user responses, allow users to search our site using keywords and search fields, or even conduct transactions over the Web—accepting credit card numbers or similar payment information in exchange for products or services.

Once the user fills in a form and sends it to your Web server to be processed, things are accomplished through what are known as CGI-BIN scripts. Created in Perl, C, and other popular scripting and programming languages, these mini-programs work behind the HTML scenes to generate on-the-fly responses to user queries (see fig. 18.5).

N O T E The CGI in CGI-BIN scripts stands for Common Gateway Interface. In essence, CGI-BIN is simply the standard way to call other programs for behind-the-scenes processing of information received through HTML forms. The programs themselves are fairly easy to create if you have any experience with UNIX shell scripting, C, Perl, or similar languages. ■

▶ **See** "Netscape Forms and CGI-BIN Scripts," **p. 557**

Part

IV

Ch

18

FIG. 18.5

Above: an HTML form being filled out. Below: the results, after a script processes the form's information.

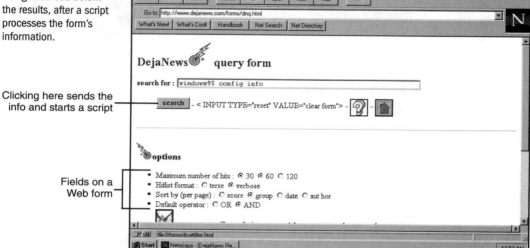

Clicking here sends the info and starts a script ────

Fields on a Web form ────

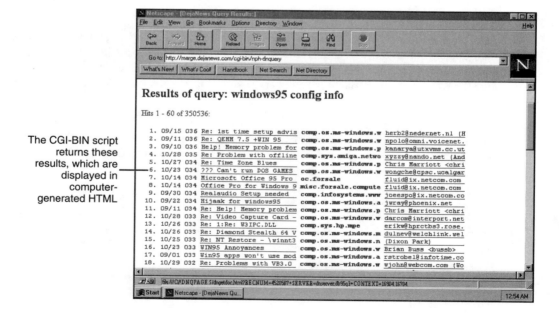

The CGI-BIN script returns these results, which are displayed in computer-generated HTML ────

Once again, Netscape is at the forefront with security and other options that make electronic commerce feasible and reasonably safe for the consumer and the Web developer. Beyond the text and graphics, the Web has emerged as a new medium for advertisement, customer service, and sales. But to get to that point takes some fairly acute HTML expertise.

> **N O T E** And then there's the next step: new Web-aware programming languages like JavaScript and Java. As these languages become more popular, CGI-BIN scripting may start to fade. See chapter 28, "Sun's Java and the Netscape Browser," chapter 29, "Java for C++ Programmers," and chapter 30, "JavaScript." ■

Setting Up Your Web Site

For the most part, new HTML developers will be creating pages that will then be made available on the Web by an Internet service provider (ISP) or an Internet presence provider (IPP). You simply write the HTML documents, create all appropriate graphic elements, and upload the finished work to your ISP. They then place the pages in the hierarchy of their Web presence, perhaps under a heading like Users' Pages or Business Pages.

> **N O T E** Organizations that call themselves Internet presence providers are generally Web publishers that don't offer Internet access. Internet service providers primarily offer Internet access (SLIP/PPP, etc.) but often offer Web sites to their users as well. ■

What becomes important here, then, are the services your ISP or IPP offer you, and how much it costs. As Web development becomes more specialized, you'll see rates for Web development that are similar to freelance design and writing costs. But what should you be paying if you do the Web development yourself?

How Much a Web Site Costs

The prices for Web site service vary dramatically from region to region and provider to provider. Those prices also tend to vary based on your needs—for instance, whether or not you'll be using the Web service for business or pleasure. For the most part, though, there are two basic factors that affect how much a Web site costs to the provider: disk space and page activity. These costs, in turn, should be passed on to you in a reasonably profitable way.

T I P Look for special deals, especially in major metro areas. Many ISPs offer free or substantially discounted Web sites in exchange for your Internet service business. Others may offer cheap Web sites as a perk when you use their service for multiple Internet accounts or higher-priced corporate accounts.

Storage Charges   You'll need to consider the size of every HTML page you create, the graphics you add to it, and any other elements you add to your site, like imagemaps or scripts. A typical Web page, with small graphics and 30-40 lines of text, will take around 20,000 bytes of storage space. This should cost you only pennies per month to maintain.

> **N O T E**   Your provider needs to be specifically set up to allow you to use imagemaps and scripts, and they may charge extra for these services. ■

Large corporate sites can be many megabytes in size, however, and depending on the ISP, charges per megabyte are generally somewhere in the $5-$10 per megabyte range. So, even if you have a very large Web site that is three megabytes in size (say, 50 highly graphical 80 KB pages), you might still be charged between only $15 and $30 a month to store that site.

Throughput Charges   Consider this, however. Many ISPs also charge you for the throughput that your site sees—that is, the amount of data that is transferred from the site across the Web to users. This number can also often be a dollar or a few dollars per megabyte. But, depending on the size of your site and the site's popularity, this arrangement can get expensive quickly. Consider a very popular corporate site that gets, for instance, 50 visitors a day—and an average visitor downloads two 25,000-byte pages:

>   50 visits * 50,000 bytes = 2,500,000 bytes per day
>
>   2.5 megabytes * $5 per megabyte = $12.50 per day

So, this site is costing you perhaps $15 a month for storage, but around $375 a month for throughput charges. Is this reasonable? It's on the high side of reasonable, to be sure. But nearly $400 a month isn't too much to spend if this site generates sales or adds a worthwhile aspect to your customer relations. In fact, it's nothing compared to a typical business' advertising costs. If it's just for fun, though, you may be paying too much—or your site may be too large.

TIP   Some providers offer flat-fee service for personal and corporate Web sites. Generally this will be a happy medium price that has a limit to the amount of space you can use (often 500 KB or 1 MB) but no real limit to throughput. If you anticipate high activity on your site, one of these plans might be your best choice.

Other Charges   Be aware, too, that many ISPs offer up other charges for your Web site. These can range significantly from an initial setup fee to a minimum monthly fee—or even a weekly or monthly maintenance fee that's a fixed, regular amount. Just make sure these fees seem reasonable. If not, shop around.

Also be aware that many ISPs and IPPs begin to act a lot like printing houses or ad agencies when it comes to creating the Web site for you. Rates of $50 to $125 an hour or more for creative services aren't uncommon. If you have graphics you need scanned, manipulated, or placed in your pages, be aware that those will cost you, too.

The key is to avoid being nickel-and-dimed on your Web site if your budget is tight. Learning a little HTML—at least enough to keep from being intimidated by it—can put you a little less at the mercy of the provider, and make you a smarter shopper. Once you realize that changing straight text into HTML documents really isn't that daunting of a prospect, you'll be much less likely to pay someone $50 or so per page to get it done.

Another big help is to pick the right provider in the first place. Like any growing industry, the Web services market is going to have its good companies, its not-so-good ones, and some failures.

Picking the Right Provider for Your Web Site

Again, choosing the right provider for displaying your Web pages has a lot to do with how and why you plan to create a Web site. Certain providers offer services that benefit the individual users, while others are more capable of filling the more demanding needs of the corporate site.

Tips for All Types of Sites   Anyone creating a Web site should take care to explore a few things about a potential provider. First and foremost should be their pricing—in fact, pricing can tell you a lot about a provider. A good provider will have straightforward, cost-based pricing that charges you for services rendered, while not forcing you to pay for services you don't need. Disk space and throughput charges are reasonable, but that doesn't mean all charges are.

The provider to be concerned about is one that has taken on more Web pages than its equipment—in this case its Web server—can handle. While shopping for a Web provider, spend some time on their Web site. Get a feel for whether or not the site reacts more slowly than other sites available locally or nationally. Do you notice a definite lag? Given that any Web server will experience occasional sluggishness, if you find that their server is regularly a bit slow, this is a good sign that their equipment isn't quite up to par.

TIP   Always be a little wary of ISPs that want or require long-term service contracts. If they offer discounts or increased services as an incentive for up-front payment, it may be worth the risk. But realize that it is a risk. There's no law that says an ISP has to stay in business.

Another sign is excessive charges for disk space, throughput, or high minimum charges for weekly or monthly Web service. A Web service company that focuses very closely on resource allocation may be doing so because their resources are limited. If things feel a bit tight at one provider, it may be in your best interest to shop around.

The Best Providers for Business Sites   Business users who intend to serve customers or generate sales from their Web site should consider that Web advertising is slightly different than most other types of advertising mediums. Why? Because customers have to seek you out. They have to know your URL and enter it in their browser (or click a link to your site) in order to see what you have to offer.

The savvy business Web site, then, is connected to a provider that actively seeks to help your Web site get hits—visits from Web users and potential customers. Sometimes a provider does this by setting up a virtual mall or an interesting home page for its users that point them in your direction (see fig. 18.6).

FIG. 18.6
Here's an attractive virtual mall site maintained by a Colorado-area Internet provider. This provides a service both to Web surfers in general and to this provider's Web site customers.

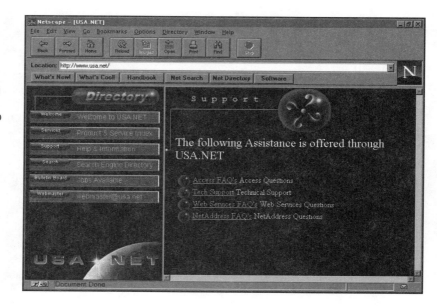

Other services they may offer you include lobbying to have your site included on popular Cool Sites or New Sites pages like those found at Netscape's Web site. Providers may also take it upon themselves to have your page registered with the Yahoo Web Directory, Infoseek, and other Web searching servers, so that your name comes up often when people all over the Web search for information and services you provide. At the very least, they should offer you some help in registering your site with these services, on your own.

Getting Your HTML Files to the Server

The final question you may ask about a provider is, how easy is it to maintain the Web site? Many providers will have you upload your pages to a central FTP server, and then they will take on the responsibility of adding or changing Web pages on your site. They may charge extra for this sort of maintenance, however, and it may take some time.

In other cases, you'll have a particular directory on the Web server to which you upload files, with the link to your page (from their virtual mall or users' home page) being a particular static file name like index.html (or index.htm for DOS-based servers). From there, you're free to create whatever links and additional pages you desire—even going so far as to create subdirectories on the site for organizing your materials. At least, you're free to do so as long as you don't go over any disk space or other limitations.

What's the best way to go? Whatever makes you most comfortable. If you'd rather have the provider take care of things, you'll probably have to pay for that service. But it may be worth it just to keep everything running smoothly.

Choosing Your Web Publishing Tools

The next step to successful HTML development is picking the right tools for the task. As HTML becomes a popular pursuit, there are more and more programs and utilities being developed to help you get a head start in HTML. Sifting through them can take some time, but you may find a gem that really is a considerable help.

You May Already Have Everything You Need!

If you're using the Netscape Gold edition, you already have an HTML editor built into Netscape. Just pull down the Window menu and choose the Editor command. This might be enough of an editor for all your HTML needs.

Even if you aren't using Netscape Gold, let me point out that you don't actually have to use any special program to create HTML pages. I've already mentioned that HTML is simply ASCII text, and it's true. So, a typical text editor (like Windows 95's WordPad, Mac's SimpleText, or UNIX's Emacs) is more than capable of creating any HTML page you can conceive.

Of course, the trick is that you need to know HTML pretty well to use just a text editor to create Web pages. That's why shareware and commercial HTML editors are popular alternatives to simple text editors. The better programs tend to make HTML creation much easier.

HTML Editor Programs

Most HTML editors improve on standard text editors in two different ways. First, they offer menu items for changing the way text appears in your HTML document, allowing you to be free from memorizing all the different HTML commands.

Second, some of these editors present HTML documents in a WYSIWYG (What You See Is What You Get) mode. If you create HTML documents in a simple text editor, you'll need to load them into Netscape to test them. With a good HTML editor program, you'll see exactly what the page will look like as you create it.

N O T E You might want to test your pages in browsers other than Netscape, too. Different browsers display pages in slightly different ways; you'll want to test your pages to make sure they look good in all of them. ■

The best of these programs do this in an intuitive way that really helps you create HTML documents quickly. Although you still need to understand how HTML works, some of the shortcuts offered by these programs will make your time spent creating HTML pages much more productive.

There are many, many HTML editors available for Windows, Windows 95, Macintosh, OS/2, and UNIX. My best suggestion would be to experiment with a few different offerings until you find one that you feel is the closest to what you need in an editor. A number of different editors for you to sample are available on the Netscape CD included with this book. The following examples aren't necessarily the programs that will be right for everyone, but they do represent some samples of what's available.

Part
IV

Ch
18

HTML Notepad   Among the most basic, and yet elegant, improvements on the simple text editor is HTML Notepad for Windows. Although the presentation is sparse, HTML Notepad is capable of creating almost any HTML or Netscape element, including tables, forms, blink, and foreign characters (see fig. 18.7). In fact, Netscape elements are found in their own menu (Netscapisms), so you'll know instantly when you're creating a Netscape-specific page.

HTML Notepad provides no special WYSIWYG features, requiring you to load pages-in-progress into Netscape to test. It automatically loads Netscape for you after every save, if you choose to do so in the Preferences menu. On top of that, HTML Notepad offers a very complete Help file that not only points you to the right menu for commands, but gives you a nice overview of HTML in general.

HTML Notepad is a product of Cranial Software (Adam Fraser and Lee Griffiths) in Great Britain. It is distributed as shareware—after a reasonable trial period, the writers ask that you mail them the $30 registration fee. The latest version of HTML Notepad can be found at **http://www.cranial.com/software/htmlnote**. It requires at least Windows 3.1 and a 386-based computer.

FIG. 18.7
HTML Notepad is a solid, small HTML editor that improves on simple text editors for HTML creation.

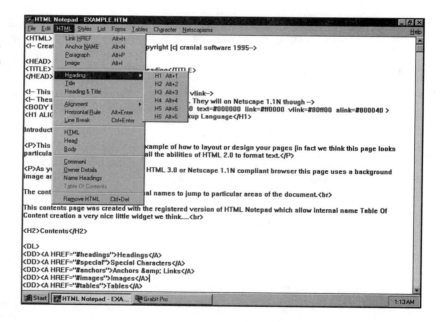

CMed   This editor is unique as one of the first to take full advantage of Windows 95, although many will follow over the next year. Taking off at full 32-bit speed, CMed has an attractive and easy-to-use interface that is especially good at handling higher-end HTML creation, like HTML 3.0 and Netscape-specific commands (see fig. 18.8).

FIG. 18.8

The CMed HTML editor, specifically designed for Windows 95.

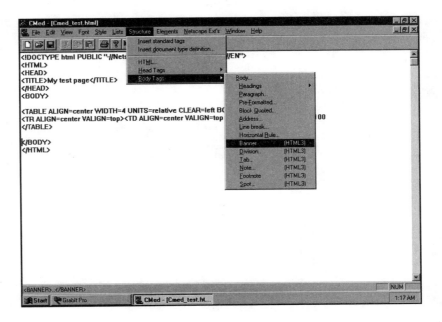

Another text-based (non-WYSIWYG) editor, CMed is aimed at the slightly more advanced HTML creator—there isn't quite as much friendly help and as many pointers here as there are with HTML Notepad. It is, ultimately, a little easier for the seasoned HTML user, and there seems to be more complete coverage of HTML 3.0 and other advanced elements.

Developed by Chad Matheson at the University of Western Australia as a school project, CMed has another distinct advantage—it's freeware. The latest version can be found at **http://www.iap.net.au/%7Ecmathes**. It requires Windows NT 3.5 or Windows 95 to operate.

HoTMetaL Free and HoTMetaL Pro   HoTMetaL Free and HoTMetaL Pro take a fundamentally different approach to HTML creation. In a nutshell, you don't have to understand HTML. HoTMetaL is a completely WYSIWYG environment that is designed to shield you from the underlying HTML codes, a phenomenon that, earlier in this chapter, I suggested we would begin to see more frequently in Web design tools.

Instead of inserting HTML commands, HoTMetaL users simply enter text on-screen, select it, and choose the formatting or linking elements from the program's menus. Like WordPerfect of old, HoTMetaL then allows you to either hide or display the resulting HTML tags. Hidden, they provide you with a WYSIWYG representation of your page—even including graphical elements (see fig. 18.9).

Part
IV

Ch
18

FIG. 18.9
HoTMetaL Free allows
you to view HTML in a
WYSIWYG environment,
with or without HTML
codes.

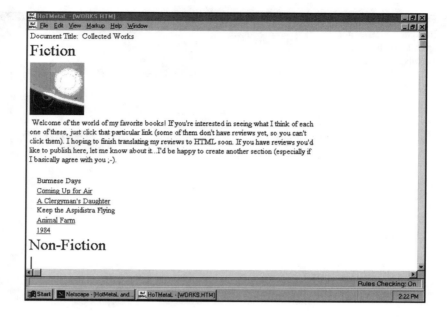

HoTMetaL Free is a scaled-down freeware version of the commerical application HoTMetaL
Pro, which retails for an astounding $195. The Pro version does, however, offer just about
everything you'd need to create HTML pages, including spell checking and thesaurus, search-
and-replace, inline graphics display, tables support, templates, and forms support. Plus, an
added bonus over many editors is the HTML parser, which actually checks to make sure your
HTML documents are valid and correctly formatted.

Both are the work of SoftQuad, Inc. The HoTMetaL Free version can be accessed via
SoftQuad's web site at **http://www.ptgs.com/links/sfq/sfqhome.html**. HoTMetaL Pro is
also available for the Macintosh, as should be HoTMetaL Free, in early 1996.

HotDog Standard   Although not a WYSIWYG editor, HotDog Standard (along with HotDog
Pro) remains an overwhelming favorite of folks all over the Web. With support for advanced
HTML features, including true HTML 3.0 elements (along with Netscape-specific elements),
HotDog is especially popular with folks on the cutting-edge of Web design.

One of the more impressive features of HotDog Standard is its built-in support for more easily
creating tables and forms using dialog boxes that guide you through the process (see fig.
18.10). Just click the Table or Forms button on HotDog's button bar, and you're presented with
a dialog box to help you create the element. This lets you avoid some of the tiresome, detailed
HTML coding usually required.

FIG. 18.10
HotDog Standard's
table editor lets you
avoid HTML.

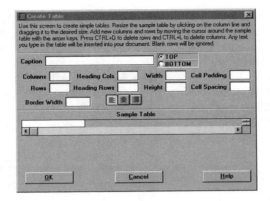

HotDog Standard is shareware, available for $29.95 from Sausage Software at **http://www.sausage.com/**. HotDog Pro is available for $99.95 and features spell checking, a built-in page viewer, HTML syntax checking, and the ability to convert ASCII files into HTML documents.

N O T E You might want to check this out: Sausage Software uses the Netscape Commerce Server to allow you to securely purchase HotDog over the Web. ▣

N O T E Web Weaver for Macintosh is a popular editor for Mac users. It's considered semi-WYSIWYG, meaning it shows you a good deal of the formatting that will appear in your browser, but not necessarily all of it. Web Weaver uses floating palette windows to give you access to common HTML tags, while the rest are available as menu commands. You can also create your own custom palettes for getting at your favorite or most used elements. ▣

Other Programs for HTML Creation

Aside from HTML editors, there are a couple of other programs you'll probably find useful for creating your Web site. Since graphics tend to be a focus on the Web, you'll want programs to deal with those. If you have access to professional graphics programs like CorelDRAW! or Adobe Photoshop, you'll definitely find good reasons to use them. There are shareware alternatives for graphics, though.

You may also want to create and make sound files available on your Web site. To do this, you may need still more shareware programs.

Graphics   LView Pro, a popular shareware image-manipulation application, is able to create transparent GIFs. (Graphics files with transparent backgrounds tend to look better on the Web; see fig. 18.11.) It is available at **ftp://oak.oakland.edu/SimTel/win3/graphics** and elsewhere.

Another very popular, and very good, shareware graphics manipulation program is PaintShop Pro. PSPro rivals some of the commercial image programs for its depth of features and ability to work with various file formats. It can be downloaded at **http://www.jasc.com/index.html**. You may also want to look into a Windows program designed to translate between common graphics file formats, like Graphics Workshop (gwswn11.zip), Image 'n' Bits (ima.zip), and Picture Man (pman155.zip), all of which are available from **ftp://gatekeeper.dec.com/pub/micro/msdos/win3/desktop/** and other popular Windows FTP sites. Because most Web browsers support only GIF and JPG formats, you'll want to convert any graphics you have in other formats to one of these two.

FIG. 18.11

A transparent GIF on the World Wide Web. Notice how the graphic seems to be sitting almost directly on the background of the page.

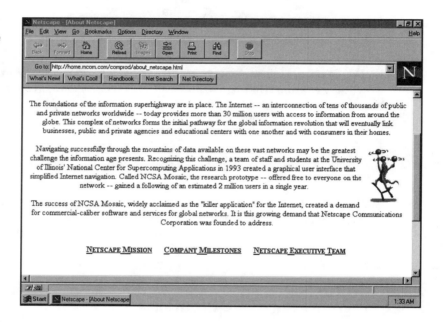

Some of these applications are also capable of rudimentary image manipulation, and can be an inexpensive way to deal with images if you don't own a professional graphics package. Another popular program for image manipulation is WinGIF (wingif14.zip), also available from **ftp://gatekeeper.dec.com/pub/micro/msdos/win3/desktop/** and others.

Sounds   As your familiarity and interest in creating Web sites continues to grow, you may also eventually want to experiment with programs that create sounds, animations, and even digital movies. Tools like these can take some learning, but, once you have your movies and sounds created, adding them to your Web site is relatively easy.

For sound, look into Gold Wave (gldwav21.zip) at **ftp://oak.oakland. edu/SimTel/win3/sound/**, a WAV to AU translation program that turns basic Windows sounds into AU format sounds—the standard file type for sounds on the Web.

Emerging Tools Page Layout and Word Processors

Not to be ignored are the growing numbers of tools and upgrades that add HTML capabilities to programs that many of us already have. Of particular interest are add-ons for common word processing programs like Microsoft Word and WordPerfect for Windows—both of which have programs available that translate text from word processing documents into HTML documents.

Also in the works are improvements and upgrades to familiar desktop publishing programs, like Adobe PageMaker and QuarkXPress, that allow HTML page creation. These are very interesting to commerical artists and other professionals who currently use these programs for publishing and advertising layout. An easy transition to HTML will be welcome by all.

The question is, do these solutions do enough? For now, you still need to know the basics of HTML, and you need some sort of editor to do much creative layout in HTML. At the moment, you'll probably have more luck creating higher-end sites with a good HTML editor and some graphics programs than you will trying to use print-oriented programs for HTML. It will take a while for those programs to fully cover the ground between print and Web publishing, while current HTML editors have been designed with the Web in mind.

That said, we may not be too far from programs that will shield users from HTML altogether. Soon, graphical interfaces and HTML conversion tools may make learning HTML codes as useful as learning embedded codes in word processing documents. Why type <bold>boldface text</bold>, when you can just select the text and click a button on the program's interface?

Part
IV

Ch
18

HTML Tools for WordPerfect Users

Ease of HTML creation is the key to most of the add-ons and functionality built into the latest versions of popular word processing and desktop publishing programs. WordPerfect for Mac 3.5, for example, is rumored to include HTML tools as part of the program.

For WordPerfect for Windows users, Novell offers the WordPerfect Internet Publisher add-on as a free download from its Web site at **http://wp. novell.com/elecpub/inttoc.htm**. This add-on turns WordPerfect into a WYSIWYG HTML editor, and even comes with a copy of Netscape for final testing.

HTML Tools for Microsoft Word Users

For Microsoft Word 95, Microsoft itself provides the Internet Assistant for MS Word 95 as a free download from its FTP site. This add-on allows you to create basic HTML pages in MS Word, then use the included translator to save your document in HTML format. The download is available at **http://198.105.232.6:80/msword/fs_wd.htm**.

TIP Internet Assistant for MS Word 6.0 (for Windows 3.1) is also available from **http://www.microsoft.com/msoffice/freestuf/msword/download/ia/ia1z/default.htm**.

For all versions of Microsoft Word, including Windows 3.1, NT, Windows 95, and Macintosh (see fig. 18.12), Jill Swift has created ANT_HTML, a template and button bar add-on to MS Word that helps you create HTML documents. It allows you to create pages without worrying about HTML codes, translate HTML pages to WYSIWYG Word documents, and insert special characters into HTML documents. It's also a great tool for translating between HTML and .DOC, ASCII, .RTF, and other file formats.

FIG. 18.12

Word for Mac users gets the same HTML functionality as Word for Windows users with ANT_HTML.

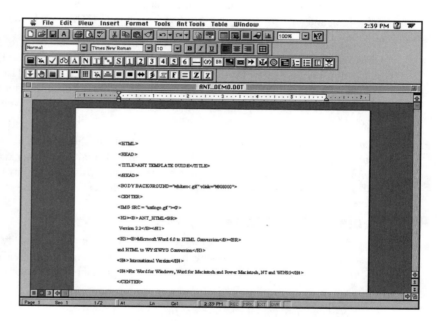

A demo of ANT_HTML (the template works for all Word 6.0 and above versions) is available at **http://www.w3.org/hypertext/WWW/Tools/Ant.html**. The commercial version of the program is $39. ●

## CHAPTER 19

Creating Web Pages with Netscape Navigator Gold

Publishing on the Web is surprisingly easy, and creating your own home page is probably the best first step. It's a great way to get a feel for how HTML works, and you'll produce something you can use, too. How do you go about producing a home page? Well, you can use any of several freeware, shareware, and commercial HTML authoring tools. But in this chapter, you're going to learn about one in particular: Netscape Navigator Gold. ■

Working with Navigator Gold

Netscape Navigator Gold contains everything that Netscape Navigator contains, plus some great authoring and editing tools that help you create a Web page from scratch or take a Web page that you like and modify it. In this chapter we've assumed that you are working with Navigator Gold. You can download it from the same place you retrieved the plain vanilla version of Navigator, Netscape's home page at **http://www.netscape.com**.

- Opening the Navigator Gold Editor
- Creating simple Web pages
- Using paragraph and text formats
- Adding links, pictures, lines, and lists
- Entering JavaScript and document properties

How Do You Open the Editor?

Navigator Gold has a special Editor window. There are two (or more) ways to open this window, as follows:

- To edit a copy of the document you are currently viewing, choose File, Edit Document or click the Edit toolbar button. You'll see a dialog box (which we'll look at in detail in a moment). Click the Save button and the browser window closes and is replaced by the Editor window, displaying the document. (You can reopen the browser window by choosing File, Browse Document, or by clicking the Browser button.)

- To create a new document from scratch from the browser window, choose File, New Document and then choose Blank, From Template, or From Wizard. If you choose Blank, the browser window closes and is replaced by a blank Editor window. The From Template and From Wizard choices only work if you're connected to the Web—they take you to pages at Netscape's Web site that feature pre-built Web page templates and a step-by-step Web page creation Wizard, respectively.

- To edit a copy of a document on your hard disk—a home page that you've created, for instance—choose File, Open File in Editor and then select a file in the Open dialog box. The Editor window opens, displaying the file you chose (the browser window remains open).

N O T E If you have both the Editor and Browser windows open, you can close one and the other will stick around. You can always open the other again by using the Browser button from the Editor, and vice versa.

Why would you want to edit an existing document? Eventually, you'll want to modify documents you created earlier, of course. But editing an existing document is also a great way to create your first Web document. Find a document that you think looks good—one that you'd like to copy—and edit that document, replacing the original headings with your headings, keeping the images and links you need, and so on. Then save the modified document on your hard disk.

N O T E   If you open a document that contains HTML code that Netscape Gold doesn't understand—
for example, Frames—that portion of the page will be displayed as straight HTML code
surrounded by "broken tag" icons. ▨

What happens when you open a document in the Editor window? If you opened a file that's
stored on your hard disk, the Editor opens and displays the document. If you chose File, Edit
Document (or just click on the Edit toolbar button), though, you'll see the dialog box shown in
figure 19.1.

FIG. 19.1

When you open a
document from the
Web, you have to tell
Navigator Gold what to
do with the links and
graphics.

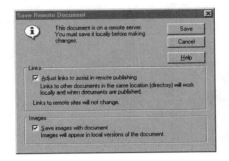

If you change your mind, simply click the Cancel button. But if you want to continue and
modify the document that is currently displayed in the browser, you must decide what to do
with the links and graphics in the document. Netscape is going to copy the document to your
hard disk, and you need to tell it how. Here are your options:

Images: Save images with document—Make sure this check box is checked if you want to
use the images in the document you are copying. Netscape will copy the HTML document
from the Web as well as the embedded images. If you know that you don't want the pictures,
clear the check box.

Links: Adjust links to assist in remote publishing—If you choose this check box,
Netscape will convert the links in the files to absolute links. For instance, say you are copying a
file that contains an HTML link like this:

> <a HREF="book.htm">Book Titles</a>

This link points to a file called book.htm—it's what's called a relative link, because it doesn't
give the full URL to that document. In effect, the link says "get book.htm, which is in the same
directory as the current document." But once the document is on your hard disk, book.htm is
no longer in the same directory, so the link won't work. If you chose this option, though,
Netscape converts the link, to something like this, for instance:

> <a HREF="http://www.bigweb.com/books/book.htm">Book Titles</a>

Now the link contains the full URL to book.htm, so it continues to work.

When you click the Save button, you'll see the dialog box in figure 19.2. This is simply a reminder that you *don't own stuff you find on the Web!* You can click the check box to tell

Netscape not to display the message next time, then click OK. Then you'll see a Save As dialog box. Find the directory in which you want to save the copied document, type a filename, then click Save.

> **CAUTION**
>
> You should understand that you don't own something you "borrow" from the Web. If you borrow something from the Web and simply keep it for your own use, there's no problem. But if you publish Web pages using pictures and text you grabbed from another Web site, you may be guilty of copyright infringement. If you use the borrowed stuff as a template, though, replacing everything in the page with your own stuff, there's no problem in most cases (though it's possible for a particular design to be copyrighted, too).

FIG. 19.2

Netscape warns you that things you find on the Web don't belong to you!

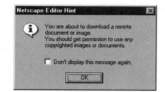

The Editor Window

Once you've opened the Editor window, you'll see something like figure 19.3. This shows the current Netscape home page inside the Editor.

The Paragraph Format toolbar

The Character Format toolbar

FIG. 19.3

The Editor window provides the tools you need to create or modify a Web page.

The File/Edit toolbar

The red bar indicates that you are in edit mode.

Notice that the mouse pointer hasn't changed to a hand because in edit mode you can't navigate via the links.

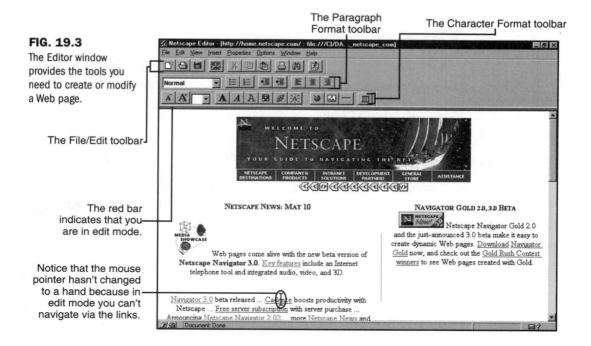

Here's a quick summary of what each button does.

New Document—Click here to open a new blank Editor window so you can begin a new document, or choose to use a Template or the Page Wizard.

Open File to Edit—Click here to open a file on your hard disk.

Save—This button saves the document on your hard disk.

View in Browser—Click here to change back to the browser window.

Cut—Highlight text in the document and click this button to remove the text, placing it in the Windows Clipboard.

Copy—This button copies highlighted text to the Clipboard.

Paste—Click here to paste text from the Clipboard to the document.

Print—This prints the document.

Find—Opens the Find dialog box so you can search the document.

Publish—Transfers your Web page and associated files to the Internet using HTTP or FTP protocol.

Paragraph Style—The Editor uses a system of styles, much like most good word processors. You can click text and modify it by selecting a style.

Bullet list—This button lets you create a bulleted list.

Numbered list—Clicking this button creates a numbered list in the document. (Well, in theory—at the time of writing it wasn't working correctly.)

Decrease indent—Use this to move indented text back to the left.

Increase indent—Click here to indent text to the right.

Align left—If a paragraph is centered or aligned to the right (right justified), click here to change it to left alignment.

Center—This button centers the selected paragraph.

Align right—This button right justifies the selected paragraph.

Decrease Font Size—Highlight text and click here to decrease the size one level. (There are seven sizes, from -2 to +4, with 0 being the default size. These are relative sizes, not directly related to point size.)

Part

IV

Ch

19

Increase Font Size—Highlight text and click here to increase the size one level.

Font Size—Highlight text and then choose a font size setting to make the text larger or smaller than the default for that text style.

Bold—Highlight text and click here to make it bold (or to remove bold, if the text is already bold).

Italic—Highlight text and click here to make it italic.

Fixed Width—Highlight text and click here to change the text to a fixed width (monospace) font, a font in which all characters take up the same space.

Font Color—Highlight text and click here to change the text color.

Make Link—Click this button to insert a link in the document.

Clear All Styles—Highlight text and click icon to remove all the text styles, changing the text back to the default font for the paragraph style.

Insert Target (Named Anchor)—Inserts a target name for frames and links to jump to inside the page.

Insert Image—This opens the Insert Image dialog box, which helps you insert a picture into your document.

Insert Horizontal Line—Click here to insert a horizontal line across the document.

Object Properties—When you click certain objects in your document (images, links, and horizontal lines) and then click this button, the appropriate properties dialog box opens. Highlight text and then click the button to modify general document characteristics (title, colors, and so on).

Entering Your Text

As an example of how to work with the Editor, let's try creating your own home page—a page that opens when you open the Netscape browser, containing all the links you need. Type the following text into a new, blank Editor window (you can see an example in figure 19.4):

```
My Home Page
This is my very own home page
Really Important Stuff
These are WWW pages I use a lot.

Not So Important Stuff
These are WWW pages I use now and again.

Not Important At All Stuff
These are WWW pages I use to waste time.
```

Right now all you have is basic text; look in the Paragraph Style drop-down list box (the list box on the left side of the Paragraph Format toolbar) and you'll see it shows *Normal*.

FIG. 19.4

Start typing the headings into the Editor; you'll find it's just like working with a word processor.

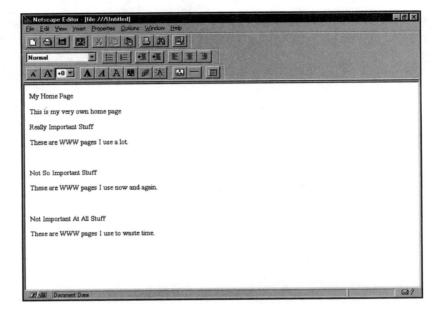

You can quickly change the paragraph styles. For instance, try the following:

1. Click the *My Home Page* text, then select Heading 1 from the Paragraph Style drop-down list box.
2. Click the Center toolbar button.
3. Click the *This is my very own home page* text, then click the Center toolbar button.
4. Click the *Really Important Stuff* text, then select Heading 2 from the Paragraph Style drop-down list box.
5. Click the *Not So Important Stuff* text, then select Heading 2 from the Paragraph Style drop-down list box.
6. Click the *Not Important At All Stuff* text, then select Heading 2 from the Paragraph Style drop-down list box.

Now what have you got? Your page should look something like that in figure 19.5.

Part

IV

Ch

19

FIG. 19.5

A few mouse clicks, and you've formatted the document.

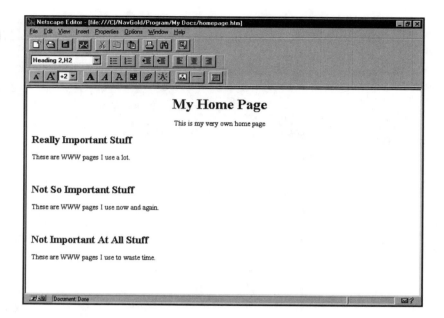

Before you go on, save what you've done: Click the Save button, type a name (homepage, if you wish), then click the Save button. The Editor will save the file with an .HTM extension.

Want to see what you've just done? Choose View, Document Source, and you'll see the HTML source document that the Editor has created for you. If you're an HTML purist and want to "tweak" your HTML code by hand, choose View, Edit Document Source instead.

Where Did My Line Breaks Go?

Did you create multiple line breaks in your document by pressing Enter? If so, when you finally view your document in the browser window, those line breaks will be gone; the Editor doesn't like multiple line breaks.

For example, try this: Place the cursor at the end of a paragraph (a paragraph that is followed by another paragraph, not the last one in the document) and press Enter several times. Several blank lines appear. Save the document, then press Ctrl+R to reload the document from the hard disk into the Editor. You'll see that the blank lines have gone!

Why? Well, this seems to be a holdover from creating a Web document by entering the HTML codes. Web browsers ignore blank lines in the HTML document. Rather, they only move text down a line when they see a special tag: the <P> or <BR> tag. Of course, there's no reason that the Navigator Gold Editor should do the same; if you entered a blank line, you probably want it there. Nonetheless, that's the way it is.

T I P If you've made changes to your document, but want to go back to the way it was the last time you saved it, simply press Ctrl+R or choose View, Reload.

However, there is a way to add a blank line. Place the cursor at the end of line and choose Insert, New Line Break. (Or simply press Shift+Enter.) A blank line appears. This time, if you save the document and then reload it, the blank line remains.

How About Links?

Now you're going to get fancy by adding an anchor, a link to another document. For example, you may want to add a link to the Netscape home page. (On the other hand, you may not; you can always choose Directory, Netscape's Home to get there, even if you are using your own home page.) Or perhaps you'd like a link to a favorite site.

N O T E The HTML tags used to create links are often known as anchors because many people refer to the links themselves in the Web documents as anchors. ▉

Click the blank line below *These are WWW pages I use a lot*, then click the Link button or choose Insert, Link. You'll see the dialog box in figure 19.6.

FIG. 19.6

Enter the text you want to see and the URL you want to link to. You can choose named targets, too.

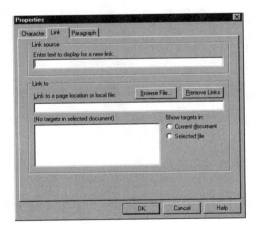

In the first text box, type the text that you want to appear in the document: the words that you will be clicking to use that link. In the second box, type the URL of the page you want to link to. The radio buttons let you list named Targets in either the Current document or Selected file. To pick one as your link, just click it and it will appear in the second text box.

Part

IV

Ch

19

You create a Target by highlighting text or placing your cursor where you want a target to appear, then clicking the Insert Target (Named Anchor) button on the bottom toolbar. You'll get a dialog that asks you for a target name. Links that jump to this target from the same page will have a destination of "#name," while links that jump in from another page will have a destination of "thispage.htm#name."

> **N O T E** You can find URLs in a number of places. You might press Alt+Tab to switch back to the browser window, then use the browser to go to the page you want and copy the URL from the Location bar. Remember also that you can right-click a link in a Web document and choose Copy This Link Location. You can also copy URLs from desktop shortcuts: Right-click the shortcut, choose Properties, click the Internet Shortcut tab and then press Ctrl+C to copy the URL.
>
> You can also get links from another document or elsewhere in the same document: Right-click a link in the Editor and choose <u>C</u>opy Link to Clipboard. ▧

Notice the <u>B</u>rowse File button; this lets you enter the URL of a file on your hard disk, which is very handy if you are creating a series of linked pages. And there's a <u>R</u>emove Links button, too. This is only active if you click inside a link in your document and then open this dialog box. Clicking the button removes the URL so you can enter a new one, or so that you can retain the document text but remove the link from it.

> **TIP** Here's another way to create a link: Highlight text that you typed into the document earlier and then click the Link button (or right-click the highlighted text and choose Create <u>L</u>ink Using Selected). The highlighted text will appear in the dialog box. All you need to do is enter the URL and click OK.

More Nifty Link Tricks

You can also create links by copying them from the browser window. Position the windows so that both are visible. Then click a link in the browser window, but hold the mouse button down. You'll notice the link turn red. Now, with the mouse button still held down, drag the link from the browser window over to the Editor window (see fig. 19.7), move the pointer to the position you want to place the link, and release the mouse button.

Finally, why not grab links from your bookmarks? You've probably already created bookmarks to your favorite sites, and you can quickly create links from them. Choose Window, Boo<u>k</u>marks to open the Bookmarks window.

Now you can drag bookmarks from the Bookmarks window onto your document in the Editor. As long as you don't click anywhere in the document—simply drag and release where you want the new link—the Bookmarks window remains above the Editor window.

> **TIP** To open a browser window containing the document you are editing so that you can test the document you've created, choose File, <u>B</u>rowse Document.

FIG. 19.7
You can drag links from the "What's Cool?" page (or any other Web document) into the Editor.

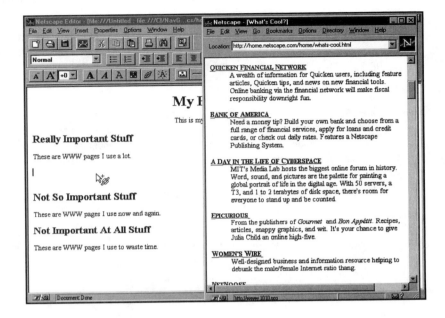

What About Pictures?

No self-respecting Web page would be complete without a picture or two, would it? Luckily, the Editor provides a way for you to insert pictures.

Place the cursor where you want the picture, then choose Insert, Image, or click the Insert Image button. You'll see the dialog box in figure 19.8.

FIG. 19.8
The Insert Image dialog box helps you place the image in just the correct manner.

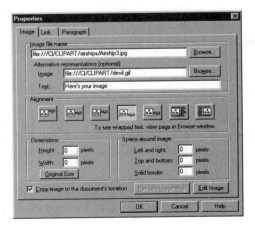

Start by clicking the Browse button right at the top of the dialog box, and select the image you want to use. (Or you may type a URL into this text box, and the Editor will go out onto the Web

Part IV

Ch

19

to grab the specified file.) If you wish, you can also enter an alternative image in the second text box. This is the image that should be used if the first image isn't available. And you can enter the alternative Text, too, into the third text box. This is the text that is shown if the browser viewing your page is not displaying inline images.

 The alternative image option doesn't work well for all browsers. If the primary image is not available, some browsers will not be able to display the alternative image, as this is a Netscape feature that has not yet been adopted by all other browser publishers. Also, if you define an alternative image, other browsers viewing your page with inline images turned off may not be able to view the alternative text. The alternative-image information in the HTML file "confuses" them and stops them reading the text.

The Copy Image to the Document's Location check box in the lower left corner of the dialog tells the Editor to copy the picture from its original location to the directory in which the document is stored.

Now take a look at the Alignment box. This is where you define how text on the same line as the image should be wrapped around the image. Each button shows a visual sample of what the image will look like with its designated alignment.

You can now tell the Editor how much space to leave around the image—or whether you want a border around it. The three text boxes under the Space Around Image heading allow you to enter a size, in pixels, between the left and right sides of the image and the text, and between the top and bottom of the image and the text. You can also define the size of a border around the text.

The text boxes under the Dimensions heading let you set the Height and Width of the displayed image. Values of "0" in each mean "original size," which you can also reset by clicking the Original Size button.

The Edit Image button lets you (logically enough) edit the image you've chosen. If you haven't already configured an image editor through the Options, Editor Preferences menu selection, you'll be given a chance to do so automatically.

Finally, how about turning the image into a link to another document? If you want the reader to be able to click the image to view another document, click the Link tab and you can create a link for the image.

When you've finished, simply click OK and the image is inserted into the document. How can you modify the image later? Many ways: double-click the image; click the picture and then click either the Object Properties or Insert Image toolbar button; or right-click and select Image Properties from the pop-up menu.

 Do you want to find some icons you can use in your documents? Go to an icon server: a Web site from which you can download icons or even link your documents across the Web to a particular icon. Try the following sites:

http://www.bsdi.com/icons
http://www-ns.rutgers.edu/doc-images

http://www.di.unipi.it/iconbrowser/icons.html
http://www.cit.gu.edu.au/~anthony/icons/

Where are you going to get pictures for your documents? You can create them yourself using a graphics program that can save in a .JPG or .GIF format (many can these days). You can also grab them from the Web, remember! Find a picture you want, right-click it, and choose Save This Image As.

 TIP   There's a special command that makes sure that text placed after an image appears below the image, not "wrapped" around it. Let's say you've aligned the picture so that the text following it appears on the right side of the picture. You can now place the cursor in the text at the point that you want to move it down below the image, and choose Insert, Break below Image(s). The text that appears after the cursor is now moved down, below the image.

Adding Horizontal Lines

Horizontal lines are handy. You can use them to underline headers, as dividers between blocks of text, to underline important information, and so on. And the Editor allows you to create a number of different types of lines, as you can see in figure 19.9.

FIG. 19.9
This dialog box helps you create a line; you can see examples in the Editor.

Part
IV

Ch
19

To place a line across the page, place the cursor on a blank line or in a line of text after which you wish to place the line, and click the Insert Horizontal Line button (or choose Insert, Horizontal Line). A line is placed across the page. But what if you don't want a line all the way across the page, or if you want a different style or thickness? You'll have to modify the line.

Select the line; with the cursor at the end of the line, simply press Shift+Left Arrow (or simply click directly on the line). The line will appear to change color or size—it will be highlighted. Now click the Object Properties button to open the Horizontal Line Properties dialog box, which you can see in figure 19.9. Double-clicking the line, or right-clicking and selecting Horizontal Line properties from the popup menu will also bring up this dialog.

There are a variety of controls in this dialog box. First, you can tell the Editor where you want the line: aligned against the Left, in the Center, or aligned against the Right. Notice, however, that by default, the line has a width of 100 percent (that is, it's 100 percent of the width of the document's window). The alignment settings have no effect until you modify the width setting. (If a line is 100 percent, how can you center it after all?)

There are actually two ways that you can adjust the line's width: by Percent or by Pixels. Both are selected from the drop-down list to the right of the Width text box. The Percent setting refers to the width of the document (when the window is maximized). So a line that has a width of 50 percent will stretch across half of the document's window.

The Pixel setting is harder to predict, though. A pixel is the smallest unit that your computer monitor can display. For instance, in VGA mode a monitor displays 640 columns and 480 rows of pixels. So if you create a line that's 60 pixels wide, it will be about 10 percent of the width of the document—in VGA mode. But what if the person viewing the document is using a different resolution—1024×768, for example? In such a case, the line that was 10 percent of the width in VGA is now about five percent of the width. Of course, this doesn't matter if you are creating a home page for your own use, but bear it in mind if you are creating documents that you plan to put out on the Web.

There are two more settings: the Height, which is measured in pixels, and 3-D Shading. The 203-D effect is created by using four different lines to create a "box,"—the left and top lines are dark gray, and the bottom and right lines are white. Clear the 3-D check box, and your horizontal line will be a single dark gray line.

Creating Tables

Navigator Gold now lets you easily create tables. Select Insert, Table from the menu and you'll get the dialog shown in figure 19.10.

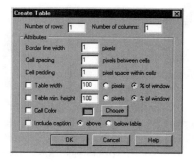

Number of rows and Number of columns each default to 1, but that doesn't make much of a table; set these to the values you want. This is all you really need to define to create a table, but the Create Table dialog also lets you set Border line width, Cell spacing (the number of pixels between cells), Cell padding (pixels of white space inside of cells), Table width, Table minimum height (these two in pixels or as a percentage of window width), and Cell Color. You can also check the Include Caption check box to put a caption above or below the table.

Once a blank table is created, you enter information into cells by clicking in them and typing. (Of course, you can also insert images or links into table cells.) You move from cell to cell using the arrow keys.

You can create "nested" tables by moving the cursor into an empty cell and creating a new table there.

Once created, you can modify a table using the menus. From the Insert menu, you can insert a new Table, Row, Column, or Cell at the cursor position. The Properties menu lets you change the properties for a Table, Row, or Cell. The Row and Cell (fig. 19.11) selections bring up dialogs which let you define text alignment and cell color (both) and column span (cell only). You can also choose Delete Table, Delete Row, Delete Column, or Delete Cell from the Properties menu.

FIG. 19.11
The Cell Properties dialog lets you customize individual table cells.

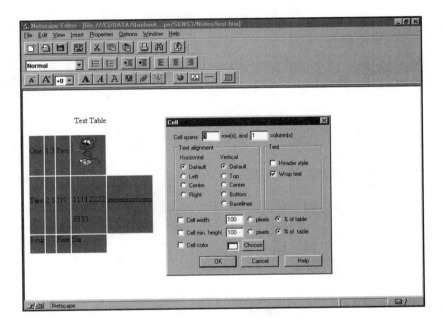

Publishing Your Work

Once you've created an HTML page, you'll probably want to publish it on the Web or on an intranet. With Gold, this is now a one-step process. Just click the Publish button on the toolbar, or choose File, Publish from the menu. You'll get the dialog shown in figure 19.12.

From this dialog, radio buttons in the Local files area let you choose to include in your upload only the Images in the Document, or All files in document's folder. A file list lets you choose individual files to include, or you can Select None or Select All using buttons.

The Publishing location box includes fields for the URL of your upload destination, as well as your User Name and Password. When these have been set, a single click on OK uploads your page to its destination.

FIG 19.12

The Publish dialog lets you publish your page on the Web.

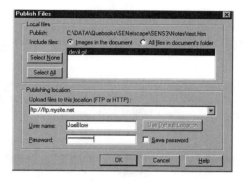

Creating Multiple Documents

You may want to create a hierarchy of documents. Create a home page, a page that appears when you open Netscape, with a table of contents linked to several other documents. In each of those documents, you could then have links related to a particular subject: one for business, one for music, one for your kids, and so on.

This is very simple to do. Create and save several documents in the Editor. (I suggest you put them all in the same directory for simplicity's sake.) Each time you finish one, choose File, New Document to clear the screen so you can create the next one. When you have all your documents completed, open your home page document again (click the Open File button or choose File, Open File), and enter links to each page, using the method previously described.

How Can I Use My Home Page?

You've created a home page; now how do you use it? Complete the following procedure:

1. Click the Open Browser button, or choose File, Browse Document. The Netscape browser opens and displays your document.
2. Click the Location text box, highlighting the URL.
3. Press Ctrl+C to copy the URL.
4. Choose Options, General Preferences, and click the Appearance tab.
5. Click the Home Page Location option button (in the Startup area).
6. Click inside the text box below this option button.
7. Press Ctrl+V to paste the URL into the text box.
8. Click OK.

Now, the next time you start your browser, you'll see your very own home page. Simple, eh?

Here's a Good One—Let's Change It

Navigator Gold provides a wonderful way to quickly create Web pages—by "borrowing" them from the Web and modifying them to your requirements. If you see a page you like—one that has many links that you'll need in your home page, for instance, or one that uses a particularly attractive format—you can open that page and make changes to it and then save it on your hard disk.

You can work in the document in the same way that you would with documents you created yourself. You can delete text and replace it with your own and change text using the formatting tools.

How do you highlight text? The Editor window works like a word processor. Simply click in the text to place the cursor, then use the arrow keys to move around in the text. You can also hold down the Shift key while you press the arrow keys to highlight text. Ctrl+Shift+Left Arrow and Ctrl+Shift+Right Arrow work (selecting an entire word at a time, though you can't do the same with the Up and Down Arrow keys). Also, you can use the mouse cursor to select text: Hold down the mouse button while you drag the pointer across text to highlight it. Or double-click a word to select it.

 As with a word processor, you don't need to highlight text in order to modify paragraph formats. If you want to change the paragraph style, indentation, or alignment, simply click once in the paragraph and then make your change.

When you've made the changes you need, click the Save button or choose File, Save and you'll be able to save the document on your hard disk. (No, you can't save it to the original location even if you own that location!)

Lots More Formatting

There are a number of formatting tools we haven't looked at yet. You can format a paragraph in many different ways by setting up indents and alignment as well as by choosing a paragraph style. And you can modify particular words or individual characters, too, by changing colors and type styles.

The Other Paragraph Styles

You've only seen a couple of paragraph styles so far, so let's take a look at the others. In figure 19.13, you can see examples of all the different Heading levels as well as Normal text, the Address style, and the Formatted style.

You can apply any of these styles by placing the cursor inside the paragraph you want to modify and then selecting the style from the drop-down list box (or by picking the style from the Properties, Paragraph cascading menu). Note that what you see depends on how you've set up Netscape; other browsers may display these styles in a different way.

N O T E   Browsers normally remove blank lines and multiple spaces when viewing a document. The Formatted style tells the browser to keep the text format as it appears in the HTML document. In fact, unless you are using the Formatted style, the Editor won't let you type multiple spaces into a document. Also, long lines of Formatted text will run off the side of the window—the text will not wrap down to the next line.

However, note that Navigator Gold currently doesn't allow you to enter multiple blank lines, even if you've selected the Formatted style.

FIG. 19.13
The headers, formatted, and address styles.

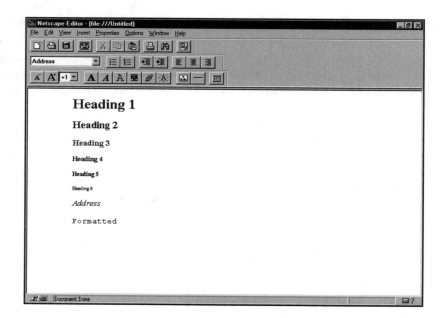

How About Creating Lists?

You can also use the Paragraph Styles drop-down list box and a couple of the toolbar buttons to create lists. You can create bulleted lists, numbered lists, and definition lists.

The quickest way to create a bulleted list is to place the cursor on a blank line and then click the Bulleted List button. You'll see a bullet (a black circle) appear at the beginning of the line. Type the first entry, press Enter, type the next entry, press Enter, and so on. When you get to the last entry press Enter and then select Normal from the Paragraph Style drop-down list box. You can see an example in figure 19.14.

You can create a numbered list in the same way by using the Numbered List button.

Another form of list is the definition list, which you can create by alternating lines between the Description Title, DD, and Description Text styles.

FIG. 19.14
You can create lists using the paragraph styles.

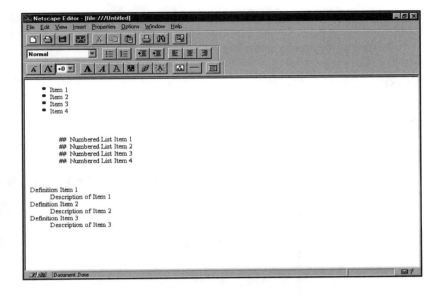

There's another way to work with lists—and other paragraph formats. Here's how to use it. Place the cursor on a blank line and then click the right mouse button. Choose Paragraph/List properties from the popup menu. You'll see the dialog box in figure 19.15.

FIG. 19.15
This dialog box allows you to format a variety of paragraph and list types.

Part
IV

Ch
19

Select the paragraph or list type you want to create in the Paragraph Style drop-down list on the left. If you've selected a List item, pick the Style from the second drop-down list. Finally, select the number or bullet type from the list on the right. Pick Left, Center, or Right alignment, then click OK and the first line is correctly formatted.

This dialog box creates not only numbered and unnumbered lists, but also several other unusual paragraph styles: Block Quotes, Directory Lists, Menu Lists, and Description Lists. Other styles may be added later, too.

Positioning Paragraphs

Now let's see how to move paragraphs around the page. You can use the five toolbar buttons on the right side of the Paragraph Format toolbar to indent paragraphs, align them to the left, center them, and align them to the right. You can combine alignment settings and indentations, too. See figure 19.16 for a few examples.

FIG. 19.16
You can position paragraphs in a variety of ways.

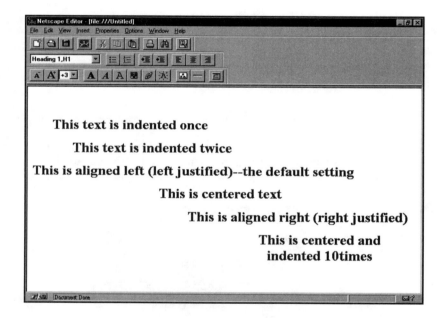

How Can I Modify Character Formats?

You have quite a bit of control over individual characters. In effect, you are telling your document to override the way in which the browser that opens your document displays the characters. A browser, for example, may have a default text color set, but you can override that color and define your own. Figure 19.17 shows a variety of character formats.

Simply highlight the characters you want to modify, then click the appropriate button (or choose the appropriate entry from the Properties, Character submenu), as follows:

Font Size—Change a character's size, ranging from –2 to +4. That is, from two "units" below the normal style size, to four "units" above. These are not absolute measurements—it's not 2 points to 4 points, for instance. Rather, they are relative sizes; the browser displaying the document simply decreases or increases the text a certain amount below or above the normal size for that paragraph style.

Decrease Font Size—Click here to decrease the size one unit.

Increase Font Size—Click here to increase the size one unit.

Bold—This changes the character to bold (or removes bold, if the text is already bold). You can combine this with italic to create bold italic.

Italic—Click here to change the text to italic (or to remove italic).

Fixed Width—This changes the text to a fixed width (monospace) font, a font in which all characters take up the same amount of space.

Font Color—You'll see a dialog box from which you can choose a color.

Clear Styles—Click here to remove all the text styles, changing the text back to the default font for the paragraph style.

FIG. 19.17

Highlight text and click the appropriate button to modify it.

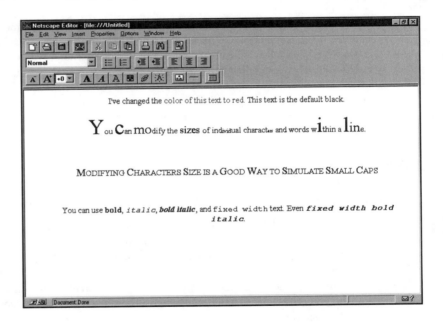

Part

IV

Ch

19

Here's an example of how to use these tools. Take a look at figure 19.14, then follow this procedure:

1. In a blank document, type all the text you see in figure 19.17. Don't worry about the different formats, simply type all the text starting at I've changed the color all the way to fixed width bold italic at the bottom.

2. Now, highlight a few words of the first line, and click the Font Color button. Click the red, then choose OK. The text will change color.

3. Select a letter or several letters on the second line. Then select a size from the Font Size drop-down list box, or click the Increase Font Size or Decrease Font Size buttons. Try several letters and different sizes.

4. You should have typed all of line three in capitals. Select the first letter of the first word,

and increase its size. Modify all the first letters that you want to "capitalize" and increase their size the same amount, to simulate a "small caps" font.

5. Highlight the word bold on the last line and click the Bold button.

6. Highlight the word italic on the last line and click the Italic button.

7. Highlight the words bold italic on the last line and click the Italic button and then the Bold button.

8. Highlight the words fixed width on the last line and click the Fixed Width button.

9. Highlight the words fixed width bold italic on the last line and click the Fixed Width button, then the Bold button, and then the Italic button.

Nonbreaking Spaces

Here's one more character format we haven't looked at yet: You can choose Insert, Nonbreaking Space to create a special space between words. This space is treated as part of the two words it divides. When you change the size of the Editor window (or when the person viewing the document changes the size of the Browser window), text has to be wrapped down onto the next line. Now, words are never split in two when Netscape does this wrapping; the text is always broken at a space. But the text won't be broken at one of the nonbreaking spaces—instead Netscape has to break the text at the first normal space that appears before the nonbreaking space.

JavaScript

There are two more character-format types which you may have noticed in the Properties, Character submenu: the JavaScript (Client) and JavaScript (Server) formats.

JavaScript is a special scripting language—a sort of fancy macro language, really. It lets you use some of the power of Java without knowing that programming language. You'll learn more about JavaScript in chapter 30. But for now, all you need to know is that you can enter JavaScript commands into your documents by choosing Properties, Character, JavaScript (Server) or Properties, Character, JavaScript (Client) formats (depending on which type of command you are entering) and then typing the command. The server commands will appear as blue text and the client commands as red text.

Document Properties—General

Web documents have a variety of properties related not to any particular paragraph or character, but to the document overall. You can modify this by choosing Properties, Document. Click the Generaltab and you'll see the information in figure 19.18.

These are the things you can modify here:

Document Property	What It Modifies
Title	The title of the document. This is displayed in the browser's title bar, in history lists, bookmark lists, and so on.
Author	This places the <meta name= "Author" content= "author name"> tag into your document. It's one of the META variables in the Head of the document (see User Variables META later in this table).
Description	A brief description of the contents of your document. This information can be helpful to readers searching for a specific topic.
Other Attributes	Keywords and Classification that you want searching services such as Yahoo to use to help users locate your document on the Web. Use category names you think best apply to your document.

FIG. 19.18

The Document Properties box lets you set colors, the document title, author name, and more.

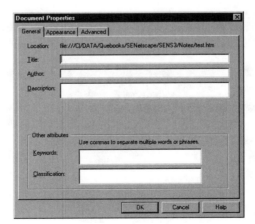

Appearance

Click the Appearance tab to see a pane. You have two option buttons at the top. You can choose to either Use Custom Colors (you'll be able to define custom colors and background for this particular document) or Use Browsers Colors (the document will use whatever colors and background are defined by the browser viewing it).

Just below the option buttons you'll see the Color Schemes drop-down list box. From this you can choose from predefined color schemes; currently, you can choose about a dozen different color schemes. Future versions will also allow you to create and save your own schemes.

Now you can select the text colors you want to use. You can modify the color of Normal Text, Link Text, Active Link Text (this is the color of a link when you point at it and hold down the mouse button), and Followed Link Text (the color of links that lead to documents that you've already been to). Clicking one of these buttons opens the Color dialog box.

Finally, you can modify the background. Either choose a Solid Color (click Choose Color button to select that color), or an Image File—click the Browse button to find a file you want to use as the background image.

Note, however, that there's something a little odd about this color selection system. The way it stands right now you can only set all or nothing. In other words, you can't define a special color for the background, yet keep the browser defaults for everything else. If you change one item, all the other items are also defined as overridden parameters. You can choose colors that are the same as the default colors for Netscape. For instance, these colors will override a reader's settings if they are different from the defaults.

Advanced Settings

Power HTML users will appreciate the settings available under the Advanced tab (see fig. 19.19).

FIG. 19.19
The Advanced tab lets you set system and user variables.

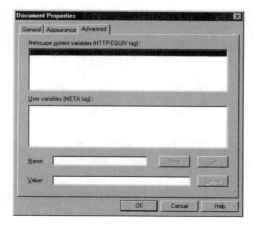

Here's what you can set in this dialog:

Document Property	What It Modifies
Netscape System Variables	This is information that is sent in a "response (HTTP-EQUIV) header" from a server. A response header is information sent to a browser or other program when it requests information about the document. The information is contained in the HEAD of the document, and may include an expiration date and keywords, for instance. You add this information by clicking in the System Variables box to select it, then typing a value into the Name and Value fields at the bottom of the dialog, and clicking the Add button.
User Variables (META)	The META variables are placed in the HEAD of the document, and are used to identify the document to servers and browsers, allowing them to index and catalog the document.
Name	Type a new user variable name here.
Value	Type the user value here, then click the Set button.

You can add more user variables. In fact you can add variables that a server may want to include in its response header. For instance, you might type Expires into the Name field, then Tue, 24 Dec 1996 into the Value field. When you click Set, the Editor adds this tag to the Head of the document: <META HTTP-EQUIV=Expires CONTENT="Tue, 24 Dec 1996">. (This is the Expires date shown in the Document Info when you select View, Document Info in the Netscape Browser.

You can also use this feature to add keywords to your document (so the document can be indexed and cataloged) and a reply-to address, to create tags such as these:

<META HTTP-EQUIV="Keywords" CONTENT="Art, Sculpture">

<META HTTP-EQUIV="Reply-to" CONTENT="robinh@sherwood.com (Robin Hood)">

Editor Options

You can set default options for the Editor. Choose Options, Editor Preferences to see the Editor Preferences dialog box. Click the Appearance tab to see the same area that we looked at a moment ago; you can use this to define the colors used by new documents you create.

Click the General tab to see the area shown in figure 19.20. This is where you define the default Author name, HTML source and Image editors, and the URL of the HTML document you'll use as a source for your templates (this defaults to a location on Netscape's Web server.

FIG. 19.20
The Editor Preferences
dialog box tells the
Editor how to set up
new documents.

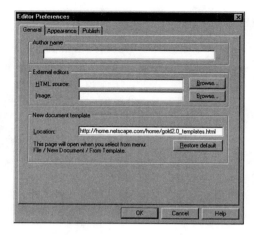

Click the Publish tab to set your Links and Images defaults.You can select the Keep Images With Document check box to tell the Editor that, when you insert an image, you want to move it to the same directory as the document into which it is being inserted. You can also tell the Editor to Maintain Links. Your choice here defines the status of the option buttons in the Save As dialog box that appears when you are opening the editor with a document you have found on the Web.

The Default Publishing Location box is where you enter information about the site where you Publish (upload) your finished pages. Enter the site address, your user name, and password information. (Only check the Save password box if you're sure no one else has access to your system!)

More to Come?

You can expect to see many more features added over the next few versions of Navigator Gold. You may find tools that help you create forms, frames, and JavaScripts. You'll also probably be able to create imagemaps—pictures with hotspots on them that lead to other Web docments—special characters, and add sounds and multimedia.

 The latest version of Netscape Navigator Gold can be downloaded for free evaluation from **ftp://ftp8.netscape.com/pub/navigator/gold/**.

## CHAPTER 20

HTML Primer

As you've worked with the World Wide Web, you've most likely come across HTML, the underlying programming language that the WWW is based upon. While not as difficult to understand or use as other computer languages out there, HTML has its own quirks and idiosyncrasies that require you to spend some time learning about it. Unlike standard programming languages, HTML is a formatting language. You start with a page of pure text, and then add special HTML attributes that tell Netscape how to display that information on-screen.

In the last chapter you learned how to prepare for building your own WWW site. That was only the first step. This chapter takes you right into HTML and serves as an introduction to build your own Web pages. In addition to learning all the basic markup tags, you'll become familiar with using horizontal lines, tables, and other popular HTML attributes.

Specifically, in this chapter you learn how to do the following:

- Use basic HTML tags
- Separate paragraphs of displayed text
- Include several types of lists in your HTML document
- Build a sample HTML document from scratch ■

Creating an HTML File

As mentioned in the last chapter, there are several tools available to make it easier to create HTML files. Some automated HTML editors take advantage of powerful drag-and-drop and WYSIWYG (What You See is What You Get) capabilities, which make writing HTML a much simpler process. Instead of memorizing dozens of different, specific HTML tags and codes, editors allow you to concentrate on how your Web pages should look, not learning a new programming language.

Even if you are interested in learning the advanced specifics of HTML, you'll still want to use a specialized editor to take care of mundane HTML authoring.

HTML editors come in two basic formats. The first, such as Internet Assistant by Microsoft (**http://www.microsoft.com**), is a complimentary add-on product that works with existing word processors. By integrating with Microsoft Word, Internet Assistant can take advantage of all the tools of a word processor—such as a spell checker and revision marking. While most add-on products are free, you've got to own the corresponding word processor before they work.

The other types of HTML editors that exist are stand-alone products that are independent of existing word processors. Popular because they are geared specifically toward creating HTML files, you'll find all the needed tags and functionality built into programs such as HoTMetaL (**http://ww.sq.com**).

 TIP Regardless of which computer platform you use, HTML editors exist for virtually every type of computer out there. Everything from the PC to the Amiga has its own HTML editor. If you have trouble locating an HTML editor for your particular machine, check out Yahoo (**http://www.yahoo.com**) for a comprehensive list of HTML editors.

How to Save HTML Files

Unlike other programming languages, an HTML document is not compiled when you are finished writing it. All HTML files are saved strictly as pure text, or ASCII. When Netscape reads the ASCII text file, it interprets the HTML tags and codes you've included, and chooses to display information based on those characteristics.

Regardless of which text editor, HTML editor, or word processor you choose to work with, ensure that your HTML files are saved in strictly ASCII/text format. Typically, text editors and HTML editors take care of this for you automatically, but word processors such as Microsoft Word may not. Before you can make your HTML page available on the WWW, you might have to export from Word into text format.

N O T E ASCII is a worldwide text standard that virtually all computer systems support. It enables any computer to read a text file and recognize all the letters, numbers, and characters stored inside. ■

Naming Conventions

By default, all HTML files should have an appropriate file extension so that both you and WWW browsers can recognize them. By following these standard naming conventions, you'll have an easier time recognizing other HTML files by their file names.

The most common way to identify your files is by using the .HTM or .HTML extension. Much as Microsoft Word recognizes files that have the .DOC extension, Netscape knows that files ending with .HTML or .HTM are specifically created for the World Wide Web.

- .HTM—the Windows 3.1 file extension
- .HTML—the file extension for HTML files created with Windows 95, Macintosh, and UNIX-based editors

Figure 20.1 shows how Lotus Word Pro automatically adds the .HTML extension to all files saved in HTML format.

FIG. 20.1

The Save As dialog box in Lotus Word Pro 96 automatically takes care of adding the proper file extension.

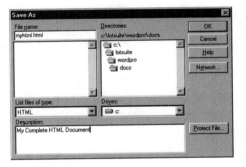

 Don't worry if you have other requirements that force you to use other naming conventions. WWW browsers use other methods to determine if a file is in HTML format when they don't recognize a file's extension. Using tags you'll learn later, Netscape recognizes HTML documents by the proper use of tags, not only the file-naming conventions. Keeping a standard file extension is more useful for you, the HTML author, when keeping track of several files. Netscape can open a file regardless of its extension or file name as long as it is in ASCII format.

N O T E Many UNIX WWW servers expect to find a file named INDEX.HTML in your main HTML directory. The server will display this file automatically when WWW visitors explore through the available directories. It's a good idea to name your initial WWW page INDEX.HTML (or INDEX.HTM) if your Web server supports this feature. Check with your Web administrator for more information. This feature of the Web is used when visitors forget to mention a specific document they want to reference within the URL. Visitors won't see the file name listed in the browser window, but Netscape knows to look for INDEX.HTML automatically. ■

In addition to ensuring that your HTML files use common extensions, it is more important that other files such as graphics, video clips, and sound clips have the correct file extension. Without the correct file extension, Netscape will not be able to properly display graphics, or load helper applications for these external media types. Table 20.1 lists several other popular file extensions that you'll use when creating HTML documents.

Table 21.1 Proper File Extensions Netscape Recognizes	
Extension	**Description**
GIF	The standard graphics format displayed with Netscape and most WWW browsers.
JPEG (JPG)	The other common graphics format used on the Web. This is a particularly good format to use with Netscape's new progressive rendering.
TIF	A less popular graphics format that requires an external helper application to view.
AU	Sound clips stored in a common audio file format that Netscape can recognize and play automatically.
WAV	The Microsoft Windows audio file format.
MPEG (MPG)	The popular video file format that was developed by the same people who created JPEG.
MOV (QT)	Apple's video file format that has quickly become one of the choice methods for providing video clips on the WWW.

Most HTML Tags Come in Pairs

Through a comprehensive set of formatting tags, Netscape knows which text to display as a headline, where to separate two paragraphs, and how to highlight vital information. Typically, these formatting tags come in pairs, surrounding the text they intend to mark up. For example, marking a title on a page looks like this:

      <TITLE> This is my Netscape title </TITLE>

When used in pairs, HTML tags are always related. The closing tag is just the initial tag with a "/" added within it.

While most tags come in pairs, you'll also encounter some HTML tags that appear alone, without a closing tag. These tags tend to separate paragraphs of text, or embed graphics on-screen, and don't change how text is formatted.

In this chapter, when a new tag is introduced, you'll always learn whether it has a corresponding closing tag, and if so, how to use the pair correctly.

Adding the <HTML> Tag

The first set of tags that you'll use in your HTML document is <HTML> and </HTML>. These tags should surround all pieces of HTML within a WWW document, indicating that HyperText Markup Language is being used. Add this set of tags so they appear like this:

- <HTML>
- </HTML>

WWW browsers use the <HTML> tags to recognize that they are reading an HTML document. Without them, a WWW browser might not recognize the other markup tags that you've included in your document. As a rule, most browsers don't require the <HTML> tag, but using it is considered good practice. While Netscape is smart enough to recognize other HTML tags without <HTML>, future versions, and other WWW browsers might require it in order to recognize standard formatting tags.

N O T E With the advent of VRML (Virtual Reality Modeling Language), Java (Sun Micro-systems advancements for the Web), and future WWW enhancements on the way, using the <HTML> and </HTML> tags is really a must. Without them, Netscape may not understand which programming language is used in a WWW document, or how to display information correctly. ■

Understanding the HTML Section Tags

With your initial tag in place, you can start typing text and information into the HTML document. Using additional tags, you should organize WWW pages into two different sections: the header and body.

Using these section tags allows Netscape to take a quick snapshot of a document and recognize that it is separated into two components. This makes it easier to display information and keep the file organized.

Using the <HEAD> Tag

The <HEAD> tag marks an HTML document's heading. By default, the heading contains the document title, indexing information, and important settings for that specific page.

Also container tags, <HEAD> and </HEAD> surround only a few lines of your file.

Netscape uses the information contained within the <HEAD> tags as a quick reference of the page while it is downloading the complete text and graphics. This allows Netscape to display the title before the rest of the document appears on-screen.

Include the <HEAD> tags within the main <HTML> tags:

<HTML>

<HEAD>

```
</HEAD>

</HTML>
```

N O T E   If you plan on taking advantage of Netscape's built-in indexing capabilities, you should include the ISINDEX keyword within the document's header. When enabled, Netscape allows documents to be completely indexed and searchable automatically. This indexing characteristic is controlled by the WWW server running at your site. Check with your Web administrator for more information on whether your site is indexed. ▧

TROUBLESHOOTING

I created a bunch of HTML documents, but I forgot to add the closing </HTML> tag to the end of each file. Netscape doesn't seem to have a problem with this. Is this causing errors that I'm not aware of within Netscape or with non-Netscape using browsers? Currently, the </HMTL> tag is not required. When Netscape gets to the end of your HTML document, there is no more information to read, so it doesn't matter whether the </HTML> tag is there or not. Other popular WWW browsers don't have any trouble with this either. It is a good idea to add the closing tag in further updates in case WWW browsers become more picky in the future, but in general, including the </HTML> closing tag is considered good practice.

Using the <BODY> Tag

Used hand inhand with the <HEAD> tags, the <BODY> and </BODY> tags signify the rest of an HTML document. These tags will surround most of your file. While the <BODY> tags don't affect how information is displayed within Netscape, they help keep the text file organized and indicate the main meat of a document.

By adding the <BODY> and </BODY> tags to your page, you have three sets of tags with no information to display:

```
<HTML>

<HEAD>

</HEAD>

<BODY>

</BODY>

</HTML>
```

Properly Titling Your Document

The first bit of text you'll type into your HTML document is the title. Like a book title, your document title is a concise statement that accurately reflects the contents of the document.

Your HTML title is the first piece of information people see when they visit a WWW page. In Netscape, the title appears in the title bar at the top of the screen, while the rest of the page is loading. Figure 20.2 shows where the HTML title appears within Netscape.

FIG. 20.2
The specified title appears in the Netscape title bar running across the top of the screen.

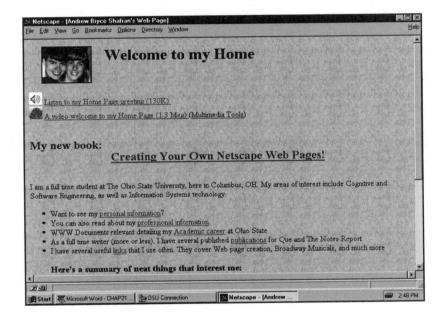

▶ **See** "Creating a Bookmark," **p. 95**, and "Deleting a Bookmark," **p. 97**

In addition to appearing in the Netscape title bar, the HTML title is also the information saved when a Netscape user adds a page to his list of bookmarks.

Part
IV

Ch
20

Using the <TITLE> Tag

Adding a title to an HTML document requires using the <TITLE> and </TITLE> tags. Embedded within the document's header, titles can be any length desired. To name a document "Andy's Home Page," add the following line of HTML to your WWW document:

<TITLE> Andy's Home Page </TITLE>

Choosing a Good Title

Like any good book title, an HTML document's title should be focused, concise, and well thought-out to pique curiosity and attract attention. When choosing a title, follow these tips:

■ Describe the page accurately. The title should be a complete phrase that describes what appears in that file. If the HTML document is a particular scene within Hamlet, then a good title would be "Shakespeare's Hamlet: Act I, Scene ii."

■ Keep the title short. Long titles may not fit in the Netscape title bar and are difficult to read and digest.

Adding Headers to Your HTML Document

Similar to using a document title, headers are also used to introduce a WWW page. Coming in six different sizes, headers are eye-catching bits of information that stand out when looking at a page with Netscape.

Add a size 1 header by surrounding text with the <H1> and </H1> tags. Figure 20.3 shows how the following tag appears within Netscape:

<H1> Dewey beats Truman!</H1>

FIG. 20.3
Headers are the real eye catchers of a WWW document.

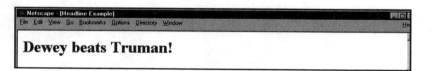

Header sizes range from 1 (the largest) to 6, and can be added by using the corresponding number tag. For example, a size 3 header uses the <H3> and </H3> tags to mark specific text.

Figure 20.4 compares the six different sizes of headers and how they are displayed within Netscape.

TROUBLESHOOTING

Is there any way I can add a more pronounced title to my HTML file to make sure people will always see the proper title? As a standard procedure, many WWW developers include a size 1 header as the first piece of displayed text within an HTML document. Similar to the document's title, this header is much larger, more noticeable, and easier to read than the small title that is included in the Netscape title bar. Make sure you don't use the exact same text in the large header and title to avoid being redundant.

FIG. 20.4
Headlines come in all sizes.

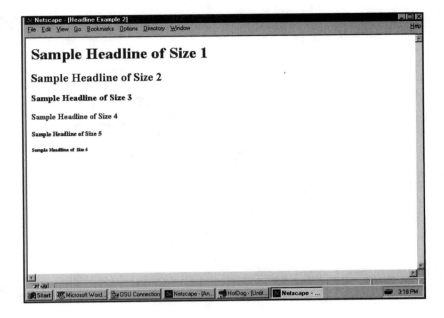

Organizing Paragraphs of Text

You're probably familiar with how a word processor works. After typing several sentences of information, you hit the Enter key and then start typing on the next line. This way you can organize your thoughts into separate paragraphs, making it easy for readers to browse through your document.

Formatting HTML doesn't work quite the same way. In an HTML file, you can use the spacebar and the Tab and Enter keys to make the source file easily readable, but without using the HTML in paragraph formatting tags, Netscape displays a jumbled mess.

Figure 20.5 shows how Netscape displays several paragraphs of text without using paragraph tags. Figure 20.6 is the same text, only formatted in a readable manner.

With these paragraph-organizing HTML tags, you can do the following:

- Organize and separate paragraphs of text on WWW pages
- Group pieces of related information together in an easy-to-read format
- Create itemized lists of information
- Focus attention on certain pieces of information on Web pages

Part
IV

Ch
20

FIG. 20.5
Not even Wordsworth
could read this mess.

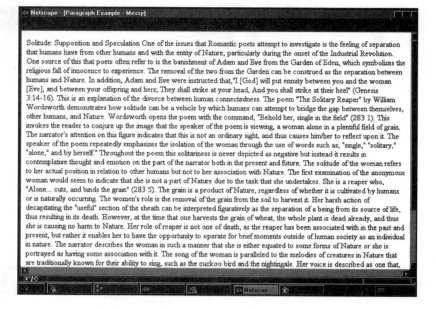

FIG. 20.6
A few short tags make
quite a readability
difference.

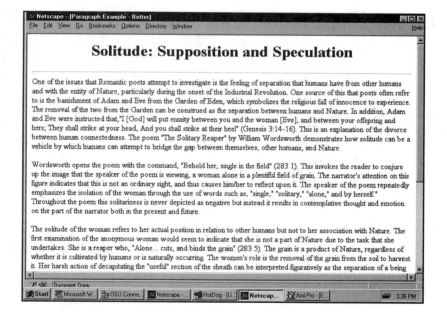

Paragraph Breaks—**<P>**

The most common paragraph tag used on WWW pages is the <P> tag. This tag separates two paragraphs of information with a blank line. To use the paragraph tag, simply add <P> to your HTML file where you want to separate two lines of text. This tag isn't a container tag and can be added anywhere within your HTML document.

Figure 20.7 shows how the <P> tag formats the following information:

Typically, you'll want to separate paragraphs of information with the HTML paragraph tag.

<P>

However, sometimes you want to use the <P> Paragraph <P> tag <P> to <P> really <P> separate <P> pieces <P> of <P> text.

FIG. 20.7
The <P> tag is the most popular paragraph separation tag.

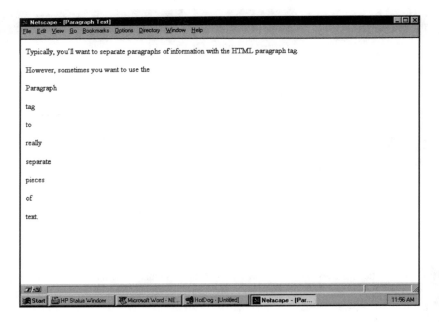

N O T E Unlike most HTML tags, the <P> tag works both as a container tag (with the closing </P> tag) and as a separate stand-alone tag. Initially, WWW browsers (including Netscape) required that each separate paragraph of text was surrounded by the <P> and </P> tags. This was quite a hassle because the closing tag was often forgotten or not used. Nowadays, Netscape allows you to separate two paragraphs of text by only using the <P> tag. ■

Line Breaks—**
**

Similar to the paragraph tag, the line break tag is also used to correctly place text on a page. The only difference is that the <BR> tag places text on the next line, without a blank line between two lines of text.

Think of the <BR> tag as hitting a carriage return on a typewriter. Whenever Netscape spots one, it automatically zings to the next line when displaying information. This tag is useful in telling Netscape where it can break up lines of text that are displayed on-screen. Figure 20.8 shows how the following snippet of HTML code appears in Netscape.

```
<H2>College Student Grocery List</H2>

Milk <BR>

Brownies <BR>

Frozen Pizza <BR>

Spaghetti <BR>

Beer <BR>
```

FIG. 20.8
The <BR> tag is popular for listing several items on subsequent lines.

The header tags automatically include a carriage return and blank line after text surrounded with the <Hn> and </Hn> tags (where the n stands for the header level as described previously) without worrying about using the line break or paragraph tags.

 N O T E HTML also includes two derivations of the <BR> tag.

The word break tag, <WBR> marks where Netscape should break up a specific word, should it need to wrap to a following line (particularly useful for long and extended medical terminology).

The opposites of <BR>, <NOBR> and </NOBR> surround text that should never be wrapped on subsequent lines automatically by Netscape. The no break tag disables word wrapping. ■

The Horizontal Rule—*<HR>*

A different way to separate and organize paragraphs of information with HTML is using the <HR>, or horizontal rule tag. The <HR> tag inserts a solid line that goes completely across the Netscape screen to separate different parts of an HTML document.

Not a container tag, adding a horizontal rule to a WWW page is as simple as typing <HR> into the HTML file. Netscape supports a variety of options that enable you to customize the appearance of horizontal lines on-screen, including the length, thickness, and alignment.

Often, the <HR> tag is used to separate the main body of a document from the title and footer. Figure 20.9 shows an example of how the solid horizontal lines clearly define the different areas of the WWW document.

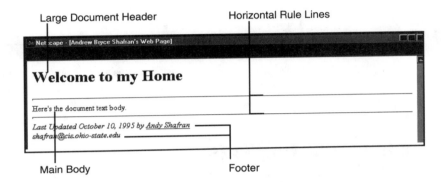

Large Document Header   Horizontal Rule Lines

FIG. 20.9
The <HR> tag is often used in WWW page layout to keep separate sections organized.

Main Body   Footer

Predefined Text—*<PRE>*

Usually, Netscape ignores how text is placed within the actual HTML text file without paragraph formatting tags. Tabs, extra spaces, and carriage returns are all ignored by Netscape when deciding how to format a WWW page.

To circumvent this, use the <PRE> and </PRE> container tags to specifically arrange preformatted text to appear in a distinct manner within Netscape.

All tabs, carriage returns, and extra spaces are displayed exactly as they appear within the <PRE> and </PRE> tags. By allowing users to predefine how text appears on-screen, Netscape lets WWW page creators create lists, tables, and specially formatted bits of info without hassling with learning advanced HTML tags.

Figure 21.10 shows how the following text appears, tabs and all, in Netscape:

```
<PRE>

<H2>How to pay for a wedding</H2>

<B>      Bride's Family      Groom's Family </B>

Reception      xxx

Alcohol                      xxx

Flowers        xxx           xxx

</PRE>
```

Other formatting tags such as headlines, italicizing, and bolding work fine within the preformatted text tags.

FIG. 20.10
Preformatted text lets you format text on-screen without using several different HTML tags.

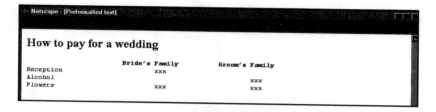

> **N O T E** When displaying preformatted text, Netscape uses a monospace font to ensure that each letter and character is the same width when displayed on the screen. This is so Netscape can guarantee that how you typed text within the <PRE> tags appears lined up correctly. ■

Basic Formatting Tags

Formatting paragraphs and chunks of text on-screen can be a harrowing task at best. In addition to organizing paragraphs of information, you've got to worry about how to make certain pieces of text stand out by using boldface, italics, text centering, and other formatting characteristics.

This section describes the popular HTML formatting tags and how they are used.

Strengthening Text—*<B>*

How often have you typed an entire paragraph, but wanted to make a single word or phrase stand out from the rest of the text? Maybe it's a special term, or the main focus of the paragraph. Either way, you want that word to jump out and catch a reader's eye on your WWW page.

Using the <B> and </B> container tags, surrounded text is displayed in boldface, making the letters appear thicker and darker on-screen compared to regular text.

> **N O T E** As mentioned in the last chapter, logical versus physical formatting is often a common debate among HTML programmers. Nowhere can this debate be better witnessed than in deciding how to make specific pieces of text stand out in bold or italics. The physical answer to this question is to use the <B> and <I> container tags to mark text as bold or italics.
>
> On the flip side, logical proponents suggest using the <STRONG> and <EM> (emphasis) tags to make text stand out. These two tags are used to describe how text should appear relative to normal text on-screen. Typically, the <STRONG> tag bolds surrounded text while the <EM> tag italicizes it, but this interpretation depends on each WWW browser's interpretation. For example, another browser might decide that <EM>phasized text should be bright red and in huge letters, while there's a much more standard approach to displaying <I>talic text—slightly slanted towards the right. With Logical Formatting tags, you're at the mercy of a WWW browser to interpret them however it likes.
>
> Nowadays, most HTML programmers tend to use the physical tags (<B> and <I>) because of the underlying uncertainty of exactly how WWW browsers will display text marked with logical tags. ■

Figure 20.11 shows how Netscape uses the `<B>` and `<STRONG>` tags to make important text stand out on a WWW page. Notice how Netscape tends to display the logical and physical tags in a virtually identical fashion.

FIG. 20.11
Boldfacing text adds significant character to specific words within paragraphs.

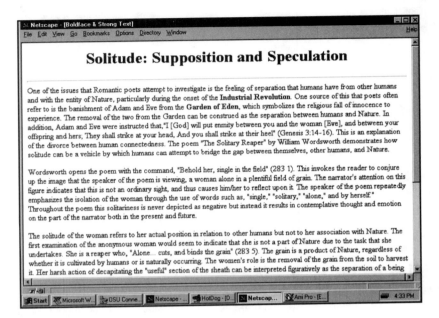

Italicizing Text—`</I>`

Another way to enhance the appearance of text within Netscape is by using the `<I>` and `</I>` italics tags. These tags indicate that text should appear italicized.

Italics can be used for highlighting a certain word or phrase, citing a published work, or for simply making a WWW page more readable. Look at figure 20.12 for an example of italicized (`<I>`) and emphasized text (`<EM>`) as listed:

```
After reading <I>The Body Farm</I> by Patricia Cornwell, I immediately had to go
out and buy her other books. <EM>Postmortem</EM> and <I>All that remains</I> are
among my favorite hair-raising whodunits!
```

N O T E You can use the italics tags alone, or in conjunction with other text formatting tags. For example, you could make some text appear boldface and italicized by surrounding it with `<B><I> YOUR TEXT </I></B>`. When embedding tags within one another, make sure you close the most recently opened tag first. Otherwise, you're more likely to forget to close a tag and have unwanted side effects. ■

T I P Some older browsers don't support recursive formatting tags. If you mark text to appear in bold and italics, older versions of Mosaic and Netscape will only use the first formatting tag encountered.

Part

IV

Ch

20

FIG. 20.12

Italics come in handy when referring to other printed works, and for highlighting certain words in a paragraph.

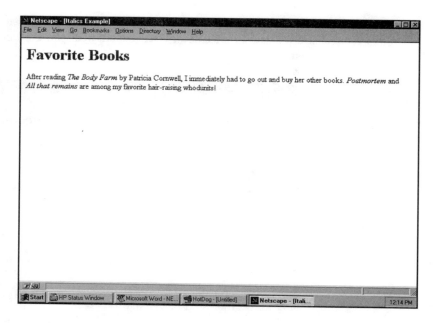

Blinking Text—*<BLINK>*

Another lesser used text formatting feature is the <BLINK> HTML tag. Using this set of container tags, displayed text intermittently blinks on and off, quickly attracting the attention of someone visiting that WWW page.

Adding blinking text to a WWW page is as simple as surrounding text with the <BLINK> and </BLINK> keywords as shown in the following example:

```
<BLINK> <H1> On the Road Yet Again </H1> </BLINK>
```

> **CAUTION**
>
> At best, blinking text should be used extremely sparingly as a text formatting feature. Prudent use of the <BLINK> tag is required unless you want to create an unwelcome eyesore on the WWW. Visitors will never forget hundreds of blinking words that make a WWW page difficult to read and unmotivating to return to.

Centering Text—*<CENTER>*

A welcome addition to the HTML text formatting tags allows you to center headlines and text in Netscape. Using the <CENTER> and </CENTER> container tags, marked text always appears horizontally in the middle of Netscape's screen. Regardless of how skinny or wide your Netscape window is, text will be automatically centered for visitors.

This flexibility allows WWW page creators to practice more page layout and design techniques, as well as use more of the available Netscape window.

Figure 21.13 shows how a previous example changes when the main header is centered.

FIG. 20.13
You'll want to take advantage of centering text on-screen to make headlines and information stand out more distinctly.

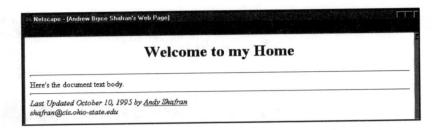

Additional Formatting Tags

In addition to bolding and italicizing text, HTML also supports several other popular text formatting tags. Table 20.2 outlines these additional HTML tags and how they make text appear in Netscape. These tags tend to be used less often and are not always supported by other non-Netscape browsers.

Table 20.2   Additional Logical Tags

HTML Tag	Tag Description
<BIG> </BIG>	Makes selected text appear logically bigger than surrounding pieces of text.
<SMALL> </SMALL>	Makes marked text smaller in comparison to other text on-screen.
<CITE> </CITE>	A popular way of citing other reference materials.
<TT> </TT>	Fixed width font that resembles a typewriter.
<BLOCKQUOTE> </BLOCKQUOTE>	Used to make references of blocks of text from another reference.

Understanding HTML Lists

Everyday you make a list to organize various pieces of information in a specific order. Whether it's creating a grocery list to go shopping, or a to-do task list, keeping track of a lot of information is vital. Within HTML, lists are one of the most widespread and powerful tools used to display text with Netscape. The following is a list of several popular reasons to include a list in your HTML document:

- You can organize a lot of different types and pieces of information in one structured, easy-to-read format.
- You can describe a complicated step-by-step process in edible chunks of information.
- Create highlights of information in a table of contents fashion that points to other more general pieces of information.

Using the several different types of built-in lists, you can handle virtually any situation. You'll learn the differences among ordered, unordered, and definition lists, as well as learn the important syntax for displaying a list within Netscape.

Figure 20.14 shows an example of what a list looks like within Netscape.

FIG. 20.14
This simple unordered list could appear on any WWW page.

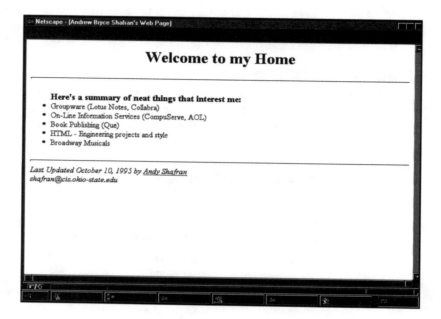

Creating Lists

In HTML, adding a list is not as easy as using a simple container tag. Several related HTML tags work together to allow you to select which type of list you want to display, how to delineate among different items within a list, and how to include a title for the list. For example, the HTML source code for the following list is shown:

```
<B>Here's a summary of neat things that interest me:
</B></LH>
<LI> Groupware (Lotus Notes, Collabra)
<LI> On-Line Information Services (CompuServe, AOL)
<LI> Book Publishing (Que)
<LI> HTML - Engineering projects and style
<LI> Broadway Musicals
</UL>
```

The tags </UL> select the list type (unordered). The </LH> tags markup the list header, or title, and the <LI> or list item tag separates each list item from one another. Together, these three parts make up a complete list. By adding each tag in a step-by-step process, your list is finished.

Next, you'll learn how to include three different types of lists within HTML documents.

Adding an Unordered List

On the WWW, the unordered list is most commonly used. This list displays each list item with a bullet preceding each item of information.

To add an unordered list, follow these steps:

1. First add the `</UL>` tags to your HTML document.

2. Within the unordered list tags, type in the text you want to appear as the list's header, and surround it with the `</LH>` tags:

   ```
   Saturday Night Live Guest Hosts</LH>

   </UL>
   ```

3. Add the list item tag `<LI>` and type in that piece of information.

   ```
   <LI> Chevy Chase
   ```

4. Repeat the third step until you have every list item typed in and accounted for. Figure 20.15 shows the final unordered list created with the following text:

   ```
   Saturday Night Live Guest Hosts</LH>
   <LI> Chevy Chase
   <LI> Steve Martin
   <LI> Jim Belushi
   <LI> Dan Akroyd
   </UL>
   ```

FIG. 20.15
This simple unordered list was created in minutes.

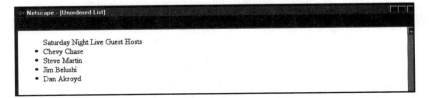

Adding a Numbered List

Similar to an unordered list, the numbered list presents separate items displayed in an organized order. The main difference between the two list types is that the numbered list automatically numbers each list item according to its order of appearance within the list.

Creating a numbered list is virtually identical to creating an unordered one. Follow these steps to build a numbered list:

1. First add the `<OL>` and `</OL>` tags to your HTML document.

2. Within the numbered list tags, type in the text you want to appear as the list's header, and surround it with the `</LH>` tags:

   ```
   <OL>
   Favorite baseball teams</LH>
   </OL>
   ```

Part
IV

Ch
20

3. Add the first list item tag `<LI>` and type in that piece of information. Remember that this first item will be numbered with a "1."

```
<LI>Cincinnati Reds
```

4. Repeat the third step until you have every list item typed in and accounted for. Figure 20.16 shows the final numbered list created in this example:

```
<OL>
Favorite baseball teams</LH>
<LI>Cincinnati Reds
<LI>Seattle Mariners
<LI>Chicago Cubs
</OL>
```

 TIP If you don't want to display the numbered list in straight numeric format, you can also number items with a letter (upper- and lowercase) or a Roman numeral. To change this Netscape-only feature, add the TYPE= keyword to the `<OL>` tag. To use Roman numerals, your `<OL>` tag becomes:

```
<OL TYPE=I, II, III...>
```

To list elements with a letter instead of a number, try:

```
<OL TYPE=A, B, C...>
```

Adding a Definition List

Unlike the other common types of lists, definition lists have two parts to each item. Much as dictionary entries have two elements, the word and the definition, the definition list has two separate terms.

To add a definition list to your HTML document, follow these steps:

1. First add the `<DL>` and `</DL>` tags to your HTML document.

2. Within the numbered list tags, type in the text you want to appear as the list's header, and surround it with the `</LH>` tags:

```
<DL>
Important Web terms</LH>
</DL>
```

FIG. 20.16
This simple numbered list is a good example of how numbered lists prioritize list items.

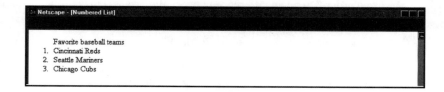

3. Unlike the other lists, which had a single component for each list item, the definition list has two. First type <DT> (short for definition term) and type in the term you want to define.

```
<DT> HTML
```

4. Next type <DD> (definition definition) and type in the term's definition.

```
<DD> Hyper Text Markup Language
```

5. Repeat the previous steps until you have every term and definition listed. Figure 20.17 shows the final definition list created in the following example:

```
<DL>
Important Web terms </LH>
<DT> HTML
<DD> Hyper Text Markup Language
<DT> WWW
<DD> World Wide Web
<DT> VRML
<DD> Virtual Reality Markup Language
</DL>
```

Notice how the definition term appears on one line, with the subsequent definition indented and on the following line.

Nesting Lists within One Another

Like most other HTML elements, you can have lists within lists, allowing you to subcategorize a single list into many different pieces. Mixing and matching lists is permitted, although be careful when embedding a list within the definition list because of the separate types of list elements.

To embed a list within another list, first create the initial list:

```
<OL>
Favorite baseball teams</LH>
<LI>Cincinnati Reds
<LI>Seattle Mariners
<LI>Chicago Cubs
</OL>
```

Then, embed the </UL> (or whichever type of list you want to use) within the original list tags. For example, an expansion of the following initial list appears in figure 20.18.

```
<OL>
<B>Favorite baseball teams</B></LH>
<LI>Cincinnati Reds
Favorite Players </LH>
<LI>Smiley
<LI>Larkin
<LI>Santiago
</UL>
<LI>Seattle Mariners
Favorite Players </LH>
```

```
<LI>Johnson
<LI>The Kid
<LI>Buhner
</UL>
<LI>Chicago Cubs
Favorite Players </LH>
<LI>Sosa
<LI>Grace
</UL>
</OL>
```

FIG. 20.17
This definition list is
only a sample of the
flexibility lists provide.

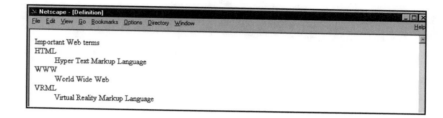

 TIP Notice how I used the <B> tags in the List Header above. This draws eyes to the description of the list before people start perusing it so they know what they are reading. Using formatting tags such as <B> or <I> are common within List Headers and List Items.

FIG. 20.18
Nested lists follow the
same rules as single
level lists.

Including Comments

In the world of programming, commenting sections of a program are virtually a required task. It is difficult to look back at work done several months ago and exactly remember the reasons you decided to display information in a certain format, or why you ignored specific conventions. Commenting within HTML is just as important.

Comments are typed bits of information that can only be seen when a visitor chooses to specifically view the page's source code. Standard comments should include the last time a file was updated, who made the modifications, and a description of recent changes. While HTML is usually straightforward, some tags can be deceptive. Commenting on how the tag works, and why you chose to use that tag is useful for future maintenance of that HTML document.

To add a comment to your document, surround the commented code with <!- and ->.

```
<!- My baseball Numbered list ->
<OL>
Favorite baseball teams</LH>
<LI>Cincinnati Reds
<LI>Seattle Mariners
<LI>Chicago Cubs
</OL>
```

> **CAUTION**
>
> Make sure you don't include private or confidential information within source code comments. Anyone who visits the page can see the original HTML text should they wish.

Building a Sample HTML Page

Now that you're finished with the HTML crash course, let's take a moment and review many of the different tags you've learned. Let's build a sample HTML document for a fictional local restaurant, trying to incorporate the many different HTML lessons learned.

1. The first step is adding the important tags that must be in all HTML documents.

   ```
   <HTML>
   <HEAD>
   </HEAD>
   <BODY>
   </BODY>
   </HTML>
   ```

2. Within the <HEAD> and </HEAD> tags, add a title to HTML document.

   ```
   <TITLE> OrangeBee's American Cuisine </TITLE>
   ```

3. Along the same lines as the title, add a large and bold header to the document.

   ```
   <BODY>
   <H1> OrangeBee's Fabulous American Cuisine on the Web </
   </BODY>
   ```

Part
IV

Ch
20

4. Type in some basic information about the restaurant. Take care to separate the paragraphs of text using the proper tags. So far your sample HTML document looks like this:

```
<HTML>
<HEAD> <TITLE> OrangeBee's American Cuisine </TITLE> </HEAD>
<BODY>
<CENTER><H1> OrangeBee's Fabulous American Cuisine on the Web
</H1></CENTER>
<HR>

Since 1991, OrangeBee's has been the fastest growing change of American cui-
sine and affordable eating. We offer a wide variety of menu items, including
several that contain under 5 grams of fat. <P>

<B>Stop by our nearest restaurants at: </B><BR>
Morse Road <BR>
Great Southern Shopping Center <BR>
Bexley <BR>
<HR>
<!- Created by OrangeBee's 1995 ->
</BODY>
</HTML>
```

5. Now the final step to this fictitious restaurant is to add a few menu items using a definition list. Try this list as an example:

```
<DL>
<B>OrangeBee's famous menu</B></LH>
<DT> Shrimp Cocktail
<DD> <I>This succulent platter of shrimp served with a tangy sauce. </I>
<DT> Fat-free Caesar
<DD> <I>Our homemade fat-free Caesar dressing makes this salad ideal.
</I>
<DT>Steak and Eggs
<DD> <I>Our cholesterol killer. This combo is everything the '90s doctors
say not to eat.</I>
</DL>
```

Figure 20.19 shows the final result of this sample WWW page. Read on to the next chapter to learn how to spice it up with graphics and links!

TIP When creating a lot of HTML files, most developers tend to create and use a standard template. This template has all the basic and necessary tags (such as <HTML> and <BODY>) already typed in, and follows a standard format (such as an unordered list). Once a template is created, all you have to do is fill in the blanks by typing the needed text, and the page is finished. Using a template saves you from always worrying about miscellaneous tags that are commonly forgotten.

FIG. 20.19
OrangeBee's now has a simple and nice-looking Web page.

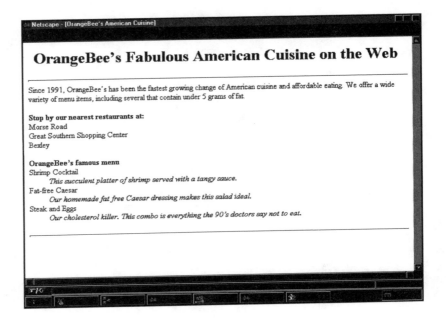

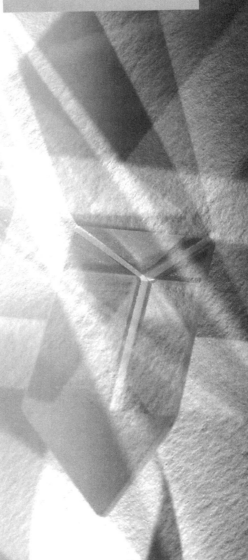

## CHAPTER 21

Adding Links, Graphics, and Tables

Learning how to place and format text on WWW pages is the important first step to getting familiar with HTML. Numerous tags exist that allow you detailed control over how information is displayed when viewed with Netscape. But HTML offers a lot more than plain text formatting.

By this point, you're probably familiar with how to use hyperlinks to jump from site to site on the WWW. In this chapter you learn how to create and include those hyperlinks in HTML documents that you've created yourself. As you'll see, links come in all different shapes, sizes, and formats.

Along with links, graphics also spice up WWW pages and make them more interesting and informative to visit. HTML allows you to include a wide variety of graphics on WWW pages.

Like lists, tables are powerful layout tools that allow you to display and compare copious amounts of information within a columnized modular format. Tables include several new HTML tags that need to be used in the proper sequence to correctly organize information on the screen.

Specifically, in this chapter you learn how to:

- Understand HTML hypertext links
- Create standard links to other WWW pages
- Link Web pages to other Internet resources
- Add images with HTML
- Understand important image customization techniques
- Learn how to use graphics as links
- Create and incorporate a table into your HTML pages ■

Explaining HTML Links

The underlying premise behind the World Wide Web was to link information from all over the globe together in a single accessible format. People browsing the WWW in Rhode Island, for example, can have immediate access to information anywhere on the Internet. To accomplish this formidable task, every file and document on the Internet was given its own unique URL (Uniform Resource Locator), or address. Similar to a mailing address, the URL tells Internet browsers where to go when looking for specific information.

Once you know an URL, you can easily link into that spot on the Internet. By linking documents and files together from across the world, you create a virtual "web" of links back and forth, inspiring the name of the WWW.

Using Links

In Netscape, hypertext links typically appear as underlined blue text (see fig. 21.1). Using your mouse, you can click the underlined text and be brought immediately to the linked document. HTML authors can link to other local HTML files, specific anchored spots within the same HTML file, WWW sites elsewhere on the Web, and even additional Internet resources such as UseNet newsgroups, Gopher, and even e-mail can be linked to with HTML.

Once visited, the linked text changes colors to indicate that you've already traversed that specific strand of the WWW. This serves as a useful reminder and map of where you've been and where you have yet to visit.

N O T E Not all hypertext links appear in blue. Using advanced HTML characteristics described below, or setting Netscape hyperlinks can appear in a variety of colors and formats. Typically though, hypertext links will be set out in a different color indicating that they are "hot" text. ■

There are no technical limitations to the number of different links available from a single HTML document. But WWW designers should be careful not to overwhelm their pages with hundreds of hypertext links to everywhere across the world—bigger is not always better.

FIG. 21.1

In general, underlined text indicates a hypertext link.

Hypertext link to
Netscape Tiger Exhibit

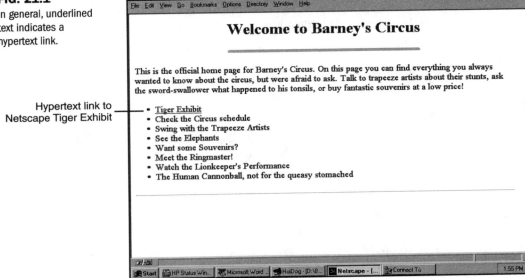

Dissecting an URL

Not surprisingly, an URL is made of several distinct elements. Much as your mailing address requires a street address, city, state, and ZIP code to receive mail correctly, an URL has its own pieces as well. In general, all URLs look like this:

Internet Service://Host Name [:port] /path/and/filename

- ■ Internet Service—The type of information Netscape is linking into. Most often you'll use http to link to other WWW documents, but e-mail, UseNet, and Gopher all have their own special name (described later). HTTP stands for HyperText Transfer Protocol and tells Netscape how to handle the linked information.

- ■ Host Name—The electronic domain on the Internet that you are trying to connect with.

- ■ [:port]—Indicates a special port on the Internet server to connect with. It is typically not required.

N O T E Most URL's don't require a specified port address because by default, Netscape knows how to specifically communicate with the WWW servers on the Internet. Port addresses are more common when you need to include a link to a different Internet resource, such as Gopher or FTP because they tell Netscape which electronic data communications port is designated specifically for Gopher or FTP access. ■

Part

IV

Ch

21

■ /path/and/filename—The complete file name of the HTML document you want to access and the path required to reach it. If no file name is specified, Netscape automatically looks for a file called "index.html" in the directory specified.

Combining all the pieces together, here's the URL for Que, the publisher for this book:

http://www.mcp.com/que/

Creating a Link

Once you know the URL you want to link to, creating the link in HTML is a relatively easy process. As with everything else in HTML, adding links requires a special tag. HTML uses the `<A>` and `</A>` tags to create a link

Follow these steps to add a hypertext link to an HTML document:

1. First identify the unique URL that you want to link to:

   http://www.mcp.com/que/

2. Add the HTML Anchor tag `<A>` `</A>` to the URL in the following fashion:

   <A HREF="http://www.mcp.com/que/"> </A>

   The HREF keyword indicates that you are creating a link to the HyperText Reference URL that you provide.

3. Indicate the text that you want to identify as "hot" in Netscape—appearing underlined and in blue, between the `<A>` and `</A>` tags.

   <A HREF="http://www.mcp.com/que/"> Link to Que Publishing </A>

Linking to Local Files

Linking WWW pages to other documents is as simple as knowing the complete URL to the linked document. However, if you want to link to other HTML documents that are located at the same site on the Internet, you can take advantage of several shortcuts

This feature is called relative addressing because it allows you to give an URL that is relative to the original document. For example, to link to an HTML file named moreinfo.html that is located in the exact same subdirectory as the original document, you can use just the file name as the URL:

```
<A HREF="moreinfo.html">Link to More Information</A>
```

Because keeping every HTML file in the same subdirectory can be confusing, with relative addressing, you can also indicate files within subdirectories as well. To link to evenmore.html in a subdirectory named INFORMATION, you can use the following link:

   <A HREF="INFORMATION/evenmore.html">Link to Even More Information</A>

Similarly, you can link to files that are one level higher than the current subdirectory in the hard drive structure:

<A HREF="../themost.html"> The Most Information </A>

Using relative addressing makes it easier to organize a WWW file structure because you don't have to type the complete URL for every linked document.

Other Types of HTML Links

HTML also handles several other popular Internet resources that exchange and share information—UseNet newsgroups, e-mail, FTP, and Gopher are the ones you'll most likely want to use in your WWW pages. Each of these different types of information can be linked directly to HTML by specifying their unique URL.

N O T E   Netscape also allows you to create hyperlinks to other different types of Internet resources including Telnet, WAIS (Wide Area Information Service), and other more obscure protocols. Each protocol requires its own unique keyword and has its own specific format. For more information on how Netscape integrates with other Internet services see chapter 6. ■

Using FTP Links

FTP traditionally allows any user to log on to an Internet domain, search through the file listings, and download the file to their personal computer. With HTML, you can directly link files to a WWW page and let visitors download a file simply by clicking the underlined link.

Follow the same steps outlined previously to add an FTP URL to an HTML document. An FTP URL looks similar to a standard URL except that it uses a different Internet service keyword. So **ftp://ftp4.netscape.com/pub/smart/SM10R2.EXE** looks like

<A HREF="ftp://ftp4.netscape.com/pub/smart/SM10R2.EXE"> Netscape's Smartmarks File</A>

when the proper tags are added. By clicking the highlighted text, Netscape automatically logs on to the Internet domain, finds the file to download, and starts retrieving it.

CAUTION

Adding an FTP URL as described previously assumes that the Internet site being connected to supports anonymous FTP logins. That allows everyone on the Internet free access to connect and download files.

Under some situations, anonymous FTP access is not allowed, and a user ID and password is necessary to connect. For those situations, the FTP URL looks like:

FTP://USERID:PASSWORD@ftp.netscape.com/file/smart.exe

Although you can include nonanonymous FTP links on a WWW page, make sure you understand the possible repercussions. Anyone who accesses that WWW page can view the HTML source code through Netscape and see the user ID and password.

N O T E Another strategy often used when linking to files via the FTP protocol is to link to a directory instead of a specific file. By linking to a directory, Netscape brings up a list of files that you can download instead of linking to a single file. This is particularly useful because Internet files tend to change file names as newer versions are released. This saves you the hassle of constantly updating your HTML documents each time a file name changes.

To link to a FTP directory instead of a file, simply leave off the file name within the URL. ▪

Using Gopher Links

As a precursor to the WWW, Gopher menus link to other worldwide menus in much the same way HTML links work. Over the years, enormous quantities of information have been placed on Gopher, and are not available in HTML format yet. Thousands of Gopher servers exist with vast information ranging from specific university information to the United States State Department Travel Advisories.

Fortunately, you can link to any Gopher server as long as you know the proper URL. Following the standard URL format, Gopher links tend to include a server port number, use extended file and directory names, and use Gopher as the Internet service keyword. The following is an example of a Gopher URL:

> **gopher://gopher.stolaf.edu:70/00/Internet%20Resources/US-State-Department-Travel-Advisories/Current-Advisories/australia**

This URL tells Netscape to connect to the gopher.stolaf.edu server using port 70 and retrieve the current travel advisory for Australia. The following is how the link appears in full HTML, and figure 21.2 shows the results of clicking this link.

```
<A HREF="gopher://gopher.stolaf.edu:70/00/Internet%20Resources/US-State-Depart-
ment-Travel-Advisories/Current-Advisories/australia">Gopher report on the US
Travel Advisory on Australia</A>
```

T I P In the preceding Gopher URL, the "%20" is used to replace a space for the WWW link. Netscape can't properly recognize spaces in URLs and the %20 string is a standard replacement for them.

TROUBLESHOOTING

I noticed the tip on replacing spaces with the %20 string, but what if I wanted to include a % sign in my Gopher (or any other) URL? Replacing the % with %25 tells Netscape to use a percent sign when interpreting an URL.

FIG. 21.2
Unlike Netscape, Gopher offers a text-only outlook on linked information from around the world.

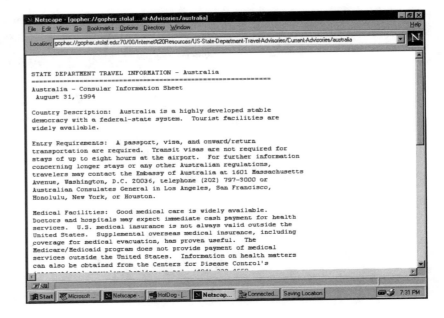

Using UseNet Links

UseNet URLs are much simpler than other types of URLs. They require the Internet resource keyword—news, a colon, and then the full name of the newsgroup:

news:alt.fan.dave_barry

UseNet URLs work differently because there is no central news Internet server. The URL tells Netscape to connect to the precustomized news server and read that newsgroup.

The following is a complete HTML link to a newsgroup. Figure 21.3 shows the Netscape newsreader reading the newsgroup.

TROUBLESHOOTING

I have a link on my WWW page to a specific UseNet newsgroup. I recently received e-mail from some people who don't have access to that newsgroup (alt.religion). They get an error message when trying to locate it. Is there a problem with my HTML encoding or any way I can help them out so they can read the newsgroup I am referring to? Every site has its load of newsgroups that it carries. Because of the massive disk space that newsgroups use, few Internet servers can afford to provide access to every newsgroup. Lesser used and varied appropriateness newsgroups (especially the alt.hierarchy) are often not available on local news servers. Contact your System Administrator to ask your site to pick up a feed from a newsgroup that isn't currently available.

FIG. 21.3

Newsgroups are another
integrated service
available with Netscape
and HTML.

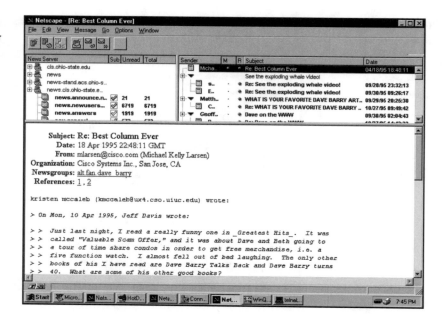

Using Mailto Links

Another important communication tool on the Internet is electronic mail. E-mail allows people
to send personal messages to other individuals all across the world. With HTML, you can
include an e-mail on a WWW page that lets visitors easily send mail to a specific address.

Using the mailto Internet services keyword, building an e-mail URL only requires knowing the
e-mail address of the recipient. For example, to build a link to shafran.5@osu.edu, you would
use the following URL:

mailto:shafran.5@osu.edu

The full HTML for the e-mail link looks like:

```
<A HREF="mailto:shafran.5@osu.edu">Sample E-mail</A>
```

When clicked upon, Netscape brings up the Netscape mail window where users can type a
message and send it on its way in a few moments (see fig. 21.4).

TROUBLESHOOTING

**I'm looking for a specific URL of a neat World Wide Web page I found while browsing one day.
Unfortunately I can't remember the complete URL or where I found the original link. Does
Netscape know how to use a partial URL when looking around the Internet?** Netscape is limited
only to the exact URLs that you supply. When looking for a specific URL to link to, try checking out

Yahoo at **http://www.yahoo.com** and searching their index of WWW links. Good luck! For more information on using search engines, see chapter 3.

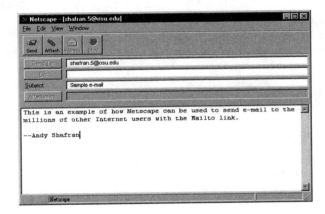

Understanding HTML Anchors and Targets

In addition to linking to other WWW files and Internet resources, HTML also has the ability to link and refer to internal points within the same document. Functioning like a table of contents, you can place multiple text anchors within an HTML document and create a centralized listing of them at the top of the file (or anywhere else). By clicking the hyperlinks, visitors aren't taken to a separate document, but to a different spot, called targets, within the same HTML file.

Primarily for large files, this internal referencing system requires two separate steps. First you've got to create the named targets within the HTML file, and then you must build the links to each of those specific targets.

Creating Named Targets

Adding named targets to WWW pages requires only a few steps. Follow these steps to add as many named targets as you want to your HTML document.

1. Choose a name for your target. This name should be succinct and to the point, but not too cryptic to be confusing.

   Mammals

2. Use the <A> and </A> tags to mark the text as a target, but instead of using the HREF keyword, use NAME instead.

   <A NAME="Mammals"></A>

3. Type in the corresponding text that you want associated with the named target. This is the text the target is attached to. Notice how other tags work within the anchor tags.

   <A NAME="Mammals">

<H3>Warm Blooded Creatures</H3

</A>

Once your named target is added, you're ready to move on to the next step and learn how to jump directly to it within the same file.

TIP You don't have to associate any text with a specific named target. Instead, you can leave a blank between the anchor tags. Netscape places that line at the top of the screen when told to link to a named target. Not associating text with a target is useful when you want to associate one with a special list, table, or graphic.

Linking to Named Targets

Linking to a named target is identical to linking to other WWW documents with one minor difference. Instead of typing a complicated URL, you simply type in the target name with a "#" in front of it.

The following is an example of how to link to the previous example:

```
<A HREF="#Mammals">Mammals - Earth's Dominant Species</A>
```

As you can see in figure 21.5, links to named targets appear the same as standard links to other HTML files.

> **CAUTION**
>
> Don't forget the "#" in front of the target name. Without it, Netscape attempts to link to a separate file (located in the same current directory) with that target name.

N O T E You can also link to specific named targets in other HTML files elsewhere on the WWW. To find out a target name, view the site's HTML source code and manually pick out the target.

Be careful, though. Named targets tend to change considerably more often than HTML file names, and have a significantly better chance of becoming obsolete or invalid. ■

Important Link Tips and Traps

There are several important stylistic situations to be aware of when linking HTML documents to one another. The following is a simple checklist to evaluate your WWW links:

- Test and retest every HTML link. Make sure that there are no typos or incorrect URLs included within your HTML documents.
- Periodically check your HTML file for outdated links. On the WWW, files occasionally move, are renamed, or are even deleted. Regularly checking WWW links ensures that they are current and constantly maintained. For example, when linking to files, remember that file names change as new versions are released.

FIG. 21.5
Whether targets or
regular links, they all
appear the same in
Netscape.

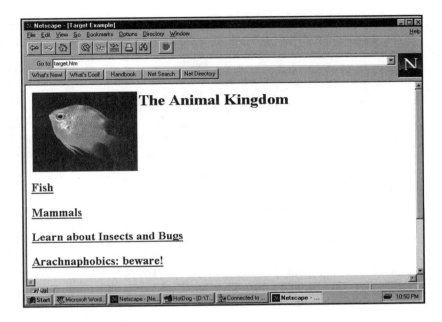

- Organize lists of links. If you need to include many links within a single document, use a list, table, or other organization technique to keep the list of links usable and readable.

- In paragraphs, links should be invisible. When linking a single word or phrase within a paragraph, the link should not affect the flow of the paragraph. Visitors should be able to read and understand the paragraph without accessing the link.

- Associate relevant information to links. Avoid linking the word "here" or other unimportant words. Pretend that you are only looking at the "hot" text. You should be able to understand where that link will take you before clicking it. The word "here" doesn't describe where the link will take you.

Adding Graphics with HTML

Creating HTML files wouldn't be complete without learning how to add exciting and colorful images and graphics to them. In the multimedia atmosphere of the WWW, graphics are important tools because they can be used to jazz up a WWW page. You'll discover that most HTML documents incorporate graphics in their design because they immediately add variety to strictly textual information.

Other than aesthetic purposes, graphics can also have functionality within your WWW pages. Images can serve as hypertext links to other WWW pages, formatting tools to organize text around, or even replace extended pieces of information with an informative graphic.

Part

IV

Ch

21

This section introduces you to embedded graphics and images with HTML. While adding an image is easy, HTML offers a multitude of customization keywords and tags that allow you to "desktop publish" WWW documents.

The Different Types of Graphics

On the WWW, there are two popular graphics file formats that are widely supported and in use today. Of these two file formats, each has its own advantages and disadvantages for certain situations.

- **GIF (Graphical Image Format)**—The GIF format was developed by CompuServe (using technology from Unisys) and has been a worldwide graphical format standard for years. GIF files use standard compression techniques to properly handle a wide variety of colors and file sizes. Because of this, GIF files tend to have a significantly larger file size, but better detail and resolution than its counterpart, JPEG. If you had to choose an image format for Michaelangelo's Sistine Chapel, you'd choose GIF for the detail.

- **JPEG (Joint Photographic Expert Group)** — With the file size limitations of GIF in mind, the JPEG format was designed to be a high compression image format that stores similar GIF images in as much as 1/3 the space. Using recursive bit construction, JPEGs shrink an image several times to achieve quicker download times. Unfortunately, as a side effect, JPEG graphics tend to lose detail, especially for larger images. Because of the fuzziness that sometimes surrounds JPEG images, Monet's masterpieces would be perfect for this file format. Netscape's enhancements are refined toward loading JPEG images progressively. Netscape loads more detail into the image over several passes, allowing you to see the image form before your very eyes.

Initially, only GIF graphics were supported in the early WWW browsers. Nowadays however, virtually every browser (including Netscape) supports both GIF and JPEG and allows you to use them interchangeably. You should feel free to use whichever of the two image types you prefer.

N O T E Be careful when including other popular image formats such as .TIF, .PCX, .PIC, or .BMP in your HTML pages. To view these images, individuals must have an external helper application built into Netscape.

This makes images of these file formats less ideal than backgrounds or embedded images, but acceptable as references to important information stored only in a specific graphical format. ■

T I P Although not quite at par with GIF quality, JPEG graphics typically are much smaller in file size, and consequently download quicker.

Using the *<IMG>* Tag

One of the most important HTML tags, the `<IMG>` tag allows you to select which graphics to include on a page and how they are sized and formatted on the screen.

Without any special formatting keywords, adding a graphic is relatively easy. For example, the picture of the fish in figure 21.5 uses the following tag:

```
<IMG SRC="FISH.JPG">
```

When placed in an HTML document, this tag tells Netscape to display the graphic entitled FISH.JPG (which is located in the same current directory as the HTML file) on-screen.

You can also link WWW pages directly to graphics at another site. For example, if the file FISH.JPG were stored on the Que site (which it isn't), you could add the following tag to link your HTML document directly to the image:

```
<IMG SRC="http://www.que.com/fish.jpg">
```

Logically, when Netscape finds this tag, it first connects to **www.que.com**, retrieves the selected image, then displays it on your WWW page.

> **CAUTION**
>
> Linking images from other Web sites can cause performance problems for Web page visitors. That's because a visitor has to wait for the information to be retrieved from another site, then sent to their PC before they can see it. Sometimes this can be quite a slowdown. For better performance, ensure that displayed images are saved on the same Internet server as the HTML file.

Another popular way to include images within HTML documents is the use of thumbnailed images. Thumbnail images are miniature versions of a larger image that take up significantly less screen size and, thus, have a much smaller file size. Thumbnailed images are then linked to the full-size version of the image. This allows individuals the option of waiting to download the full-size image, or just being satisfied with the small, thumbnail version.

> **N O T E** Graphics can be stored and organized in separate subdirectories just like linked files. Using the method outlined previously in this chapter, you can direct Netscape to graphics stored in directories both higher and lower in the hard drive structure with no complications. ■

When placing graphics on WWW pages, the `<IMG>` tag offers a great deal of flexibility regarding how the image appears and is formatted on-screen. The following sections explain most popular `<IMG>` keywords that allow you to customize image placement in Netscape.

Part
IV

Ch
21

Alternative Text

Not all WWW browsers are created equal. While Netscape is by far the most robust and popular, others such as Lynx, are text only, and don't have the ability to display graphics and images

Additionally, Netscape also allows users to customize whether or not to display graphics when visiting new WWW pages, because often times it takes too long to download and display all the embedded images.

To handle nongraphical browsers and Netscape's flexibility, it is standard practice to include alternative text in the <IMG> tag, which is displayed when the graphic isn't downloaded.

Use the ALT="" keyword to specify the alternative text to display instead of a graphic. Figure 21.6 shows how Netscape displays alternative text in the following example.

```
<IMG SRC="FISH.JPG" ALT="A cool picture of a colorful fish">
```

FIG. 21.6

Instead of the graphic, Netscape can display the alternative text.

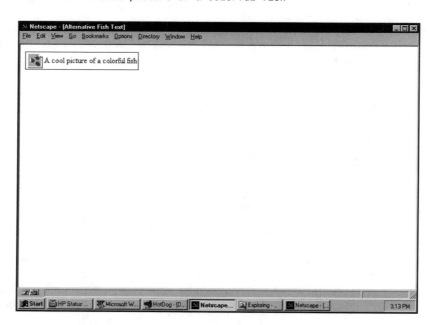

Alignment and Image Placement Options

When including graphics on a WWW page, you have several different choices of where they are placed in the Netscape window. These alignment options are set with the ALIGN= keyword. With this keyword you specify not only where the image is aligned on-screen but also how text appears in relation to displayed images.

Table 21.1 lists the five unique ALIGN keywords and how they display graphics and text accordingly.

Table 21.1   HTML Alignment Options

Keyword	Definition
LEFT	Places the graphic on the left side of the screen. Text is displayed to the right.
RIGHT	The opposite of LEFT, the graphic is placed on the right margin with text on the left.
TOP	Lines up the graphic to the tallest item on the same line.
MIDDLE	Aligns the top of the text to the middle of a placed graphic.
BASELINE	Aligns the bottom of the graphic with the bottom of the line of text.

Although there are other ALIGN keywords, they are repetitive and not commonly accepted. For example, the BASELINE keyword is interchangeable and virtually identical to the BOTTOM and ABSBOTTOM keywords—just a different syntax for the same effect.

Figure 21.7 shows how the graphics are displayed on-screen using the following snippet of HTML:

```
<IMG SRC="fish.jpg" ALIGN=LEFT> Left Alignment<P>

<IMG SRC="fish.jpg" ALIGN=RIGHT> Right Alignment<P>

<IMG SRC="fish.jpg" ALIGN=TOP> Top Alignment<P>

<IMG SRC="fish.jpg" ALIGN=MIDDLE> Middle Alignment <P>

<IMG SRC="fish.jpg" ALIGN=BASELINE> Baseline Alignment <P>
```

N O T E   Another popular way to control graphics placement on-screen is to use Netscape tables. By using a table, you have more exact control on the position and area the graphic takes up on the screen. ■

Height and Width

Another advanced graphic option allows you to control exactly how wide and tall images appear within Netscape. By using the WIDTH and HEIGHT keywords, you can specify how many pixels of the screen an image should appear, regardless of what the original file's resolution was.

The HEIGHT and WIDTH keywords are typically used to create smaller, icon-sized versions of images that are easier to view on a WWW page. Using these two keywords is also an additional performance benefit within Netscape. Traditionally, Netscape must download all of the embedded images before it can format the text on-screen accordingly. When the WIDTH and HEIGHT keywords are used, Netscape knows exactly how much space to allocate for an image on-screen, and formats the page while the image(s) are downloading.

Part

IV

Ch

21

FIG. 21.7
With graphic alignment
options, HTML
designers have
significantly more
control over the
appearance of their
WWW pages.

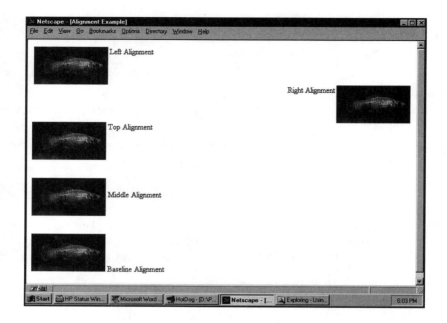

Use HEIGHT and WIDTH just like you would use the other IMG keywords described in this
section. For example, to set an image to display exactly 300 pixels wide and 150 pixels tall, type
in the following HTML:

```
<IMG SRC="FISH.JPG" HEIGHT=150 WIDTH=300>
```

Figure 21.8 shows an example of the same image with three different height and width dimensions.

> **CAUTION**
>
> Make sure you limit your HEIGHT and WIDTH pixel ranges to under 600 × 440. A standard VGA monitor
> displays 640 × 480 pixels across the screen, and anything larger virtually guarantees that visitors won't be
> able to easily see the entire graphic. 600 × 440 is the maximum recommended size to give clearance for
> standard Netscape options such as the title and scroll bars.

Vertical and Horizontal Distance

The next image placement keywords to become familiar with are HSPACE and VSPACE.
These two keywords specify a specific horizontal and vertical distance away from an image that
is blank space. This ensures that text remains a reasonable distance from the image by allowing the specified white space.

Similar to the HEIGHT and WIDTH keywords, VSPACE and HSPACE require numeric values
in the form of pixels. As good practice, try to keep at least a 10-pixel border between an image

and associated text. The following HTML example shows how to use the HSPACE and VSPACE keywords to provide a standard 10-pixel radius around an image:

```
<IMG SRC="FISH.JPG" VSPACE=10 HSPACE=10>
```

FIG. 21.8
All three sizes of this image are based on the same original graphic.

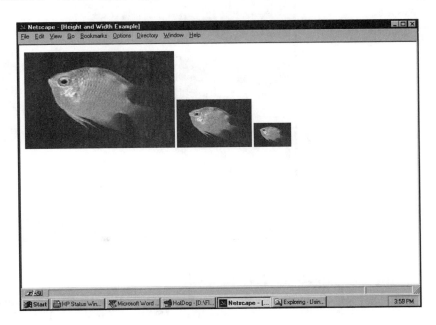

Borders

The last image customization tag is the BORDER width keyword. With this setting, you can have Netscape automatically create a thick (or thin) black border around any image included on your WWW pages.

Using the BORDER keyword, you can have a border thickness ranging from 0-10 (the default is 0). The following example sets your image border thickness to 5.

```
<IMG SRC="FISH.JPG" BORDER=5>
```

Figure 21.9 shows a sampling of five different border thicknesses ranging from 1 to 9.

The *EMBED* Tag

Netscape has proposed an extension to HTML that allows you to embed an arbitrary file type into your Web page. This extension, the <EMBED> tag, functions similarly to the <IMG> element. It has a SRC attribute used to specify the file to use, and HEIGHT and WIDTH attributes to control the size. It's still being worked on, so it may have more attributes in the future. Currently, the <EMBED> element is used to insert file types that plug-ins will use. Examples of such file types are Macromedia Director files, Live 3D worlds, and AVI multimedia files.

Part
IV
Ch
21

FIG. 21.9

Adding an outline black border to your images frames them on your WWW pages.

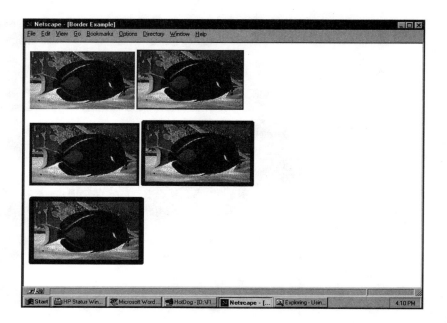

Wiring Graphics as HTML Links

Not only do graphics serve as pure visual eye candy, but they can also do double duty and work as hypertext links. By adding the proper HTML tags, embedded graphics and images can serve as links to other WWW documents and pages across the world.

Making an image serve as a link is a two step process. First you add the image along with the appropriate settings into the WWW document:

```
<IMG SRC="arrows.gif" ALIGN=LEFT>
```

Once you've added the image, now add a hypertext link in the same manner as you did earlier in this chapter, only instead of making a text phrase "hot" and surrounded by the link <A> and </A> tags, surround the IMG tag. You can also include text as well, so both the image and a text phrase link you to the same HTML document:

```
<A HREF="dir.html"><IMG SRC="arrows.gif" ALIGN=LEFT> <H2>Directions to my
House<H2></A>
```

Figure 21.10 shows how graphics can be used to link to different HTML documents. A blue outline border surrounds the graphics that are linked to other documents. By clicking upon the graphic, users are hyperlinked to the associated file.

> **N O T E**   Advanced Web developers tend to use graphics and images often to represent links to other WWW sites and pages. By using smaller icons to represent clickable buttons, WWW developers can create a graphical interface to their set of Web documents. ∎

FIG. 21.10
HTML flexibility allows
graphics to also serve
as links to other WWW
documents.

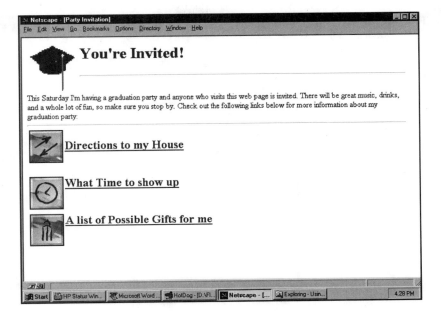

Creating Tables

Besides using standard lists and formatting tags, tables are another powerful tool for displaying information within HTML documents. Emulating the look and feel of a spreadsheet, tables allow you to specify rows and columns of information that are displayed within Netscape.

Tables are similar to lists (described in the previous chapter) because they allow a lot of information to be easily displayed in a small area. The main difference is that tables allow multiple columns of information—making it easier to compare and organize data.

Figure 21.11 shows an actual table from within Netscape.

> **CAUTION**
>
> Although tables are popular with Netscape, their formal definition has not been accepted in HTML version 3, yet. The final HTML tags and codes that are accepted by all browsers could change slightly when HTML 3.0 is finally approved.

Adding a Table

Adding a table within HTML can be confusing because there are several different tags that need to be used in conjunction with one another. You've got to specify each cell of every row and column individually, as well as the table's header and other information.

Part
IV

Ch
21

FIG. 21.11

This easy-to-make table lets you compare facts in a readable and efficient manner.

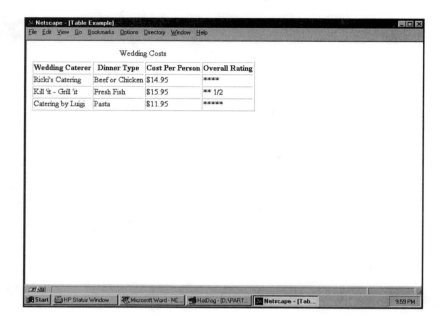

Follow these steps to add a basic table to your HTML document:

1. First type the <TABLE> and </TABLE> container tags. This set of tags must surround the entire table. You can tell Netscape to draw the lines separating each cell of information from one another using the BORDER keyword:

   <TABLE BORDER=1>

   </TABLE>

2. Next type in the Table's Caption. This is a simple identifier that serves as a label for the table in general.

   <CAPTION> Wedding Costs </CAPTION>

N O T E   You can specify whether or not you want the table's caption to appear above or below the table by using the ALIGN keyword. By default, the caption appears above the table. To instruct the caption to appear below the table, you would use the <CAPTION> tag in the following way:

<CAPTION ALIGN=BOTTOM> Wedding Costs </CAPTION> ■

3. Next type in the tags identifying each row of the table. The <TR> and </TR> tags surround every cell of information that appears within a single row. The number of <TR> row tags specifies the number of rows within your table.

4. Within the Table Row (<TR>) tags, you've got to specify the data in each cell with the <TD> tags. The number of <TD> and </TD> container tags indicates the number of columns within your table. Type the information for that cell within each set of <TD> container tags:

```
                    <TR>
                                    <TD>Ricki's Catering</TD>
                                    <TD>Beef or Chicken</TD>
                                    <TD>$14.95</TD>
                                    <TD>****</TD>
                    </TR>
```

5. When you are finished typing in each row and column, check out your table within Netscape. Make sure that each row has the same amount of columns and is lined up correctly.

N O T E   As a separate tag, you can also specify which cells of data should be boldface and serve as the Table Headers. Typically the first row and/or column of information is marked as a column or row header. Using the and </TH> tags instead of <TD>, Netscape automatically marks those cells in boldface so they standout. In this sample table, the first row of information uses the tags as below:

```
<TR>
Wedding Caterer</TH>
Dinner Type</TH>
Cost Per Person</TH>
Overall Rating</TH>
</TR>
```

The complete HTML code for the table shown in figure 21.11 is listed below:

```
<TABLE BORDER=1>
<CAPTION ALIGN=top>Wedding Costs</CAPTION>
<TR>
Wedding Caterer</TH>
Dinner Type</TH>
Cost Per Person</TH>
Overall Rating</TH>
</TR>
<TR>
<TD>Ricki's Catering</TD>
<TD>Beef or Chicken</TD>
<TD>$14.95</TD>
<TD>****</TD>
</TR>
<TR>
<TD>Kill 'it - Grill 'it</TD>
<TD>Fresh Fish</TD>
<TD>$15.95</TD>
<TD>** 1/2</TD>
</TR>
<TR>
<TD>Catering by Luigi</TD>
<TD>Pasta</TD>
<TD>$11.95</TD>
<TD>*****</TD>
</TR>
</TABLE>
```

Advanced Table Features

As a robust formatting language, HTML offers significant flexibility and customizability in creating tables that fit all sorts of different situations. A simple table forces you to ensure that every cell is typed in and offers a single straightforward format.

This section describes several ways to customize and modify how tables appear within Netscape using several different keywords. You'll learn how to create cells that span multiple rows and columns, customize the border thickness, and set text alignment within each cell.

Cells that Span Multiple Columns   Sometimes you'll want a particular set of information to be spread across more than one column. To accomplish this, you've got to add the COLSPAN keyword to the <TD> tag for the cells you want to affect.

For example, in the sample table above, here's the following HTML to create a multiple column set of information (fig. 21.12):

```
<TR>
<TH COLSPAN=2>General Info </TH>
<TH COLSPAN=2>Hard Numbers </TH>
</TR>
<TR>
Wedding Caterer</TH>
Dinner Type</TH>
Cost Per Person</TH>
Overall Rating</TH>
</TR>
```

FIG. 21.12
Spanning multiple columns lets you organize information hierarchically.

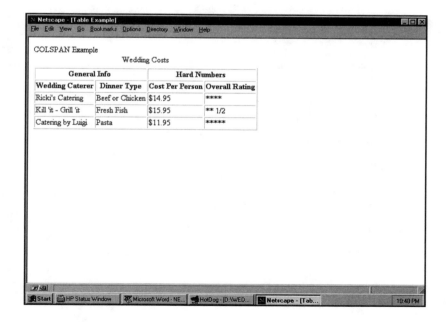

> **CAUTION**
>
> When using the COLSPAN and ROWSPAN keywords (described below), make sure you correctly calculate the correct number of rows and columns that you combine. An incorrect number creates a disproportionate-looking table within Netscape.

Cells that Span Multiple Rows   Similar to the COLSPAN keyword described above, table cells can also be spread across multiple rows of information. Using the ROWSPAN keyword, you can specify how many rows a cell of information should span.

Figure 21.13 shows the multiple row spanning cells described below:

```
<TR>
<TD ROWSPAN=2>Ricki's Catering</TD>
<TD>Beef</TD>
<TD>$14.95</TD>
<TD>****</TD>
</TR>
<TR>
<TD>Ricki's Catering</TD>
<TD>Chicken</TD>
<TD>$12.95</TD>
<TD>**</TD>
</TR>
```

FIG. 21.13
Multiple row spanning saves you from typing the same information twice.

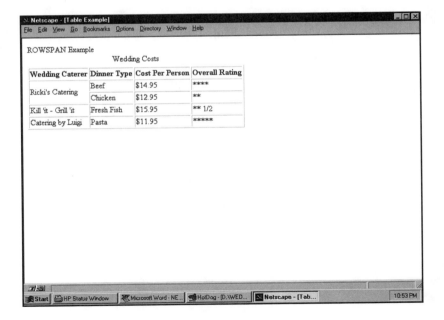

Cell Alignment   Like other text and image elements within HTML, you can also customize the text alignment within each cell of the table. By adding the appropriate keyword to the <TD> tag you can specify both the horizontal and vertical alignment of data within the cell.

To set the horizontal alignment within a cell, use the ALIGN keyword. You can set alignment to be LEFT, RIGHT, and CENTER:

```
<TD ALIGN=CENTER>
```

To set the Vertical alignment, use the VALIGN keyword. VALIGN can be set as either TOP, MIDDLE, or BOTTOM:

```
<TD ALIGN=MIDDLE>
```

Vertical alignment is sometimes necessary when one column of information within a row has several lines of information.

N O T E   You can also embed graphics, other tables, and all types of lists within a specific table cell. By using the appropriate set of tags, images, lists, and tables are just as easy to include within a cell as straight data. ▩

## CHAPTER 22

Advanced Graphics

World Wide Web pages benefit from the use of graphical elements, yet sophisticated graphics can significantly slow down the transfer of a site. Developing an attractive, and still responsive, site is the focus of this chapter. In addition to providing information on designing and choosing existing images, this chapter focuses on different image formats used on the Web and emphasizes the benefits and drawbacks of each. We explore the inherent graphical capabilities of Netscape, which allow the designer to make the best use of image download time through the use of thumbnail images. Finally, we look at Netscape's capability to modify a document's background and text colors.

In this chapter, you learn:

- Guidelines for developing graphics
- Which file formats are best for your Web site
- How to make interlaced and transparent GIFs
- How to convert images to progressive JPEGs
- Guidelines to optimize image download time
- How to develop and use thumbnail images
- How to modify backgrounds and text colors
- How to align images and wrap text

Developing Graphics for the Web

Developing graphics for use on the World Wide Web is significantly different from designing for the printed page. A closer analogy can be drawn between multimedia and the Web, because visitors to a Web page do not merely read information, but actually interact with the medium. In order to facilitate this interaction, care must be taken to develop an interface for a Web site that is useful and attractive. The ability to mix graphical elements with text and other media is much more limited in HTML than in other types of multimedia authoring. Often, WWW pages are limited to the constraints of HTML, which was designed to display information in a vertical list. WWW page designers are also limited by differences in the user's connection to the Internet and his choice of browser. The popularity of Netscape is due in large part to its capability to allow designers with more options for placing elements on the page as well as its excellent presentation of graphics.

Options for Developing Your Own Images

There are a number of excellent software products on the market for developing graphics. While shopping for these, pay particular attention to those designed specifically for working with graphics for the screen. As mentioned previously, developing images for print and screen are two separate issues.

Graphics programs are usually designed to produce either vector or raster image files. Vector files contain mathematical equations describing the makeup of the image. This equation describes the relationship between objects in the image. For this reason, vector graphics are frequently used for Computer-Aided Design (CAD) and images that contain distinct geometric shapes. Vector graphics were developed to print cleanly, much like the PostScript fonts. Raster files, also known as bitmapped graphics, store information about the individual placement and color of pixels in the image. Bitmapped graphics are primarily developed to be viewed on the computer screen. Printing bitmapped graphics is similar to printing bitmapped fonts in that they appear to be more jagged around the edges than their vector counterparts.

The image files currently supported by Netscape are all bitmapped graphics files. For this reason it is recommended that you purchase a graphics program that is capable of developing bitmapped images. The most popular graphics program for the World Wide Web is Adobe Photoshop. This piece of software has been the leading graphics design package for years due to its capability to produce original bitmapped images as well as touch up existing images. Other leading bitmapped graphics programs include Deneba Canvas, Fractal Design Painter, and Fauve Matisse.

Options for Using Existing Images

Many times you will want to use graphics and images in your site that already have been developed. For example, you might want to include a professionally designed logo on your company home page, or maybe a photo of your cat on a personal profile Web page. Many times these images have to be converted to a digital format and possibly retouched in an image-processing program before they can be used on the Web. There are a number of options available to help you with this process.

Desktop Scanners   A growing number of relatively inexpensive scanners on the market can capture photographs, line art, transparencies, slides, prints, and other two-dimensional images. Once captured, these images can be enhanced and resized in an image-processing program such as Photoshop or Paintshop Pro, and saved in a format that can be used with graphical browsers.

Service Bureaus   A graphics service bureau or color separation house can scan images with a much higher degree of precision than is possible with desktop scanners. Some of these agencies may also convert your existing files to formats used on the World Wide Web. The use of a service bureau is generally the most expensive option for converting images to digital formats. Prices range considerably for individual services and between different locations in the country. You should explore the other possibilities first and if there is a particular need to have a high-resolution image scanned for your site, contact a number of service bureaus for price quotes.

Kodak PhotoCD   If the images you want to use are photographs, slides, or negatives, and you do not have access to a desktop scanner, consider having them placed on a PhotoCD. This method does require that you have an extended architecture CD-ROM drive and software capable of reading this type of compact disc; and most dual-speed, multi-session CD-ROM drives are compatible with this standard. Check the documentation of your graphics software to see if it can read the image format used for this process. PhotoCDs are capable of holding up to 100 photographs on each CD-ROM. The photos are scanned and saved on the CD in five different resolutions ranging from 128×192 pixels to 2048×3072 pixels. PhotoCDs can be ordered just about anywhere you can have prints made. The compact disc itself costs between $10.00 and $20.00, and each photo added to the CD costs between $1.00 and $2.00.

Digital Cameras   A number of cameras have appeared on the market in recent years that record images directly to disk in a digital format. These cameras are still relatively expensive, averaging around $700.00, and the images produced are generally of lesser quality than that of photographs converted by one of the previous scanning methods. The advantage to using digital cameras is the fact that they store the photographs directly in a digital format and the photos can be used immediately.

Stock Photo and Clip Art CDs   This option allows you to work with images that are already in a digital format. As a last resort, stock photo and clip art collections allow you to include some graphical elements into your Web pages where there would otherwise be none. There are a number of sites on the Web where you can download individual or libraries of clip art in file formats ready to use for your own site. For instance, Sandra's Clip Art Server at **http:// www.cs.yale.edu/home/sjl/clipart.html** archives a number of clip art collections. When using clip art from the World Wide Web or from CD-ROM, always read the copyright notice; although most can be used royalty-free, some require payment or simple acknowledgment.

Image File Formats

World Wide Web browsers support a limited number of file formats for inline images, and not all browsers are capable of displaying every type of image format within the same window as the HTML document. The two most popular formats supported by Netscape and most other graphical browsers are GIF and JPEG. Although the TIF and X-Bitmap formats can be used by some browsers, it is recommended that you use only GIFs or JPEGs.

> **N O T E** More and more Netscape plug-in modules allow the displaying of inline images saved as new and different formats, including sound, video, and vector graphics. While using GIF and JPEG will ensure maximum compatibility, plug-ins will let you use different file formats when the situation calls for it. ■

Guidelines for Using GIF and JPEG Images

The Graphics Interchange Format, or GIF, was developed by CompuServe to provide an efficient way of storing and exchanging image files across platforms (see fig. 22.1). A file in this format can contain a maximum of 256 colors, or 8-bits per pixel. GIFs are the most popular images to use as inline images because they are supported by all graphical browsers. They are also the only format that supports transparent backgrounds and interlaced display.

The GIF format is best suited for the following types of images:

- Black-and-white line art and text
- Images with a limited number of distinct colors
- Graphics that have sharp or distinct edges—most menus, buttons, and graphs
- Graphics that are overlaid with text

The JPEG format was developed by the Joint Photographers Expert Group as a means of compressing images with a color palette of 24-bits per pixel, or 16.7 million possible colors.

For more information on GIF, JPEG, and other image formats, consult the World Wide Web FAQ at **http://www.boutell.com/faq/**.

The JPEG format is best suited for the following types of images:

- Scanned photographs and ray-traced renderings
- Images that contain a complex mixture of colors
- Any image that requires more than a 256-color palette

FIG. 22.1
GIF is the best graphics format to use for images such as buttons and menus.

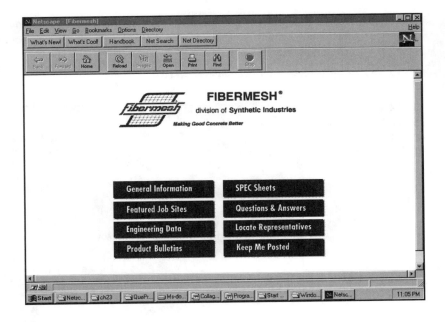

Using Interlaced GIFs

During download, a GIF file that is saved without the interlaced option appears on the viewer's Netscape window starting with the top of the image and filling down as it is received and decoded. The Netscape browser has been enhanced to take advantage of interlaced GIFs. An interlaced GIF stores the image in a sequence of nonadjacent sets, or what you might think of as layers. Netscape begins to process and display the image as it is received, which results in a gradual emergence of the image. Because the whole image appears in Netscape's window in sections rather than gradually filling in from the top down, viewers of the page can see much of the image before the download is complete. Interlaced GIFs should be used for all large graphics to allow the viewers of your page to see the entire image size immediately.

You can convert images to interlaced GIFs by using any of a number of commercial and shareware programs. The shareware program LView Pro, developed by Leonardo Loureiro, includes the option to open a number of common file formats and save them as interlaced GIFs. The file formats that can be converted to and from GIFs and JPEGs using LView Pro include JPEG, Windows bitmap, OS/2 bitmap, GIF, TARGA, PCX, PPM, and TIFF. To convert images to interlaced GIFs in LView Pro, follow these steps:

1. Open LView Pro by double-clicking its icon.
2. Choose File, Open, and in the Open Image File dialog box, highlight the image file you want to convert. Click Open.
3. After the image is open, choose File, Properties, GIF, and check the box titled Save Interlaced (see fig. 22.2).

4. Save the image as an interlaced GIF by selecting File, Save As. In the Save Image As dialog box, rename your image with the .GIF extension and select the GIF89a file type. Then click the Save button.

The image is now saved as an interlaced GIF.

FIG. 22.2

Check the interlaced GIF option when converting an image in LView Pro.

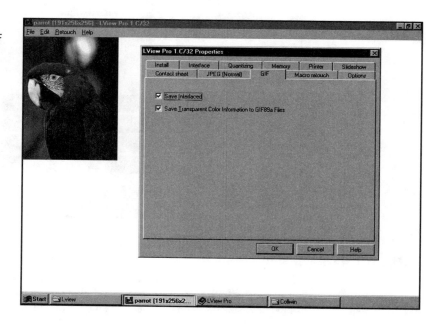

Using Transparent GIFs

An update to the original GIF format is GIF89a, which allows the image file to designate one of the colors in the image as transparent. Netscape supports the display of transparent GIFs, such as the one on the right in figure 22.3. Images that do not specify one of the colors as transparent are always displayed with a background on the browser's screen. This is fine if all your graphics are rectangular, but if you want to give your site a more polished look, you will want to include images that appear to be part of the background.

As with interlaced GIFs, there are a number of shareware utilities that convert images to transparent GIFs. To do so using LView Pro, follow these steps:

1. Open LView Pro by double-clicking its icon.

2. Choose File, Open; and in the Open Image File dialog box, highlight the image file you want to convert, and then click OK.

3. Select Retouch, Color Depth. To save as a GIF, your image must be a palette image. Converting from True Color to Palette Image in LView changes the color depth of your image to a maximum of 256 colors. In the Color Depth dialog box, select the Palette Image radio button (see fig. 22.4). Next you see options for palette creation and quantizing. Select 256 colors, uncheck the Dithering option, and click OK.

FIG. 22.3

Using transparent GIFs, such as the one on the right, gives your site a more polished look.

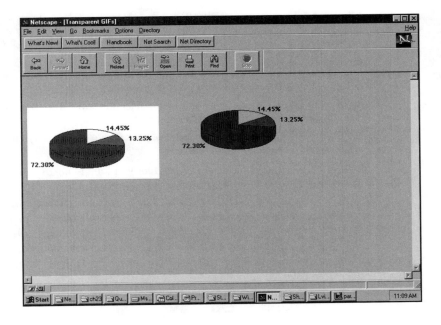

NOTE A GIF image can contain up to 256 different colors specified in its color lookup table. In order to convert images with more than 256 colors in LView Pro, you must first select the Palette Image option to create a 256-color lookup table for the image. It is best to use the 256 colors (including Windows palette) option when creating the palette unless you are sure that your image will look acceptable in 16 colors or simply black and white.

Often in the process of creating a 256-color palette for an image, some colors in the original do not find a perfect match. The Enable Floyd-Steinberg Dithering option instructs LView Pro to recolor an image using a technique that creates the look of more colors than the image actually has. Dithering should be avoided if possible because more complex images take longer to download. ▨

FIG. 22.4

To make a transparent GIF, the image must first be converted to a palette image.

4. Now you're ready to identify the transparent color. Select Retouch, Background Color and you see the Select Color Palette Entry dialog box. This window provides you with the color palette used by the image (see fig. 22.5).

5. If you can identify the color you want to make transparent, click once on that color in the Select Color Palette Entry dialog box, and check the Mask selection box with either the white or black option. This masks your selection with either black or white, which enables you to see if the correct color for transparency was chosen. Don't be alarmed; the mask does not change the color of your image—it's just a helpful way of showing you the transparent selection.

6. If you have trouble seeing the exact color you want to make transparent, click the Dropper button in the Select Color Palette Entry dialog box. The dropper, shown in figure 22.6, allows you to click directly on the image to indicate where you want the color to be transparent. Be careful: When the dropper is clicked on the screen, it disappears. However, the color that you clicked will be highlighted in the Select Color Entry Palette dialog box. You can test it by masking the selected color with black or white. If this is the correct color, choose OK; otherwise, select the Dropper button again and click the desired color.

FIG. 22.5
The Select Color Palette Entry dialog box shows which colors are used in the image.

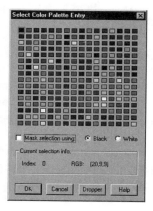

FIG. 22.6
The Dropper can be used to identify the color for transparency.

7. To save the image as a transparent GIF, select File, Save As; and in the Save Image As dialog box, select the GIF89a file type, as shown in figure 22.7.

More information about transparent and interlaced GIFs can be found on the World Wide Web at The Transparent/Interlaced GIF Resource Page **http://dragon.jpl.nasa.gov/~adam/ transparent.html**.

 When creating images to be used as transparent GIFs, be sure that the desired transparent color is used only in those areas you want to hide.

FIG. 22.7
Transparent GIFs must
be saved as GIF89a.

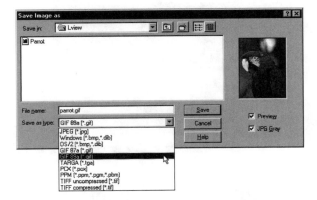

Converting Images to Progressive JPEGs

Beginning with version 2.0, Netscape includes support for a recent implementation of JPEG compression called the Progressive JPEG. Prior to version 2.0 of Netscape, use of inline JPEG images was limited to simple, or baseline, JPEGs. Baseline JPEGs store the image information as a top-to-bottom scan of the image. Baseline JPEGs appear in Netscape's window beginning at the top of the image and fill downward as image data is received. The progressive JPEG is similar to the interlaced GIF in that the image is stored as a series of scans. The first scan, or layer, of a progressive JPEG appears in the Netscape window as soon as the download begins.

The advantage of using progressive JPEG images in your Web site is that viewers of your page will begin to see the full size of images in rough detail as soon as the download begins. Existing baseline JPEGs must, however, be converted to the progressive format to take advantage of its features. To save images with progressive JPEG compression in LView Pro, follow these simple steps:

1. Open LView Pro by double-clicking its icon.

2. Choose File, Open; and in the Open Image File dialog box, highlight the image file you want to convert, and then click OK.

3. When the image is open choose File, Properties, JPEG (Normal), and check the Progressive compression box as seen in figure 22.8.

4. To save the image as a progressive JPEG, select File, Save As; and in the Save Image As dialog box, select the JPEG file type.

For more information on JPEG, consult the JPEG, image compression FAQ at the URL **http:// www.cis.ohio-state.edu/hypertext/faq/usenet/jpeg-faq/top.html**.

FIG. 22.8

Images can be saved with progressive JPEG compression in LView Pro by checking the Progressive compression option.

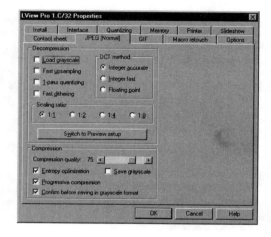

Bandwidth Considerations for Image Use

When designing images for use on the Web, it's important to think about who the end user is and what type of setup he has for viewing pages. Basic information relating to who is accessing your site can be found in the http log maintained by your server software. This log file records data about each visitor to your site. Log file statistics are generally no more than the date and time of access and the user's IP address. Unfortunately, http logs usually provide no information about the user's Internet connection, computer system, or monitor size and settings, all of which are important to consider when developing the graphics for your site.

A number of demographic reports and surveys have been published to present a better understanding of the general Web "surfer." These findings reveal the following:

■ Over 90 percent are using graphical browsers

■ Nearly 70 percent use the Netscape browser

■ There is a fairly even distribution of Windows, Macintosh, and UNIX users

■ Most users have a 14" monitor with a 256-color palette

Guidelines for Image Sizes

Because the majority of users are set up to view the Web on a 14" monitor capable of displaying a 256-color palette, you should consider that to be the standard for designing graphics for your site. The typical screen size of a 14" monitor is 640 pixels wide by 480 pixels high. When developing images to fit within this size, you should first consider that the user's browser will take up part of that viewing area. Depending on how it is configured, a browser may leave as little as 600 × 400 pixels as the viewing area. Also remember that Macintosh and UNIX browsers do not generally take up the entire width of the screen. As a general rule, the maximum width of any image on your site should be less than 500 pixels wide and 300 pixels high—a variety of image sizes are shown in figure 22.9. Images larger than this will not fit on most users' screens. They will also take longer to transfer.

FIG. 22.9
Images wider than 500 pixels may not appear in full on all viewers' screens.

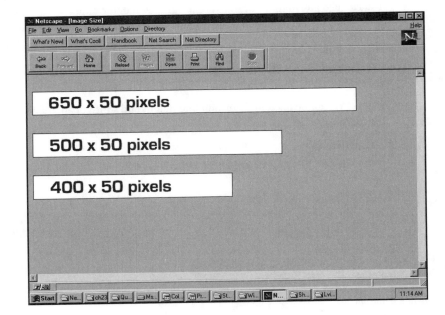

Using the Image Tag with Height and Width Attributes

One way to reduce the amount of time someone waits for your inline graphics to load is to tell the browser the size of the image in advance. Netscape uses this information when interpreting the final page layout; when it receives an HTML document, it spends a bit of time deciphering where to place the different elements on the screen. By knowing the exact dimensions of an incoming graphical element, Netscape can immediately lay out the text areas relative to where the graphic will eventually be.

▶ **See** "Using the <IMG> Tag," **p. 471**

As you recall from chapter 20, the Image tag in an HTML document is comprised of two necessary elements: IMG and SRC. IMG signifies that it is an image, SRC denotes the source or path to the image. Netscape can take advantage of the Image tag appended with the height and width of the inline image to which it refers. This is done by adding HEIGHT and WIDTH attributes to the <IMG SRC> tag. The height and width of an image are measured in pixels. The use of this tag for an image with a height of 100 pixels and a width of 300 pixels would be written like this:

```
<IMG SRC="path_to_image" HEIGHT=100 WIDTH=300>
```

It doesn't matter whether the HEIGHT or WIDTH attribute comes first, but they must both be included along with the IMG and the SRC elements.

You can use any number of software programs to determine the dimensions of an inline image. Most professional paint and draw programs provide information about the dimensions of an open document. You may, however, have to change the preferences in a specific program to show the dimensional units in pixels rather than inches or centimeters because the Image tag elements must be written in pixels. Check the user manual for the specific paint program you are using to determine a document's height and width information.

LView Pro can be used to determine the height and width of an image in pixel coordinates in the following way:

1. Open LView Pro by double-clicking its icon.

2. Choose File, Open; and in the Open Image File dialog box, highlight the image you want to measure.

3. When the image is open choose Edit, Resize (Ctrl+R). You see the Resize Image window shown in figure 22.10. The size, in pixels, of the open image is reported at the top of this dialog box. The image width is the first number followed by the height.

FIG. 22.10
LView Pro's Resize Image option shows the size of the open image and allows you to increase or decrease the size proportionately.

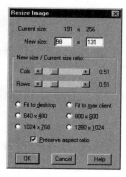

 When you have determined the size of an image, write it down on a scrap of paper or add it to your HTML document immediately. Whatever you do, don't write down something like 137 × 281; if you're anything like me you'll forget which number is the height and which is the width. Getting these numbers reversed will change the shape of your image on Netscape's screen.

N O T E Text is transferred much more quickly than images are. If width and height information is included for images, Netscape will begin to lay out text as soon as it is received. Always include the width and height of an inline image in the HTML of the page so the reader can read the text on-screen while the image is loading. Paying attention to download time will increase satisfaction of those who visit your Web site. ■

Using and Developing Thumbnail Images

Thumbnail images on a Web page are small representations of larger graphics (see fig. 22.11). They are particularly useful on index pages as graphical links to the full-sized image. Because of the reduced size, thumbnails transfer to a user's browser more quickly than the full-sized graphics.

The easiest way to create a thumbnail is to reduce the size of the original image in a paint or image processing program. Photoshop and other image-processing packages do an excellent job of proportionately reducing the size of an image. Many of the lower-end paint programs have options to scale images; however, the result will most likely not produce a professional-looking image. LView Pro, however, does an excellent job of resizing images for use as thumbnails.

To produce a thumbnail image in LView Pro, follow these steps:

1. Open LView Pro by double-clicking its icon.

2. Choose File, Open; and in the Open Image File dialog box, highlight the image from which you will create a thumbnail.

3. When the image is open choose Edit, Resize (Ctrl+R). You will see the Resize Image window shown in figure 22.11. The size, in pixels, of the original image is reported at the top of this dialog box. The image width is the first number, followed by the height. To change the height or width of the image, simply type the height or width of the desired thumbnail image or use the slider bars below New Size/Current Size Ratio to adjust the percent of scaling. Be careful to check Preserve aspect ratio option if you want the image to be reduced in size proportionally.

4. Save the thumbnail image as either a GIF or JPEG by choosing File, Save As, and renaming the image.

 If the images you want to make thumbnails of are photographs, consider having them put on a Kodak PhotoCD. This process not only scans the images into digital files, but also provides you with duplicates of the images in a number of sizes.

As I mentioned earlier, Netscape and a few other browsers enable you to adjust the size of an image simply by changing the HEIGHT and WIDTH attributes in the Image tag. Although this could be used to decrease the size of an image on the screen, the entire graphic still must be transferred to the user's browser. If your goal is to decrease the frustration time of potential viewers, this method will not help.

FIG. 22.11

Thumbnails are an efficient use of screen size and bandwidth.

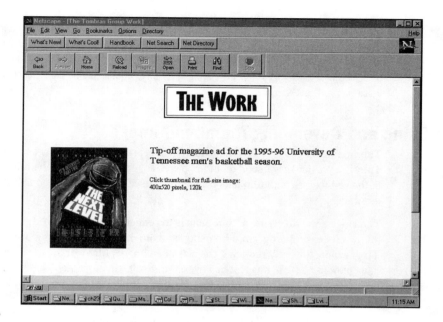

The image HEIGHT and WIDTH attributes can be used to alter the size of an image in the following ways:

- To reduce the size of an inline image, make its height and width proportionately smaller. For instance, an image 200 pixels high by 200 pixels wide can be displayed at half this size in the following way:

```
<IMG SRC="path_to_image" HEIGHT=100 WIDTH=100>
```

- To increase the size of an inline image, make its height and width proportionately larger. For instance, the same 200 × 200 image can be displayed at twice this size in the following way:

```
<IMG SRC="path_to_image" HEIGHT=400 WIDTH=400>
```

- It is also possible to increase or decrease an image size relative to the viewer's Netscape window. In this case, the percent of increase or decrease is provided for either the HEIGHT or WIDTH or for both. For instance, an image can be displayed at half of Netscape's window size in the following ways:

```
<IMG SRC="path_to_image" HEIGHT=50%>
```

The image in this case will occupy 50 percent of the height of the Netscape window. The width will remain proportional to the height of the image, not to the window size.

```
<IMG SRC="path_to_image" WIDTH=50%>
```

This image will occupy 50 percent of the width of the Netscape window. The height will remain proportional to the width of the image, not to the window size.

```
<IMG SRC="path_to_image" HEIGHT=50% WIDTH=50%>
```

The image in this case will occupy 50 percent of the height and 50 percent of the width of the Netscape window.

> **CAUTION**
>
> Because individual users configure their browser windows to their own preferences, changing the aspect of an image with both a WIDTH and a HEIGHT percent will most likely distort your image.

Making Use of Cached Images

The Netscape cache function allows repeat images to appear more quickly than they did when they were first loaded. The browser's capability to store recent items can be used to decrease download time for graphics by using the same images on each page of your site for things such as title bars, menus, buttons, and bullets.

As you develop graphics for your Web site, consider taking advantage of the browser's cache. When Netscape downloads an image during a session, it keeps a copy of that image in your hard drive's cache. Subsequent requests for that image result in a faster display because the image is now stored in Netscape's cache and doesn't have to be retrieved from the server.

Images that appear on multiple pages on your site should be developed to take advantage of the viewer's cache. Designing shared navigation items such as menu buttons and image maps common to all pages not only increases the ease of use, but also decreases the amount of time a viewer will spend waiting for images to load; for instance, if you develop a series of images that are used as clickable buttons in your Web site.

 To best keep track of images used on your Web site, it is best to keep them all in a common images directory. This practice can help eliminate multiple copies of the same image that can slow down your site by not taking advantage of images in the user's cache.

Design Tips for Graphical Web Pages

When developing graphical Web pages you can take advantage of Netscape's additions to HTML that affect the background and text of your page. Table 22.1 lists the additions to the BODY tag that include the use of background images and colors, as well as the designation of text and link colors. HTML extensions such as these make it easier to design pages that have visual impact.

Table 22.1 Additions to the *BODY* Tag

Attribute	Result
BACKGROUND	Loads an image to use as a background
BGCOLOR	Specifies the browser's background color
TEXT	Specifies the text color
LINK	Specifies the link color
ALINK	Specifies the active link color
VLINK	Specifies the visited link color

Using Backgrounds and Text Colors

A welcome set of improvements to assist graphical development are extensions to the `<BODY>` tag. In Netscape it is possible for the designer of a Web page to distinguish the color and appearance of the end user's window, as well as specify the document's text and link colors. Most of the BODY attributes make use of the viewer's browser to change the page's appearance, thereby costing no more download time for viewing. The BACKGROUND attribute is an exception to the rule, it requires the use of an image to display as a background.

The *BACKGROUND* Attribute   Netscape and a growing number of graphical World Wide Web browsers support the BACKGROUND attribute of the BODY tag. As mentioned previously, this extension does require the use of an image to be displayed as a background for the specific page. A GIF or JPEG image is appended to the tag in the following way:

```
<BODY BACKGROUND=<"url_of_image">
document
</BODY>
```

An image used as the background is tiled across and down the viewer's window. Because they are tiled in this fashion, background images must be created to appear in the browser's window without visible connection points—their edges must appear seamless. Textured graphics can be made seamless with the help of image-processing software such as PhotoShop. There are also a growing number of WWW sites dedicated to background images, and many of the better ones include high-quality seamless images you can download and use on your own site. Figure 22.12 shows one such site at the URL **http://funnelweb.utcc.utk.edu/~wallace/textures/textures.html**.

> **CAUTION**
>
> Background images require Netscape to fetch and download the specified graphic before the rest of the page is displayed. To minimize download time, always use the smallest image possible for backgrounds. A 100 × 100 pixel image should be the largest background image used.

FIG. 22.12

There are a number of WWW sites dedicated to background images.

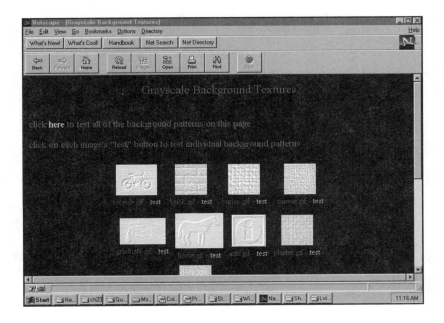

N O T E Background images—like an inline image—are stored in Netscape's cache. You can increase access time to your site by using a common background image for all pages.

The *BGCOLOR* Attribute   The BGCOLOR attribute for the BODY tag is recognized by Netscape and a limited number of other graphical browsers. It differs from the BACKGROUND attribute in that the BGCOLOR changes the window color of a viewer's browser. This attribute does not require a viewer's browser to download and tile an image. For this reason, use of the BGCOLOR changes the window's background color immediately upon receiving the HTML tag and doesn't delay layout of the document. The primary drawback of using BGCOLOR is that there are a limited number of browsers that recognize it.

You use the BGCOLOR in the BODY tag like this:

```
<BODY BGCOLOR=#RRGGBB>
document
</BODY>
```

#RRGGBB refers to the hexadecimal color code made up of red, green, and blue. This code is interpreted as a color value in hexadecimal format. The red value of the desired color occupies the first two units, followed by two for green and two for blue. Each of these two color components must consist of one of 16 characters—numbers 0 through 9 followed by A through F—where 0 is the lowest value and F is the highest.

Table 22.2 outlines eight basic color combinations in hexadecimal code. Table 23.1 in chapter 23, "Using Imagemaps," contains the code for numerous other combinations.

Table 22.2   Hexadecimal RGB Color Codes

Color	Code
White	#FFFFFF
Red	#FF0000
Green	#00FF00
Blue	#0000FF
Cyan	#00FFFF
Magenta	#FF00FF
Yellow	#FFFF00
Black	#000000

 TIP   When developing transparent GIFs for use as background images or colors, it is best to use the same background color as the image background when creating the image.

Text and Link Attributes   In addition to controlling the background color of a user's browser, it is possible to change the text and link colors. These extensions to the BODY tag use the same hexadecimal color code as BGCOLOR. The attribute for changing the color of a document's text is TEXT followed by a specific color code. For example, to change a document's body text to green, the BODY tag would read:

```
<BODY TEXT=#00FF00>
document
</BODY>
```

Similarly, colors can be assigned to links as outlined in table 22.1. LINK specifies the color to be used for links that have not been followed. The ALINK attribute is the color a link momentarily flashes as it is clicked, or activated. VLINK is a link that has previously been activated, or visited.

N O T E   If one or more of the body attributes for text and link colors are not specified, the default color for those attributes is used: LINK=blue, ALINK=red, and VLINK=purple. ■

An example of the BODY tag with all attributes designated—BGCOLOR set to black, TEXT set to white, LINK set to yellow, ALINK set to magenta, and VLINK set to green—is written like this:

```
<BODY BGCOLOR=#000000 TEXT=#FFFFFF LINK=#FFFF00 ALINK=#FF00FF VLINK=00FF00>
document
</BODY>
```

 TIP   You should always use the BGCOLOR attribute if you use BACKGROUND in the BODY tag. If the image specified in BODY BACKGROUND fails to load or a user chooses to not load images, all text and link colors will be displayed in their default colors. By including a BGCOLOR that is similar in appearance to the BACKGROUND image, the text and link colors will appear as you intended.

There are a number of excellent resources on the World Wide Web for previewing colors in hexadecimal code. Consult the following references on the World Wide Web for more information on background colors and images:

- Controlling Document Backgrounds: **http://home.netscape.com/assist/net_sites/ bg/index.html**
- Yahoo's Index on Backgrounds: **http://www.yahoo.com/Computers_and_Internet/ Internet/World_Wide_Web/Programming/Backgrounds/**
- Background Color Index: **http://www.infi.net/wwwimages/colorindex.html**

Image Alignment and Borders

By far the most influential feature of the Netscape browser is its unique extensions to HTML that allow text and inline images to be laid out on the screen in an aesthetic fashion (see fig. 22.13). The additions to the IMG tag cause an image to float in relationship to other elements on the screen, hence they are referred to as floating images. The ALIGN attributes can be found in table 22.3, along with a brief description of the desired result. These recent additions are by far the most finicky elements in HTML. They are also the most important elements to master.

FIG. 22.13

An addition to the IMG tag allows images to be aligned on the right border.

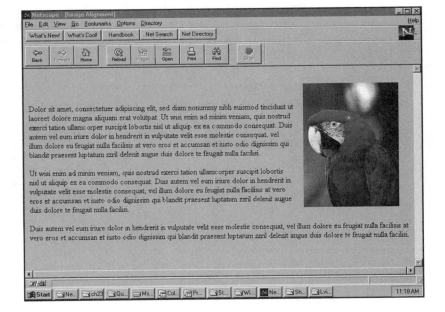

Table 22.3 **Additions to the _IMG_ Tag**

Attribute	Result
ALIGN=LEFT	Aligns an image on the browser's left margin
ALIGN=RIGHT	Aligns an image on the browser's right margin
ALIGN=TOP	Aligns an image with the top of the tallest item on the same line, whether it is text or another image
ALIGN=MIDDLE	Aligns the middle of an image with the baseline of elements on the same line
ALIGN=BOTTOM	Aligns the image with the baseline of elements on the same line
BORDER=pixel size	Places a border around the image of the specified pixel size

The ALIGN attributes are used with the IMG tag. For example, to align an image on the browser's left margin, the tag would be used in the following way:

```
<IMG SRC="url_of_image" ALIGN=LEFT>
```

The image in this instance aligns itself on the left margin of Netscape's window. Elements specified after the IMG tag are positioned to the right of the floating image. The BR tag and its attributes are needed to end the effect of a floating image. These will be discussed in more detail in the following section.

N O T E Only one form of the ALIGN attribute can be used with each image. If two or more are included with the IMG tag, only the first one in the line will be used. ■

Wrapping Text Around Images

Netscape's additions to the IMG tag offer developers the ability to wrap text around floating images (see fig. 22.14). This is an important component to developing both an attractive and useful site, because the World Wide Web was not initially developed with screen layout in mind. Prior to these attributes, using inline images with text resulted in a linear-looking page. Now it is possible to dictate the position of images in respect to text elements and graphics.

To wrap text around an image on a Web page, it is necessary to use one of the ALIGN attributes with the IMG tag. The desired text should then be included directly after the IMG tag. The result will vary with the attributes as follows:

■ ALIGN=LEFT causes the image to align with the left margin of Netscape's window; text following this tag wraps to the right of the floating image.

■ ALIGN=RIGHT causes the image to align with the right margin of Netscape's window; text following this tag wraps to the left of the floating image.

FIG. 22.14
Images and text can be positioned in sophisticated ways using the `IMG ALIGN` attributes.

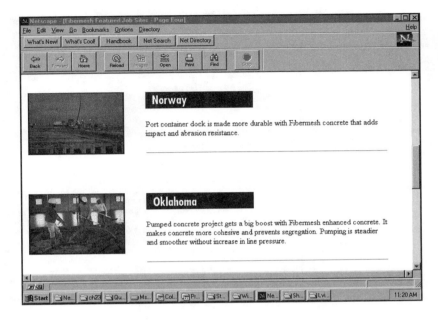

- `ALIGN=MIDDLE` causes the image to align with the left margin of Netscape's window; text following this attribute begins on the right side of the image at the middle point. Only the amount of text that fits between the right side of the image and the left margin of the window aligns with the middle of this floating image. All remaining text continues at the left margin below the image.

- `ALIGN=TOP` causes the image to align with the left margin of Netscape's window; text following this attribute begins on the right side of the image aligned with the top edge. Only the amount of text that fits between the right side of the image and the left margin of the window aligns with the top of this floating image. All remaining text continues at the left margin below the image.

- `ALIGN=BOTTOM` causes the image to align with the left margin of Netscape's window; the base line of text begins on the right, aligned with the bottom edge of the floating image (see fig. 22.15).

To get good results with floating images with text requires practice with extensions to the `BR` tag. The basic `BR` tag employed with text following an `ALIGN` attribute will merely break the line without stopping the effect of the floating image. In order to break the line and clear the margin to the right or left of the floating image, you must use one of the additions to the `BR` tag. These attributes are outlined in table 22.4. The `BR` tag with a `CLEAR` attribute is used at the point where you want to clear the right or left margin of a floating image. For example, if we aligned an image on the left with text wrapped to the right, it would be necessary to clear the left margin before another element could be placed there. The HTML would be:

```
<IMG SRC="url_to_image" ALIGN=LEFT>
text
<BR CLEAR=LEFT>
```

FIG. 22.15
ALIGN=BOTTOM allows an image to serve as a part of the running text.

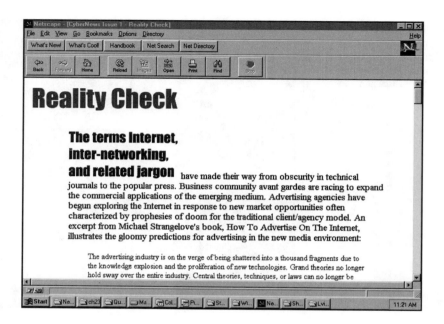

When in doubt as to which CLEAR attribute to use, begin with CLEAR=ALL. This clears both margins and allows you to safely add new elements to the page.

Table 23.4   Additions to the *BR* Tag

Attribute	Result
CLEAR=RIGHT	Breaks the line and clears the right margin
CLEAR=LEFT	Breaks the line and clears the left margin
CLEAR=ALL	Breaks the line and clears both margins

CAUTION
Aligning two images on the same margin without the appropriate BR attribute between them will cause one image to appear on top of the other.

## CHAPTER 23

Using Imagemaps

One feature you'll see in some of the more advanced home pages are imagemaps. These are simply pictures with certain designated areas that go to different URLs. Imagemaps are inherently easier to use than regular text links because there's no need to explain what the link does. A person doesn't have to read where a link might take him, he just sees it.

Though this may sound like imagemaps should be used everywhere, that's not true. There are some things to consider before using imagemaps. You also have to make sure it makes sense to put in imagemaps where you want them. All the information you'd want to know about imagemaps is covered in this chapter.

In this chapter, you learn:

- What imagemaps are and how they work
- How to choose appropriate imagemap graphics
- How to create an imagemap definition file
- How to reference your imagemap in HTML
- Guidelines for using imagemaps
- Basic elements of laying out your imagemap ■

What Are Imagemaps?

Imagemaps allow for a friendly way for users to go to different Web pages by pointing and clicking in a picture. One of the big advantages of the Web over other Internet-related stores of information is that it's graphically advanced, which makes it more approachable to use. Instead of bland text menus, such as with Gopher clients, users can see what they want to get information on (see fig. 23.1).

FIG. 23.1

Instead of having people imagine what the Colossus might look like, you can use imagemaps to show them.

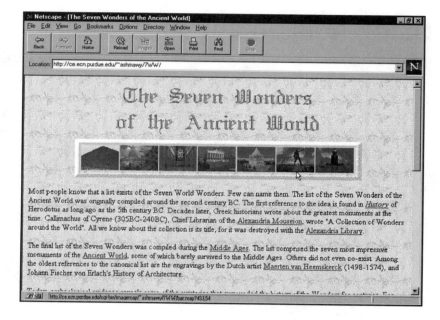

Imagemaps are simply pictures with areas that users can click on to go to different Web pages. Typically, the user sees an image which indicates where to click to go to different Web pages. There are a lot of different ways that the image can indicate clickable areas. Usually there is a border or something in the picture that indicates where users should click to go somewhere.

When the user clicks on the imagemap, Netscape sends the location of where the mouse click occurred in the image to the Web server. The server looks up which URL is referenced at that point and travels there. An imagemap that you may be familiar with is on the Netscape home page (see fig. 23.2).

FIG. 23.2
The first imagemap almost everyone comes across is the one on the Netscape home page. Notice that when you move the mouse, different numbers appear at the bottom.

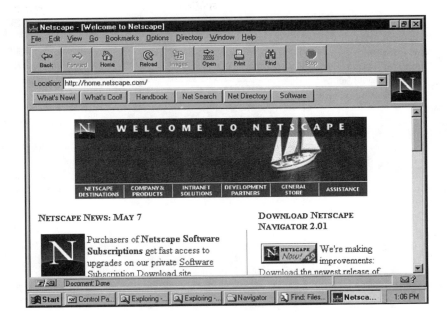

Strengths and Weaknesses of Imagemaps

There are some good and bad points to using imagemaps. Most are aesthetic points, but a few are technical. Understanding the advantages and disadvantages of imagemaps is important if you want a popular Web site.

Advantages to Using Imagemaps

Imagemaps are most useful in the following situations:

- To represent spatial links, such as geographical coordinates, which would be difficult to lay out using single-image buttons or text links (see fig. 23.3).

- As a top-level menu bar that appears on each page in your Web site. The use of imagemap menus offers users the option of going anywhere in your site at any time (see fig 23.4).

- Creating the above mentioned common menu bar graphic for your site will save time in developing HTML documents, as this graphic will refer to the same imagemap reference file. Consistent menus also present a consistent look to a site, which will ease user navigation. Instead of having to go into each page and put in links to other parts of your home page, you can just refer to the common menu bar graphic.

FIG. 23.3

Imagemaps make it easy to represent spatial links, such as the area codes for North America.

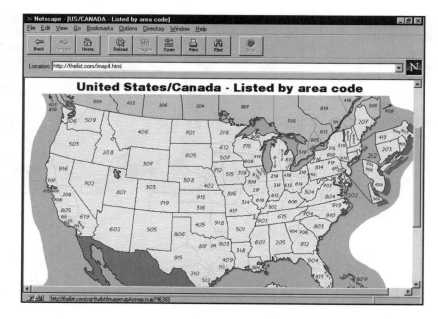

FIG. 23.4

No matter where you go in the Internet Movie Database, you can always go to the most important parts.

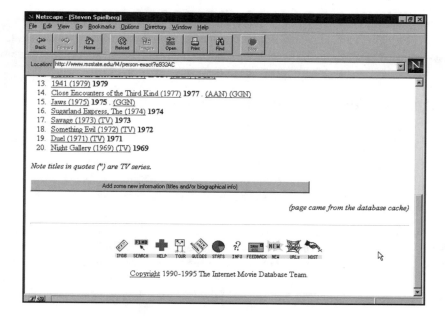

Disadvantages of Using Imagemaps

Obviously imagemaps aren't the end-all feature of Web pages, or else everyone would use them. There are certain situations where you shouldn't use imagemaps. There are also some technical considerations before using them.

Imagemaps have a number of inherent drawbacks:

- Imagemaps cannot be used when running your site locally off a hard drive. This is only true if the server you're running locally doesn't have CGI scripts to support the imagemap. Also, some Web servers come prebuilt with imagemap support. If you're not running one of these "smart servers," you can't use imagemaps on your site.
- You can't test your imagemap until the HTML document is placed on a server. Because Netscape is merely an interface between the user and a Web server, CGI scripts are never used by it. Thus even things like imagemap interpretations are impossible without a Web server.
- Unless you provide an alternative text menu, there is no means of navigation for users who cannot load graphics or have turned graphics loading off (see fig. 23.5).
- Imagemaps tend to be larger than single-image buttons and, therefore, take longer to download.
- Use of a single imagemap menu for your site offers users the option of clicking on the reference to the page they are presently viewing. This can cause confusion in navigation.

Part IV Ch 23

FIG. 23.5
This text menu provides a navigational alternative for the imagemaps that did not load.

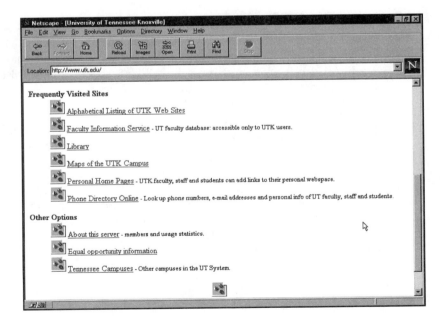

Client-Side Imagemaps

Client-side imagemaps allow all map information to be specified in the HTML file that includes the image, while server-side imagemaps send a request to the server for the page address and then replies back with that information. You know this can take quite a bit of time. With client-side imagemaps the number of times a server is accessed is reduced, increasing the speed of the links. They can also be modified locally, without the need of a server. For example, add the image as an inline image to your HTML document along with the name of the map definition associated with the image,

<IMG SRC="logo.gif"> USEMAP="image.html #testlogo">

As a user moves the pointer over a client-side mapped area, the associated URL is displayed in the status bar at the bottom of your Netscape browser. Server-side imagemaps will not display the URL because that information is located on the server that is not accessed until the user clicks on the imagemap. What I like most about client-side imagemaps (a necessity) is that you can also define them as server-side imagemaps for those browsers that don't support client-side images by adding the ISMAP attribute to the IMG element and by adding a map configuration file on the server. For example,

<A HREF="http://www.brown.edu/testmap/logo.map">
<IMG SRC="logo.gif" USEMAP="#logo" ISMAP>

Imagemaps and CGI

There is more involved in adding an imagemap to your Web site than simply creating an interesting graphic and referencing it in HTML. First of all, the use of an imagemap requires that your HTML document is located on a World Wide Web server. Its use also requires that the server is configured with an imagemap Common Gateway Interface (CGI) program, which will handle the mouse-click request from the user.

When a user clicks one of the hotspots of your imagemap graphic, the mouse's relative position on the image is sent to the Web server. Figure 23.6 shows an imagemap with buttons that represent the hotspots and take users to different URLs.

▶ **See** "Netscape Forms and CGI-BIN Scripts," **p. 557**

There are two primary types of imagemap definition file configurations, CERN and NCSA. They both hold the same information in an imagemap definition file, but it is presented differently. Both use the same region types (see "Elements of Imagemaps" later in this chapter) and the same coordinates. For this reason, you should check with the system administrator about the particular imagemap setup of the server you are using. For the following discussion we will assume that you have access to a Web server.

FIG. 23.6
An imagemap on this home page allows visitors easy access to chief information areas.

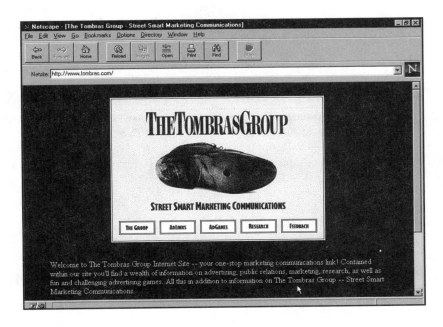

What the CERN Format Is

CERN is a group of European engineers who research a wide variety of topics. During the course of their research, they came up with the concept of the World Wide Web. They were the starting point for all sorts of WWW development and are rightfully labeled as "the birthplace of the Web." When the demand came for imagemap definition files, CERN came up with the following format:

region_type coordinates URL

The coordinates must be in parentheses and the x and y coordinates must be separated by a comma. The CERN format also doesn't allow for comments about hotspot regions. Here's an example of a CERN imagemap definition:

rect (56,47) (357,265) **http://www.rectangle.com/**

How NCSA Is Different

The University of Illinois' National Center for Supercomputing Applications (NCSA) is also very important for its contributions to the Web. It's at NCSA that the first popular graphical Web browser, Mosaic, was born. They presented a slightly different format than CERN's for the imagemap definition file. Their format is:

region_type URL coordinates

The coordinates don't have to be in parentheses, but they do have to be separated by commas. Here's an example of an NCSA imagemap definition:

rect http://www.rectangle.com/ 56,47 357,265

Changing Things...Again

The standard-setting Netscape Navigator has taken a bite out of the complexity of imagemaps. Netscape Navigator 3.0 supports client-side imagemaps, which means that as a Web author, you don't need CGI scripts to figure out where you clicked. Netscape does the mouse interpretation and sends the correct coordinates to the Web server. However, you'll probably still need an imagemap definition file as it's the only thing that knows where the hotspots are.

Elements of Imagemaps

Several elements contribute to creating and using imagemaps effectively.

Imagemap, Image Map, Area Map, and Clickable Map

All of these terms are synonymous with what we refer to in this chapter as the imagemap concept: The use of an inline image in an HTML document that is configured to contain one or more predetermined hotspots or regions, which represent active URL links. The imagemap is the complete embodiment of all the other elements of the imagemap itself.

Imagemap Graphic

An imagemap graphic is the actual inline graphic image that is displayed on your Web page. These images must be of the GIF graphics format and can be either interlaced or noninterlaced. It's also possible to have the imagemap graphic have a transparent background color (see "Choosing Imagemap Graphics," later in this chapter).

Imagemap Definition File

An imagemap definition file is a text file, usually denoted with the extension .MAP, that contains the coordinates for each hotspot of a specific imagemap graphic. This file also contains the resulting URL associated with each region. Active regions may be made up of rectangles, circles, polygons, or points. Imagemaps may contain any combination of these figures. This file can also specify one default URL in the event that the user clicks inside an imagemap graphic that doesn't have a specified region. Be sure to find out from your system administrator whether the Web server accepts the CERN or NCSA format.

Imagemap Program

An imagemap program is a Common Gateway Interface (CGI) program running on a World Wide Web server. This program determines what URL to return to the browser depending upon where the user clicked on the imagemap graphic relative to the coordinates in the definition file. Some Webmasters don't let people run CGI scripts, so check with your system administrator before you begin.

The Imagemap Definition File Itself

The imagemap definition file is a text file which contains information about the active regions of a specific imagemap graphic. For this reason, a separate definition file will be necessary for each imagemap graphic you wish to use. The definition specifies the type of region located in the graphic as either a rectangle, circle, polygon, or point (see fig. 23.7).

These regions, obviously, reflect the geometric shape of the active region. Their coordinates are determined as pixel points relative to the upper left-hand corner of the imagemap graphic. The following list identifies basic imagemap shapes and their required coordinates.

- rect—Indicates that the region is a rectangle. The coordinates required for this type of shape are the upper left-hand and lower right-hand pixels in the rectangle. The active region is the area of the rectangle.

- circle—Indicates that the region is a circle. Coordinates required for using a circle are center-point and edge-point pixels. The active region is calculated as the area of the circle.

- poly—Indicates that the region is a polygon. Coordinates are required as a list of vertices for the polygon. A polygon region can contain up to 100 vertices. The active region is the area within the polygon.

- point—Indicates that the region is a point on the image. A point coordinate is one specific pixel measured from the upper left-hand corner of the imagemap graphic. A point is considered active if the click occurred closest to that point on the graphic, yet not within another active region.

- default—Indicates all of the area of an imagemap graphic not specified by any other active region.

The rect Region Type

This element indicates that the region is a rectangle. Coordinates required for using a rectangle are center-point and edge-point pixels. The active region is calculated as the area of the rectangle.

The circle Region Type

This type indicates that the clickable region is a circle. Coordinates required for using a circle are center-point and edge-point pixels for NCSA servers. The CERN servers require the center-point of the circle and its radius. The active region is calculated as the area of the circle.

The poly Region Type

When you want to specify any multisided region, you use the poly region type. Coordinates are required as a list of vertices for the polygon. A polygon region can contain up to 100 vertices. The active region is the area within the polygon.

The point Region Type

Small dots can be indicated with the point region type. A point coordinate is one specific pixel measured from the upper-left corner of the imagemap graphic. A point is considered active if the click occurred closest to that point on the graphic, yet not within another active region.

The default Region Type

What all other regions don't cover, the default region will. If a user clicks inside an imagemap and it's not within the bounds of any other region, the default URL will be retrieved.

FIG. 23.7
You can easily see three of the five region types. The point region is very hard to see and the default region is everything else not already covered.

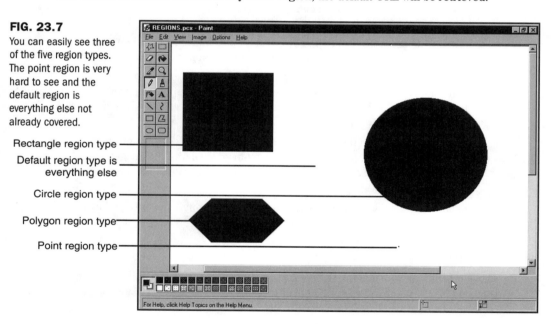

Rectangle region type

Default region type is everything else

Circle region type

Polygon region type

Point region type

CAUTION

An imagemap definition file should never contain both a point and a default region. The point region is activated by a click on the graphic closest to that point. The problem is that since the point region is so small, it's too easy for a user to not click it. As a result, the user could spend a lot of time trying to click on a point region and always getting the default URL.

Following each type of region in the imagemap definition file is the URL which will be returned to the user when a click within that area is recorded. The URL can be written as either a relative or an absolute path. Bear in mind that relative URL paths must be specific to the location of the definition file, not to the imagemap graphic. Active regions in the definition file are read from the first line down. If two regions overlap in their coordinates, only the one referenced first will be activated by the imagemap program.

On each line after the type of region and resulting URL there must be the integer pixel coordinates of the region. Figure 23.8 shows a sample imagemap definition file with the different region types and coordinates. The coordinates are all measured in pixels, starting from the upper left-hand corner of the imagemap graphic. The first number indicates the number of pixels the point is to the right of the left edge. The second number is the pixel measured down from the top edge.

Part

IV

Ch

23

FIG. 23.8

An imagemap reference file contains information about the shape, resulting URL, and coordinates of active regions on the imagemap graphic.

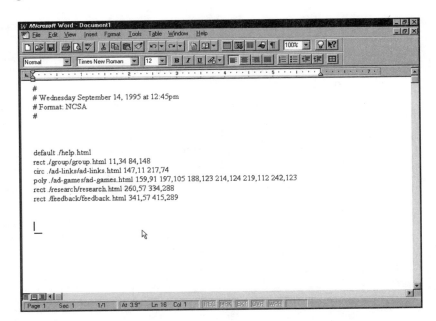

 An imagemap definition file should, whenever possible, be configured with a default HTML link. The default link will take the user to an area that isn't designated as being an active link. This URL should provide the user with feedback or helpful information about using that particular imagemap.

N O T E The pound sign or hash character (#) can be used to comment a line in the imagemap definition file. Any line with the hash character at the beginning will not be executed by the imagemap program. It's useful for adding information such as the date of creation, the physical path to the imagemap graphic, or specific comments about the server configuration. ▪

The Imagemap Process

An imagemap application can be one of the most confusing components in your site's development. For the most part, difficulties with the use of imagemaps result from a lack of understanding of the imagemap process. Therefore, let's look at what happens from the time you click your mouse on a spot in an imagemap graphic to when you are taken to the resulting URL (see fig. 23.9).

1. Let's assume you have clicked your mouse on one of the specified areas of an imagemap graphic.

2. Your browser will then send the location of the click back to the server. This information is sent using the HTTP GET method, the most common way of transferring information between Netscape and the server. You will notice that in Netscape's Location Window the URL is followed by a question mark and also the coordinates of where you clicked on the imagemap graphic. These numbers are referred to as integer pixel coordinates. They represent the distance in pixels from the upper left-hand corner of the imagemap graphic to the point where your mouse clicked. For instance, a pixel coordinate of 102,217 is 102 pixels to the right of the left edge and 217 pixels down from the top of the imagemap graphic.

3. The server receives the query from your browser and hands over the request to the imagemap program. This common gateway interface (CGI) program is given both the integer coordinates of where you clicked, as well as the location of the imagemap definition file. This file is essentially a lookup table for that particular imagemap graphic. It contains coordinates for the active regions in the graphic and their resulting action.

4. The imagemap program analyzes the click coordinate against the predetermined regions indicated in the imagemap definition file.

5. If the spot where you clicked matches with a region in the imagemap definition file, the imagemap program returns the resulting URL to the server. In the event that there is no match, an error message is sent to the server.

6. The server takes the information returned from the imagemap CGI and processes it. Typically, it sends the result back to your browser, which reacts by requesting the specified URL. If there was an error in the imagemap program or it failed to find a match for your request, the server sends an error message to your browser.

Obviously imagemaps don't just magically appear on a home page, they have to be created. To create an imagemap, you're going to need an image and a tool to create the clickable regions. Since all of this information is going to be stored on a Web server, you'll need to know some information about it.

Things You'll Need on the Web Server

Since imagemaps depend heavily on pictures, you're going to need to know how much disk space you have on the server. For those who want to run a home page from their own Internet account, be sure to watch your disk quotas. Most service providers charge you money if you go over a certain limit.

It's also very important that you find out what type of Web server your home page is going to be running on.

You should contact your system administrator and find out if the Web server supports NCSA or CERN definition files. You should also find out if there are special restrictions for setting up your own home pages. Your service provider may have all their users' Web pages in one central location. This is information you'll need to know.

Part

IV

Ch

23

FIG. 23.9

The Macmillan Computer Publishing home page presents the user with several possible places to go. All the possible locations have clear and distinct borders around them.

Different hotspot regions go to different places

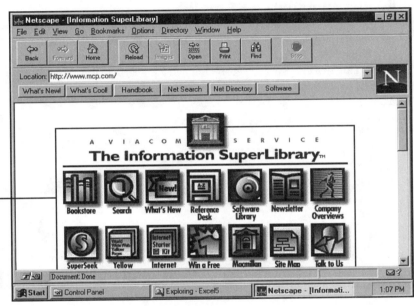

Mapping Tools

Obviously, one other thing you're going to need when creating imagemaps is a program that creates the imagemap definition file. These programs allow you to draw clickable regions on an image and then specify which URLs to go to. There are a number of mapping tools available for Windows 95 and Macintosh and a short description of each wouldn't do them justice. Mapedit is a good Windows 95 imagemap editor that you can get from **http://www.boutell.com/mapedit/mapedit.zip**. A good Macintosh imagemap editor is WebMap, which can be found at **http://www.city.net/cnx/software/webmap2.0b9.sea.hqx**.

Most map editing programs are the same. They all let you create and modify imagemap definition files, typically with the graphic loaded. They all provide for the three basic region types—rect, circle, and poly. The slightly more sophisticated ones also support the point and default region types directly. The only thing to really watch out for with imagemap editing programs is if it feels right for you. If the user interface is awkward, throw it out. There are many alternatives.

Creating an Imagemap

So far, we've been talking about everything related with the imagemap, it's time to talk about creating the imagemap itself. You should get a good idea of what type of imagemap you want to use. Do you want a menu bar that's everywhere? Do you want all your pages to have large imagemaps?

Choosing Imagemap Graphics

Now that you have a basic understanding of how the imagemap process works, it's time to begin thinking about using an imagemap in your own World Wide Web site. The best place to begin is by choosing an inline image to be used as the imagemap graphic. Figure 23.10 is an example of choosing the correct image for a particular imagemap.

FIG. 23.10

Creating links to geographic information is a common use for imagemaps.

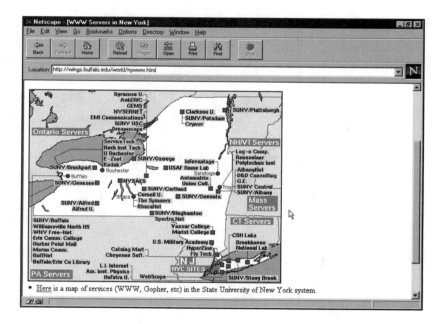

In chapter 21 you were introduced to guidelines for developing graphics for use in World Wide Web sites. Many of these ideas are also useful when deciding upon the graphics to use for an imagemap. Let's review some of the more important issues with respect to inline images:

- Inline images should be saved in the GIF file format whenever possible, as it is the only format supported by all graphical World Wide Web browsers.

- Save or convert images to be interlaced GIFs. Saving or converting pictures as interlaced GIFs depends on which program you use, but most paint programs will do it. This format allows the graphic to be displayed in "layers" as it is transmitted from the server. That is to say the image is presented in ever-increasing detail as it's being received by Netscape.

Users will begin to see the entire image area, without waiting for the entire image to download.

■ Develop graphics to be no more than 500 pixels wide and 200 pixels high. Most users will be viewing your site on a 14-inch monitor. Graphics that exceed the size of this recommendation cannot be easily viewed without scrolling for Macintosh users.

■ Graphics will download faster if they are created with a limited number of colors. Scanned images should be retouched to eliminate dithering. Dithering is the process where an image has more colors than can be displayed. When retouching a scanned image, simply change as many similar colors to a common color. For example, if you have a picture with three shades of red and they look very similar, then just change them all to one color.

N O T E Transparent GIFs used as imagemaps present a problem with user navigation. Transparent GIFs are images where the background color is specified by Netscape. This makes the transparent image appear to have no border and to "float" on the home page. Some of the active graphics will not be apparent to the user, so these imagemaps should contain some form of feedback or help as the default URL setting (see fig. 23.11). ■

FIG. 23.11
Yahoo's main masthead
is a transparent GIF
and the main user
navigational interface.

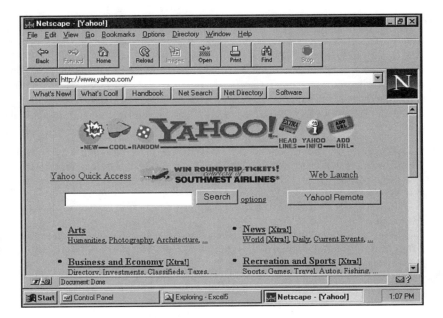

Creating the Imagemap Reference File

Developing the imagemap definition file will be the most difficult part of creating an imagemap for your Web site. Fortunately there are a number of shareware and freeware utilities to help you with this process.

An excellent utility for creating imagemap definition files for Windows 95 is the shareware program Mapedit developed by Thomas Boutell. Mapedit allows you to create definition files in the NCSA and CERN formats, as well as tools for defining active coordinate regions in the shape of polygons, rectangles, and circles. This program even gives you an opportunity to test your links prior to installing your document on a server.

To create an imagemap definition file using Mapedit 1.4, follow these steps:

1. To create a new imagemap definition file, first open Mapedit 1.4.

2. From the File Menu select Open/Create. Figure 23.12 shows the resulting dialog box that pops up.

3. Click on the Browse button to open an existing .MAP file. To create a new definition file, type in a name for this file in the Map Filename text box.

FIG. 23.12

Mapedit's Open/Create
Map dialog box.

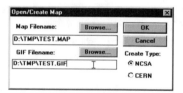

N O T E Most imagemap programs require the definition file to end with the extension .MAP. If this is the case with your server be sure to add this extension to all new definition files you create. ▨

4. Under GIF Filename, click the Browse button and find the GIF image you wish to use for an imagemap graphic. Once you have chosen an image, the path to this graphic will appear in the GIF Filename window.

5. Click on either NCSA or CERN as the definition map format, then choose the OK button.

6. If you are creating a new imagemap definition file, Mapedit will display a Confirmation dialog box asking if you really would like to create this text file. Choose the OK button to continue.

7. Mapedit will open your imagemap GIF graphic in a window. To begin mapping active regions on this image choose one of the selections from the Tools Menu.

8. Selecting the Tools, Polygon Tool, Mapedit allows you to create the coordinates of a polygon on your image. To do so, click with the left mouse button onto the image where you would like to begin drawing out a polygon. You will notice that a line will stretch from the tip of your cursor to where you clicked on the image. Drag this line to the first vertex of your polygon and click the left mouse button again. The line will now be attached to that vertex. You will continue to click and stretch in this fashion around the area of your graphic to enclose the polygon—clicking the left mouse button on each vertex (see fig. 23.13). When you've reached the point where your polygon began, click the right mouse button.

FIG. 23.13
Click the vertices of a
polygon to create the
coordinates.

9. A window titled Object URL will appear asking for the URL to be associated with this region. In the text-area below URL for Clicks on This Object, type in a relative or absolute path to the desired URL.

   Comments may also be added in the text box below Comments on This Object (see fig. 23.14). When you have typed in a URL and added a comment, click OK.

FIG. 23.14
Type in the resulting
URL and comments for
each region.

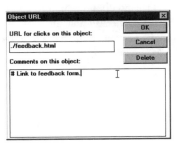

10. You may now continue creating additional regions on your imagemap graphic. The Circle Tool draws the radius of a circle out from where you click the left mouse button. Click the right mouse button to add a URL and comment to the circle region. Likewise, the Rectangle Tool traces a rectangle from the point where you click the left mouse button. To finish the rectangle, click the right mouse button. You may cancel any shape by pressing the Esc key or by clicking on the Cancel button in the Object URL window.

11. When you have finished mapping out the regions on an image, Mapedit allows testing of the active links. To test an imagemap, select Tools, Test+Edit. Clicking on an active region in this mode will highlight the region and open the Object URL window. If there are changes to be made in the URL or comments for this region, add this information to what appears in the Object URL window. Choose OK to continue testing your imagemap definition file. The Test+Edit functionality of Mapedit is built into the program itself and is not being run off the Web server. Also, there's no guarantee that any other imagemap creation programs will have this feature.

12. If you wish to include a default URL in your imagemap definition file choose File, Edit Default URL. This will allow you to specify a URL to be returned in the event that none of the regions match where the user clicked on the imagemap graphic. When you have specified a default URL, choose the OK button.

13. The last step is to save this document as a imagemap definition file. Choose File, Save. In Mapedit's Confirmation window choose OK.

 A separate imagemap definition file is necessary for each imagemap graphic used in your Web site. A good rule of thumb is to keep the imagemap definition file and the related imagemap graphic in the same directory with a similar name, for example, main_menu.gif and main_menu.map.

Referencing the Imagemap in HTML—The ISMAP Tag

As you recall from chapter 22, the Image tag <IMG SRC> can contain a number of attributes which determine the border, alignment, and alternative text name for the image. The Image tag is also the element in an HTML document that triggers the imagemap process.

The imagemap graphic must be made an active link in your Web page, much like the use of a single image button. As you will remember from chapter 20, inlined images can be used as clickable items as long as they are enclosed in the Anchor tag. That is, if you were to use an image named feedback_button.gif to link from your home page to a document in the same directory named feedback.html, the HTML would be:

```
<A HREF=feedback.html>
<IMG SRC=feedback_button.gif>
</A>
```

This tells the server that when the feedback_button.gif is clicked, a document named feedback.html is returned to the browser.

The ISMAP attribute appended to the <IMG SRC> tag builds upon the previous process, and activates the imagemap. The link in the case of an imagemap is not to a specific document, such as feedback.html, but to an imagemap definition file containing the coordinates for all the hot-spots of an imagemap graphic. The definition file, usually denoted with the extension .MAP, is analyzed by the imagemap CGI program on the requested server along with the coordinates of where the imagemap graphic was clicked.

N O T E   The physical location of your imagemap definition file will be subject to the configuration of your World Wide Web server. Most Netscape Commerce and Secure servers allow these files to be located anywhere within the http or Netsite directories. However, it is best to check with the system administrator on how your particular server is configured to handle imagemaps. ■

Regardless of your server's imagemap configuration, use of an imagemap in your HTML document must include the Image tag <IMG SRC> with the attribute: ISMAP. For instance, to reference an image on your home page named my_map.gif as an imagemap using the coordinates in the definition my_map.map, the HTML would be:

```
<A HREF=my_map.map>
<IMG SRC=my_map.gif ISMAP>
</A>
```

The link in this instance is not another HTML document, but the imagemap definition file which contains the coordinates for each region of the imagemap graphic, my_map.gif. The server receives the request for the definition file and the coordinates of the user's click in the form of a HTTP GET request. From there the imagemap CGI program is executed in order to interpret the request.

N O T E   It's acceptable to combine other Image attributes with ISMAP, however, it is customary to place the ISMAP as the final attribute. For instance:

```
<IMG align=left border=0 SRC=my_map.gif alt=My Map ISMAP> ■
```

Using Netscape to Test Your Imagemap

Once you've made your imagemap, the only thing left to do is to test it out. While most map editing programs let you test the imagemap regions you've outlined, nothing beats using Netscape. Testing it out as if you were an actual user, instead of the designer, is useful because there are things users catch that designers won't.

The best way to test your imagemap is to put it on your Web server. By testing the imagemap with Netscape, you'll see just how fast your imagemap comes through your modem and how distinct each clickable region is. It's also a good idea to have a friend at another service provider try out your imagemap, so you can check for valid URLs. No matter how detailed your imagemap might be, it's always a good idea to try it out a few times as if you were an ordinary user.

Providing an Alternative

While it's great to have imagemaps, you must also consider other people. There is a significant number of people browsing the Web who are using text-based browsers. You should provide for some means of letting them navigate around your home page. You can put in a separate section with a description of the links and the corresponding URLs. You can also have a link that takes the user to a text-only menu that has the same links as the imagemap. Whichever approach you take, be sure to put in an alternative for text-only users. ●

## CHAPTER 24

Netscape-Specific and Future HTML Commands

Having seen quite a bit of HTML, we're ready to look at the different levels of HTML (Netscape, HTML 2.0, and HTML 3.0) and consider whether you want to use these elements. In the previous few chapters you've been introduced to elements that fall under the purview of the HTML 2.0 standard. There's more to it than that, though.

Of particular concern in this chapter are two other types of HTML commands: Netscape-specific and HTML 3.0. Netscape-specific commands are HTML elements that have been introduced by the Netscape Corp. as proprietary elements that its browsers support for Web design. This doesn't necessarily mean that other browsers aren't able to deal with these elements. But it does mean there's a good chance that they can't.

HTML 3.0 is the emerging new standard for Web design. It hasn't yet been completely pounded out, but many of the elements that programmers assume will be included have already been recognized and included in browsers by Netscape and others.

In this chapter, you learn:

- The difference between Netscape and HTML 3.0 elements
- What the Netscape elements are and how to add them to your Web pages
- How to design your Web site so that Netscape and non-Netscape users can both access it
- How to design your pages for both Netscape and HTML 3.0
- The future of HTML ■

Netscape Versus HTML Commands

While not yet official, the HTML 3.0 standard for HTML elements is beginning to come into widespread use. Some of these elements are commands that Netscape (and others) have recognized for quite some time. In fact, Netscape is very active in the creation of the standard, and many elements that have been considered Netscape-specific for the last year or so will probably be included in the HTML 3.0 standard.

For now though, it's important for us to distinguish between Netscape and HTML 3.0 commands. As the HTML 3.0 standard comes into shape, we'll see where the standard deviates from Netscape-specific commands, and which will be included as they stand. And that will be important to you as a Web designer.

Why? While Netscape does control a considerable majority of the browser market, there are others out there. For that reason, it's important that you decide whether you're going to include any of these elements in your pages. Some browsers may not be able to view documents that include these tags, and others may, but with less than satisfactory results.

As other browsers begin to lean toward the HTML 3.0 standard, they may have less reason to try to implement Netscape commands—especially where the two overlap. So for the best results, you'll want to stay as close to the HTML 3.0 standard as you can.

Adding Netscape-Only Commands to Your Pages

Netscape additions to HTML are of basically two kinds: extensions of the HTML 2.0 standard elements and new Netscape-only elements. Let's start with the extensions to HTML 2.0, then we'll look at the new types of elements you can include in Netscape-only pages.

Netscape's HTML 2.0 Extensions

Nearly all of Netscape's extensions work as attribute tags that are added to standard HTML elements—and, they are just about all designed to give the user more control over the look and feel of the page. This is, in fact, where Netscape tends to diverge from the spirit of HTML. These very specific tags allow you to decide with precision how the browser displays the HTML element. For the most part, the theory of HTML works against this—each individual browser should be left to doing the formatting on its own.

But, with 70 percent of the browser market, Netscape has made the ultimate overture to the more artistic of Web designers—more control over the page.

 T I P Remember, you should not use any of these Netscape-specific elements and tags if your goal is to create HTML 3.0 compatible pages. We'll talk about HTML 3.0 later in this chapter.

The _<HR>_ Element   <HR> generally returns a horizontal rule in Netscape and other browsers. In Netscape, the default for this element is a shaded, engraved-looking line. But, thanks to new Netscape attributes, you can change this with the SIZE, WIDTH, ALIGN, and NOSHADE tags (see fig. 24.1).

FIG. 24.1
The <HR> Netscape extensions in action.

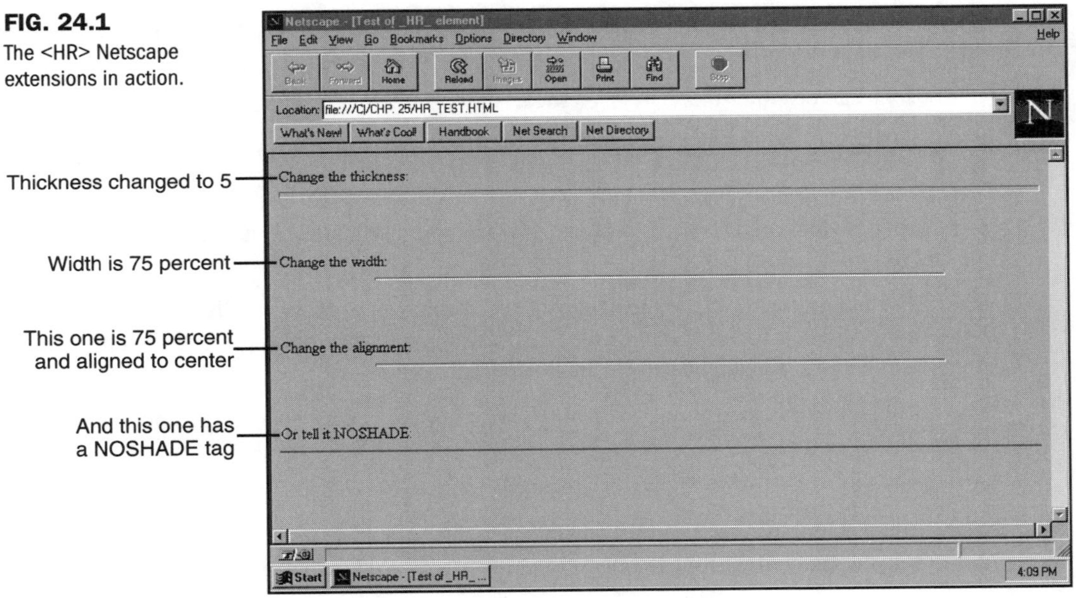

Thickness changed to 5

Width is 75 percent

This one is 75 percent and aligned to center

And this one has a NOSHADE tag

To change the size of an <HR> tag, the format is

```
<HR SIZE=number>
```

where number is the thickness of the horizontal rule.

Similarly, you can change the width of the <HR> tag from the default (whatever the width of the page is) to something more specific by formatting the tag as

```
<HR WIDTH=number>
```

where number is the exact length in pixels that you'd like the horizontal rule to be. You can also use a percentage (for example, 75 percent) to indicate that you want the line to be a percentage of the available window.

Part
IV

Ch
24

To align the horizontal rule on the page (this is only really useful if you've changed the WIDTH), the align tag is formatted as

```
<HR ALIGN=direction>
```

where direction is either left, right, or center. This, respectively, pushes the line up against the left margin of the available window or the right margin of the window, or it centers the line on the page.

The final tag, NOSHADE, takes no variables, simply following the format <HR NOSHADE>.

HTML Lists   Another set of fully cosmetic tags can be added to the HTML elements: <BL> (bulleted list) and <OL> (ordered list) (see fig. 24.2).

To change the bullet style for lists, you can add the TYPE tag

```
<UL TYPE=style>
```

where style can be either disc, circle, or square.

Changing ordered list styles is very similar:

```
<OL TYPE=style>
```

In this case, style can be A for capital letters, a for lowercase letters, I for large roman numerals, or i for small roman numerals.

The <LI> element can also take the above tags, allowing you to change bullet types or order types in the middle of a list. For instance, <LI TYPE=a> changes this item's and all subsequent items' numbers (in an <OL> list) to lowercase letters.

The <LI> element can also accept the VALUE tag, allowing you to reset the number count in ordered lists, so that

```
<LI VALUE=5>
```

as the first element in an ordered list would cause the list to start counting from 5 (or V or E, depending on the type tag for that list).

▶ **See** "Adding Links, Graphics, and Tables," **p. 459**

N O T E   For the most part, an incorrect tag added to an HTML element returns that element to its default style in Netscape. For instance, adding the tag TYPE=circle to an ordered list causes the list to revert to standard numbers (for example, 6,7,8) even if the ordered list had been previously assigned a style tag for letters or roman numerals. ■

The <*IMG*> element

The image <IMG> element has a number of refinements that allow you to align the image with text, specify dimensions for images, decide how wide the border (or frame) for the image will be, and decide how much space should be left between images and text.

▶ **See** "Adding Links, Graphics, and Tables," **p. 459**

FIG. 24.2

The different ways to show bullets and numbers in lists.

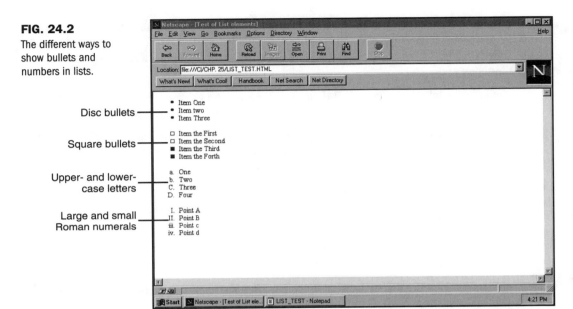

Disc bullets ——————

Square bullets ——————

Upper- and lower-case letters ——————

Large and small Roman numerals ——————

When you include the image in a line of text (that is, within the same paragraph), you can use the ALIGN tag, like

```
<IMG ALIGN=direction>
```

to specify a number of different ways to align the image. The following are the different ways you can align the image:

- left—Image aligns with the left margin in the next available space down. Subsequent text is wrapped around the right margin of the image.
- right—Image aligns with the right margin of the page, and text wraps around its left side.
- top—The image aligns itself with the tallest item in the current line.
- texttop—Aligns the image with the tallest text in the line.
- middle—Aligns the middle of the image with the baseline of the current line.
- absmiddle (Absolute middle)—Aligns the image with the middle of the current line.
- baseline and bottom—Both of these align the bottom of the image with the baseline of the current line.
- absbottom (Absolute bottom)—Aligns the bottom of the image with the bottom of the current line.

You may ask, why the distinction between baseline and bottom? Or tallest item and tallest text? Because they can be slightly different, depending on the particular line of HTML coding in question, and that can be a little annoying to the HTML perfectionist.

Baseline is the bottom of a line of text that does not take into consideration the descenders in letters like y, j, q, and g. Notice that the bottom of the letters c and g are different, even on this page. The absolute bottom, then, is the bottom of the lowest letter in a line, generally one of these descending letters.

Similarly, the tallest item in an HTML line might easily be a graphic file, while the tallest text generally is a capital letter. Figure 24.3 shows why this might make a difference.

Aside from the ALIGN tag, the <IMG> element can also take five other tags: WIDTH, HEIGHT, BORDER, VSPACE, and HSPACE. Width and height generally appear together

```
<IMG WIDTH=number HEIGHT=number>
```

where each number is the dimension in pixels. This tag is essentially used to speed up the loading of a page—Netscape determines width and height when it loads the graphic, but it takes a second or so longer.

To change the size of a border, add the border tag

```
<IMG BORDER=number>
```

where number is the size of the border in pixels. Remember, the border is what changes colors when an image is used as a hypertext link, so setting BORDER=0 may confuse your users into thinking that the image is not a link.

When you use the left and right ALIGN tags for images, you create what's called a floating image that isn't attached to a particular line, but simply fills the space left over by text. So, to keep these images from pressing up against the text (and get a nice, clean word-wrap around the image) use the VSPACE and HSPACE tags

```
<IMG VSPACE=number HSPACE=number>
```

where the number for VSPACE is the number of pixels above and below the image that are to be kept clear of text, while the number for HSPACE is the number of pixels for the left and right margins of the image.

**
**   Adding some variety to the line break <BR> tag is the CLEAR attribute, which, in the case of left- or right-aligned images, makes sure that the text coming after the <BR> appears below the aligned image. For example

```
<BR CLEAR=left>
```

will make sure text begins in the clear space below an image that is aligned left.

New Elements

Netscape has also added some completely new Netscape-only elements that can be used just like HTML 2.0 elements, but can only be viewed by the Netscape Navigator browser or any Netscape-compatible browser.

Embedded Objects   Netscape plug-ins are essentially specially written code modules that integrate seamlessly into your browser. For example, a Netscape plug-in for playing MPEG movies would, once installed, allow Netscape to display MPEG movies inline, without having to launch an external helper application. This is exciting, because it makes Netscape infinitely expandable, and means that multimedia content may finally become commonplace on the Web. For the full low-down on plug-ins, see chapter 9.

FIG. 24.3
Aligning an image to texttop ignores non-text elements in an HTML line.

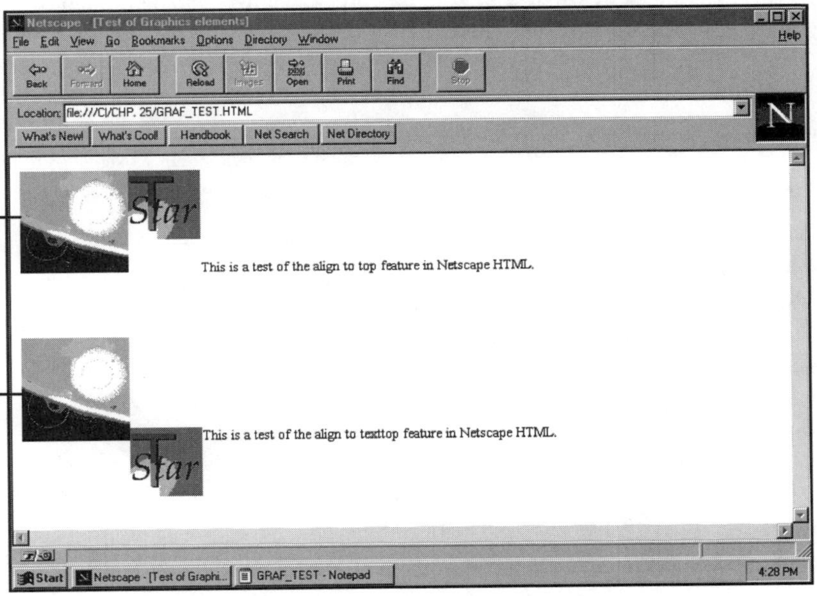

This graphic is aligned to top

This one is aligned to texttop

Live objects for these new plug-ins can be presented inline on a Web page using the new EMBED tag. Here is a typical use:

```
<EMBED SRC="video.avi" WIDTH=100 HEIGHT=200 AUTOSTART=TRUE LOOP=TRUE>
```

This line of HTML code would embed a Video for Windows movie called "video.avi" in place on the Web page. When the page is displayed, the plug-in that is configured for playing .avi files launches invisibly in the background. The WIDTH and HEIGHT attributes create a playback area 100 pixels wide and 200 pixels high in the browser window. The AUTOSTART=TRUE command starts the video playing automatically, while the LOOP=TRUE attribute indicates that the video should play in a loop until stopped. These EMBED tag attributes are defined for a specific fictional plug-in. Each real plug-in has its own attribute syntax, defined by the plug-in publisher.

If you plan to support Netscape plug-ins on your Web pages, you'll have to find out the EMBED tag attributes for specific viewers.

<NOBR> and <WBR> <NOBR> is a new element that allows you to create text that cannot be broken into a new line by the end of the Netscape window. It follows the format

```
<NOBR>text</NOBR>
```

where text is any text in which you do not want Netscape to create a line break. <NOBR> is especially effective when you have a series of words that you do not wish broken within a paragraph of text (like, for instance, a URL address).

The new element <WBR> is used in the rare instance that you have a <NOBR> section and you know exactly where you want it to break, if it needs to be broken by the Navigator window. You can also use it if you want to let Netscape know when a particularly long word can be broken, if it needs to be. Notice that <WBR> is only used if Netscape needs to create a line break in a particular line.

TIP The <PRE>, </PRE> HTML element can also be used to create unbroken lines of text (like using <NOBR> and <WBR> in conjunction), with the additional benefit of allowing all white space and returns to remain intact.

Font and Basefont Size   Another new element created by Netscape gives you the ability to determine relative font sizes for normal text (see fig. 24.4). This is accomplished using the <FONT SIZE> tag, as in

```
<FONT SIZE=number>
```

where number is between 1 and 7 (3 is the default size). But, there is also another element, called <BASEFONT SIZE>. Why have the two different elements? Well, the <FONT SIZE> element can actually be made relative to the <BASEFONT SIZE> by using a plus or minus in front of the number, like this example

```
<BASEFONT SIZE=2>
<FONT SIZE=+2>
```

Now the font size for this particular text will actually be 4, which is the basefont's 2 plus the increase in the font size element. What good is this? By using relative <FONT SIZE> values throughout your HTML page, you can change the size of all fonts by simply changing the <BASEFONT SIZE> value.

You need to use a new <FONT SIZE> tag for every change in font size. In the example pictured in figure 24.4, there are eight different <FONT SIZE> tags in that one line of text!

TIP Another way to make text stand out on the page is to use Netscape's <BLINK> text </BLINK> element, which causes a blinking gray box to appear and disappear over the enclosed text. Be aware, however, that there is fairly universal scorn for this silly little blink among the Web elite. Many folks find it annoying.

<CENTER>   Our final Netscape addition to HTML 2.0 is the <CENTER> element. Using this element, you can center any amount of text on the page, following the format

```
<CENTER>text</CENTER>
```

where text can be a word, many lines, or even multiple paragraphs. In fact, the <CENTER> tag centers just about anything at all, including lists, images, and other elements (see fig. 24.5). Also, realize that Netscape inserts a line break at the end of the </CENTER> tag.

FIG. 24.4
You can change font size as much as you want, but for each change you need a <FONT SIZE> tag.

This is standard-sized text

The font size is increased for every letter

Back to standard size

Here the font size is decreased for every letter

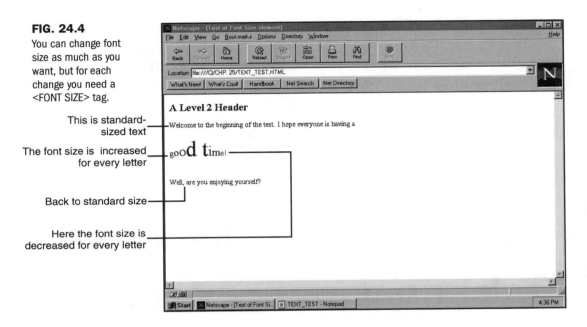

N O T E Most ALIGN tags overrule the <CENTER> element, so if your images are set with <IMG ALIGN> they will continue to appear as they should, although the text that wraps around them will still be centered against the page. ■

FIG. 24.5
With the entire page set between <CENTER> and </CENTER>, you get some interesting results.

Creating Tables with Netscape Elements

Once again you should note that Netscape tables are not the same as HTML 3.0 tables. To their credit, Netscape has been trying to implement tables that match the HTML standard for some time now, but the standard has been changed a few times.

What is a table? In HTML, creating a table allows you to present data in a way that is very similar to the way a spreadsheet looks. You have labels, rows, columns, and cells for your table that make information—especially reference data and financial and scientific findings—a little easier for your reader to consume.

With Netscape HTML, you start by creating a table, then adding a row and placing the header data (or titles of columns) in that row. Then you create more rows, and within each row you enter the data for the table. Each separate data entry creates a cell in the table (see fig. 24.6).

FIG. 24.6
A table created using Netscape-specific HTML elements.

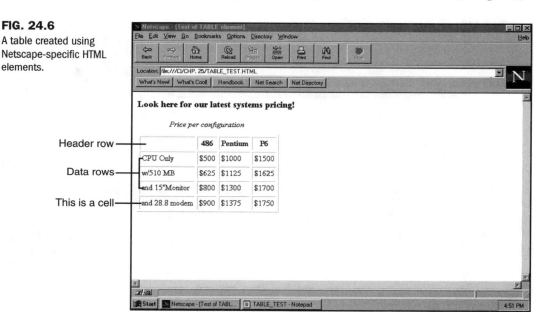

The **<TABLE> element**   To start your table you'll need to begin with the <TABLE> element, which wraps around all other table tags as such:

```
<TABLE>
...all other table elements...
</TABLE>
```

In Netscape 1.1, the <TABLE> element has an implied line break before and after the table is shown. This changed with Netscape 2.0, however, in anticipation of the HTML 3.0 standard for tables.

The <TABLE> element can also take a number of attributes, including the BORDER, CELLSPACING, CELLPADDING, and WIDTH attributes. All of these follow the format

```
<TABLE attribute_tag=number>
```

where `attribute_tag` is one of the four listed, and number represents how much of the attribute is applied. In the case of WIDTH, the number may also be a percentage, for example, 75 percent.

What do these attributes do? The BORDER attribute is used to determine the size of the border around the table and between cells. CELLSPACING determines the amount of space that is placed between individual cells in the table. CELLPADDING determines the distance between a cell's data and the cell border. The WIDTH attribute determines the width of the table (default is whatever fits on the page). If you use a number for WIDTH, then it represents the number of pixels for the table; a percentage means the table should take up that portion of the available browser window.

Creating Rows of Data   The next step, after creating the table, is to fill it with rows. Beginning with a row for header information (if desired), rows are entered using the following element:

```
<TR> data cells </TR>
```

where data cells are Netscape HTML data elements as described by the <TD> or tag (explained in a moment). The <TR> element can take either an ALIGN or VALIGN attribute, which becomes the default for all the cells in that row, so that

```
<TR ALIGN=Center> data cells </TR>
```

causes data to be aligned in the center of the data cells that you create for that row.

And how do you create data cells? With the (header cell) and <TD> (standard data cell) elements, such as

```
<TD> data </TD>
```

in which case, the data is any valid body HTML markup or text. A simple table, including a header row and a few data rows, might look something like this:

```
<TABLE BORDER=2 CELLSPACING=4 CELLPADDING=3>
<TR> Job</TH>Tues.</TH>Wed.</TH>Thurs.</TH> </TR>
<TR> <TD>Clean</TD><TD>Bob</TD><TD>Joe</TD><TD>Beth</TD> </TR>
<TR> <TD>Trash</TD><TD>Beth</TD><TD>Bob</TD><TD>Joe</TD> </TR>
<TR> <TD>Dishes</TD><TD>Joe</TD><TD>Beth</TD><TD>Bob</TD> </TR>
<CAPTION ALIGN=bottom><H3>Mid-week chore list</H3></CAPTION>
</TABLE>
```

N O T E   You might appreciate knowing that table data elements don't require the closing tag (for example, </TD> or </TH>)—especially if you type in your HTML manually. It's good form to include them, though.

Part
IV

Ch
24

Notice the last major element for a Netscape table there at the end—the CAPTION element. This allows you to create a quick identifying line for your table, taking an ALIGN attribute (if desired) to align to the top or the bottom of the table (default is the top of the table). Netscape can accept any valid HTML between <CAPTION> and </CAPTION>, and the caption always appears centered with respect to the table (see fig. 24.7).

 T I P For a blank cell, enter <td> </td> instead of just a blank space (like <td> </td>). This preserves the cell borders, making your table appear more complete.

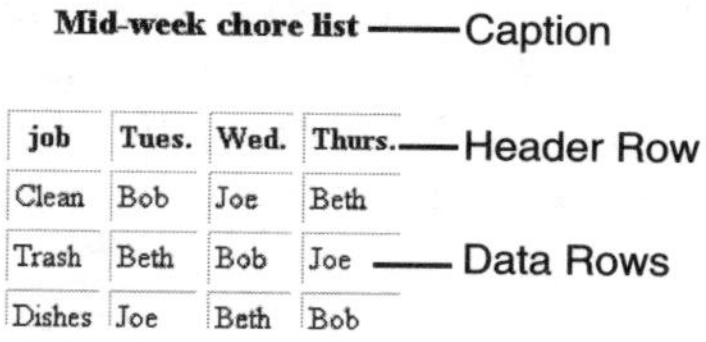

FIG. 24.7

Assign your family chores over the Web? Well, maybe you can come up with a better reason for a Netscape table.

Mid-week chore list ——Caption

| job | Tues. | Wed. | Thurs. |——Header Row
| Clean | Bob | Joe | Beth |
| Trash | Beth | Bob | Joe |—— Data Rows
| Dishes | Joe | Beth | Bob |

Background Graphics and Page Colors

Netscape HTML allows you to define certain graphics to tile behind your HTML codes, or colors to specify for the background and foreground. HTML 3.0 also allows you to add graphics to the background for Web pages, but doesn't follow Netscape's conventions for changing background colors. Again, it's up to you to decide if you should use these commands—just recognize that only Netscape-compatible browsers see these pages correctly.

Background   To add a background image to your HTML page, you simply add the BACK-GROUND attribute to the BODY element

```
<BODY BACKGROUND=path/graphic.ext>
...HTML document...
</BODY>
```

where path is the directory path to the graphic file on your server (either relative or absolute) and the name of the graphic file, with an appropriate extension, follows the path. (Of course, you don't necessarily need a path statement if your graphic resides in the same directory as your HTML page.) This causes the graphic to be tiled behind your text and other graphics so that the background graphic is displayed over and down the screen until the background is filled, depending on the size of the graphic (see fig. 24.8).

N O T E There's a little file-size paradox here with background images—the smaller the image, the faster the page loads, but the larger the image, the faster it appears. So, if you use a single graphic background for your entire site, it's not too awful to have it a little on the large side; it will load once and the image appears quickly from the cache. If you have many different backgrounds throughout your site, keep them smaller. ▪

FIG. 24.8

A Web page with a background graphic. Notice that, since the graphic is smaller than the page, it is tiled to fill the screen.

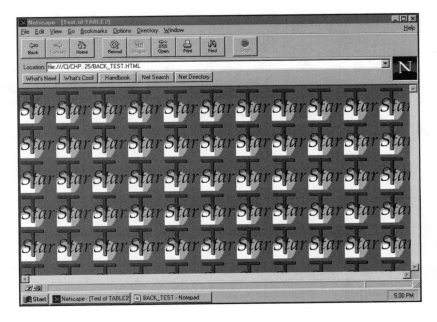

For Netscape only, you can define a background color for a page, and depending on the user's browser settings, it may or may not display. This is done with the BGCOLOR attribute to the BODY element

```
<BODY BGCOLOR=#rrggbb>
...HTML document...
</BODY>
```

where #rrggbb is the number sign and three hexadecimal numbers representing red, green, and blue. An example might be

```
<BODY BGCOLOR=#000000>
```

which results in a black background. #FFFFFF would be a white background, #FF0000 for red, #00FF00 for green, #0000FF for blue, and so on.

N O T E Here's a quick lesson in hexadecimal numbers. Hexadecimal means base-16, not base-10 (normal counting numbers), so each place past the one's column represents a multiple of 16, not ten. Since there are no single-digit numerals past 9 in our base-10 counting system, hexadecimal uses letters (A–F) to represent the remaining digits (10–15). An F in the 16's place, then, is 15*16=240. An F in the one's place represents 15, so the hexademical number FF equals the decimal number 255 (240+15). ▨

Foreground Once you've changed the background of your document, you might have a good reason to change your foreground colors, too—especially the color of your text and links. To do this, you use another attribute to the BODY element. For regular text, that attribute is TEXT, as in

```
<BODY TEXT=#rrggbb>
...HTML document...
</BODY>
```

where #rrggbb is another three hexadecimal numbers. You can also change the colors of links, realizing that there are actually three different link attributes: LINK, VLINK, and ALINK. LINK is the link before being selected, VLINK is a visited link, and ALINK is an active link. These are also attributes for the BODY element

```
<BODY LINK=#rrggbb VLINK=#rrggbb ALINK=#rrggbb>
```

where, once again, you enter the number sign and three hexadecimal numbers. Default for these values is blue for LINK, purple for VLINK, and red for ALINK.

> **N O T E** You may be wondering how you can see an active link (ALINK). This is the color the link changes to right after you've selected it, while the next page loads. It's also the color of a link to a sound, movie, or other file that you're in the process of downloading. ■

Realize that whether or not your users see these colors depends on how their browser is designed. If they don't Auto Load Images, for instance, then the background image won't be loaded, and (if you haven't also set a background color) Netscape will also ignore your link color attributes, working on the assumption that your changed colors may look bad on the default gray background.

New Design, Style, and Layout Enhancements

The most recent Netscape Navigator 3 release along with the Netscape Navigator Gold 3 have several new features that add increased functionality with new layout capabilities. These new enhancements include a new column feature that allows for multicolumn text layout along with the new Spacers feature which helps control both the vertical and horizontal white space, pixel by pixel. Also, a new font style tag adds font support to HTML Web pages. Below is a more detailed overview of these new Netscape enhancements.

Multicolumn Design

You use the new tag MULTICOL, to create multiple columns similar to columns found in the newspaper. COL, GUTTER, and WIDTH are attributes that you use along with the MULTICOL tag necessary to control the number of columns, the space between the columns and the column width.

See the following for MULTICOL tag syntax and attributes.

- ■ MULTICOL—The MULTICOL tag is the container. Text displayed in the multicolumn format would include all HTML text between the starting and ending tag. Multicolumn tags can also be nested endlessly.

- ■ COLS—The COLS attribute is mandatory and will set the number of columns. If the WIDTH attribute is not used, the width is adjusted to fit the page.

■ WIDTH—The WIDTH attribute sets the same width for all columns.

■ GUTTER—The GUTTER attribute defaults to 10 and sets the amount of white space in pixels.

> **N O T E** The page-breaking algorithm breaks the columns to look aligned with any left- or right-aligned images. In some cases, it won't find a section to column break. In this instance, you might end up with one very long column. ■

New Spacers

Web designers can now have quite a lot of control over the vertical and horizontal white space that appears on HTML documents. The new SPACER tag has five attributes; TYPE, SIZE, WIDTH, HEIGHT, and ALIGN. The TYPE attribute also has values HORIZONTAL, VERTICAL, and BLOCK. The BLOCK value lets you create discretionary white space along margins or within a line of text. The following example puts white space as an indent (30 pixels) in a paragraph of text.

```
<SPACER TYPE=HORIZONTAL SIZE=30>
```

The SPACER tag can also be used like an invisible IMG tag and could set width, height, and align attributes. Using this tag along with the MULTICOL tag, HTML documents can now have the appearance of professionally designed page layouts similar to the look of desktop publishing.

Font Enhancements

The FONT FACE tag allows Web page designers to specify fonts that could be loaded on a user's system and would then display the font. Multiple font choices can be set. If no specified font is found, it will display a default font. The syntax for the FONT FACE tag would look similar to the example below.

```
FONT FACE="1st fontname,2nd fontname,3rd fontname"
```

> **N O T E** Underline (U tag) and strikeout (S tag) text are now supported with Netscape Navigator 3. Strikeout was already supported (STRIKE tag) in Netscape Navigator 2. ■

Designing Web Sites for Netscape and Non-Netscape Users

Among Web designers who create pages with Netscape-specific commands, there are basically two different trains of thought. The first group, the others-be-darned group, designs pages with Netscape and HTML 3.0 commands, graphics, and area maps without concern for users who use other browsers; their emphasis is on the look of the page, not (necessarily) the content of the page. If you can read it, good. If not, get Netscape.

It's hard to condemn these folks—after all, Netscape commands give you the most artful control over your pages. In fact, many of them are even willing to offer a link to Netscape so you can download the browser for yourself. That's nice of them, but there is another way.

By using a front door to your Web site, you can give users a choice (see fig. 24.9). If you'd like, you can design sites that offer the same pages in two different formats: Netscape-specific and non-Netscape specific. Sometimes, for instance, with tables it takes a little creativity to create a non-Netscape page that still communicates everything you want it to. But, for the most part, Netscape additions are just cosmetic. It's easy enough to create pages that work for both Netscape users and non-Netscape users.

FIG. 24.9
A front door can let users decide whether or not they want to view pages that use Netscape-specific commands.

Netscape users can select this link

Others have this choice

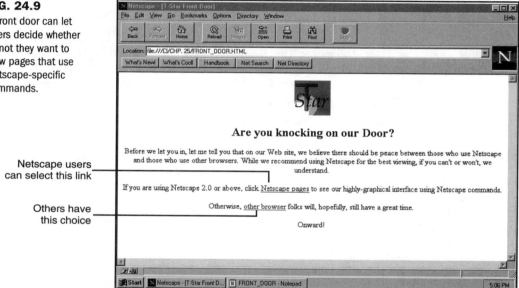

All you really need to do for your front door is offer two different links—one to an index page for your Netscape site, and another for your text-only or HTML 2.0-only site. Then, duplicate your pages for both types, taking any Netscape-specific elements or attributes out of one set of pages.

 TIP If you're developing a site for your business, it's almost imperative that you offer your users a choice of browsers. If not, you're cutting out 30 to 40 percent of your market!

Is there any way around this duplication? Actually, yes. Develop your pages without Netscape-specific commands. If that seems too limiting, consider developing your pages according to the HTML 3.0 standard instead of Netscape's HTML extensions. As time wears on, HTML 3.0 should be received very quickly by the folks who create Web browsers. You may have to give up a particular Netscapism or two, but that's a price to pay for reaching everyone who uses the Web.

For an exceptional Web-based reference for achieving Netscape-specific results using only HTML 3.0 standard elements and attributes, point your browser at Andrew B. King's pages at **http://webreference.com/html3andns/**.

Introduction to HTML 3.0

It's been said often enough that HTML 3.0 is an emerging standard. But that does lead us to a couple of disclaimers that are important to make at this point; they are as follows:

- HTML 3.0 may not yet be supported by all browsers. At least for a while, you may have the same problems using HTML 3.0 elements that are new since HTML 2.0. It will take browsers a little while to catch up, although I imagine that the big names (Netscape, Mosaic, MS Internet Explorer) will support HTML 3.0 by the end of 1996, assuming the standard stays relatively stable.

- HTML 3.0 may change. As has happened a few times over the last couple of months, the HTML 3.0 standard may change a bit from what's presented here.

If you're interested in watching the progress of HTML 3.0 on the Web, you might want to check in at **http://www.w3.org/hypertext/WWW/MarkUp/html3/CoverPage.html**.

HTML 3.0 Versus Netscape HTML

Before we look at the new elements that HTML presents us with, let's look at a few that have already been implemented in Netscape's version of HTML and figure out where the two disagree.

There's a rule of thumb here. Netscape, in general, errs on the side of more control over the layout of a page. Netscape also tends to create additional element tags for layout functions, whereas HTML 3.0 leans toward adding attribute tags to existing elements for layout—for instance, the Netscape <CENTER> tag.

Aligning Things in HTML 3.0 You may remember that the Netscape <CENTER> element tag is a catchall—anything between the <CENTER> and </CENTER> tags gets centered, except for images that overrule that with their own <ALIGN> tags. HTML 3.0 doesn't offer the <CENTER> tag, however, since it's a purely aesthetic tag. HTML prefers to use the <ALIGN> attribute tag, added to different existing tags, such as

```
<P ALIGN=direction> Text </P>
```

where direction is left, right, center, or justify (solid left and right borders). This <ALIGN> attribute can also be added to the header tags (for example, <H1>, <H2>, and so on), <TABLE> tag, <TR> (table row) tag, and others.

But isn't this leaving something out? After all, the Netscape <CENTER> tag allows you to center any amount of anything that you want to center. That's more convenient, right?

Well, HTML 3.0 lets you center big chunks, too, with the <DIV> element tag. By adding the <ALIGN> attribute tag, you get something like

```
<DIV ALIGN=direction>
...a section of HTML...
</DIV>
```

where direction is, again, left, right, center, or justify. The <DIV> tag is creating a division within the body of the document. In essence, you're telling the browser that this is a particular portion of the body elements that needs to be treated in this special way. Advantage over Netscape HTML? It gives you more choices, while staying with the HTML 3.0 theory of no appearance-only element tags.

Creating HTML 3.0 Tables   If you've read through the process for creating Netscape tables, you may notice that HTML 3.0 tables aren't completely different. Most of the commands are the same; where the two diverge is basically in cosmetic differences. HTML 3.0 and Netscape tend to use different attribute tags for such things as centering text in cells.

Here's a quick sample of an HTML table:

```
<TABLE BORDER=1 ALIGN=CENTER>
<TR>PayTuesdayWednesdayThursday</TR>
<TR><TD>Luis<TD>$25.00<TD>$40.00<TD>$30.00</TR>
<TR><TD>Marcia<TD>$15.00<TD>$30.00<TD>$50.00</TR>
<TR><TD>Rick<TD>$20.00<TD>$20.00<TD>$20.00</TR>
<TR><TD>Ellis<TD>$35.00<TD>12.00<TD>$40.00</TR>
<CAPTION ALIGN=BOTTOM>Pay per day for employees</CAPTION>
</TABLE>
```

As mentioned in the last section, the HTML 3.0 <TABLE> element takes the attribute <ALIGN>, which can be either left, right, or center. The <TABLE> element can also accept the BORDER, WIDTH, CELLPADDING, and CELLSPACING attributes as explained for Netscape tables.

The other differences are somewhat petty—if you get deep into creating tables, you'll want to explore them. In general, HTML 3.0 offers slightly fewer (and slightly different) attribute tags for the lowest level of table alignment and appearance.

Other Issues of Appearance   How about a couple more differences? HTML 3.0 does not recognize any of the text color and background color attributes that Netscape does (those hexadecimal numbers for colors). In fact, the <BODY> element can only be used to load a background graphic—you can't change any colors within it. So, our only choice here is

```
<BODY BACKGROUND=path/filename.ext>
...HTML document
</BODY>
```

where path is the directory path to the background file and filename.ext is the name of the background graphic and the appropriate extension.

HTML 3.0 also doesn't recognize the additional attribute tags for bulleted lists, ordered lists, and the <HR> tag that Netscape offers. It does offer customizing attributes for these, but no browser currently supports them.

The <BLINK>, <NOBR>, and <FONT SIZE> elements are also lacking in HTML 3.0. In the last case, though, HTML does offer the <SMALL>, <SUB>, <SUP>, and <LARGE> tags for text, which (respectively) allow you to format text as smaller than the standard text, a subscript, a superscript, and larger than standard text on the page (see fig. 24.10).

FIG. 24.10
HTML 3.0 offers these alternatives to Netscape's <FONT SIZE> element.

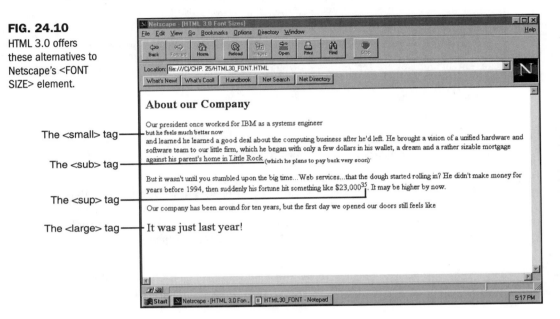

The <small> tag

The <sub> tag

The <sup> tag

The <large> tag

T I P It's a good idea to continue to use the header tags (<H1>, <H2>, and so on) when you're actually creating a header within your document. Use <SMALL> and <LARGE> only for body text.

Finally, HTML 3.0 doesn't recognize most of the ALIGN characteristics for <IMG> elements that Netscape has added to HTML 2.0, like texttop, absmiddle, baseline, and absbottom.

The Coming Elements of HTML 3.0

In essence, HTML 3.0 is designed to add three major requests from the Web world: tables (discussed previously), text-wrap around figures, and the ability to show mathematical formulas in HTML documents. In addition to this, there are a number of appearance issues that HTML 3.0 addresses including the new <BANNER> element for more control of the top of a document, allowing you to fix corporate logos, back/forward controls, and other elements to keep them from scrolling as the rest of the page is scrolled.

The <FIG> element

This is basically a replacement for the <IMG> tag, although, of course, the <IMG> tag remains for the sake of backward compatibility. The new <FIG> element has three basic reasons for being.

- Text flows around a <FIG> defined image.
- A text-based description is part of the basic definition of the <FIG> tag, allowing nongraphical Web users to still get the gist of a graphic on the page (and access it if it happens to be a hypertext link).
- The <FIG> element allows you to create hotzones for client-side imagemaps.

Current imagemaps are server-based—you create the imagemap in a special program and, when accessed, it calls a map server program to determine where the user has clicked the graphic. That, in turn, determines which link it follows.

▶ **See** "Using Imagemaps," **p. 505**

For client-side maps, then, no server interaction is required. The HTML describes what part of the graphics has been clicked, the browser interprets that click into the appropriate URL, and that URL is accessed.

Math in HTML 3.0   This element can get really complicated, and if you're a math person, that might just be heaven. The <MATH> element for HTML 3.0 gives Web pages a standard way to represent complex mathematical formulas within lines of text. Up until now, the only choice for representing formulas in HTML has been to include them as graphics—perhaps creating them in a word processor or advanced math program first.

Although an amazing range of formulas and equations can be represented, I'll stick to a fairly simple example. Using the <MATH> tag, you can render the integral from a to b of f(x) over 1+x as

```
<MATH>&int;<SUB>a</SUB><SUP>b</SUP><BOX>f(x)<OVER>1+x</BOX>dx </MATH>
```

or

```
<MATH>&int;_a_^b^{f(x)<OVER>1+x} dx </MATH>
```

Look complicated? It does to me. But, if this is the sort of thing you want to represent in HTML, you'll soon find that it's not terribly difficult. Notice that the first example uses the full HTML tags for the various different attributes you want assigned to the equation's variable (<SUB> for subscript, <SUP> for superscript). The second example uses HTML shortref characters for those same mark-up tags (_for <SUB>, ^ for <SUP>).

As the standard emerges, more information on markup and attributes for the <MATH> tag will be ready for you to use in your pages. To keep tabs on developments, check out **http://www.w3.org/hypertext/WWW/MarkUp/html3/maths.html**.

Non-Scrolling Elements   This tag is very interesting to serious Web designers. Using the <BANNER> tag in the <BODY> section of your page, you force the top of your page to be non-scrolling, allowing you to keep a corporate logo, back/forward controls, or a button-bar interface at the top of the screen at all times.

And, it's easy to implement! An example <BANNER> looks like

```
<BODY>
<BANNER>
```

```
<P ALIGN=Center>
<IMG SRC=logo.gif ALT=T-Star Consulting>
</BANNER>
...HTML document...
</BODY>
```

This results in a section at the top of our document that remains fixed, while the rest of the text scrolls as it normally would.

Frames

It seems like everywhere you surf on the Net these days, you find sites all gussied up with frames—at least, you do if you're using a frames-capable browser like Netscape 3.0.

Frames create independently changeable and (sometimes) scrollable windows that tile together to break up and organize a display so that it is not only more visually appealing, but easier to work with.

Frames are similar in many ways to HTML tables. If you understand how tables work, frames will be second nature to you.

However, unlike tables, frames not only organize data, they organize your browser's display window, too. In fact, they break up the window into individual, independent panes or frames. Each frame holds its own HTML file as content, and the content of each frame can be scrolled or changed independently of the others. In a way, it's almost as though each frame becomes its own "mini-browser."

Let's dive in headfirst, and take a look at an entire block of HTML markup code that creates a frame document of medium complexity:

```
<HTML>
<HEAD>
</HEAD>
<FRAMESET ROWS="25%,50%,25%">
<FRAME SRC="header.htm">
<FRAMESET COLS="25%,75%">
<FRAME SRC="label.htm">
<FRAME SRC="info.htm">
</FRAMESET>
<FRAME SRC="footer.htm">
</FRAMESET>
<NOFRAMES>
Your browser cannot display frames.
</NOFRAMES>
</HTML>
```

This example produces the frames page shown in figure 24.11. As you can see, this HTML code produces four frames. The top frame spans the page and includes a header. There are two central frames, one for a label on the left, which takes up 25 percent of the screen width, and one for information on the right, which takes up the remaining space. Another frame fills the entire width of the bottom of the screen and contains a footer.

FIG. 24.11

This is the frame document produced by the preceding HTML code, as displayed by Netscape.

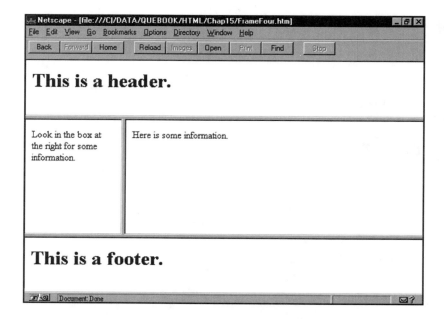

The FRAMESET Container

Frames are contained themselves in a structure called a FRAMESET, which takes the place of the BODY container on a frames-formatted Web page. A Web page composed of frames has no BODY section in its HTML code, and a page with a BODY section cannot use frames.

CAUTION

I Ain't Got No BODY

If you define a BODY section for a page that you compose with FRAMESET and FRAME commands, the frame structure will be completely ignored by browser programs, and none of the content contained in the frames will be displayed.

Because there is no BODY container, FRAMESET pages can't have background images and background colors associated with them. (These are defined by the BACKGROUND and BGCOLOR attributes of the BODY tag, respectively.)

Make sure you don't accidentally use BODY and FRAMESET on the same page.

The <FRAMESET></FRAMESET> container surrounds each block of frame definitions. Within the FRAMESET container you can only have FRAME tags or nested FRAMESET containers.

The FRAMESET tag has two attributes: ROWS and COLS (columns). Here's a fully decked-out (but empty) generic FRAMESET container:

```
<FRAMESET ROWS="value_list" COLS="value_list">
</FRAMESET>
```

You can define any reasonable number of ROWS or COLS, or both, but you have to define something for at least one of them.

CAUTION

FRAMEs Come in Sets Only

If you don't define more than one row or column, browser programs will ignore your FRAMES completely. Your screen will be left totally blank. In other words, you can't have a FRAMESET of just one row and one column—which would just be a single window, anyway. If you've defined at least two ROWS or COLS, however, you can safely omit the other attribute, and a value of "100%" will be assumed for it.

Part
IV
Ch
24

The "value list" in our generic FRAMESET line is a comma-separated list of values that can be expressed as pixels, percentages, or relative scale values. The number of rows or columns is set by the number of values in their respective value lists. For example,

```
<FRAMESET ROWS="100,240,140">
```

Defines a frame set with three rows. These values are an absolute number of pixels. In other words, the first row is 100 pixels high, the second 240 pixels high, and the last 140 pixels high.

Setting row and column height by absolute number of pixels is bad practice, however. It doesn't allow for the fact that browsers run on all kinds of systems on all sizes of screens. While you might want to define absolute pixel values for a few limited uses—such as displaying a small image of known dimensions—it is better practice to define your rows and columns using percentage or relative values like this:

```
<FRAMESET ROWS="25%,50%,25%">
```

This example would create three frames arranged as rows, the top row taking up 25 percent of the available screen height, the middle row 50 percent, and the bottom row 25 percent. If the percentages you give don't add up to 100 percent, they will be scaled up or down proportionally to equal 100 percent.

Proportional values look like this:

```
<FRAMESET COLS="*, 2*, 3*">
```

The asterisk (*) is used to define a proportional division of space. Each asterisk represents one piece of the overall "pie." You get the denominator of the fraction by adding up all the asterisk values (if there is no number specified, "1" is assumed). In this example, the first column would get 1/6 of the total width of the window, the second column would get 2/6 (or 1/3), and the final column would get 3/6 (or 1/2).

Remember that bare numeric values assign an absolute number of pixels to a row or column, values with a % sign assign a percentage of the total width (for COLS) or height (for ROWS) of the display window, and values with an * assign a proportional amount of the remaining space.

Here's an example using all three in a single definition:

```
<FRAMESET COLS="100, 25%, *, 2*">
```

This example assigns the first column an absolute width of 100 pixels. The second column gets 25 percent of the width of the entire display window, whatever that is. The third column gets 1/3 of what's left, and the final column gets the other 2/3. Absolute pixel values are always assigned space first, in order from left to right. These are followed by percentage values of the total space. Finally, proportional values are divided up based on what space is left.

CAUTION

Don't Be So Absolute

Remember, if you do use absolute pixel values in a COLS or ROWS definition, keep them small so you are sure they'll fit in any browser window, and balance them with at least one percentage or relative definition to fill the remainder of the space gracefully.

If you use a FRAMESET with both COLS and ROWS attributes, it will create a grid of frames. Here's an example:

```
<FRAMESET ROWS="*, 2*, *" COLS="2*, *">
```

This line of HTML creates a frame grid with three rows and two columns. The first and last rows each take up 1/4 of the screen height, and the middle row takes up half. The first column is 2/3 as wide as the screen, and the second is 1/3 the width.

<FRAMESET></FRAMESET> sections can be nested inside one another, as we showed in our initial example. But don't get ahead of yourself. You need to look at the FRAME tag first.

The *FRAME* Tag

The FRAME tag defines a single frame. It must sit inside a FRAMESET container, like this:

```
<FRAMESET ROWS="*, 2*">
<FRAME>
<FRAME>
</FRAMESET>
```

Note that the FRAME tag is not a container so, unlike FRAMESET, it has no matching end tag. An entire FRAME definition takes place within a single line of HTML code.

You should have as many FRAME tags as there are spaces defined for them in the FRAMESET definition. In this example, the FRAMESET established two rows, so we needed two FRAME tags. However, this example is very, very boring, since neither of our frames has anything in it! (Frames like these are displayed as blank space.)

The FRAME tag has six associated attributes: SRC, NAME, MARGINWIDTH, MARGINHEIGHT, SCROLLING, and NORESIZE. Here's a complete generic FRAME:

```
<FRAME SRC="url" NAME="window_name" SCROLLING=YES|NO|AUTO MARGINWIDTH="value"
MARGINHEIGHT="value" NORESIZE>
```

Fortunately, frames hardly ever actually use all of these options.

The most important FRAME attribute is SRC (source). You can (and quite often, do) have a complete FRAME definition using nothing but the SRC attribute, like this:

```
<FRAME SRC="url">
```

SRC defines the URL of the content of your frame. This is usually an HTML format file on the same system, so it usually looks something like this:

```
<FRAME SRC="sample.htm">
```

Note that any HTML file called by a frame must be a complete HTML document, not a fragment. This means it must have HTML, HEAD, and BODY containers, and so on.

Of course, the source can be any valid URL. If, for example, you wanted your frame to display a GIF image that was located somewhere in Timbuktu, your FRAME might look like this:

```
<FRAME SRC="http://www.timbuktu.com/budda.gif">
```

If you specify an URL that the browser can't find, space will be allocated for the frame, but it won't be displayed and you will get a nasty error message from your browser. Note that the effect is quite different than simply specifying a FRAME with no SRC at all. <FRAME> will always be created, but left blank; <FRAME SRC="unknown URL"> will not be created at all—the space will be allocated and left completely empty. The former will fill with background color, while the latter will remain the browser's border color.

> **CAUTION**
>
> **No Content Allowed**
>
> Plain text, headers, graphics, and other elements cannot be used directly in a FRAME document. All of the content must come from HTML files as defined by the SRC attribute of the FRAME tags. If any other content appears on a FRAMESET page, it will be displayed and the entire set of frames will be ignored.

The NAME attribute assigns a name to a frame that can be used to link to the frame, usually from other frames in the same display. This example:

```
<FRAME NAME="Joe">
```

creates a frame named "Joe," which can be referenced via a hyperlink like this:

```
<A HREF="http://www.yoursite.net" TARGET="Joe">Click Here to Jump to Joe</A>
```

Note the TARGET attribute that references the name of our frame.

If you don't create a name for a frame, it will simply have no name, and you won't be able to use links in one frame to open documents or images in another. All frame names must begin with an alphanumeric character.

MARGINWIDTH and MARGINHEIGHT give you control over the width of the frame's margins. They both look like this:

```
MARGINWIDTH="value"
```

The value is always a number, and always represents an absolute value in pixels. For example:

```
<FRAME MARGINHEIGHT="5" MARGINWIDTH="7">
```

would create a frame with top and bottom margins 5 pixels wide, and left and right margins 7 pixels wide. Remember, we're talking margins here, not borders. MARGINWIDTH and MARGINHEIGHT define a space within the frame within which content will not appear. Border widths are set automatically by the browser, not your HTML code.

Your frames will automatically have scrollbars if the content you've specified for them is too big to fit the frame. Sometimes this ruins the aesthetics of your page, so you need a way to control them. That's what the SCROLLING attribute is for. Here's the format:

```
<FRAME SCROLLING="yeslnolauto">
```

There are three valid values for SCROLLING: "Yes," "No," and "Auto." "Auto" is assumed if there is no SCROLLING attribute in your FRAME definition. "Yes" forces the appearance of a scrollbar. "No" keeps them away at all costs. For example, this FRAME definition turns on scrollbars:

```
<FRAME SCROLLING=YES>
```

Frames are normally resizable by the user. If you move the mouse cursor over a frame border, it turns into a resize gadget that lets you move the border where you want it. This always mucks up the look and feel of your beautifully designed frames. You will therefore always want to use the NORESIZE attribute to keep users from resizing your frames. Here's how:

```
<FRAME NORESIZE>
```

That's it. No values. Of course, when you set NORESIZE for one frame, none of the adjacent frames can be resized, either. Depending on your layout, using NORESIZE in a single frame will usually be enough to keep users from resizing all the frames on the screen.

NOFRAMES

"All of this is well and good," you say, "and I really, really want to use these keen new features on my Web pages. But I can't help feeling guilty about all those users who don't have frames-capable browsers. They won't be able to see my beautiful pages!"

Don't worry. Here's where you can provide for them, too.

The <NOFRAMES></NOFRAMES> container is what saves your donkey. By defining a NOFRAMES section and marking it up with normal HTML tags, you can provide an alternate Web page for those without forms-capable browsers. This is how it works:

```
<NOFRAMES>
All your HTML goes here.
</NOFRAMES>
```

You can safely think of this as an alternative to the BODY structure of a normal Web page. Whatever you place between the <NOFRAMES> and </NOFRAMES> tags will appear on browsers without frames capability. Browsers with frames will throw away everything between these two tags.

Some Frame Examples

Frames are very flexible, which means they can get complicated fast. This section presents a few examples of real-world frame definitions.

The simplest possible frame setup is one with two frames, like this

```
<HTML>
<HEAD>
</HEAD>
<FRAMESET ROWS="*, 2*">
<FRAME SRC="label2.htm">
<FRAME SRC="info.htm">
</FRAMESET>
</HTML>
```

FIG. 24.12

Netscape displays the simple two-row FRAMESET defined by the HTML code above.

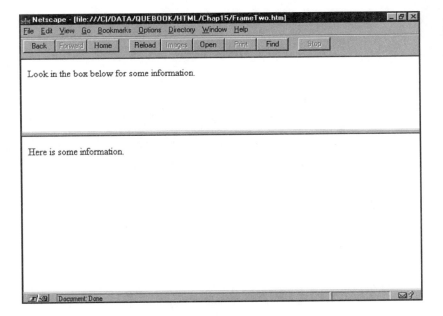

This code defines a page with two frames, organized as two rows. The first row takes up 1/3 the height of the screen and contains the HTML document "label2.htm," and the second takes up the other 2/3 and contains the document "info.htm." Figure 24.12 shows how Netscape displays this page.

We could just as easily create ten or more rows, or use the same syntax substituting the COLS attribute to create two (or ten) columns. However, ten columns or rows is too many for any browser to handle gracefully. Your pages should never have more than three or four rows or columns.

Too Much Is Too Much

If you want to display more information than three or four rows or columns, you should probably be using tables rather than frames. Remember, frames are most useful when you want to add an element of control in addition to formatting the display. Tables are best if all you want to do is format data.

A regular rectangular grid of rows and columns is just about as easy to implement:

```
<HTML>
<HEAD>
</HEAD>
<FRAMESET ROWS="*, 2*" COLS="20%, 30%, 40%">
<FRAME SRC="labela.htm">
<FRAME SRC="labelb.htm">
<FRAME SRC="labelc.htm">
<FRAME SRC="info.htm">
<FRAME SRC="info.htm">
<FRAME SRC="info.htm">
</FRAMESET>
</HTML>
```

This example creates a grid with two rows and three columns (see fig. 24.13). Since we defined a set of six frames, we've provided six FRAME definitions. Note that they fill in by rows. That is, the first FRAME goes in the first defined column in the first row, the second frame follows across in the second column, and the third finishes out the last column in the first row. The last three frames then fill in the columns of the second row, going across.

Also note that the math didn't work out very well, because the percentage values in the COLS definition only add up to 90 percent. No problem, because the browser has adjusted all the columns proportionally to make up the difference.

A bit tougher is the problem of creating a more complex grid of frames. For that, return to the example that opened this section:

```
<HTML>
<HEAD>
</HEAD>
<FRAMESET ROWS="25%,50%,25%">
<FRAME SRC="header.htm">
<FRAMESET COLS="25%,75%">
<FRAME SRC="label.htm">
<FRAME SRC="info.htm">
</FRAMESET>
<FRAME SRC="footer.htm">
</FRAMESET>
<NOFRAMES>
Your browser cannot display frames.
</NOFRAMES>
</HTML>
```

This example makes use of nested FRAMESET containers. The outside set creates three ROWS, with 25 percent, 50 percent, and 25 percent of the window height, respectively:

```
<FRAMESET ROWS="25%,50%,25%">
```

FIG. 24.13
This 2 × 3 grid of frames was created by the previous HTML example.

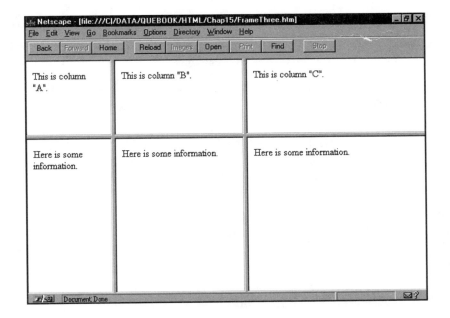

Within this definition, the first and last rows are simple frames:

```
<FRAME SRC="header.htm">
<FRAME SRC="footer.htm">
```

Each of these rows runs the entire width of the screen. The first row at the top of the screen takes up 25 percent of the screen height, and the third row at the bottom of the screen also takes up 25 percent of the screen height.

In between however, is this nested FRAMESET container:

```
<FRAMESET COLS="25%,75%">
<FRAME SRC="label.htm">
<FRAME SRC="info.htm">
</FRAMESET>
```

This FRAMESET defines two columns that split the middle row of the screen. The row these two columns reside in takes up 50 percent of the total screen height, as defined in the middle row value for the outside FRAMESET container. The left column uses 25 percent of the screen width, while the right column occupies the other 75 percent of the screen width.

The FRAMEs for the columns are defined within the set of FRAMESET tags, which include the column definitions, while the FRAME definitions for the first and last rows are outside the nested FRAMESET command, but within the exterior FRAMESET, in their proper order.

This is not as confusing if you think of an entire nested FRAMESET block as a single FRAME tag. In our example, the outside FRAMESET block sets up a situation in which we have three rows. Each must be filled. In this case, they are filled by a FRAME, then a nested FRAMESET two columns wide, then another FRAME.

By now (if you are a perverse programming-type person) you may be asking yourself, "Self, I wonder if it is possible for a FRAME to use as its SRC a document that is, itself, a FRAMESET?" The answer is "Yes." In this case, you simply use the FRAME tag to point to an HTML document which is the FRAMESET you would have otherwise used in place of the FRAME.

Recall the previous example (which used nested FRAMESETs) in terms of referenced FRAME documents instead. Of course, this takes two HTML files instead of one, because you're moving the nested FRAMESET to its own document. Here's the first (outside) file:

```
<HTML>
<HEAD>
</HEAD>
<FRAMESET ROWS="25%,50%,25%">
<FRAME SRC="header.htm">
<FRAME SRC="frameset.htm">
<FRAME SRC="footer.htm">
</FRAMESET>
<NOFRAMES>
Your browser cannot display frames.
</NOFRAMES>
</HTML>
```

And here's the second file, called "frameset.htm."

```
<HTML>
<HEAD>
</HEAD>
<FRAMESET COLS="25%,75%">
<FRAME SRC="label.htm">
<FRAME SRC="info.htm">
</FRAMESET>
</HTML>
```

In this case, the top and bottom rows behave as before. But the second row is now just a simple FRAME definition like the others. However, the file that its SRC points to is "frameset.htm," which you just created with a FRAMESET all its own. When inserted into the original FRAMESET, it will behave just as if it appeared there verbatim. The resulting screen is identical to your original example (see fig. 24.14).

CAUTION

Infinite Recursion

Though it's possible to create nested FRAMESETs using FRAME tags that call the same URL, it certainly isn't a good idea. This is called infinite recursion, and creates an infinite loop in a computer that consumes all memory and crashes the machine. Fortunately, frames-aware browsers check for this—if an SRC URL is the same as any of its ancestors it's ignored, just as if there were no SRC attribute at all.

FIG. 24.14
FRAMESET containers can be nested, or can call other documents containing their own FRAMESETs. The end result is the same.

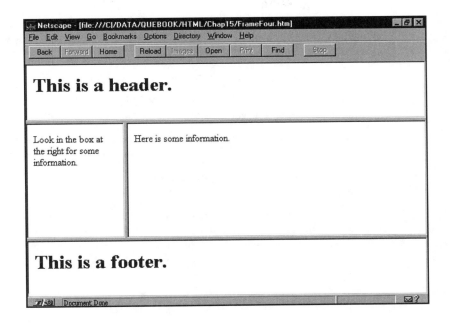

By using nested FRAMESET containers in clever combinations, it is possible to create just about any grid of frames you can dream up. But remember that you're trying to create a friendly, useful interface, not show off how clever you can be with frames.

N O T E Navigating a Site with Frames

There are three things you need to know about navigating through a site that uses frames.

1. The Back button doesn't back you out of a frame, it backs you out of the whole FRAMESET to the previous page. To back out of a frame, first point your mouse to the frame you want to back out of. Then click the right mouse button (the Mac only has one button, so use it). You'll get a pop-up menu and can select Back in Frame.

2. If you're in a window with frames and you move on to one that's outside the FRAMESET, your frames will disappear. They'll return if you use the Back button.

3. You can bookmark a frame by choosing Add Bookmark for This Link from the same pop-up menu mentioned in point one. If you simply choose Add Bookmark from your browser's main menu, you'll get a bookmark for the original FRAMESET, which may not be exactly where you are now. ■

Finding HTML 3.0 Info on the Web

If you've got a handle on which Netscape tags you plan to use, whether or not you're going to use a front door, and if you keep in mind the ways that HTML 3.0 might change Web design in the near future, then you've gotten the most out of this chapter. From here, you'll probably want to head out on the Web for the latest in developments for both Netscape-specific and HTML 3.0 commands.

Check out the following good Web sites for this type of information:

http://home.netscape.com/assist/net_sites/index.html to keep abreast of changes and additions to new versions of Netscape and Netscape-specific HTML elements.

http://www.w3.org/hypertext/WWW/MarkUp/html3/CoverPage.html to watch the HTML 3.0 specification change, shape up, and become a formal standard.

http://webreference.com/html3andns/ for great advice from Andrew King on getting Netscape HTML and HTML 3.0 to work together on your pages.

Next up in this book you'll finish the discussion of the advanced Web site with a look at some of the programming that goes on under the hood, and a summary of the best elements and design techniques that make for the world-class site. Then it's on to some more emerging Web technology—a new programming language called Java. ●

## CHAPTER 25

Netscape Forms and CGI-BIN Scripts

The Web can seem a constantly changing, dynamic place. Netscape can give you a feeling of almost unlimited freedom and endless possibilities—a full tank of gas; wide, rough tires; and a wide, colorful horizon spreading off as far as you can see.

But sometimes, there's something more. Some sites on the Web seem thriving, somehow, even more exciting than the usual. It's hard to pin down, but some outposts in cyberspace seem almost alive.

What is it? What's the thing that separates these sites from thousands of others?

They're interactive! You can enter data and receive customized responses. You can make choices and alter the site as you like. You aren't just reading information, you're controlling it.

True interactivity—sites that let users do more than just browse—is the one thing that sets one bus stop on the Information Superhighway apart from another, that really defines the World Wide Web as a new medium. You use this interactivity all the time, probably without thinking twice about it—but it sticks in your mind as something special, something worth remembering.

In this chapter, you learn

- How CGI scripts and forms interrelate
- How to write CGI scripts in Bourne shell, Perl, or other languages
- What HTML tags are used to create forms
- The dangers you must be aware of when creating scripts and forms
- Where to go to get publicly available code for creating your own interactive Web site ■

Creating Web Interactivity

Two elements go into making interactivity on the Web possible: CGI scripts and forms. While these elements are probably two of the most misunderstood—and confusing—aspects of creating a Web site, they are also the two most powerful. With them you can do anything from asking the user to guess a number to taking an order for a pizza to offering free searches of your comprehensive Web database, as shown in figure 25.1.

FIG. 25.1
What makes Yahoo! special? One thing is the ability to interactively search the entire site—something only CGI scripts and forms make possible.

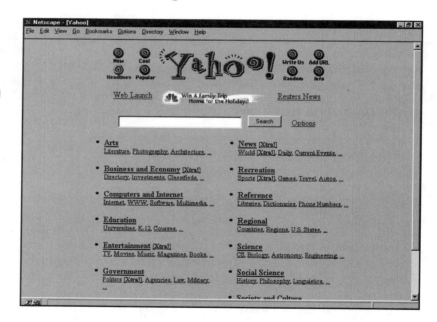

To get true interactivity on the Web, you need to understand and use both CGI scripts and forms, as they make up two halves of the same coin. Forms allow the user to enter data—information about himself, his request, his purchase order, or anything else—into Netscape and send it through the World Wide Web to your server. This is a "front end" that users see and interact with.

CGI scripts make up the "back end." They take the information sent to the server through the Web and process it—querying databases, placing orders, or simply logging accesses. It all happens behind the scenes, but it's where the real work takes place. The results are then passed back. Figure 25.2 is an illustration.

Though it can seem confusing, CGI scripts and forms are worth the trouble. They can transform your site from something static and predictable to something dynamic and exciting.

FIG. 25.2

Information is passed from a form to Netscape through the Web, to the server and ends up at a CGI script. The response is passed back through to the server, through the Web and back to Netscape.

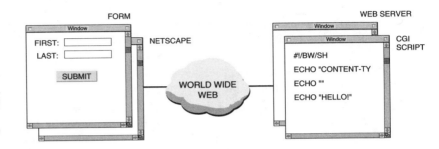

CGI Scripting

The Common Gateway Interface is the full name of CGI, and it is a way for your Web server to extend its capabilities by running external programs—much the way Netscape uses helper applications to display a Word document, for example. CGI is a "gateway" to functionality not preprogrammed into your server, and allows you to use all of your computer's capabilities, instead of just those that are already part of the HTTP server software.

To a user, a link to a CGI program looks like a link to any other URL. It can be clicked like any other link and results in new information being displayed, just like any other link.

But a CGI program, under the hood, is much more than a normal Web page. When a normal URL is selected, a file is read, interpreted, and displayed by Netscape. When a URL to a CGI program is selected, it causes a program to be run on the server system, and that program can do just about anything you want it to: scan databases, sort names, send mail. CGI scripts allow for complex "back-end" processing.

CGI changes the definition of what Netscape can do. While normal pages are static and unchanging, CGI programs allow a page to be anything it wants to be.

Part
IV
Ch
25

Scripts versus Programs

What's the difference between a CGI script and a CGI program? Semantics, mostly. The term script is left over from the early days of the Web, when it ran exclusively on UNIX machines. A UNIX script is a list of commands that are run in sequence, a lot like DOS batch files. The first CGI programs were written using these scripts, so the name CGI scripts caught on. Later, true programs (written in Perl or C, usually) were used to perform the same functions. There is no functional difference between scripts and programs—neither the user nor the server software can tell them apart—and both terms are used interchangeably in this chapter.

Setting Things Up

Before you can begin to use CGI scripts, you must take care of a few preliminaries. Because what follows really has nothing to do with Netscape—CGI scripts live and run on the server— we will just touch on the requirements. The following are some of these requirements:

- You must have access to a Web server, or the ability to install and configure one. This can be a complicated, tedious job and you should ask your company or school's system administrator or Webmaster if the facility is already set up.

- You must know at least some UNIX. Though Web servers exist for many different platforms and the concepts discussed in this chapter apply to all of them, the details contained here are UNIX-specific.

- You must know a computer language. CGI scripts are not written in HTML like normal Web pages. Instead of static instructions to be interpreted by the Netscape browser, they are actual computer programs. This gives them a flexibility that normal Web pages don't have, but also increases their complexity. Before you can write CGI scripts, you must know how to program.

  While you can use almost any language to write your CGI scripts, the most popular are Bourne shell (on UNIX), batch files (on Windows NT and Windows 95), Perl, and C. Each has strengths and weaknesses, and while a discussion of each is beyond the scope of this book, there are many excellent references available.

  For smaller CGI scripts, UNIX Bourne shell scripts or Windows NT or 95 batch files are a good choice. They are easy to write, easy to test, and don't take much of a time investment. If a simple script needs to evolve into something more complex—maybe it needs the ability to search a text file—you can use the command-line tools, like grep, awk, sed, or any number of others.

  For medium-sized CGI scripts, Perl is a good choice. It's fast, flexible, and easy to program. You can set variables, call subroutines, and do everything a "real" language allows, without a lot of the hassle.

  For large or time-critical CGI scripts, the most common choice is a true C program. While C can be difficult to use and even harder to debug, it is incredibly flexible and often the only way to get to external functionality—Microsoft's Telephony API (TAPI), for instance, can only be used from C.

- You must have permission to correctly install your script on the server. For UNIX Web servers, by default, there is a subdirectory off of where the HTTP software itself is installed called cgi-bin. All CGI scripts go in this directory, though you will need specific UNIX permissions to access it. Again, talk to your system administrator or Webmaster for details.

CGI URLs

After the Web server is installed and you have correct access, the CGI script can be accessed like any other URL. A script called demo.sh, if placed right in the cgi-bin directory, would have a URL like

> http://www.server.com/cgi-bin/demo.sh

Subdirectories can be used as well, allowing for URLs like

> http://www.server.com/cgi-bin/marketing/demo/start.sh

These examples use the standard HTTP protocol to communicate with the CGI script. The Netscape Navigator, when connected to Netscape's Commerce Server, allows secure communication with CGI scripts by using the https URL type, like this:

> https://www.server.com/cgi-bin/demo.sh

Sample CGI Scripts

Now that all the preliminaries are out of the way, the best way to see what CGI scripts can actually do is by writing a few and seeing how they perform. Following are four simple examples that demonstrate some of the power that CGI scripts give to Web pages.

Sending a Simple Message While many CGI programs are extremely complex, they don't have to be. Probably the simplest example possible is the UNIX shell script in listing 26.1. This code produces figure 26.3.

Listing 25.1 A Very Simple CGI Script

```
#!/bin/sh
echo "Content-type: text/html"
echo ""
echo "<HTML><HEAD><TITLE>Listing 26.1</TITLE></HEAD>"
echo "<BODY>This is a <EM>simple</EM> CGI script.</BODY></HTML>"
```

Part

IV

Ch

25

A lot is happening in that five-line CGI program, and all of it is vital for the script to work as intended.

FIG. 25.3
Listing 25.1 creates a
page that looks like
normal HTML.

The first line of this program tells UNIX that this script is to run in the Bourne shell, one of the many available in UNIX. Bourne is the most common, however, and the only one that every UNIX ships with, so it is the most often used. If this program were a Windows NT or 95 batch file, this first line could be left off.

The second line tells Netscape what kind of information it is about to receive. The Content-type: is required for all CGI scripts and it must correspond to a valid, well-known MIME type.

MIME (or Multipurpose Internet Mail Extensions) is a method for delivering complex binary data over networks, and Web browsers like Netscape use it to invisibly encode and decode that data. The two most common MIME types used by CGI scripts are text/html for HTML output, and text/plain for flat ASCII text.

The third line is simply an empty space to tell the server that what follows is the data described by the Content-type. You must include this empty line, or there will be nothing to separate this header information from the main body of the message.

CAUTION

One common error when writing CGI scripts is to have an incorrect Content-type for the type of data that is being sent. If your script sends HTML, as listing 25.1 does, but the Content-type: is text/plain, none of the HTML tags will be interpreted by Netscape, leaving your page looking like HTML source code.

N O T E While Content-type: is far and away the most common header sent from CGI scripts, Netscape (and most other browsers) understand another one as well.

If you have a Location: URL line, Netscape will automatically ignore any following content and jump to the new URL. This is how certain links can send you to a random URL—a CGI script picks from a database of URLs and returns a randomly generated Location: line. ■

The fourth and fifth lines are the actual HTML data that is to be sent to the Netscape Navigator. These lines are passed through the server and interpreted, just as the same instructions would be if they'd been read from an HTML file.

TROUBLESHOOTING

I keep getting errors when I try to run my CGI program. What do they mean? And what's the best way to debug my script? The most common error is 500 Server Error and it means that you either forgot to send the Content-type: line before your data or your CGI program failed somehow part way through. Both cases mean you have some debugging to do. If you get 403 Forbidden, you need to set certain permissions on your CGI script. When a Web server is installed, it is owned by a specific user on the system (usually root), and that user must be able to read and execute the CGI script itself and traverse the directories that contain it. Talk to your system administrator or Webmaster to correct this problem. The best way to debug CGI programs is to execute them from the command line instead of through the Web server. Set any appropriate environment variables by hand—environment variables are discussed later in the chapter—and simply run your program. This allows you to see any errors your script generates instead of the generic 500 Server Error message.

Sending a Dynamic Message   Of course, the simple CGI program above only outputs static data—no matter how many times you call it, the output doesn't change—and a user wouldn't be able to tell it from a normal Web page. The real power of CGI scripts can be seen when they go beyond this, when they start generating dynamic data—something that's impossible for a normal page to do.

This CGI script displays a new fortune each time you jump to it (see listing 25.2). The output is shown in figure 25.4.

Listing 25.2 A Dynamic CGI Script

```
#!/bin/sh
echo "Content-type: text/html"
echo ""
echo "<HTML><HEAD><TITLE>Fortune</TITLE></HEAD>"
echo "<BODY>Words of wisdom:<HR><PRE>"
FORTUNE=/usr/games/fortune
if [ "$FORTUNE" = "" ]; then
        echo "A wise system administrator installs 'fortune' for his
                _users."
        echo "        — Anon"
else
        echo $FORTUNE
fi
echo "</PRE></BODY></HTML>"
```

FIG. 25.4
Web users are given new words of advice from the UNIX fortune command each time they jump to this script.

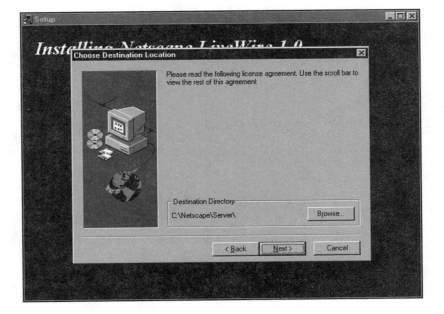

Instead of just printing out a predefined message, this script—through the UNIX fortune command—shows dynamic information each time it is run. If a user selects the link that runs this script twice in a row, it produces totally different results.

Just about any UNIX utility, or combination of utilities, can be used in place of the fortune command in the previous example. The real power of CGI scripts is to allow the entire capability of the computer to go into generating the Web page, and this example only hints at the possibilities.

If you're feeling adventurous—and know UNIX Bourne shell scripting—try modifying this script to do something other than print a fortune. Use finger to show who is currently logged on, or uptime to show how long the server has been running, or any command that you can think of. Be creative!

Using Server-Provided Information   While dynamic Web pages can be powerful, they can be even more so if they use some of the information that the server provides every CGI program. A CGI script that uses server information isn't doing anything special to get the server to provide that information, it's just taking advantage of what is always there.

When a CGI script is run by the server, several environment variables are set, each containing information about the server software, the browser the request came from, and the script itself. These variables can then be read by the CGI program and used in various ways.

For example, the program in listing 25.3 greets each user with the name (or Internet address) of his machine, and the name of the browser software he is using—Netscape, in our case. The results of this script are shown in figure 25.5.

Listing 25.3   A CGI Program That Uses Server Information

```
#!/bin/sh
echo "Content-type: text/html"
echo ""
echo "<HTML><HEAD><TITLE>Greetings\!</TITLE></HEAD>"
if [ "${REMOTE_HOST}" == "" ]<îthen
    REMOTE_HOST=${REMOTE_ADDR}
fi
if [ "${HTTP_USER_AGENT" == "" ]; then
    HTTP_USER_AGENT="a browser I don't know about"
fi
echo "<BODY>You are running ${HTTP_USER_AGENT}, on ${REMOTE_HOST}."
echo "</BODY></HTM L>"
```

FIG. 25.5

This CGI program not only tells a user that you know where he lives, but what he's running, too.

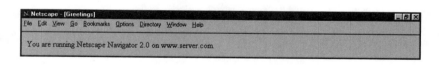

This program uses three environment variables set by the server to find out the name of the machine running the browser: REMOTE_HOST, REMOTE_ADDR, and HTTP_USER_AGENT. REMOTE_HOST normally contains the Internet host name of the browser's machine—for example, my.server.com. But if, for some reason, this variable is empty, REMOTE_ADDR always contains the Internet address of the browser—123.45.67.123, for example. HTTP_USER_AGENT, if set, is an arbitrary string that describes the browser software the user is running—Netscape Navigator 2.0, for example.

That's all this program does—gets this information, does a little checking on it, and returns it to the user.

There are many variables like these. The most common are listed in table 25.1.

Table 25.1 CGI Environment Variables

Variable	Contents
REMOTE_HOST	The Internet name of the machine the browser is running on; may be empty if the information is not known
REMOTE_ADDR	The Internet address of the machine the browser is running on
SCRIPT_NAME	The program currently running
SERVER_NAME	The Internet name or address of the server itself
HTTP_USER_AGENT	The browser software that the user is running

A complete list of CGI environment variables is available at **http://hoohoo.ncsa.uiuc.edu/docs/cgi/env.html**.

By using these environment variables creatively, you can do all sorts of neat things. Combining SERVER_NAME and SCRIPT_NAME can produce a URL to the currently running script, allowing it to reference itself.

Sending Continuous Data   Finally, there is another type of CGI script: the server push. When the user clicks a URL that points to a server push CGI script, the script does not simply send data to Netscape and shut down. It maintains the connection, and constantly pumps new data into the browser allowing such neat tricks as animating icons.

Writing server push CGI scripts is a complicated business, involving the creation of multi-part MIME documents, and it is well beyond the scope of this chapter. Fortunately, server push is losing favor as Java becomes the standard. While just as hard to program, Java animations are smoother and faster, as they don't depend on the speed of the network.

Part
IV

Ch
25

Creating HTML Forms

While CGI scripts are interesting in and of themselves and allow Web pages to come alive—through variation, personalization, and animation—their real power comes when they're combined with specific information received from the user himself. This is where forms come in.

Forms allow you to pose specific questions to a Netscape user and answer him based on the processing done in a CGI script. A form can be as business-like or as informal as you need it to be (see fig. 25.6). They can even add to the flavor of your site by being professional, friendly, or full of attitude. It's up to you.

FIG. 25.6

A site poses a specific question to a Netscape user.

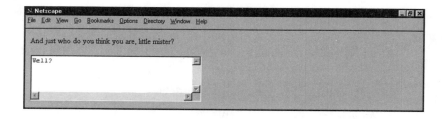

If CGI scripts are the "back end" of Web interactivity—taking care of all the processing behind the scenes—forms are the "front end," the pretty, GUI view that users see. CGI scripts and forms are two sides of the same coin and to get the maximum use out of either, you must understand both.

A form in Netscape is almost exactly like a form in real life: it's made up of spaces to enter text information in, lists of choices to check off, and options to select from. But while a paper form must then be turned in or mailed off, a Netscape form is instantly submitted—and instantly responded to.

There are four form tags that Netscape 3.0 understands, and they're used just like any tags. The first, FORM, simply defines the beginning and end of a form, and how and where the information collected in it will be sent. The other three—TEXTAREA, SELECT, and INPUT—make up the part of the form the user sees and interacts with, the actual text entry areas, menu selections, and push buttons.

FORM

The <FORM> tag is used to mark the beginning of a form, while its complement, </FORM>, is used to mark the end. All the other form tags—TEXTAREA, SELECT, and INPUT—are ignored outside of a <FORM>/</FORM> pairing, so you must be sure to delineate both the beginning and the end of your forms.

 TIP It's good practice to add a </FORM> tag immediately after you create a <FORM>, then go back and fill in the contents. This helps eliminate accidentally leaving the end form tag off after you've finished.

The <FORM> tag has three attributes, and they define how a particular form behaves. While the contents of the form are set by the remaining tags, these three attributes determine where the information entered by the user goes and how it is sent there.

The first attribute is ACTION. A form's ACTION defines what URL the information entered into a form is sent to. It appears inside the FORM tag in the format:

```
<FORM ACTION="URL">
...
</FORM>
```

URL may be any URL, though for the data entered into the form to be processed correctly, URL should point to a CGI script that is designed to handle that particular form. If an ACTION is omitted, the URL of the page containing the form is used by default.

The FORM tag's second attribute is its METHOD. A form's METHOD defines how the information collected by that form is sent to the ACTION URL, and may be one of two choices, either GET or POST. The GET method is the simpler of the two, while POST allows far more data to be transmitted. Which METHOD you choose depends entirely on how the CGI program that processes the form data is written, but a well-written CGI program can handle both. METHOD has no effect on the form itself, only how the gathered information is sent.

N O T E As the Web becomes bigger and the data sent across it more complex, the GET method is falling out of favor. Though it's easier to use, GET limits the amount of data that can be transmitted and does not hide that data from others using the machine the Web server is running on. For new or important Web sites, POST is the way to go. ▣

 T I P It is almost always a good idea, when writing CGI scripts, to use a library that parses form data automatically, no matter which METHOD you use. These libraries are covered later in the "Encoding" section.

The METHOD attribute is used inside the FORM tag like this:

```
<FORM METHOD="POST">
...
</FORM>
```

CAUTION

Though it's possible to leave off a form's METHOD and have it work perfectly well, it's not generally a good idea. You should be as explicit as you can with your HTML, both to remind you what you intended to do in a specific case and to avoid relying on defaults that may change in the future or be different for non-Netscape browsers.

The third attribute—ENCTYPE—is rarely used. ENCTYPE defines the MIME content type that is used to encode the contents of the form when they are sent to the server. The default ENCTYPE is application/x-www-form-urlencoded, which is the standard URL encoding.

Of course, any or all of these attributes may be set for any particular form. For example, the following use of ACTION and METHOD is very common:

```
<FORM ACTION="http://my.server.com/cgi-bin/form.sh" METHOD="GET">
...
</FORM>
```

Once your form has defined how it will be used with the FORM tag, you must fill it with controls that the user can see and interact with.

TEXTAREA

The TEXTAREA tag allows users to enter free-form text information, in an open-ended edit field. This is useful for doing anything from sending comments to telling a story.

Part

IV

Ch

25

TEXTAREAs are defined with a beginning <TEXTAREA> and a closing </TEXTAREA>, with the default contents held between them:

```
<FORM ACTION="/cgi-bin/form.sh" METHOD="POST">
Type your comment here:<BR>
<TEXTAREA>
Everything was wonderful!
</TEXTAREA>
</FORM>
```

This code sample produces figure 25.7.

FIG. 25.7

A TEXTAREA can be created with defaults.

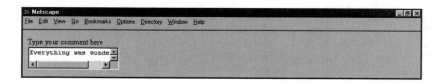

CAUTION

No HTML tags used inside a TEXTAREA pair are interpreted. If you use, say, the italics tag, <I>, you get three characters—less than, capital I, and greater than—instead of italics.

Like FORM, TEXTAREA also has attributes that may be set inside the initial tag.

The first attribute is NAME, and it defines the name of the TEXTAREA. What you set a TEXTAREA's name to is paired with the contents of the area when the user finishes his editing and submits the form. You must always give a NAME, as this is how the control is identified and its value retrieved.

The next two attributes are ROWS and COLS, each defining how big the TEXTAREA is to be, in character heights and widths. If left off, Netscape sets ROWS to one and COLS to 20, only allowing a very small typing area.

For example:

```
<TEXTAREA NAME="comment" ROWS=4 COLS=60>
I love your product!
I wish I had found it sooner.
</TEXTAREA>
```

This snippet of HTML results in the TEXTAREA shown in figure 25.8.

FIG. 25.8

This TEXTAREA is named "comment," and is 60 columns wide and four rows tall.

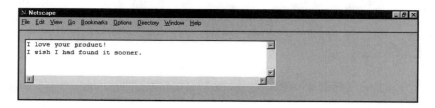

The final attribute is WRAP. WRAP affects how text appears within a TEXTAREA and may be set to OFF (which is the default) or to PHYSICAL or VIRTUAL.

If WRAP is omitted or set to OFF, the user must decide where each line entered into the TEXTAREA ends. If they continually type without hitting Return, the text will remain confined to the first line and the TEXTAREA will scroll to accommodate it. If WRAP is set to PHYSICAL or VIRTUAL, the text will wrap around to the next line, like it does when you type into a word processor.

The difference between PHYSICAL and VIRTUAL only becomes apparent when the data is sent to a CGI script. If WRAP is set to PHYSICAL, linebreaks are added to the end of each line, as if the user had pressed Return there. If set to VIRTUAL, the text is delivered as if it had been entered all on one line.

SELECT

While TEXTAREAs allow users to enter free-form text information, it's often more desirable to allow them to make limited choices from a predefined list—just what the SELECT tag was designed to do.

The SELECT tag itself is simple, just a <SELECT>/</SELECT> pair with three attributes: NAME, SIZE, and MULTIPLE.

TROUBLESHOOTING

What happened? Everything after my prompt text is gone! You forgot to include a closing </SELECT> tag. If left off, no other HTML tags are interpreted until the </FORM>.

NAME, like TEXTAREA, defines a name that is paired with whatever value the user selects.

SIZE defines the height of the list of selections to show the user. If it's left off, or if it's set to 1, the user is shown his choices as a pop-up menu, as in figure 25.9.

FIG. 25.9
Only the current
selection is shown if
SIZE is set to 1.

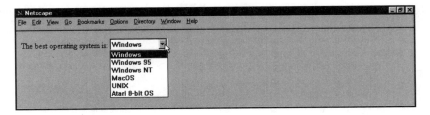

If SIZE is set to greater than one, the choices are shown as a list that the user may select from. If SIZE is greater than the number of actual choices available, empty spaces are displayed after the choices, as in figure 25.10.

Part
IV

Ch
25

FIG. 25.10
With SIZE set to 7, the
entire list—including
empty spaces—is
displayed.

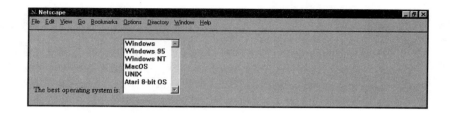

The next attribute, MULTIPLE, takes no value and simply defines if this SELECT group allows multiple selections at one time. If omitted, the user is only able to make one choice from the list; if included, the user is able to make any number of choices, including zero. Also, as a side-effect of specifying MULTIPLE, the list is shown as scrollable, even if SIZE is set to 1.

After the SELECT entity is defined, OPTIONs must be defined within it. The OPTION tag defines each individual choice that the user will see and is only recognized inside a <SELECT>/</SELECT> pair. Like the LI tag, an OPTION's text does not need to be closed with </OPTION>, though it doesn't hurt:

```
<FORM METHOD="GET">
Select your favorite food:
<SELECT NAME="food">
<OPTION>Cold pizza
<OPTION>Cold Chinese
<OPTION>Cold fried chicken
</SELECT>
</FORM>
```

The OPTION tag has two attributes itself: VALUE and SELECTED.

The VALUE of an OPTION is what is associated with the NAME, if that option is chosen by the user. This is used by the CGI script to identify the option, but does not need to correspond to the text the user sees. Creative use of this can make selections easier to deal with from the CGI side of a form. If VALUE is omitted, it is defaulted to the text that follows the OPTION.

The second flag, SELECTED, simply defines which OPTIONs are selected by default when the choices are first displayed. If SELECTED is not sent on any OPTIONs, none of them are chosen; if more than one is marked as SELECTED, those are all marked. Usually, the single most common selection should be set as the default.

> **CAUTION**
> The SELECT tag's MULTIPLE flag only comes into play if the user selects something other than the default selections you have defined. If your SELECT is not MULTIPLE, it is still possible to have multiple selections returned—if more than one OPTION is marked as SELECTED by default.

If you want to allow customers to rate your service people, you might use something like the following. Note that the VALUEs of the OPTIONs relate to your scoring system, rather than the actual text of the OPTION.

```
<FORM ACTION="/cgi-bin/service_logger.sh" METHOD="GET">
Please rate the service you received:
<SELECT NAME="service">
<OPTION VALUE="100">Excellent
<OPTION VALUE="75" SELECTED>Good
<OPTION VALUE="60">Fair
<OPTION VALUE="50">Poor
</SELECT>
</FORM>
```

This result of this is shown in figure 25.11.

FIG. 25.11

Web sites can offer two-way communication, both providing information to visitors and generating it for you.

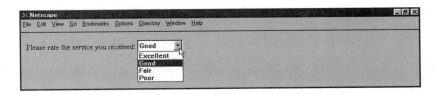

INPUT

The final tag, INPUT, is far and away the most flexible and the most complex. While TEXTAREA produces editable fields and SELECT produces lists of choices, INPUT can be used to create six different input methods: TEXT, PASSWORD, CHECKBOX, RADIO, HIDDEN, RESET, and SUBMIT.

Each kind of input is specified by an attribute of INPUT called TYPE. All the other attributes to INPUT are based on what TYPE is set to.

TEXT The TEXT attribute produces a single-line text entry field, like a single row TEXTAREA.

If the TYPE of an INPUT is TEXT, a NAME must be specified, along with three other optional attributes: SIZE, MAXLENGTH, and VALUE.

The SIZE of a TEXT INPUT is how many characters wide the text-entry field will be; MAXLENGTH specifies the maximum number of characters a user may enter into the field. If SIZE is bigger than MAXLENGTH, the text field will scroll to allow the user to enter more data. If SIZE is excluded, the default is 20 characters; if MAXLENGTH is excluded, there is no limit on the amount of text that may be entered.

The final attribute, VALUE, may be set to the default contents of the field, or left off entirely if there are none. For example:

```
Please enter your name, first then last:
<INPUT TYPE="TEXT" NAME="first" SIZE="15" MAXLENGTH="13" _VALUE="John">
<INPUT TYPE="TEXT" NAME="last" SIZE="20" MAXLENGTH="18" _VALUE="Smith">
```

This result is shown in figure 25.12.

Part

IV

Ch

25

FIG. 25.12

Default values can be used to show the format of the requested data if no realistic defaults are possible.

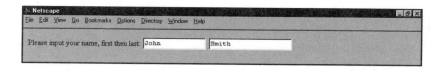

PASSWORD PASSWORD is a lot like TEXT—they share the same attributes—except that any characters typed into a PASSWORD TYPE are hidden. This, of course, allows passwords and other secret data to be entered:

```
Password: <INPUT TYPE="PASSWORD" NAME="pass" SIZE="8" MAXLENGTH="8">
```

If the user enters this code snippet, it appears like figure 25.13.

FIG. 25.13

No matter what characters are typed in, a PASSWORD field hides them from prying eyes.

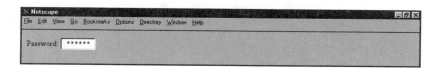

> **CAUTION**
>
> It is important to remember that even though a PASSWORD field prevents your secret data from being read off the screen, it is still passed over the network as plain, unencrypted text. It can even appear in the URL that way. Don't let PASSWORD lull you into a false sense of security.

CHECKBOX A CHECKBOX is simply a toggle; it can be either on or off. CHECKBOX is great for the simple, yes/no choices on your form.

CHECKBOX has three attributes: NAME, VALUE, and CHECKED.

NAME is the name that is delivered to the Web server, paired with the VALUE, if the check box is selected when the form is submitted. If VALUE is left off, it is automatically set to "on." If the final attribute, CHECKED, is included, the default state of the box is on instead of off.

```
Select the condiments you would like:
<INPUT TYPE="CHECKBOX" NAME="mayo" CHECKED> Mayonaise
<INPUT TYPE="CHECKBOX" NAME="mustard" CHECKED> Mustard
<INPUT TYPE="CHECKBOX" NAME="relish"> Sweet Relish
```

This HTML produces the check boxes shown in figure 25.14.

FIG. 25.14

CHECKBOXes allow for yes/no choices that are independent of each other.

RADIO RADIO is a lot like CHECKBOX, but only one toggle in a group may be selected at a time. All RADIOs in a single form that share a NAME are considered members of the same group, and if one is chosen by the user, any selected button is cleared. Otherwise, RADIO functions exactly like CHECKBOX, even down to the attributes it uses.

You may notice that this functionality sounds a lot like a non-MULTIPLE SELECT, and they accomplish almost exactly the same thing. Which one you choose depends largely on the look and feel you want your page to have.

The following code demonstrates the RADIO TYPE:

```
Select the type of bread:
<INPUT TYPE="RADIO" NAME="bread" VALUE="white" CHECKED> White
<INPUT TYPE="RADIO" NAME="bread" VALUE="wheat"> Wheat
<INPUT TYPE="RADIO" NAME="bread" VALUE="roll"> French Roll
<INPUT TYPE="RADIO" NAME="bread" VALUE="rye"> Rye
```

The result is shown in figure 25.15.

FIG. 25.15
RADIOs are designed for when you want the user to be able to make one selection from several choices.

> **CAUTION**
> As with SELECTs that are missing a SELECTED entry, if you don't specify a default value, it's possible that no member of a RADIO group will be CHECKED if you don't initially define a default. Always be sure to mark the most common choice as the default, with CHECKED.

Part
IV

Ch

25

HIDDEN Different from all the other INPUT TYPEs, HIDDEN does not produce any graphics on the screen. It exists simply to allow the CGI script to receive a NAME and a VALUE that is guaranteed not to have been edited by the user.

There are several reasons to want to do this, but the most common is to maintain some sort of transaction number between server accesses. If, for instance, a CGI script generates a page that it wants to identify again, it inserts a HIDDEN element—containing some checksum, identification number, or password—that it can check for in the future.

RESET The RESET TYPE creates a push button on the screen that clears the form and returns all the settings to their original default values. Its only attribute, VALUE, may be set to the text that you want the button to have. VALUE may also be left off, resulting in the text "Reset."

Consider this small bit of HTML:

```
<INPUT TYPE="RESET">
<BR>
<INPUT TYPE="RESET" VALUE="Clear Choices">
```

Its result is shown in figure 25.16.

FIG. 25.16
The top button is the default text for the RESET TYPE.

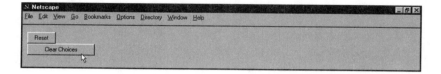

SUBMIT   The final TYPE, SUBMIT, works a lot like RESET but achieves an entirely different result—exactly the opposite, as a matter of fact. While RESET clears a form of user-entered values, SUBMIT gathers them up and sends them off to the Web server for processing, to the URL specified back in the ACTION. A SUBMIT button is the "Go" switch that every form must have to let the user say when he is done editing.

The only attribute to SUBMIT is VALUE, which sets the text of the push button. If excluded, the default is "Submit Query."

For example:

```
<INPUT TYPE="SUBMIT">
<BR>
<INPUT TYPE="SUBMIT" VALUE="     OK     ">
```

This code shows up as in figure 25.17.

FIG. 25.17
The top button uses the default text; the bottom, custom.

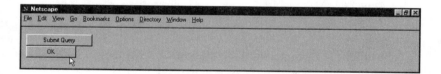

> **CAUTION**
> If the text of a button is very short, say "OK," the button usually ends up looking ugly. You can avoid this by padding the VALUE of the button with an equal number of spaces on both sides to widen it.

Bringing CGI and Forms Together

Now that you've got some basic background on both CGI scripts and forms, you're ready to bring them together to allow true user interaction with your Web site. The combination of CGI scripts and forms can bring a Web page to life, turning what was a static display of information into a customized and dynamic experience.

The program in listing 25.4 is a guestbook, an electronic version of the familiar visitor log used by hotels and museums. It first displays a list of signees, then uses a form to ask the current user to add his signature. It is written in Perl and uses a form-input library called cgi-bin.pl to parse—untangle—the data sent from Netscape. The result of the program is shown in figure 25.18.

Listing 25.4 A CGI Program to Process Form Input

```perl
#!/usr/local/bin/perl
print "Content-type: text/html\n\n";
# Load the library
do "cgi-bin.pl" || die "Fatal Error: Could not load cgi-bin.pl";
&ReadParse;
# Set the location of the guestbook
$guestbk = "guestbk.gbk";
# Get the sign-ins name
$name = $in{'name'};
# Only add to the log if they entered something
if (length($name) > 0) {
    open(FILE,">>$guestbk");
    print FILE "$name\n";
    close FILE;
}
# Show the current sign-ins
print "<HTML>\n<HEAD><TITLE>Guestbook</TITLE></HEAD>\n";
print "<BODY>\n<H1>Guestbook</H1>\n<H2>Current signees:</_H2>\n<HR>\n\n";
open(FILE,"<$guestbk") || print "You'll be the first\!\n";
while (<FILE>) {
    print "<LI>$_";
}
close FILE;
print "</UL>\n";
# Request new sign-ins
print "<HR>\n<FORM METHOD=\"GET\" ACTION=\"$ENV{'SCRIPT_NAME'}\">";
print "Your name: <INPUT TYPE=\"text\" NAME=\"name\" SIZE=\"20\">";
print "<INPUT TYPE=\"submit\" VALUE=\"Sign in\!\"></FORM>\n</_BODY>\n</HTML>\n";
```

There are a few things to note about this CGI script. The first, and probably most important, is that it is not only a CGI script—it does processing, like a normal script, but it also generates its own form. The last three lines, in the "Request new sign-ins" section, generates the HTML to request more information from the user.

This neat trick, where a CGI script also generates a form, is becoming standard practice on many Web sites. It allows a single program to both request and process the data—it could even be expanded to generate its own error message pages, too.

Secondly, you should note that the program uses the cgi-bin.pl library to extract the information the user has typed into the form. By using this utility, the user-entered information is pulled out of the request, decrypted, and stored in a Perl table called $in, easily and conveniently. You can get the VALUEs of each form INPUT by asking $in for it, by referencing its NAME. For instance, if a form INPUT has the NAME "address," the following line of Perl code would return the value the user entered:

```
$addr_variable = $in{'address'};
```

FIG. 25.18

A guestbook is a nice way to make your site more personal.

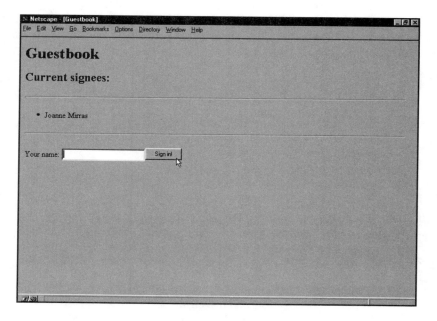

Of course, before you can use $in, you must have loaded cgi-bin.pl and called the library routine that sets up the table—lines four and five in listing 25.4.

> **CAUTION**
>
> When creating forms and CGI scripts, you should be aware that, normally, none of the data passed between the Navigator and the Web site is encrypted. This means that any private data (credit card numbers, love letters, and so on) can be "sniffed" by machines between the sender and receiver. Keep this in mind not only when designing your own forms and CGI scripts, but when using others.
>
> Luckily, the Netscape Navigator, when used with its counterpart, the Commerce Server, has the ability to automatically encrypt data. If a connection is secure, Netscape makes the small key icon in the lower-right of the window whole instead of broken—making it impossible for intermediate machines to view the information you're sending. (Information on Netscape's secure Commerce Server is available at **http://www.netscape.com/comprod/netscape_commerce.html**.)

stdin and stdout

So far, we've glossed over the details of how a CGI script accepts input from, and sends output to, the Web server. There are a few reasons for this, but the main one is that quite a lot can be done without ever having to understand how the mechanism works. Every one of the previous examples works without special knowledge of how the transfer is performed.

But in some rare instances, you need to know how this transfer takes place.

Every program running on UNIX has two channels, stdin ("standard in") and stdout ("standard out"). These two channels are how normal processes communicate with the world, and if the program is run from the UNIX command line, stdin reads from the keyboard and stdout writes to the screen.

But when a CGI script is executed from a Web server, it redirects these two channels away from the screen and the keyboard and takes control of them itself. This allows the server to send specific data into the script and receive answers back.

Every one of the previous examples, for instance, just echos or prints its output. Normally, this would just send the text to the screen, but because the script is run from the server, the output is captured and sent through the server to Netscape for viewing. Simple!

Reading input is a more complicated matter. While utility libraries like cgi-bin.pl automatically take care of the complexities of decoding input, you can do it yourself if you're feeling adventurous.

GET and POST

There are two ways to read the form data submitted to a CGI script, depending on the METHOD the FORM used. The type of METHOD the form used—either GET or POST—is stored in an environment variable called REQUEST_METHOD, and based on that, the data should be read in one of the following ways:

- If the data is sent from a GET METHOD FORM, the input stream is stored in an environment variable called QUERY_STRING. As noted above, this input stream usually is limited to about one kilobyte of data, which is why the GET METHOD is losing popularity to the more flexible POST.

- If the data is submitted from a POST FORM, the input string waits on stdin, with the number of bytes waiting stored in the environment variable CONTENT_LENGTH. POST can accept data of any length, up into the megabytes, though this is not very common yet.

> **CAUTION**
> While the GET METHOD is simpler for CGI scripts to handle, it limits the amount of data that can be sent, usually to slightly less than one kilobyte. If there is any chance that your form will generate more data than that, you should use the POST METHOD.

Parsing

After your CGI script has read the submitted data, it must parse it to pull out each NAME and VALUE that was sent from the form.

When a user clicks the SUBMIT button on a form, Netscape gathers all the user's choices and strings them together in NAME=VALUE pairs, each separated by an ampersand character.

```
<FORM ACTION="/cgi-bin/form.sh" METHOD="POST">
<INPUT TYPE="TEXT" NAME="first">
<INPUT TYPE="TEXT" NAME="last">
<INPUT TYPE="SUBMIT">
</FORM>
```

This code snippet, if edited and submitted by Curly Howard, could produce the following data waiting on a CGI scripts stdin:

```
first=Curly&last=Howard
```

For your CGI script to actually use this information, it first must search for each ampersand to get each NAME/VALUE pair, then split the pair at the equal sign.

Encoding

There is more to getting the data a user enters into a form than simply reading and parsing it. The submission is encoded to protect it from 7-bit network layers that might silently strip significant bits from the data, damaging it in the process.

> **CAUTION**
>
> You should be careful not to confuse encoding with encryption. When data is submitted from a normal form, it is encoded simply to protect the integrity of the data while it travels over the network. This does not prevent it from being discovered, and decoded, by prying eyes.

The encoding format used when Netscape submits a form to a CGI script is determined by the ENCTYPE of the FORM, by default the MIME content type "application/www-x-form-urlencoded." This encoding format simply replaces spaces with the plus character and translates any other possibly troublesome character (control characters, the ampersand and equals sign, some punctuation, and so on) to a percent sign followed by its hexadecimal equivalent. So, using "application/www-x-form-urlencoded"-style encoding, the string

```
Here I am!
```

becomes

```
Here+I+am%21
```

After your script has read the submitted data, parsed it into NAME and VALUEs, it must finally decode it into the actual data that the user entered into the form. Then it is ready to use.

Protecting Yourself and Your Users

While programming CGI scripts and their forms is fun, the following are several things you should keep in mind—to protect yourself and your users.

■ Elegantly handle the submission of an empty form—If a user just presses the SUBMIT button without entering any information into your form, what does your CGI script do? A well-written program handles this situation gracefully, without even trying to process the submission.

When you receive an empty request, you should either return an error telling the user what he did wrong or—even better—return the form that needs to be filled out. That way, as with the guestbook example, a single CGI script can both request and process the data, guaranteeing that both situations are handled. This is also handy for the first time the URL is jumped to, when the CGI script automatically presents the form to request data.

■ Always be careful about trusting the data sent to you—There are people out on the Web who would love nothing more than to cause you trouble. Purely out of a sense of vindictiveness, they will try to make your life as hard as it can be. Your CGI scripts need to take this into account.

For example, cleverly written queries can be used to gain privileges on your server that you never intended to grant. One common trick involves sending a shell command appended to some piece of requested data, so that when the CGI program uses that piece of data in an external command, the "piggy-back" command is executed as well.

Imagine a user entering curly@stooges.com;rm -rf / into a form. If you know UNIX, you'll recognize rm -rf / as the command that will delete everything on the computer. A badly written CGI script might simply add "finger" to the front of the request and execute it as a shell command, causing finger curly@stooges.com to be executed first, followed by rm -rf /.

Or, even worse, an unfriendly user could enter curly@stooges.com;cat '+ +' > ~/.rhosts and give the world login access to your Web server—the cat '+ +' > ~/.rhosts command removes password protection from a UNIX account.

■ Be mindful that your users might not have a secure connection, and warn them if you are requesting sensitive data—while both the Netscape Navigator and Commerce Server allow secure communication, most browsers don't; and there's no guarantee that the people who use your forms and run your CGI scripts will be using Netscape. At the very least, you should be wary of requesting sensitive data—bank account numbers, passwords—and, if you must, explicitly warn the user of the possibility (no matter how remote) of the data being sniffed.

Part

IV

Ch

25

Using Secure Forms

To ensure the security of any data submitted from a form, you must use Netscape's "secure HTTP" URL type, https.

If you know that a form will be sending data to a CGI script running on a Netscape Commerce Server, you simply need to change the "http" that starts the FORM's ACTION URL to "https" and the data will be encrypted and indecipherable to anybody "sniffing" the network. For example,

http://www.megaco.com/order.sh

becomes

https://www.megaco.com/order.sh

Any transactions made with the second URL are completely secure—the little key icon in the lower-left corner of the Navigator has become whole (see fig. 25.19). No other changes are needed, either to your form or CGI script.

 T I P Remember, https only works with Netscape's Commerce Server!

▶ For more information on these security features mentioned in this chapter as well as on other security features like VeriSign personal certificates and Secure Sockets Layer (SSL) 3.0, **see** chapter 5 "Forms and Transaction Security" **p. 111**

FIG. 25.19
When operating securely, Netscape makes the key icon whole.

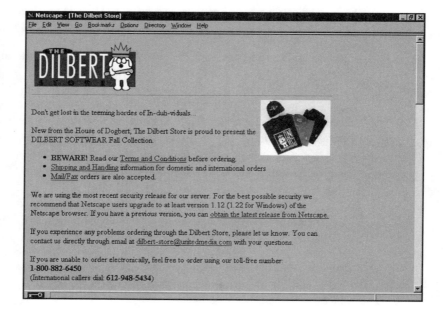

Using the Public Domain

Form and CGI programming can be frustrating in the beginning. There are many rules to follow, most of which can be obscure or complex. Even getting a simple script up and running can be a chore.

One of the best ways to get over these first few hurdles and start CGI programming is to look at existing code. By reviewing (or simply using) already existing CGI scripts, you can not only save yourself a lot of time, but teach yourself new techniques.

Existing code almost always makes a good base to expand from. Instead of implementing a new script from scratch, an older program can often be expanded (or shrunk) to suit your needs. The earlier "guestbook" program, for example, could be modified to automatically add the name of the computer the user is connecting from, if that's what you wanted your guestbook to do.

Often rivaling the abilities of commercial offerings, many public domain CGI programs exist, free for the taking. Even if these scripts are too general for your specific needs, they can be mined for techniques and methods that you can then use in your own programs.

Also, experienced CGI programmers are almost always happy to share their code and talents with you. They've probably already solved any problem you might have and can save you hours of frustration with a word or a clue. Just ask.

And be sure to return the favor when you become an expert!

Available Resources

You can find many public domain CGI references and scripts on the Web itself. Good places to begin looking are:

> **http://www.yahoo.com/Computers_and_Internet/Internet/World_Wide_Web/Programming/CGI**
>
> **ftp://ftp.ncsa.uiuc.edu/Web/httpd/Unix/ncsa_https/cgi**
>
> **news:comp.infosystems.www.authoring.cgi**

Because every CGI program that receives data from a form must go through the bothersome decoding and parsing steps to get the information the user entered, common libraries have been created to handle the trouble for you. It is much, much easier to use this existing code than to go to the trouble of writing your own decoding and parsing routines, as these existing libraries come tested and are free.

> **ftp://ftp.ncsa.uiuc.edu/Web/httpd/Unix/ncsa_httpd/cgi/cgi-lib.pl.Z** (for Perl)
>
> **ftp://ftp.ncsa.uiuc.edu/Web/httpd/Unix/ncsa_httpd/cgi/ncsa_default.tar.Z**
> (for C)

If you're adventurous (or you want to use an ENCTYPE other than "application/x-www-form-urlencoded," which all of these libraries are written for), you can try writing your own routines, but there really is no reason to—these work great! ●

Part
IV

Ch

25

Building World Class Web Sites and Servers for Netscape

## CHAPTER 26

LiveWire

Netscape Communications Corporation has created a professional development environment for authoring, customizing and managing online applications for enterprise networks and the Internet. With LiveWire, you can easily develop and maintain next-generation online application systems. This chapter will briefly acquaint you with Netscape's LiveWire visual development environment and will illustrate the new level of interactivity that LiveWire brings to developers for integrating live online information.

In this chapter:

- Why the need for LiveWire?
- LiveWire requirements and platform compatibility
- What is the LiveWire visual development environment?
- How LiveWire and Java are related
- How LiveWire Pro works with Informix ■

What Is LiveWire?

Netscape Communications Corporation first introduced LiveWire in September of 1995. The product was released in the second quarter of 1996. LiveWire was created to enable developers to easily construct and maintain online applications through a simple point-and-click, drag-and-drop visual environment.

Experienced Web page developers understand how difficult and time consuming it is to create and maintain Web sites with various links, Web pages, and graphics. A Web page can contain numerous links to other Web pages and data files, which then can link to many more pages and files. When making modifications to a Web site, many links end up not being updated correctly. Designing and maintaining a Web site is a very formidable project. Server administrators can modify URLs (Universal Resource Locators) without notification to the Web page developer. It is with this in mind that Netscape has developed LiveWire and LiveWire Pro, a visual development tool that easily modifies Web sites with the aforementioned drag-and-drop feature.

While Netscape Navigator Gold 3.0 allows users to develop and edit JavaScript language scripts, LiveWire allows JavaScript programs to be installed, executed, and maintained on Netscape servers. In addition, LiveWire Pro provides for JavaScript interconnectivity to most standard relational databases such as Microsoft, Sybase, Oracle, and Informix for easy information management. With LiveWire Pro, developers can devise applications that allow Netscape Navigator users to navigate, revise, and search relational databases.

The platforms mentioned below are the only ones currently supported by the current LiveWire release. See Table 26.1 for platform processor requirements.

Intel (x86) and UNIX based:

- Windows NT

    Version 3.51 or higher allows for full utilization of the LiveWire visual development environment.

- Windows 95

    As yet, Netscape has not developed a server for Windows 95 scripting language. The compiler and Application Manager are not functional under this platform; however, the web site can be brought under management control with LiveWire's Site Manager.

- Sun SPARC

    Solaris 2.4 and 2.5 allow for full utilization of the LiveWire visual development environment.

- Silicon Graphics

    IRIS 5.3 and 6.2 allow for full utilization of the LiveWire visual development environment.

Table 26.1 displays LiveWire platform processor requirements.

Table 26.1   LiveWire—Processor Requirements

Platform/Processor/ Disk Space/ Memory Requirements	Minimum/(Recommended)
LiveWire:	
Windows 95/486/10MB	12MB/(16MB)
Windows NT/486/10MB	12MB/(16MB)
UNIX/10MB	12MB/(16MB)
LiveWire Pro:	
Windows 95/486/50MB	16MB/(32MB)
Windows NT/486/85MB	16MB/(24MB)
UNIX/85MB	16MB/(24MB)

Supported languages

- U.S. English
- French
- German
- Japanese

There are many common uses and advantages with Netscape's LiveWire. Corporate networks and Intranets share information with employees as well as customers and vendors. Many large MIS departments are providing user interface and database interconnectivity by developing and deploying applications that can be shared among their corporate network. Applications can be created that increase the functionality of company departments such as payroll, human resources, order inventory, as well as business and finance departments.

Across company Intranets, Web users can easily manage and share projects and interactive documents, including spreadsheets, charts, and graphs, over the company Web. LiveWire lets developers build applications that tie HTML pages together, including JavaScript programs, embedded HTML documents, as well as database applications. It becomes easier to create and manage company information and data collection through this LiveWire development environment.

Downloading and Installing LiveWire

Currently, there is no Netscape server for Windows 95. If you are running Windows 95, you can access Netscape Navigator Gold and the LiveWire Site Manager only.

Part
V

Ch
26

Configuring LiveWire

There are four important configuration recommendations to consider before you install LiveWire. First, you need to decide where you plan to locate your development environment. Development done on the production server will considerably slow down server resources.

Second is the development server. This is for running LiveWire applications that are still under the development process. This is where you should install your Netscape Navigator and LiveWire programs. You would use this platform for all your Web authoring and script compiling.

Third is the deployment server. Users deploy finished applications from this server.

Lastly, if you plan on accessing a database server, you must install the client software for the database on your database server, as well as on both your deployment and development servers. This database server, however, can be on the same platforms as the development server or on another server entirely.

Steps to follow for downloading and installing LiveWire:

Windows NT and Windows 95

1. If you plan on using Netscape Navigator Gold, it must be installed first before LiveWire.

   ▶ For information on installing, **see** appendix B, "Loading and Configuring Netscape,"
   p. 749

2. LiveWire currently works with Netscape FastTrack and Netscape Enterprise 2.0 servers. You must run the server's setup.exe and install before you install LiveWire.

3. Netscape's LiveWire is located at Netscape's pub/livewire/ directory at their FTP mirror sites (ftp2.netscape.com - ftp20.netscape.com). Soon you should be able to download this program, l32e10b3.exe from Netscape's home page at **http://home.netscape.com/**.

4. Download the file l32e10b3.exe to a temp directory. It is a self-extracting file that takes you into LiveWire's setup installation wizard. You will be prompted through the installation (see fig. 26.1).

N O T E Documentation is provided in HTML format online in the /doc directory in the LiveWire program folder. The index.html file points to all other documentation, including the release notes. ■

5. After accepting the license agreement, you will be prompted for the cluster you wish to configure. It will default to your current network (see fig. 26.2).

CAUTION

When installing LiveWire on Windows 95, you will receive an error message that your http server could not be found. Just click "OK" and LiveWire will continue its installation.

6. The destination directory defaults to \Netscape\Server\. You can browse and select another directory.

FIG. 26.1

The LiveWire
Installation Wizard
screen

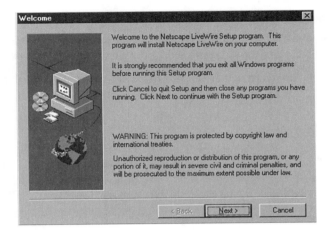

7. LiveWire finishes its installation by copying its files to the destination directory that you selected in step 6.

8. To run database applications, you need to install the Informix software. See the section on How LiveWire Pro Works with Informix? | Installing Informix Server | Installing Informix Client.

FIG. 26.2

The Cluster
Configuration screen

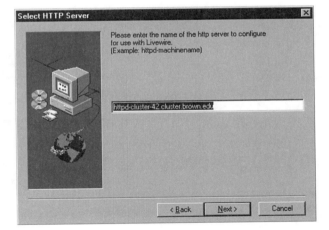

TROUBLESHOOTING

What is absolutely necessary in terms of internet connection, to run LiveWire, along with Navigator Gold? You must have direct Internet connection. There are three requirements that must be met: a direct Ethernet connection, or a dial-up SLIP or PPP account from an Internet service provider; TCP/IP stack; and Netscape Navigator Gold and LiveWire software.

Part
V

Ch
26

Solaris

1. From the FTP site, download the file lw-b3-export.sparc-sun-solaris5.4.tar.
2. Un-tar this file to create installation files in the subdirectory "lw."
3. Run setup from the "lw" directory. This will run the LiveWire installation script. You will be prompted to enter the server directory. Enter your server's top-level directory.
4. Add the following line to magnus.conf:

```
KeepAliveTimeOut 0
```

> **CAUTION**
>
> You can not use the server administration tool to change the server setting. You must add "KeepAliveTimeOut 0" to your magnus.conf file manually.

5. Restart your Netscape server before you run LiveWire's Site Manager or Application Manager from the Navigator.

N O T E   To run the LiveWire compiler from another directory, add <server_rootdir>/livewire/bin to your PATH variable. ■

IRIX

1. From the FTP site, download the file lw-b3-export.mips-sgi-irix5.3.tar.
2. Follow Solaris steps 2-5 above.

 T I P   For LiveWire to run on Windows NT and UNIX systems, remember to restart the server after running LiveWire's installation. This does not apply to Windows 95, where there is no Netscape server yet available.

The LiveWire Visual Development Environment

The LiveWire visual development environment consists of:

- ■ Netscape Navigator Gold
- ■ LiveWire Site Manager
- ■ LiveWire JavaScript Compiler
- ■ LiveWire Database Connectivity Library

In addition, LiveWire Pro includes:

- ■ Informix OnLine Workgroup high-performance SQL database
- ■ Crystal Software's Crystal Reports Professional Version 4.5 (for Windows NT only)

Netscape Navigator Gold is a next-generation software tool that allows users to simplify the designing and modification of live online documents. In a WYSIWYG (what-you-see-is-what-you-get) environment, developers can devise advanced page content, including Live Objects.

Version 3.0 is only being distributed as a 32-bit window program. To run the 32-bit Navigator, you need to have a 32-bit TCP/IP stack. Both Windows NT and Windows 95 have 32-bit TCP/IP stacks that you can set up.

N O T E To use LiveWire along with Navigator Gold, you must install Navigator Gold first, and then you can install and setup LiveWire. ■

LiveWire Site Manager is a visual point-and-click, drag-and-drop visual development tool. Developers can design and depict their Web sites in graphical form. Site Manager will preserve and update any links that have been changed, due to creating, editing, or deleting any Web pages. You can also actually view your hypertext links between pages, and modify them simply by the point-and-click use of a mouse. You can create site indices and can verify links to see if they are still active.

In Windows NT, to start Site Manager, double-click the Site Manager icon in the LiveWire program group; single-click in a UNIX environment. In Windows 95, double-click the file sitemgr.exe in the LiveWire folder (see fig. 26.3).

LiveWire JavaScript Compiler lets users readily produce live applications. This simplified scripting language was based on Java—a language that is very much like C/C++. However, LiveScript is simpler and is useful for developing small scripts and programs when building server and client applications.

▶ **See** chapter 29, "Java for C++ Programmers," **p. 675** and chapter 30, "JavaScript," **p. 697**

LiveWire Database Connectivity Library lets developers create server-side applications that allow Web clients to browse and modify relational databases (Informix, Oracle, Sybase, and Illustra) on enterprise networks and across the Internet.

Part
V

Ch
26

FIG. 26.3
LiveWire Site Manager window

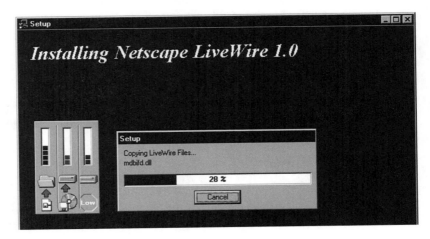

Informix OnLine Workgroup Database is a developer version that is licensed for one Web server with no limit on the number of users. It is designed for quick and easy configuration with full support for multiprocessor and parallel systems. Figure 26.4 displays a sample application.

FIG. 26.4

Sample Database
Application screen

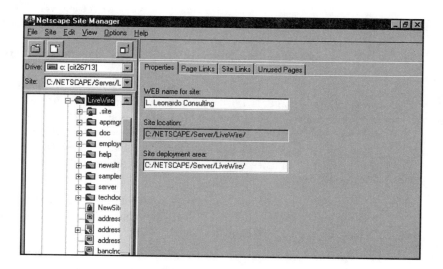

Crystal Reports Professional Version 4.5 runs on Windows NT LiveWire Pro version only and utilizes a visual graphic interface. It comes with predefined form templates that allow for complete customization including cross tabulation and complex graphs.

LiveWire Site Manager Terminology

LiveWire's visual development environment allows for a graphical panorama appearance and transformation of a Web site. All links and references to pages and files are automatically updated as changes are made to a site. Existing sites can be imported into LiveWire's environment and managed locally for additional modifying. See below for LiveWire Site Manager terminology as well as table 26.2 on LiveWire's attributes and what they do.

- External Target—A document that is on another site
- Invalid Link—A link that the site manager does not find
- Link—A hypertext pointer to a document, graphics file, or sound file

- Pagemark—A fixed location in a document
- Site—An assortment of files on a World Wide Web server that are linked together and have the same root directory
- Target—A file referenced by a hyperlink
- Unreachable Target—A file not referenced by a hyperlink

Table 26.2 displays the many LiveWire attributes available.

Table 26.2   LiveWire Attributes—What LiveWire Can Do

LiveWire Development	Function
Visual Site Management	Can view and modify an entire Web site in graphical format
Automatic Link Reorganization	When modifications are made within a Web site, automatically updates all corresponding links
External Link Checker	Ascertains if external links are still active
Wizards and Templates	Directions and forms for easy Web page creation
Document Conversion Support	Support for many standard formats like MS Word, FrameMaker, and Novell WordPerfect
Image Conversion Support	Support for many standard formats like PCX, BMP, TIFF, and PICT
Runtime/Interpreter	For executing scripting language
Installation and Update	Can install and update Web pages from any site
Java Compatibility	Easy to use with little training; similar to Visual Basic
Augments Multiple Languages	Enhances or replaces multiple-scripting languages (like CGI) with Java-compatible scripting language (LiveScript)
Compiler	Creates executable script code
Multiple-User Management	Manages client information across multiple transactions

Part

V

Ch

26

Creating and Managing a Web Site

If you have an existing Web site (i.e., /NET), you must first bring it under management control of the Site Manager. This, of course, is what lets you manage hyperlinks in documents on that site. External links can also be assessed to determine their position.

1. Start LiveWire's Site Manager by double-clicking sitemgr.exe in your LiveWire directory. Click the top-level directory that contains your main index.html file. In figure 26.5, I selected the /NET folder.

FIG. 26.5

Site / Manage screen

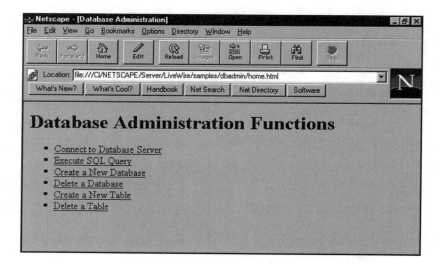

2. Select Manage from the Site menu. If the directory is on a remote server, just enter the URL in the Site box also shown in figure 26.5. For example, you could enter **http://www.remote.com/directory**. Answer "Yes" to the warning message to begin this management process.

3. Give your site a name.

4. LiveWire Site Manager will import all HTML files, scripts, and any multimedia files from the top-level directory down to all subdirectories. All hyperlinks to these files are included as well.

Creating a New Web Site

Several different site types and templates are included with LiveWire's Site Manager.

1. From the Site menu, select New and choose "Create a new site from a template" (see fig. 26.6).

FIG. 26.6

Creating a New Site
Screen

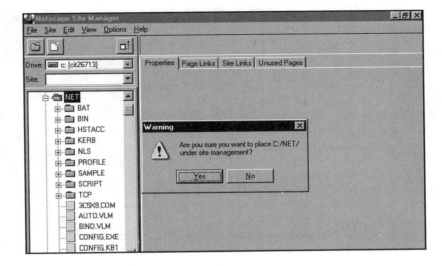

2. Select the directory which is the top-level containing the main index.html file (see fig. 26.7).

FIG. 26.7

Working Directory
screen

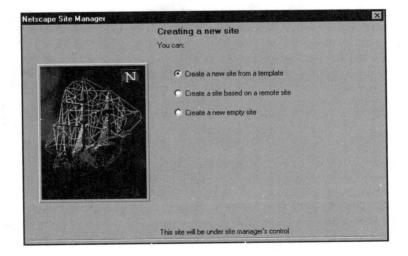

3. Choose the kind of site type, from one of several, that you wish to create (see fig. 26.8).

4. Choose your site template you wish to create (see fig. 26.9).

5. After you finish entering all the site information, the Site Manager creates and loads your customized Web site.

Part

V

Ch

26

FIG. 26.8

Kind of Site Type screen

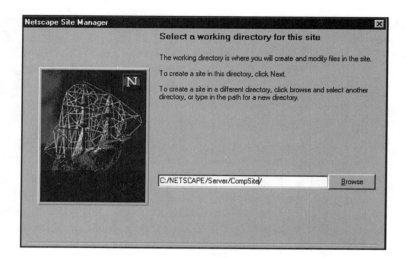

FIG. 26.9

Site Template screen

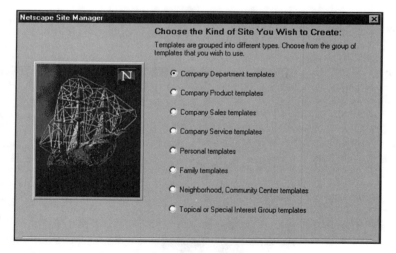

By choosing Open from the Site menu and selecting a .site file, Site Manager will open and load that file. The site is shown in directory format from top-level down. See Site Links in figure 26.10.

Clicking any "+" shown to the left of a particular folder will display the contents of that folder. You will also find a target icon displayed in files that contain internal links. Click the file that you want to display all the internal targets. Again, see figure 26.10. You can choose to display page links as well (see fig. 26.11).

FIG. 26.10
Site Manager—Site
Links screen

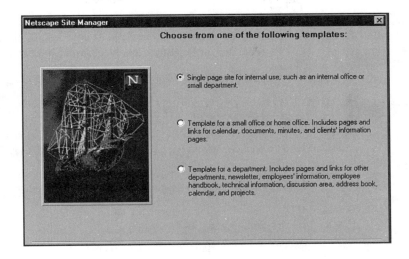

FIG. 26.11
Site Manager—Page
Links screen

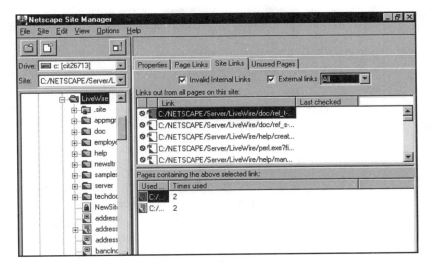

There are shortcut buttons you can use on selected directories and documents. Click a directory or document you wish to select. Click your Right mouse button to bring up a menu of shortcuts. The menu lets you

- rename the directory or file
- delete the directory or file
- launch the Navigator or Navigator Gold browser to edit a file.

You can also move files within a site by using the "drag-n-drop" feature. To do this, select a file, keep the mouse button depressed, and drag the file to its new desired directory (or folder). Whether moving a file, renaming, or deleting a file, LiveWire's Site Manager will update all hyperlinks to that file.

Developing Applications with LiveWire

The LiveWire Application Manager enables you to create LiveWire applications. You create, run, modify, and delete applications on your server all from within the LiveWire Application Manager.

A LiveWire application can contain three types of source files:

- Standard HTML—Has the file extensions of either .html or .htm
- Script embedded HTML—Has the file extensions of either .html or .htm
- JavaScript functions only—Has the file extension of .ls

An executable file with a .web extension is created when the files are compiled by LiveWire. This .web application should be installed on the Netscape server that has the LiveWire run-time files. The application is then run by accessing its URL **http://your_server.domain/ appmgr/home.html** from the Netscape Navigator where <your_server.domain> is your server and domain names (see fig. 26.12).

To delete or modify an existing application, click "Modify" or "Delete" at the listed application. Click "Restart" and then click the URL prefix to re-run an application. To create a new application, click "Add New LiveWire Application."

LiveWire comes with some sample applications. One sample application is "Hello World." To run this application, do the following:

1. Start the Application Manager by loading from your Navigator: **http:// your_server.domain/appmgr/home.html**.
2. From the Application Manager window, click Restart next to the application "/livewire/samples/world/hello.web."
3. Next click URL Prefix /world (see fig. 26.13).

This application provides a form to enter your name and displays your IP address, how many times you have accessed this page, and how many times the page has been accessed by all.

1. Type in your name and click "Enter." Now you will see the number of times and access numbers incremented by "1."

2. Type in another name and click "Enter." Now you will see the "Last time you were previous name" and now "This time you are current name," and notice the numbers are incremented again.

FIG. 26.12

LiveWire Application Manager window

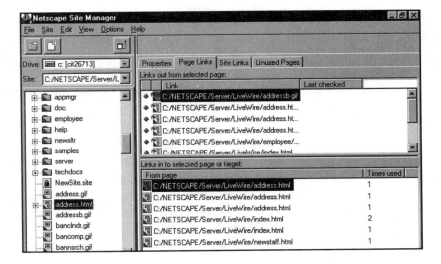

FIG. 26.13

Hello World window

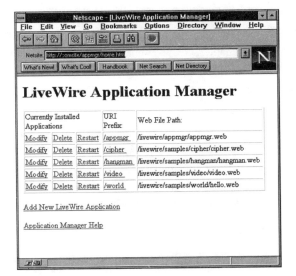

Now we are going to change this sample form. Use any text editor you prefer to edit this file.

1. Change the title "Hello World" to a title of your choice.
2. Move "This time you are," so that it appears before "Last time you were."
3. Save changes and exit the text editor.

A little further along in this chapter, we will rebuild the Hello World application using LiveWire Site Manager. You will then see the changes you have made to the application (see fig. 26.12).

1. Start the Application Manager by loading from your Navigator: **http://your_server.domain/appmgr/home.html**.
2. To add a new application, choose "Add New LiveWire Application" (see fig. 26.14).
3. Enter the URL prefix for the application. If you're creating a "Hello Galaxy" application then the prefix could be /world. Of course, you would have already created galaxy.html.
4. Enter an Object file path. If your root directory is /livewire, then your path would be /livewire/samples/world/galaxy.html.
6. Enter a default URL for the application. If a user does not identify the page, then a default URL could be index.html.
7. Enter the initial URL for the application. This is the URL address that is run from the Application Manager.
8. Enter the client context mode (i.e., client-URL, server-IP, server-URL).
9. Exit the Netscape Navigator.

Again, further along in the chapter, you will build the new Galaxy.html with LiveWire Site Manager. Then the "Hello Galaxy" application will be ready to run.

To build applications using the Site Manager:

1. Start the Site Manager by double-clicking the Site Manager icon.
2. Open the "Hello World" site by choosing Open from the Site menu and select this html file from the livewire\samples directory.
3. Rebuild this application by choosing Build Now from the Make menu (see fig. 26.14).
4. Exit the Site Manager and load this URL from your Navigator: http://your_server.domain/world/restart where <your_server.domain> is your server and domain names. You could also start the Application Manager and select restart next to the "Hello World" application.
5. To see the changes you made previously, run the applicaton by loading the URL http://your_server.domain/world/hello.html or from the Application Manager, click the URL's prefix.

Hooray, you should now be able to see the changes you made to the application. You can also build the new application that we created called "Hello Galaxy." Follow steps 1-5 listed previously, except remember the site is "Hello Galaxy," and the application URL is http://your_server.domain/world/galaxy.html.

FIG. 26.14

LiveWire Site Manager / Build Now screen

Part

V

Ch

26

TROUBLESHOOTING

I'm sure I'm using the correct URLs and I ran the external link checker; however, users are being told by the server that the pages aren't found. What's wrong? Check the permissions on the page. The page must be readable by the user who the server is running as. A sure way to fix this problem would be to set the file as world-readable.

LiveWire also allows for the maintenance of data across multiple transactions by using predefined objects (see table 26.3).

Table 26.3 displays LiveWire's predefined objects.

Table 26.3   LiveWire's Predefined Objects

Object	Contains
Request	Data particular to a transaction and changes with each new request of the client
Client	Data particular to a client and changes with each unique client
Project	Data for the whole application and can be shared among several clients
Server	Global data for the whole server and can be shared among several applications and clients

Debugging and Executing an Application

You can trace how a LiveWire application executes by running the /trace URL. If you are running "Hello World" at http://your_server.domain/world, you can run the trace by loading http://your_server.domain/world/trace (see fig. 26.15).

FIG. 26.15

Netscape-Trace
Information screen

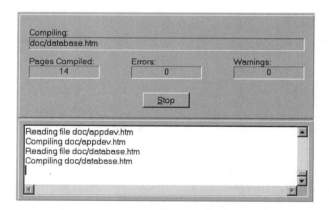

By tracing an application, object variables and properties are exhibited as debug functions.

Again, you would run an application by loading the application URL in your Netscape Navigator browser. When an application runs, LiveWire performs up to eight steps in processing each hyperlink request (see table 26.4).

Table 26.4 displays LiveWire's processing routine.

Table 26.4   LiveWire's Processing Routine

Routine	Function
Server authorization	Performs authorization based on how the server was installed and configured
Client new request object	Initializes all built-in client requests (i.e., IP address)
Create/Restore client object	Locates pre-existing client object or creates a new one
Save client object properties	Saves all client object properties before page output
Output HTML	For static pages, the server transfers the HTML Web page and LiveWire performs the application to create the HTML to the client for dynamic pages
Save/destroy client object	LiveWire saves or destroys the client object
Destroy request object	LiveWire destroys the request object
Server data logging	The server performs data logging as part of the initial server installation and configuration

N O T E   Since LiveWire saves client object properties before outputting the Web page, any
JavaScript statements that require client object properties should come before any
`print()` statements. ▪

JavaScript Enhancements

Generating HTML with the `print()` function and executing a JavaScript statement are the two
ways you would use JavaScript embedded HTML.

You can embed JavaScript into an HTML file in two ways: the <server> tag or by using
back quotes (').

This tag is similar to a standard HTML tag. Each JavaScript statement is preceded by a
<server> tag and then followed by a </server> tag. Do not use a <server> tag
inside another HTML tag.

You can use JavaScript embedded in HTML two ways: to generate HTML with the `print()`
function and to execute a JavaScript statement. An example of using the `print()` function is
below:

```
&lt;P&gt; Username logged on
&lt;server&gt;print(new.username);
old.username=new.username;&lt;/server&gt;
```

You use back quotes (') to enclose JavaScript expressions and to replace an HTML name or value attribute. An example of using back quotes (') follows:

```
&lt;img src='"images/comp" + employee.num + ".gif"'&gt;
```

This line generates a picture or image of a company employee based on their employee number. The back quote encloses the JavaScript expression and concatenates the string "images/comp" with the numeric value of employee.num and the ".gif." The final result would show a HTML statement such as this:

```
&lt;img src="images/comp().gif"&gt;
```

or

```
&lt;img src="images/comp(1).gif"&gt;
```

JavaScript Dynamic Images and Animations

Netscape Navigator 3.0 has the ability to change images right from within an HTML document. This is done without reloading that HTML. Creating a dynamic image is simple. First, note the image number you wish to change in brackets, and second, choose the dynamic .gif such as this to fade an image:

```
document.images[1].src = "fade.gif";
```

The image can dynamically fade and then reappear again using simple if/then statements such as this:

```
which_one = 0;
                        function change()
                        {
                                if (which_one == 0)
                                {
                                document.images[1].src = "fade.gif;
                                        which_one = 1;
                                }
                                else
                                {
                                document.images[1].src = "plain.gif";
                                                which_one = 0;
                                }
                        }
```

You create animated images in much the same way; however, you need to create a sequence of images. Once you have created all your images to be used in the animation you will need to create those variables and functions that will then animate your images. With the example below, the first line chooses the delay rate of the animation (.1 second). The second line is again the image number in brackets.

```
delay = 100
imagenumber = 1;
loadnumber = 1;
ignore = 0;
```

You now need to create two functions that will animate the image and control the frame rate. The first function below switches the sequence of the images. "Golf," for example, refers to all the images relating to a golfer swinging his club as the image number increases by ten frames.

```
function Switch ()
{
name = "golf" + imagenumber;
document.images[1].src = name + ".gif";
imagenumber++;
        if (imagenumber > 10)
        {
        imagenumber = 1;
        }
}
```

To set the frame delay rate for the animation

```
function animate()
{
Switch();
setTimeout ("animate()", delay);
}
```

To run the animation, the images must be loaded (repeats every four seconds)

```
function loadimages()
{
        if (ignore == 0)
        {
        loadname = "golf" + loadnumber;
        document.images[1].src = loadnmae + ".gif";
        loadnumber++;
                if (loadnumber >10)
                {
                ignore = 1;
                setTimeout ("animate()", 4000;
                }
        }
}
function load()
{
loadimages();
setTimeout ("load()", 4000);
}
```

Of course, if you don't golf, any images can be animated by following, in order, all the source code in the above section.

▶ For information on JavaScript Objects, **see** chapter 28, "Sun's Java and the Netscape Browser," **p. 655**

▶ For information on JavaScript, **see** chapter 30, "JavaScript," **p. 697**

Part
V

Ch

26

Inline Plug-Ins

Plug-ins are software applications that impart Netscape Navigator with certain capabilities. Some enable users to create and view dynamic images quickly and easily. While others, more commonly, allow for playing audio and video clips from within the Navigator. Current plug-ins that are available today incorporate Audio and Video, 3D and Animation, Image Viewers and Presentations, as well as Business and Utility programs. Most plug-ins are available across many platforms such as Windows 95, Windows NT, Windows 3.1 and the Macintosh.

Plug-ins enhance Netscape's Navigator in such a way as to build their browser into an Internet "platform." This platform has moved the Web industry into the next generation. Netscape's Navigator Java classes enable JavaScript and applets, in addition to inline plug-ins, to be accessible in the their browser environment. Never before has communication been more reciprocated through the use of interactive HTML Web pages. For inline plug-in product information, see Netscape's product page at **http://home.netscape.com/comprod/products/navigator/version_2.0 /plugins/index.html**.

▶ For information on inline plug-ins, **see** chapter 9, "Netscape Browser Plug-Ins," **p. 219**.

How LiveWire and Java Are Related

As visual application development tools, LiveWire and LiveWire Pro were created for the swift design and deployment of Java-compatible scripting language. Netscape LiveWire permits the installation, output, and operation of JavaScript programs on Netscape servers along enterprise networks and the Internet.

Netscape's latest Live Objects technology links their Navigator to external Java applets. You can jump from one media viewer program to another across the Web and view your document perfectly.

Jointly created by Netscape and Sun, this technology enables developers to devise and run interactive hypermedia content and Live Objects which are intrinsic to their applications. Netscape's support for Java and JavaScript in client and server products, along with their developmental tools, made this joint effort an actuality.

Netscape's incorporating support for Java and JavaScript into their Netscape products will ensure a more unified client-server-development tool environment. Subsequently, through the notability of both Java and Netscape LiveWire, an interactive Internet has moved past the personal computer into the forefront of technology.

▶ **See** chapter 28, "Sun's Java and the Netscape Browser," **p. 655**; chapter 29, "Java for C++ Programmers," **p. 675**; and chapter 30, "JavaScript," **p. 697**.

How LiveWire Pro Works with Informix

As of this writing, Netscape Communications Corporation and Informix Database, Inc. announced on February 6, 1996 a joint venture that will allow Informix to combine their relational database and developmental tools with Netscape's client, server, and visual development environment. This leading technology will enable developers to manage information that reaches across global enterprises.

Informix's relational database technology is included as part of Netscape LiveWire Pro, as well as in Netscape Internet Applications(TM). Users can now manage elaborate and extensive amounts of data currently found in Web applications across the Internet. Applications can be developed that allow users to browse, modify, and search SQL databases from the Netscape Navigator client on a network and across the Internet.

When utilizing the LiveWire visual development environment, you only need to install the Informix software if you want to create database applications for the Web. You must install both the server and the client. The server can be installed on the same machine that is running LiveWire or any other machine that is part of the network. The client should only be installed on the same machine that is running LiveWire.

Installing Informix Server

Informix OnLine-Workgroup Database is constructed for swift configuration and easy maintenance. It provides multi and parallel processing system support and is entirely in accordance with Informix's database architecture. The database is bundled with LiveWire Pro. It is licensed as a single developer copy with a limitless number of users. If you want to develop database applications, you must install Informix. You install the client on the machine that is running LiveWire. The server can be installed on the same machine or on a different machine entirely.

Windows NT (not compatible with Windows 95):

1. Create a temp directory on your server and download the file informix.zip from the NT/Informix directory.

2. Unzip the file. This will create a setup.exe file.

3. Run setup.exe to install the Informix server. You must install the Informix server on an NTFS disk partition.

4. Enter the following:

   - Server license serial number: AAB#A287805

   - Key: TSJLJV

5. Click the check box for "Enable Role Separation" to DE-SELECT (disable) this option.

6. Stop your Netscape server.

7. By default, the Netscape HTTPD service runs as a system service. To use Informix, you must change the HTTPD service to run as a user service. To do this, in Control Panel | Services, select the "Netscape Httpd-80" service and select "Startup." In the dialog box that appears, choose "Log On As - This Account," and enter your account name. Make sure you are currently logged on to NT under that user name.

8. Stop and restart your Netscape server.

CAUTION

The Informix database server must be installed on a disk with an NTFS partition. The client can be installed on either an NTFS or FAT partition.

UNIX   The first four steps below will normally require assistance from your system adminis-trator. About 40MB of disk space and 8MB of shared memory is required to install Informix.

1. Your system configuration file (/etc/system) should include the following minimum values:

    ```
    set enable_sm_wa = 1
    set shmsys:shminfo_shmmax=16777216
    set semsys:seminfo_semmap=64
    set semsys:seminfo_semmni=4096
    set semsys:seminfo_semmns=4096
    set semsys:seminfo_semmnu=4096
    set semsys:seminfo_semume=64
    set shmsys:shminfo_shmmin=100
    set shmsys:shminfo_shmmni=100
    set shmsys:shminfo_shmseg=100
    ```

    Your system administrator should add them to your system and reboot the machine.

2. Add the following entry to /etc/services:

    ```
    online  1535/tcp   # Informix Online 7.10
    ```

    If another entry uses the number 1535, make sure that no one online is using this number.

3. Create an informix group (/etc/group). The suggested group id is 2002, which is what the tar file uses.

4. Create a user Informix (/etc/passwd) with group informix.

    The suggested userid is again 2002. Create the C shell and create the Informix home directory (/usr/informix).

5. Login as user "root" and execute the following steps:

    (a) Set the INFORMIXDIR environment variable to the Informix

    ```
    home directory:
    C shell:
    setenv INFORMIXDIR /usr/informix
    Bourne shell:
    INFORMIXDIR=/usr/informix;export INFORMIXDIR
    ```

    (b) Go to the informix home directory

    ```
    cd $INFORMIXDIR
    ```

    uncompress informix.tar.Z

    tar xvf informix.tar

    (e) rm informix.tar

(f) execute install online (./intallonline)

```
serial number: AAB#A287805
key      : TSJLJV
```

6. Login as user "informix" and do the following:

    (a) Create or modify .cshrc to include:

    ```
    setenv INFORMIXDIR /usr/informix (as explained above)
    setenv INFORMIXSERVER on_test   (or choose name)
    set path=($path $INFORMIXDIR/bin)
    ```

    (b) Make sure these values are set in your environment:

    ```
    source .cshrc
    ```

    execute installdbs (./installdbs). This script performs these statements:

    ```
    mkdir dbs
    touch dbs/rootdbs
    chmod 664 dbs/rootdbs
    ```

    cd to the INFORMIXDIR/etc directory, and modify the

    ```
    onconfig file:
    ROOTPATH: full path of the dbs/rootdbs file, e.g.
    /usr/informix/dbs/rootdbs
    ROOTSIZE: space for databases in KB (at least 20000)
    MSGPATH : fullpath of a file in INFORMIXDIR that will contain server
    messages, e.g. /usr/informix/online.log
    DBSERVERNAME: value of INFORMIXSERVER (e.g. on_test)
    ```

    (e) Modify the sqlhosts file to add an entry with the values:

    ```
    INFORMIXSERVER ontlitcp <machine-name> online
    where INFORMIXSERVER is the value chosen above and <machine-name> is
    the name of your machine. You can obtain this by typing "uname -n"
    at the SunOS prompt, e.g. uname -n bigserver on_test ontlitcp bigserver
    online
    ```

    (f) Then enter the command:

    ```
    oninit -iy
    ```

This will bring up and initialize Informix Online. To bring down the Informix Online server enter:

```
onmode - ky
```

To start up the Informix Online server subsequently type:

```
oninit
```

NOTE Consult the Informix documentation for further information on the Informix Online Server. ■

Part
V

Ch
26

FIG. 26.16
Database Configuration
chart

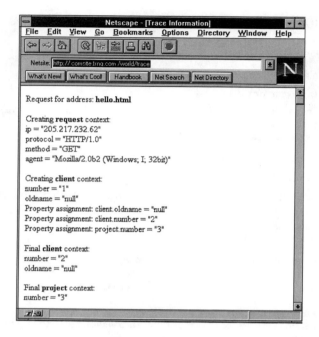

Installing Informix Client

For Windows NT (not compatible with Windows 95) you must install the client on the machine running LiveWire.

1. Create a temp directory and download the file client.zip from the NT/Informix/Client directory.

2. Un-zip the file. This will create a setup.exe file.

3. Run setup.exe to install the Informix client. You may install the client on either an NTFS or a FAT disk partition.

4. When prompted, enter the following:

   - Client license serial number: AAA#M440727

   - Key: RIMAJG

   Configuring the Informix Client

N O T E On the Informix client, you must add <informix_client>\bin to your system PATH, where <informix_client> is your informix root directory.

Now reboot your system from the Control Panel | System application. ▪

Run the Informix Setnet application on the client and enter:

- The name of the Informix server and the InformixDir directory.
- All required information for the server. Choose "Edit Server Information" and enter:
  1. Informix server: <your server name>
  2. Hostname: <your host name>
  3. Username: informix
  4. Servicename: turbo
  5. Protocolname: olsoctcp
  6. Password:
- Choose "Edit NLS Information" and enter:
  1. Client Locale: English
  2. DbNls: 2
  3. Lc_Collate: C

 TIP You should stop and restart your server, after you install the Informix server and client. This should be done through the Control Panel | Services application

LiveWire Visual Development Resources

Professionals working with Informix can check out Dataspace Consulting Informix Resources (see figure 26.18) at: **http://www.dataspace.com.au/index.html**.

You can reach the FAQ (Frequently Asked Questions) site on Informix at: **http://mathcs.emory.edu/pub/informix**. This site also contains Informix Archives.

If you're looking to access an Informix user group, you can reach the Washington DC Area Informix User Group at: **http://www.access.digex.net/~lester/waiug.html**. You can also reach the International Informix Users Group at: **http://www.iiug.org/**.

Of course, you can reach Informix Database, Inc. at their home page **http://www.informix.com/**.

You can go directly to the Netscape Home Page, located at: **http://www.netscape.com/**.

From this site, you can go on to one of many mirrored Netscape ftp sites and download the Netscape Navigator Gold 3.0. The Netscape LiveWire product should be fully released sometime in the second quarter of 1996.

Go directly to Netscape's store at: **http://merchant.netscape.com/netstore/index.html**.

Reach Netscape user groups (NUGgies) at: **http://www.netscape.com/commun/netscape_user_groups.html**.

For help on creating net sites, check out **http://www.netscape.com/assist/net_sites /index.html**.

FIG. 26.17
Dataspace Consulting
Informix Resources Web
site

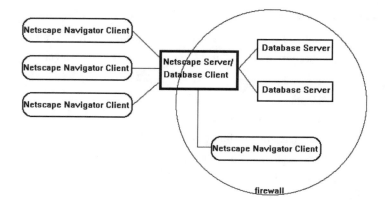

FIG. 26.18
The Netscape Assist
Net_Sites Web page

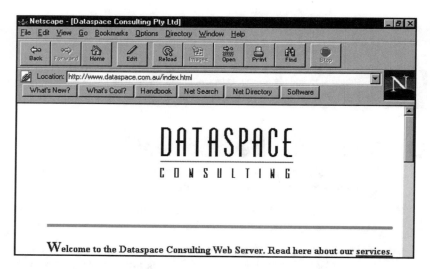

When trying to find reference material on any Netscape product or tool, go to: **http://www.netscape.com/newsref/ref/index.html** or to access documentation, **http://www.netscape.com/newsref/std/index.html**.

Sun Microsystems is available on the Web at: **http://www.sun.com** or for Java information at: **http://java.sun.com/**.

For additional information on Netscape Communications Corporation, send e-mail to info@netscape.com or call 415-937-2555.

Live Wire Bugs

You can report LiveWire bugs with the LiveWire online bug report form located at **http://www1.netscape.com/cgi-bin/auto_bug.cgi**.

You can also send e-mail to livewire@netscape.com and the message will be posted to newsgroup mcom.dev.client_livewire.

To report bugs with the LiveWire Site Manager, send e-mail to sitemgr.feedback@netscape.com.

Part
V

Ch
26

## CHAPTER 27

Testing the Netscape Commerce Server

One of the features that caused Netscape Navigator to make such a big splash when it was first introduced was its capacity to conduct secure transactions over the Internet. For businesses and others who wanted to transact private business using the Internet, this was a major step forward; the introduction of Netscape's secure transaction capabilities led many organizations to finally venture out onto the Net.

The Navigator software is only one half of the security solution created by Netscape. The other half resides with the software that runs the Web site, called the server.

Netscape actually produces several variations of its server products. In this chapter, we'll cover the basics of "test-driving" the Netscape Commerce server, which is used to handle secure transactions.

In this chapter, we discuss:

- Netscape's offer to let you try their server for 60 days without charge
- The technical requirements for setting up a Netscape Commerce server
- How Netscape's Secure Sockets Layer security works

- Getting a copy of the software
- Installing the software
- Basic configuration of your server software
- Setting up security on your server
- How activating security affects the way users see a Web site ■

> **CAUTION**
>
> Obviously, there's more involved in setting up and configuring a Web server than we could possibly hope to cover in one chapter. Our goal here is to provide the basic information that someone (either with a fairly good idea of how Web servers work, or a fairly good book on the subject of setting up Web servers available as a reference) would need to get and try the Commerce server software. This chapter assumes that you have familiarity with either Windows NT or some variant of UNIX at a server management level.
>
> Nevertheless, even if you don't have advanced experience with running NT or UNIX servers, you may find the information on how the Web server interacts with Netscape Navigator to be interesting or at least helpful in understanding how your transactions are protected when you sign on to a secure server.

Have They Got a Deal for You!

Whereas Netscape's Navigator Web browser is a relative bargain for the level of increased functionality it brought to the Web at under $40 for a licensed copy, Netscape's server software is generally seen as a fairly high ticket item—a single copy of the Commerce server generally costs an organization over $2,000 (and that's in addition to what you pay for the machine and the connection to the Internet!).

Because most organizations aren't willing to lay that much money down on a product sight unseen, Netscape has created a way for companies to test out their server software before they purchase it, following the same "shareware" concept they employed to make their Navigator software the de facto standard of Web browsers.

Netscape calls their "try-before-you-buy" offer the Test Drive program. The deal is pretty straightforward; after filling out and submitting an application form to Netscape (which can be done over the Web), you receive an account name and password that can be used to download a copy of the server software.

The copy of the software that you receive is fully functional. Unlike many shareware producers, Netscape does not disable any of the features in their Test Drive version.

Sometime shortly before the two months are over, you are contacted by a member of Netscape's sales staff, who reminds you that if you don't purchase their server software, you need to stop using it when the 60 days are up. Netscape banks on the fact that by the time the 60 days are over, you won't be able to think about parting with their server software, and you'll be much more willing to part with the cash instead.

The only key feature that you don't get through the test drive offer is support from Netscape's technicians. In order to get support for Netscape's server products, you must buy a support contract, and you must have a licensed copy of a Netscape server to purchase the support contract.

Netscape does offer some help facilities for its test drive customers. Netscape has established in-house newsgroups (called Netscape User Groups, or NUGgies) that promote the exchange of information among users of Netsape's products. Many of the questions you may have about the configuration of your system can be answered by participants in these newsgroups.

You can also order a copy of the documentation for the particular type of server you're using. There are two manuals for the Netscape Communications and Commerce servers; there's a Server Administration Guide and a Programmer's Guide for each. Unless a change has been made recently, the only difference between the Communications Server guides and the Commerce Server guides is the cover. Although the documentation is a little thin, you may want to order copies of both the Administration Guide and the Programmer's Guide as a reference.

Test Drives on Most Netscape Servers Available

Netscape's offer is not limited to just their Commerce server software. If you want a more robust regular Web server but don't need the security capabilities of the Commerce server, you might consider trying the Communications server. If you need to set up a secure firewall for a collection of systems, you may want to use the Test Drive offer to try the Netscape Proxy server.

The difference between the Commerce server and the Communications server is that the Commerce server includes programs necessary to do secure transactions and the Communications server software does not. In terms of administration and configuration, the two types of servers are practically identical. A copy of the Commerce server can be used to transmit insecure documents the same way a Communications server would. You are also allowed to run more than one copy of the server software on a machine at a time (provided that your machine is powerful enough to handle it). Therefore, if you needed to transmit both secure and insecure documents from your server, you could run two copies of the Commerce server—one with security turned on and the other with it turned off—rather than buying two different versions of the server software.

Part

V

Ch

27

Requirements for Running a Netscape Commerce Server

In order to be able to run a Netscape Commerce server, you're going to need access to some heavy-duty resources (that is, beyond the scope of your average home user). Before you go to the trouble of downloading the software, let's take a minute to review the minimum requirements for setting up a Commerce server. These requirements can be broken into three main categories: operating system, hardware, and Internet connection.

Operating System Requirements

At the time of this writing, Netscape only produces versions of its server product that run under Windows NT (3.5 or later) and commercial variants of UNIX produced by Digital (OSF/1 2.0), Hewlett-Packard (HP-UX 9.03, 9.04), IBM (AIX 3.2.5, 4.1), Silicon Graphics (IRIX 5.2, 5.3), Sun (Sun OS 4.1.3, Solaris 2.3, 2.4), and Berkeley Systems Design (BSDI 1.1, 2.0). Therefore, a user running Windows 3.1, 3.11, 95, or a Macintosh running some version of the MacOS, won't be able to run this software.

NOTE Not only must you have access to a system running one of these operating systems, you must be able to access this system as a privileged user. (On UNIX-style systems, you will probably need root access.) If you are only one user on a system with multiple users, you may want to ask your system administrator to install a version of the Commerce server for you. System administrators can configure the Netscape server software to give individual users the ability to set up personal Web sites, which can use many of the Netscape server features. For security reasons, however, it is quite likely that your system administrator will prohibit you from using the server's most interactive features, especially those that require running programs.

Windows NT may be more familiar to a novice Webmaster, especially if you have limited knowledge of the UNIX operating system at the administrator level. Choosing NT as your operating system might be the right choice if your organization lacks the in-house knowledge necessary to maintain a UNIX-based system.

Nevertheless, you should be aware that running a Netscape server on a Windows NT system somewhat limits its functionality. Many programmers find that it is much more difficult to get NT to perform the types of variable exchanges most frequently employed in CGI scripts.

For these reasons, if in-house programming and UNIX system administration help is available (or if you are the in-house programming and system administration expertise), you may want to lean towards a UNIX-based system.

NOTE Although Linux is dearly loved by many, there is, at the time of this writing, no port of the Netscape server software for Linux. If you plan to run a Netscape server on a PC, you'll have to use either Windows NT or BSDI.

Hardware Requirements

There are a number of considerations that should go into the selection of the hardware platform for your Netscape Commerce server Web site. The type of system to use, amount of memory, and the kind of connection you have all play important roles—depending upon your objectives for your server.

Intel 386, 486, or Pentium-based PC   You have two big options with respect to running a Netscape server on a PC—Windows NT or UNIX. Windows NT may provide a familiar operating environment that makes the leap onto the Web easier, but our experience shows that PCs running BSDI perform quite valiantly as servers. A particularly bulked-up machine (such as a high-speed Pentium with a lot of available memory) functions nearly as well as much more expensive equipment options.

Digital Alpha   A Digital Alpha system can run either Windows NT or OSF/1, Digital's variant of UNIX. According to Netscape's specifications, a DEC Alpha running Windows NT 3.5 only requires 16MB of memory to run the server. We still recommend having more, but if you're in a pinch and are limited on resources for your test, this is an option.

Silicon Graphics   Silicon Graphics (SGI) actually offers several configurations of their machines, called the WebFORCE product line, which come bundled with a bunch of tools for creating HTML documents and graphics for Web sites. A copy of any version of the Netscape server software can be added to the package at a discount from Netscape's own price. Our experience setting up servers on SGI equipment has been extremely positive. SGI's X Window desktop is a very intuitive, very user-friendly interface that, in our experience, has proven to be a great help for beginner-to-intermediate level system administrators who want to focus more on the operation of the Web site than on the maintenance of their machine.

Furthermore, SGI has taken substantial steps to provide support for their customers by publicly announcing the solutions to complex technical problems, such as getting a server to answer to several distinct IP addresses so that multiple Web sites can be run on one machine. However, unless you happen to have a spare SGI system just lying around, this can prove to be a fairly expensive solution. (A low-end system can still cost more than $10K.) While I wouldn't suggest buying one for your test drive, you might very well consider purchasing one as your permanent server if your test drive is successful.

Sun Systems   Like Silicon Graphics, Sun Systems has bundled systems aimed at organizations getting onto the Internet. Once they are set up, Sun's SPARCstations and Netra servers perform well as servers. Users who are unfamiliar with UNIX (and even some experienced users) may find Sun's X Window interface clunky and cumbersome. Sun's systems remain aimed at more advanced system administrators, but because they comprise a larger percentage of Sun's market, you will also find a larger number of ready-to-use tools that have already been debugged and compiled for Sun systems.

Hewlett-Packard PA and IBM RS/6000   Whereas Silicon Graphics and Sun have engaged in public alliances with Netscape to support their server products, IBM and Hewlett-Packard have not, which probably explains why many corporate users don't necessarily think of these platforms when planning their corporate online presence. Nevertheless, Netscape's server products work on these platforms. If available, they are a fine platform for your test drive.

Necessary Memory   Memory plays an important factor in figuring out how many people will be able to connect to your site at any one time. Each connection consumes a certain percentage of your system's memory resources. When these resources are fully allocated, your server refuses to take any additional connections. Therefore, it's important to be sure that you have sufficient memory to accommodate a reasonable number of users simultaneously.

According to Netscape, the minimum memory necessary to run their server under Windows NT is 16MB. However, 16MB is a little light just for running Windows NT, let alone a heavy-duty server. 32MB should be your minimum for running your system; 64MB is common for sites that receive moderate traffic. If you are planning for your site to have a very high volume of traffic, you probably need to plan for even more memory to handle the burden.

Similarly, Netscape lists the minimum memory configuration for UNIX-based servers at 32MB. During configuration, you need to set the maximum number of processes that can be run by Netscape to serve users. This number is limited by the amount of available memory on your system. While 32MB of memory may be sufficient for the purposes of testing your new server, you probably want more memory on your completed system.

Necessary Internet Connectivity   Theoretically, any type of connection to the Internet that provides the server with its own unique IP address can be used to provide access to a Web server. There are, however, some practical considerations that make certain types of connections more practical than others.

To be successful, your site needs to have its own unique name and IP address. Your server should therefore be attached to a system where it is given a unique and unchanging IP address.

Likewise, there needs to be a sufficient amount of available bandwidth for users to reach your site. The term bandwidth refers to the amount of information that can be transferred to and from any particular site on the Internet at any point in time. Moreover, the connection needs to be stable and dependable, or users become frustrated while trying to access your site and may never come back.

It is therefore no surprise that the most successful Web sites are on networks with high-speed connections to the Internet, such as a T1 line, or a fractional T1 line. For smaller organizations and businesses with only moderate traffic on their Web site, a 256K connection (one-fourth of a T1 line) may be sufficient. Web sites with higher volumes of traffic may require even more bandwidth. Just remember that it makes no sense to invest in high-end server software and a powerful machine to run it if no one can connect to your site.

CAUTION

Some Internet Service Providers (ISPs) offer plans that provide a minimum amount of bandwidth regularly, with the option to automatically bump up to a higher volume of bandwidth if demand requires it.

Because these pricing models tend to be based on the maximum bandwidth demanded at any one point during a month, this is a particularly dangerous strategy for a Web site.

Web sites can become popular almost instantaneously; mention of your site on the right index or UseNet newsgroup can generate a tremendous amount of interest literally overnight. Therefore, demand for access to your site could skyrocket, far outstripping the amount of bandwidth that you had budgeted to support.

Be sure to choose a plan that lets you define the maximum amount of bandwidth being provided so you don't end up with a surprisingly high bill at the end of the month. Choose an ISP that provides you with regular reports of your bandwidth usage. If you find that you are regularly using the maximum amount of bandwidth available, you may want to consider increasing your connection. Just don't put that decision into the hands of the users who decide to visit your site.

Getting the Software

Once you've set up the machine on which you'll be running your server, you can start the process of getting a copy of the software. The process has the following three steps:

1. Apply to participate in the Test Drive program.
2. Receive a username and password from Netscape.
3. Log in to Netscape's Test Drive system and download the appropriate version of the software for your system.

The next few pages guide you through the process of applying for the Test Drive program and downloading the software. Most of the directions that you need are available on the Test Drive pages of Netscape's Web site.

Submitting an Application

The first step is submitting an application to participate in the Test Drive program. To do this, you should open up Netscape Navigator and connect to their site at **http://test-drive.netscape.com/**.

There are three main portions to the application. The first phase asks for contact information for the person downloading and using the software. Netscape uses this information to contact you to see if you want to purchase the software when your 60 days are nearly over.

N O T E Sometimes people are tempted to enter incomplete or inaccurate information in these forms, primarily because they don't want to be bothered in the future by solicitations. This is probably one of those situations where that's not such a good idea. Think of it this way, if the nice salesman were letting you take a $50,000 car out for a spin, you would think it completely reasonable that they'd want to know how to reach you. ■

The most important part of this segment of the application is your e-mail address. Double- and triple-check to ensure that it's properly entered. Netscape uses this e-mail address to send you the access password you need to download the software.

The second section of the application asks for contact information of a Value-Added Reseller of Netscape products. If you've already been dealing with a specific reseller of Netscape products, you should enter this person's information. Then he will be the person bothering you in 60 days instead of someone from Netscape in Mountain View.

Part

V

Ch

27

> **N O T E** There are two ways to buy Netscape's products: directly from Netscape or through an intermediary company called a Value-Added Reseller, or VAR. Some organizations, such as government agencies, may be required to purchase all of their software through one or another VAR. In this case, you should identify who that VAR is, as that salesperson probably knows more about special arrangements for pricing of software than a more general salesperson for Netscape.
>
> VARs can also be a secondary source for support of the products that they sell; although Netscape doesn't provide technical assistance for Test Drive users, a VAR may very well have a technician who can help you work out problems to get your site set up and running. ▪

The third phase of the application is a participant survey. These questions are aimed at providing Netscape with a better consumer profile so they can better target the development of new products. Answer all of the questions, and then click the Submit button to send the information to Netscape.

Getting a Password and Downloading the Software

Shortly after you submit your application (within a few hours to a few days), you should receive an e-mail message to the account listed in your application, giving you a username and password to use to download the Netscape server software.

TROUBLESHOOTING

It's been over a week and I still don't have a password! If you've submitted an application and haven't heard anything back within a week, that probably means that the application didn't make it through. That doesn't mean that they don't love you and won't let you try their software, it just means that somewhere along the line the form didn't process properly.

Go back and re-submit your application. This time, be sure to very carefully check your e-mail address before you submit the application. If after a few days you still haven't received a password, try calling the Test Drive program directly. They can probably take an application from you directly over the phone.

To download the software, follow these steps on the computer that will serve as the Web site:

1. Log in to the Test Drive server at the address listed in your response e-mail; the address is probably **http://test-drive.netscape.com/download/**.

2. Once you connect, you should see a dialog box that looks like the one in figure 27.1.

   Enter your username as indicated in your e-mail from Netscape (probably your e-mail address) and your password where prompted. Be careful when typing the password to specify capitals and lowercase letters exactly as you received them from Netscape.

3. Read the Test Drive License Agreement. If you agree, click the button that says you agree to move on. If you don't agree, the process of downloading the software will end, and you'll be returned to Netscape's home page.

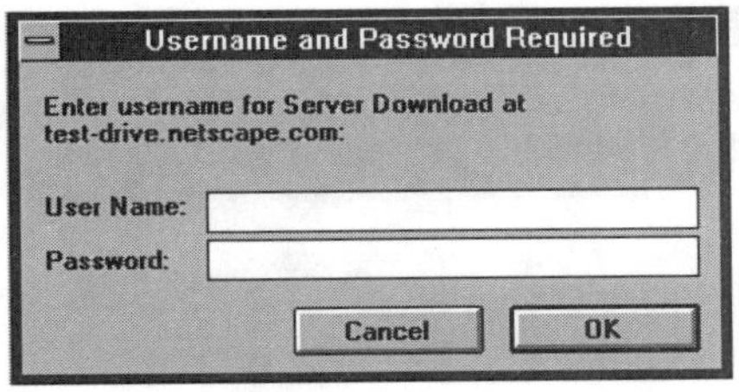

FIG. 27.1

The Test Drive download login dialog box.

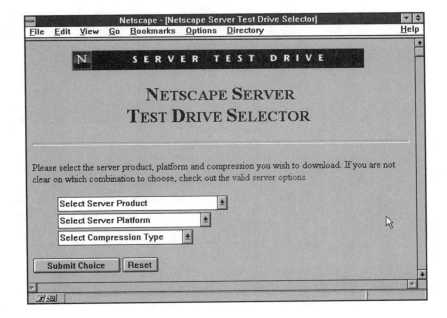

4. After you agree to the License Agreement, a form like the one shown in figure 27.2 appears.

FIG. 27.2

The Test Drive Download Request form.

5. Select the operating system that you'll be using.

6. Select the type of server (Communications, Commerce, Proxy) that you want to download.

7. Select the compression type that you want. For NT servers, you can choose either .EXE or .ZIP compression types; for UNIX, you can choose between .Z and .gz compression. Choose a compression type that you know is usable on the computer that will be running the server.

8. Click the Submit button. This opens a dialog box that allows you to specify where the file should be stored. In the dialog box is the name of the specific file that Netscape will be sending (usually PICK.CGI); you need to replace this generic name with the full path of the working directory where you will be unpacking the file and the full name of the file provided by Netscape in the Downloader form, as shown in figure 27.3.

FIG. 27.3

The Downloader form.

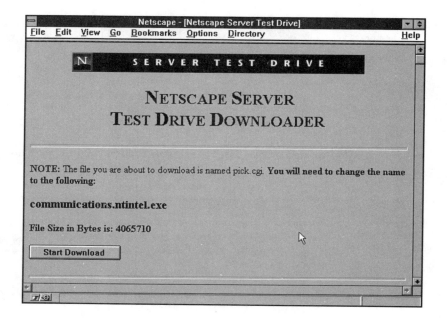

> **CAUTION**
>
> The name of the file as it's stored on Netscape's server, where it must be distinguished from all of the other versions of the software, is different from the name of the archive as it should be stored on your computer to let the installation scripts work. Therefore, you must change the name of the file when it is downloaded to the name specified by Netscape. This will likely be COMMERCE.EXE, COMMERCE.ZIP, commerce.tar.gz, or commerce.tar.Z, depending on which compression type you've chosen.

N O T E Netscape starts the clock on your 60-day test drive from the first time you try to download the files. So before you start the download, make sure that you have sufficient hard drive space on your machine to hold the file. The download is about 2.5MB; when uncompressed, the files may take up to 30MB. ■

9. Click the Accept button. This should start the download process. Keep an eye on it, and shut down the connection when the file is done transferring.

Installing the Netscape Commerce Server Software

Once you've downloaded the software, you'll need to unpack and install it. On both UNIX and NT systems, this is simply a matter of running a simple script, which copies files to the appropriate directories and automatically starts a special installation server so you can perform whatever configuration needs to be done.

The next section has separate sets of instructions for starting the Installation server on NT and UNIX systems. Once Netscape appears and the installation server is started, skip forward to the section "Configuring Your Netscape Test Drive Web Server."

Starting the Installation Server on an NT System

To start the installation process on an NT server, follow these steps:

1. Decompress the files into a working directory. When you started the download, you specified which type of compression you wanted to use. If you chose .EXE, you can simply type the name of the file at a DOS prompt or double-click the file name in File Manager and the archive will be decompressed.

   If you chose .ZIP as your compression style, use your favorite .ZIP utility (such as WinZip) to uncompress the files into a working directory.

   N O T E Name your working directory something other than \NETSCAPE. The \NETSCAPE directory is where the install program will want to put the completed files; it will have a hard time if the installation files are in the same directory. ▪

2. Run the program SETUP.EXE from your working directory. When prompted, click the Continue button to install the server files.

3. At this point, you need to specify a path to store the server files. By default, the SETUP program wants to put the files under a subdirectory called \NETSCAPE. Unless there's a big reason not to use this default, you should use it. It doesn't matter if your current version of Netscape is already stored there; the Netscape server needs the Navigator client to finish configuration. The path that you specify at this point is what is called the server root. Remember this path because you need it while configuring your server.

4. You will then be asked whether there is an existing Domain Name System (DNS) entry for your server through a dialog box like the one shown in figure 27.4. The DNS is a cross-referencing database of computers by name and IP address. If the administrator of your domain has already given you the name of your server, click the DNS Configured button. If you do not have a specific domain name for your system, click the No DNS Entry button.

Part

V

Ch

27

FIG. 27.4
The DNS Configuration
dialog box.

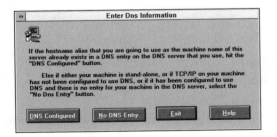

5. If you clicked the DNS Configured button, you will be prompted through a dialog box to enter the DNS name of your server.

    If you clicked the No DNS Entry button, you will be prompted through a dialog box like the one shown in figure 27.5 to enter your system's IP address.

FIG. 27.5

Enter your system's IP address in this dialog box if your server doesn't have a DNS entry.

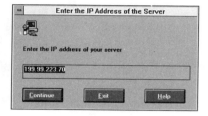

6. Once you've entered the requested information, you should see a dialog box like the one shown in figure 27.6 telling you that the files have been successfully installed.

7. Click the OK button. This should start a copy of Netscape and bring up a screen that looks like the one shown in figure 27.7. You should now skip forward to the section on configuring your server.

FIG. 27.6

The installation server files have been successfully installed.

Starting the Installation Server on Your UNIX System

Starting the installation of the Netscape Server on your UNIX system is a matter of running a simple script. On a UNIX system, you need to create a user that will own the processes created by the server system. Create your new user before you start the installation.

To run the QuickStart installation script, follow these steps:

1. Decompress and untar the file you downloaded from Netscape.

    If you have gzip on your system, type the following command:

    gzip -d filename

    where filename is replaced by the name of the file that you downloaded from Netscape.

FIG. 27.7

The Netscape Server Installation home page.

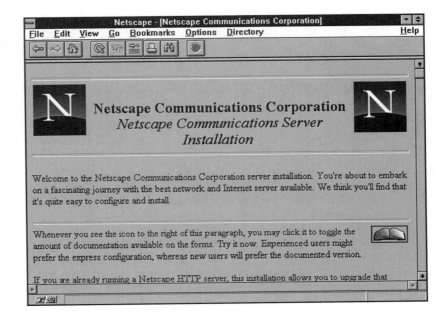

2. You should now have a .TAR archive file in your working directory. To unpack the .TAR file, type

   tar -xvf whatever.tar

   where whatever.tar is the name of the tar file that resulted when you decompressed the file in step one.

3. When you untar the file, you should end up with a directory called either httpd, if you're test driving the Communications Server, or https, if you're testing the secure server. The installation script is stored in a subdirectory called install under this directory. Change into this directory by typing either **cd httpd/install** or **cd https/install** depending on which one applies.

4. Once you're in the install directory, type **./ns-setup** to start the installation script.

5. When prompted, enter the full name of the server, complete with the domain name.

6. You will then be prompted to indicate what browser you will be using to configure the server. If you are at the terminal that controls the server, you can just press Enter, and a copy of Netscape will connect to the Installation Server and appear on your screen.

   If you are installing the server software remotely or on a system that does not have its own monitor, type *NONE* at the network navigator prompt. You will need to access the Installation Server through a copy of Netscape on your remote system. To access the server, enter the URL **http://servername:portnumber** where servername is the name of the server that you entered in step five, and where portnumber is the port number that the installation script points you to before prompting you for the name of your browser.

Part

V

Ch

27

7. At this point, the installation server should be running, and you should see a screen that looks like the one in figure 27.7. You can now proceed to the next section on configuring your server.

Configuring Your Netscape Test Drive Web Server

There is little difference between the configuration of a UNIX-based server and an NT-based server. Both use Netscape as the user interface, and the forms for the two systems are practically identical.

There are three sections to the configuration of a Netscape server. These are Server configuration, Document configuration, and Administrative configuration.

If you follow these steps, you can easily complete all three sections and get your server configured right away.

1. From the introductory page, select the option Install a New Netscape Server from Scratch and click the Start the Installation! button.

2. This brings up the Installation Overview page, as illustrated in figure 27.8. Although you can do the three parts of the configuration in any order, it's probably best to do them left to right, as shown on the page. Click the Server Config button.

FIG. 27.8

The Installation Overview form.

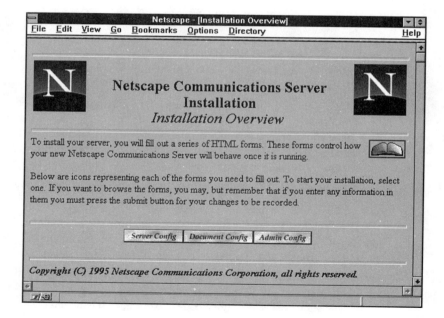

3. The Server Configuration form shown in figure 27.9 lets you enter information about the server itself.

- Server Name: Check the server name and make sure it's the same as the one you entered when you started the setup program.

- IP Address: Enter the IP address of your system. This information is used primarily for systems that are running multiple Web sites off the same computer through a process where one computer answers to multiple IP addresses. Even if that's more complicated than you want to get right now, enter your IP address so that if you want to run multiple servers down the line, that option will be available without having to shut down and reinstall your original server.

FIG. 27.9
The Server Configuration form.

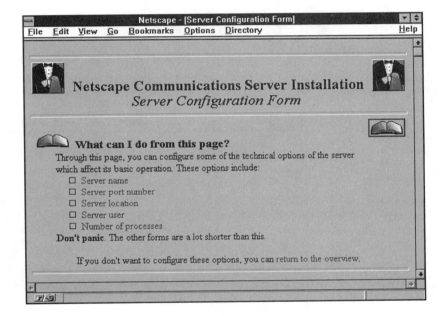

- Server Port: The regular port for a Web site is port 80. Unless you really have a need to change this, leave it on 80.

- Server Location: This is the server root directory. The default server root on a UNIX system is /usr/ns-home; the default root on an NT system is \NETSCAPE\HTTPD.

- Server User: On UNIX systems, you need to specify the name of the user that you created that will own the server's processes. For a variety of reasons, you should not leave the default username "nobody" as the user. Create a real user and enter that name in this slot.

Part
V

Ch
27

- Number of Processes/Threads: Unless you know that your use is going to be either very light or very heavy, you should leave these numbers as they are.

- Recording Errors: By default, the Netscape server logs its errors to its own error file. If it is more convenient for you to have them directed to the system error log, you can indicate that here.

- Hostname Resolution: If you leave this option turned on, the Server will attempt to resolve the hostnames of users entering your system. This can be very helpful for monitoring your system's usage.

- Access Logging: By default, the server keeps a log of all users who access the site. If you're extremely short on disk space or if you expect that the volume to your site is going to be so large that trying to keep a record would not be of any value, you can shut the logging off at this point.

4. When you're done entering the Server Configuration information, click the Make These Changes button. This takes you to the Document Configuration form.

5. The Document Configuration form shown in figure 27.10 lets you tell the server where your HTML files will be stored and how to present files to users.

FIG. 27.10

The Document Configuration form.

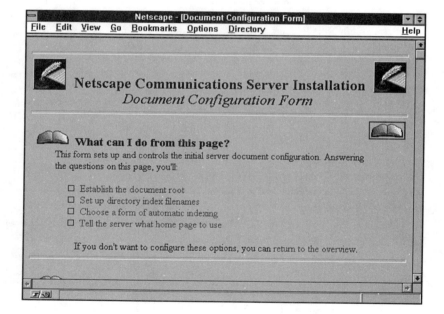

- Document Root: Enter the name of the directory where you have stored the HTML files for your server.

- Index Files: When a user asks for a specific directory, the server usually sends an index of the directory. On Web sites, there is usually an HTML document that spells out the contents of a specific directory called the index file. These files are usually named index.html, but if you want to call them something else you can. Just enter the name of your first page documents in this line.

- Automatic Indexing: When a user asks for the index of a directory that does not have an index.html file, they get a listing of the files that the server has available in that directory. If you leave Fancy Indexing checked, the Netscape server will send little icons to indicate the file type as well as the name of the file. Checking Simple Directory Indexing provides the user with only a directory of files.

- Home Page: This option lets you specify a particular document that will be the first thing users see when they come to your site. Normally this is the index.html file stored in the server root, but Netscape allows you to specify any document you'd like.

6. When you have completed entering your document configuration information, click the Make These Changes button to continue to Administrative Configuration.

7. Netscape servers have a lot of features beyond those that you configure during installation. All the administrative features are handled by another smaller server, called the Administrative Server. The Administrative Configuration form shown in figure 27.11 lets you configure this server so you can access the more advanced options of your Netscape server.

FIG. 27.11

The Administrative Configuration form.

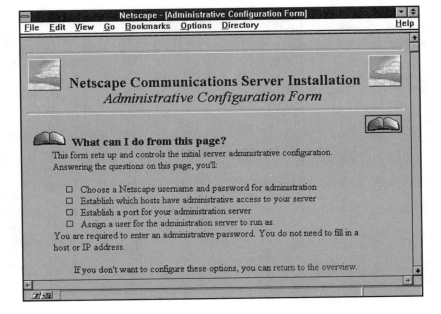

Part

V

Ch

27

- Administrative Username and Password: Pick a username and a password that you'll use when accessing the Administrative server. Remember these, or you'll pretty much have to reinstall the server software to reconfigure the Administrative server.

- Administrative Access Control: By default, the only place you can access the Administrative server is from the server console. If you want to be able to access the server remotely, enter the specific domain names or IP numbers in this slot.

- Administrative Server Configuration: You will be prompted to enter a port and the user ID of a real system user that will own the processes generated by the Administrative server. Just as the traditional Web server port is 80, the traditional Web server administration port is 8080. The administrative user should probably be a user on your system that can run system-wide processes. You may want to make it the root user on a UNIX system or the administrative user on an NT system.

8. When you're done configuring the Administrative server, click the Make These Changes button.

9. You should now see a form that indicates all the information you've entered for your server (see fig. 27.12). Check through it to make sure there are no mistakes, and then click the link that says "Go for it!!!"

FIG. 27.12
The Server Configuration summary.

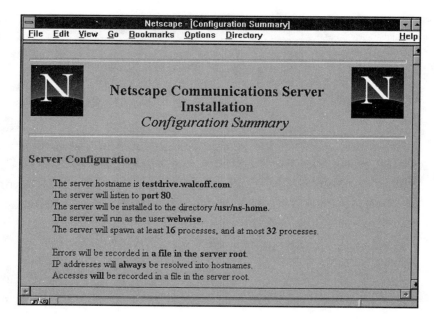

10. The Installation server will copy the server files to their appropriate locations and start your Web server. When the process is complete, you will see a page that starts with the image shown in figure 27.13.

FIG. 27.13
The server has been successfully installed.

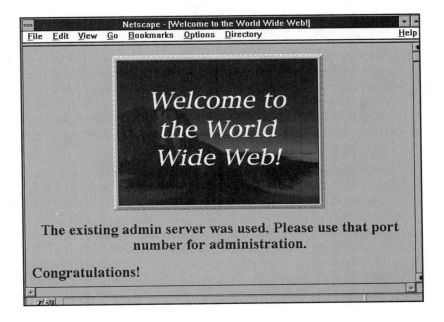

Your server is now up and running. You have successfully started your test drive.

Setting Up Security on Your Commerce Server

In order to make transactions with their Commerce server "secure," Netscape has employed a strategy called the Secure Sockets Layer (SSL). The Secure Sockets Layer uses a three-part approach to make sure that messages are transmitted securely between a user and the Web server. These three steps are authentication, encryption, and data integrity.

The first two steps of this strategy, authentication and encryption, depend on a fairly fundamental concept in current computer security called public key encryption. Before we examine how Netscape implements public key encryption in its own software, let's take a look at how it works generally.

What Is Public Key Encryption?

The types of code making and breaking that most people are familiar with are called secret key encryption. In secret key encryption, both the sender and receiver know what the "key" is in

Part
V

Ch

order to decrypt the message. The problem with secret key encryption is that both the sender and the receiver need to be in agreement as to what the key is. Usually, somehow you need to get the key from one person to another; thus, the plots of hundreds of spy movies involving codebooks and microfiche hidden in teeth are created. Obviously, the problem with secret key codes is that once the secret key is no longer a secret, all messages sent using that key are compromised.

In 1976, Whitfield Diffie and Martin Hellman created a new system of cryptography that they called public key cryptography. In public key encryption, three separate mathematical factors are used. Two of these factors, called a public key pair are made available publicly. The third factor is actually the result of a particular mathematical relationship involving the other two factors. This third factor, called the private key, is protected and not made available to anyone except for the user who receives information. The text of the message itself becomes a fourth factor in a very complex mathematical equation.

When the text of a message is processed in relation to the public key factors, it results in a value that can only be retrieved by someone who knows the private key factor or by someone who has sufficient computer resources to try all possible factor combinations until the private key factor is determined and the original message is decoded. The theory is that, given sufficiently complex factors, the amount of resources necessary to factor out the private key and the message text from the result of the mathematical relationship is far greater than the value of the information contained in the message.

Sending and Receiving Messages Using Public Key Encryption

Suppose that a sender wants to issue a private message to a receiver. In cryptography, the original message is called the plaintext. The sender retrieves the receiver's public key pair (two of the three factors) and encrypts the message using these two factors. The resulting encrypted message, or ciphertext, can only be decoded if the third factor, the private key, is also known. Since the private key factor is only known by the receiver, he should be the only person capable of decoding the message. When the message is sent through the system, it can be intercepted, but unless the third factor is known, it cannot be read.

> **CAUTION**
>
> Obviously, this system depends on the fact that the private key is kept private and is not made generally available. When your private key is known, all three factors are available to the person who wants to read messages intended for you. Later in this chapter, we'll discuss some common sense approaches to keeping your information secure.

Avoiding Message Tampering Through Authentication

The second problem of sending messages through an open system (after the possibility of private information being intercepted) is the problem of ensuring that a received message is actually from the person who supposedly sent it.

On the Internet, the process of verifying that the sender of a message is actually who they claim to be is called authentication.

Public key encryption can also be used as a system for authentication. Using the private key, a sender does a computation involving the private key and the message itself. The result of this computation is attached to the message and both are sent. When the message is received, the receiver performs another computation using the message, the signature, and the sender's public key. While this computation does not yield the private key factor, it does show whether or not the factors could exist within the mathematical relationship that should exist among the known factors. If the mathematical relationship does not hold, either the signature or the message may have been altered.

N O T E For more information on data encryption, check out RSA's Web site at **http:// www.rsa.com**. Lists of answers to Frequently Asked Questions about cryptography, public key encryption, and digital signatures can be found at **http://www.rsa.com/rsalabs/faq/**. ▪

How Is Public Key Encryption Used by Netscape?

In 1977 Ron Rivest, Adi Shamir, and Leonard Adelman invented a type of public key encryption that they named RSA (using the first initial of each of their last names). This process was patented and is licensed by a variety of companies for use in products that maintain secure transmission of materials.

Netscape has licensed the RSA public key system for use in its server and client products. Netscape has incorporated the RSA encryption mathematical formulas or algorithms into their message transmission security system, which they called the Secure Sockets Layer. As we mentioned earlier in this chapter, the Secure Sockets Layer actually involves three separate strategies: authentication, encryption, and data integrity verification.

Authentication The first step of the Secure Sockets Layer approach is a variation of the public key authentication discussed earlier. When a user tries to connect to a Web site, the user's copy of the Netscape Navigator Web browser client sends a request for information to the Commerce server. When a Netscape Commerce server receives this request for information, it sends the Netscape Navigator client software a package of information, including the server's public key pair and a copy of a signed digital certificate. A signed digital certificate is an electronic document from a trusted third party (called a Certification Authority) stating that the public key pair sent is authentic and actually belongs to the server that the user is trying to reach.

As the name suggests, the signed digital certificate contains its own public key information. When the Netscape Navigator client receives this information, it authenticates the signed digital certificate by checking it against the public key pair at the Certification Authority. It then checks the content of the server's public key pair. Once the public key pair has been mathematically verified by the Netscape Navigator client, the server has been authenticated.

At this point, the Netscape Navigator client then generates a session key, or a temporary public key. Using the server's public key, the client encrypts this session key and sends it to the server.

Encryption   Once the client has received and authenticated the server's public key and sent a copy of its session key to the server, both sides have copies of the other's public key. Information can now be transferred between the server and the client using standard public key encryption techniques. Encrypted information, while available to many other systems on the Net, is of little value without the factors necessary to decipher it.

Data Integrity   Like most Internet transmission protocols, Netscape's Secure Sockets Layer system uses an integrity checker to ensure that data hasn't been tampered with or warped in transmission between the server and client. SSL's Message Authentication Codes (MACs) work much like the system that FTP uses to ensure that a packet has been properly received.

Why Go to All This Trouble?

Let's suppose someone figures out how to fool the DNS system into sending requests for a server at www.goodguy.com to a server at www.thief.com. Since, like most Internet client applications, the Netscape Navigator software depends on the DNS system for navigation, as far as it's concerned, www.thief.com looks exactly like www.goodguy.com.

Let's also say that our thief is particularly diligent and has made copies of all of the available files on the www.goodguy.com site. This means that the site looks exactly like www.goodguy.com.

Here's the thief's problem: If the thief uses the public key pairs from www.goodguy.com (which he could get), he can't decrypt any of the information he received without the www.goodguy.com private key.

If the thief tries to resolve this problem by creating his own set of public keys, they won't match the signature on the signed digital certificate, and the client will know that it's not talking to the right server.

The Great Netscape Security Debacle of 1995

In September of 1995, Netscape faced a public relations nightmare when two Berkeley students (Ian Goldberg and David Wagner) announced to computer hacker groups and the press that they had figured out a way to crack the public key encryption system used by Netscape. (Check out **http://www.tezcat.com/web/security/items/ssl-news.txt** to read the announcement.)

Unlike the server's public/private key set, which is generated only about once a year, the Netscape Navigator client generates a new session key each time it encounters a new secure server. Versions of the Netscape Navigator client up to version 1.1 used a limited set of variables to generate the client's session key.

Armed with some limited knowledge about the origin of these variables and their eventual use, these students were able to use sheer computing power to eventually crack a session key. Once the session key was known, it was possible to decrypt messages from the server to the client, revealing a potential flaw in the security system.

Netscape responded by raising the number of variables used to create the session key from 30 to 300, thus raising the number of potential combinations considerably and making this particular type of attack much less feasible. Versions of the Netscape Navigator client 1.2 and above incorporate this feature. An upgrade patch was also sent to users of the Netscape Commerce server software that prevents users of versions prior to 1.2 from logging in to a Netscape Commerce server.

Establishing SSL Security on Your Commerce Server

The process of setting up security on your Netscape Commerce server is less an exercise in computing skills than it is a challenge to get through red tape. The following are four steps to establishing security on your server:

1. Generate your private and public keys.
2. Request a signed digital certificate from a Certification Authority.
3. Install your signed digital certificate.
4. Activate security through your administrative server.

Before you get started, do the following to get your server ready to handle secure data:

■ Get rid of any programs that aren't absolutely necessary to run the Commerce server. Users should only be accessing this computer through the Commerce server.

■ If this is a system that lets users log in through accounts, get rid of all of them except for the account that runs the server. If certain accounts need to be left in place for server maintenance, make sure they have passwords and have all external accesses locked out.

■ Eliminate physical access to the system as much as possible.

■ Place the server in a locked, climate-controlled computer server room, if possible, and limit access as much as possible.

■ Set up an adequate backup system that copies all relevant files to tape on a regular basis. (These tapes also need to be protected, as they contain copies of your private key file.)

N O T E Why go through all the bother of taking these precautions? If the information that is stored on this system is sensitive enough to require protection through encryption, you'll want to make sure that unauthorized parties are blocked at all potential entrances. After all, once the data gets to your server, it's no longer encoded and can be viewed clearly by someone who can get access to your system. ■

Generating Private and Public Key Pairs

The first step to setting up SSL is generating public and private keys for your server. Early versions of the Netscape Commerce server allowed the administrator to generate key pairs using a form that could be viewed through a Netscape Navigator client attached to the administrative server. This system used a set of conditions on the system to generate a set of random numbers that provided the basis for the keys. This system was later discovered to be insufficiently secure.

The new method of generating key pairs requires input from the server administrator to serve as the random seed for generating the key pair. Once you run the program, you are prompted to enter input at the keyboard. The key generating program records the random lengths of time between input keystrokes and uses them as the random seed for generating the key pair.

To start the key generation program on a UNIX system follow these steps:

1. Log in as root by entering the command su root. When prompted, enter the root password.

N O T E If you are Telnetting to the server, you should not be able to log in directly as root. Log in through another account with permission to access the server and use the superuser (su) command to log in as root. If you are able to Telnet in to the server as root, go back and disable root login through Telnet before continuing. If you are unsure how to do this, check your server administration manual. ■

2. Change to your server's root directory. This is not the directory where your HTML documents are stored but rather where the server programs are kept. If you did a standard installation of your Commerce server, these files are found in the directory /usr/ns-home. To change to this directory, type **cd /usr/ns-home**.

3. The key generation program is stored in the directory bin/https/admin/bin. Change to this directory by **typing cd bin/https/admin/bin**.

4. Run the key generation program by typing **./key**.

5. At this point, you can begin generating the key pair files.

To start the key generation program on an NT system, follow these steps:

1. Through a DOS window, change directories to where the key generation program is stored.

2. Run the key generation program by typing **key**.

3. Begin generating the key pair files.

Generating the Key Pair Files   Once the key script has been started, you are prompted to provide a path for the new key pair file. Usually, this file is stored in the secure server's configuration directory. If you did a standard installation of your Commerce server, this directory would be /usr/ns-home/https-443.###.###.###.###/config (where ###.###.###.### is replaced by the IP address of the server) on a UNIX system or \netscape\https\config on an NT system. The default name for the key pair file is SERVERKEY.DER.

N O T E   You may change the default locations of these files if you want. In fact, changing these locations may be desirable if you feel fairly confident in your skills with UNIX. Placing the files in an unorthodox location makes it harder for system intruders to find the files should they manage to somehow gain access to your system. If you decide to place this file in a location other than the default, be sure that the directory where you put it is accessible only by root (and don't forget where you put it). ▪

Once you've entered the path for your key files, you are presented with a progress meter above your command line. When prompted, begin to type on your keyboard. You can type anything; the text isn't really important, though I'd avoid "The Quick Brown Fox." Any text you're not familiar with (even this paragraph) will do. The program reads the time between your keystrokes and uses them as the random seed for generating your key files.

N O T E   Do not use the automatic repeat feature by holding down a single key to fill up the progress meter. The time between keystrokes of a held-down key is not random and makes your resulting keys much more vulnerable to attack. ▪

Once you have filled up the progress meter, the program uses your random input to generate a key pair file.

After the key pair file is generated, you are prompted to enter a keyfile password. This password should be at least eight characters long and should include at least one non-alphabetic character. The password should also not be found in any regular dictionary of terms. Birthdates, family member names, and the like are all bad choices because someone might be able to use this information to crack your keyfile password. Once you select a password, you should memorize it and not write it down. You also need to remember it; should you forget your keyfile password, you'll need to generate a new key pair and request a new signed digital certificate (for which the Certification Authority will probably charge a fee to your organization).

N O T E   When you request a signed digital certificate from a Certification Authority, they ask for the name of one key Web administrator who has responsibility for the security of the system. This should be the person who creates and knows the keyfile password.

In many organizations, it's considered regular business practice to make sure a copy of your password is available should something happen to you and someone needs to access your files. This should be an exception.

The worst that can happen if something happens to you or the keyfile is somehow "lost" is that a new key pair needs to be generated and someone needs to have a new signed digital certificate produced by the Certification Authority, proving the validity of the new key pair. Though frustrating, the total potential loss is some downtime on your server and the cost of a new signed digital certificate (about $100).

continues

continued

By contrast, if the integrity of the keyfile password is violated, the information on your server can be vulnerable for an indefinite period before you discover that someone else is copying and decrypting your data. These potential costs by far outweigh the cost of generating a new keyfile password. ■

> **CAUTION**
>
> Whenever the secure server is restarted, the administrator is prompted to enter the keyfile password so the keyfile can be decrypted into the public and private keys for use by the server. Since the keyfile password is required to be entered, secure servers must be restarted manually, unlike Communications servers which can be started by a script when the server starts up.

Once you have generated the keyfile, you can request a signed digital certificate from a Certification Authority.

Requesting a Signed Digital Certificate

There's some paperwork you need to do before you can perform the computer side of this task. The red tape involved with getting a signed digital certificate is largely related to proving that you are who you say you are.

Certification Authorities are companies whose job it is to verify that a given public key actually belongs to the company that purportedly owns it. Through their digital signature on your digital server certificate, users are able to authenticate that the server they've reached is the one they think they're addressing.

What Is Verisign?   Verisign is the Certification Authority most generally affiliated with Netscape Commerce servers. The directions in this chapter assume that you are getting your signed digital certificate from Verisign. If you get your certificate from another Certification Authority, the process may vary slightly, but the requirements are generally the same.

> **N O T E**   You can find out more about Verisign's signed digital certificate services at their Web site, **http://www.verisign.com/**. ■

Documenting Your Server   Before Verisign will process your request for a signed digital certificate, they require that you send them the following information:

- The name, address, and contact information of the person who will be serving as Webmaster of the secure server, as well as the name of the specific server that will be running the Commerce server software. Verisign usually requires that this information appears on corporate letterhead above the signature of someone with authority to delegate this authority on behalf of the company. This information proves that the person interacting with Verisign is authorized by the stated company to do so.

N O T E A template for generating this letter is available on Verisign's Web site at **http://www.verisign.com/netscape/index.html**. ▓

- The company's business license or articles of incorporation. This information proves that the company has the right to engage in commercial transactions.
- A purchase order or check for the cost of issuing the signed digital certificate.

In order to expedite the processing of requests for signed digital certificates, Verisign asks that applicants fax a copy of this information to them before submitting the request for the certificate. Verisign begins processing the request but does not issue the certificate until the hard copy of all materials reaches them by mail.

N O T E Certification Authorities tend to be very strict about their rules. It can take up to two months for a Certification Authority to issue a signed digital certificate, depending on the ease with which they can validate the information submitted with the certificate request.

This stringency is actually good for everyone, as it helps to prevent fraudulent behavior that could damage online commerce for everyone. If the CA requests additional verification or supporting information, do your best to provide the information as soon as possible.

If it is impossible to provide a specific piece of information requested by the CA, contact them and explain why. There is usually an alternate form of proof that the CA finds acceptable. ▓

Requesting a Signed Digital Certificate from a Certification Authority

Once the proper documentation has been submitted to your selected Certification Authority, you can issue your online request for a signed digital certificate. This is done through a form accessible through the Administrative server.

Starting the Administrative Server

To start the Administrative server on a UNIX machine, follow these steps:

1. Log in as root by typing the following at a command prompt: **su**. When prompted, type in the server's root password.
2. Change the server's root directory. For a standard installation of the Netscape Commerce server where the root is stored in the directory/usr/ns-home, type the following command: **cd /usr/ns-home**.
3. Run the Administrative server program by typing the following: **/start-admin**.

    The server returns a message that tells you the port through which the Administrative server can be reached.

To start the Administrative server on a Windows NT machine, follow these steps:

1. Change to the directory where the Netscape server programs are kept.
2. Run the Administrative server program by double-clicking it.

Accessing the Administrative Server   Once you have started the Administrative server, you can access the security configuration forms using the Netscape Navigator client. To do this, follow these steps:

1. Start a copy of Netscape.

2. Open a connection to the Administrative server. You can open a dialog box to enter the Administrative server's address by clicking the Open tool, or you can enter the address into the Location field below the Netscape toolbar.

   The administrative server's address is the name of the server followed by a colon and the number of the port through which the Administrative server can be accessed.

N O T E   The Administrative server tells you at what port it can be reached when you start it; the default setting is port 8080. The name should look like this: **http://www.servername.com:8080** ▧

Once you enter the Administrative server's address, you are presented with a dialog box asking you for the name of the Administrative user and password, as illustrated in figure 27.14.

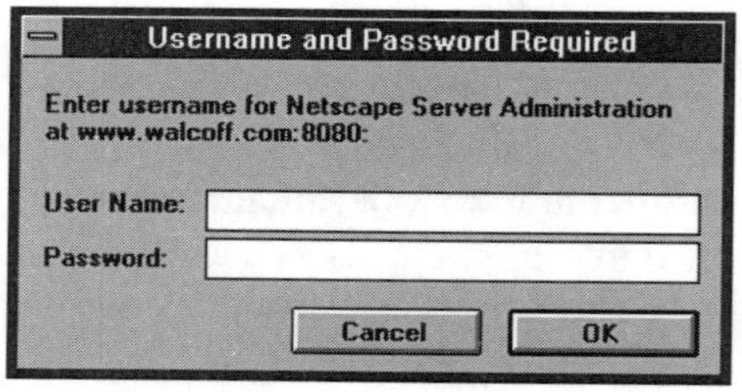

FIG. 27.14
The Administrative
server login dialog box.

N O T E   The username and password requested at this point are the administrative username and password you entered when you first installed the server software. If you have forgotten this name and password, you may need to remove the software and reinstall it. ▧

When the appropriate username and password are entered, you see an HTML document that looks like the one shown in figure 27.15.

3. Scroll down to the section titled Security Configuration, as illustrated in figure 27.16.

   Click the Request or Renew a Certificate link. This brings up the form shown in figure 27.17.

FIG. 27.15
The Administrative
server index page.

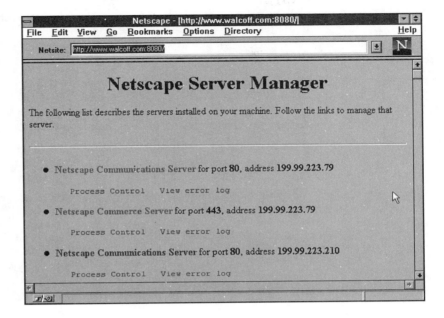

FIG. 27.16
Options for establishing
security on your server.

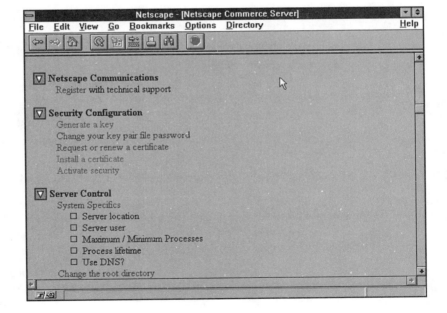

FIG. 27.17

Use this form to request a signed digital certificate.

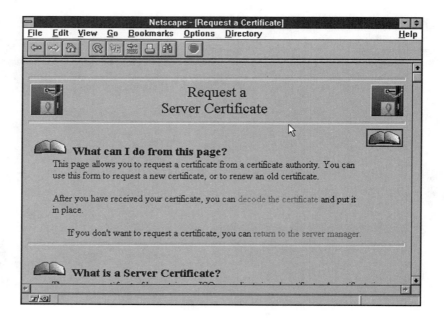

4. Fill out the form to request your certificate.

   You need to enter the following information:

   - The e-mail address of your Certification Authority
   - The path to your keyfile
   - Your keyfile password (used to decrypt the keyfile so a copy of the public key can be sent to the Certification Authority)
   - The "distinguished name" of the server that will be running the secure server
   - A phone number so the Certification Authority can contact you if any problems arise

5. Once you have entered the appropriate information, click the Make These Changes button.

The Administrative server then runs a script that decrypts your keyfile and attaches a copy of your public key to a message that is sent to the Certification Authority using the e-mail address you supplied.

Shortly after you submit your request, you should receive a confirmation by e-mail that your request has been received. Before you can do anything else, you need to wait for the Certification Authority to validate your information. Within a few days or a few weeks, you will receive a second e-mail message containing the signed digital certificate. Then you can proceed to install it and activate security on your server.

Installing a Signed Server Certificate

Once the Certification Authority has verified the authenticity of your request for a signed digital certificate, they send you an e-mail containing your server certificate.

The critical piece of this e-mail is marked with lines that say

— BEGIN CERTIFICATE —

and

— END CERTIFICATE —

This is your signed digital certificate that is used by clients to authenticate your server. You can either edit the e-mail and save this text in a file, or you can cut and paste this text directly into the appropriate form.

To install the certificate, follow these steps:

1. Start the Administrative server. (This is covered in detail in the previous section.)

2. Log in to the Administrative server through your Netscape Navigator software.

3. From the Server Manager index page, click the link called Install a Server Certificate. This opens up the hypertext document shown in figure 27.18.

FIG. 27.18
The Server Certificate installation form.

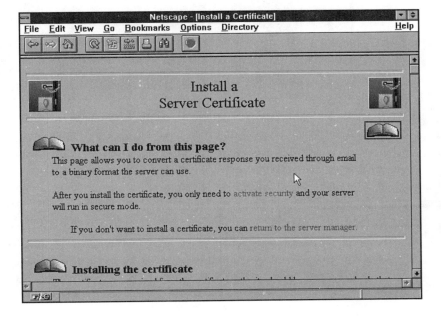

Part
V

Ch
27

4. Insert the text of the certificate from the e-mail message. If you have already saved the contents of the certificate into a file, specify the full path of the file where the file can be found. If you have decided to cut and paste the certificate contents, open up your e-mail program in a window and copy the lines saying Begin, End, and everything in between, and paste them into the section of the form designated for this purpose, as shown in figure 27.19.

FIG. 27.19

The contents of a server certificate pasted into the installation form.

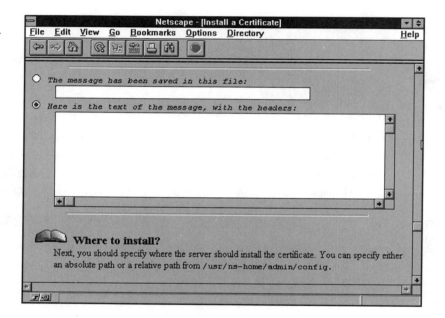

N O T E As discussed earlier in this chapter, server certificates are related to specific keyfiles. If you requested server certificates for several servers at the same time, be absolutely sure that the server certificate you install matches the keyfile and the server. ■

5. Specify where the certificate file will be kept. As a default, the file is called SERVERCERT.DER and is stored below the directory where the main server files are stored in a subdirectory called /admin/config.

N O T E If you are running a UNIX system and decide not to store the file in the default location, make sure that the SERVERCERT.DER file is not kept in the root directory or in another generally accessible directory. Although many clients access and read this file, you don't want anyone to be able to tamper with it. If this file is tampered with, users of your site will be unable to authenticate your server and will therefore be unable to log in. ■

6. Click the Make These Changes button. A script runs, and your server certificate is installed in the appropriate directory.

Now that the certificate is installed, you need to tell your server to turn its security features on.

Activating Security and Enabling (/Disabling) Ciphers   Once you install the server certificate, the server's response should provide you with an opportunity to proceed and activate security on the server.

If you elected not to follow this option at the time you installed the server certificate, or if for some reason you decided to leave security deactivated, you can get to the Security Activation form by following these steps:

1. Activate the Administrative server, as discussed previously in the section on generating a key pair.
2. Log into the Administrative server using your Netscape Navigator client.
3. From the Server Manager index page, select Activate Security or Enable a Cipher. This reveals the HTML document shown in figure 27.20.

Once you have entered the Activate Security or Enable a Cipher form, you have to supply the basic information that the server needs to pull all of the previous efforts together. Follow the next series of steps to fully activate security on your server:

1. Select the option that says you want to run in secure mode.

N O T E   Once you have activated your server's secure mode, users with Web clients that do not support SSL are no longer able to communicate with the server. At this time, only users running Netscape Navigator can access your secured server. These users will also experience some changes to their interface that alert them to the fact that they are communicating with a secure server. These interface changes are discussed in the next section of this chapter. ■

FIG. 27.20
This form allows you to turn on your server's security features.

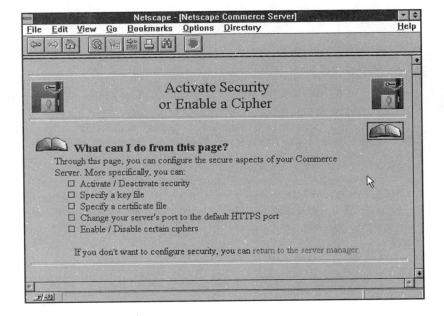

2. Select a port number for your server. The default selection is 443; this port is the standard for secure Web servers. Unless you have a really good reason to change it, you should probably leave it alone.

3. Enter the path of the keyfile that you generated before you requested your server certificate. This points users to your public keyfile to enable the encryption section of SSL.

4. Specify the path to the server certificate that was installed in step 3. This allows users to authenticate your public key by verifying your keyfile with the Certification Authority.

5. Select which ciphers you want to activate. Unless you have a specific reason to shut one off, you might as well choose to leave them all turned on.

6. When you have supplied all of this information, click the Make These Changes button.

Once the Administrative server runs the appropriate script, the security features of your server are activated.

How Users See a Secure Server

Once security is activated on your server, users who can access the site will notice several key changes in the way their Netscape Navigator responds to your site.

The most important change is that any users who had previously connected to your server using software other than Netscape Navigator (or some other SSL-compliant Web browser) will no longer be able to access your site.

N O T E   The patch to the Commerce server that solved the security problem related to key generation also added an option for redirecting users who do not have either SSL software or a version of Netscape Navigator beyond 1.1 to another HTML document. If you are running an insecure Communications server on the same machine as your secure Commerce server, these users can be redirected to an insecure version of your site (which does not accept credit card numbers or exchange other sensitive information). ▨

Second, the prefix to the URL of your site will change from http:// to https://. Thus the insecure server **http://www.walcoff.com/** would become **https://www.walcoff.com/**. This new URL tells the host (**www.walcoff.com**) two key things: First it connects to the machine at the secure port (number 443); second, the preliminary request to the server activates the sequence of exchanging keys that is necessary for secure communications.

Third, users will notice some changes to the look of their Netscape Navigator window that indicate the activation of secure communications. These include the addition of a blue bar below the toolbar, and the "joining" of the broken key into a dark blue key in the lower-left corner. Both of these modifications are illustrated in figures 27.21 and 27.22.

Additionally, if the user has not deactivated them, dialog boxes will appear as the user moves in and out of secured documents, alerting them to the transition from insecure to secure communications.

If all of these features are working, then you have correctly installed your Commerce server. The question of whether you like the software well enough to buy a copy is up to you, but if you do decide to buy it, your installation and signed digital certificate are still valid. No further configuration is necessary; all that is required is the payment of the appropriate fees to Netscape.

New Server Product Software from Netscape

SuiteSpot

SuiteSpot is an integrated suite of client/server software. It will be available sometime in the second quarter of 1996. Using standard protocols, SuiteSpot utilizes and shares information across the Internet as well as within the Intranet. It maintains a client/server solution that includes providing a universal client on the desktop. Live online applications can be deployed from anywhere on the enterprise network. Support for protocols like Secure Sockets Layer (SSL) allows for message encryption and data veritable checks.

LiveWire is one component that is included with SuiteSpot. It provides its own database, however, it also provides Client Library Interface (CLI) access to Informix, Oracle, Sybase, and Microsoft databases. Other components can be licensed as part of SuiteSpot. These include Netscape's Enterprise Server, Catalog Server, Proxy Server, Mail Server, and News Server. Pricing, from $3,000-5,000, is flexible depending on what servers you choose to include. SuiteSpot runs on SPARC, MIPS, RS/6000, PA, DEC Alpha, and Intel x86/Pentium systems. It supports both Unix and Windows NT.

Directory Server

If you're looking for a way to manage user names and proprietary information, Netscape's Directory Server may be what you need. It is designed to scale to the Internet. What this means is that it can support thousands of users, while making information accessible to anyone on the Internet using a standard protocol called Lightweight Directory Access Protocol (LDAP). This enables directory queries on user names and other information within a company's Intranet as well as across the Internet.

Netscape's Directory Server supports existing X.500-based management systems, naming conventions included, that support Directory Access Protocol (DAP). Other vendors, like Novell, plan to be compatible with the server by supporting DAP as well. The server also supports both Unix and Windows NT.

Part V
Ch
27

Architecturally, Secure Sockets Layer (SSL) is supported by the Directory Server, so companies can provide secure access both locally as well as over the Internet. This product won't be released until sometime in the third quarter of 1996. No pricing information is available as yet.

Certificate Server

Netscape's Certificate Server allows for companies to manage secure communications over the Internet as well as their own Intranet. A company with multiple Web servers can issue a digital ID certificate to allow access to multiple servers using the same username and password. The server supports both UNIX and Windows NT.

Some of the many features include standard RSA digital signature for software signing, an online certificate management database, and templates that can be customized to meet the company's specifications including JavaScript applets that illustrate certificate management. All open standards are supported including X.509v3 certificates, HTML, HTTP, PKCS 10, and directory servers using LDAP. The Certificate Server can also be managed remotely, while still maintaining data encryption and authorization integrity. Pricing is not available at this time. You should expect to see Netscape's Certificate Server released sometime in the third quarter of 1996.

FIG. 27.21

Connections to insecure servers are marked with a broken key in the lower left hand corner.

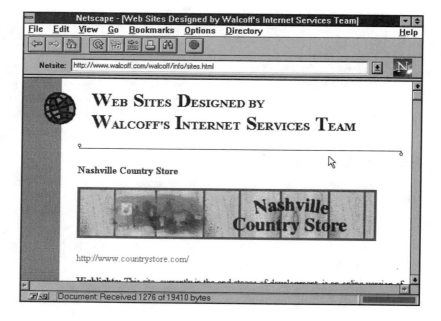

FIG. 27.22

A connection to a secure server is marked with a solid key in the lower-left corner, a blue bar underneath the location line, and the prefix https before the site address.

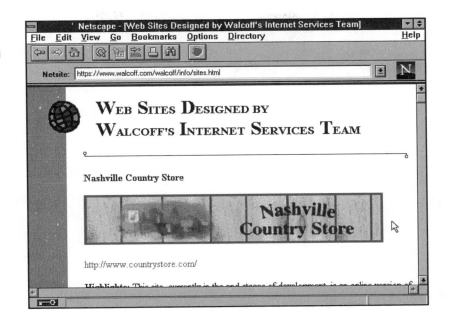

Advanced Netscape Customization

## CHAPTER 28

Sun's Java and the Netscape Browser

Java is a new programming language created by Sun Microsystems, and has created a lot more excitement than new programming languages usually generate. Programmers are excited about Java because the language supports many useful features, such as an object-oriented structure, intuitive multithreading, and built-in network support. The language also avoids many of the pitfalls of C++. Where C++ forces the programmer to keep track of the memory that he uses, a Java programmer doesn't need to worry about using memory reserved for the system or not freeing up memory appropriately.

Java programmers don't need to worry about how memory is utilized because of how a Java program is run. Java is a semi-compiled language. When you program in a compiled language like C++, the compiler takes your source code and creates a file that is ready for the system to execute. A Java compiler doesn't work this way. Instead, it creates a file that contains bytecodes. This file is then handed to an interpreter that sits on your computer. That interpreter executes the program. The interpreter keeps track of how memory is used, and can let the programmer know if something has gone wrong. This is different from an errant C++ program, which simply stops, sometimes after crashing the system. Because of this, it is much harder to debug C++ programs than programs written in Java.

But these advantages aren't the only reasons that Java is generating so much excitement. Its semi-compiled nature allows the language to be architecture neutral, which means that you can compile your Java program once and it is ready to run on many different platforms. But the real brilliance of Java is that it is designed with distributed systems in mind. Part of this is the built-in networking support. The more important part is that a Java program can be transferred across the Internet to your computer and the interpreter can make sure that it doesn't do anything bad to the system.

But you are probably asking, "Why does this interest me, a Netscape 3.0 user?" The reason that it should is that Netscape 3.0 has a Java interpreter built in, which means that instead of just downloading pictures, sound, and text, Netscape 3.0 can download small programs called applets, which are then run on your computer. These applets, which are written in Java, can display animations, allow you to play games, or get stock prices from a remote computer. Whatever these applets do, you don't have to worry about them crashing your system, spreading a virus, or wiping out your hard drive.

In this chapter, you learn

- What a Java Applet is
- How Java Applets are changing the Web
- How Java works in Netscape
- What people have been designing Java Applets to do
- Where to find a wealth of online Java resources ■

Why Java Is Waking Up the Internet

In the Spring of 1995, Sun Microsystems released a Web browser called HotJava. This Web browser was written in a new programming language called Java. This language was originally intended to handle such tasks as interactive television and coordination of household appliances. The explosion of the Web in 1994 revealed the real opportunity for Java, and work on the Web browser commenced.

Though this Web browser was rough around the edges, it could do some things no other Web browser at that time could. With this Web browser, a user could see animation, play games, and even view a ticker tape of their up-to-date stock prices. Almost immediately after its release, Netscape decided to license HotJava's technology and incorporate it into its browsers. Netscape's incorporation of this technology into Netscape 3.0 makes this technology available to a much wider audience than before. This wider audience, along with the capabilities that Java provides, is revolutionizing the Web.

What Is a Java Applet?

Netscape 3.0 can run Java Applets, which are small programs that are downloaded from a Web server. There isn't anything special about how it does this; it downloads a Java Applet in precisely the same manner as it downloads any file. Just as any browser displays an image as it is received, a Java-capable browser runs the Java Applet. When the Java Applet runs, it is much (but not exactly) like any other program that can run on your computer. It can take input from your keyboard, mouse, or even a remote computer. The output displays on your screen.

But there are differences between a Java Applet and the applications that sit on your desktop. You wouldn't want Netscape 3.0 to download a virus. At the same time, you wouldn't want to have to check every program that came down, because most programmers have no interest in harming your computer. Because of the way that the Java language is structured, you don't have to worry about a Java Applet harming your computer.

But this does mean that there have been some restrictions placed on Java Applets. In fact, a Java Applet knows next to nothing about your computer. It can't look or write to any file in your file system. It can use your computer's memory, but not directly. These restrictions on a Java Applet keep your computer safe from harm, and also protect your privacy.

How a Java Applet Is Different from the CGI Program

Anyone who has been around the Web for a while knows that programs can be run on the Web without Java. One of the reasons the Web, without Java, has become so popular is that the Web allows simple interaction across the Internet. It does this through the Common Gateway Interface (CGI). The CGI underlies electronic forms, imagemaps, and search engines. Basically, it runs a program that resides on the server. The program, called a CGI program, outputs a Web page, and that Web page is sent back to the client (see fig. 28.1).

The Common Gateway Interface puts the Web a step above other information protocols such as FTP and Gopher because it allows you to tell a remote computer to do things for you. It is great for information providers because they can let you do very specific tasks without having to give you, and the rest of the world, the run of their machines.

CGI programs are great for a lot of things. For instance, let's say that you are an officer of a club that is running a Web server. Through the use of a simple CGI program, you can give your members a way to keep their mailing addresses up to date. You can put an electronic form on your Web site, and if someone moves, she can just access that form and enter her new address. Then, the CGI program takes that information and updates the database.

However, there are many limitations of CGI programs that applets overcome (see table 28.1).

Table 28.1   Differences Between CGI Programs and Java Applets

Property	Java Applet	CGI Program
Get information from remote computer	Yes	Yes
Computer that it runs on	Client	Server
How it handles input and output	Instantaneously across the Internet	Only after transmission

FIG. 28.1
How programs are transmitted over the Web.

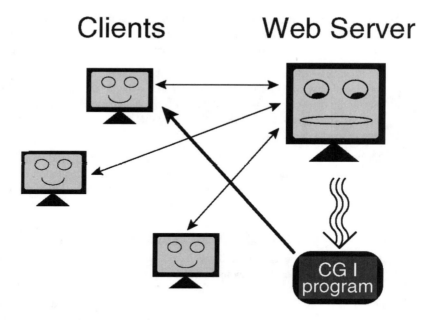

The limitations of CGI programs are outlined in table 28.1, but let's also look at something that has been done with both a CGI program and a Java Applet. Figure 28.2 shows a tic-tac-toe game that was done using a Java Applet. Tic-tac-toe also has been done many times using CGI programs, and looks a lot like this.

For both the CGI implementation and the applet implementation, you simply click where you want the X to go.

First, let's look at how the CGI implementation handles the input. Your Web browser takes that information and transmits it to the Web server. The Web server runs the CGI program. The CGI program figures out the best response and writes a Web page indicating this. That page is then transmitted back across the Internet.

FIG. 28.2
Tic-tac-toe with a Java Applet.

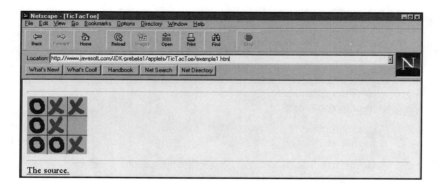

When tic-tac-toe is implemented using a Java Applet, the Java Applet figures out the best move. Because no communication takes place across the Internet, it is much faster.

Of course, for something as simple as tic-tac-toe, one could argue that speed isn't very important. But for something like Tetris, speed is important (see fig. 28.3). It would be a boring game of Tetris if you had to wait several seconds between each move of a piece. Because a Java Applet runs on your computer, it provides real-time animation. Also, when you interact with the applet by clicking the mouse or pressing a key, the applet knows about it immediately. A CGI program can only know after the data has been transmitted across the Internet.

There are many other examples of Web applications that are best done by an applet. For instance, an applet can ticker the current prices of your stocks across your screen. A virtual world can be downloaded in the form of an applet, and if that virtual world is changed by someone else, your view of it is immediately updated.

Java Applets are faster because they don't have to transmit input and output across the Internet. They are also better than CGI programs for many applications because the server doesn't have to process anything. This was a big problem with Netscape's first attempt at animation and interactivity. This attempt was called Server Push and Client Pull and it was based on the Common Gateway Interface. After the page was loaded, a CGI program would hold the connection open and update the page as necessary. This allowed a Web page designer to make a page dynamic and interactive.

But Tetris, for example, would have two distinct disadvantages as a CGI program. First, playing the game is slower, because input and output still have to be transmitted across the Internet. Second, the increased load resulting from such rapid-fire contact slows down the server enough that other clients experience the delay, as we see in figure 28.4.

Because Server Push and Client Pull have such an ill effect on the server, many Web sites have banned their information providers from using it. This is a real shame because any machine powerful enough to run a graphical Web browser could easily be a Web server. The processing power of the client machine sits idle while a busy server handles the computation.

The use of applets means that your machine can do processing that the server doesn't have to do, leaving the server to concentrate on its real purpose: serving information. Even in cases where speed might not be crucial, it is still better to use Java Applets for interactivity. The processing is more evenly balanced, as shown in figure 28.5.

CGI Programs Versus Java Applets—When to Use What

If you are a Web page designer, you are probably wondering when a Java Applet is appropriate and when a CGI program is. For two reasons, applets do not completely replace the Common Gateway Interface. First, not all Web browsers are able to run applets. Unless you can be guaranteed that the users of your particular service are going to have a Java-enabled version of Netscape or some other browser, you should consider providing an alternative version of your service.

FIG. 28.3

Tetris with a Java Applet.

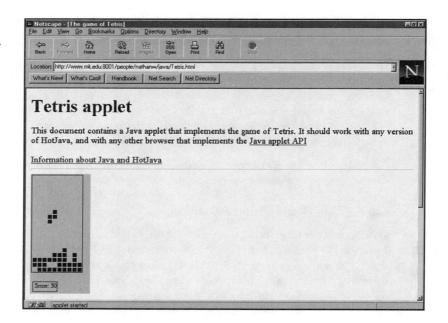

FIG. 28.4

Interactivity through the Common Gateway Interface.

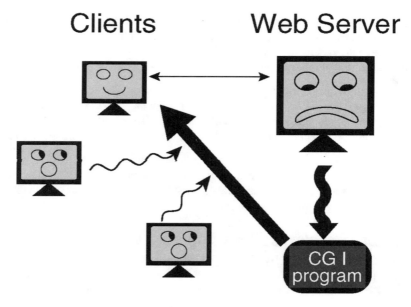

FIG. 28.5
Processing responsibilities balanced with use of Java Applets.

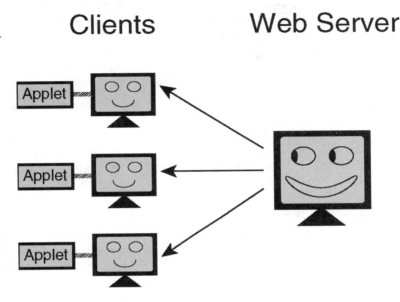

Clients   Web Server

Second, if your program is using a central database, you should use a CGI program. For example, a search engine should function as a CGI program. Advanced search engines, such as WAIS, Lycos, and Harvest, maintain a database of keywords. Instead of directly searching Web pages for some keyword, a CGI program simply looks in the database. An applet couldn't act as a search engine nearly as well because it would have to traverse the network looking for some keyword.

In the search engine example, the database is only read. Since an applet isn't allowed to write to any file system, you can't use an applet to modify a database, either. If you want visitors to your Web site to fill out a survey, you would probably want to use a CGI program.

Unless you are dealing with a central store of information, you should consider using Java Applets. They reduce the load on the Web server and allow more interactivity. They also make more dynamic Web pages.

Remember, Java Applets and CGI programs are not mutually exclusive. Let's look back at the search engine example. We definitely don't want an applet to search the entire Web when a CGI program can just do a quick lookup in its database. But by writing an applet that communicates with the CGI program, we can provide superior interactivity. The CGI program can generate the raw results of the search, while the applet provides an advanced interface. Instead of just providing a list of pages containing a keyword, an applet can display a map for each of those pages. That map can show the pages that are directly linked from a certain page containing that keyword. Then, you can focus your energies on those parts of the Web where the information you want is most centralized.

Also, an applet can easily keep track of what a user has done. Let's go back to the example of someone modifying a database that resides on your Web server. If you want people to be able

Part
VI

Ch
28

to make a lot of modifications, you have to assume that they are going to make some mistakes. An applet can easily keep track of what they have done and correct any mistakes with the press of a button. However, a CGI program has a hard time providing this functionality, because it is responsible for answering many users. It is quite difficult for a CGI program to keep track of who has done what, and even more difficult for it to provide an intuitive interface.

Let's expand this example a bit. Let's say that there are many databases on different machines that need to be manipulated by some user. An applet can make it appear that all of them are the same. When the user wants information from a certain one, the applet figures out which CGI program to connect to. This is much more intuitive and less time-consuming than forcing the user to link directly to the CGI program. Still, the applet can provide interactive features like an Undo key.

How Java Allows the Web to Evolve Itself

Java allows applet writers to build on the Web's current infrastructure. If there is some capability that a Web browser doesn't have, a Java Applet can often be written to give the Web browser that capability. Such possible capabilities include interactive features that you expect from your normal desktop applications and the capability to understand new protocols. The applet writer doesn't have to write an entire Web browser. This is important, because it is hard to expect the entire Internet to adapt to a new way of doing things, even if it is a great idea.

If a new way of compressing video data were to be invented, the inventors wouldn't have to convince everyone that it was great. Instead, they could just write an applet that utilizes their new method. They wouldn't have to distribute software that everyone would then have to install on their computers. They wouldn't have to wait for Web browser makers to adopt their technology. The applet could simply be downloaded at the same time the data is. If they decide to add a feature, they could just do it, and their improved software would be available instantly.

Java allows the Web to become a programming platform. Without Java, new network programs have to be developed from the ground up. Before, if you wanted to develop an Internet-wide conferencing system, you had to develop an application that would run on the user's desktop. Your users would have to acquire the software and install it themselves. With a Java-ized Web, you would simply write an applet and put it on your Web site. Anyone with a Java-enabled browser, such as Netscape 3.0, would have whatever level of access to the software that you allow. Your distribution costs drop to nothing. Also, the development would be easier because the Java language was designed for distributed network computing.

This is what makes Java, in the words of Mark Andresseen, "as revolutionary as the Web itself." Given a Web server, anyone who can write a Web page can add information to the Web. With Java, any programmer can add to the Web's very infrastructure. The Web will not grow only in terms of content. It now has the capability of evolving itself. Instead of your bank or travel agent merely having information online, the future will see you being able to do all your banking and booking an entire trip from your computer. The applets that you will use will have interfaces of equal or better quality than any other application on your desktop. Plus, you won't have to download them and install them on your computer; they will be instantly downloaded when you access the particular Web site.

What Java Can Do Beyond the Web

It is important to know that Java is not just a part of the Web. It is a complete, object-oriented, programming language designed to overcome some of the limitations of C++.

Right now, applets as we know them can only run in some Web browsers. But applets aren't bound just to Web browsers. Any application that sits on your desktop can be upgraded to connect to the Web and make use of special applets.

Imagine that your spreadsheet program can deal with special applets. One of these special Java Applets can talk to a server sitting on Wall Street. When the price of one of your stocks changes, the server tells the Java Applet, and the Java Applet updates your spreadsheet automatically.

Now your formulas that deal with stock prices always deal with live data. They deal with live data because when you open up your spreadsheet, it downloads this applet that puts the appropriate stock prices into the places they are supposed to be. No longer do you have to look up the prices and enter them into your spreadsheet. They are already there, and they are current. When you take your report to your meeting, the data is as current as when you printed it out.

Still, this isn't the end of what Java can do for the Internet and the programming world. You may or may not turn your computer off when you leave for home. Could you be persuaded to leave your computer on all night if it could help solve some massive problem, like global warming?

Consider the following scenario: A central computer checks with your computer at some appointed time, a few hours after you go home. If it isn't busy, it sends an applet across the Internet. Your computer runs that applet all night. When you come in the next morning and press a key, your computer sends the applet back across the Internet to the central "problem server." The problem server takes the data that has been crunched and incorporates it into a database. With the help of your computer and thousands of others, the problem is eventually solved. Better yet, the research institution working on this problem didn't have to purchase several supercomputers to solve it. And you were able to help solve a problem like global warming by simply going home.

The thrust of these examples is based on a simple fact: There is a lot of information and a lot of processing power on the millions of computers all over the world. What Java does is allow computers to access and deal with all of that information safely. There is no reason that you should have to manually insert data into a program when it is available on the Internet. Your computer is capable of getting the data and inserting it. Along the same lines, there is no reason that your computer should sit idle when there are pressing problems to be solved. The use of Java in software not only makes the end user's life easier, but also brings all of the computers on the Internet into a true working community.

Part
VI

Ch
28

How Java Works in Netscape 3.0

Netscape 3.0 has the ability to run Java Applets. Because of how it is set up, a Java Applet knows next to nothing about your computer. This means that you don't have to worry about a Java Applet doing damage to your computer. But if you just want to see cool applets, you don't need to know anything about it. If this is all you want to do, just read the following section, "How to Access Java Applets with Netscape 3.0," and start exploring.

> **N O T E**   Netscape 3.0 improved Java and JavaScript, adding security enhancements, support for Macintosh, Windows 3.1, IBM AIX and BSDI platforms, and support for additional languages, such as Chinese, Japanese, and Korean. With JavaScript, users can now change GIF and JPEG images on the fly as well as detect which plug-ins are loaded on a page.
>
> In addition, Netscape 3.0's new LiveConnect protocol allows Web developers to script, link, and control live objects such as plug-ins, Java applets, and HTML objects. ▪

How to Access Java Applets with Netscape 3.0

There is nothing complicated about accessing applets with Netscape 3.0. After your browser is set up correctly, you don't need to configure anything to enable Java. To the user, an applet is simply a part of a Web page, just as an image or text can be. In the case that a page contains an image, the browser takes care of getting that image and displaying it. With a Java-enabled browser, the same is true with applets. When you access a Web page that has an applet embedded in it, the browser fetches the code and takes care of running it.

Running an applet is not hard. It takes no advanced planning or configuring. As long as your version of Netscape 3.0 is Java-enabled, you can just point your Web browser at a page that contains the applet you want. There is a list of Web sites at the end of this chapter that have Java Applet pages. As long as these Java pages don't tell you that your browser doesn't support Java, you are ready to start exploring the Java-ized Web.

> **CAUTION**
> Some Java Applets cannot be accessed by Netscape 3.0, even if your version supports Java Applet handling. This is because many Java Applets were written while Java was still being developed. Those Java Applets are not compatible with the current standard.

How Netscape Runs Java Applets

Now let's look at the technical issues involved in running an applet. When Netscape encounters an HTML page with an APPLET tag, it retrieves the compiled Java classes from the remote server in the same way that it retrieves any other object. After the applet has been downloaded across the network onto your machine, it is subjected to various security checks before it is actually loaded and run. These checks are performed by the Java verifier. After the code is checked, it is loaded into its own place in the Netscape's applet runtime environment. This is done by the Java class loader. This loading is done in such a way that an applet is kept separate from system resources and other applets.

> **N O T E** In object-oriented languages, classes are the definitions of objects. When a programmer is writing his program, he writes a class. When the program is run, the computer takes that definition and creates an object. ▪

Because Java code is platform independent, it must be interpreted, or translated, into instructions that your machine can understand. This translation is performed by the Java interpreter. The Java interpreter can be thought of as a special viewer application that allows Netscape 3.0 to run applets inline.

This whole process disallows the applet from harming your computer in any way. This is explained further in the next section on Java and safety, "Why Java Applets Won't Harm Your Computer."

Why Java Applets Won't Harm Your Computer

The idea of your machine executing code fragments downloaded from a public network most likely makes your stomach a bit uneasy. People often ask if a Java Applet could erase their files or propagate a virus into their computer. Luckily, safe execution was a major consideration from the very start of making Java.

The Java language, and the technology Netscape 3.0 uses to run applets, provides many defenses against malicious applets. These strict language security mechanisms, coupled with Netscape 3.0's watchful eye, create an environment in which code can be run on your machine with virtually no chance of it accessing your private data or starting a virus.

The Java Console Window

Many programmers write their applets so that they print out messages while they are executing. Usually, this information helps the programmer see whether or not an applet is encountering problems. In Netscape 3.0, the Java Console window provides a way for you to view the direct output of an applet as it is running. Just select Show Java Console Window from the Options menu. The Java Console window pops up as shown in figure 28.6.

Later, if you write your own applets, this window is your way of keeping tabs on your applet during the development process. If you need to, you can copy from this window and paste in another document.

The Four Layers of Defense

Java contains multiple layers of security, each serving to filter out harmful code. This section will provide you with a firm understanding of how Java's security layers serve to protect your machine. At the same time, this section will give you the security background necessary to program your own applets.

FIG. 28.6
The Java Console
window.

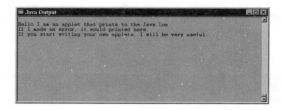

The four layers of security built into Java and Netscape are as follows:

- The Java language and compiler
- Java bytecode verification and strong type information
- Java's class loader
- Restrictions on local file system and network access

Safety Layer One—The Java Language's Defenses   The first layer of safety in the Java language comes from its lack of the harmful language and compiler features that C and C++ both possess. Java does not allow the programmer to directly manipulate memory. C and C++, however, do allow direct manipulation of memory, which means that a careless programmer can manipulate memory that the system has reversed for its use. This is the usual cause for a system crash. A malicious programmer can also use this weakness to propagate a virus.

Let's focus on how the Java Applet interacts with Netscape 3.0 after it is downloaded. The fundamental line of defense is that Netscape 3.0 keeps the Java Applet from dealing with a specific memory address on your computer. Of course, a Java Applet does use your computer's memory. It is just that Netscape 3.0 won't let an applet look at or write to a specific memory address. If the applet needs to change something in that data, it hands its changes back to Netscape 3.0 (see fig. 28.7). Netscape 3.0 actually changes the data in memory.

Unlike C and C++, the structure of the Java language requires this interpreter. With a C or C++ program, the programmer might not be malicious or careless and maybe he used an advanced compiler that won't produce evil programs. You don't have to hope that a Java program won't harm your computer; the interpreter simply won't allow it. Because a Java program must access memory through the interpreter, that interpreter is in complete control. Netscape 3.0 acts as a firewall between a Java Applet and your computer. It does this by isolating the program from the rest of the system and acting as its guardian. By forcing a Java program to obey its guardian, the Java language itself keeps the program from misbehaving and harming your system.

Besides direct memory manipulation, the Java language also deals very carefully with casting. Casting allows a programmer to change one data type to another, even if this shouldn't be done. In C++, a programmer is able to cast a complex object to a much simpler type, like an array of bytes. Generally, doing this is an error and causes the program to crash. However, a malicious programmer can use this to change the object itself. He can overwrite the individual bytes that make up the object so that it does something that the language doesn't allow. The Java language only allows the programmer to cast between types when it makes sense to cast.

It checks all attempts to cast very carefully, while C and C++ allow the programmer to cast between literally any two data types. Java's strong checking of casting closes the back door on the type of memory manipulation described earlier.

These are the ways that the Java language itself assures a certain degree of safety for all Java programs. But these features aren't enough to prevent an applet from harming your computer. This layer is just the foundation for the other layers of safety in the Java environment. You will now see why this layer means very little without the support of the following layers.

Safety Layer Two—Making Sure the Applet Isn't Faking It   After a Java, C, or C++ program is written, the author compiles it. For C and C++, the compilation process produces an executable file. This file can be loaded into your computer's memory and run. Most programs on your desktop have been created through this process.

FIG. 28.7
How a Java Applet accesses memory.

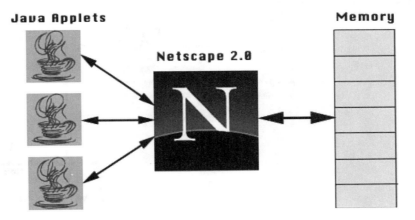

Java is a semi-compiled language, and its compilation process is different. When Java is compiled, the compiler produces platform-independent machine instructions called bytecodes. These bytecodes are what Netscape retrieves from a remote server, and then executes on your machine (see fig. 28.8). Because a compiler can easily be altered to bypass the first level of security, these bytecodes must be subjected to strong tests before being executed on your machine.

The second layer of safety accomplishes this. When Netscape 3.0 downloads an applet, the bytecode of that applet is examined by your browser's verifier. The verifier subjects each code fragment to a sequence of tests before it is allowed to execute. It first looks to see that the bytecode has all of the information about the different data types that are going to be used. There is actually more of this type of information than strictly necessary. This excess of information helps the verifier analyze the rest of the bytecode.

It is possible for a malicious programmer to write a Java compiler that doesn't follow all the rules of the Java language. He could write it so that it produces code that tricks the compiler into harming your computer. The verifier ensures that no such code ever reaches the interpreter. It checks to make sure that the bytecode plays by the rules of the Java language, and protects the integrity of the interpreter.

Part
VI

Ch
28

N O T E An example of an alternative Java compiler is Borland's C++ Development Suite, version 5.0. While it is by no means "malicious" in any way, it will compile Java bytecode all by itself, but it is still checked by the verifier for security. For more information, check out **http://www.borland.com**. ■

Safety Layer Three—Keeping an Applet Separate The class loader offers Java's third line of defense. As independent pieces of code are loaded and executed, the class loader makes sure that different applets can't interfere with each other. It also means that each and every applet is completely separate from the Java objects already resident that it needs to actually run. This means that an applet can't go and replace parts of Netscape 3.0 needed to run applets.

FIG. 28.8

How Java Applets run.

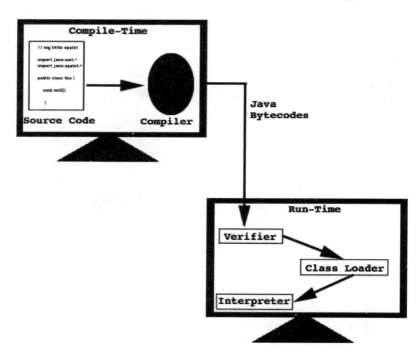

If it could replace these parts, all layers of safety could be undermined. All applets depend on the interpreter to provide it with some of the basic constructs of the Java language. If the applets aren't kept strictly separate, an applet can override some of these basic constructs. By overriding these basic constructs, the applet can violate the integrity of the Java language itself, and trick the interpreter into hurting your system.

Netscape 3.0 Includes Borland's Java JIT Compiler

Netscape enhanced its Java support when they struck a deal with Borland International Inc. to include the Borland JIT compiler, APP*Accelerator*, for Windows 95.

Although the Java programming language produces dynamic live Web pages, users and developers have complained of its slow compile time. App*Accelerator* translates Java bytecodes into machine code (Intel in this case) allowing programs to execute 5-10 times faster. The JIT compiler will entice more developers to create Java programs and, given its fast compile time, will enable users to quickly use Java applets without further time delays.

Safety Layer Four—Protecting Your File System   The fourth level of defense against harmful applets comes in the form of file system access protection. Applets are restricted from any access to the local file system, so they can neither read your files, overwrite your existing files, nor generate new ones. This not only protects your privacy, but also prevents your files from being corrupted or infected by viruses.

The interpreter protects your computer's safety by simply disallowing all Java language calls that deal with files. The Java language itself, being equivalent to C++, does have the ability to deal with a file system. But the interpreter in Netscape 3.0 won't allow applets to have that capability. If an applet tries to open a file, the interpreter just tells the applet that the file system does not exist.

N O T E   The Java language ensures that a Java program can only affect your system in safe ways. Even if someone troubled himself to write a fake Java compiler, the verifier in Netscape 3.0 would figure it out and refuse to run the applet. The class loader makes sure that applets are kept separate from your system and other applets. To top it all off, the interpreter doesn't even allow an applet to access the file system. This means that an applet only knows about the Netscape 3.0 applet runtime environment, and can't access any part of your computer beyond that. ▨

Including Java Applets in Web Pages—The APPLET Tag

Including an applet in a Web document is accomplished via an extension to HTML called the APPLET tag. This tag, along with the PARAM tag, allows the Web page designer to include and configure executable content in documents. The general syntax for including an applet in a Web page is as follows:

```
<APPLET CODEBASE=codebaseURL  CODE=appletFile.class WIDTH=pixels HEIGHT=pixels>
<PARAM NAME=someAttributeName VALUE=1st_attributeValue>
<PARAM NAME=someOtherAttributeName VALUE=Nth_attributeValue>
{Alternate HTML displayed by non-java enabled browsers}
</APPLET>
```

The following are the definitions of the various tags:

- APPLET—Signifies that an applet is to be included in the document.
- CODEBASE—The path, to the classes directory containing the Java code. If this field is omitted, then the CODEBASE is assumed to be the same as the document's URL.
- CODE—The name of the applet to be included in your page. This file always ends in .class, which indicates that it is a compiled Java class. It should be noted that this variable is relative to the applet's base URL and should not be given as absolute.

- HEIGHT and WIDTH—The dimensions in units of pixels that the applet takes up on your Web page.
- PARAM—Used to pass a parameter to an applet.
- NAME—The name of the parameter. This name must be understood by the applet.
- VALUE—The value that corresponds to a given name. This is where you may enter your configurations.

As shown above, alternative HTML can be included between the open and close APPLET tags. This code is intended to be displayed if the person who accesses your page is not using a Java-enabled browser, such as Netscape 3.0. If Netscape 3.0 can't download the Java Applet, it shows the alternative HTML.

If the browser can run the Java Applet, then the alternative text is not shown. This feature comes in very handy when designing pages for an audience mixed between Java-enabled and non-Java-enabled browsers.

TIP When including applets in your Web pages, use alternative HTML inside the APPLET tag as a courtesy to people whose browsers are not Java-enabled.

The PARAM tag makes it possible for Web page designers to configure an applet to their special needs. This feature allows applets to be written as generalized tools that can be configured to work in many different situations. Someone who has no desire to learn all of the details of programming applets can customize other people's Java Applets to fit his own needs. For example, a simple animation applet can be told which sequence of images it should load and display. Because such an applet can be configured, many people can run different animations using the same code. You can imagine that without the PARAM tag, using Java would become much more difficult for designers. If applets were not configurable, in the case of the animation applet, individual designers would each have to customize their own copy of the program.

Let's look now at a simple example that shows how to include a configurable applet in a Web page. For simplicity, we will use the Blinking Text example from the Java Product Development Team. This applet displays a text string in multiple colors and then blinks each word at random. It takes two parameters; lbl is the text string that is displayed and speed is the rate at which the text blinks.

To include this applet in one of your Web pages, add this code:

```
<HR>
<APPLET
CODEBASE="http://www.javasoft.com/JDK-prebeta1/applets/Blink/"
CODE="Blink.class" WIDTH=300 HEIGHT=130>
<PARAM NAME=lbl VALUE="Configuring Applets is easy and very useful.
with Netscape 3.0, we can make an applet do what WE WANT!">
<PARAM NAME=speed VALUE="4">
Sorry, you should be using Netscape 3.0. <BR>
Your browser is not Java enabled!!!!
</APPLET>
<HR>
```

Figure 28.9 shows what you should see when you load your page, if you are using Netscape 3.0.

FIG. 28.9
Results of configuration.

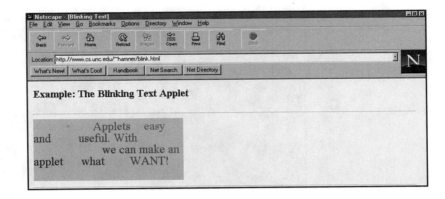

In this example, the Blinking Text Applet is loaded from a remote site (**http://www.javasoft.com**, in this case). This shows that you are not obligated to download the applet onto your own machine just to include it on a Web page. As always, when including someone else's work in your pages, you should make sure you have the permission of the author first.

N O T E It is impossible to describe, generally, how Java Applets should be configured. It is totally up to the author of a Java Applet to decide how the applet may be configured and to provide documentation for the applet user. ■

Examples of Java Applets on the Internet

In the short time that Java has been alive, the World Wide Web has come to life with clever Java programs. Here are a few examples that show the kind of stuff that Java can do for the Web. Be sure to point Netscape 3.0 at the URLs to see them in action.

Entertainment and Games on the Web

Because so much of the Web is designed to entertain, it isn't surprising that people have been writing applets to further the cause. Many applets are designed to spice up Web pages. Probably the most common example is the use of applets to embed animation into a Web page.

Many applets let us play games over the Web. For example, applets for mine sweeper and tic-tac-toe have been written. The applet shown in figure 28.10 lets you fill in a crossword puzzle. It has a couple of advantages over the crossword puzzle in your daily newspaper. First, you don't have to strain to find the clue; you just click the mouse in the box. The clue appears at the top. Second, it gives you feedback. Incorrect responses are displayed in red, while correct ones are shown in black.

Crossword purists may not consider these improvements, but it is a good example of how applets add interactivity to the Web.

FIG. 28.10
Java crossword puzzle.

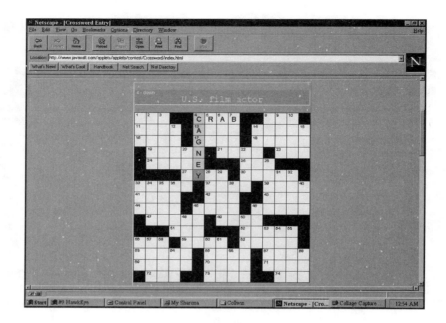

Educational Java Applets

Java is providing new opportunities in education that were never before possible. Now an educator can write an applet that demonstrates some complex subject. His demonstration can be interactive and instantly available to a worldwide audience.

A great example of the educational potential of Java is the applet shown in figure 28.11.

This applet walks us through the Pythagorean Theorem. In case you don't remember your geometry, the Pythagorean Theorem is the one that proves that the lengths of the sides of a right triangle are related.

Real-World Business Applications

The ease with which applets can deal with data on a remote computer makes them a good fit with the information needs of companies. Additionally, applets can also provide a good interface to services provided by a company.

The example shown in figure 28.12 was created by the Java Product Development Team. For this particular demo, the stock prices are randomly generated by a remote server. They could just as easily come from a server that has the correct data. We can expect that a service providing real stock prices will be available soon from some enterprising Web site.

FIG. 28.11

Interactive mathematical proof.

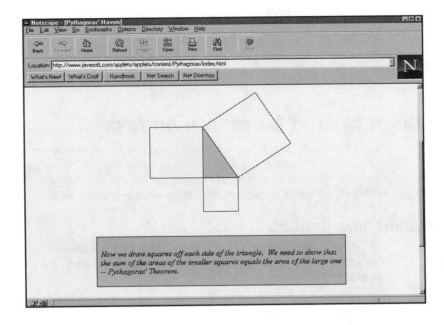

FIG. 28.12

Real-time financial portfolio.

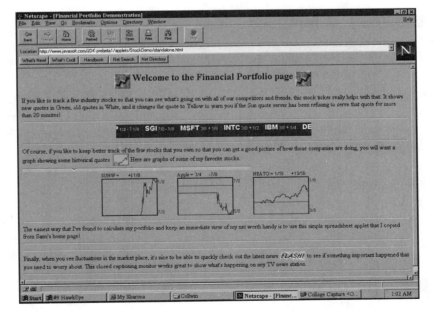

Many companies outside the software industry are exploring the usefulness of Java. Some of these include:

- Dow Jones
- Internet Underground Music Archive
- NBC
- Random House

Where to Find More Info on Java

Sun maintains a complete set of documentation on Java at **http://www.javasoft.com**. At this site, you can find everything from language documentation to tutorials. Yahoo has a rather extensive index of pointers to Java resources. You can find this listing at **http://www.yahoo.com/Computers_and_Internet/Languages/Java**.

Finding Java Applets

If it is Java Applets you seek, then check out the Gamelan site at **http://www.gamelan.com/**. This site acts as a registry of applets. It contains links to hundreds of applets, all categorized by subject.

The Java Development Team also maintains its own listing of applets, which can be found at **http://www.javasoft.com/Applets**.

Language References

The definitive overview of the Java language is the Java Language White Paper, written by the Java Development Team. It is at **http://www.javasoft.com/whitePaper/javawhitepaper_1.html**.

The Java Development Team also has an online overview of the security features inherent to applets. It is available at **http://www.javasoft.com/1.0alpha3/doc/security/security.html**.

Newsgroups and Mailing Lists

For information specific to Java, you should regularly read the newsgroup **comp.lang.java@news:comp.lang.java**.

Sun Microsystems, the inventor of Java and applets, also maintains a mailing list concerning Java. To subscribe, send mail to **majordomo@www.javasoft.com**, and enter **subscribe java-interest@www.javasoft.com** <your email address> in the body of the message. Replace <your email address> with your full Internet e-mail address.

Other Resources

Digital Espresso, produced by Mentor Software Solutions, is a well-formatted, easy-to-read summary of the newsgroups and mailing lists pertaining to Java and Java Applets. Information is updated weekly and broken down into categories. You can find Digital Espresso at **http://www.io.org/~mentor/JavaNotes.html**. ●

## CHAPTER 29

Java for C++ Programmers

Java is a new language and set of class libraries developed by Sun Microsystems. In its white paper on the language, Sun defines Java as "a simple, object-oriented, distributed, interpreted, robust, secure, architecture-neutral, portable, high-performance, multithreaded, and dynamic language." That's quite a definition! We'll look at exactly what Sun means by it in this chapter.

There is no way to cover every component of the Java language in one chapter. This chapter gives an introduction to the Java language and takes a look at its basic structure and classes.

In this chapter, you learn:

- Java fundamentals
- How Java differs from C and C++
- A basic Java program
- Java syntax
- Java's class library

The World According to Java

Until now, the various pages on the Web have been fairly static in their ability to interact with the user. With the current conventional Web tools, it's not easy to provide real-time interaction for a user without performing a lot of CPU processing on your Web server. For example, animation sequences require server push operations to send the new images out to the client browser program.

Another problem with the current paradigm is that you, the user—or your poor system administrator—have to keep up with all the different helper applications that you need to really use Netscape to its fullest. Now, how many of you have the latest versions of all your helper apps installed and configured?

Sun Microsystems raised the ante in the Web game when it introduced the Java language and the HotJava Web browser. The goal of Java is to provide a development language that is uniquely suited to developing Web applications. At the same time, Java gives you the ability to deliver both data content and a small application that manipulates the data to the client browser in real time. These small applications, known as applets, are downloaded to a user's computer and activated by his Web browser transparently whenever the user views a page that contains an applet. This keeps the promise of no longer needing to download and configure helper applications for all the different types of data that you want to view.

Java is uniquely suited for developing Web applications, and provides support for parallelism by supporting multithreading. Also, Java is a multi-platform language: Any Java applet or application will run directly on any platform that supports the Java runtime system. We'll look at how this works later in the chapter.

Current Java Information

Since Java is a new language with lots of new features, it can be difficult to get current information on Java. As this book is being written, the Java Development Kit, from Sun Microsystems, is in beta release. It has gone through both an alpha and pre-beta incarnation stage. Supposedly, the methods for building applets and the API for the Java classes have been finalized—but be prepared for future changes, just in case.

The best source for up-to-the-minute information on Java and the Java development tools is the Sun Microsystem Java Web site. It can be found on the Web at **http://java.sun.com/**. From this location, you can get the Java Development Kit (JDK), the documentation for the JDK in both HTML and PostScript format, all the documentation for programming the JDK API, and a whole series of lessons on learning to program in Java.

Java Language Features

Java was designed to be an object-oriented language similar to C++ to make it familiar to a large number of programmers. As you see later in the chapter, the syntax of Java is very similar to C++. Because Java is an object-oriented language, this chapter assumes that you are familiar with basic object-oriented concepts, such as classes and inheritance.

N O T E In Java, the basic object-oriented programming element is the class. A class is a collection of related data members and functions, known as methods, that operate on that data. Everything in Java exists within a class—there are no global variables or global functions. ■

In developing Java, Sun chose to leave out several C++ language features. Specifically, Java does not support multiple inheritance, operator overloading, or extensive automatic coercion. Java also takes steps to make pointer operations much safer. Java's pointer model does not allow memory overwrites and data corruption. In fact, Java does not allow pointer arithmetic at all. It supports true arrays with bounds checking. You cannot change an integer to a pointer via a cast operator. In short, Java eliminates many of the confusing, often misused aspects of C++ and creates a smaller, easier to understand language.

Let's look at some of the new features that Java adds. The language has support for automatic garbage collection, so you no longer have to explicitly delete an object. Objects are automatically deleted whenever they are no longer needed. Java has extensive support for distributed applications. It has native support for the TCP/IP protocols, which allows programmers to easily work with objects such as URLs.

Because Java was designed with native support for client/server applications, security is obviously an issue. Java has extensive security support to allow you to create tamper-free systems. Java uses a public-key encryption scheme to provide authentication, and its new pointer model makes it impossible to overwrite secure areas of memory.

If you look back to Sun's definition of Java, you are probably wondering about the architecture-neutral and portable part. Well, Java is really a bytecode-based interpreted language.

Bytecodes are essentially the components of a machine language. They are similar to the object files that you get when you compile a C++ program with your favorite compiler. However, the "machine" language that these bytecodes represent isn't a real machine at all. Bytecodes are really elements of a machine language for an imaginary machine.

By turning a Java program into bytecodes for an imaginary machine language, the bytecodes are not tied to any one computer hardware platform. In fact, they need a special interpreter program to convert them into actual machine instructions for the destination computer.

Why do it this way? For a couple of different reasons. First, by not having the bytecodes represent an actual machine, the compiled Java file is not restricted to any one type of computer. Second, because the bytecode machine language is for an imaginary machine, the designers were able to avoid design problems that are specific to the various types of computers. They were able to design their machine language in a very efficient way, so that even though Java files must be run through an interpreter, they are still very efficient.

When a Java program is compiled, it creates a bytecode image that is interpreted by a Java runtime system. Because this bytecode image has nothing to do with the architecture that the Java program was built on, it will run on any platform that has a Java runtime environment. This means that you only have to write a Java program once—that one version is portable to any platform with the Java runtime environment!

In addition to being architecture-neutral, Java eliminates all platform-specific data types that have plagued C programmers for years. None of the primitive data types are architecture dependent. All of them have specified sizes and arithmetic operations. For example, a float is always an IEEE 754 32-bit floating point number—on any platform.

A common problem with object-oriented development is that when a company releases a new version of a library, all client software that uses that library will have to be recompiled and redistributed. Java was designed to allow classes to add new methods and instance variables with no effect on the client applications.

As you can see, Java truly is an object-oriented distributed language that solves a lot of the problems that plague current object-oriented technology.

Java Development

In order to develop Java applets and applications, you need a copy of the Java Development Kit (JDK). At the time this book went to press, the JDK is in Beta release and is available on Windows 95, NT, and Sun Solaris 2.x platforms. A Macintosh port of the JDK is under development. You can get the JDK from the Sun Microsystems Java Web site at **http://java.sun.com/**.

The process of turning Java source code into compiled Java bytecodes is performed by the Java compiler, javac. To compile a Java program, write your code using your favorite text editor and save it in ASCII text format. The name of the file must have a .JAVA extension. Then, compile the file by typing

```
javac filename.java
```

where `filename.java` is the name of your Java source code file. For each class that is defined in your Java source file, the `javac` compiler generates a file named classname.class where classname is the name of the particular class. For complete details of the Java compilation process, see the online documentation for Java programmers at **http://java.sun.com/doc/programmer.html**.

N O T E   Java places exactly one class in each bytecode compiled .class file.

After you have compiled your Java application into a .class file, you can run the file with the Java bytecode interpreter, which is, coincidentally, named `java`. To do this, you run the `java` command followed by the name of the .class file that has the `main()` method for your Java application. For example:

```
java myclass.class
```

This command would start the Java runtime environment and cause it to execute the file `myclass.class`.

Much of Java's functionality is encapsulated in prewritten collections of classes known as `packages`. These packages are provided with the Java development environment. Each of these packages contains several different classes that are related to a particular topic.

Table 29.1 lists the packages in the Java development library at the time this book was written. Packages prefixed with java are actual Java language classes. The other classes are HotJava classes, used in the development of Sun's HotJava browser.

Table 29.1 Java Packages in the Development Library

Package Name	Description
java.lang	Basic language support classes
java.util	Utility classes such as encoders and decoders
java.io	Different types of I/O streams
java.awt	A platform-independent windowing system
java.awt.image	Class for handling images in the AWT windowing system
java.applet	Class for building applets to run within Web browsers
java.net	Support for TCP/IP networking

Hello World

We start our exploration of Java with an example that almost all good programming languages use—the Hello World program. In Java, there are two different types of programs: applications and applets. An application is designed to run directly in the Java runtime environment. An applet is designed to run as a component of a network browser, such as Netscape Navigator. Of the two, applications are a bit simpler in structure.

The concept of the "Java runtime environment" gets fuzzy here. As you saw in the previous section, there is a stand-alone Java interpreter, Java, that executes a byte code-compiled file. This is how applications are executed. Applets, on the other hand, are designed to run within the context of a Web browser like Netscape. Applets require more complicated programming than applications because they are actually running within the context of another program. This other program, Netscape in this case, actually has a version of the Java interpreter embedded within it. This means that when Netscape executes a Java applet, it is actually acting as the Java runtime environment for the applet.

Here is the Java code for the Hello World application:

```
class HelloApp
{
public static void main(String args[])
{
System.out.println("Hello World!");
}
}
```

In Java, all functions and variables exist within a class object; there are no global functions or variables in a Java application. So, the first line of this sample application defines a class named `HelloApp`.

Inside `HelloApp`'s definition, there is one method called `main`. The `main` method is the method that is invoked when the application's execution is started in the Java runtime environment. Because you have to specify the class that you want to execute in the Java runtime environment, Java invokes the `main` method for that class.

The `main` method is declared to be `public static void`. The `public` keyword means that the `main` method is visible to all other classes outside this class. The `static` keyword indicates that `main` is a static method, which means that `main` is associated directly with the class `HelloApp` instead of with an instance of `HelloApp`. Without the `static` keyword, `main` would have been an instance method—a method that is associated with an instance of a class. We'll look at another example in a minute.

The next line of code in the `main` method appears to print the "Hello World" string as output. So what exactly is `System.out.println`? `System` refers to Java's `System` class. The word `out` is an instance variable in the `System` class, and `println` is one of `out`'s methods. Notice that we never declared an instance of the `System` class; we just called `out.println` directly. That is because `out` is a static variable of the `System` class. We can refer to it directly by just referring to the class itself.

Command Line Arguments

You'll notice that the arguments to `main` are different than they are in a regular C or C++ program. Instead of the traditional `argv` and `argc` arguments, Java gives you an array of strings that contain the command line arguments. This is not an array of pointers as it is under C and C++, but an array of real strings. You can get the length of the array with the `.length` function of the `String` class. For example, the length of the command line argument array is `args.length`.

Another major difference between Java and C++ is that the name of the application program is not passed in the command line argument array. The name of the application program is always the same as the class name where the `main` method is defined. So, while under C++, for example:

```
foo arg1 arg2
```

Running the program foo with two arguments would make the first entry in the command line argument array "foo." While under Java:

```
java foo arg1 arg2
```

The word `java` invokes the runtime environment, and the word `foo` is the class that has `main` defined. Thus, the first argument in the command line arguments array, `args[0]`, is "arg1."

Introduction to Classes

Classes form the basic program component in Java. Every function and variable must be contained in a class. There are no global functions or variables supported by Java. Here is an example of a Java class declaration:

```
/** latitude and longitude of a location **/
public class Location
{
int lat, long;    //latitude and longitude
...
}
```

This Java code segment declares a class named Location, which contains two instance variables that hold the latitude and longitude of some location.

> **NOTE** In this example, the ellipsis (...) just means that there could be additional members or variables—we just didn't write them in the example. ▪

You might have noticed that this class doesn't appear to have any parent class. In Java, all classes are subclasses of the class Object. So the above code sample is identical to:

```
/** latitude and longitude of a location **/
public class Location extends Object
{
int lat, long;    //latitude and longitude
...
}
```

In this example, the extends keyword is used to indicate that the new class, Location, is a subclass of the class Object. In effect, it extends the Object class by adding new features. We'll look at this more in the next section.

Subclassing and Inheritance

A subclass is a class that is derived from another class. To create a subclass, you use the extends keyword. This allows a new class to be created that adds or changes functionality from its base class. Take our example of the Location class:

```
/** latitude and longitude of a location **/
public class Location
{
int lat, long;    //latitude and longitude
...
}
```

Let's create a subclass of Location that knows how to print the location. So, we then have:

```
/** printable Location **/
public class PrintLocation extends Location
{
void print()
{
```

```
...
    }
}
```

This example simply creates a subclass of Location called PrintLocation and adds a print method.

Access Specifiers

C++ programmers will, by now, be wondering how Java supports class access specifiers. Java uses the public, private, and protected access specifiers like C++.

An access specifier states how visible an entity is during execution. In Java, these specifiers can be applied to a class, method, or variable. If an entity is declared public, it can be accessed from any class. If it is declared private, it can only be accessed from within the same class. A declaration of protected means that the variable can be accessed by the same class and any of its subclasses, but not by any external classes. If no access specifier is given, the entity is given public access within the package in which it is defined. We look at packages in a bit more detail later in the chapter.

Using *this* and *super*

Java provides two special variables to a class, which are known as this and super. The this variable is a reference to the current object. It is typically used when an object needs to pass a reference to itself to another method. For example:

```
/** latitude and longitude of a location **/
public class Location
{
int lat, long;    //latitude and longitude
...
void Plot(AnotherObject foo)
{
...
foo.DoSomething(this);
}
}
```

In this example, the Plot method of the Location class calls the DoSomething method of foo, an object of class AnotherObject. Location passes a reference to itself, via the this variable, to foo.DoSomething().

The super variable works the same way, except that it is a reference to a class's superclass. Remember that in Java there is no multiple inheritance, so there can be only one superclass for every class. In C++, there can be multiple superclasses, so there would be no way to know which class you are referring to with a super variable in C++.

Let's recap: In Java, the Object class is the ultimate superclass of all other classes. Each class can have, at most, one direct superclass, which can be referred to by the super keyword.

Constructors

A constructor is a special method that is used to initialize an object. It is indicated by being a method with the same name as the class itself and having no return value. A class can have more than one constructor, as long as they differ in the number or type of parameters. A constructor that takes no parameters is known as the default constructor. As in C++, a constructor is automatically called when an object is created.

You can call the constructor of a class's superclass by using the `super` special variable. You can explicitly place the call in your class's constructor. This is how you initialize the superclass's instance variables, for example. If you don't place an explicit call to a superclass constructor, Java will call the superclass's default constructor for you. Let's look at an example:

```java
/** latitude and longitude of a location **/
public class Location
{
int lat, long;    //latitude and longitude

Location(int x, int y)    //constructor with 2 parameters
{
lat = x;
long = y;
}

Location()              // default constructor
{
lat = 0;
long = 0;
}
}
/** printablelocation **/
public class PrintLocation extends Location
{
int foo;
PrintLocation(int x, int y)
{
super(x,y);    // Calls Location(x,y)
foo = 0;
}
PrintLocation()
{
foo=0;         // implicit call to Location()
}
void print()
{
...
}

}
```

This example is a little bit more complicated than what you've seen before. We have expanded the `PrintLocation` class so that it subclasses the `Location` class. Both `PrintLocation` and `Location` each have two different constructors. If we create an instance of `PrintLocation` so that its default constructor is called, as in:

```
blah = new PrintLocation();
```

the default constructor sets the `foo` instance variable of `PrintLocation` to be 0. Because there is no explicit call to `PrintLocation`'s super class, Java calls the superclass's default constructor automatically.

On the other hand, if we create an instance of `PrintLocation` like this:

```
blah = new PrintLocation(10,40);
```

the `PrintLocation(x,y)` constructor is called instead. This constructor makes a call to `super(x,y)`, which calls `PrintLocation`'s superclass constructor that takes two integer parameters. The default constructor of `Location` is not called in this case.

Types, Arrays, Identifiers, and Operators

Now that you've seen how the basic class structure of Java works, it's time to look at some of the nuts and bolts of the language. You've already seen several of these components in the previous examples.

Types

Java supports four basic data types: integers, floating points, characters, and Booleans. You could argue that arrays are really a data type and should be discussed in this section. However, because arrays are also closely linked to Java classes, we will get to them in the next section.

Java supports four different sizes of integer data. All Java integers are signed. Unlike integers in other languages, none of the Java integer sizes are platform dependent. In Java, an 8-bit integer value is known as a byte, a 16-bit integer is a short, a 32-bit integer is an int, and a 64-bit integer is a long.

For floating point data types, Java supports both 32-bit single precision, floating point and 64-bit double precision, floating point. In order to preserve significant digits in floating point calculations, any operation that has at least one of its floating point operands as a double will give a result that is a double. Table 29.2 shows the numeric types in Java with their sizes.

Table 29.2 Sizes of the Java Numeric Data Types

Name	Type	Size
byte	integer	8 bits
short	integer	16 bits
int	integer	32 bits
long	integer	64 bits
float	floating point	32 bits
double	floating point	64 bits

The Java character set follows the Unicode standard character set. Unicode is an international character set standard that allows for direct support of non-Latin character sets, such as Chinese and Arabic. As such, all Java characters are 16-bit unsigned integers.

The Boolean data type in Java denotes the result of logical Boolean operations. This data type has two values: `true` and `false`.

> **N O T E** Booleans in Java, unlike C and C++, are not numbers. You cannot cast a Boolean data type to be a number in Java. ■

Arrays

In some ways, Java arrays are similar to the arrays in C and C++, but there are very significant differences. Java uses arrays to replace pointer arithmetic. It is not possible to manipulate the pointer to an array and have it point somewhere else. Also, in Java, all arrays have bounds checking enabled, which prevents you from overwriting the end of your array and unintentionally creating self-modifying code!

> **N O T E** Under C++, you can do things like:
> ```
> int myarray[10];
> myarray[15] = 10;
> ```
> This code segment writes beyond the end of the allocated array and will probably crash your program. Java does not allow you to do this and will throw an exception if you try. ■

Java arrays are really classes, being a subclass of the `Object` class. As such, arrays are created explicitly with the `new` operator. For example,

```
int myint[] = new int[3];
```

creates an array of three integers named `myint`.

> **N O T E** Java arrays, like those in C and C++, are 0-based. This means that in an array of three integers, the elements will have subscripts: `myint[0]`, `myint[1]`, and `myint[2]`. ■

Java does not allow explicit multidimensional arrays. Instead, you create arrays of arrays. For example,

```
int myint[][] = new int[3][5];
```

is used to simulate an integer array with dimensions 3×5.

Identifiers

An identifier is a symbolic indicator, such as a variable, that represents some value. In Java, identifiers must start with an underscore (_), a dollar sign ($), a character in the set "A" to "Z" inclusive, a character in the set "a" to "z" inclusive, or a Unicode character with a value greater than 00C0.

After the first character, the identifier can include digits and any character that is not reserved as a Unicode special character.

Operators

Java has a rich set of operators. You will find that they are very similar to operators in C++. Table 29.3 shows the order of precedence of operators in Java.

Table 29.3   Operator Order of Precedence from Highest to Lowest
Operators
. [] ()
++ —— ! ~ instanceof
* / %
+ −
<< >> >>>
< > <= >=
== !=
&
^
|
&&
||
?:
= op=
,

Integer Operations   When performing operations on integer values, if any element in the operation is a long the result will be a long. Table 29.4 lists the operations for integers.

Table 29.4 Operations for Integers	
Operator	**Definition**
−	Unary negation
~	Bitwise compliment
++	Auto increment

Operator	Definition
——	Auto decrement
+	Addition
−	Subtraction
*	Multiplication
/	Division
%	Modulus
<<	Shift left
>>	Shift right
>>>	Shift right with zero fill
&	Bitwise AND
|	Bitwise OR
^	Bitwise XOR

Boolean Operations   Boolean, or logical, operations work virtually identically to those in C. The bitwise logical operators &, |, and ^ force evaluation of both sides of a logical expression. You can shortcut the evaluation of the right side of the expression by using the && and || operators. Table 29.5 shows the Boolean operations available under Java.

Table 29.5   Boolean Operations in Java

Operator	Definition
&	Bitwise AND. Forces evaluation of both sides of operation.
|	Bitwise OR. Forces evaluation of both sides of operation.
^	Bitwise XOR. Forces evaluation of both sides of operation.
&&	Shortcut AND. Does not force evaluation of both sides of operation.
||	Shortcut OR. Does not force evaluation of both sides of operation.
!	Logical negation.
==	Logical equality.
!=	Logical inequality.
&=	Logical AND and assignment.
|=	Logical OR and assignment.

continues

Table 29.5   Continued

Operator	Definition
^=	Logical XOR and assignment.
?:	If-then-else ternary operator.

Comments

In Java, there are three different ways to specify a comment in a source file. You can use the original C syntax of /* */ to bracket your comments, in which all characters between the two comment indicators are ignored. You can also use the C++ style comments indicated by // . This causes Java to ignore all characters following the // to the end of the current line.

The third style of comments is indicated by bracketing text with the /** and **/ symbols. All text between these symbols is ignored. This style of comment should only be used immediately before a declaration. The comments between the /** and **/ symbols are used in automatically generated documentation and are taken to be a description of the immediately following code.

Literals

A literal is an entity that represents the actual value of an integer, Boolean, string, floating point, or character value.

Integer Literals

For integer literals, Java supports literals in base-10 (decimal), base-8 (octal), or base-16 (hexadecimal). A decimal literal is a sequence of numbers without a leading 0. If a number has a leading 0 and only the digits 0 through 7, Java interprets it as an octal number. Hexadecimal numbers are prefixed by 0x and can include the digits 0 through 9 and the letters A through F.

Floating Point Literals

A floating point literal uses scientific notation to represent the number. It consists of a decimal integer, a decimal point, another decimal integer representing a fraction, the letter e or E, an integer exponent that may be signed, and a type suffix. Java supports both single and double precision floating point.

A d or D character as the type suffix indicates a double precision floating point value. If the type suffix is an f, F, or is not specified, the number is a single precision floating point value.

To simplify things, here is an example:

```
2.0E14, 3.1e3f, 3.6e-6F single precision
3.1e4D, 0.12E3d double precision
```

Character Literals

Java supports `character literals` by enclosing the character in single quotes. Like C and C++, Java also has support for a set of special, nongraphical characters. Table 29.6 shows the special characters that you can use in Java.

Table 29.6   Java Special Character Support

Character	Definition
\b	Backspace
\f	Form feed
\n	Newline
\r	Carriage return
\t	Tab character
\ddd	Octal value
\xddd	Hexadecimal value
\uddddd	Unicode value

In addition, you can represent the backslash, single quote, and double quote characters as character literals by prefixing the character with a backslash. So, a backslash literal is \\, a single quote literal is \', and a double quote literal is \".

String Literals

A string literal is represented as a sequence of characters enclosed in double quotes. Every string literal is an instance of the `String` class. String literals can be continued as multiline strings by using a \ character as a continuation.

Boolean Literals

Of all the literals, Booleans are the simplest. Boolean literals consist of two values, `true` and `false`.

Statements

Okay, you've fought your way through all that information about literals, operators, and identifiers. Now it's time to start learning how the various parts of Java work together.

Declarations

A declaration is an indicator to the Java compiler that you are going to use a data type. You are declaring that a certain variable is of a particular data type. For example:

```
inti;
float myFloat;
```

are both declarations for simple data types. In this case, they declare variables of type `int` and `float`, respectively.

Declarations are also used to define variables that are class objects or arrays. In these cases, the declaration does not allocate any space for these objects. You must use the `new` operator to actually create an object. For example:

```
Location myLocation;
```

does not actually create an object of type `Location`. To do that, you would need to write

```
Location myLocation;
myLocation = new Location();
```

Similarly,

```
int myInt[];
```

does not create an array of integers. To actually create the array, you would need to write

```
int myInt[];
myInt = new int[10];
```

Java declarations can appear anywhere that statements can appear, and have a scope that is valid for the duration of the enclosing block. The enclosing block is denoted by the surrounding curly braces { and }.

Control Statements

Java gives you a variety of control structures to specify the flow of control through your program. Most of these are virtually identical to those found in C.

The conditional statement structure is identical to the `if` structure in C and C++. For example:

```
if (a==1)
{
// do something
}
else
{
// do something else
}
```

The Java multi-way conditional branch is the `switch` statement. As in C, you switch on a variable and have a `case` entry for each possible value. There is a `default` label that matches if none of the other case labels match. For example:

```
switch(foo)
{
case 1:
break;       // do something;
case 2:
break;       // do something else;
```

```
case 3:
break;     // do something really strange;
default:
break;     // panic completely
}
```

Java supports three different looping structures, the syntax of which is identical to C. The Java for loop:

```
for (initial condition; while true; each iteration)
{
// loop body
}
```

provides for loop indices, and looks like the following example:

```
for (i=0; i<5; i++)
{
// do something over and over
}
```

The while loop has the following syntax:

```
while (boolean expression is true)
{
// loop body
}
```

and looks like the following example when implemented:

```
while (i<6)
{
i++;
}
```

The third loop structure is the do-while loop, which has the following syntax:

```
do
{
// loop body
} while (boolean expression is true);
```

and looks like the following example when implemented:

```
do
{
i++;
} while (i<5);
```

> **N O T E** The primary difference between the while loop and the do-while loop is that, in the
> do-while loop, the loop body is guaranteed to be executed at least once, since the test
> condition for the loop is at the beginning of a while loop and at the end of a do-while loop. ▪

Java also supports the concept of labeled statements and labeled breaks. We saw the break statement in the example of the Java switch statement. The break statement breaks out of the immediately enclosing control structure. If a control structure is marked with a label, and a labeled break is used, control flow can break out of several levels of control structures at once. For example:

```
escape:
for (i=0; i<10; i++)
{
for (j=5; j<20; j++)
{
...
break escape;
}
}
```

The `break` statement in the above example causes the flow of control to break out of the labeled loop—in this case, the outer loop labeled `escape`.

To complete the Java control structures, the language includes the `continue` statement, which simply causes execution to continue when encountered, and the `return` statement, for returning from method calls.

Interfaces and Packages

Java includes two mechanisms for logically grouping and working with classes. These are the interface and the package.

Interfaces

An interface is a collection of method definitions without providing the method implementation. A class can implement an interface by providing method bodies for all the methods in the interface definition. Interfaces can be defined to be either public or private. All methods in an interface are public. Java uses interfaces to provide some of the features of multiple inheritance in C++.

The following code segment defines two interfaces:

```
public interface Test1
{
Method1();
Method2(int x);
}

public interface Test2
{
Foo1(float myFloat);
}
```

A class can then choose to implement either or both of these interfaces. For example:

```
public class IntfExample implements Test1, Test2
{
Method1()
{
... // method body
```

```
}
Method2(int x)
{
... // method body
}
Foo1(float myFloat)
{
... // method body
}
}
```

In this example, the class IntfExample implements both the Test1 and Test2 interfaces by providing method bodies for each method defined in the interface.

By using interfaces, you can specify an interface as a data type in a parameter list. This allows you to pass an object in the parameter list, as long as the object implements the specified interface. You don't have to know the exact class details of the object—only that it implements the interface. For example:

```
public class Blah
{
void TestMethod(Test1 x)
{
...
}
}
```

In this example, the name of an interface, Test1, is used as a parameter type in the method TestMethod. This means that any object that implements the Test1 interface can be passed as a parameter.

Packages

A package is a Java construct that is used to manage the program namespace. It is a collection of classes and interfaces. Every class is contained in a package. If no package name is explicitly given, the class is contained in the default package. You may remember, from the earlier section on classes, that if a class does not give an access specifier to a method, it is considered public for its enclosing package.

To define a package for a compilation unit, you use the package statement. This statement must be the first statement in the file.

> **N O T E** A compilation unit is the basic compiled unit in Java. It is a file that contains one or more classes. ■

Sun's convention for Java packages is that they be named with period separated names. You should put the name of the organization that developed the package as the leftmost item in the package name.

The easiest way to use a class that is in another package is through the use of the `import` statement. With the `import` statement, you can import a specific class from a package, or you can import every public class at once.

Assume we have the package `test.package` that contains the classes `Location` and `Mapper`. If we want to use all the public classes from `test.package` in our current compilation unit, put the line

```
import test.package.*
```

at the top of your code, right after the statement defining your current package. The * character tells Java to import all the public classes in `test.package`. To import just one specific class, such as `Location`, use the following line instead:

```
import test.package.Location
```

You are now able to create and use objects of the `Location` class as if it were a local class.

Exception Handling

In order to manage runtime errors, Java supports runtime exception handling. When a statement causes some type of runtime error, it throws an exception. A special segment of code, called an exception handler, is said to catch the exception. Java has many different runtime exceptions defined. It is also possible to define your own exceptions and exception handlers.

Throwing Exceptions

You can define your own exceptions and exception handlers in order to cope with runtime error conditions in your code. In order to throw an exception, you must first define an exception class. The `throw` statement takes a class as a parameter. By convention, your custom-defined exception class should be a subclass of `Exception`. For example, we can define our own exception called `PanicCompletely` with the following very simple code segment:

```
class PanicCompletely extends Exception
{
}
```

Then, we can throw the exception when an error occurs in a class that is subject to a runtime error. For example:

```
class CausesErrors
{
void Problem()
{
...
if (/* no error occurred */)
{
// do nothing special
}
else /* we have error */
{
```

```
throw new PanicCompletely();
  }
 }
}
```

Now, when someone executes `CausesErrors.Problem()` and an error occurs, the
`PanicCompletely` exception will be thrown.

Catching Exceptions

Throwing exceptions is only half the battle. In order for them to be effective, you must have an
exception handler to catch the exception. To create an exception handler, we use the `try-`
`catch` control structure.

To use `try-catch`, bracket the code that is likely to cause an exception with a `try` statement,
and then put multiple `catch` statements below it, one for each exception that could be thrown.
Let's look at an example:

```
try
{
CausesErrors myClass = new CausesErrors();
myClass.Problem();    // can throw a PanicCompletely exception
}
catch (PanicCompletely exc)
{
// handle the PanicCompletely exception
}
catch (Exception exc)
{
// handle any object of class Exception
}
catch (Object obj)
{
// handle any improperly created exception
}
```

In the above code, there are three `catch` statements. The first one is for the `PanicCompletely`
exception, which we know that `myClass.Problem()` can throw. The second `catch` statement
catches all objects of class `Exception`. This should catch any other exceptions that we didn't
explicitly write a `catch` statement for. The third `catch` statement catches all objects of type
`Object`. If someone designed an exception that was not a subclass of `Exception`, it would be
caught by this `catch` statement.

N O T E Remember that all objects, even exceptions, are subclasses of the `Object` class. ■

Java also provides another keyword, `finally`, that is used to mark code in an exception handler
that will get executed whether or not an exception occurs. If we add a `finally` statement to the
previous example:

```
try
{
CausesErrors myClass = new CausesErrors();
```

```
    myClass.Problem();      // can throw a PanicCompletely exception
    }
    catch (PanicCompletely exc)
    {
    // handle the PanicCompletely exception
    }
    catch (Exception exc)
    {
    // handle any object of class Exception
    }
    catch (Object obj)
    {
    // handle any improperly created exception
    }
    finally
    {
    // this always gets executed
    }
```

The code in the `finally` block is always executed, no matter what exception is thrown by `myClass.Problem()`, even if no exception is thrown. ●

## CHAPTER 30

JavaScript

You already know that Web pages are written using the HyperText Markup Language, or HTML. You may also know that Netscape introduced a number of HTML extensions in the 1.x releases of Netscape Navigator. With the release of Navigator 2.0, Netscape has added a powerful new capability: JavaScript, a language that lets you write programs that Navigator executes when users load or browse your pages. This chapter teaches you how to use JavaScript to power up your Web pages.

In this chapter, you learn:

- What JavaScript is capable of doing
- How the programming elements of JavaScript are used, what they're for, and their relationship to Netscape and HTML
- The properties and uses of JavaScript objects, events, expressions, and operators
- Sample applications you can program using JavaScript ■

Introduction to JavaScript

JavaScript allows you to embed commands in an HTML page; when a Navigator user downloads the page, your JavaScript commands will be evaluated. These commands can be triggered when the user clicks on page items, manipulates gadgets and fields in an HTML form, or moves through the page history list.

N O T E You've probably heard JavaScript called by its earlier-version name, LiveScript; at the time of this writing, most of JavaScript's capabilities are based on the functionality of LiveScript. As more and more HTML page designers and enterprise application developers create scripts that define the behavior of objects to run on both clients and servers, you'll continue to see improvements and changes for the better in JavaScript. Just as Java (and any other software, for that matter) becomes better in response to its programmers' and developers' imaginations, so will JavaScript. If you're interested in following up on the latest revisions and additions, keep Netscape's home page (**http://home.netscape.com**) at the top of your bookmarks list. ■

Some computer languages are compiled; you run your program through a compiler, which performs a one-time translation of the human-readable program into a binary language that the computer can execute. JavaScript is an interpreted language; the computer must evaluate the program every time it's run. You embed your JavaScript commands within an HTML page, and any browser that supports JavaScript can interpret the commands and act on them.

Don't let all these programming terms frighten you off—JavaScript is powerful and simple. If you've ever programmed in dBase or Visual Basic, you'll find JavaScript easy to pick up. If not, don't worry; this chapter will have you JavaScripting in no time!

N O T E Java offers a number of C++-like capabilities that were purposefully omitted from LiveScript. For example, you can only access the limited set of objects defined by the browser and its Java applets, and you can't extend those objects yourself. For more details on Java, see chapter 28, "Sun's Java and the Netscape Browser," and chapter 29, "Java for C++ Programmers." ■

Why Use a Scripting Language?

HTML provides a good deal of flexibility to page authors, but HTML by itself is static; once written, HTML documents can't interact with the user other than by presenting hyperlinks. Creative use of CGI scripts (which run on Web servers) have made it possible to create more interesting and effective interactive sites, but some applications really demand client-side scripting.

JavaScript was developed to provide page authors a way to write small scripts that would execute on the users' browsers instead of on the server. For example, an application that collects data from a form then POSTs it to the server can validate the data for completeness and correctness before sending it to the server. This can greatly improve the performance of the browsing session, since users don't have to send data to the server until it has been verified as correct. The following are some other potential applications for JavaScript:

- JavaScripts can verify forms for completeness, like a mailing list registration form that checks to make sure the user has entered a name and e-mail address before the form is posted.

- Pages can display content derived from information stored on the user's computer—without sending that data to the server. For example, a bank can embed JavaScript commands in their pages that look up account data from a Quicken file and display it as part of the bank's page.

- Because JavaScripts can modify settings for applets written in Java, page authors can control the size, appearance, and behavior of Navigator plug-ins, as well as other Java applets. A page that contains an embedded Director animation might use a JavaScript to set the Director plug-in's window size and position before triggering the animation.

Part

VI

Ch

30

What Can JavaScript Do?

JavaScript provides a rich set of built-in functions and commands. Your JavaScripts can display HTML in the browser, do math calculations (like figuring the sales tax or shipping for an order form), play sounds, open new URLs, and even click buttons in forms.

 TIP A function is just a small program that does something, and a method is a function that belongs to an object. For more lingo, see chapter 28, "Sun's Java and the Netscape Browser."

Code to perform these actions can be embedded in a page and executed when the page is loaded; you can also write methods that contain code that's triggered by events you specify. For example, you can write a JavaScript method that is called when the user clicks the Submit button of a form, or one that is activated when the user clicks a hyperlink on the active page.

JavaScript can also set the attributes, or properties, of Java applets running in the browser. This makes it easy for you to change the behavior of plug-ins or other objects without having to delve into their innards. For example, your JavaScript code could automatically start playing an embedded QuickTime or .AVI file when the user clicks a button.

What Does JavaScript Look Like?

JavaScript commands are embedded in your HTML documents, either directly or via a URL that tells the browser which scripts to load. Embedding JavaScript in your pages only requires one new HTML element: <SCRIPT>...</SCRIPT>.

The <SCRIPT> element takes two attributes: LANGUAGE, which specifies the scripting language to use when evaluating the script, and URL, which specifies a URL from which the script can be loaded. The LANGUAGE attribute is always required, unless the SRC attribute's URL specifies a language. LANGUAGE and SRC can both be used, too. Here are some examples:

```
<SCRIPT LANGUAGE="LiveScript">...</SCRIPT>
<SCRIPT SRC="http://www.fairgate.com/scripts/common.LiveScript">...</SCRIPT>
<SCRIPT LANGUAGE="LiveScript" SRC="http://www.fairgate.com/scripts/common">...
</SCRIPT>
```

JavaScript itself resembles many other computer languages; if you're familiar with C, C++, Pascal, HyperTalk, Visual Basic, or dBase, you'll recognize the similarities. If not, don't worry; the following are some simple rules that will help you understand how the language is structured:

- JavaScript treats all letters as lowercase (except for quoted strings), so document.write and DOCUMENT.WRITE are the same.
- JavaScript is pretty flexible about statements. A single statement can cover multiple lines, and you can put multiple short statements on a single line—just make sure to add a semicolon (;) at the end of each statement.
- Curly braces (the { and } characters) group statements into blocks; a block may be the body of a function or a section of code that gets executed in a loop or as part of a conditional test.

Figure 30.1 shows a small piece of JavaScript code embedded in an HTML page; the frontmost window shows the original HTML file, and the Navigator window shows its output.

JavaScript Programming Conventions

Even though JavaScript is a simple language, it's quite expressive. In this section, we'll cover a small number of simple rules and conventions that will ease your learning process and speed your JavaScripting.

Hiding Your Scripts   You'll probably be designing pages that may be seen by browsers that don't support JavaScript. To keep those browsers from interpreting your JavaScript commands as HTML—and displaying them—wrap your scripts like this:

```
<SCRIPT LANGUAGE="LiveScript">
<!— This line opens an HTML comment
document.write("You can see this script's output, but not its source.")
<!— This line opens and closes a comment —>
</SCRIPT>
```

The opening <!— comment causes browsers to disregard all text they encounter until they find a matching —>, so they won't display your script. You do have to be careful with the <SCRIPT> tag, though; if you put your <SCRIPT>...</SCRIPT> block inside the comments, Navigator will ignore it!

FIG. 30.1
The foremost window shows a small piece of JavaScript code embedded in simple HTML file; the Navigator window shows the result of loading that page (which executes the JavaScript).

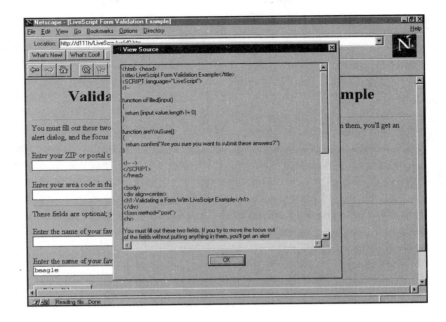

Comments   It's usually good practice to include comments in your programs to explain what they do; JavaScript is no exception. The JavaScript interpreter will ignore any text marked as a comment, so don't be shy about including them. There are two types of comments: single-line and multiple-line.

Single-line comments start with two slashes (//), and they're limited to one line. Multiple-line comments must start with /* on the first line, and end with */ on the last line. Here are a few quick examples:

```
// this is a legal comment
/ illegal — comments start with two slashes
/*     Multiple-line comments can
be spread across more than one line, as long as they end. */
/* illegal— this comment doesn't have an end!
// this comment's OK, because extra slashes are ignored //
```

The JavaScript Language

JavaScript was designed to resemble Java, which in turn looks a lot like C and C++. The difference is that Java was built as a general-purpose object language, while JavaScript is intended to provide a quicker and simpler language for enhancing Web pages and servers. In this section, you learn the building blocks of JavaScript and how to combine them into legal JavaScript programs.

Using Identifiers

An identifier is just a unique name that JavaScript uses to identify a variable, method, or object in your program. As with other programming languages, JavaScript imposes some rules on what names you can use. All JavaScript names must start with a letter or the underscore character ("_"), and they can contain both upper- and lowercase letters and the digits 0–9. (Remember, JavaScript doesn't distinguish between cases, so UserName, userName, and USERNAME all refer to the same thing in a JavaScript program.)

JavaScript supports two different ways for you to represent values in your scripts: literals and variables. As their names imply, literals are fixed values that don't change while the script is executing, while variables hold data that can change at any time.

Literals and variables have several different types; the type is determined by the kind of data that the literal or variable contains. The following is a list of the types supported in JavaScript:

- Integers, or positive whole numbers—Integer literals are made up of a sequence of digits only; integer variables can contain any whole-number value from 0 to more than 2 billion.

- Floating-point, or numbers with fractional parts—10 is an integer, but 10.5 is a floating-point number. Floating-point literals can be positive or negative, and they can contain either positive or negative exponents (which are indicated by an e in the number.) For example, 3.14159265 is a floating-point literal, as is 6.02e24 (6.02×10^{24}, or Avogadro's number).

- Strings, or sequences of characters—Strings can represent words, phrases, or data, and they're set off by either double (") or single (') quotes. If you start a string with one type of quote, you must close it with the other.

- Booleans, or true or false values—Boolean literals can only have values of either TRUE or FALSE; other statements in the JavaScript language can return Boolean values.

Using Functions, Objects, and Properties

Before we go any further, let's talk about functions, objects, and properties. A function is just a piece of code that does something; it might play a sound, calculate an equation, or send a piece of e-mail. An object is a collection of data and functions that have been grouped together. The object's functions are called methods, and its data are called its properties. The JavaScript programs you write will have properties and methods, and they'll interact with objects provided by Navigator and its plug-ins (as well as any other Java applets you may supply to your users).

 TIP A simple guideline: an object's properties are things it knows, and its methods are things it can do.

Using Built-In Objects and Functions
Individual JavaScript elements are objects; for example, string literals are string objects, and they have methods that you can use to do things like change their case. JavaScript also provides a set of useful objects to represent the Navigator browser, the currently displayed page, and other elements of the browsing session.

You access objects by specifying their name. For example, the active document object is named document. To use document's properties or methods, you add a period and the name of the method or property you want. For example, document.title is the title property of the document object, and "Navigator".length would call the length member of the string object named "Navigator." Remember, literals are objects too!

Using Properties   Every object has properties—even literals. To access a property, just use the object name followed by a period and the property name. To get the length of a string object named address, you can write

```
address.length
```

and you'll get back an integer which equals the number of characters in the string. If the object you're using has properties that can be modified, you can change them in the same way. To set the color property of a house object, just write

```
house.color = "blue"
```

You can also add new properties to an object just by naming them. For example, let's say you define a class called customer for one of your pages. You can add new properties to the customer object like this:

```
customer.name = "Joe Smith"
customer.address = "123 Elm Street"
customer.zip = "90210"
```

Finally, it's important to know that an object's methods are just properties, so you can easily add new properties to an object by writing your own function and creating a new object property using your own function name. If you wanted to add a Bill method to your customer object, you could do so by writing a function named BillCustomer and setting the object's property like this:

```
customer.Bill = BillCustomer;
```

To call the new method, you'd just write

```
customer.Bill()
```

Array and Object Properties   JavaScript objects store their properties in an internal table that you can access in two ways. You've already seen the first way—just use the properties' name. The second way, arrays, allow you to access all of an object's properties in sequence. The following function prints out all the properties of the specified object:

```
function DumpProperties(obj, obj_name) {
result = ""        // set the result string to blank
for (i in obj)
result += obj_name + "." + i + " = " + obj[i] + "\n"
return result
}
```

You'll see this code again in the "Sample JavaScript Code" section, and we'll explain in detail what it does. For now, it's enough to know that there are two different, but related, ways to access an object's properties.

HTML Elements Have Properties Too Navigator provides properties for HTML forms and some types of form fields. JavaScript is especially valuable for writing scripts that check or change data in forms. Navigator's properties allow you to get and set the form elements' data, as well as specify actions to be taken when something happens to the form element (as when the user clicks in a text field, or moves to another field). For more details on using HTML object properties, see the later section "HTML Objects and Events."

JavaScript and the Netscape Navigator

Now that you understand how JavaScript works, let's talk about how Navigator supports JavaScript.

When Scripts Get Executed

When you put JavaScript code in a page, Navigator evaluates the code as soon as it's encountered. As Navigator evaluates the code, it converts it into a more efficient internal format so it can be executed later. When you think about it, this is similar to how HTML is processed; browsers parse and display HTML as they encounter it in the page, not all at once.

However, functions don't get executed when they're evaluated; they just get stored for later use. You still have to explicitly call functions to make them work. Some functions are attached to objects, like buttons or text fields on forms, and they are called when some event happens on the button or field. You might also have functions that you want to execute during page evaluation; you can do this by putting a call to the function at the appropriate place in the page, like this:

```
<SCRIPT language="LiveScript">
<!—
myFunction()
<!—  —>
</SCRIPT>
```

Where to Put Your Scripts

You can put scripts anywhere within your HTML page, as long as they're surrounded with the <SCRIPT>...</SCRIPT> tag. Many JavaScript programmers choose to put functions that will be executed more than once into the <HEAD> element of their pages; this provides a convenient storage place. Since the <HEAD> element is at the beginning of the file, functions and JavaScript code that you put there will be evaluated before the rest of the document is loaded.

Sometimes, though, you have code that shouldn't be evaluated or executed until after all of the page's HTML has been parsed and displayed. An example is the DumpURL() function described in the "Building a Link Table" section later in the chapter; it prints out all the URLs referenced in the page. If this function is evaluated before all the HTML on the page has been loaded, it'll miss some URLs, so the call to the function should come at the page's end.

Navigator Objects and Events

In addition to recognizing JavaScript when it's embedded inside a <SCRIPT>...</SCRIPT> tag, Netscape Navigator also exposes some objects (and their methods and properties) that you can use in your JavaScript programs. Also, Navigator can trigger methods you define when the user takes certain actions in the browser.

Browser Objects and Events

Many things that happen in a Navigator browsing session aren't related to items on the page, like buttons or HTML text. Instead, they're related to what's happening in the browser itself, like what page the user is viewing.

The *location* Object   Navigator exposes an object called location, which holds the current URL, including the hostname, path, CGI script arguments, and even the protocol. Table 30.1 shows the properties and methods of the location object.

Table 30.1   Navigator's location Object Contains Information on the Currently Displayed URL

Property	Type	What It Does
href	String	Contains the entire URL, including all the subparts; for example, **http://home.netscape.com/comprod/ products/navigator/version_2.0/script/script_info/ lsnn.html**
protocol	String	Contains the protocol field of the URL, including the first colon; for example, http:
host	String	Contains the hostname and port number; for example, home.netscape.com:80
hostname	String	Contains only the hostname; for example, home.netscape.com
port	String	Contains the port, if specified; otherwise, it's blank.
path	String	Contains the path to the actual document; for example, comprod/products/navigator/version_2.0/script/ script_info/lsnn.html
hash	String	Contains any CGI arguments after the first "#" in the URL.
search	String	Contains any CGI arguments after the first "?" in the URL.
toString()	Method	Returns location.href; you can use this function to easily get the entire URL.
assign(x)	Method	Sets location.href to the value you specify.

The *document* Object   Navigator also exposes an object called document; as you might expect, this object exposes useful properties and methods of the active document.location only refers to the URL of the active document, but document refers to the document itself. Table 30.2 shows document's properties and methods.

N O T E   Because Navigator was still changing as this was written, Netscape may have defined additional properties in the document object. Please see their JavaScript documentation at **http://home.netscape.com/comprod/products/navigator/version_2.0/script/script_info/** for full details. ■

Table 30.2   Netscape's document Object Contains Information on the Currently Loaded and Displayed HTML Page

Property	Type	What It Does
title	String	Contains title of the current page, or "Untitled" if there's no title.
URL or Location	String	Contain the document's address (from its history stack entry); these two are synonyms.
last	Modified	Contains the page's last-modified date.
forms[]	Array	Contains all the FORMs in the current page.
forms[].length	Integer	Contains the number of FORMs in the current page.
links[]	Array	Contains all HREF anchors in the current page.
links[].length	Integer	Contains the number of HREF anchors in the current page.
write(x)	Method	Writes HTML to the current document, in the order in which the script occurs on the page.

The History Object   Navigator maintains a list of pages you've visited since running the program; this list is called the history list. Your JavaScript programs can move through pages in the list using the properties and functions shown in table 30.3.

Table 30.3   Netscape's History Object Contains Information on the Browser's History List

Property	Type	What It Does
previous, back	String	Contains the URL of the previous history stack entry (that is, the one before the active page). These properties are synonyms.
next, forward	String	Contains the URL of the next history stack entry (that is, the one after the active page). These properties are synonyms.

Property	Type	What It Does
go(x)	Method	Goes forward x entries in the history stack if x > 0; else, goes backward x entries. x must be a number.
go(x)	Method	Goes to the newest history entry whose title or URL contains x as a substring; the string case doesn't matter. x must be a string.

The window Object   Navigator creates a window object for every document. Think of the window object as an actual Windows or Macintosh window, and the document object as the content that appears in the window. Navigator provides the following two methods for doing things in the window:

- alert(string) puts up an alert dialog box and displays the message specified in the string. Users must dismiss the dialog box by clicking the OK button before Navigator will let them do anything else.

- confirm(string) puts up a confirmation dialog box with two buttons (OK and Cancel) and displays the message specified in the string. Users may dismiss the dialog box by clicking Cancel or OK; the confirm function returns TRUE when users click OK and FALSE if they click Cancel.

HTML Objects and Events

Navigator represents some individual HTML elements as objects, and these objects have properties and methods attached to them just like every other. You can use these objects to customize your pages' behavior by attaching JavaScript code to the appropriate methods.

Properties for Generic HTML Objects   The methods and properties in this section apply to several HTML tags; note that there are other methods and properties, discussed after the following table, for anchors and form elements. Table 30.4 shows the features that these generic HTML objects provide.

Table 30.4   These Properties and Methods Allow You to Control the Contents and Behavior of HTML Elements

Property	Type	What It Does
onFocus	Function	Called when the user moves the input focus to the field, either via the Tab key or a mouse click.
onBlur	Function	Called when the user moves the input focus out of this field.
onSelect	Function	Called when the user selects text in the field.
onChange	Function	Called only when the field loses focus and the user has modified its text; use this function to validate data in a field.

continues

Table 30.4   Continued

Property	Type	What It Does
onSubmit	Function	Called when the user submits the form (if the form has a submit button).
onClick	Function	Called when the button is clicked.
focus()	Function	Call to move the input focus to the specified object.
blur()	Function	Call to move the input focus away from the specified object.
select()	Function	Call to select the specified object.
click()	Function	Call to click the specified object, which must be a button.
enable()	Function	Call to enable (un-gray) the specified object.
disable()	Function	Call to disable (gray out) the specified object.

Note that the focus(), blur(), select(), click(), enable(), and disable() functions are methods of objects; to call them, use the name of the object you want to affect. For example, to turn off the button named Search, you'd use form.search.disable().

Properties for Anchor Objects   Hypertext anchors don't have all the properties listed above; they only have the onFocus(), onBlur(), and onClick() methods. You modify and set these methods just like others. Remember that no matter what code you attach, Navigator's still going to follow the clicked link—it will execute your code first, though.

Properties for Form Objects   Table 30.5 lists the properties exposed for HTML FORM elements; the later section "HTML Events" also presents several methods that you can override to call JavaScript routines when something happens to an object on the page.

Table 30.5   HTML Forms Themselves Have Special Properties That You Can Use in Your JavaScript Code

Property	Type	What It Does
name	String	Contains the value of the form's NAME attribute.
method	Integer	Contains the value of the form's METHOD attribute: () for GET or 1 for POST.
action	String	Contains the value of the form's ACTION attribute.
target	Window	Window targeted after submit for form response.
onSubmit()	Method	Called when the form is submitted; this method can't stop the submission, though.
submit()	Method	Any form element can force the form to be submitted by calling the form's submit() method.

Properties for Objects in a Form   One of the best places to use JavaScript is in forms, since you can write scripts that process, check, and perform calculations with the data the user enters. JavaScript provides a useful set of properties and methods for text INPUT elements and buttons.

You use INPUT elements in a form to let the user enter text data; JavaScript provides properties to get string objects that hold the element's contents, as well as methods for doing something when the user moves into or out of a field. Table 30.6 shows the properties and methods which are defined for text INPUT elements.

Table 30.6   These Properties and Methods Allow You to Control the Contents and Behavior of HTML INPUT Elements

Property	Type	What It Does
name	String	Contains the value of the element's NAME attribute.
value	String	Contains the field's contents.
default	Value String	The initial contents of the field; returns "" if blank.
onFocus	Method	Called when the user moves the input focus to the field, either via the Tab key or a mouse click.
onBlur	Method	Called when the user moves the input focus out of this field.
onSelect	Method	Called when the user selects text in the field.
onChange	Method	Called only when the field loses focus and the user has modified its text; use this function to validate data in a field.

Individual buttons and check boxes have properties, too; JavaScript provides properties to get string objects containing the buttons' data, as well as methods for doing something when the user selects or deselects a particular button. Table 30.7 shows the properties and methods that are defined for button elements.

Table 30.7   These Properties and Methods Allow You to Control the Contents and Behavior of HTML Button Elements

Property	Type	What It Does
name	String	Contains the value of the button's NAME attribute.
value	String	Contains the VALUE attribute.
onClick	Method	Called when the button is pressed.
click()	Method	Clicks a button and triggers whatever actions are attached to it.

Radio buttons are grouped so that only one button in a group can be selected at a time. Because all radio buttons in a group have the same name, JavaScript has a special property, index, for use in distinguishing radio buttons. Querying the index property returns a number, starting with 0 for the first button, indicating which button in the group was triggered.

For example, you might want to automatically put the user's cursor into the first text field in a form, instead of making the user manually click the field. If your first text field is named "UserName," you can put this

```
form.UserName.focus()
```

in your document's script to get the desired behavior.

Programming with JavaScript

As you've seen in the preceding sections, JavaScript has a lot to offer page authors. It's not as flexible as C or C++, but it's quick and simple. Most importantly, it's easily embedded in your WWW pages, so you can maximize their impact with a little JavaScript seasoning. This section covers the gritty details of JavaScript programming, including a detailed explanation of the language's features.

Expressions

An expression is anything that can be evaluated to get a single value. Expressions can contain string or numeric literals, variables, operators, and other expressions, and they can range from simple to quite complex. For example,

```
x = 7;
```

is an expression which uses the assignment operator (more on operators in the next section) to assign the result 7 to the variable x. By contrast,

```
(quitFlag == TRUE) & (formComplete == FALSE)
```

is a more complex expression whose final value depends on the values of the quitFlag and formComplete variables.

Operators

Operators do just what their name suggests: they operate on variables or literals. The items that an operator acts on are called its operands. Operators come in the two following types:

- Unary operators only require one operand, and the operator can come before or after the operand. The — operator, which subtracts one from the operand, is a good example. — count and count— will both subtract 1 from the variable count.

- Binary operators need two operands. The four math operators you learned in elementary school (+ for addition, — for subtraction, * for multiplication, and / for division) are all binary operators, as is the = assignment operator we saw earlier.

Assignment Operators   Assignment operators take the result of an expression and assign it to a variable. JavaScript won't allow you to assign the result of an expression to a literal. One feature that JavaScript has that most other programming languages don't is that you can change a variable's type on-the-fly.

```
function TypeDemo()
{
var pi = 3.14159265
document.write("Pi is ", pi, "\n")
pi = FALSE
document.write("Pi is ", pi, "\n")
}
```

This short function first prints the (correct) value of pi. In most other languages, though, trying to set a floating-point variable to a Boolean value would either generate a compiler error or a runtime error. JavaScript and Java happily accept the change and print pi's new value: FALSE.

The most common assignment operator, =, simply assigns the value of an expression's right side to its left side. In the example above, the variable x got the integer value 7 after the expression was evaluated. For convenience, JavaScript also defines some other operators that combine common math operations with assignment; they're shown in table 30.8.

Table 30.8   These Assignment Operators Provide a Shorthand Way to Do an Assignment and a Math Operation at the Same Time

Operator	What It Does	Two Equivalent Expressions
+=	Adds two values	x+=y and x=x+y
	adds two strings	string = string + "HTML" and string += "HTML"
-=	Subtracts two values	x-=y and x=x-y
*=	Multiples two values	a*=b and a=a*b
/=	Divides two values	e/=b and e=e/b

Math Operators   The previous sections gave you a sneak preview of the math operators that JavaScript furnishes. You can either combine math operations with assignments, as shown in table 30.8, or use them individually. As you'd expect, the standard four math functions (addition, subtraction, multiplication, and division) work just as they do on an ordinary calculator.

The negation operator, —, is a unary operator that negates the sign of its operand. To use the negation operator, you must put the operator before the operand.

JavaScript also adds two useful binary operators: — and ++, called, respectively, the decrement and increment operators. These two operators do two things; they modify the value of their operand, and return the new value. They also share a unique property: they can be used either before or after their operand. If you put the operator after the operand, JavaScript will return the operand's value, then modify it. If you take the opposite route and put the operator before the operand, JavaScript will modify it and return the modified value. The following short example might help clarify this seemingly odd behavior:

```
x = 7;  // start x as 7
a = —x;        // set x to x-1, and return the new x; a = 6
b = a++;     // set b to a, so b = 6, then add 1 to a; a = 7
x++;   // add one to x; ignore the returned value; a = 7 again
```

Comparison Operators   It's often necessary to compare the value of two expressions to see whether one is larger, smaller, or equal to another. JavaScript supplies several comparison operators that take two operands and return TRUE if the comparison's true, and FALSE if it's not. (Remember, you can use literals, variables, or expressions with operators that require expressions.) Table 30.9 shows the JavaScript comparison operators.

Table 30.9   These Comparison Operators Provide a Shorthand Way to Do an Assignment and a Math Operation at the Same Time

Operator	Read It As	Returns TRUE When:
==	Equals	The two operands are equal
!=	Does not equal	The two operands are unequal
<	Less than	The left operand is less than the right operand
<=	Less than or	The left operand is less than equal to or equal to the right operand
>	Greater than	The left operand is greater than the right operand
>=	Greater than or	The left operand is greater than or equal to the right operand

 The comparison operators can be used on strings, too; the results depend on standard lexicographic ordering, but comparisons aren't case-sensitive.

It may be helpful to think of the comparison operators as questions; when you write

```
(x >= 10)
```

you're really saying, "Is the value of variable x greater than or equal to 10?"

Logical Operators   Comparison operators compare quantity or content for numeric and string expressions, but sometimes you need to test a logical value—like whether a comparison operator returned TRUE or FALSE. JavaScript's logical operators allow you to compare expressions that return logical values. The following are JavaScript's logical operators:

- &&, read as "and." The && operator returns TRUE if both its input expressions are true. If the first operand evaluates to FALSE, && returns FALSE immediately, without evaluating the second operand. Here's an example:

```
x = TRUE && TRUE;      // x is TRUE
x = FALSE && FALSE;    // x is FALSE
x = FALSE && TRUE;     // x is FALSE
```

- ||, read as "or." This operator returns TRUE if either of its operands are true. If the first operand is true, || returns true without evaluating the second operand. Here's an example:

```
x = TRUE ¦¦ TRUE;      // x is TRUE
x = FALSE ¦¦ TRUE;     // x is TRUE
x = FALSE ¦¦ FALSE;    // x is FALSE
```

- !, read as "not." This operator takes only one expression, and it returns the opposite of that expression, so !TRUE returns FALSE, and !FALSE returns TRUE.

Note that the "and" and "or" operators won't evaluate the second operand if the first operand provides enough information for the operator to return a value. This process, called short-circuit evaluation, can be significant when the second operand is a function call. For example,

```
keepGoing = (userCancelled == FALSE) && (theForm.Submit())
```

If userCancelled is TRUE, the second operand—which submits the active form—won't be called.

Controlling Your JavaScripts

Some scripts you write will be simple; they'll execute the same way every time, once per page. For example, if you add a JavaScript to play a sound when users visit your home page, it won't need to evaluate any conditions or do anything more than once. More sophisticated scripts might require that you take different actions under different circumstances; you might also want to repeat the execution of a block of code—perhaps by a set number of times, or as long as some condition is true. JavaScript provides constructs for controlling the execution flow of your script based on conditions, as well as repeating a sequence of operations.

Testing Conditions   JavaScript provides a single type of control statement for making decisions: the if..else statement. To make a decision, you supply an expression which evaluates to TRUE or FALSE; which code is executed depends on what your expression evaluates to.

The simplest form of if..else uses only the if part. If the specified condition is true, the code following the condition is executed; if not, it's skipped. For example, in this code fragment

```
if (document.lastModified.year < 1995)
document.write("Danger! This is a mighty old document.")
```

the message will only appear if the condition (that the document's Last Modified field says it was modified before 1995) is true. You can use any expression as the condition; since expressions can be nested and combined with the logical operators, your tests can be pretty sophisticated:

```
if ((document.lastModified.year >= 1995) &&
(document.lastModified.month >= 10))
document.write("This document is reasonably current.")
```

The *else* clause allows you to specify a set of statements to execute when the condition is FALSE.

Repeating Actions   If you want to repeat an action more than once, you're in luck! JavaScript provides two different loop constructs that you can use to repeat a set of operations.

The first, called a *for* loop, will execute a set of statements some number of times. You specify three expressions: an initial expression that sets the values of any variables you need to use, a condition that tells the loop how to see when it's done, and an increment expression that modifies any variables that need it. Here's a simple example:

```
for (count=0; count < 100; count++)
document.write("Count is ", count);
```

This loop will execute 100 times and print out a number each time. The initial expression sets our counter, count, to zero; the condition tests to see whether count is less than 100, and the increment expression increments count.

You can use several statements for any of these expressions, like this:

```
for (count=0, numFound = 0; (count < 100) && (numFound < 3); count++)
if (someObject.found()) numFound++;
```

This loop will either loop 100 times or as many times as it takes to "find" three items—the loop condition terminates when count >= 100 or when numFound >= 3.

The second form of loop is the *while* loop. It executes statements as long as its condition is true. For example, you could rewrite the first for loop above like this:

```
count = 0
while (count < 100) {
document.write("Count is ", count) }
```

Which form you prefer depends on what you're doing; for loops are useful when you want to perform an action a set number of times, and while loops are best when you want to keep doing something as long as a particular condition remains true.

JavaScript Reserved Words

JavaScript reserves some keywords for its own use. You may not define your own methods or properties with the same name as any of these keywords; if you do, the JavaScript interpreter will complain.

TIP Some of these keywords are reserved for future use (hint: think Java!) JavaScript might allow you to use them, but your scripts may break in the future if you do.

abstract	double	instanceof	super
boolean	else	int	switch
break	extends	interface	synchronized
byte	false	long	this
byvalue	final	native	threadsafe
case	finally	new	throw
catch	float	null	transient
char	for	package	true
class	function	private	try
const	goto	protected	var
continue	if	public	void
default	implements	return	while
delete	import	short	with
do	in	static	

Part

VI

Ch

30

Command Reference

This section provides a quick reference to the JavaScript commands that are implemented in Navigator 3.0. The commands are listed in alphabetical order; many have examples. Before we dive in, here's what the formatting of these entries mean:

- All JavaScript keywords are in monospaced font.
- Words in italics represent user-defined names or statements.
- Any portions enclosed in square brackets ([and]) are optional.
- {statements} indicates a block of statements, which can consist of a single statement or multiple statements enclosed by curly braces.

break The break statement terminates the current while or for loop and transfers program control to the statement following the terminated loop.

Syntax

```
break
```

Example:

The following function scans the list of URLs in the current document and stops when it has seen all URLs or when it finds a URL that matches the input parameter searchName.

```
function findURL(searchName) {
var i = 0;
for (I=0; i < document.links.length; i++) {
if (document.links[i] == searchName)
{
document.write(document.links[i])
break;
}
}
```

continue   The continue statement stops executing the statements in a while or for loop, and skips to the next iteration of the loop. It doesn't stop the loop altogether like the break statement; instead, in a while loop it jumps back to the condition, and in a for loop it jumps to the update expression.

Syntax

```
continue
```

Example:

The following function prints the odd numbers between 1 and x; it has a continue statement that goes to the next iteration when i is even.

```
function printOddNumbers(x) {
var i = 0
while (i < x)
{
i++;
if ((i % 2) == 0     // the % operator divides & returns the remainder
continue
else
document.write(i, "\n")
}
}
```

for Loop   A for loop consists of three optional expressions, enclosed in parentheses and separated by semicolons, followed by a block of statements executed in the loop. These parts do the following:

- The starting expression, initial_expr, is evaluated before the loop starts. It's most often used to initialize loop counter variables, and you're free to use the var keyword here to declare new variables.

- A condition is evaluated on each pass through the loop. If the condition evaluates to TRUE, the statements in the loop body are executed. You can leave the condition out, and it will always evaluate to TRUE. If you do this, make sure to use break in your loop when it's time to exit.

- An update expression, update_expr, is usually used to update or increment the counter variable or other variables used in the condition. This expression is optional; you can update variables as needed within the body of the loop if you prefer.

- A block of statements is executed as long as the condition is TRUE. This block can have one or multiple statements in it.

Syntax

```
for ([initial_expr;] [condition;] [update_expr])
{
statements
}
```

Example:

This simple for statement prints out the numbers from 0 to 9. It starts by declaring that a loop counter variable, i, and initializes it to zero. As long as i is less than 9, the update expression will increment i, and the statements in the loop body will be executed.

```
for (var i = 0; i < 9; i++)
{
document.write(i);
}
```

for...in   This is a special form of the for loop that iterates the variable variable-name over all the properties of the object named object-name. For each distinct property, it executes the statements in the loop body.

Syntax

```
for (var in obj)
{
statements
}
```

Example:

The following function takes as its arguments an object and the object's name. It then uses the for...in loop to iterate through all the object's properties; when done, it returns a string that lists the property names and their values.

```
function dump_props(obj, obj_name) {
var result = ""
for (i in obj)
result += obj_name + "." + i + " = " + obj[i] + "\n"
return result;
}
```

function   The function statement declares a JavaScript function; the function may optionally accept one or more parameters. To return a value, the function must have a return statement that specifies the value to return. All parameters are passed to functions by value—the function gets the value of the parameter, but cannot change the original value in the caller.

Syntax

```
function name([param] [, param] [..., param])
{
statements
}
```

Example:

```
//This function returns TRUE if the active document has the title
//specified in the theString parameter and FALSE otherwise
function PageNameMatches(theString)
{
return (document.title == theString)
}
```

if...else   The if...else statement is a conditional statement that executes the statements in block1 if condition is TRUE. In the optional else clause, it executes the statements in block2 if condition is FALSE. The blocks of statements may contain any JavaScript statements, including further nested if statements.

Syntax

```
if (condition) {
statements
} [else {
statements}]
```

Example:

```
if (Message.IsEncrypted()) {
Message.Decrypt(SecretKey); }
else {
Message.Display();
}
```

return   The return statement specifies the value to be returned by a function.

Syntax

```
return expression;
```

Example:

The following simple function returns the square of its argument, x, where x is any number.

```
function square( x ) {
return x * x;
}
```

this   Use this to access methods or properties of an object within the object's methods. This always refers to the current object.

Syntax

```
this.property
```

Example:

If setSize is a method of the document object, then this refers to the specific object whose setSize method is called:

```
function setSize (x, y) {
this.horizSize = x;
this.vertSize = y;
}
```

This method will set the size for an object when called as follows:

```
document.setSize (640, 480);
```

var   The var statement declares a variable varname, optionally initializing it to have value. The variable name varname can be any JavaScript identifier, and value can be any legal expression (including literals).

Syntax

```
var varname [= value] [, var varname [= value] ] [..., var varname [= value] ]
```

Example:

```
var num_hits = 0, var cust_no = 0;
```

while   The while statement contains a condition and a block of statements. while evaluates the condition; if condition is TRUE, it executes the statements in the loop body. It then reevaluates condition and continues to execute the statement block as long as condition is TRUE. When condition evaluates to FALSE, execution continues with the next statement following the block.

Syntax

```
while (condition)
{
statements
}
```

Example:

The following simple while loop iterates until it finds a form in the current document object whose name is "OrderForm," or until it runs out of forms in the document.

```
x = 0;
while ((x < document.forms[].length) &&
 (document.forms[x].name != "OrderForm"))
{ x++; }
```

with   The with statement establishes object as the default object for the statements in block. Any property references without an object are then assumed to be for object.

Syntax

```
with object
{
statements
}
```

Example:

```
with document {
write "Inside a with block, you don't need to specify the object.";
bgColor = gray;
}
```

Sample JavaScript Code

It can be difficult to pick up a new programming language from scratch—even for experienced programmers. To make it easy for you to master Java-Script, this section presents some examples of JavaScript code and functions that you can use in your own pages. Each of them demonstrates a practical concept.

Dumping an Object's Properties

In the earlier section "Array and Object Properties" you saw a small function, DumpProperties(), that gets all the property names and their values. Let's look at that function again now to see it in light of what you've learned.

```
function DumpProperties (obj, obj_name) {
var result = ""      // set the result string to blank
for (i in obj)
result += obj_name + "." + i + " = " + obj[i] + "\n"
return result
}
```

As all JavaScript functions should, this one starts by defining its variables using the var keyword; it supplies an initial value, too, which is a good habit to start. The meat of the function is the for...in loop, which iterates over all the properties of the specified object. For each property, the loop body collects the object name, the property name (provided by the loop counter in the for...in loop), and the property's value. We access the properties as an indexed array instead of by name, so we can get them all.

Note that this function doesn't print anything out. If you want to see its output, put it in a page (remember to surround it with <SCRIPT>...</SCRIPT>!), then at the page's bottom, use

```
document.writeln(DumpProperties(obj, objName))
```

where obj is the object of interest and objName is its name.

Building a Link Table

You might want to have a way to automatically generate a list of all the links in a page, perhaps to display them in a separate section at the end of the page, as shown in figure 30.2. DumpURL(), shown in listing 30.1 below, does just that; it prints out a nicely formatted numbered list showing the hostname of each link in the page.

Listing 30.1 DumpURL( ) Displays a Numbered List of All the URLs on a Page

```
function DumpURL()
{
// declare the variables we'll use
var linkCount = document.links.length
var result = ""

// build our summary line
result = "<hr>\nLink summary: this page has links to <b>" + linkCount  + "</b>
```

```
hosts<br>\n"
result += "<ol>\n"

// for each link in the document, print a list item with its hostname
for (i=0; i < linkCount ; i++)
result += "<li> " + document.links[i].hostname + "\n"

// add the closing HTML for our list
result += "</ol><hr>\n"
return result
    <LX>}
```

This function starts by declaring the variables used in the function. JavaScript requires that you declare most variables before using them, and good programming practice dictates doing so even when JavaScript doesn't require it. Next, you build the summary line for your table by assigning a string literal full of HTML to the result variable. You use a for loop to iterate through all the links in the current document and add a list item for each to the result variable. When you finish, add the closing HTML for your list to result and return it.

Updating Data in Form Fields

There have been several mentions of the benefits of using JavaScript to check and modify data in HTML forms. Let's look at an example that dynamically updates the value of a text field based on the user's selection from one of several buttons.

To make this work, you need two pieces; the first is a simple bit of JavaScript that updates the value property of an object to whatever you pass in. Here's what it looks like:

FIG. 30.2

The DumpURL ( ) function adds a numbered list of all the links in a page at the end of the page.

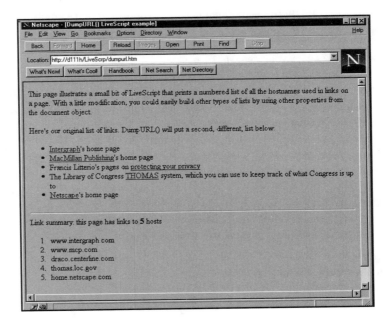

```
function change(input, newValue)
{
input.value = newValue
}
```

Then, each button you want to include needs to have its onClick method changed so that it calls your change() function. Here's a sample button definition:

```
<input type="button" value="Mac"
onClick="change(this.form.display, 'Macintosh')">
```

When the button is clicked, JavaScript calls the onClick method, which happens to point to your function. The this.form.display object points to a text field named display; this refers to the active document, form refers to the form in the active document, and display refers to the form field named display.

Of course, this requires that you have a form INPUT gadget named display!

Validating Data in Form Fields

Often when you create a form to get data from the user, you need to check that data to see if it's correct and complete before sending mail, or making a database entry, or whatever you collected the data for. Without JavaScript, you have to POST the data and let a CGI script on the server decide if all the fields were correctly filled out. You can do better, though, by writing JavaScript functions that check the data in your form on the client; by the time the data gets posted, you know it's correct.

For this example, let's require that the user fill out two fields on our form: ZIP code and area code. We'll also present some other fields that are optional. First, you need a function that will return TRUE if there's something in a field, and FALSE if it's empty:

```
function isFilled(input)
{
return (input.value.length != 0)
}
```

That's simple enough! For each field you want to make the user complete, you'll override its onBlur() method. onBlur() is triggered when the user moves the focus out of the specified field. Here's what your buttons look like:

```
<input name="ZIP" value=""
onBlur="if (!isFilled(form.ZIP)) {
alert('You must put your ZIP code in this field.');
form.ZIP.focus() }">
```

When the user tries to move the focus out of the ZIP code button, the code attached to the onBlur() event is called. That code in turn checks to see if the field is complete; if not, it nags the user and puts the focus back into the ZIP field.

Of course, you could also implement a more gentle validation scheme by attaching a JavaScript to the form's submit button, like this:

```
<script language="LiveScript">
function areYouSure()
{
return confirm("Are you sure you want to submit these answers?")
}
</script>
<input type=button name="doIt" value="Submit form"
onClick="if (areYouSure()) this.form.submit();">
```

Part
VI

Ch
30

Figure 30.3 shows your finished page, including the politely worded dialog box that tells the user to go back and finish filling out the form.

A Pseudo-Scientific Calculator

If you ask any engineer under a certain age what kind of calculator she used in college, the answer is likely to be "a Hewlett Packard." HP calculators are somewhat different from ordinary calculators; you use reverse Polish notation, or RPN, to do calculations.

FIG. 30.3
The fields on this page are tied to JavaScript functions that keep the user from moving the input focus until the user supplies a value.

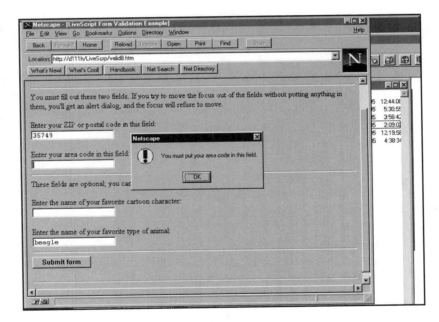

With a regular calculator, you put the operator in between operands. To add 3 and 7, you push 3, then the + key, then 7, then = to print the answer. With an RPN calculator, you put the operator after both operands. To add 3 and 7 on an HP-15C, you have to push 3, then Enter (which puts the first operand on the internal stack), then 7, then +, at which time you would see the correct answer. This oddity takes a bit of getting used to, but it makes complex calculations go much faster, since intermediate results get saved on the stack.

Here's a simple RPN example. To compute $((1024 * 768) / 3.14159)^2$, you'd enter:

```
1024, Enter, 768, *, 3.14159, /, x²
```

to get the correct answer: 6.266475×10^{10}, or about 6.3 billion.

Netscape provides an RPN calculator as an example of JavaScript's expressive power. Let's take a detailed look at how it works. Listing 30.2 shows the JavaScript itself (note that these are really in the same file; we've just split them for convenience.) Figure 30.4 shows the calculator as it's displayed in Navigator.

FIG. 30.4

Navigator displays the RPN calculator as a table of buttons, with the accumulator (the answer) and the stack at the top.

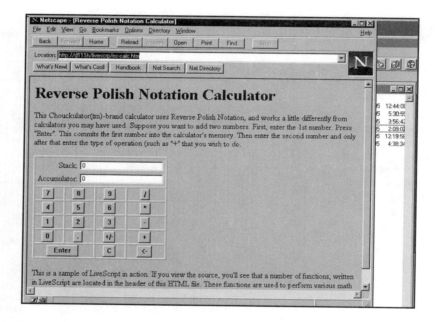

The HTML Page   Listing 30.2 shows the HTML for our calculator's page. For precise alignment, all the buttons are grouped into a table; the accumulator (where the answer's displayed) and the stack (where operands can be stored) are at the top.

Listing 30.2   The HTML Definition for the RPN Calculator Example

```
<table border="0">
<tr>
<td align=right>Stack:</td><td><input name="stack" value="0"></td>
</tr>
<tr>
<td align=right>Accumulator:</td><td><input name="display" value="0"></td>
</tr>
</table>

</td>
</tr>
```

```
<tr align=center>
<td>
<input type="button" value=" 7 "
onClick="addChar(this.form.display, '7')">
</td>
<td>
<input type="button" value=" 8 "
onClick="addChar(this.form.display, '8')">
</td>
<td>
<input type="button" value=" 9 "
onClick="addChar(this.form.display, '9')">
</td>
<td>
<input type="button" value=" / "
onClick="divide(this.form)">
</td>
</tr>

<tr align=center>
<td>
<input type="button" value=" 4 "
onClick="addChar(this.form.display, '4')">
</td>
<td>
<input type="button" value=" 5 "
onClick="addChar(this.form.display, '5')">
</td>
<td>
<input type="button" value=" 6 "
onClick="addChar(this.form.display, '6')">
</td>
<td>
<input type="button" value=" * "
onClick="multiply(this.form)">
</td>
</tr>

<tr align=center>
<td>
<input type="button" value=" 1 "
onClick="addChar(this.form.display, '1')">
</td>
<td>
<input type="button" value=" 2 "
onClick="addChar(this.form.display, '2')">
</td>
<td>
<input type="button" value=" 3 "
onClick="addChar(this.form.display, '3')">
</td>
<td>
<input type="button" value=" - "
onClick="subtract(this.form)">
```

continues

Listing 30.2   Continued

```
</td>
</tr>

<tr align=center>
<td>
<input type="button" value=" 0 "
onClick="addChar(this.form.display, '0')">
</td>
<td>
<input type="button" value=" . "
onClick="addChar(this.form.display, '.')">
</td>
<td>
<input type="button" value="+/-"
onClick="changeSign(this.form.display)">
</td>
<td>
<input type="button" value=" + "
onClick="add(this.form)">
</td>
</tr>

<tr align=center>
<td colspan="2">
<input type="button" value=" Enter " name="enter"
onClick="pushStack(this.form)">
</td>
<td>
<input type="button" value=" C "
onClick="this.form.display.value = 0 ">
</td>
<td>
<input type="button" value=" <- "
onClick="deleteChar(this.form.display)">
</td>
</tr>

</table>
 <LX>    <LX>   </form>
```

Notice that each button has an onClick() definition associated with it. The digits 0 through 9 all call the addChar() JavaScript function; the editing keys, C for clear and <- for backspace, call functions that change the value of the accumulator. The Enter key stores the current value on the stack, and the +/- button changes the accumulator's sign.

Of course, the operators themselves call JavaScript functions too; for example, the * button's definition calls the Multiply() function. The definitions aren't functions themselves; they include function calls (as for the digits) or individual statements (as in the "clear" key.)

The JavaScript   Of course, all these onClick() triggers need to have JavaScript routines to call! Listing 30.3 shows the JavaScript functions that implement the actual calculator.

Listing 30.3   The JavaScript Code That Makes the RPN Calculator

```
<script language="LiveScript">
<!— hide this script tag's contents from old browsers

// keep track of whether we just computed display.value
var computed = false

function pushStack(form)
{
form.stack.value = form.display.value
form.display.value = 0
}

// Define a function to add a new character to the display
function addChar(input, character)
{
// auto-push the stack if the last value was computed
if(computed) {
pushStack(input.form)
computed = false
}

// make sure input.value is a string
if(input.value == null ¦¦ input.value == "0")
input.value = character
else
input.value += character
}

function deleteChar(input)
{
input.value = input.value.substring(0, input.value.length - 1)
}

function add(form)
{
form.display.value = (0 + form.stack.value) + form.display.value
computed = true
}

function subtract(form)
{
form.display.value = form.stack.value - form.display.value
computed = true
}

function multiply(form)
{
```

continues

Listing 30.3   Continued

```
form.display.value = form.stack.value * form.display.value
computed = true
}

function divide(form)
{
var divisor = 0 + form.display.value
if(divisor == 0) {
alert("Don't divide by zero, pal...");
return
}
form.display.value = form.stack.value / divisor
computed = true
}

function changeSign(input)
{
// could use input.value = 0 - input.value, but let's show off substring
if(input.value.substring(0, 1) == "-")
input.value = input.value.substring(1, input.value.length)
else
input.value = "-" + input.value
    <LX>}
```

As you saw in the HTML listing above, every button is connected to some function. The addChar() and deleteChar() functions directly modify the contents of the form field named display—the accumulator—as do the operators (add(), subtract(), multiply(), and divide()).

This code shows off some subtle but cool benefits of JavaScript that would be difficult or impossible to do with CGI scripts. First, notice that the divide() function checks for division by zero and presents a warning dialog box to the user.

More importantly, in this example, all the processing is done on the client—imagine an application like an interactive tax form, where all the calculations are done on the browser and only the completed, verified data gets POSTed to the server.

A Note About LiveWire

At the time of this writing, Netscape has announced LiveWire and LiveWire Pro. These two products are intended for Web site providers who want to add JavaScript objects to their servers. Instead of embedding JavaScript in HTML pages and letting the client execute it, these products offer the tantalizing potential to put JavaScript scripts on the server and have them executed in response to client actions.

Unfortunately, the products, though announced, haven't been released, even in beta form, so we don't know exactly what they'll do or how they'll work. ●

Appendixes

Connecting to the Internet

Getting a connection to the Internet can seem to be an overwhelming problem. There are literally hundreds of Internet service providers (ISPs), many different types of connections, different levels of support, and different pricing plans. How are you supposed to sort through all of it so that it makes sense?

In this chapter, we tackle the major issues related to getting connected to the Internet and show you how to evaluate the various considerations. In particular, we look at:

- Determining the type of Internet connection you need
- Pricing and services
- How to choose an Internet service provider
- Setting up Windows 95 for PPP ■

TCP/IP Basics

Before we dive into the details of setting up an Internet connection, we need to talk about a few details of the protocols that make the Internet work. In order to understand all the issues involved with an Internet connection, you need to understand the basics of TCP/IP, domain names, and IP addresses.

The History of TCP/IP

The suite of widely used protocols known as Transmission Control Protocol/Internet Protocol (TCP/IP) has become increasingly important because international networks such as the Internet depend on it for their communications.

In the mid-1970s, the U.S. Department of Defense (DOD) recognized an electronic communication problem developing within its organization. Communicating the ever-increasing volume of electronic information among DOD staff, research labs, universities, and contractors had hit a major obstacle. The various entities had computer systems from different computer manufacturers, running different operating systems, and using different networking topologies and protocols. How could information be shared between all of them?

The Advanced Research Projects Agency (ARPA) was assigned to resolve the problem of dealing with different networking equipment and topologies. ARPA formed an alliance with universities and computer manufacturers to develop communication standards. This alliance specified and built a four-node network that is the foundation of today's Internet. During the 1970s, this network migrated to a new, core protocol design that became the basis for TCP/IP.

No matter what version of Netscape you are running, they all require a TCP/IP protocol stack to be present in order to communicate with the Internet. TCP/IP is the "language" that computers on the Internet use to speak to each other.

Domain Names

With millions of computers on the Internet, how do you specify the one that you want to interact with? You must know the name of the computer, just as you must know the name of someone you want to send a letter to. These names are specified by a convention called the domain name service (DNS).

A domain name typically gives a hierarchical structure for a computer or group within an organization. The portion of the name to the far right, the domain field, provides the most general category. The United States has eight domain fields, which are listed in table A.1.

Table A.1   Listing of U.S. Domains

Domain	Description
arpa	ARPANET members (obsolete)
com	Commercial and industrial organizations
edu	Universities and educational institutions
gov	Non-military government organizations
mil	Military
net	Network operation organizations
org	Other organizations
us	United States ISO domain

When you hook up to the Internet, you are a part of some domain, whether it is your own domain or that of your company or service provider. You also give your computer a name to identify it as part of your domain. For dial-up accounts with an Internet service provider, you can usually pick the host name for your computer yourself.

Let's look at an example. Assume that you have a personal account through a fictional Internet service provider named SpiffyNet. SpiffyNet's domain name is spiffy.net. SpiffyNet allows you to pick the name for your computer, so in a fit of creativity, you choose to call your computer viper. Thus, the full host and domain name of your computer would be viper.spiffy.net.

IP Addresses

Just as you have a name to identify a computer, your computer also has a number that uniquely identifies it to the rest of the world. This number is known as the IP address of your computer. Let's look a little closer at how IP addresses work.

An IP address is a 32-bit value that is divided into four 8-bit fields, each separated by a period. This means that the address would look something like 192.1.5.1. Each computer has exactly one IP address for each physical interface that it has connected to a network.

N O T E   In networking terminology, an 8-bit field is known as an octet. ■

The IP address of a computer is divided into two parts: a network section, which specifies a particular network, and a host portion, which identifies a particular machine on the network. Now there are five categories of IP addresses based on the type of network address. These are referred to as Class A through Class E.

In a Class A address, the first octet has a value between 1 and 126, and the network portion consists of the first octet. This obviously limits the number of Class A networks to 126; however, each network can have more than 16 million computers. Class A networks are limited to major corporations and network providers.

Class B networks use the first two octets to specify the network portion and have the first octet in the range of 128 to 191. This leaves the last two octets free for the host ID. The Class B network space provides for 16,382 network ID numbers, each with 65,534 host IDs. Large companies and organizations such as universities are typically assigned Class B addresses.

Class C addresses use three octets to specify the network portion, with the first octet in the range from 192 to 223. This provides for more than 2 million different Class C networks, but only 254 hosts per network. Class C networks are usually assigned to small businesses or organizations.

In Class D addresses, the first octet is in the range from 224 to 239 and is used for multicast transmissions.

Class E addresses, with the first octet in the range of 240 to 247, are reserved for future use.

When computers communicate using TCP/IP, they use the numeric IP address. DNS names are simply a device that helps us humans remember which host is which and what network it's connected to. When the Internet was first formed, the number of hosts on the Net was very small. As a result, each host had a complete list of all host names and addresses in a local file. For obvious reasons, this system quickly became unwieldy. When a new host was added, it was necessary to update every host file on every computer. With the explosive growth of the Internet, the host files also grew quite large. The mapping of DNS names to IP addresses is now accomplished via a distributed database and specific software that performs the lookup.

Static Versus Dynamic IP Addresses

As you've probably figured out by now, your computer has to have an IP address to communicate on the Internet. How does it get it? Well, in most cases it is assigned by your ISP when you set up your account. Even if you are setting up a whole network of computers, your ISP will probably handle everything for you.

For direct Internet connections, the IP address of your computer is permanently assigned to you. It never changes. These are known as static IP addresses. Most Internet service providers, however, use a scheme known as dynamic IP addressing.

Because most ISPs typically have many more dial-up customers than they do modems, only a fraction of their dial-up customers can be online at any given moment. This usually isn't a problem, unless you want to sit in front of your computer and run Netscape 24 hours a day! In short, this means that an ISP can "recycle" IP addresses by only assigning them when your system dials up to connect to the service. This allows ISPs to get by with far fewer IP addresses than if they were statically assigned.

How does this affect you, the network user? First, you have to configure your networking software differently depending on whether you have a static or dynamic IP address. Second, there are a few things that you just can't do if you have a dynamic IP address. Specifically, because your IP address is dynamic—it changes every time you log in—your host name cannot be registered in a domain name service database along with your IP address. Basically, this prevents anyone out on the Internet from being able to initiate contact with your computer. You won't be able to run an FTP server or a Web server if your computer has a dynamic IP address. Similarly, some commercial database services limit access to specific IP addresses based on subscription. Obviously, if your IP address is changing all the time, this scheme won't work.

Although these limitations don't really affect a lot of people, they can be a real problem if you really want to run an FTP or Web server. Some ISPs charge extra for static IP addresses—sometimes a lot extra! If having a static IP address is a real issue for you, make sure you check with your ISP before signing a service contract.

Types of Internet Connections

Depending on how much money you want to spend, you can get many different levels of connection to the Internet. These connection levels primarily differ in the amount of data you can transfer over a given period of time. We refer to the rate at which data can be transferred as the bandwidth of the connection.

There are two categories of Internet connections: dial-up and direct connections. A dial-up connection uses a modem to dial another modem at an Internet service provider, perform some connection sequence, and bring up the TCP/IP network. A direct connection uses a dedicated, data-grade telephone circuit as the connection path to the Internet. Let's look at these in a bit more detail.

Dial-Up Connections

When you sign up for a dial-up Internet account, you use a modem to dial a telephone number for an Internet service provider. After the modems connect, your computer performs some type of login sequence and the computers start to communicate via TCP/IP.

> **N O T E** For Netscape to be usable with a dial-up connection, you need, at a minimum, a 14.4KBps modem. A faster modem, such as a 28.8KBps model, is recommended. ■

The login sequence that your system performs depends on the requirements of your particular ISP. Most of the time, these login sequences are automated by a script file. (For more information on script files, see "Setting Up Windows 95 for PPP" later in this Appendix.)

We use a bit of smoke and mirrors when we refer to "starting TCP/IP networking." What this really means is that the remote system told us that you want to start communicating via TCP/IP instead of just via ASCII terminal emulation. This is accomplished via a dial-up connection that uses a protocol such as PPP.

PPP, the Point to Point Protocol, and SLIP, the Serial Line Internet Protocol, allow you to use TCP/IP communications over a dial-up connection. While either of these protocols works for serial TCP/IP, most ISPs are migrating to PPP, as it is newer and has more robust features. For this discussion, we are assuming you use PPP.

The way you start PPP varies depending on your ISP. In some cases, it starts automatically for you when you log in. In other cases, you may have to execute a command from a login shell on the ISP. Still another way is to make a selection from an interactive menu. It really depends on your ISP.

Direct Connections

The other major way of connecting to the Internet is through a direct connection. This method is typically used by large offices and companies to tie their internal networks into the Internet. Quite simply, it requires a lot of money.

A direct connection consists of a dedicated, data-grade telephone line that runs between your location and your service provider. Depending on the bandwidth of this line, the charges from your phone company can be several thousand dollars per month! In addition to this charge, you also have the recurring monthly charge from your ISP, which can also be very expensive. Add to that the cost of the network hardware required, and this option quickly prices itself out of the reach of individuals and small companies.

But let's assume for a second that you have the money to set up a direct Internet connection. How do you do it and what does it buy you? Well, the main things that it gives you are the ability to have a large pipe into the Internet through which to pump data, the ability to assign IP addresses to a whole network of computers, and static IP addressing. As for setting up the connection, most established ISPs have a setup package where they order your phone line, provide the hardware, register your domain name, and get your IP addresses for you—all for a flat fee. It's best to check with the ISP of your choice for more information.

Types of Services

Now that we've gotten the basics out of the way, let's look at what services you can get from an ISP. Most ISPs provide dial-up and direct connect services, with a whole menu of services that you can select from.

Dial-Up IP

For most ISPs, the basic level of dial-up IP gives you PPP-based, dynamic IP addressing on a public dial-up number. This number is connected to a modem bank, and rotates to the next available modem when you dial in— if there is a modem available. For most ISPs, busy signals are a common problem, especially during the prime evening and weekend hours.

Some ISPs provide a couple of levels of service above the basic dial-up PPP account. For example, you may be able to pay an additional fee to dial into a restricted number that has a better user-to-modem ratio. For even more money, the ISP may provide you with a dedicated dial-up line—a phone line that only you can dial in on. It's important to decide what type of dial-up account you are going to need, because this is one of the primary factors that affects the cost of your Internet service.

E-mail

If you've managed to get this far and set up an Internet connection, you probably want e-mail, right? By using a dial-up PPP account, you can read and send e-mail via the Post Office Protocol (POP). To do this, you get an e-mail client program such as Eudora for your PC and configure it with your e-mail account information and the IP address of your network mail server. If you have a dial-up account, your network mail server is a computer located at your ISP's offices.

N O T E E-mail is transferred between systems on the Internet using a protocol known as the Simple Mail Transport Protocol, or SMTP. POP is the protocol that a local e-mail client program uses to retrieve mail from a mail server. ■

Most personal dial-up accounts provide you with at least one e-mail address. Some ISPs even provide as many as five different addresses for personal or family accounts. Other ISPs make you pay an additional monthly charge for extra e-mail IDs. Business accounts usually have a fixed number as well. If you have more than one person who will be using e-mail from your system, you might want to shop around to see what the ISP policies on multiple e-mail addresses are in your area.

News

Just as with e-mail, if your Internet service provider gives you access to UseNet news, you can probably read and post news from your PC by using a newsreader, such as Netscape, that supports the Network News Transport Protocol (NNTP). To do this, simply configure your newsreader with the names or addresses of your mail and news hosts—the computers that you exchange e-mail and news with. Most ISPs provide UseNet news as part of the basic dial-up PPP account service.

Shell Access

Another service that is often available with a dial-up account is shell access. This refers to the ability to access a command-line processor on the remote ISP system.

N O T E Because most ISPs use a UNIX system to provide Internet access, and UNIX command-line processors are known as shells, the term shell access has become rather common. ■

Your ISP may or may not provide shell access as part of your basic network package. Most people can get by fine without having shell access. It is useful for accessing your account over the Internet, via Telnet or FTP from another location, as well as doing things like compiling C code. But if you are just running Netscape from home, you can probably survive without it.

N O T E   Be aware that some ISPs sell a "shell-access-only" account as a dial-up account. Typically, you cannot run PPP or SLIP from this type of account. Because Netscape needs TCP/IP to run, you need to make sure that you get the right type of service from your ISP. ■

Web Servers

The Web is a hot item—obviously, or you wouldn't be reading a book about Netscape! Another service provided by many ISPs is access to a Web server. Web servers allow you to put home pages on the Web so they can be accessed by people with Web browsers like Netscape. Figure A.1 shows an example of a Web page.

FIG. A.1

The home Web page for Macmillan Computer Publishing.

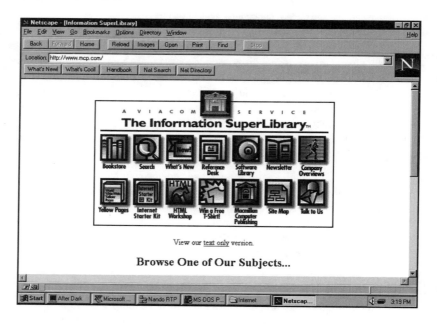

N O T E   Don't confuse Netscape with a Web server—you can still surf the Net with Netscape even if you don't have Web server access. ■

Having access to a Web server means that you can write Web pages in HTML and make them available on the Web. Many ISPs provide their personal account customers the ability to create personal Web pages. Businesses usually have to pay an additional fee for the service.

N O T E   Companies that have a direct connection to the Internet can simply set up their own Web server on one of their own machines. ■

If your ISP doesn't provide Web server access, don't give up hope. There are many companies that provide Web services alone, without providing any type of interactive access to the Internet. Basically, you pay a monthly fee to have the Web provider's site place your pages in the World Wide Web. These Web service providers also typically offer consulting and design services to help you create effective Web pages.

Virtual Domains

If you are setting up a business account, you may want to use your own domain name instead of simply using the name of your ISP. A domain name that is actually a directory on an ISP's server is commonly referred to as a virtual domain.

In order to set up a virtual domain, you must register your domain name with the Network Information Center (NIC). The NIC acts as the clearinghouse for all Internet domain names. You can reach the NIC by Telnet at rs.internic.net, on the Web at http://rs.internic.net, by e-mail at question@internic.net, or by telephone at 1-703-742-4777. You must fill out a domain name registration template and submit it to the NIC. Currently, the NIC charges a fee of $100 to register a domain, and $50 per year to use the domain. The $100 fee covers the first two years.

As part of the registration process, you must provide information about which network name servers advertise your domain name. In short, this means that you have to find an ISP that provides virtual domains, and have it enter your domain name in its name server.

As with everything else, most ISPs charge an additional fee for supporting virtual domains. If this is a service that you require, make sure you shop around and ask questions.

Finding an Internet Service Provider

With the explosive growth of the Internet, there are now a lot of ISPs to choose from. The services, cost, and customer satisfaction of ISPs vary widely. Some are terrible—a few are wonderful—most fall somewhere in the middle.

National Providers

You can divide ISPs into categories based on whether they have a national presence or they are mainly a local company. If you think about it, any ISP has a national presence in the sense that it is connected to the Internet and can be reached from anywhere. What we are referring to is the ability to contact the ISP via a local telephone call. Several of the larger ISPs have local dial access in many different locations, effectively making them national providers.

There are pros and cons to using a national provider. The company is usually larger—not a basement operation—and it usually has competent technical support people working for it. Also, national providers usually have a better uptime percentage than local providers, and also have a better price structure. On the other hand, because national ISPs tend to be larger, it may be harder to reach a technical support person when you have a problem. You may find that their policies are less flexible than local providers, and that they are less willing to make exceptions and work with you. If you are setting up a business connection, your ISP's office may be hundreds or thousands of miles away. If you are the kind of person that values working with a local company, this could present a problem for you.

Regional and Local Providers

Local and regional providers are ISPs that serve a regional market instead of having a national presence. Like national providers, there are pros and cons here, too. You will probably find that local providers are more flexible on their services and policies. For business, you are usually able to meet face to face with someone in the office to discuss your Internet needs. On the down side, the service quality of local ISPs tends to be less reliable. Sometimes these companies are very small operations, with limited hardware and technical support. You may find that it is difficult to connect due to busy signals during certain times of the day.

Local and regional ISPs are notorious for expanding their customer base faster than their hardware will support. When their servers get overloaded, response creeps to a crawl and uptime suffers. Phone lines are continually busy. If this happens to an ISP, it has to respond immediately or its systems will become unusable.

A Word About Private Information Services

Most people are aware of private national information services like CompuServe or America Online. While these services do provide Internet access, including Web access, they did not, when this book was written, provide routed IP access to the Internet. In short, this means that you have to use their tools and interfaces to access the Net. Because you will not have a routed IP connection, you cannot use the network tools of your choice, such as Netscape, via one of these services.

Service Levels and Cost

As you have seen, there are a lot of things to consider when selecting an ISP. The level of service you need is probably the main thing that affects the cost of your connection. Dial-up modem connections in the general public modem pool are usually cheapest. A restricted modem group is more expensive. A dedicated dial-up line costs even more. Direct connections via leased lines are among the most expensive.

In addition to service level, many ISPs offer different connection pricing plans. Some plans give you a fixed number of connect hours per month and charge you for extra hours. Other plans may give you unlimited hours during a certain time period, and charge you for hours outside of that window. Still other plans give you unlimited connect time for your fee.

Before choosing an ISP, take time to evaluate how you are going to use the service and what level of service you need. Check with computer users in your area to see if they can recommend a local service or a national service that works well.

Netscape and Windows 95

There are several different ways that you can use Netscape to connect to the Internet. You can connect over Microsoft's TCP/IP, a third-party TCP/IP package, or you can purchase one of the bundled starter kits, such as the Earthlink Netscape Total Access package. In this section, we look at how to set up Netscape to run under Windows 95.

Setting Up Windows 95 for PPP

If you're using Netscape under Windows 95, you're in luck. Windows 95 includes support for PPP, which enables Netscape to access the Internet. Assuming that you have an account already set up with an Internet service provider, it's not too difficult to configure Windows 95 so that it provides you dial-up PPP support.

There are several bits of information that you need to correctly configure PPP for Windows 95. Your ISP should provide all this information when you set up your account. If you don't know some of these items, contact your ISP for help. You need to know:

- The username that you use to login to your ISP
- The password for your ISP account
- The telephone number for your ISP
- The host name for your computer
- The network domain name for your ISP
- The IP address of your ISP's default gateway or router
- The IP subnet mask of your ISP's network
- The IP address of your ISP's DNS name server
- Whether you have a static or dynamic IP address
- The IP address of your computer, if you have a static address

After you gather all the above information, you're ready to start installing PPP for Windows 95. You probably didn't install all the components for PPP when you installed Windows 95, so you need to check to see what's already there and install the ones that are missing.

Dial-Up Networking, the Dial-Up Adapter, and TCP/IP

The dial-up networking and dial-up adapter items are necessary to set up a dial-up account to the Internet. Make sure you have your installation media handy throughout this process. For simplicity, I'll assume that you are installing from a CD-ROM. To check that dial-up networking is installed:

1. Click the Start button and choose Settings, Control Panel.
2. Double-click the Add/Remove Programs icon.
3. Select the Windows Setup tab. This brings up the section of the Add/Remove Programs dialog box that allows you to install or change various components of Windows 95.

4. Select the Communications option.

5. Click the Details button. This brings up the Communications dialog box showing current configuration of your Windows 95 communications system.

6. Make sure the Dial-Up Networking entry is selected. If it is not selected, select it and click OK.

Now that the dial-up networking package is installed, you need to check for the dial-up adapter. Basically, this program allows Windows 95 to use your telephone to make a network connection. To check that the dial-up adapter is installed:

1. Click the Start button, and choose Settings, Control Panel.

2. Double-click the Network icon. This brings up the Network control panel, which allows you to configure your network setup.

3. Select the Configuration tab. This portion of the Network dialog box allows you to add new network protocols and adapters to your Windows 95 environment. Figure A.2 shows the Network dialog box.

4. Look for TCP/IP and Dial-up Adapter in the list.

FIG. A.2
The Network dialog box for configuring your network environment.

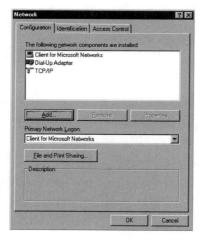

If you don't see the Dial-Up Adapter in the Network dialog box:

1. Click the Add button. This brings up the Select Network Component Type dialog box, which is where you tell Windows 95 what sort of networking item you want to add to your computer.

2. Double-click Adapter. This brings up the Select Network adapters dialog box. We want to add the Dial-Up Adapter so that we can use dial-up networking.

3. The lefthand scroll box is labeled Select Network Component Type. Scroll this box until you see the Microsoft entry.

4. Select Microsoft from the Select Network Component Type scroll box. Choose Dial-Up Adapter from the righthand scroll box labeled Network Adapters.

5. Click OK.

If you don't see TCP/IP in the Network dialog box:

1. Click the Add button to add the protocol to your computer.

2. Double-click Protocol. TCP/IP is a networking protocol and that is what we need to add. This brings up the Select Network Protocol dialog box.

3. Scroll the left scroll box, labeled Manufacturers, until you see the Microsoft entry.

4. Select Microsoft in the left scroll box and then choose TCP/IP in the right scroll box, labeled Network Protocols.

5. Click OK.

At this point, you should see both TCP/IP and the dial-up adapter in the Network dialog box. Click Properties and then Bindings and verify that the TCP/IP box is selected.

Dial-Up Scripting

You will probably want to create a script that handles logging you in to your ISP's system. This way, you can just double-click an icon and have Windows 95 dial your ISP, log you in automatically, and start PPP. We'll come back to scripting in a bit, but first you need to verify that the Dial-Up Scripting program has been installed.

1. Click Start and choose Programs, Accessories.

2. Look for an entry for the Dial-Up Scripting Tool.

If the Dial-up Scripting Tool isn't installed:

1. Click the Start button, and choose Settings, Control Panel.

2. Double-click the Add/Remove Programs icon.

3. Select the Windows Setup tab. Remember, this is where you add components to your Windows 95 system. We need to install the Dial-Up Scripting Tool from your Windows 95 CD.

4. Click the Have Disk button. This tells Windows 95 that you need to install something from the CD.

5. You will need to enter the path to the dial-up scripting program on your Windows 95 CD. For example, if your CD is drive G:, you would enter G:\admin\apptools\dscript.

6. Click the OK button.

Entering the Address Information

Okay, at this point you should have all the drivers and other programs installed so that you can configure TCP/IP with your network information. A couple of steps in this section depend on whether you have a static or dynamic IP address, so pay attention!

1. Click the Start button, and choose Settings, Control Panel.
2. Double-click the Network icon, and select the TCP/IP Protocol entry.
3. Click the Properties button.
4. If you have a static IP address, select the option labeled Specify an IP Address, type your IP address into the box, and fill in the Subnet Mask box with your subnet mask.

   If you have a dynamic IP address, choose the Obtain an IP Address Automatically option.
5. Select Disable WINS Resolution.
6. In the section marked Gateway, type the IP address for your ISP's gateway or router, and then click the Add button.
7. Select the Enable DNS option.
8. Type the host name of your computer in the Host box.
9. Enter the domain name of your ISP in the Domain box.
10. In the DNS Server Search Order section, enter the IP address of your ISP's DNS server.
11. Type the domain name for your ISP in the Domain Suffix Search Order section, and then click the Add button.
12. Double-check all your entries, and then click OK.
13. Windows 95 asks you to reboot your computer. Click Yes.

At this point, your Windows 95 environment should have support for Dial-up Networking, TCP/IP, and the Dial-up Scripting Tool. Hopefully, you were able to successfully add any of those components that were not already installed.

Setting Up a Connection Icon

Now we're almost ready to log on. The connection icon is the icon that you use to initiate your PPP connection. To start configuring it, double-click the My Computer icon on your desktop. Next, double-click the Dial-Up Networking icon, and then double-click the Make New Connection icon. This brings up a wizard box that helps you set up a new connection entry. Simply follow these steps:

1. Enter the connection name that you want to use into the dialog box.
2. Click the Configure button, and then select the General tab.
3. In the Maximum Speed box, set the port speed for your modem. In general, 57600 is a good setting.
4. Make sure that the box marked Only Connect at This Speed is not checked.
5. If you are not going to use a script to automate your login process, select the Options tab. From here, you can have PPP open a login window for you so that you can manually log in to your server.
6. Click OK, and then press Next in the wizard dialog box.

7. Enter the area code and phone number of your ISP in the dialog box and click Next.

8. Click Finish

At this point, you should see a new connection icon, with the name that you specified, on your system. There are just a couple of more things to do before it's ready to use.

1. Click the right mouse button on your connection icon. This brings up a pop-up menu for the connection icon.

2. Choose Properties from the pop-up menu.

3. Click the Server Type button, and then PPP from the list box.

4. Verify that the TCP/IP box in the Allowed Network Protocols section is checked, and make sure that the Log on to Network box is not selected.

5. Click OK.

6. Click OK again.

We're done configuring TCP/IP! If you want to set your modem to automatically redial, you can do so from the Settings option on the Connections menu in the Dial-Up Networking folder.

Basic Scripting

As mentioned earlier, using a script to automate your login process makes things a lot easier. You can start your connection session and run to the fridge while Windows 95 retries your ISP dial-up line and logs you in. Also, scripting is very easy. You can think of a script as telling Windows 95 what to look for from the ISP server. Just as you might look for a login: prompt to type your username, you can have your script do the same thing. Use the Dial-Up Scripting Tool to create scripts to control your dial-up network session. Figure A.3 shows the Dial-Up Scripting Tool.

FIG. A.3
The Windows 95 Dial-Up Scripting Tool.

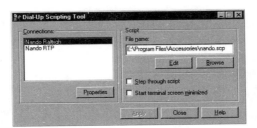

To make a script, follow these steps:

1. Click the Start button; select Programs, Accessories.

2. Select the Dial-Up Scripting Tool.

3. Click the Edit button to start editing a script.

All scripts start with the line

```
proc main
```

and end with the line

```
endproc
```

Between these two statements, you enter the commands that tell Windows 95 what to transmit and what to wait for. There are three basic commands that you need to know in order to write a script: `delay`, `waitfor`, and `transmit`.

The `delay` statement causes your script to wait for a specified number of seconds. For example:

```
delay 3
```

causes the script to pause for three seconds.

The `waitfor` statement makes the script wait until the specified string is received. For example:

```
waitfor "ssword"
```

waits for the string "ssword" to be received by your system.

The third statement, `transmit`, transmits a string to the remote system. It does not automatically send a carriage return at the end of the string. To send a carriage return, you need to transmit the string "^M" to the remote system. Here is an example of a script:

```
proc main
delay 1
transmit "^M"
delay 1
transmit "^M"
delay 1
transmit "^M"
waitfor "name>"
transmit $USERID
transmit "^M"
waitfor "ssword>"
transmit $PASSWORD
transmit "^M"
waitfor "enu:"
transmit "3"
transmit "^M"
endproc
```

N O T E It is usually a good idea to only use the last part of a string in a waitfor statement, in case the first character or two gets garbled by the network. For example, you should use waitfor "ssword>" instead of waitfor "password>". ■

The previous script waits for one second and then sends a carriage return to the remote system. It then repeats this sequence two more times. The script then waits for the string name> from the remote system. It sends the contents of the special variable $USERID, which contains the user ID that you enter when you start the network connection program. It follows the user ID with a carriage return.

The script then waits for the ssword> prompt from the remote system and sends the contents of the $PASSWORD variable. This variable contains the password that you enter when you start the network connection program. It follows the password with a carriage return. It then waits for the string enu:, and sends the number 5 and a carriage return. That's all there is to it!

Once you have written your script, save it with a .SCP extension. Then, in the Dial-Up Scripting Tool, select the network connection that you want to attach the script to and click Apply. Your script is now associated with that network connection and will be executed automatically any time you run that particular network connection.

You can also select the Step through Script box to be able to step through the script one line at a time to debug it. By selecting the Start Terminal Screen Minimized box, you will see no terminal box displaying the progress of your script. Uncheck this box if you want to watch your script execute as it runs.

Netscape and Earthlink

An Internet service provider, Earthlink, has teamed up with Netscape to provide an Internet access package that is easy to set up. The Earthlink Total Access software package comes with an automatic setup program, and also provides Netscape and the Eudora electronic mail program.

To obtain Total Access for Windows 95, you can download it from a variety of sites. It is available via anonymous FTP from www.earthlink.net, or you can contact Earthlink directly at 1-800-395-8425.

Once you have the software, it is easy to install. Just run the setup program that comes with the installation kit. For example, if Total Access is in drive A:, type:

    a:\setup

This brings up an installation wizard that guides you through the installation process. When the installation wizard prompts you for the installation directory, enter the name of the directory where you want Total Access installed. Total Access is installed in the specified directory, and a program group is added to Windows 95.

After you complete the installation process, registration with Earthlink is very straightforward. You are prompted to create a new account or use an existing account, fill out a form with your name and address, and choose a username and password. You then get a choice of a couple of different connection pricing plans, and you enter your credit card number for billing purposes. Total Access then dials out to Earthlink via your modem and creates your account for you. Once your account is created, you are ready to take your virtual surfboard in hand and join your fellow Net citizens on the Internet. ●

Loading and Configuring Netscape

In chapters 1 and 2 we discussed the history of the World Wide Web, its uses, the direction in which it is developing, and the many methods of connecting to it. But we have yet to access the Web's bounty of information. The Web has become one of the most common methods of finding specific information about any topic under the sun. In fact, Netscape, the most popular World Wide Web browser, is used by almost 80 percent of all households and businesses connected to the Internet. That number is pretty amazing when you consider the abundant number of World Wide Web browsers available, many of which are free.

When considering the purchase of any product, you try to look at all the options available so you can get the best value for your money. Now, the fact that Netscape is so widely used may assist you in making the decision to purchase Netscape.

Other World Wide Web Browsers have some very nice features, or may cost less, but none offer the diversity and power of Netscape. When you are using Netscape, the hard part is figuring out where you want to go.

In this appendix, you learn how to:

- ■ Install Netscape from the CD-ROM with this book
- ■ Download Netscape from the Internet
- ■ Get on the Web for the first time
- ■ Get help with Netscape products ■

Loading Netscape

Of course, you have to install the program before you can catch that first wave. But don't worry; Netscape has included a wizard that guides you through the entire installation process. Netscape has a few system requirements that you must meet to complete the installation and run the program effectively.

Installation Requirements

The following list shows all the requirements for installing and running Netscape 3.

- ■ Mouse
- ■ Windows 95, Windows NT (3.5 or higher), or Windows 3.1
- ■ 386sx or compatible machine
- ■ 2MB of hard drive space
- ■ 4MB of memory (8MB recommended)
- ■ LAN or a SLIP/PPP connection to the Internet

> **CAUTION**
>
> These are just the minimum requirements to run Netscape 3 under Windows. Keep in mind that you need more hard drive space if you keep a large list of sites you have visited or if you download lots of images and other files.
>
> The minimum requirements only take into consideration the amount of hard drive space and memory that is required to load and run the program in most situations. When you visit a Web site that has an extraordinary amount of graphics on it, the page takes a long time to load if you only have the "minimum" amount of RAM.

Installing the Netscape Browser

The installation process is relatively quick and painless. Because Netscape uses a wizard to walk you through the installation, most of your questions are answered right on-screen. If you experience problems during the installation, call the Macmillan phone number listed in the section titled "Getting Help for Netscape Products" later in this chapter.

1. Close any Windows or DOS programs that are running. Sometimes other programs use files or memory that Netscape needs to use during the installation process.

2. Click the Start button or press Ctrl+Esc and select Run.

3. From Windows Explorer, go to the \netscape directory on the CD-ROM. In this directory, there are subdirectories for Windows 95, Windows NT, and Windows 3.1. Change to the directory for your operating system version and double-click the file there. Once the installation files are extracted, the setup wizard (which guides you through the installation process) is installed. Once the wizard's initialization is complete, an introduction and a warning on Netscape appear. Click Next.

4. Netscape requires a specific destination directory, as shown in figure B.1. This is the directory that stores the main portion of Netscape. You can either use the default directory, or you can enter your own directory name.

Part

VII

App

B

FIG. B.1

The default installation directory for Netscape 2.0 is C:\Program Files\ Netscape\Navigator\.

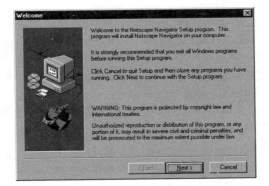

To specify your own directory, click Browse. You see a list showing your current directory structure, as shown in figure B.2. Select the directory you want to place Netscape into, or type the name of a new directory, and click OK.

FIG. B.2

You can easily select an alternative directory from this Choose Directory dialog window.

N O T E The examples in this book use the default path. If you install Netscape in another directory, please go to that location when you see a reference to c:\Program Files\Netscape. ▪

Whether you choose to create your own directory, or use the predefined directory structure, you need to click Next to continue.

5. Netscape now copies the files from the temporary directory to Netscape's permanent location on your hard drive. The scales shown in figure B.3 enable you to keep track of the installation process. When it is done, the wizard creates a program group folder and shortcut icons that allow you to run Netscape directly from your Start menu.

FIG. B.3

Netscape makes it easy to see how your installation is progressing by providing a setup status bar and checks on your available disk space.

6. When you see the short prompt requesting that you finish the Netscape setup by going to their Setup Site, click yes. You will be greeted with the How to Setup Netscape page on Netscape's site.

Travelling through the setup site, you will be asked to register your product and purchase the rights to use this program. Note that the copy of Netscape on the CD with this book includes the rights for you to use the program. You do not have to pay Netscape to use it.

NOTE   The README.TXT file is full of useful information. It guides you through setting up Netscape to deal with Win32s, and lets you know how to procure and load the appropriate WINSOCK.DLL file. The README.TXT file also gives some basic pointers on where to get more information if you encounter problems using Netscape. Although it does not provide very much helpful information for individuals that are first-time users of Netscape, it may help some old pros fix a new problem. ■

Now you have Netscape 3 installed. This is the latest shipping version that is currently available.

Downloading Netscape from the Internet

Netscape is frequently updated and there may come a time when you want to get a new version. These new versions are available on the Internet. The best way to download a new version if you ever need one is to use the current version you installed from the CD-ROM with this book to go to the Netscape web site (**http://home.netscape.com**) and download it from there.

1. Go to the Netscape home age at **http://home.netscape.com** and click the Netscape 3 Now button shown in figure B.4. (This number on the button may change when there are new versions.) You can go directly to **http://home.netscape.com/comprod/ mirror/client_download.html** and skip step 2. This is the address of the Web page for downloading Netscape 3.

FIG. B.4

The Netscape Communications Corporation's World Wide Web home page.

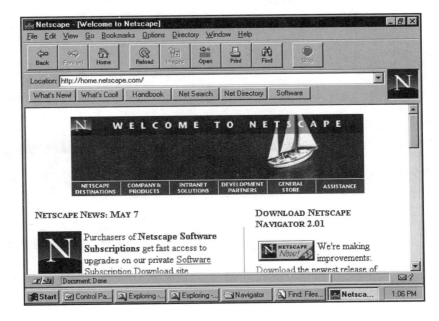

2. Scroll through the document shown in figure B.5 until you find the Netscape Navigator category which then links you to the Web page for downloading Netscape (see fig. B.6).

FIG. B.5

The Netscape Communications Corporation's product page.

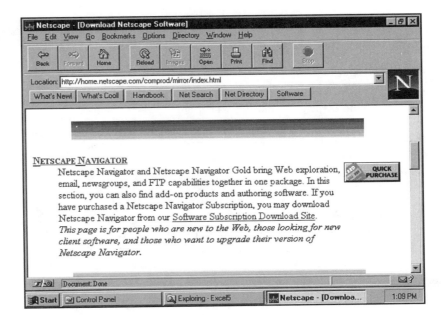

3. Netscape asks a series of questions about the product that you want to download.

- Desired product
- Operating system
- Desired language
- You need to select Netscape, or Netscape Gold, if you want to look at the latest enhancements in Netscape software.

FIG. B.6

Netscape 3.0
Download Page

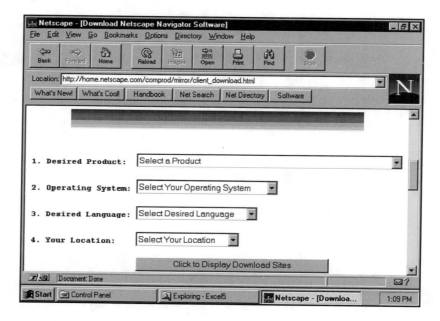

4. Once you have filled in the previous requests for information, you need to click the Click to Display Download Sites button.

5. A list of locations from which you can download Netscape appears. This list includes the majority of the mirror sites listed in the later section titled "The Netscape Mirror Site List." Select the site closest to your current computer location.

6. Once you have downloaded Netscape, close your Web browser.

Because most of the sites holding Netscape store the program as a self-extracting executable file, you can run the executable by double-clicking it in Windows Explorer. This extracts the compressed files and starts the installation of Netscape. From this point you can follow the instructions in the earlier section entitled "Installing the Netscape Browser" to install it. You simply need to refer to the directory to which you copied the Netscape executable file.

N O T E It is always nice to start a new project with some idea about the amount of time that it is going to involve. The following table shows the average download time I experienced when transferring this file several times while preparing this book. These times should be close to what you will experience, although you should not worry if your times are a bit longer or shorter. These times will vary if the file size of newer versions changes dramatically.

Connection Type	Total Transfer Time
14,400 Modem	1 hour
28,800 Modem (at least a 24,000 baud carrier)	30 minutes
57,600 Network	15 minutes
T1 Cable	1 minute

The Netscape Mirror Site List   Netscape allows only a few sites to mirror its information. The following list shows you all the official sites from North America. Of course, you can always download a copy of Netscape from the Netscape Communications Corporation site, listed in the North American section, from anywhere in the world.

Since the most logical place to get a program is from the company that makes it, it would stand to reason that this corporation would have the busiest file servers. This reasoning holds true for the Netscape FTP sites. You will often find that the main Netscape site is busy, even though they have several servers available from which you can download programs. The solution to this information bottleneck lies in the development of mirror sites. Mirror sites provide easy access to information by having copies of files from other computers that could be located across the continent, or on the other side of the globe. Mirror sites draw away from the pool of people that are waiting to get onto the main file server.

- Netscape Communications Corp—**ftp://ftp.netscape.com/pub/navigator**
- Washington University, St. Louis—**ftp://wuarchive.wustl.edu/packages/www/ Netscape/navigator**

 T I P   Netscape changes their directories on a regular basis. You can find Netscape 3 in the subdirectories under the "Navigator" directory.

- University of Texas at Austin—**ftp://ftp.the.net/mirrors/ftp.netscape.com/pub/ navigator**
- University of Texas at Dallas—**ftp://lassen.utdallas.edu/pub/web/netscape/pub/ navigator**
- Central Michigan University, Computer Center—**ftp://ftp.cps.cmich.edu/pub/ netscape/navigator**

Getting on the Web for the First Time

The World Wide Web is considered one of the best places to get information on any subject, at any time. To reach this large body of information, you first need to connect to the network of computer systems that makes up the Internet. Use the information in the following sections to connect to your Internet service provider or to your company's network. If you have problems attaining these connections, chapter 2 provides you with more detailed information.

Connecting to Your Service Provider

Although the term service provider usually refers to a dial-up SLIP or PPP connection, you can also use a standard TCP/IP LAN connection. There are specific details in appendix A, "Connecting to the Internet," that discuss how to set up a working Internet connection for all the operating systems used by Netscape products. The following section covers only the basic steps in the setup process for Windows 95.

Making a LAN Connection   When using a Local Area Network (LAN) to connect to the Internet, you must make sure that your computer is correctly configured to use the specific type of network to which it is physically attached. You have to know the specific type of network card that your computer uses and the names of the drivers that are required to run your card. Once this information is obtained, you must load those drivers, or tell your computer to do it automatically for you each time it starts, before you can connect to the network. The following steps guide you through the process of getting these drivers loaded and running properly.

1. Open the Control Panel and select the Networks icon.
2. On your Network Properties screen, make sure that you have a TCP/IP protocol loaded for your network card.

N O T E   This protocol needs configured with the following information:

- Your network IP address
- The address of your Internet gateway
- The address of the Domain Name Servers (DNS) used by your facility

Complete the configuration by choosing Properties and filling out the forms on the tab dialog box that appears. See appendix A for detailed information on how to configure these settings. ▮

3. Choose the OK button to exit this screen once you have ensured that the proper drivers are loaded.
4. Double-click the Netscape icon on your desktop. If you do not find this icon, you can open the Start menu, select Programs, and then the Netscape folder, and choose the Netscape icon located on this menu to start the program.

Netscape finds your network and travels through it and out onto the Internet to find Netscape's home page. Once you are there you can travel across the Net to anywhere.

TROUBLESHOOTING

Every time I open Netscape I get an error message telling me that I have a Winsock error.
Generally you get this error when you do not have your TCP/IP protocol properly loaded. Go back
to the Control Panel's Network Properties dialog box and ensure that the appropriate TCP/IP and
network drivers for your network card are loaded. If you have selected the wrong network card, you will
load inappropriate drivers and receive this message. If you just installed your network drivers, you must
restart your computer for them to load. Windows 95 does not automatically load the drivers into your
computer's memory after you have installed them.

Making a SLIP/PPP Connection   Very few home users and relatively few businesses have a
direct connection to the Internet, which leaves the majority of the world connecting to the
Internet through a SLIP or PPP connection and a modem. Because Netscape does not provide
you with a dialing program, you have to use the one that comes with Windows 95, or another
third party dial-up connector. Before you attempt to use Netscape the first time, check your
dial-up program. It will save you time in the long run.

1. Open the Control Panel and select the Networks icon.
2. Check to ensure that you have the dial-up adapter and a TCP/IP protocol loaded for that
   adapter. If you do not have these items in your list of network components, refer to
   appendix A for assistance in configuring these drivers.
3. Open the Start menu and choose the Programs option, and then choose the Accessories
   option. This opens the Accessories pop-up menu on which you will find an icon labeled
   Dial-Up Networking. This is the utility that dials your phone connection for you.

N O T E   The dial-up networking utility actually dials your phone and can log you into your service
provider. ▇

4. Open the Start menu, select the Programs option, and then choose the Netscape group
   option.
5. Choose the Netscape option from the resulting menu.

Netscape automatically starts the dial-up networking client, which calls your service provider
and establishes a connection. Depending on how you have installed the dial-up client, you
might have to manually enter your name and password. When you establish your connection,
all the features of Netscape are available.

Getting Help for Netscape Products

Because Netscape is used by such a large base of Internet users, you can get product support
quickly and easily from a variety of sources. If you are using the copy of Netscape provided
with this book, your technical support will be provided through QUE and Macmillan Computer
Publishing. Netscape Communications Corporation provides technical support to its licensed

customers. UseNet newsgroups discuss how to use and configure Netscape to work in various situations. Listserv discussion groups also discuss the use of Netscape and how to make it perform specific required tasks. And once again, there is the World Wide Web. The Web has many sites specifically designed to be viewed with Netscape. Many of these site owners will assist you in configuring Netscape to view their sites in the best possible fashion. You can generally contact the site owners by sending an e-mail message to *webmaster@the.site.name*.

Receiving Technical Support from Netscape

Netscape Communications Corporation provides its customers with many ways to get in touch with technical support. These methods include e-mail, World Wide Web pages, its online Help system, a printed handbook (for registered users), and technical voice support over a telephone.

Contacting QUE and Macmillan Computer Publishing   If your copy of Netscape is from the CD-ROM included with this book, you must call or e-mail Que for technical support. Please send questions via e-mail to **support@mcp.com** or call 317-581-3833. Unless you have purchased a copy of Netscape from Netscape, you cannot use the Netscape technical support numbers listed in this appendix.

Using E-Mail   In this world of fast paced, practically instantaneous communication, electronic mail is becoming the best way to get information to and from your associates. Technical support services are also starting to jump on this bandwagon. Netscape has quite a few e-mail addresses from which you can get information (see table B.1). Some of them respond with a generic letter full of other important information and answers to the most common questions that people ask. Others respond individually by qualified support or sales personnel.

Table B.1   Netscape Corporation Electronic Mail Addresses

For Help on...	Department Name	E-mail Address
The Netscape Test-Drive Servers	Technical Support	**test-drive@netscape.com**
Netscape 3.0 for licensed customers	Technical Support	**client@netscape.com**
Getting information about purchasing products	Sales—automated	**sales@netscape.com**
General product questions and answers	Sales—automated	**info@netscape.com**
Licensed Netscape Servers	Technical Support	**server@netscape.com**

For Help on...	Department Name	E-mail Address
Netscape Training programs information		**training@netscape.com**
Bug reports from X Windows users	Technical Support	**x_cbug@netscape.com**
Bug reports from Windows users	Technical Support	**win31_cbug@netscape.com** **win95_cbug@netscape.com** **winnt_cbug@netscape.com**
Bug reports from Macintosh users	Technical Support	**mac_cbug@netscape.com**

Part
VII

App
B

When using a manually monitored system, include your name, return e-mail address, and product registration number in your message. Netscape provides support only to individuals who provide this information.

Referring to Netscape's Help System   Netscape's help system uses a series of linked HTML pages, some of which are located on your local computer, while others are located at Netscape's Web site. The Help menu in Netscape allows you to jump directly to important product support pages for your version of Netscape (see fig. B.7). These pages include the Release Notes for your version, the related FAQs for Navigator, a Netscape Handbook, and a series of articles on how to get assistance and give feedback on Netscape's products. You can generally answer most, if not all, of your questions by reading these documents.

FIG. B.7

The available Netscape Help utilities located in the Help menu.

Using Netscape's World Wide Web Pages   Netscape uses its Web site to provide much of its product support, not to mention sales and marketing pushes. You can reach the Technical Support pages by clicking the Assistance portion of the main Netscape image map located at the top of the Netscape home page. The address of Netscape Communications Corporation's Technical Support home page is **http://help.netscape.com**. Figure B.8 shows you what to expect.

When you get to this page, you are greeted with product FAQs, search engines, a storefront, and a list of all the services Netscape provides for its products. You simply need to find the most appropriate services for the product you have questions on, click its link, and continue down your path to a completely working product.

FIG. B.8

The main Technical Support Web page for Netscape.

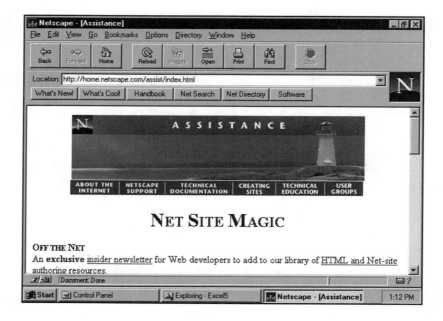

The Web site contains layers upon layers of information. If you see a topic that just might be helpful, jump to it and read it. If the site does not contain the information you are looking for, choose Back and continue on to your next option. You never know when a document is going to provide you with that one clue that solves your problem. Even if it doesn't solve your problem today, it might keep you from having another problem in the future.

Using Netscape Phone Support   For those of you who have purchased a Netscape product from Netscape, you can get product support over the telephone. There are quite a few numbers you can call depending on the type of questions that you want to ask (see table B.2).

Table B.2   Netscape Corporation's Support Phone Numbers

For Questions About...	Department	Phone Number
Problems with any Netscape Servers-UNIX	Technical Support	415-528-2727
Problems with any Netscape Servers-Windows NT	Technical Support	800-542-5134
Problems with a licensed version of Netscape	Technical Support	800-320-2099
Purchasing a product or checking on an order	Sales	415-937-3777

For Questions About...	Department	Phone Number
Purchasing - Corporate	Sales	415-937-2555
Purchasing - Federal	Sales	415-937-3678
For assistance with Netscape Personal Edition	Technical Support	503-626-5475

Getting Help from UseNet Newsgroups

As mentioned earlier, UseNet newsgroups are one of the best ways for people with common interests to get together. There are many different newsgroups that discuss Netscape products. The following list names a few UseNet searching tools with some of the known sites that you can use to get into a UseNet discussion. I have also included specific instructions on how to use Dejanews, a UseNet newsgroup message searching utility that I have found helpful.

- Launch Pad—**http://sunsite.unc.edu/**

  alt.fan.mozzila

  comp.infosystems.www.browsers
- TileNet—**http://www.tile.net/tile/news/index.html**

  comp.infosystems.www.misc

  comp.infosystems.www.users
- Dejanews—**http://www.dejanews.com**

  comp.infosystems.www.browsers.ms-windows

The Dejanews system is very easy to use. The following steps enable you to search its entire message database for information specific to your problem with Netscape.

N O T E Please remember that vocabulary and spelling are very important. You may refer to "e-mail" in a search, while someone else calls it "email," and another individual uses the phrase "Internet mail." Your search will not find the messages left by those other individuals. To do a thorough exploration, you need to search as many different phrases and spellings as you can to get the broadest range of information out of your search.

1. In Netscape, enter the previous URL as the address you want to visit.
2. Choose the Power Search! option.
3. Set your search criteria.
   - Keywords Match (All/Any)
   - Usenet database (Current/Old)
   - Max. number of hits (30/60/120)
   - Hitlist detail (Concise/Detailed)

- Hitlist format (Listed/Threaded)
- Sort by (Section/Newsgroup/Date/Author)
- Article date bias (Prefer New/Prefer Old)
- Article date weight (Some/Great/None)

4. Enter your search criteria, such as **Netscape**, and choose the Find button, as shown in figure B.9.

5. Choose Continue from the Security Warning dialog box.

Your screen now changes to a listing of all the messages and UseNet newsgroups that are currently discussing Netscape. This screen should be similar to the one shown in figure B.10. You can read the UseNet discussions by double-clicking the highlighted message subject.

FIG. B.9

The main Dejanews search utility screen configured to perform a search for all discussions of Netscape.

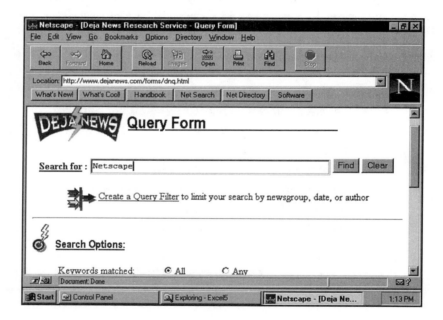

> **N O T E**   If you would like more details on using UseNet newsgroups with Netscape, please see chapter 9. To go directly to a UseNet newsgroup, type the address preceded by news: in the URL: field at the top of your Netscape screen.
>
> For example, if you want to look at the comp.infosystems.www.browsers.ms-windows newsgroup, place your cursor in the URL: field on your main Netscape screen and type **news:comp.infosystems. www.browsers.ms-windows**. Press Enter to tell Netscape to search for that address. ■

FIG. B.10

The list of the most recent discussions about Netscape that the Dejanews service could find.

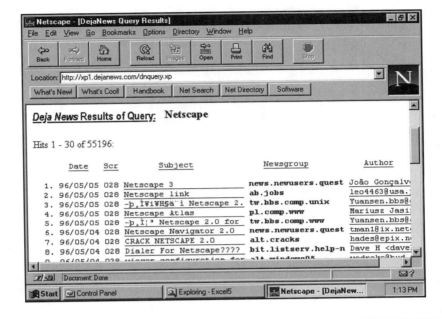

T I P Netscape also maintains a set of newsgroups devoted to help with Netscape products. These are called the Netscape User Groups and are easiest to reach by using Navigator to open this web address: **http://home.netscape.com/commun/netscape_user_groups.html**. Here you will find a list of groups and links. Clicking a link will open that group in a Netscape new window. Be sure to post any messages to only the appropriate newsgroups. For example, questions about Netscape Navigator are appropriate in the NETSCAPE GENERAL TOPICS USER GROUP or NETSCAPE NAVIGATOR USER GROUP but not in groups related to security, server software, or development products.

Netscape Administration Kit

We can't end this chapter without bringing your attention to a new Netscape navigator product, the Administration Kit, which enables site administrators to customize Netscape 3.0 settings such as preference parameters, directory buttons, and URLs. Before disbursing Netscape 3.0 to end users, this kit enables site administrators to customize 3.0 for better suitability and overall control of their Internet as well as Intranet applications. These customized settings can be locked to ensure a secure and consistent site.

The Administration Kit is priced at $1995.[00] and is purchased separately from Netscape 3.0. Figures B.11 and B.12, from Netscape's Administration Kit Web page, display the many features of this product. This site can be reached at **http://home.netscape.com/comprod/ products/navigator/version_3.0/enterprise/index.html**.

FIG. B.11

The Netscape Administration Kit Web page—Customization Features.

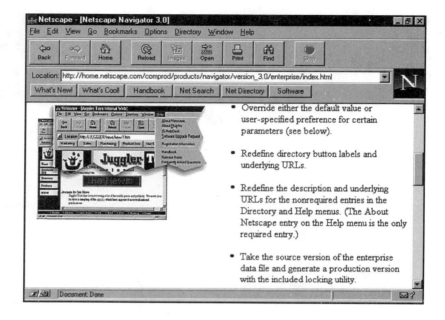

FIG. B.12

The Netscape Administration Kit Web page—Parameters that can be specified and locked.

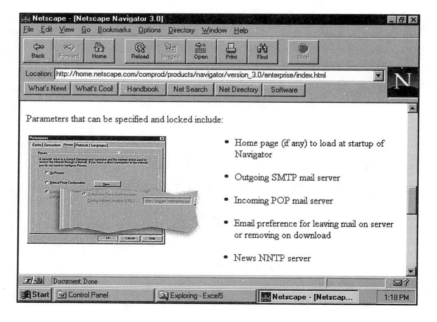

General Troubleshooting

There are more "little" problems experienced every day than all the technical support departments across the country can fix. So when you do have to call or write for technical support, have the following information handy to help the process along:

▶ **See** "A UseNet Primer," **p. 198**

- Your name and registration number. Most technical support services will not assist you unless you have a registered product.

- Version of the software you are using. This narrows down the list of known problems so the support specialist can quickly switch gears to help you best with your product version.

- A short description of the problem. For example, "I am able to connect to my service provider, John Doe's Internet Connections, but once I start Netscape I constantly get the following error message: Netscape is unable to locate server: www.yahoo.com. This server does not have a DNS entry. Check the server name in the location (URL) and try again." With this information the technician will know if your dial-up PPP connection is working properly, allowing them to narrow down the possible sources of your problem. They will also know the error messages that you are receiving in case this is a known problem they can fix in just a few minutes. When Technical Support personnel have to dig for information on a problem, it needlessly takes more of your time and causes you, and them, more frustration than the problem is worth.

- The name and version of your operating system. If you are running a product designed for Windows 3.1 under Windows 95, you may be having a known conflict with the operating system.

- The type of Internet connection you are using: SLIP/PPP or LAN.

- If you have a SLIP/PPP connection, know the brand and speed of your modem, and the name of the TCP/IP stack you are loading.

  If you have a LAN connection, know the name of the TCP/IP stack you are loading, the type of network card you are using, and the type of connection your network has to the Internet (e.g., T1 cable, 57,600 baud line, and so on).

- Try other Internet applications, such as Ping or Telnet, and let the support technician know if they work properly.

- Know when the problem first started, and whether you recently added any new software to your computer around that time. Sometimes installing new software makes your old software not run properly. Many software packages come with their own versions of hardware drivers, and a new software package will often overwrite the version of the driver installed and used by a previously installed package.

Knowing this information in advance helps the technician to diagnose your problem, and get you off the telephone and back onto the Web faster. Without this type of information, you will be extending the time involved in solving your problem. Technical support personnel are highly trained individuals that really know their jobs. Remember that they are people, too, and can't read your mind, nor can they see your computer screen. They are dependent on your descriptions of a situation, or a screen to direct them to a solution. By providing them with as much information as you can, you are helping yourself and all the other people that are waiting on the phone lines. ●

Loading and Configuring Netscape for the Macintosh

The Internet has traditionally been difficult to understand and use for two reasons: it's vast, and it's arcane.

The size of the Internet is easy to see. When Valvoline advertises its Web page address (**http://www.valvoline.com/**) during televised stock car races in the southeast United States, you realize that the Internet has spread into parts of our lives unimaginable 10 or more years ago. No one expects the Internet to become any less pervasive any time soon, if ever.

In the early days of the Internet, Internet access was difficult. Everyone involved in the Internet received access through their professional careers in academia and the military. Because the Internet was built primarily by linking computer systems that spoke various flavors of UNIX, UNIX knowledge became the required passport. When the Internet grew large enough that people could not hope to find what they needed just casting about by themselves, search tools were created with names like FTP, Telnet, Gopher, Archie, and Veronica. These tools were created for use by computer professionals, and were not designed for today's average user of the Internet.

Since 1990, the World Wide Web has been created as a user-friendly way to link many of these information resources and search engines together. The first Web browser, NCSA Mosaic, was a wonderful improvement in ease-of-use of the Internet. Since Mosaic's first version, many other Web browsers, including Netscape, have been developed. While there are many Web browsers, one study in the spring of 1995 estimated that three-quarters of all Web access was through a Netscape browser. This chapter discusses how to get Netscape 3.0 running on your Macintosh computer.

In this chapter, you learn the following:

- How to get Netscape onto your Macintosh
- What communications software you need in addition to Netscape, and where to get it
- How to configure Netscape ■

Getting Netscape

The two most likely ways for you to install Netscape on your Macintosh are either by downloading a newer version of Netscape with an already-installed older version of Netscape or other World Wide Web browser, or using floppy disks or CD-ROMs from a purchased copy of Netscape. If you are installing Netscape from a set of floppy disks or CD-ROMs, follow the instructions provided.

If you are using Netscape or another Web browser, the URL for downloading the most current version of Netscape is **http://home.netscape.com/comprod/products/navigator/version_3.0**. You then click the Netscape Navigator option button.

If you have FTP (File Transfer Protocol) software, you can look for the FTP site **ftp.netscape.com**. After you get through to the FTP site, look for the folder the files are stored in. As of this writing, the path for the 3.0 release of Netscape is **ftp.netscape.com/pub/navigator/3.0**. Check the subdirectory for the appropriate Macintosh version. (This directory may change slightly when there is a new version).

The Netscape Now! page is where you always find the most current version of the Netscape software (see fig. C.1).

N O T E   If you already have Netscape and are installing a newer version, find Netscape on your Macintosh and note what folder the application is in. If you are downloading Netscape with an older edition of Netscape, choose the General Preferences command from the Options menu, and then look at the Applications dialog box to see the default Temporary Directory used for downloading. If the default directory is the same folder your current Netscape is located in, change the download folder to another folder. If you do not change the default download directory, you will overwrite your currently installed version of Netscape. ■

Follow Netscape's instructions on the following pages of its Web site. You will be asked to specify which version you'd like as your operating system, the language you use, and your location. You will then be given a list of sites to choose from. After you download the file, you need to uncompress the compressed file.

FIG. C.1
Netscape Now! page.

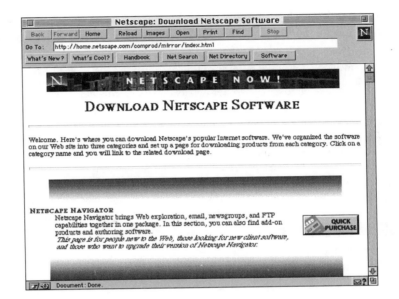

NOTE You will be given the option of choosing the Maximum version or the standard version with Chat, Phone, and 3D. The standard version is reccormended if you have enough RAM and free hard disk space. ▪

Installation Requirements

In order to install Netscape, you need a Macintosh that has a 68020 processor or better, can run System 7.0 or later, and has at least 5MB of free RAM and about 5MB of hard disk space.

NOTE Netscape will not run on the Mac Plus, SE, Classic, Portable, or Powerbook 100. ▪

Any helper applications or plug-ins you install will also want additional memory, from less than 400KB for StuffIt Expander to 2.5MB or more for Whurlwind. You also need at least a 14,400 baud modem.

The previous paragraph discussed the minimum requirements for Netscape on the Macintosh. A more realistic setup would have a Macintosh with the following:

- Either a 68040 or PowerPC processor
- At least 10MB of total RAM (not free RAM, although 16MB is recommended and will be needed to run some plug-ins)
- A color monitor (to take advantage of the image display capability of Netscape)
- The fastest modem you can find (28,800 external modems for the Macintosh are available for under $150 as of this writing)

Netscape, like almost every other application, performs better with more memory. For better performance and reliability, a good general rule for Macintosh software is to set the "minimum size" memory requirement to 25 percent higher than its default setting. Also, you can set Netscape's cache value higher, so that more images and Web pages are stored on your hard disk, which gives you a faster response when jumping to a Web page you've visited in that session. With a large cache, your newsreader and electronic mail requirements, several plug-ins (sound, video, uncompressing files, VRML, and so on), and your Netscape and plug-ins folder could easily reach 6MB or more of memory and 20MB or more of hard disk space.

Installing Netscape

After you have the Netscape installer icon on your Macintosh desktop, double-click the icon to display the Netscape Installer window shown in figure C.2.

FIG. C.2

The Netscape Installer window.

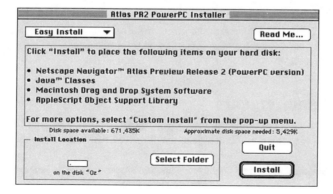

The Easy Install option, shown as the default selection of the pop-up menu in the upper left of the window, installs a version of Netscape appropriate to your Macintosh (either a PowerPC-native version, or a version capable of running on 68000-series Macintoshes).

If you have multiple disks attached to your Macintosh, use the Switch Disk button in the bottom center of the window to select the desired installation disk. Selecting the name of the disk next to its icon in the Installer window displays a pop-up list of the available disks and an option to select a folder of the current disk. If there is not enough disk space to install Netscape (about 3.5-4.5MB), the Installer will not allow you to install to that disk, and will display a message that you should select another disk. After you have decided where to install Netscape and checked to see if the chosen disk has enough memory, click the Install button in the lower-right corner of the window. An Installing window appears with a progress bar that fills in as the files are installed. A dialog box appears if installation is successful, and prompts you to quit the Netscape Installer or perform further installations. You will then be given the option of registering your copy offline (see fig. C.3). Choose the option you prefer and continue.

FIG. C.3
The Netscape Installer window after a successful installation.

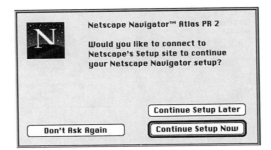

Macintosh Prerequisites: MacTCP/Open Transport and FreePPP

Depending on your operating system, either open transport or MacTCP. MacTCP is the Macintosh version of TCP/IP (Transmission Control Protocol/Internet Protocol) used by research organizations, universities, and the Internet to allow different types of computers to connect with each other over a network.

SLIP (Serial Line Internet Protocol) and PPP (Point-to-Point Protocol) are protocols that use TCP/IP to make your personal computer a part of the Internet as long as the link to your ISP (Internet service provider) stays open.

N O T E   If you have Netscape or another World Wide Web browser running on your Macintosh already and are just upgrading your version of Netscape, you have MacTCP or Open Transport and some form of SLIP/PPP working already. Skip ahead to the "Configuring Netscape Preferences" section of this appendix for information on how to customize your version of Netscape to work best for you. ■

If you are using an operating system before 7.5.3, but after 7.5, MacTCP is included, but was not installed if an Easy [System] Install was performed. If MacTCP is not in your Macintosh's System Folder, install the control panel with the following steps:

1. Insert Disk 1 of your set of System 7.5 floppy disks (or the CD, if your System disk shipped as a CD-ROM), and click the Continue button in the Welcome to System 7.5 window.

   2. Click the Easy Install option in the upper-left of the Installer window, and select Custom Install from the pop-up list (see fig. C.4).

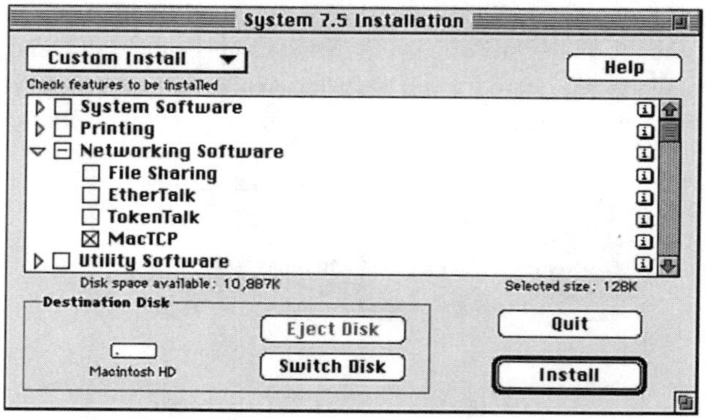

FIG. C.4

Custom Install.

   3. Click the triangle to the left of Networking Software to show the items in that folder. Click the checkbox to the left of MacTCP, and then click the Install button.

   4. If you are using a CD-ROM, wait until you see a dialog box that says Installation was successful, and then click the Restart button to restart the Macintosh.

   5. If you are using System 7.5.3., Open Transport is preinstalled.

You also need either SLIP or PPP software to allow Netscape for Macintosh to talk to MacTCP or Open Transport. Apple does not supply SLIP or PPP software, but there are several shareware and freeware packages available.

N O T E   SLIP has almost entirely died out; almost everyone is using a PPP connection. SLIP software (such as InterSLIP) tends to be found in the same archive location as PPP software, so if you need SLIP, just follow my pointers to PPP software. ■

One place to find PPP packages such as MacPPP, ConfigPPP, and FreePPP is the Info-Mac HyperArchive. The URL of the TCP/IP-related software directory is **http://hyperarchive.lcs.mit.edu//HyperArchive.html**.

After you download and uncompress the file, the PPP software will be a control panel with a README file. Install the PPP software by dragging the icons onto the closed System Folder, and then restart your Macintosh.

If you are installing MacTCP and ConfigPPP or FreePPP, you need several pieces of information from your Internet Service Provider or system administrator. If they support Macintoshes at all, they may have a set of instructions prepared for configuring MacTCP, ConfigPPP or FreePPP, and Netscape.

For MacTCP, you need to know the following information to enter into the window that appears when you select the More button from the MacTCP or TCP/IP window (see figs. C.5 and C.6).

FIG. C.5
The MacTCP 2.0.6 More window.

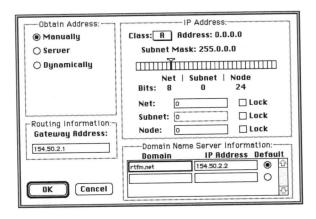

FIG. C.6
The TCP/IP window.

- How your system obtains the IP address—Indicate this by choosing one of the radio buttons in the upper-left corner of the window. In Open Transport, this is the configure field.

- Gateway address—This is typically four sets of one to three numbers with periods between the sets. A gateway address looks like this: 151.2.46.2. Open Transport calls this the Router address.

- Class of the server—The A that is visible is a drop-down menu from which you can select A, B, or C. This is not entered using Open Transport.

- Net, subnet, and node values—These are three (normally) single-digit numbers. Only an optional subnet mask is required with Open Transport.

- Domain name and IP address—The domain is typically going to be the hostname of your Internet service provider, and normally is two or more words separated by periods. The IP Address field is the IP address corresponding to your ISP's domain name, and will look like the gateway address. Domain names are not required in Open Transport, although your Domain Name Server IP address is.

For ConfigPPP and FreePPP, you need the following information to enter in the Config window:

- PPP server name (you can call this whatever you want)
- Port speed of your Macintosh and modem
- Flow control to use
- Type of telephone line (tone dial or pulse dial)
- Telephone number to dial
- Modem Init string
- Connect script for establishing connection

If you have difficulty configuring MacTCP and ConfigPPP or FreePPP, note these tips:

- If you are trying to enter values into the More window of MacTCP and the only fields you can enter values in are the Domain Name and IP addresses in the lower-right corner, you should set the Obtain Address buttons in the upper-left corner to Manually. Once you are done entering values in this window, remember to set the Obtain Address button to the correct choice.

- If you've entered all your information and you're having problems connecting, double-check everything. People often have trouble with typing errors. Get a friend or coworker to verify that all the information you have on-screen is correct.

- If you're still having trouble and there's another Macintosh that works with the network or service provider, find whoever is responsible for that Macintosh and double-check your settings with the settings on the working Macintosh. Remember that the connection script entered into ConfigPPP can include the username and password, so let the person responsible for that Macintosh preserve his privacy. You might ask him to make a copy of the Control Panels you need, delete his passwords from the copies, and give them to you on a floppy disk. Copying their setup to your Macintosh eliminates most of the setup this section describes.

Configuring Netscape Preferences

Netscape can be customized in many ways. Most of the Preferences options ask you to choose which you prefer, more graphics or more speed. The Options menu contains controls for you to set many parameters of Netscape's appearance and behavior. There are four major windows and five toggled controls that can be selected from the Options menu.

The General Preferences Window

To view the General Preferences window, go to the Options menu and select the General command (see fig. C.7).

FIG. C.7
The General Preferences window.

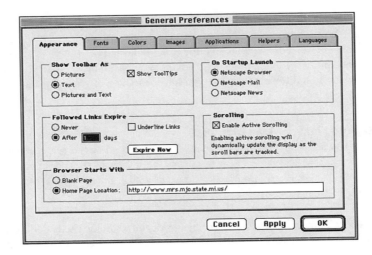

The General Preferences window has seven screens that let you control many aspects of how Netscape operates on your Macintosh. These seven screens are the following:

- Appearance
- Fonts
- Colors
- Images
- Applications
- Helpers
- Languages

The Appearances Screen The Appearances screen contains five panels: Toolbars, Startup, Link Styles, Scrollbars, and Starting URL. The Toolbars panel controls whether the buttons on the main Netscape toolbar appear as text-only, picture-only, or pictorial buttons with text labels. If you want the window for your Web page viewing to be as large as possible, set this for text-only.

The Startup panel controls what Web page Netscape loads when it is first started, and what windows (for Web, mailbox, or UseNet news) are launched on startup. You can enter any URL (Universal Resource Locator) you like for the startup page.

One tip to speed Netscape's startup is to have your startup page be a page local to your computer, which doesn't have to be downloaded over your network connection. If you set the startup page to a local HTML file on your hard disk, Netscape typically takes less time to access a hard disk than to download a Web page over its Internet connection.

Link Styles controls whether or not you want links to appear on Web pages as underlined or not, and how long you want Netscape to keep a record of you following a given link. The default value of this Followed Links Expire option is 30 days, but you can set the time from 0 (a followed link never looks different from one you haven't looked at) to Never (a followed link will always look different than one you haven't looked at). You can also enable active scrolling from this screen.

Expired Links as Trail Markers?

About now, somebody is thinking, "I can use these expired links as markers of where I've been!" True, but it's probably more efficient to mark your trail at just the interesting points, not every step along the path. On the other hand, expired links could be used in an experiment to research how people search for information.

The Fonts Screen   The Fonts screen allows you to define the encoding format, the fixed fonts, and the proportional fonts used to draw the pages. You can also choose the display size of the fonts. If you find yourself leaning close to your monitor to read the words, and the text is in high contrast to the background, you could enlarge the text with these controls.

The Colors Screen   The Colors screen lets you set the colors for new links, links you haven't looked at yet, the text color, and the background color. For contrast and ease of reading, keep the text color dark and the background color light, or vice versa, unless you like trying to read purple text on a black background. Instead of a color, you can set a background image file as the default background: a useful option if you are setting up Netscape for a presentation and want the company logo as a faint watermark-like image in the background of every page that does not have a defined background.

The Images Screen   The Images screen includes a choice that might improve Netscape's performance: Display Images either While, or After Downloading them. The default setting is to display an image as it downloads. If you are on a slow-to-medium speed connection, this lets you see the part of an image that has been downloaded, giving you the choice of whether to stop the download. If your computer is on a high-speed Internet connection, choosing the While Downloading option can be slower than After Downloading. Typically, a computer is idle between pieces of a downloading image. If the connection is faster than the computer can process the received information, you may have better performance if you choose After Downloading.

The Applications Screen   The Applications screen of the General Preferences window lets you select the supporting applications to use with a Telnet session, a TN3270 session (TN3270 is a fancy version of Telnet), and the application to choose to view the HTML source of a Web page. On a Macintosh, this is usually Simpletext. However, you can set the View Source application to any word processor or HTML editor you might have. This screen also allows you to define your download folder.

The Helpers Screen   This screen lets you determine what "Helper" applications to use. From this window, you can define which applications to use to unstuff archives, process images, audio and video, as well as how to handle executables.

The Languages Screen   This screen lets you choose which language you are using. You probably won't need to use this screen if you downloaded the correct version of the software for the language you use. The languages screen simply allows you to enable Java and JavaScript processing. The Protocols screen gives you the option of accepting Cookies (a way for Web sites to put a "marker" on your computer that other servers can read indicating that you have visited them), sending your e-mail address for anonymous FTP connections, and submitting forms via e-mail. It is recommended to keep Cookies disabled while enabling the other two options.

The Mail and News Preferences Window

The Mail and News Preferences window of the Options menu presents you with five ways to customize Netscape for sending and receiving electronic mail and reading UseNet newsgroups (see fig. C.8). Chapters 6, "Accessing Other Services with Netscape," and 8, "Reading UseNet Newsgroups with Netscape," cover this screen and its options in detail, so this section only covers the basics of what you need to do in order to get connected to your mail and news.

Part

VII

App

C

FIG. C.8

The Mail and News Preferences window.

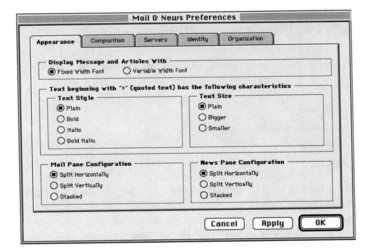

N O T E   You will need to have the names of the computers, or servers, your Internet connection uses as the SMTP server, the POP server, and the NNTP server. You can get these names from your Internet service provider or system administrator. ■

To set Netscape's required preferences so that you can send and receive mail and read and post to UseNet newsgroups, follow these steps:

1. First, select the Servers tab. In the Mail panel of the screen, enter the name of the SMTP (Simple Message Transaction Protocol) Server and the Mail POP (Point-of-Presence) Server in the first two fields at the top of the screen. The two servers may be the same, but they don't have to be. You should also include your e-mail ID under POP user ID.

2. In the News panel at the bottom of the Servers screen, enter the name of the news server.

3. Select the Identity tab. The Identity screen contains information Netscape uses to identify you to the outside world when you send a message.

4. Enter your name. This is the name you want the rest of the Internet to know you as, and does not have to be your real name.

5. Enter your e-mail address so messages you send can have a return address attached to them. Your e-mail address will look like words_or_numbers@more_words_or_numbers. Your POP user ID is the part of your e-mail address to the left of the @ symbol. Your reply-to address does not have to be the same as the address of the account you are sending from.

6. Click OK. To save your work, from the Options menu, choose Save Options.

The Network Preferences Window

The Network Preferences window contains settings that affect your connection to the network. The three screens of the Network window are the following (as shown in fig. C.9):

- Cache
- Connections
- Languages
- Protocols
- Proxies

The Cache screen lets you set the size of the cache Netscape uses on the local hard disk of your computer, and where you want the cache to be on your Macintosh. Netscape's cache does not have to be in the same folder or even the same disk drive where Netscape is located. If you decide to go back to a Web page that you've already downloaded, Netscape will look at the version you downloaded five minutes ago, instead of reconnecting to the network and downloading the page again (which probably hasn't changed in five minutes). Loading the page from your hard disk will always, except in very special circumstances, be faster than reloading the page from your network connection.

FIG. C.9

The Network Preferences window.

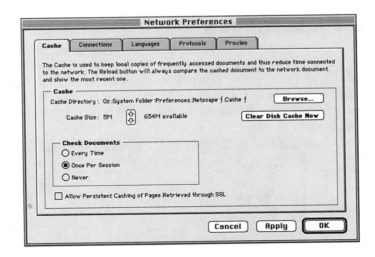

NOTE If you think the page has changed in the last five minutes (for example, there are several people who have wired digital cameras to their Internet connections and updated their Web pages every minute with snapshots of their offices), select the Reload button to load the page from your network connection, rather than from the cache. ■

Netscape's default setting for the cache is 5MB, and you can change this to a higher or lower value. Reducing the cache size to below 1MB is not recommended, as some individual Web pages and files can exceed 1MB in size. Reducing the cache too low causes Netscape to act as if it has no cache, which can severely limit performance.

The Connections screen lets you set the number of simultaneous connections Netscape can keep operating at any moment. When you connect to a Web page with many images, Netscape is actually trying to load four (the default setting) of the images at the same time. The only difficulty is that because your network connection doesn't grow in size as you raise the number of simultaneous connections, Netscape takes as long to download a Web page four connections at a time as it does to download the same page one connection at a time. You can probably avoid this screen and leave the default value of four in place, and never worry about changing the value.

Proxies are applications that are substitutes (that is, they act as a stand-in) for your same type of application. Proxies are rarely present for any other reason than to act as guards on the firewall on a network. You will need to ask your system administrator if there are any proxies present for use across a firewall, and what settings you need to make in Netscape in order to use them.

The Securities Window

Individuals have different concerns over their privacy and personal security. While one resident of an apartment building may use only the latch lock on her door and leave the windows open all day, her neighbor may have two deadbolt locks on each door and bars on the windows. Netscape lets you choose how often you want to be shown an alert when the security level of the page you are looking at changes (see fig. C.10).

FIG. C.10

The Security window.

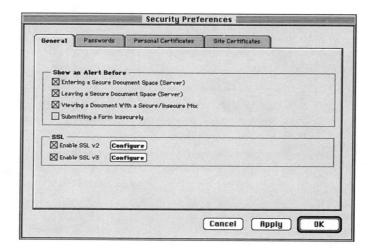

N O T E   Netscape's security is always working whenever you connect to a secure Web site. You cannot turn it off, either intentionally or accidentally. ▩

The Security panel of the Options menu lets you choose how often you want to be alerted of changes in the security of your transaction. The four choices in the amount you want to be alerted are:

- Entering a Secure Document Space (Server)—When this option is on, Netscape displays a dialog box every time you enter a Netscape Commerce Server.
- Leaving a Secure Document Space (Server)—When this option is on, Netscape displays a dialog box every time you leave a Netscape Commerce Server.
- Viewing a Document With a Secure/Insecure Mix—When this option is on, Netscape displays a dialog box every time you enter a Netscape Commerce Server.
- Submitting a Form Insecurely—When this option is on, Netscape displays a dialog box every time you send a form response to an insecure server.
- In addition, you can define options for secure servers.

If you have all these options off, you can still detect if you are connected to a secure or insecure Web page by looking at the bottom left of the Netscape window and finding the key. If the key is broken, you are looking at an insecure site. If the key is a single piece, you are connected to a secure site. If the key image is enough for you, you can turn all of the options off. However, if the key image is small and unobtrusive enough that you might not remember to check the security status of your connection, you can turn on any or all of the various warning boxes.

The Passwords option allows you to set a password, and tell Netscape how often to request it, for access to your copy of Netscape. This option is particularly helpful if you are using Netscape over a network or in a public setting.

Certificates are generally needed to operate a server securely. This setting will generally be of interest only to system administrators so you should not have to touch these settings.

The Preferences Menu Commands

Below the Preferences menu entries for the General, Mail and News, Network, and Security windows, the next portion of the Options menu is a set of five settings that can be toggled from this menu. If the command has a check next to it, the command is on. These commands are as follows:

- Show Toolbar—Shows the toolbar across the top of the Netscape window. If you don't need the buttons, turning off this option gives more area within the Netscape window to display images.

- Show Location—The field that displays the URL of the current Web page is optional. I keep this field for use in helping diagnose problematic URLs.

- Show Java Console—This toggle allows your Java control console to always be displayed if selected.

- Show Directory Buttons—As with the toolbar, if you want a thinner top border to the Netscape window, turn this command off by leaving it unchecked.

- Auto Load Images—This command can be important for performance. If you're in a hurry, or if you don't care about pretty colored buttons, background textures and the full-page image of the Web page creator's favorite hermit crab, turn this option off to (often substantially) reduce the amount of time it takes to download a page.

- Show FTP File Information—When you look at an FTP site with Netscape, you see icons of folders and files with file information (size, date created or last changed, and so on). If you don't want to see this information, turn this option off.

The Document Encoding command lets you choose the document encoding standards. These options provide for more international use than earlier versions of Netscape.

The final command is important—Save Options preserves the changes you've made in this menu for the next time you start Netscape.

Where to Go for Technical Support

This appendix should be able to help you with most of your questions about where to find Netscape, how to install Netscape, and what you need in order to configure and run Netscape. In case you need some more assistance, here are some pointers.

If you have a problem with installing the MacTCP system extension, call Apple Computers at 1-800-SOS-APPL.

If you have a problem with ConfigPPP or another shareware or freeware PPP or SLIP system extension or control panel, look for the README file that comes with the software. If there is no README or Help file, throw it into the Trash, delete the file, and find another connection package.

The most likely problem you may have with getting Netscape is getting through to its site to download the software, especially if an updated version of the software was recently released. Look to the URL **http://home.netscape.com/comprod/mirror/index.html** for a list of mirror sites—not operated by Netscape Communications—that have the most current publicly available version of Netscape.

If you can connect to the Internet using Netscape, look in your application's menus (Netscape for the Macintosh moved the Help menu underneath the Apple Guide or Balloon help menu item in the System menu bar) for the entry Release Notes. This command takes you to the most recent official release notes for your version of Netscape.

For general assistance, Netscape has a large amount of information on its Web site. Netscape's technical support is on the Web at **http://home.netscape.com/assist/support/index.html**. In general, if you have a purchased version of Netscape, consult the materials you received with your purchase for consulting with technical support. Another good source of help is the UseNet newsgroup comp.infosystems.www.browsers.mac. If you are having problems connecting with Netscape and can't see the Web page in order to request technical assistance, technical support is available for Netscape Navigator Personal Edition at 503-626-5475. Telephone support is available for the LAN Edition of Netscape Navigator at 1-800-320-3099.

> **N O T E** As of this writing, Netscape Communication's support policy is free telephone support for 90 days to purchasers of the LAN Edition. If you did not purchase the LAN Edition within the last 90 days, telephone support is billed to your credit card (have it with you when you call) at $25 for the first 15 minutes and $2 per minute after the first 15. ■

You can also contact other people in your area (for example, within your office or university, or the local area Macintosh User Group) for advice and assistance. Your network system administrator or Internet Service Provider (ISP) technical support should also be able to help.

A final piece of advice: If you expend a great deal of effort solving a problem and succeed, write down how you did it. Preferably, write it down where you can find it again easily. Even if you choose not to be helpful to someone else if they run into the same problem, consider how much trouble you will have reinventing your solution. ●

Loading and Configuring Netscape for UNIX

While Netscape on UNIX systems is much the same as it is on Windows PCs and the Macintosh, there are a number of significant differences, particularly with respect to installing and configuring the package. UNIX systems are multiuser, multitasking systems, and are considerably more complex than PCs. You may need help from your UNIX system administrator to get Netscape set up on the system.

In this chapter, you learn:

- The different available versions of Netscape

- How to download Netscape over the Internet using standard UNIX utilities and/or a Web browser

- How to install Netscape from the archive package you download over the Internet

- How to install Netscape you purchase from the CD-ROM distribution media

- How to configure Netscape to set it up so all users on your UNIX system can use it
- How to set up your own Netscape configuration so it looks and acts the way you want it to

You'll also want to look at chapter 10, "Configuring Helper Applications," where the setup of Netscape helper applications is covered for more UNIX-specific configuration instructions. Chapter 10 also describes some UNIX software on the CD-ROM that you can use as Netscape helper applications.

N O T E   Although Netscape is freely available for download over the Internet, you need to be aware that the downloadable version is substantially different than the version you might purchase in a computer store or directly from Netscape Communications Corporation. As we discuss in chapter 18, Netscape can communicate with some World Wide Web servers using data encryption to implement security in transactions, and hide confidential information such as credit card numbers, sensitive corporate information, or any other data you want to protect from Internet snoopers.

The version of Netscape available on the Internet is considerably less secure than the one you can purchase. If you plan to use Netscape for the transmission of confidential information over the Internet, or you are otherwise concerned about the security of your Internet transactions with Netscape, you are well advised to purchase the secure version directly from Netscape Communications or in a computer store. The more secure version is not accessible on the Internet because it contains enhanced data encryption technology that the U.S. government considers to be a weapon of war. Consequently, this version cannot be exported. If you are in the U.S., you can, and probably should, purchase the secure, non-export version. ■

Downloading Netscape Over the Internet

Although you can purchase Netscape in computer stores or directly from the manufacturer, you can also get a copy over the Internet using anonymous FTP or a World Wide Web browser, such as NCSA Mosaic or an earlier release of Netscape.

Getting Netscape with Anonymous FTP

If you don't already have some sort of World Wide Web browser working on your system but are on the Internet, you can use your system's FTP utility to download a copy. The TCP/IP file transfer protocol (FTP) is a standard part of virtually all UNIX systems; if your system is on the Internet, your system has the FTP utility. Although there are some graphical FTP tools available here and there for UNIX systems, they're not part of any vendor's standard UNIX installation, so I focus on the non-graphical user interface all provide. Later on, I cover how to use a Web browser to download Netscape.

The UNIX FTP utility is a non-graphical one, so you'll need to run it from the shell in a terminal window, such as a Sun cmdtool, AIX aixterm, HP-UX hpterm, standard X Windows xterm, or any ordinary terminal session. Figures D.1 and D.2 show the process of downloading Netscape using standard anonymous FTP.

In figure D.1, you start up the FTP utility from the UNIX shell prompt, log in to Netscape's anonymous FTP server, named ftp.netscape.com, using the login name anonymous. For a password, type in your Internet e-mail address, such as yourname@yourcompany.com.

FIG. D.1

Accessing Netscape's
anonymous FTP server.

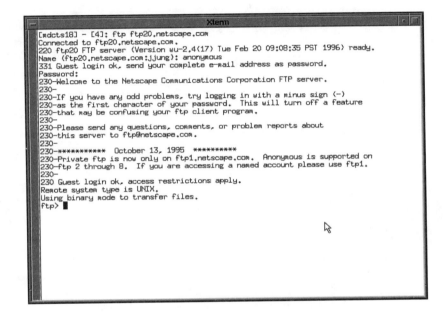

```
Xterm
[mdcts18] - [4]: ftp ftp20.netscape.com
Connected to ftp20.netscape.com.
220 ftp20 FTP server (Version wu-2.4(17) Tue Feb 20 09:08:35 PST 1996) ready.
Name (ftp20.netscape.com:jjung): anonymous
331 Guest login ok, send your complete e-mail address as password.
Password:
230-Welcome to the Netscape Communications Corporation FTP server.
230-
230-If you have any odd problems, try logging in with a minus sign (-)
230-as the first character of your password.  This will turn off a feature
230-that may be confusing your ftp client program.
230-
230-Please send any questions, comments, or problem reports about
230-this server to ftp@netscape.com.
230-
230-********** October 13, 1995 **********
230-Private ftp is now only on ftp1.netscape.com.  Anonymous is supported on
230-ftp 2 through 8.  If you are accessing a named account please use ftp1.
230-
230 Guest login ok, access restrictions apply.
Remote system type is UNIX.
Using binary mode to transfer files.
ftp> █
```

Part
VII

App
D

Figure D.2 shows a directory listing from the server's /pub/navigator/standard subdirectory with the several different versions of Netscape displayed. Several of the listing's lines are too wide for the screen shot so they are shown wrapped. Figure D.2 also shows the actual download taking place.

In figure D.2, note the use of the FTP pwd (print working directory) command to show we've switched to the unix/standard subdirectory, and the bin (binary transfer mode) command. Finally, get **http://home.netscape.com/comprod/mirror/client_download.html** downloads the Solaris 2.4 version of Netscape, retaining its original file name. (The figure shows we've used the standard X Windows cut-and-paste to highlight the file name, then paste it onto the get command line_a nifty trick with long, complex file names like this one.) You can, of course, change the file name by specifying a new file name on the command line. At this point, you can download additional versions of Netscape if you have other UNIX systems from other vendors. To end the FTP session, just type bye.

FIG. D.2

Downloading a copy of
Netscape for UNIX.

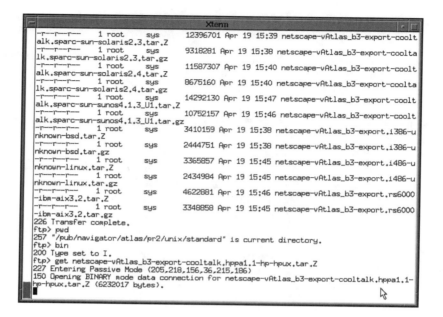

Downloading Netscape with NCSA Mosaic

If you already have a Web browser installed on your system, you can use it to retrieve Netscape over the Internet. For example, in NCSA Mosaic, pull down the File menu and select Open URL. When the dialog box opens, type in the URL **ftp://ftp.netscape.com/pub/navigator**. This will take you directly to the subdirectory on Netscape's anonymous FTP server containing the various UNIX versions. Figure D.3 shows this directory. Note the similarity to figure D.2, with the same file names shown. Note also the display of graphical icons here; I discuss these icons and how they got into your display in chapter 10, "Configuring Helper Applications."

To download a copy, pull down Options and select Save to Local Disk, then click the version you want. You'll see a running count of the bytes downloaded displayed in the lower-left corner of the Mosaic window. After the download is complete, a dialog box opens, prompting you to enter the file name to save the download under; enter any name you want. Continue to click any other versions you want to download. Exit from Mosaic, or iconify it, when you're finished. (If you plan to continue to use Mosaic in this session, be sure to click Options, then Save to Local Disk, to turn off the auto-download.)

FIG. D.3
Using NCSA Mosaic to access Netscape's FTP server.

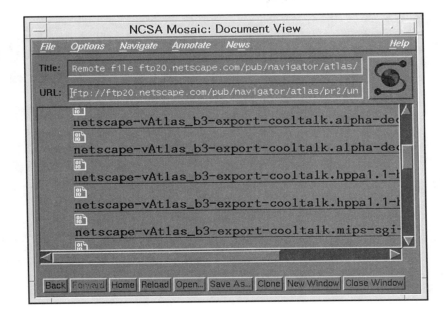

Downloading Netscape with Netscape

If you're already using Netscape, you can use it to download a later version. Click Open, then type in the URL **ftp://ftp.netscape.com/pub/navigator**. This takes you directly to the subdirectory on Netscape's anonymous FTP server containing the various UNIX versions. Figure D.4 shows this directory. (Of course, you can also reach this page from the Netscape home page at **http://home.netscape.com**, which can be accessed by clicking the large N icon in the upper-right corner of the Netscape window. From the Netscape home page, click the Netscape Now icon, and then follow the prompts.)

To download a copy of the latest Netscape, click the version you want. Netscape pops up a window, asking you to enter a name for the file you're downloading; the default is the same name under which it is stored on the FTP server. After you've entered a file name, or accepted the default name, the download starts.

N O T E Version 3.0 now pops up a separate Download window in which the progress of an FTP file download is tracked (see fig. D.5). (This new window also appears when data is being passed to a Netscape helper application as discussed in chapter 10, "Configuring Helper Applications.") You can use your mouse to drag the Download window out of your way and continue to use your main Netscape window while the download is taking place, scrolling the displayed page, or following other links on it. When the download completes, the separate Download window closes. ■

After your download is complete, you can exit Netscape or iconify (minimize) it.

FIG. D.4

Using Netscape to access Netscape's FTP server.

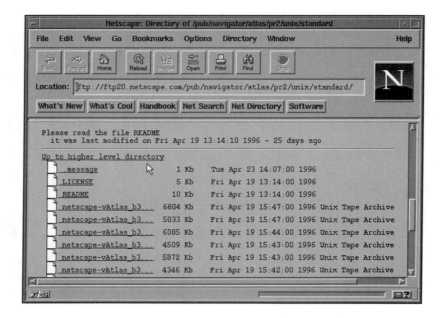

FIG. D.5

Netscape version 3.0 Download window.

Installing Netscape on a UNIX System

Although you can install Netscape in your own user directory on a UNIX system, you or your system administrator will probably want to install it so it's accessible to everyone using the system. However you decide to do the installation, these are the steps to perform.

First, make a temporary directory into which to unpack the Netscape distribution. Be sure there's enough disk space available in the file system you pick; you'll need about 5MB of free work space. You'll be able to remove the work directory later. The example that follows creates the directory /tmp/netscape. (The hash mark (#) signifies the superuser, or root, shell prompt; yours may be a dollar sign, or a customized prompt of some sort.)

```
# mkdir /tmp/netscape
```

After you've created the directory, you can unpack the compressed Netscape distribution archive into it, using the commands that follow. Netscape is distributed in a simple compressed

UNIX tar archive. The following commands assume you are working with superuser authority, have stored the downloaded Netscape tar archive in the directory /home/netscape, and have created the /tmp/netscape temporary directory.

```
# cd /home/netscape
# uncompress netscape-v20b1N-export.sparc-sun-solaris2.4.tar.Z
# cd /tmp/netscape
# tar xfv /home/netscape/netscape-v20b1N-export.sparc-sun-solaris2.4.tar
```

 Experienced UNIX users will recognize that the uncompress and tar commands can be combined into a single pipeline of commands. (Utilizing the vertical bar, or pipe, symbol (|), UNIX pipelines allow the output of one command to serve as the input to the next command in the pipeline.) Here's the above sequence using this approach:

```
# cd /tmp/netscape
# zcat /home/netscape/netscape-v20b1N-export.sparc-sun-solaris2.4.tar.Z | tar xfv -
```

In either case, the unpacking of the archive will generate several files in the /tmp/netscape directory. Among them, you'll find a README file with detailed installation instructions. You can view this file online with the UNIX more or pg commands, or print it for reference. Also, you'll find a file named license.txt. Be sure to read this file so you understand Netscape's licensing terms. Use of Netscape is free to many users (primarily users in educational and nonprofit institutions), but others (primarily commercial users) are required to pay for it beyond the initial evaluation period.

Extracting Netscape from CD-ROM

Before moving into the actual installation of Netscape from the temporary directory you've created, let's take a side trip and bring those of you who've purchased Netscape up to the same point we reached in the preceding section. After we've done so, we'll return to the final Netscape installation instructions, which apply both to the Internet-download and CD-ROM purchase situations.

> **CAUTION**
> The CD-ROM we are discussing here is the Netscape Communications CD and not the one inserted in this book.

Rather than providing a separate CD-ROM for each supported UNIX system, Netscape distributes a CD-ROM containing versions for several different UNIX systems:

- Sun Microsystems (SunOS 4.1.x and Solaris 2.x for Sun SPARC hardware, though not for Solaris 2.x on x86)
- IBM RISC System/6000 (AIX 3.2.5, but not AIX 4.1.x)
- BSDI and Linux (two versions of UNIX for IBM-compatible PCs)
- Digital UNIX (formerly called OSF/1)

■ Silicon Graphics (IRIX 5.x)

■ Hewlett-Packard (HP-UX 9.x)

Here's a UNIX-style directory listing of the CD-ROM's top-level directory:

```
-r_r_r_ 1 root 6074 Apr 21 01:27 _readme.txt
dr-xr-xr-x 2 root 2048 Apr 21 01:12 aix.32
drwxr-xr-x 2 root 2048 Apr 24 12:40 bsdi
dr-xr-xr-x 3 root 2048 Apr 21 01:16 common
dr-xr-xr-x 2 root 2048 Apr 21 01:15 dec_osf1.20
dr-xr-xr-x 2 root 2048 Apr 21 01:15 hpux.903
dr-xr-xr-x 2 root 2048 Apr 21 01:15 irix.52
-r_r_r_ 1 root 9351 Apr 19 11:40 license.txt
drwxr-xr-x 2 root 2048 Apr 24 12:15 linux
dr-xr-xr-x 2 root 2048 Apr 21 01:15 solaris.23
dr-xr-xr-x 2 root 2048 Apr 21 01:15 sunos.413
```

Each of the supported systems has a different procedure for mounting the CD-ROM. You don't need a CD drive on every system, because you can install Netscape from one machine to another over your local area network using network file transfers, including using NFS-mounted file systems. After the CD-ROM is mounted, the procedure for installing Netscape is pretty much the same on all systems. Let's get the CD-ROM mounted first, then turn to the final installation instructions.

N O T E UNIX device names for CD-ROMs (and other devices) vary, depending on the type of device, its type of hardware connection, the device configuration, and other matters. All the examples below use the default device name for the CD-ROM on the example system; your own device names may be different depending on your hardware setup. Check with your system administrator on the exact device name you should use on your system. ■

Mounting the CD-ROM on Sun Systems On a Sun system running SunOS 4.1.x (also called Solaris 1.x), you'll need access to the root, or superuser, account to mount the CD-ROM. Insert the CD-ROM into its caddy and place it in the CD player, then type the following commands (as with the examples above, the # symbol represents the super-user prompt; you don't enter it):

```
# mkdir /cdrom
# mount -rt hsfs /dev/sr0 /cdrom
```

The system may tell you the /cdrom directory already exists when you type the first command; you can ignore this message. In the second command, the command-line arguments tell the mount command to mount the high-speed type file system device /dev/sr0 read-only on the /cdrom directory mount point. You can check to see that the mount succeeded by asking for a directory listing with the command ls /cdrom.

On a Sun system running Solaris 2.x (also called SunOS 5.x), you may or may not need superuser authority to mount the CD-ROM, depending on how the system was configured when it was installed. Ask your system administrator if the Solaris Volume Management feature is enabled. Volume Management is a new feature of Solaris 2.x that allows any user to mount and unmount CD-ROMs and floppy disks. If the package was installed, you can simply slip the CD-ROM into the drive and the system will automatically mount it for you. After a couple of minutes, you'll be able to change to the /cdrom/cdrom0 directory and see the Netscape CD-ROM. (This mount point is the default one used by Volume Management; your system administrator may have changed this default, so check with her if the /cdrom/cdrom0 directory doesn't appear within a minute or so.)

Volume Management

Although instructions for mounting the Netscape CD-ROM in the absence of this package are provided below, Solaris Volume Management is a useful feature. You can check to see if Volume Management is running by searching the output of the UNIX ps command, like this:

```
# ps -ef | grep vold
```

If you get nothing back, it's not running. Check to see if it has been installed with this command:

```
# pkginfo | grep -l volume
```

If it isn't installed, you'll get back nothing but your shell prompt. You or your system administrator can install Volume Management from the Solaris distribution CD-ROM, using the pkgadd command.

If Volume Management is not running on your Solaris 2.x system, mounting the CD-ROM requires superuser access. Use the following commands:

```
# mkdir /cdrom
# mount -o ro -F hsfs /dev/dsk/c0t6d0s2 /cdrom
```

Mounting the CD-ROM on an IBM AIX System   IBM's UNIX, called AIX, also requires superuser authority to mount CD-ROMs. Here are the commands:

```
# mkdir /cdrom
# crfs -v cdrfs -p ro -d cd0 -m /cdrom
# mount /cdrom
```

You can also use the AIX System Management Interface Tool, using the smit command. Start up smit, select Physical and Logical Storage, Filesystems, Add/Change/Show/Delete Filesystems, and, finally, CDROM File Systems. Fill in the blanks, then click DO to mount the CD-ROM.

Mounting the CD-ROM on a Silicon Graphics System   SGI's UNIX, called IRIX, automatically senses and mounts the CD-ROM when it is placed into the CD drive. Just pop the CD-ROM in, and it will be mounted on the directory /CDROM.

Mounting the CD-ROM on an HP-UX System   HP-UX 9.x requires manual mounting of CD-ROM file systems.

```
# mkdir /cdrom
# mount -rt cdfs /dev/dsk/c201d2s0 /cdrom
```

As with the other examples in this section, this command uses the default device name for the CD-ROM device in HP-UX. Your hardware setup may differ, so see your system administrator if this command doesn't work.

Mounting the CD-ROM on a BSDI System   BSDI requires manual mounting of CD-ROMs by the superuser:

```
# mkdir /cdrom
# mount_cd9660 /dev/sd6a /cdrom
```

Mounting the CD-ROM on a Linux System   Linux requires manual mounting of CD-ROMs by the superuser.

```
# mkdir /cdrom
# mount -rt iso9660 /dev/scd0 /cdrom
```

Mounting the CD-ROM on a Digital UNIX System   Digital UNIX requires manual mounting of CD-ROM file systems.

```
# mkdir /cdrom
# mount -rt cdfs /dev/rz6c /cdrom
```

Unpacking the CD-ROM Distribution   Having mounted the CD-ROM on your UNIX system, you can unpack the distribution for your particular release of UNIX. We'll assume you've mounted the CD-ROM on the /cdrom mount point in the previous examples, and that you'll unpack the distribution into the temporary directory /var/tmp/netscape. As the earlier directory listing shows, there is a subdirectory on the CD-ROM for each of the supported UNIX versions, such as aix.32, bsdi, and so on. We'll use the convention ostype in our example commands; that is, where /cdrom/ostype is used, substitute the subdirectory name from the CD-ROM for your UNIX version for ostype. With the exception of Solaris 2.x, the command to unpack the distribution is exactly the same on all other UNIX systems:

```
# cd /tmp/netscape
# tar xfv /cdrom/ostype/netscape.tar
```

If your UNIX system is Solaris 2.x, substitute this command for the second one shown previously:

```
# tar xfv /cdrom/cdrom0/ostype/netscape.tar
```

At this point, the Netscape distribution has been unpacked into the temporary directory and you can unmount the CD-ROM, then proceed to the final installation.

Final Netscape Installation

Whether you've downloaded Netscape over the Internet or purchased it on CD-ROM, you're now ready for the final installation of the package. With some small differences, which are explained in context (later in the chapter) as they arise, the procedure is the same on all the supported UNIX systems.

You now have several files in your working directory, including the following:

- readme.txt, or README
- license.txt, or LICENSE
- netscape

- Netscape.ad
- XKeysymDB
- hot-convert.sh.

We'll cover these files in the order listed. As noted, the README and LICENSE files provide installation instructions and licensing information, respectively.

The file named netscape is the Netscape executable program. Move the Netscape executable program into a directory accessible to all users on your system. A common place is the /usr /local/bin directory. Here's the command:

```
# mv netscape /usr/local/bin
```

Move the Netscape application defaults file Netscape.ad into a central location on the system:

```
# mv Netscape.ad /usr/lib/X11/app-defaults/Netscape
```

If you can't find the /usr/lib/X11 directory, you're probably on a Sun system, on which the app-defaults directory is /usr/openwin/lib/X11/app-defaults. Place the file in this directory instead. Since Netscape is an X Windows program on UNIX systems, you can control some of its behavior and on-screen appearance using X Windows Resources; the application defaults file contains those which pertain to Netscape. See "Netscape X Resources" later in this chapter for more information.

Move XKeysymDB, the key symbols file, into a central location on the system:

```
# mv XKeysymDB /usr/lib/X11 (or /usr/openwin/lib/X11)
```

This is a particularly important file for Sun users, since Netscape is a Motif application. The SunOS-supplied XKeysymDB file is set up for the (non-Motif) OpenWindows graphical user interface. The XKeysymDB file provided with the Netscape distribution contains the needed Motif keyboard bindings, linking various keystrokes to Netscape commands. If you don't install this file, Netscape will generate a large number of error messages on startup and some of the keystrokes may not work properly (or may not work at all). See your X Windows documentation for more information about the XKeysymDB file.

If you or other users on your system have been using NCSA Mosaic for Web browsing, you'll want to translate your Mosaic Hotlist into Netscape Bookmarks. The shell script hot-convert.sh can be used to do this. Install the supplied conversion file in a location accessible to all:

```
# mv hot-convert.sh /usr/local/bin
```

Later, users can run this script to do the conversion of Hotlist files into a Netscape Bookmarks file. The original Hotlist files are not changed.

That's it. You're done installing Netscape. You'll need to exit from your current X Windows session and start a new one before you start Netscape to put all the changes into effect.

Making Netscape Look Like You Want it To

There are a number of ways you can personalize the look of Netscape on your screen. These range from the size and position of the Netscape window to the font styles and sizes Netscape uses. In addition, you can control Netscape's background color and maximize the amount of information it can display.

Displaying More in Your Netscape Screen

Netscape uses a lot of on-screen real estate to display its various bells and whistles—in particular, the toolbar, directory buttons, and location. All these features of Netscape are convenient when you're just starting out. After a while, however, you might want to suppress the routine display of one or more of them, especially since they're all available from Netscape's pull-down menus. When you do, you gain a lot more space in the Netscape window for actual Web documents.

Removing the Toolbar, Directory Buttons, and Location   Figure D.6 shows the Netscape Options menu. Notice the middle group of items set off by the horizontal lines—Show Toolbar, Show Location, and Show Directory Buttons. You can suppress the display of any of these by clicking the one(s) you want to suppress. Notice how the shading changes on the checkboxes beside the ones you select for suppression. To make your changes permanent, select Save Options.

FIG. D.6
The Netscape Options menu.

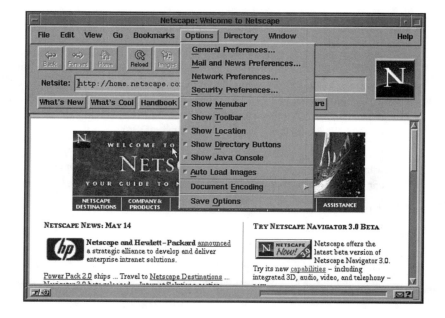

Installing CoolTalk

Netscape 3 comes with the CoolTalk plug-in which allows for Internet telephone and conferencing ability. On Windows 95 machines, CoolTalk is automatically installed for you when you install Netscape. People who use Netscape on UNIX machines, however, will need to install CoolTalk manually. Simply go into the Netscape installation directory and the CoolTalk subdirectory. Next, simply run the install.sh program.

Installing CoolTalk is a simple matter of specifying where you want CoolTalk installed (see fig. D.7). The installation script will copy all the necessary files into the correct locations.

FIG. D.7
UNIX users must install
CoolTalk after installing
Netscape.

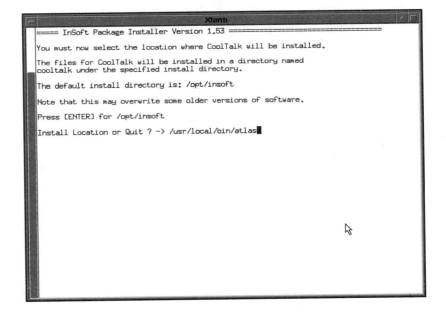

Part
VII

App
D

> **CAUTION**
> CoolTalk requires that the root user install the CoolTalk plug-in. This is because InSoft, the makers of CoolTalk, assume that only the system administrator will want to install Netscape or CoolTalk. Unfortunately, for many Unix users, this makes the CoolTalk installation more troublesome than necessary.

> **N O T E** CoolTalk requires that the computer you're installing CoolTalk on has audio capability.
> Additionally, some flavors of UNIX require certain OS-level patches to be applied before CoolTalk will work. Contact your system administrator to ensure that your system meets all the requirements of CoolTalk. ▦

Changing Fonts, Window Size, and Colors

UNIX Netscape provides some Preferences for selecting the font, window sizes, and colors used to display text. In addition, there are a couple of other simple ways of setting fonts, windows and/or colors, along with some more complex ones:

- Font Selection—Netscape's General Preferences, Fonts dialog box allows a choice of several font sizes.

- Window Size—You can change the size of your running Netscape window by dragging a corner of the window, the same as you do with any other X Windows program. To start Netscape with a particular window size, use a command-line option. If your workstation has a large, high-resolution monitor, you might start Netscape in a large, 1024 × 768 pixels window, like this (be sure to include the equal (=) sign, as well as a blank space between it and the word geometry):

    ```
    Netscape -geometry =1024x768 &
    ```

    If you'd like to position your Netscape window precisely at startup, try this, which places it at the upper-left corner of your screen:

    ```
    Netscape -geometry =1024x768+0-0 &
    ```

Command-Line Options

Like most UNIX programs, you can control the behavior of Netscape by giving it options on the command line when you start it. Experienced X Windows users, you may want to add a startup line for Netscape with your preferred command-line options to your X Windows startup file so it starts up every time you start X Windows. You'll find a list of the options Netscape knows about in the Frequently Asked Questions document, available on the Netscape Help pull-down.

- Colors—UNIX Netscape has only one easy way to let you change on-screen colors. You can select the background color with another command-line option at startup time. The figures in this chapter were made with Netscape using a white background to enhance their appearance. Here's how to start Netscape from your shell prompt with a white background:

    ```
    Netscape -bg white &
    ```

Netscape X Resources   Besides command-line options, Netscape supports a large number of X Windows Resources, with which you can control many aspects of its operation and on-screen appearance. Installing Netscape X Resources allows you to make permanent changes such as background color, screen size, and many others, saving you from having to enter command-line options every time you start the program.

Netscape X Resources are listed in the Netscape.ad file distributed with the software and installed on your system. A common location for this file is the /usr/lib/X11/app-defaults directory; Sun, however, puts it in /usr/openwin/lib/X11/app-defaults. The file is named Netscape. You'll find a lot of documentation in this file in the form of comments. While these comments strongly suggest you not make extensive changes in this file, an example change might be to turn off Netscape's irritating (to many) use of the HTML <blink> attribute. As with other X Windows Resources, you can make changes in your Home directory, or make them system-wide. To do the former, create the file Netscape (note the initial cap) in your Home directory, containing just this single line:

```
*blinkingEnabled:      False
```

Save the file, then exit from your editor and run the following command at your shell prompt:

```
$ xrdb -merge Netscape
```

Some users prefer a single X resources file in their Home directory, usually named .Xdefaults (or .Xresources), containing all their customized X resources, rather than separate files for each application. If you're one of these folks, add the following line to your .Xdefaults file:

```
Netscape*blinkingEnabled:      False
```

As you can see, you must include the application name (Netscape) in the .Xdefaults file; since this file refers generically to X Windows programs, you have to specify which one each entry in the file applies to. Once you've added the line, run the following command at your shell prompt:

```
$ xrdb -merge .Xdefaults
```

Earlier, I noted a Netscape command-line option that starts up Netscape with a white background. If you have tried this, you know that only part of the Netscape background actually comes up white (just the toolbar, Location, and the other housekeeping parts of the Netscape window). The rest of your window continues with the default Netscape gray background. If you'd like a completely white background, including not only the standard icons and the background of the actual text windows, use the *DefaultBackground Netscape X Resource. Do this in either the Netscape file in your Home Directory or .Xdefaults file, as follows:

```
*DefaultBackground:      #FFFFFF
```

You may recognize the right side of this entry as three hexadecimal (base 16) numbers, hex FF being equivalent to decimal 255. This entry uses a pure white background, and has been used for the figures in this chapter, to enhance their appearance. You can locate other available colors in the file /usr/lib/X11/rgb.txt on your system (/usr/openwin/lib/X11/rgb.txt on Sun systems). Each entry contains a color name and a set of three numbers referring to the respective amounts of red, green, and blue that make up the color. For example, the following are several entries from this file for shades of white:

248 248 255	ghost white
245 245 255	white smoke
255 250 240	floral white
250 235 215	antique white
255 222 173	navajo white
255 255 255	white

As you can see, white is shown with the three decimal color attributes 255, 255, and 255 in the rgb.txt file. You need to convert these numbers to hexadecimal to use them for this purpose. Decimal 255 is hex FF, so the entry FFFFFF represents white, while floral white would be FFFAF0 (255, 250, and 240 in decimal, per the rgb.txt file).

If you or your system administrator want to make Netscape X Resource changes effective system-wide, make the changes in the /usr/lib/X11/app- defaults/Netscape file (/usr/openwin/lib/X11/app-defaults/Netscape on Sun systems). Users need to quit and restart Netscape to pick up the new settings. ●

What's on the CD-ROM

The CD-ROM included with this book is packed full of valuable programs and utilities. This appendix gives you a brief overview of the contents of the CD. For a more detailed look at any of these parts, load the CD-ROM and browse the contents. ■

Netscape Navigator 3

This CD-ROM contains a complete, fully licensed copy of Netscape Navigator 3.0. This is the full-featured one-button Web browser/client described throughout this book. Que has licensed this for your use and paid the licensing fee so that you are no longer limited by the Netscape 90 day trial or educational and government usage requirements.

You'll find Netscape in the \netscape directory on the CD-ROM.

Netscape Plug-Ins

Plug-ins are great. You've seen them described in some detail in chapter 9 of this book and you've seen what they can do. But finding and downloading these can be a hassle and is definitely time-consuming. So, as an added convenience, we've added 30 plug-ins to this CD-ROM.

Each of the following plug-ins has its own subdirectory in the \plugins directory:

- Acrobat Amber
- CMX Viewer
- Envoy
- IChat
- Inso Cyberspell
- Inso Word Viewer
- Inso Quick View

- Lightning Strike
- Macromedia Shockwave for Authorware
- Macromedia Shockwave for Freehand
- Sizzler
- TrueSpeech Player
- VRealm
- Web Active
- WIRL Virtual Reality Browser

- ASAP WebShow
- DWG/DFX
- FIGLeaf Inline
- History Tree
- InterCAP Inline
- Look@Me
- Macromedia Shockwave for Director

- NetInstall
- PowerMedia
- Scream
- StreamWorks
- Table of Contents
- VDOLive
- VRScout

HTML Editors and Utilities

There are dozens of good HTML editors and related utilities available with so many to choose from, you may not know where to start. To help you, we've included a selection of the best of these here. Look for these in the subdirectories in the \html directory.

- Color Manipulation Device
- Fountain

- ColorWiz
- Hot Dog Standard

- HoTMetaL
- HTMLed
- HTML Writer
- Kenn Nesbitt's WebEdit
- Map This!
- WebForms

- HTML Assistant
- HTML NotePad
- Iconovex Web Anchor
- LiveMarkup
- Webber
- WebMania

Web Utilities, Helper Applications, and Other Useful Utilities

This final section of software on the CD-ROM includes a carefully selected collection of the best additional utilities that you may find useful when using Netscape. These are in the \util directory

- Cool Edit
- Eyor
- MidiGate
- MPEGPlay
- PaintShop Pro
- QuickTime VR Player
- WebWatch
- WinZip

- Indexer
- Java Developers Kit (JDK)
- MOD4Win
- NetDate
- QuickTime Player
- VuePrint
- WinCode
- Video for Windows Runtime (use for Windows 3.1 only)

Part
VII

App
E

Free HTML Versions of Popular Que Books

The final piece of this CD-ROM makes owning this book like getting four books in one. The CD-ROM contains the entire text of three popular best-selling books from Que in HTML format. The chapters and sections are all hyperlinked and an HTML index is included for each book to make using them even easy. (The index is generated by Iconovex's Web Anchor indexing program, a free trial version of which is included on the CD-ROM in the HTML Editors and Utilities section.)

The three free books included are:

- *Special Edition Using Java*
- *Special Edition Using HTML, 2nd Edition*
- *Special Edition Using JavaScript*

We think that you'll find each of these books in HTML to be valuable additions to your reference library. You'll find these books in the \quebooks directory. ●

Index

BEFOUR	AFTER

e-mail 's great. Problm is i look like an idoit if iv'e got lots of misspellings, my net conventions are wrong. I'm a lowsy proofreader (too

.fool

boring). so i only send e-male when I know quality's no issue. in fact i type lots more msitakes so the reader' wil know i'm not dumb -- just in too much a hurry to be anal about this stuff. Besides who'll notice teh diffrence?

After I purchased CyberSpell my confidence level soared. Now, I can deliver important messages with assurance that they don't contain foolish

.cool

mistakes. CyberSpell is cybersavvy, so it even checks all my e-mail conventions — like FTP + http addresses and emoticons. I never imagined a spelling tool could be so powerful. It's a real time saver for sending polished e-mail. :->

CyberSpell can transform your e-mail beyond standard spell checking by providing error **correction for punctuation, formatting, spacing, capitalization, and more!** And it's so easy to use — just load CyberSpell trialware from the enclosed CD-ROM or download it from our web site. Don't make another foolish mistake. If you want correct e-mail on the Net, order CyberSpell today!

330 North Wabash, 15th Floor, Chicago, Il 60611 Tel (800) 333-1395 Fax (312) 670-0820 E-mail: saleschi@inso.com

http://www.inso.com

Copyright © 1996 INSO Corporation. The Inso logo is a registered trademark and CyberSpell and the CyberSpell logo are trademarks of INSO Corporation.

INTRODUCING A UTILITY THAT WORKS OVERTIME SO YOU MAY NOT HAVE TO.

Quick View Plus. The unbelievably productive utility for Windows 95.

Few things can help you blaze through the day like Quick View Plus. Based on the award-winning Outside In technology, Quick View Plus helps you make the most of the Windows 95 operating system and Netscape Navigator so you can work more productively.

View Everything. Do Anything.

Quick View Plus integrates with Windows Explorer and Microsoft Exchange so you can look at files and attachments without launching, or even having, the original applications.

Quick View Plus lets you view over 200 file formats-from Windows, DOS, and Macintosh programs-including PKZIP, HTML and UUE. It's like having hundreds of applications on your desktop!

And it's WYSIWYG, so what you see is what you get. Quick View Plus gives you instant, fully formatted

display of any file, so you can view text, graphic, database and spreadsheet documents just as they were created in the original applications.

What's more, you can print anything you can see with Quick View Plus. You'll get fully formatted output, with fonts, tables, embedded graphics and OLE objects intact.

Plug in to Netscape.

Quick View Plus plugs in to Netscape Navigator so you have the power to view, copy, print and manipulate virtually any native file from within the Navigator browser window – including word processing, graphic, presentation and compressed formats.

The built-in productivity tool.

Quick View Plus is easy. Quick View Plus is powerful. Most of all, Quick View Plus lets you concentrate on using information instead of acquiring it.

So you can spend your work hours actually working. And your free time doing what you want.

ôInso®
CORPORATION

330 North Wabash, 15th Floor, Chicago, IL 60611
Toll-free: 800.333.1395, 312.329.0700, fax: 312.670.0820, e-mail: saleschi@inso.com
http://www.inso.com

Starting today, you can feel at home on the Internet

Introducing AT&T WorldNet℠ Service

AT&T

A World of Possibilities...

With AT&T WorldNet℠ Service, a world of possibilities awaits you. Discover new ways to stay in touch with the people, ideas, and information that are important to you at home and at work.

Make travel reservations at any time of the day or night. Access the facts you need to make key decisions. Pursue business opportunities on the AT&T Business Network. Explore new investment options. Play games. Research academic subjects. Stay abreast of current events. Participate in online newsgroups. Purchase merchandise from leading retailers. Send e-Mail.

All you need is a computer with a mouse, a modem, a phone line, and the software enclosed with this mailing. We've taken care of the rest.

If You Can Point and Click, You're There.

Finding the information you want on the Internet with AT&T WorldNet Service is easier than you ever imagined it could be. That's because AT&T WorldNet Service integrates a specially customized version of the popular Netscape Navigator™ software with advanced Internet directories and search engines. The result is an Internet service that sets a new standard for ease of use — virtually everywhere you want to go is a point and click away.

Choose the Plan That's Right for You.

If you're an AT&T Long Distance customer signing up in 1996, you can experience this exciting new service for 5 free hours a month for one full year. Beyond your 5 free hours, you'll be charged only $2.50 for each additional hour. Just use the service for a minimum of one hour per month. If you intend to use AT&T WorldNet Service for more than 5 hours a month, consider choosing the plan with unlimited hours for $19.95 per month.*

If you're not an AT&T Long Distance customer, you can still benefit from AT&T quality and reliability by starting with the plan that offers 3 hours each month and a low monthly fee of $4.95. Under this plan you'll be charged $2.50 for each additional hour, or AT&T WorldNet Service can provide you with unlimited online access for $24.95 per month. It's entirely up to you.

If you're not currently an AT&T Long Distance customer, but would like to become one, please call 1 800 431-0800, ext. 21624.

*The 5 free hours is limited to one AT&T WorldNet Account per residential billed telephone presubscribed to AT&T for "1+ area code + number" long distance dialing. Unlimited usage offers limited to one logon per account at any time. Other terms and conditions apply. Prices quoted are current as of 4/22/96 and are subject to modification by AT&T at any time. Local, long distance, or 800 number access charges and additional access charges and/or taxes that may be imposed on subscribers or on AT&T WorldNet Service will apply to all usage.

Minimum System Requirements

To run AT&T WorldNet Service, you need:

- An IBM-compatible personal computer with a 386 processor or better
- Microsoft Windows 3.1x or Windows 95
- 8MB RAM (16MB or more recommended)

- 11MB of free hard disk space
- 14.4 bps (or faster) modem (28.8 bps is recommended)
- A standard phone line

We're With You Every Step of the Way. 24 Hours a Day, 7 Days a Week.

Nothing is more important to us than making sure that your Internet experience is a truly enriching and satisfying one. That's why our highly trained customer service representatives are available to answer your questions and offer assistance whenever you need it — 24 hours a day, 7 days a week. To reach AT&T WorldNet Customer Care, call **1 800 400-1447**.

Installation Tips and Instructions

- If you have other Web browsers or online software, please consider uninstalling them according to vendor's instructions.
- At the end of installation, you may be asked to restart Windows. Don't attempt the registration process until you have done so.
- If you are experiencing modem problems trying to dial out, try different modem selections, such as Hayes Compatible. If you still have problems, please call Customer Care at **1 800 400-1447**.
- If you are installing AT&T WorldNet Service on a PC with Local Area Networking, please contact your LAN administrator for set-up instructions.
- Follow the initial start-up instructions given to you by the vendor product you purchased. These instructions will tell you how to start the installation of the AT&T WorldNet Service Software.
- Follow the on-screen instructions to install AT&T WorldNet Service Software on your computer.

When you have finished installing the software you may be prompted to restart your computer. Do so when prompted.

Safeguard Your Online Purchases

By registering and continuing to charge your AT&T WorldNet Service to your AT&T Universal Card, you'll enjoy peace of mind whenever you shop the Internet. Should your account number be compromised on the Net, you won't be liable for any online transactions charged to your AT&T Universal Card by a person who is not an authorized user.*

Setting Up Your WorldNet Account

The AT&T WorldNet Service Program group/folder will appear on your Windows desktop.

- Double click on the AT&T WorldNet Service registration icon.
- Follow the on-screen instructions and complete all the stages of registration.

After all the stages have been completed, you'll be prompted to dial into the network to complete the registration process. Make sure your modem and phone line are not in use.

*Today cardmembers may be liable for the first $50 of charges made by a person who is not an authorized user, which will not be imposed under this program as long as the cardmember notifies AT&T Universal Card of the loss within 24 hours and otherwise complies with the Cardmember Agreement. Refer to Cardmember Agreement for definition of authorized user.

Registering With AT&T WorldNet Service

Once you have connected with AT&T WorldNet online registration service, you will be presented with a series of screens that will confirm billing information and prompt you for additional account set-up data.

The following is a list of registration tips and comments that will help you during the registration process.

I. Use the registration code:
- Code for current AT&T Long Distance Customers: L30QIM631
- Code for other long distance customers: L30QIM632

II. We advise that you use all lowercase letters when assigning an e-Mail ID and security code, since they are easier to remember.

III. Choose a special "security code" that you will use to verify who you are when you call Customer Care.

IV. If you make a mistake and exit the registration process prematurely, all you need to do is click on "Create New Account". Do not click on "Edit Existing Account".

V. When choosing your local access telephone number, you will be given several options. Please choose the one nearest to you. Please note that calling a number within your area does not guarantee that the call is free.

Connecting to AT&T WorldNet Service

When you have finished registering with AT&T WorldNet Service you are ready to make online connections.

- Make sure your modem and phone line are available.
- Double click on the AT&T WorldNet Service icon

Follow these steps whenever you wish to connect to AT&T WorldNet Service.

Explore our AT&T WorldNet Service Web site at: http://www.att.com/worldnet

The enclosed software is not for export outside the U.S. and Canada.

Registration Codes

When installing and registering the AT&T WorldNet℠ Service software, please use the following registration codes:

- Code for current AT&T Long Distance Customers: L30QIM631
- Code for other long distance customers: L30QIM632

Please see the previous pages if you need information about subscribing to AT&T Long Distance service.

Upgrading AT&T WorldNet Service Software to Netscape 3

The version of AT&T WorldNet Service software included on this CD-ROM installs a previous version of Netscape Navigator. In order to use the copy of Netscape Navigator 3 provided by Que on this CD-ROM along with AT&T WorldNet Service, please follow these directions:

I. Follow all of the steps to install the AT&T WorldNet Service software included on the previous pages. You must install the software, set up your account, and register with AT&T WorldNet Service before installing Netscape Navigator 3.

II. Once you have successfully set up your account and registered, install Netscape Navigator 3 by following the directions found in the section "Loading Netscape" in the appendix "Loading and Configuring Netscape" in this book. Windows 3.1 users should select the "Use old Netscape ini file" option when prompted. Choose your WorldNet directory when prompted for the destination path (c:\worldnet). Select the "AT&T WorldNet Services" folder for new items when prompted.

If you choose to use Netscape 3 with AT&T WorldNet Service, you should not call AT&T WorldNet Service customer support for problems relating to Netscape. You will still call them for any support needs related to AT&T WorldNet Service at the number listed earlier under "We're With You Every Step of the Way." For Netscape 3 support, you will call or e-mail Macmillan Technical Support at 317-581-3833 or **support@mcp.com.**

Windows 3.1 users: After following the directions above, use the following steps to configure mail in Netscape 3.

I. Run Eudora light by double-clicking the Eudora light e-mail icon and select the **Special** pull down menu.

II. Select **Settings**.

III. Select the **Getting Started** category.

IV. Write down your POP account information.

V. Cancel the settings and close Eudora Light.

I. Now open Netscape Navigator 3.

II. Select the **Options** pull down menu.

III. Select **Mail and News Preferences...**

IV. Select the **Servers** tab.

V. Select the box to the right of **Incoming Mail (POP3) Server:**

VI. Enter everything after the @ symbol from your Eudora Light POP account information. For instance, if your account information was "Jdoe@postoffice.worldnet.att.net" you would enter "worldnet.att.net" in the box.

VII. Tab to the **POP3 User Name:** box.

VIII. Enter everything before the @ symbol from your Eudora Light POP account information. For instance, if your account information was "Jdoe@postoffice.worldnet.att.net" you would enter "Jdoe" in the box.

IX. Select the **OK** button at the bottom of the Preferences window.

X. You are now ready to use Netscape for e-mail.

After confirming the mail portion of Netscape is configured properly, you may delete the Eudora Light folder from your WorldNet directory, if you choose not to use Eudora Light.

Remember, you can use the copy of Netscape 3 on this CD-ROM with any Internet service provider you choose. AT&T WorldNet Service software is provided as an option for you if you don't currently have an internet provider or would like to switch to AT&T's WorldNet Service.

AT&T WorldNet is a service name of AT&T Corp

EXHIBIT B

SOFTWARE LICENSE for QuickTime

PLEASE READ THIS LICENSE CAREFULLY BEFORE USING THE SOFTWARE. BY USING THE SOFTWARE, YOU ARE AGREEING TO BE BOUND BY THE TERMS OF THIS LICENSE. IF YOU DO NOT AGREE TO THE TERMS OF THIS LICENSE, PROMPTLY RETURN THE UNUSED SOFTWARE TO THE PLACE WHERE YOU OBTAINED IT AND YOUR MONEY WILL BE REFUNDED.

1. **License.** The application, demonstration, system, and other software accompanying this License, whether on disk, in read-only memory, or on any other media (the "Software"), the related documentation and fonts are licensed to you by Macmillan Computer Publishing. You own the disk on which the Software and fonts are recorded but Macmillan Computer Publishing and/or Macmillan Computer Publishing's Licensors retain title to the Software, related documentation, and fonts. This License allows you to use the Software and fonts on a single Apple computer and make one copy of the Software and fonts in machine-readable form for backup purposes only. You must reproduce on such copy the Macmillan Computer Publishing copyright notice and any other proprietary legends that were on the original copy of the Software and fonts. You may also transfer all your license rights in the Software and fonts, the backup copy of the Software and fonts, the related documentation, and a copy of this License to another party, provided the other party reads and agrees to accept the terms and conditions of this License.

2. **Restrictions.** The Software contains copyrighted material, trade secrets, and other proprietary material. In order to protect them, and except as permitted by applicable legislation, you may not decompile, reverse engineer, disassemble, or otherwise reduce the Software to a human-perceivable form. You may not modify, network, rent, lease, loan, distribute, or create derivative works based upon the Software, in whole or in part. You may not electronically transmit the Software from one computer to another or over a network.

3. **Termination.** This License is effective until terminated. You may terminate this License at any time by destroying the Software, related documentation and fonts, and all copies thereof. This License will terminate immediately without notice from Macmillan Computer Publishing if you fail to comply with any provision of this License. Upon termination you must destroy the Software, related documentation and fonts, and all copies thereof.

4. **Export Law Assurances.** You agree and certify that neither the Software nor any other technical data received from Macmillan Computer Publishing, nor the direct product thereof, will be exported outside the United States except as authorized and as permitted by the laws and regulations of the United States. If the Software has been rightfully obtained by you outside of the United States, you agree that you will not re-export the Software nor any other technical data received from Macmillan Computer Publishing, nor the direct product thereof, except as permitted by the laws and regulations of the United States and the laws and regulations of the jurisdiction in which you obtained the Software.

5. **Government End Users.** If you are acquiring the Software and fonts on behalf of any unit or agency of the United States Government, the following provisions apply. The Government agrees:

    (i) if the Software and fonts are supplied to the Department of Defense (DoD), the Software and fonts are classified as "Commercial Computer Software" and the Government is acquiring only "restricted rights" in the Software, its documentation and fonts as that term is defined in Clause 252.227-7013(c)(1) or the DFARS; and

    (ii) if the Software and fonts are supplied to any unit or agency of the United States Government other than DoD, the Government's rights in the Software, its documentation and fonts will be as defined in Clause 52.227-19(c)(2) of the FAR or, in the case of NASA, in Clause 18-52.227-86(d) of the NASA supplement to the FAR.

6. **Limited Warranty on Media.** Macmillan Computer Publishing warrants the diskettes and/or compact disc on which the Software and fonts are recorded to be free from defects in materials and workmanship under normal use for a period of ninety (90) days from the date of purchase as evidenced by a copy of the receipt. Macmillan Computer Publishing's entire liability and your exclusive remedy will be replacement of

the diskettes and/or compact disc not meeting Macmillan Computer Publishing's limited warranty and which is returned to Macmillan Computer Publishing or a Macmillan Computer Publishing authorized representative with a copy of the receipt. Macmillan Computer Publishing will have no responsibility to replace a disk/disc damaged by accident, abuse, or misapplication. ANY IMPLIED WARRANTIES ON THE DISKETTES AND/OR COMPACT DISC, INCLUDING THE IMPLIED WARRANTIES OF MERCHANTABILITY AND FITNESS FOR A PARTICULAR PURPOSE, ARE LIMITED IN DURATION TO NINETY (90) DAYS FROM THE DATE OF DELIVERY. THIS WARRANTY GIVES YOU SPECIFIC LEGAL RIGHTS, AND YOU MAY ALSO HAVE OTHER RIGHTS WHICH VARY BY JURISDICTION.

7. **Disclaimer of Warranty on Apple Software.** You expressly acknowledge and agree that use of the Software and fonts is at your sole risk. The Software, related documentation and fonts are provided "AS IS" and without warranty of any kind and Macmillan Computer Publishing and Macmillan Computer Publishing's Licensor(s) (for the purposes of provisions 7 and 8, Macmillan Computer Publishing and Macmillan Computer Publishing's Licensor(s) shall be collectively referred to as "Macmillan Computer Publishing") EXPRESSLY DISCLAIM ALL WARRANTIES, EXPRESS OR IMPLIED, INCLUDING, BUT NOT LIMITED TO, THE IMPLIED WARRANTIES OF MERCHANTABILITY AND FITNESS FOR A PARTICULAR PURPOSE. MACMILLAN COMPUTER PUBLISHING DOES NOT WARRANT THAT THE FUNCTIONS CONTAINED IN THE SOFTWARE WILL MEET YOUR REQUIREMENTS, OR THAT THE OPERATION OF THE SOFTWARE WILL BE UNINTERRUPTED OR ERROR-FREE, OR THAT DEFECTS IN THE SOFTWARE AND THE FONTS WILL BE CORRECTED. FURTHERMORE, MACMILLAN COMPUTER PUBLISHING DOES NOT WARRANT OR MAKE ANY REPRESENTATIONS REGARDING THE USE OR THE RESULTS OF THE USE OF THE SOFTWARE AND FONTS OR RELATED DOCUMENTATION IN TERMS OF THEIR CORRECTNESS, ACCURACY, RELIABILITY, OR OTHERWISE. NO ORAL OR WRITTEN INFORMATION OR ADVICE GIVEN BY MACMILLAN COMPUTER PUBLISHING OR A MACMILLAN COMPUTER PUBLISHING AUTHORIZED REPRESENTATIVE SHALL CREATE A WARRANTY OR IN ANY WAY INCREASE THE SCOPE OF THIS WARRANTY. SHOULD THE SOFTWARE PROVE DEFECTIVE, YOU (AND NOT MACMILLAN COMPUTER PUBLISHING OR A MACMILLAN COMPUTER PUBLISHING AUTHORIZED REPRESENTATIVE) ASSUME THE ENTIRE COST OF ALL NECESSARY SERVICING, REPAIR OR CORRECTION. SOME JURISDICTIONS DO NOT ALLOW THE EXCLUSION OF IMPLIED WARRANTIES, SO THE ABOVE EXCLUSION MAY NOT APPLY TO YOU.

8. **Limitation of Liability.** UNDER NO CIRCUMSTANCES INCLUDING NEGLIGENCE, SHALL MACMILLAN COMPUTER PUBLISHING BE LIABLE FOR ANY INCIDENTAL, SPECIAL, OR CONSEQUENTIAL DAMAGES THAT RESULT FROM THE USE OR INABILITY TO USE THE SOFTWARE OR RELATED DOCUMENTATION, EVEN IF MACMILLAN COMPUTER PUBLISHING OR A MACMILLAN COMPUTER PUBLISHING AUTHORIZED REPRESENTATIVE HAS BEEN ADVISED OF THE POSSIBILITY OF SUCH DAMAGES. SOME JURISDICTIONS DO NOT ALLOW THE LIMITATION OR EXCLUSION OF LIABILITY FOR INCIDENTAL OR CONSEQUENTIAL DAMAGES SO THE ABOVE LIMITATION OR EXCLUSION MAY NOT APPLY TO YOU.

In no event shall Macmillan Computer Publishing's total liability to you for all damages, losses, and causes of action (whether in contract, tort [including negligence] or otherwise) exceed the amount paid by you for the Software and fonts.

9. **Law and Severability.** This License shall be governed by and construed in accordance with the laws of the United States and the State of California, as applied to agreements entered into and to be performed entirely within California between California residents. If for any reason a court of competent jurisdiction finds any provision of this License, or portion thereof, to be unenforceable, that provision of the License shall be enforced to the maximum extent permissible so as to affect the intent of the parties, and the remainder of this License shall continue in full force and effect.

10. **Complete Agreement.** This License constitutes the entire agreement between the parties with respect to the use of the Software, the related documentation and fonts, and supersedes all prior or contemporaneous understandings or agreements, written or oral, regarding such subject matter. No amendment to or modification of this License will be binding unless in writing and signed by a duly authorized representative of Macmillan Computer Publishing.

Netscape Navigator End-User License Agreement

BY CLICKING ON THE "ACCEPT" BUTTON OR OPENING THE PACKAGE, YOU ARE CONSENTING TO BE BOUND BY THIS AGREEMENT. IF YOU DO NOT AGREE TO ALL OF THE TERMS OF THIS AGREEMENT, CLICK THE "DO NOT ACCEPT" BUTTON AND THE INSTALLATION PROCESS WILL NOT CONTINUE, AND, IF APPLICABLE, RETURN THE PRODUCT TO THE PLACE OF PURCHASE FOR A FULL REFUND.

NETSCAPE END-USER LICENSE AGREEMENT

REDISTRIBUTION NOT PERMITTED

This Agreement has 3 parts. Part I applies if you have not purchased a license to the accompanying software (the "Software"). Part II applies if you have purchased a license to the Software. Part III applies to all license grants. If you initially acquired a copy of the Software without purchasing a license and you wish to purchase a license, contact Netscape Communications Corporation ("Netscape") on the Internet at **http://www.netscape.com**.

PART I—TERMS APPLICABLE WHEN LICENSE FEES NOT (YET) PAID

(LIMITED TO EVALUATION, EDUCATIONAL, AND NONPROFIT USE)

GRANT. Netscape grants you a non-exclusive license to use the Software free of charge if (a) you are a student, faculty member, or staff member of an educational institution (K-12, junior college, college, or library) or an employee of an organization that meets Netscape's criteria for a charitable nonprofit organization; or (b) your use of the Software is for the purpose of evaluating whether to purchase an ongoing license to the Software. The evaluation period for use by or on behalf of a commercial entity is limited to ninety (90) days; evaluation use by others is not subject to this ninety (90) day limit. Government agencies (other than public libraries) are not considered educational or charitable nonprofit organizations for purposes of this Agreement. If you are using the software free of charge, you are not entitled to hard-copy documentation, support, or telephone assistance. If you fit within the description above, you may use the Software in the manner described in Part III under "Scope of Grant."

DISCLAIMER OF WARRANTY. Free of charge Software is provided on an "AS IS" basis, without warranty of any kind, including without limitation the warranties of merchantability, fitness for a particular purpose, and non-infringement. The entire risk as to the quality and performance of the Software is borne by you. Should the Software prove defective, you and not Netscape or its suppliers assume the entire cost of any service and repair. In addition, the security mechanisms implemented by Netscape software have inherent limitations, and you must determine that the Software sufficiently meets your requirements. This disclaimer of warranty constitutes an essential part of this Agreement. SOME JURISDICTIONS DO NOT ALLOW EXCLUSIONS OF AN IMPLIED WARRANTY, SO THIS DISCLAIMER MAY NOT APPLY TO YOU AND YOU MAY HAVE OTHER LEGAL RIGHTS THAT VARY BY JURISDICTION.

PART II—TERMS APPLICABLE WHEN LICENSE FEES PAID

GRANT. Subject to payment of applicable license fees, Netscape grants to you a non-exclusive license to use the Software and accompanying documentation ("Documentation") in the manner described in Part III under "Scope of Grant."

LIMITED WARRANTY. Netscape warrants that for a period of ninety (90) days from the date of acquisition, the Software, if operated as directed, will substantially achieve the functionality described in the Documentation. Netscape does not warrant, however, that your use of the Software will be uninterrupted or that the operation of the Software will be error-free or secure. In addition, the security mechanisms implemented by Netscape software have inherent limitations, and you must determine that the Software sufficiently meets your requirements. Netscape also warrants that the media containing the Software, if provided by Netscape, is free from defects in material and workmanship and will so remain for ninety (90) days from the date you acquired the Software. Netscape's sole liability for any breach of this warranty shall be, in Netscape's sole discretion: (i) to replace your defective media or Software; or (ii) to advise you how to achieve substantially the same functionality with the Software as described in the Documentation through a procedure different from that set forth in the Documentation; or (iii) if the above remedies are impracticable, to refund the license fee you paid for the Software. Repaired, corrected, or replaced Software and Documentation shall be covered by this limited warranty for the period remaining under the warranty that covered the original Software, or if longer, for thirty (30) days after the date (a) of shipment to you of the repaired or replaced Software, or (b) Netscape advised you how to operate the Software so as to achieve the functionality described in the Documentation. Only if you inform Netscape of your problem with the Software during the applicable warranty period and provide evidence of the date you purchased a license to the Software will Netscape be obligated to honor this warranty. Netscape will use reasonable commercial efforts to repair, replace, advise or, for individual consumers, refund pursuant to the foregoing warranty within thirty (30) days of being so notified.

THIS IS A LIMITED WARRANTY AND IT IS THE ONLY WARRANTY MADE BY NETSCAPE OR ITS SUPPLIERS. NETSCAPE MAKES NO OTHER EXPRESS WARRANTY AND NO WARRANTY OF NONINFRINGEMENT OF THIRD PARTIES' RIGHTS. THE DURATION OF IMPLIED WARRANTIES INCLUDING, WITHOUT LIMITATION, WARRANTIES OF MERCHANTABILITY AND OF FITNESS FOR A PARTICULAR PURPOSE, IS LIMITED TO THE ABOVE LIMITED WARRANTY PERIOD; SOME JURISDICTIONS DO NOT ALLOW LIMITATIONS ON HOW LONG AN IMPLIED WARRANTY LASTS, SO LIMITATIONS MAY NOT APPLY TO YOU. NO NETSCAPE DEALER, AGENT, OR EMPLOYEE IS AUTHORIZED TO MAKE ANY MODIFICATIONS, EXTENSIONS, OR ADDITIONS TO THIS WARRANTY. If any modifications are made to the Software by you during the warranty period; if the media is subjected to accident, abuse, or improper use; or if you violate the terms of this Agreement, then this warranty shall immediately terminate. This warranty shall not apply if the Software is used on or in conjunction with hardware or software other than the unmodified version of hardware or software with which the Software was designed to be used as described in the Documentation. THIS WARRANTY GIVES YOU SPECIFIC LEGAL RIGHTS, AND YOU MAY HAVE OTHER LEGAL RIGHTS THAT VARY BY JURISDICTION.

PART III—TERMS APPLICABLE TO ALL LICENSE GRANTS

SCOPE OF GRANT.

You may:

- use the Software on any single computer;
- use the Software on a network, provided that each person accessing the Software through the network must have a copy licensed to that person;

- use the Software on a second computer so long as only one copy is used at a time;
- copy the Software for archival purposes, provided any copy must contain all of the original Software's proprietary notices; or
- if you have purchased licenses for a 10 Pack or a 50 Pack, make up to 10 or 50 copies, respectively, of the Software (but not the Documentation), or, if you have purchased licenses for multiple copies of the Software, make the number of copies of Software (but not the Documentation) that the packing slip or invoice states you have paid for, provided any copy must contain all of the original Software's proprietary notices. The number of copies on the invoice is the total number of copies that may be made for *all* platforms. Additional copies of Documentation may be purchased from Netscape.

You may not:

- permit other individuals to use the Software except under the terms listed previously;
- permit concurrent use of the Software;
- modify, translate, reverse engineer, decompile, disassemble (except to the extent applicable laws specifically prohibit such restriction), or create derivative works based on the Software;
- copy the Software other than as specified above;
- rent, lease, grant a security interest in, or otherwise transfer rights to the Software; or
- remove any proprietary notices or labels from the Software.

TITLE. Title, ownership rights, and intellectual property rights in the Software shall remain in Netscape and/or its suppliers. The Software is protected by copyright and other intellectual property laws and by international treaties. Title and related rights in the content accessed through the Software is the property of the applicable content owner and may be protected by applicable law. The license granted under this Agreement gives you no rights to such content.

TERMINATION. This Agreement and the license granted hereunder will terminate automatically if you fail to comply with the limitations described herein. Upon termination, you must destroy all copies of the Software and Documentation.

EXPORT CONTROLS. None of the Software or underlying information or technology may be downloaded or otherwise exported or reexported (i) into (or to a national or resident of) Cuba, Iraq, Libya, Yugoslavia, North Korea, Iran, Syria, or any other country to which the U.S. has embargoed goods; or (ii) to anyone on the U.S. Treasury Department's list of Specially Designated Nationals or the U.S. Commerce Department's Table of Denial Orders. By downloading or using the Software, you are agreeing to the foregoing and you are representing and warranting that you are not located in, under the control of, or a national or resident of any such country or on any such list.

In addition, if the licensed Software is identified as a not-for-export product (for example, on the box or media or in the installation process), then the following applies: EXCEPT FOR EXPORT TO CANADA FOR USE IN CANADA BY CANADIAN CITIZENS, THE SOFTWARE AND ANY UNDERLYING TECHNOLOGY MAY NOT BE EXPORTED OUTSIDE THE UNITED STATES OR TO ANY FOREIGN ENTITY OR "FOREIGN PERSON" AS DEFINED

BY U.S. GOVERNMENT REGULATIONS, INCLUDING WITHOUT LIMITATION, ANYONE WHO IS NOT A CITIZEN, NATIONAL OR LAWFUL PERMANENT RESIDENT OF THE UNITED STATES. BY DOWNLOADING OR USING THE SOFTWARE, YOU ARE AGREEING TO THE FOREGOING AND YOU ARE WARRANTING THAT YOU ARE NOT A "FOREIGN PERSON" OR UNDER THE CONTROL OF A FOREIGN PERSON.

LIMITATION OF LIABILITY. UNDER NO CIRCUMSTANCES AND UNDER NO LEGAL THEORY, TORT, CONTRACT, OR OTHERWISE, SHALL NETSCAPE OR ITS SUPPLIERS OR RESELLERS BE LIABLE TO YOU OR ANY OTHER PERSON FOR ANY INDIRECT, SPE-CIAL, INCIDENTAL, OR CONSEQUENTIAL DAMAGES OF ANY CHARACTER INCLUD-ING, WITHOUT LIMITATION, DAMAGES FOR LOSS OF GOODWILL, WORK STOPPAGE, COMPUTER FAILURE OR MALFUNCTION, OR ANY AND ALL OTHER COMMERCIAL DAMAGES OR LOSSES. IN NO EVENT WILL NETSCAPE BE LIABLE FOR ANY DAMAGES IN EXCESS OF THE AMOUNT NETSCAPE RECEIVED FROM YOU FOR A LICENSE TO THE SOFTWARE, EVEN IF NETSCAPE SHALL HAVE BEEN INFORMED OF THE POSSI-BILITY OF SUCH DAMAGES, OR FOR ANY CLAIM BY ANY OTHER PARTY. THIS LIMITA-TION OF LIABILITY SHALL NOT APPLY TO LIABILITY FOR DEATH OR PERSONAL IN-JURY TO THE EXTENT APPLICABLE LAW PROHIBITS SUCH LIMITATION. FURTHER-MORE, SOME JURISDICTIONS DO NOT ALLOW THE EXCLUSION OR LIMITATION OF INCIDENTAL OR CONSEQUENTIAL DAMAGES, SO THIS LIMITATION AND EXCLUSION MAY NOT APPLY TO YOU.

HIGH RISK ACTIVITIES. The Software is not fault-tolerant and is not designed, manufactured, or intended for use or resale as on-line control equipment in hazardous environments requiring fail-safe performance, such as in the operation of nuclear facilities, aircraft navigation or com-munication systems, air traffic control, direct life support machines, or weapons systems, in which the failure of the Software could lead directly to death, personal injury, or severe physi-cal or environmental damage ("High Risk Activities"). Netscape and its suppliers specifically disclaim any express or implied warranty of fitness for High Risk Activities.

MISCELLANEOUS. If the copy of the Software you received was accompanied by a printed or other form of "hard-copy" End User License Agreement whose terms vary from this Agree-ment, then the hard-copy End User License Agreement governs your use of the Software. This Agreement represents the complete agreement concerning the license granted hereunder and may be amended only by a writing executed by both parties. THE ACCEPTANCE OF ANY PURCHASE ORDER PLACED BY YOU IS EXPRESSLY MADE CONDITIONAL ON YOUR ASSENT TO THE TERMS SET FORTH HEREIN, AND NOT THOSE IN YOUR PURCHASE ORDER. If any provision of this Agreement is held to be unenforceable, such provision shall be reformed only to the extent necessary to make it enforceable. This Agreement shall be gov-erned by California law (except for conflict of law provisions). The application of the United Nations Convention of Contracts for the International Sale of Goods is expressly excluded.

U.S. GOVERNMENT END USERS. The Software is a "commercial item," as that term is de-fined in 48 C.F.R. 2.101 (Oct. 1995), consisting of "commercial computer software" and "com-mercial computer software documentation," as such terms are used in 48 C.F.R. 12.212 (Sept. 1995). Consistent with 48 C.F.R. 12.212 and 48 C.F.R. 227.7202-1 through 227.7202-4 (June 1995), all U.S. Government End Users acquire the Software with only those rights set forth herein.

Before using any of the software on this disc, you need to install the software you plan to use. See Appendix E, "What's on the CD-ROM," for directions. If you have problems with the *Special Edition Using Netscape 3* CD, please contact Macmillan Technical Support at (317) 581-3833. We can be reached by e-mail at **support@mcp.com** or by CompuServe at **GO QUEBOOKS**.

Please note that technical support for the copy of Netscape Navigator included on the CD is provided through Macmillan Technical Support at the number or e-mail address listed above. Do not contact Netscape Corporation for technical support with this product.